BIOGRAPHICAL DICTIONARY OF THE YOUNGS

BIOGRAPHICAL DICTIONARY

of the

YOUNGS

(Born 1653-1870)

FROM TOWNS UNDER THE JURISDICTION OF
STRAFFORD COUNTY, NEW HAMPSHIRE
BEFORE **1840**

*A Listing of All Proprietors,
Pioneers, Land Owners, Heads of Family,
Soldiers and Sailors, Brides, Widows and Orphans
by the Family Name of Young*

Compiled by

Louise Ryder Young

HERITAGE BOOKS
2014

HERITAGE BOOKS
AN IMPRINT OF HERITAGE BOOKS, INC.

Books, CDs, and more—Worldwide

For our listing of thousands of titles see our website
at
www.HeritageBooks.com

Published 2014 by
HERITAGE BOOKS, INC.
Publishing Division
5810 Ruatan Street
Berwyn Heights, Md. 20740

Heritage Books by the author:

*Biographical Dictionary of the Youngs (Born Circa 1600–1870): From Essex
and Old Norfolk Counties, Massachusetts Bay Colony, Which Once
Contained Parts of Rockingham County, New Hampshire*

*Biographical Dictionary of the Youngs (Born 1653–1870): From Towns Under
the Jurisdiction of Strafford County, New Hampshire before 1840*

*Biographical Dictionary of the Youngs (Born Circa 1625–1870):
From Towns Under the Jurisdiction of York County, Maine*

International Standard Book Numbers
Paperbound: 978-1-55613-285-8
Clothbound: 978-0-7884-8426-1

CONTENTS

PREFACE

I confess to holding strong emotional ties to the State
of New Hampshire. My husband and I can count two family
branches out of four which stemmed from Sandwich and Wakefield
when both towns belonged to old Strafford County before 1840.
The third branch stemmed from Dunbarton, Hillsborough County.
Of course I married into the Young family and these are the
ties that bind. They help to explain my abiding interest over
these past twelve years in tracing the Youngs of Strafford
County.

Research on the Youngs began in a leisurely fashion the
summer of 1977, with no thought in mind except the writing of
a personal family history on my husband's branch. The idea
of a biographical dictionary somehow evolved about four or
five years ago when it dawned on me that the collection of
notes then taken on all Youngs county-wide could easily be the
backbone for a dictionary on all the independent branches of
the family. From that point on, there was not a doubt in my
mind as to the direction I wanted to take, that the task of
compiling a biographical dictionary would certainly be
demanding, but at the same time, very rewarding. Viewed in
this new light, the research project would provide a much
wider application for others searching for Young connections
in New Hampshire. When research was completed this past
summer, I was grateful for having taken this direction.
Having said that I now express the hope that errors have been
kept to a minimum. Much care was taken to cross-reference,
cross-check, and index all names and dates, but human errors
can be made. I offer my apology in advance for any error of
omission or commission.

The mode which I used to present alphabetical listings
of the Youngs from all independent branches was adapted from
Freemont Rider's "trace system" of cross-indexing as presented
in his encyclopedic biographical dictionary entitled: Preliminary Materials For A Genealogy Of The Rider (Ryder) Families
In The United States, Arranged According To The "Rider Trace"
System of Presentation. Godfrey Memorial Library, Middletown,
Connecticut (1959), 3 Vols., n.p. Full credit and acknowl-
edgement are given Mr. Rider as the originator of this "trace
system."

Heartfelt thanks are due all my family for being audience
and critics on this project, but special thanks go to:

My husband Richard who set up genealogical filing systems
on the word processor, made composite maps of the three

counties involved, and printed out the manuscript, without whose help the manuscript would not have seen the light of day.

Our daughter Susan A. Stiles of Falls Church, Virginia who encoded the index of the Youngs and allied families from the text on her personal computer, a labor of love!

Richard's uncle Alden N. Young of East Wakefield, New Hampshire, who in 1977 handed down to us the oral tradition of Young ancestors who stemmed from Dover and Wakefield.

Colleague Dorothy Aleshire of the Howard County Genealogical Society, Columbia, Maryland for reading over the manuscript, not once but twice, and for all her suggestions.

The staff of the Latter Day Saints Family History Library, Columbia, Maryland, for their assistance and encouragement in the research project. Thousands of hours were spent here in reading microfilms from the early 1980s on.

Special acknowledgments and thanks are due these faithful researchers working on their own branches of Young families of Strafford County who responded to my ad placed in the New England Historic and Genealogical Society **NEXUS**, February-March 1989, Vol. VI, No. 1. I am indebted to them for their generous exchanges of information from family bibles and personal files: Ms. Nancy L. Dodge of Colebrook, New Hampshire; Thomas P. Doherty of Wilmington, Delaware; Mrs. Marjorie S. Heaney of DeLand, Florida; Granvyl Hulse of Colebrook, New Hampshire; Jerry Ortell of Bellerose Terrace, New York State; and Ms. M. Elaine Woodward of Beaverton, Oregon.

Louise Ryder Young

Ellicott City, Maryland
October 1989

LIST OF ABBREVIATIONS

Admin.	Administration
	Administrator
	Administratrix
aka	also known as
Assoc.	Association
b	born
bp	baptism, baptized
Biog.	Biographical
BR	Birth Records
ca	circa
Cem.	Cemetery
Cert.	Certificate
Ch.	child, children
CR	Church Records
Co.	Company, County
CT	Connecticut
cont.	continued
d	died
D.A.R.	Daughters of the American Revolution
d-o-b	date of birth
d.y.	died young
d/o	daughter of
Exec.	Executor, Executrix
Gen.	Genealogy
gr.d/o	granddaughter of
gr.s/o	grandson of
IGI	International Genealogical Index
LDS	Latter Day Saints
m	married
MA	Massachusetts
Mil.	Military
ME	Maine
Nat'l.	National

N.B.	New Brunswick
n.d.	no date given
n.e.	northeast
NHVR	New Hampshire Vital Records
n.p.	no page numbers given
n.w.	northwest
N.S.	Nova Scotia
p	page
poss.	possibly
prob.	probably
Prov.	Provincial
rec'd	received, recorded
Recs.	Records
Reg.	**Register**
Regt.	Regiment
res.	resided
s/o	son of
s.e.	southeast
s.w.	southwest
TMs	typed manuscript
TR	Town Records
VA	Virginia
VR	Vital Records
V	Volume
VT	Vermont
y-o-b	year of birth

Brackets [ ] were used: (1) to enclose citation of a document; (2) to enclose interjectory comments believed to be true on statements found within documents.

TOPOGRAPHY

The table below lists the thirty towns under the jurisdiction of Strafford County, New Hampshire before 1840 where
records were found on the dozen or so independent branches of
the Youngs. Included are the dates of incorporation, names
of local landmarks often referred to in land deeds and probate
papers and other matters of historic interest. Acknowledgments should be given the following sources of material: N.H.
State Papers, "Township Grants," Vols. 27,28; Gazetteer of New
Hampshire, by Merrill & Merrill; and Mary P. Thompson's
Landmarks in Ancient Dover, New Hampshire.

Alton, Belknap Co. Once
known as New Durham Gore as
part of Strafford Co, the
town was granted 16 June
1796, after the Revolution;
it fronts on Alton Bay on
Lake Winnipesaukee and borders on New Durham; a portion
of the town was annexed to
Barnstead in 1840 when county
lines were redistricted; annexed to Belknap Co. in this
move.

Back River. Situated on the
west side of Dover Neck,
above which it was called
Bellamy's Bank River. As a
district, it includes the
whole territory between Back
River itself and the Durham
line.

Barbadoes. District on the
present borders of Dover and
Madbury that comprised Barbadoes Marsh, Plain, Pond,
Spring and Woods.

Barnstead, Belknap Co. Formerly of Strafford Co., town

was granted 20 May 1727, an-
nexed to Belknap Co. in 1840.
Local landmarks are Barnstead
Parade Cemetery and Barnstead
Center Cemetery.

Barrington, Strafford Co.
Granted 10 May 1722, the town
was originally about 13 miles
long by 6-1/2 miles wide.
The western part of the town
was set off and became known
as Strafford, inc. 17 June
1820.

Beauty Hill. Situated n.e.
of Bodge's Pond, in the Two-
Mile Streak, Barrington.
Beauty Hill Road leads NNW
off of present-day Route 125.

Bellamy Bank River, aka Bell-
amine's Bank. Rises at Chesley's lower pond, lower Barrington and flows into Madbury; flows along the west
side of Dover Neck to empty
into the Piscataqua River.

Belmont, Belnap Co. Previously known as Upper Parish,

Belmont, cont.
Gilmanton inc. 29 June 1859; its name was changed to Belmont when it was inc. 24 Jun 1869.

Blind Will's Neck. At the s.w. part of Rochester near the Dover line, at or near marshes called "Long Marsh" and "Great Marsh."

Brookfield, Carroll Co. Originally a section of Middleton, set off and inc. 30 Dec 1794. Neighboring towns are East Wolfeboro and Wakefield.

Center Harbor, Belknap Co. Set off from New Hampton, inc. 7 Dec 1797, when it belonged to Strafford Co. It is situated in the lake district of Winnipesaukee and Squam Lakes.

Cochecho. Settlement in Dover around the lowest falls on the Cochecho river, as opposed to the settlement on Dover Neck. This is now Dover proper.

Colonial Period, 1641–1679. The towns of Exeter, Dover, Hampton and Portsmouth were under the jurisdiction of the Bay Colony of Massachusetts during this era. Citizens were governed by general laws of that colony and the terms observed. The union of the four New Hampshire towns with Massachusetts was enacted by law by the General Court 9 August 1641.

Dover Common. Land between Fresh Creek and the Cochecho River, set aside "forever" in 1675 for grazing of live-stock. As unimproved land in Dover became scarcer, shares of the Common became true assets.

Dover, Strafford Co. Settled in 1623, inc. as town of Dover in 1641 and as a city in 1855. It continues as the County Seat of Strafford Co. Old Dover included present-day Durham, Lee, Madbury, Newington, Rollingsford, and Somersworth. For date of incorporation on sister cities, see individual town.

Dover Neck. Strip of land two miles long and half a mile wide between Fore and Back Rivers to the main body of the Piscataqua. The first pioneers settled in this section.

Durham, Strafford Co. Town was originally known as a parish of Dover. It also went by the name of Oyster River Plantation. When town was inc. 15 May 1732, it adopted the name of Durham, home of many early Dover settlers.

Effingham, Carroll Co. Originally called Leavittstown, the town was granted 28 Jun 1749, inc. 18 Aug 1778. Town of Freedom was set off 16 Jun 1831; the town abuts Maine state line which separates Effingham from Parsonsfield, Maine.

Farmington, Strafford Co. Located on Cochecho River, it used to be called the "West Parish" of Rochester. Set off 1 Dec 1798, the name may have been derived from its farms and fertile land.

Freedom, Carroll Co. Originally known as North Effingham when inc. 16 Jun 1831; inc. as Freedom 6 Dec 1832.

Gerrish's Mills. Paul and Timothy Gerrish inherited two mills from their father Capt. John Gerrish who acquired exclusive water privileges on the Bellamy Bank River. One-sixteenth shares of their third mill located in Madbury, s.w. of Barbadoes Pond, were treated in land deeds as negotiable assets.

Gilford, Belknap Co. Formerly part of Gilmanton as part of Strafford Co. under the name of Gunstock Parish, it was inc. as Gilford 16 Jun 1812. The town contains Meredith Bridge Village and Lake Village.

Gilmanton, Belknap Co. Of old Strafford Co., the town was granted and inc. 20 May 1727. The first region settled was Lower Gilmanton. East Gilmanton contains Smith Meeting House, the first Congregational Church, a local landmark. The village of Gilmanton Iron Works was named for deposits of iron ore found in neighboring Suncook or Lougee Pond. The Center Village or Academy Village has been the social and literary center of the town, their Academy erected in 1796. Two villages, set off to become towns in their own right, were Gilford in 1812 and Belmont in 1869, both cited elsewhere.

Green Hill. Neighborhood adjacent to Toll End Road of East Barrington and near the Dover-Rochester head line. Situated in the Two-Mile Streak, it was one of the first areas of Barrington to be settled.

Greenland. A parish of old Dover lying on the western side, at the bottom of Great Bay on the Piscataqua River.

Haven's Hill, aka Rochester Hill. An area in Rochester on the main road from Dover to Norway Plains, around which the first settlers gathered. Norway Plains refered to the large sandy plain on which the city of Rochester now stands. Here were located the town's first cemetery for the early settlers and first meeting house as of 1731.

Horne's Woods. Known by this name since the early 1700s, they are in the heart of the Lubberland district below the present road from Durham village to Newmarket.

Lamprey River. There were many variations in the spelling of it: see also Lamprill, Lampereel, Lamprel. In 1652 it was declared to be the lawful boundary between Dover and Exeter; it crosses the Durham line where it unites with Piscassic River from New Market and empties into the Great Bay.

Lee, Strafford Co. Situated in south part of the county; formerly a part of Dover, it became an off-shoot of Durham, known as the Parish of Lee in 1766, and inc. as a town 16 Jan 1767. Several rivers criss-cross the town.

Littleworth. A district in Dover near the Madbury line between the Cochecho River and Barbadoes Pond, its name known as early as 1721. One highly-priced piece of real estate in this area was called "Littleworth" owned by James and Elizabeth Young before 1821. On Littleworth Road is located the John Young Cemetery.

Lubberland. The name given to the upper shore of Great Bay, south of Newmarket. It is situated below Packers Fall District, Durham, in itself a district of Durham.

Madbury, Strafford Co. Once a part of Dover, it was made a parish for religious purposes 31 May 1755; parish was made a town 26 May 1768. Curiously enough the town held no village center.

Meredith, Belknap Co. Known first as Palmer's Town, once part of Strafford Co., town was granted 31 Dec 1748, inc. 30 Dec 1768. A section was set off and inc. as Laconia on 14 Jul 1855; annexed to Belknap Co. in 1840.

Middleton, Strafford Co. Was granted 27 Apr 1749, inc. 4 Mar 1778. One section was severed to become known as Brookfield in 1794. Once it was considered the "head-lands" of greater Dover in 1750.

Milton, Strafford Co. Originally part of Rochester, this section was set off and inc. 11 June 1802; by 1858 a part of the town was annexed to Wakefield. Many of its residents came from Maine on the eastern side of Salmon River.

New Durham, Strafford Co. Granted as Cochecho Township 5 May 1749, and inc. by the name of New Durham 7 Dec 1762. The town was settled for the most part by residents of Durham, hence its name.

Moultonboro, Carroll Co. Granted 17 Nov 1763, inc. 27 Nov 1777. There are two villages, Moultonboro P.O. and Lakeview P.O.

Newfields, Rockingham Co. Name given to South Newmarket, inc. 27 June 1849, formerly a parish of Exeter; many Youngs relocated from here to neighboring town of Durham.

New Hampton, Belknap Co. It was first named "Moultonboro Addition" by grant of 24 Jan 1765; town inc. 27 Nov 1777. Center Harbor was set off from this town in 1797.

Newington, Rockingham Co. Originally known as Bloody Point settlement, inc. as a parish of old Dover 16 Jul 1713.

Ossipee, Carroll Co. Under the jurisdiction of Strafford Co. before 1840; present-day County Seat for Carroll Co. The town was inc. 22 Feb 1785. In Dec 1800, its southern section abutting northern Wolfeboro became known as the Wolfeboro Addition and then was absorbed into its neighbor town soon after.

Packer's Falls. Known by this name as early as 1718, it is a locality situated on both sides of Lamprey River, extending to Newmarket on its western side and to Lee on its northern side. A private Young cemetery is located here on David Davis farm.

Pine Grove Cemetery. Located between Oak Hill and the intersection of Routes 9 and 125, Two-Mile Streak, Barrington.

Pine Hill Cemetery. Public cemetery in Dover at the lower end of the city near the former Meeting House. One-1/2 acres were granted by the town fathers 29 Mar 1731 to establish the cemetery. Here the old settlers of Dover were buried. It has grown considerably larger according to Frost's Pine Hill Cemetery Records (1976).

Province Road. Often mentioned in old deeds as points of abutment. Today it is called Route 9, originating in Dover, running north and n.w. through Madbury and Barrington to merge with Route 202 in Northwood.

Rochester, Strafford Co. Inc. 10 May 1722, it was settled mainly by people of Dover. The western part of it became Farmington, inc. 1 Dec 1798. Milton was set off and inc. 11 June 1802.

Royal Province, 1680-1775. The four towns of Exeter, Dover, Hampton and Portsmouth, N.H. were taken from the jurisdiction of Massachusetts and inc. as a Royal Province in 1680, enduring up through 1775.

Rollingsford, Strafford Co. Was set off from Somersworth and inc. 3 July 1849.

Sanbornton, Belknap Co. Granted 31 Dec 1748, inc. by this spelling 1 Mar 1779.

Sandwich, Carroll Co. Inc. at same time of grant, 25 Oct 1763. There are two villages, Sandwich P.O. and North Sandwich P.O.

Somersworth, Strafford Co. First known as the parish of "Summersworth," it was set off from Dover, inc. 22 Apr 1754. One section by the name of Rollingsford was created in 1849. Forest Glade Cemetery is a local land mark.

State Government, 1784 to Present Day. From first Constitution enacted in 1784 to State Government formed in 1792, the state has been a federally constituted one, subject only to federal law and its own laws enacted for city, county and state.

Strafford, Strafford Co. The western part of Barrington was cut off and inc. 17 Jun 1820. The town includes the areas of Bow Lake and Crown Point. The latter was the first settlement of the town made before the Revolutionary War.

Strafford County. For full roster of townships within this county before 1840, see Introduction. After redistricting county lines in 1840

Strafford County, cont. thirteen towns remained: Barrinton, Dover, Durham, Farmington, Lee, Madbury, Middleton, Milton, New Durham, Rochester, Rollingsford, Somersworth, and Strafford.

Tamworth, Carroll Co. Originally part of Strafford Co., granted 14 Oct 1766. Parts of the town had been annexed from Sandwich and Ossipee; town lines were settled by 23 Jun 1859.

Tole End, aka Tolend. A district on the south side of the Cochecho River above the second or Tolend falls; also the name given to road often cited in deeds, stemming from Dover via Madbury into eastern Barrington.

Tuftonboro, Carroll Co. Once under jurisdiction of Strafford Co. Granted 11 Dec 1750, inc. 17 Dec 1795; named in honor of John Tufton Mason. Originally a township in Strafford Co., annexed to Carroll County in 1840. Melvin Village and Tuftonboro Center are P.O. addresses.

Two-Mile Streak, aka Two-Mile Strip, Barrington. Often mentioned in old deeds, the area was 2 miles in width and 6-1/2 miles in breadth. Head line of Lee, Madbury and Dover was the southern boundary. It was included in the original grant of Barrington in 1722 for the inducement of iron-ore production badly needed at that time. It was hoped that the area would be settled by its workers. The area drew pioneers from all over, but most of its set-

tlers came from old Dover and Portsmouth.

Wakefield, Carroll Co. Under jurisdiction of Strafford Co., it was annexed to Carroll Co. in 1840. Township was granted 27 Apr 1749. Once known as East Town by old land deeds, it was inc. 30 Aug 1774. Most of its earliest settlers came from Dover and Somersworth. The town includes the villages of Sanbornville, Union and the Pine River settlement in North Wakefield. The section north of Province Road was annexed to Effingham in 1820.

Wolfeboro, Carroll Co. Town charter was granted 5 Oct 1759. Some of those who helped to settle Wolfeboro were former residents of Durham and Newfields.

Wolfeboro Addition, Carroll Co. Formerly under jurisdiction of Strafford Co. A portion of Ossipee Gore was annexed to Wolfeboro 4 Dec 1800, and named "Wolfeboro Addition." Merrill's Carroll Co., p282, gives a graphic description of the "Addition": "It extended the n.e. line of the town [of Wolfeboro] one mile and 70 rods to North Wakefield village, then ran n.w. three miles and 230 rods, where there was a setoff of 83 rods towards Wolfeboro; then the n.w. line continued 1-3/4." In the Addition, there were five lots, two of which held 500 acres each.

INTRODUCTION

HISTORIC STRAFFORD COUNTY, NEW HAMPSHIRE PRE 1840

Scope of Research. A concerted effort was made over a five-year period to search out any and all references to Youngs from among the towns which fell under the jurisdiction of Strafford County, New Hampshire before the annexations of 1840. The federal census returns from 1790 on served as a checklist on the towns which held Young inhabitants. This produced findings from among thirty townships after eliminating a handful of towns whose returns did not pertain. All avenues of research were systematically sought out for state, county and town. All types of resource materials, both primary and secondary, were researched: land deeds and probate papers, both provincial and county; land grants and charters; State vital records on births, brides, marriages and deaths; town and county histories; town records; cemetery records; military and pension records; census records from 1732 up through 1900; county maps; gazetteers; family histories on allied families; and state sources for research. See bibliography for complete listing.

Thirty Townships Defined. The townships under consideration became the focus of research for the periods both before and after the annexations of 1840 which created Belknap and Carroll Counties. After county lines were redrawn in 1840 thirteen towns remained in Strafford County: Barrington, Dover, Durham, Farmington, Lee, Madbury, Middleton, Milton, New Durham, Rochester, Rollingsford, Somersworth and Strafford. Belknap County after annexations in 1840 contained eight towns all told from the original thirty. Seven of the eight were drawn from the 1850 federal census: Alton, Barnstead, Gilford, Gilmanton, Meredith, New Hampton and Sanbornton. The eighth town, Upper Gilmanton, would emerge on the 1860 census for this county, only to have its name changed to Belmont per the 1870 census. Carroll County, as drawn from the 1850 federal census after annexation, contained ten of the original thirty towns: Brookfield, Effingham, Freedom, Moultonboro, Ossipee, Sandwich, Tamworth, Tuftonboro, Wakefield and Wolfeboro.

See topography for dates of incorporation, local land marks, and matters of history. See also appendix for maps of present-day Strafford County, Belknap County and Carroll County which depict the thirty towns originally of old Strafford County containing Youngs.

METHODS OF APPROACH TO RESEARCH

The Whole Family Approach. One statistic from the late 1970s on the family name of Young tells us it is the eleventh most common name in the United States. That would give anyone much pause for thought in undertaking a biographical dictionary on one family name. The requirement was clearly spelled out according to Cameron Allen, genealogist and lecturer at the August 1988 Federation of Genealogical Societies Conference in Boston under the auspices of the New England Historic Genealogical Society. Mr. Allen's talk was entitled "Resolving Discrepancies: Applying Principles of Genealogical Evidence" [Recording #T-38]. Mr. Allen advised that when researching one family name and especially one that is very common, "the whole family approach will have to be taken, testing out anyone bearing the name so that safer conclusions can be made from the preponderance of evidence....The collection of facts becomes very significant." Using this approach one family unit could be traced from one community to another after cross-checking for similarities and crucial differences. A measure of reliance and trust can thus be built up from the findings obtained from the preponderance of evidence.

"Preliminary Materials" Approach. Influenced by the term "preliminary materials" as coined by Freemont Rider in his biographical dictionary on the Rider family cited above, I felt that his approach should also be considered to obtain a balanced picture. According to Mr. Rider, the basic data presented by his main entries were to be considered as "preliminary." This allowed for the fact that family records could still be lacking on many a family unit. It admits that certain problem areas had to be left unresolved with the hope that the reader may be able to provide additional information on that branch from family bibles and personal papers. His approach was adopted. In truth this relieved me of the necessity of forcing things to fit just so. Further along when differences of opinion cropped up with other authorities, both sides of the issue were expressed, yielding respect of course for the other's point of view. Conclusions were often expressed in such terms as "it is believed," "most likely," "more than likely," "probably," and so on, which should leave the reader no doubt as to the measure of certitude. And when conflicting evidence existed, variants of records were given.

FRAMEWORK FOR BIOGRAPHICAL DICTIONARY

Criteria on Main Entries. It is implicit that place or location is the State of New Hampshire, unless otherwise noted. A male Young earned a main entry when he fell into one or more of the following categories: native son, proprietor, land owner, listed head of family or taxpayer, married man, soldier or sailor. A female Young had her own entry when these conditions were met: a married daughter provided that date of marriage was known or a widow of a male Young who was not identified. Data on wife and allied family was contained under the husband's entry, being fully cross-indexed between maiden and married name of Young. Main entries were given for those cases when only dates of birth or death were known. An exception to the rule on unmarried children was made when extensive documents were found for them. In this situation it was felt a main entry was warranted. Entries were confined to births from 1653-1870. Data found on children born after 1870 was entered whenever possible under the parents' entry, but no effort was made to trace further.

Formula For Determining Age When Not Known. Some rule of thumb had to be used to assign year of birth, however arbitrary the system may be, when vital records were lacking. Take for instance old marriage records and census returns up to 1840. For generations it has been traditional wisdom that the male married around the age of 25 and the female at the age of 20 [give or take a few years]. Thus if a couple married in 1830, the male's year of birth would be set at circa 1805, the female, at circa 1810. With respect to census returns between 1790-1840 when age of head of household was merely bracketed, the year of birth given a male in the 40-50 year group, for example, was set at circa 1795. Land deeds helped in determining rough approximations of ages. Generally speaking a male would become a man of means or property usually when in full adulthood, age at least 30-35 years. Exceptions to this rule were found in land deeds which stated that the purchaser was a minor, or had just reached the age of 21. This statistical system allowed time for the parent figure to settle property upon the son as was so often the case upon the son's marriage or time for the parent figure to settle property upon his own retirement. It also allowed time for the young man to build up a stake when credit was almost non-existent. If the date of signing on a land deed was given as 25 Jul 1825 for a Young principal, then lacking other data, year of birth was given as circa 1790. Guardianship papers on minor children proved somewhat easier in determining age inasmuch as probate papers set forth age of minors by brackets: under the age of seven, or either under or over the age of fourteen.

Entry, Its Order and Form. A main entry is presented first in alphabetical order, then by sequence of birth and then, all things being equal, by name of town, and occasionally, by date of marriage. It is to be noted that titles such as Jr., 2nd, II, 3rd, Gent., Ens. and so on were recorded after the christian name by noting "also known as" or "aka." Inasmuch as titles were deemed to be of a transitory nature, they were not a factor either in the alphabetical listings of entries or Index. Uniformity of entry was stressed, to contain in this order the following elements whenever known: vital records on male or female entry, vital records on spouse, findings from all other reference sources, listings

3

of children with place and dates of birth, and lastly, full documentation with ready reference to entries under bibliography. For instance, NH State Papers, V28, p101; Merrill's Carroll Co., p204; or Twombly's Wakefield Cem., TMs.

On Finding Ancestors Or Descendants Using The "Rider Trace System" of Cross-Indexing. Dates of birth and parentage were fully cross-indexed whenever known according to Freemont Rider's "trace system." As an adaptation to this trace system, the sign (+) was added under the parents' entry beside the names of married sons who carried on the family line and daughters by married name, indicating that these children had entries of their own. This system allows the reader to follow the lineage either backward or downward. In scrolling backward to the main entry on the father per name and date of birth, the father's parentage will be found, and so on. In reverse order, identification of the married children by name+ and date of birth enables the reader to scroll downward to their main entries and following generations. Lineage extends as far back or as far forward as information is available.

Cross-Referencing of Major Documents. To avoid duplication of effort citations of land deeds between Young grantors and Young grantees have been cross-referenced only by date of signing and recording, holding full citation of county deed and witnesses to the grantor. Wills are cross-referenced between testator and heirs-at-law as to date of signing and date of probate, reserving complete terms of will, citation and names of witnesses to the testator. Probate papers such as guardianships, petitions and letters of administration were cross-referenced only with interested parties by dates of signing and approval, saving citation and names of witnesses to the principal Young. Census returns were only cited under the father's or widowed mother's entry.

DISCOVERIES OF INDEPENDENT BRANCHES

Identities of Pioneers and Progenitors of the Earliest Towns From 1653-1785. Land deeds and probate papers were mainly instrumental in providing evidence of a dozen or more independent branches whose progenitors came primarily from England, and as a close second, from Scotland, during the seventeenth and eighteenth centuries. Emigrants during the nineteenth century stemmed from Ireland and Canada. From the preponderance of evidence it was possible to identify nine progenitors of independent branches and a handful of pioneers whose branches may no longer be extant. They settled by the late seventeenth century up through the mid-eighteenth century in the towns of Barnstead, Dover, Durham, Gilmanton, Parish of Madbury, Barrington and Rochester.

Barnstead: The earliest Young to settle here was Jonathan [b 1756] of Kingston who became progenitor. He and wife Sarah (Clifford) Young had three sons who headed respective branches.

Barrington: Two independent branches of Youngs were found here. The first was headed by Ebenezer Young of Newington [born 1724] and wife Elizabeth (Bickford) Young. Their descendants became farmers and pillars of the community headed by Isaac [b 1754] and his two wives. The other progenitor was James Young of Scotland [b ca 1720] who came to Barrington via Philadelphia. His son William [b 1749] and wife Charity (Howe) Young established a branch here known for its affluence and prestige down through the generations.

Dover: There were three known progenitors. The earliest branch was headed by Thomas Young, an indentured servant born 1653, who settled on Dover Neck in the 1680s and became freeman. His descendants from the principal branch headed by Jonathan and Abigail (Hanson) Young of Cochecho Parish, later to be known for its inherited wealth, settled in Dover, Madbury, Durham and Rochester. The second independent branch was headed by Benjamin Young [b ca 1730], who moved in the early 1750s to that section of Barrington which became Strafford; his son Winthrop [b 1753] was one of the pioneers of the town of Canterbury. Son Jonathan [b 1761] established an individual branch in Strafford, part of which relocated in Farmington by the 1840s. The third independent branch was headed by Capt. Thomas Young [b 1730s] whose background was unknown. His five sons helped to carry on the family line in Ossipee, Wakefield, Farmington and Dover.

Durham: Joseph [b 1726], son of Thomas and Sarah (Folsom) Young of Salisbury, Mass. and New Market, N.H., first wife Anna (Folsom) Young and second wife Mary (Foss) Young headed a prolific independent branch which is extant today. Joseph and Mary settled in Durham on or about 1760 and eight sons carried on the family name in Strafford County. Younger sons Henry [b 1773] and William [b 1777] remained in Durham. The other six sons settled after the Revolutionary War in Ossipee, Tuftonboro, Wakefield, Wolfeboro Addition, and Wolfeboro. One other distinct branch at Oyster River was headed by Rowland Young Jr. [b ca 1648], whose wife was Susannah (Matthews) Young. Their stay at Oyster River was brief. They later established their home in York, York County, Maine.

Gilmanton: Dudley Young of Kingston was the earliest of the Youngs to settle here circa 1762, becoming head of an independent branch with five sons to carry on the family line. One pioneer was Joseph of Kingston [b 1749], whose wife was Anna (Folsom) Young (not be confused with namesakes from Durham). They settled here by 1770. Their one grown son died by 1797; however there were married daughters.

Parish of Madbury: The earliest of the Young pioneers of this town was Eleazer [b 1691], son of Thomas Young of Dover Neck mentioned above. He and wife Alice (Watson) Young were progenitors of many generations headed by son Solomon [b ca 1730] and wife Kezia (Hanson) Young. A cousin of Solomon, Nathaniel [b 1720], son of Jonathan and Abigail (Hanson) Young, and wife Mary (Kimball) Young established their home here. Descendants of their branch were identifiable in the 1850s.

Rochester: One pioneer was Jonathan Young Jr., son of Jonathan and Abigail (Hanson) Young cited above; he received acreage on Blind Will's Neck from his father. An independent branch was headed by Thomas and Anna (Roberts) Young who made their home on or near Haven's Hill in the 1750s. Son James [b 1758] and wife Mary (Kimball) Young became pioneer settlers in Wakefield.

Progenitors of the Post-Revolutionary War Period. There were four independent branches of the Youngs from this post-revolutionary war period. In addition to these there were offshoots of the first settlers mentioned above who helped in the aftermath of the Revolutionary War to settle the towns of Alton, Effingham, Ossipee, Wakefield, Tuftonboro, Wolfeboro and Wolfeboro Addition. Since their numbers were legion, it was deemed feasible to list only the independent heads of these four branches who settled in the above-mentioned towns.

Effingham: Timothy [b 1776] of York, York County, Maine was the earliest of the Youngs to settle here circa 1796 and became progenitor. His parents Jonathan and Mercy came from England. Son Jonathan [b 1805] carried on the family line.

Upper Gilmanton: Two independent branches of Youngs were discernible in this area that later was called Belmont. The progenitor of the first branch was Eleazer [b 1757] of Barrington and wife Hannah (Bailey) Young who settled here circa 1790. Son Bailey and wife Polly (Rundlet) Young headed a family branch. The second progenitor of this town was Joseph [b 1760], of Kingston, whose wife was Betsey (Shaw) Young. They settled here at least by 1787. Six sons carried on the family line as residents of this town.

Ossipee: There were as many as three branches of Youngs here, and ironically the settlers were all known by the name of John Young. Only John the Highlander [b ca 1755] of Scotland, name of wife not known, headed an independent branch after receiving a grant of land here in 1785. Son John C. Young continued the Ossipee branch.

BIOGRAPHICAL DICTIONARY OF THE YOUNGS (BORN 1653-1870) FROM TOWNS UNDER THE JURISDICTION OF STRAFFORD COUNTY, NEW HAMPSHIRE BEFORE 1840

AARON, b 30 Nov 1793, Barrington, s/o William and Charity (Howe) Young, d testate, widower, 4 Apr 1854, native town; m 1816, Barrington, Lydia Daniels [b 30 Mar 1790, Barrington, d/o Clement and Esther (Danielson) Daniels, d 11 Sep 1847, home town]. Aaron was listed as head of household in Barrington from 1830-1850, in the latter year a widower. In 1840 his age was 40-50, as was his spouse; members of family were four males between the ages of 5-20, and two females age 20-30. Members of household in 1850 were sons Jacob D., Aaron Jr., and Andrew H., also Eliza Henderson, age 26 [b 1824]. He was chosen to represent Barrington in the New Hampshire State Legislature and served on the town board as Selectman. He and his family were affiliated with the Congregational Church. The extensive properties he held in Barrington and Dover were devised to his four sons by will drawn 5 Mar 1850, codicil dated 2 Dec 1850, proved 2 May 1854, with sons Jacob D. and Andrew H. named as Co-Execs. and residuary legatees; witnesses Solomon Pearl, John D. Pierce and Sarah Robinson [Strafford Co. Probate 66:209]. His Co-Execs. posted bond of $6,000.00 on day of probate with sureties Elijah Austin of Madbury and William H. Young of Barrington [Strafford Co. Probate 68:61].

Aaron's estate in Barrington included the Waldron lot, David Hall lot, Wingate lot, and Broke aka Brock lot with all the buildings; these properties were devised equally to sons Jacob D. and Andrew H. An individual bequest to eldest son Jacob D. was the Daniels lot adjoining lands of John Ricker and William H. Young on the north side of the long bridge road in Barrington; to Andrew H. he gave exclusively all the land called the Fowler field in Barrington which he bought from the heirs of Jonathan Young and Nicholas Brock, whose wives in turn received this parcel of land from Stephen Young of Barrington; and also devised to Andrew H. the Kingman lot of ten acres, the Winkley lot of eight acres, the Daniels lot of about two acres and the Woodman lot located in Barrington owned by himself, Jonathan Young and Solomon Pearl, as well as his share in the Meserve sawmill. Sons Aaron Jr. and George W. were to receive moieties of the house and lot he owned in Dover at the corner of Atkinson and St. Thomas Streets. Settlements of $100.00 were to be made by each of his four sons upon each of his two daughters, Esther, wife of

John S. Buzzell, and Sophia A., wife of George Hanson. A codicil to Aaron's will, appended 2 Dec 1850, instructed that although he had already deeded to son Andrew the one-half of his homestead prior to probate, all the terms of his will still held good "as if the deed had not been given." Aaron and Lydia were buried at Pine Grove Cemetery, Barrington.

    Ch. b Barrington: Esther Daniels+ (Young) Buzzell, b 12 May 1817; Sophia Abigail+ (Young) Hanson, b 4 Feb 1820; Jacob Daniels+, b 28 Dec 1823; Aaron George+, b 16 Jun 1827, twin; Andrew Huckins+, b 16 Jun 1827, twin; and George William+, b 24 Jul 1830. (Ham Gen., p25,43,65; NHVR-Births, Deaths; Barrington Graveyards, Lot 12-8W, p132,133; Census Strafford Co., 1830, p28; 1840, p479; 1850, p523; Biog. Review, XXI, p89; Wiggin's Barrington, p102)

    AARON, b 12 Jan 1794, Barnstead, s/o Jonathan and Sarah (Clifford) Young of Kingston, alive 1830, home town; m 8 Dec 1816, Barnstead, Betsey Bickford [b ca 1795, Barnstead, d 1843, buried at old Beauty Hill Cemetery, home town]. When his father died in 1807, Aaron was a minor under the age of fourteen. In that year he was made the ward of David Edgerly Esq. of Gilmanton. After his mother's dower rights were set off, he received a one-third share of Lots 88 and 89, 2nd Div. in Barnstead, sharing equally with his two brothers. Aaron was first listed as head of household in Barnstead in 1830 under the age of 40, with family of spouse, two sons and four daughters. Ch. b Barnstead: Lucy Walker, b 8 Jul 1817; Sarah Ann, b 11 Feb 1819; Aaron George+, b 3 Apr 1821; Mary Elizabeth, b 8 Mar 1828. (Census Strafford Co., 1830, p15; NHVR-Births, Marr; LDS I.G.I. BR; Merrill's Barnstead, p330)

    AARON B., b 1815, Gilmanton, s/o Dudley and Sally (Jacobs) Young, merchant, d 10 Sep 1883, Concord; m2 8 Feb 1839, Loudon, Louisa Lovering [b 1815, res. of Loudon, alive 1860, Gilmanton]. Aaron B. was named son and heir of Dudley Young of Gilmanton by his will signed 20 Jun, proved 21 Jul 1863. Aaron was resident of Lowell, MA up through 1854. By 1860 he and second wife Louise lived in Gilmanton with household containing Aaron's three daughters Josephine, Laura P., and Florence A., and teenager Charles Mason [b 1844, MA]. Ch. b MA by first wife: Josephine, b 1830. Ch. b Lowell, MA by Louisa: Laura A., b 31 Aug 1843; Florence A., b 1854. (Census Belknap Co., 1860, p231; Biog. Review, XXI, p354,355; NHVR-Deaths, Marr; LDS I.G.I. VR of MA)

    AARON G., b Jul 1861, Wakefield, s/o James C. and Rosemandel (Gill) Young, d 1938, Wakefield; m ca 1895, Wakefield, Celia F. Lilley [b Mar 1879, Stoneham, MA, alive 1900, Wakefield]. Aaron and wife lived in Wakefield as of 1900; child at home, Joseph, age 2. By deed of 7 Sep, rec'd 21 Sep 1899, Aaron bought out the family homestead in Wakefield from his widowed mother Rosemandel. Aaron was buried at the Aaron Young Cemetery, Pray Hill Road, Wakefield. Ch. b MA: Joseph B., b Jun 1897, not traced further. (Twombly's Wakefield Cem., TMs; 1900 Soundex)

AARON GEORGE, b 3 Apr 1821, Barnstead, s/o Aaron and
Betsey (Bickford) Young, d testate pre 17 Apr 1894, Laconia;
m ca 1860, poss. Meredith, Priscilla aka Purcilla F. Boardman
[b 1830, Meredith, alive 1900, Laconia]. In 1859 his homestead farm was Lot 86, 2nd Div., Barnstead, which had been
passed from father to son ever since grandparents Jonathan and
Sarah (Clifford) Young of Kingston purchased it circa 1783.
Aaron George and Priscilla lived in Laconia as early as 1886
according to his will drawn up 7 Dec 1886, proved 17 Apr 1894;
he named son Fred A. as sole Exec.; witnesses Stephen Vittum,
Frank J. Brown, Walter S. Peaslee [Belknap Co. Probate #5233].
He devised to wife Priscilla all his personal estate for ever,
and all real estate for her natural life. These bequests were
made to children: son George G., $1.00; daughter Sarah E.
Sackett, $1.00; sons Fred A. and Erle B., each a one-half
share of the family homestead in Barnstead upon the remarriage
or death of their mother. In 1900 Priscilla, widow, and son
Earl B. were listed on the 1900 census returns for Laconia;
the census listed her d-o-b as June 1839. Ch. b Barnstead:
George G., b ca 1860, alive 1886, Laconia; Sarah E. (Young)
Sackett, b 1860s, alive 1886, Laconia; Fred A.+, b Aug 1866;
and Earl B., b 3 Jun 1878, alive 1886, Laconia. (NHVR-Marr,
Births; Merrill's Barnstead, p330; 1900 Soundex)

    AARON GEORGE, b 16 Jun 1827, Barrington, twin, s/o Aaron
and Lydia (Daniels) Young, d 23 Dec 1903, Portsmouth; m 25 Apr
1853, Manchester, Louisa Blaisdell Page aka Paige [b 2 Jul
1831, Barrington, d/o Osgood and Martha (   ) Page, d 14 Mar
1893, Manchester]. Aaron's legacy from his father was a
one-half share of a house and lot in Dover by his father's
will signed 2 Dec 1850, proved 2 May 1854. In the early 1850s
he moved to Manchester; by the 1870s, Aaron and family resided
in Portsmouth where he worked for the Custom House and later
for the Internal Revenue Service, a career man up to the time
of his death. The 1900 census listed Aaron as resident of
Portsmouth; members of household were daughter Alice R., son
Philip and domestic Christine McDonald [b July 1876, Nova
Scotia]. Aaron, wife and children were buried at Pine Hill
Cemetery, Dover. Ch. b Manchester: Alice Richardson, b 1 Mar
1858, d 19 Dec 1904, Portsmouth. Ch. b Portsmouth: Philip,
b 16 Nov 1874, twin, d 20 Jun 1946, Dover; and Aaron Jr., b
16 Nov 1874, twin. (NHVR-Births; Ham Gen., p43,59; Frost's
Dover Cem., V1, #535; LDS I.G.I. BR; N.H. Men, p286; 1900
Soundex)

    AARON W., b Feb 1846, Alton, s/o Henry and Sarah (Witham)
Young, shoemaker, widower pre 1882, alive 1900, home town; m1
ca 1850, Alton, Martha (   ) [b 1850, of Alton, d pre 1882,
same town]; m2 25 Dec 1882, Gilmanton, Lulla aka Luella
(Stevens) Gilkerson, divorced [b Aug 1853, Stannard, VT, d/o
George and Naomi (   ) Stevens, alive 1900, Alton]. In 1860
he lived with his parents in Alton at age 15. By 1870 Aaron
and first wife Martha lived by themselves in Alton where he
worked for a shoe factory; no known children. In 1900 he and

second wife Lulla made their home in Alton; members of household were her three sons by a previous marriage. It should be noted that NHVR-Marr gave his d-o-b as 1835. Ch. b VI by Luella's first marriage: Harry Gilkerson, b Sep 1878; William H. Gilkerson, b Aug 1882; and Ernest L. Gilkerson, b Jul 1890. (Census Belknap Co., 1870, p28; 1900 Soundex; NHVR-Marr)

ABBIE, b ca 1860, Wakefield, m 1879, Wakefield, John N. Glidden [b ca 1860, Wakefield, s/o Jerome A. Glidden, gr.s/o Abigail (Young) Glidden and John H. Glidden]. (NHVR-Brides)

ABBY M., b 10 May 1858, Ossipee, youngest d/o Thomas C. and Abigail (Wiggin) Young of Wolfeboro; m 26 Oct 1890, Wolfeboro, Charles G. Nute [b ca 1855, Wolfeboro]. Abby M. was named the sole legatee of the estate of her sister Martha H. Young of Ossipee by Martha's will drawn 6 Feb 1888, proved 5 Mar 1889. Since Abby M. was still single at time Martha's will was proved, she received the full bequest left to her; for further details see parents' entry. (NHVR-Brides; Wiggin Gen., p176)

ABIAL, b Feb 1833, ME, s/o Daniel and Betsey (Cook) Young of Wakefield, d 1909 Dover, shoemaker; m ca 1860, Sarah F. (   ) [b Jul 1832, of Wakefield, d 1913, Dover]. Abial lived with parents in 1850 in Wakefield. He and wife Sarah lived alone in Durham from 1860-1900. No known children. Abial and Sarah were buried at Pine Hill Cemetery, Dover. (Census Strafford Co., 1860, p574; 1900 Soundex; Frost's Dover Cem., V1, Plot #658)

ABIGAIL, b 15 Sep 1723, Dover, d/o Jonathan and Abigail (Hanson) Young, d 1 Dec 1804, Barrington; m ca 1747, Benjamin Hayes [b 12 Mar 1723/24, Dover, s/o Peter and Sarah (Wingate) Hayes, d 14 Apr 1797, Barrington]. Abigail was baptized with parents and siblings at First Church, Dover on 31 Jan 1742, upon which occasion they were blessed by "owning the covenant." She was named as heir and known by her married name of Hayes in Jonathan's will drawn 1 Jul 1752, proved 29 Sep 1756. She and husband Benjamin lived in Barrington on the 100 acres which he received by deed of gift from his father in 1746. In 1764 Benjamin Hayes bought Lot 108, 1st Div., at Blind Will's Neck, for 5,000 pounds lawful money [Hayes Gen., V1, p74-76]. This lot was made a gift to son Joseph Hayes who would later marry first cousin Abigail Young. Abigail was the daughter of Nathaniel Young, brother to this subject entry. Widow Abigail Hayes of Barrington, sister and one of many heirs of Isaac Young of Dover, quitclaimed on date of 14 Apr, rec'd 8 Feb 1802, all rights in a small property on the "easterly side of the Main road from Dover Meeting House to Portsmouth," which had originally been owned by Isaac Young late of Dover [cited by Hayes Gen. above]. Abigail and spouse were buried at the Hayes family plot, Pine Grove Cemetery, Barrington. Ch. b Barrington: Joseph Hayes, b 1748; Sarah Hayes Young [see husband Peter Young of Barrington], bp 14 Feb 1751, twin; Ebenezer Hayes, bp 14 Feb 1751, twin, prob. d.y.; Andrew Hayes, b 2 Jan 1757. These four children were not mentioned in their father's will: Benjamin Hussey Hayes, Elizabeth Hayes, Rachel Hayes, and Job Hayes. (Heritage's Dover VR, p23,24, 148; Adam's Madbury, n.p.; Barrington Graveyards, p48)

ABIGAIL, bp 23 Oct 1757, Madbury, d/o Nathaniel and Mary (Kimball) Young, d 12 Nov 1840, Rochester; m 1775, Joseph Hayes, first cousin [b 1748, Barrington, s/o Benjamin and Abigail (Young) Hayes, d pre 7 Feb 1817, Rochester]. Abigail was named as single daughter and heir of her father Nathaniel by his will signed 29 Jan, proved 26 May 1762. In 1790 Joseph Hayes was head of household in Rochester in that section that became Milton with family consisting of one male over 16 years, three males under 16, and five females. For disposition of Abigail Hayes' share in the estate of Isaac Young of Dover, see Ezra Young [brother] of Dover. Joseph, Abigail and ten children resided on 80 acres at Blind Will's Neck, Rochester, Lot 108, 1st Div., which Joseph's father Benjamin deeded to him prior to Benjamin's will of 3 May 1797. This land was quite near the Dover line between the Isinglass and Cochecho Rivers [Hayes Gen., V1, p75,132]. Ch. b Rochester: Nathaniel Hayes, b 15 Mar 1776; Benjamin Hayes, b 11 Jan 1778; Abigail Hayes, b 23 Apr 1782, twin; Mary Hayes, b 23 Apr 1782, twin, d 2 Apr 1864, age 82; Sarah Hayes, b 21 Feb 1785; David Hayes, b 28 May 1787; Elizabeth Hayes, b 20 Apr 1790; Susan Hayes, b 9 Dec 1792; James Young Hayes, b 29 May 1797; and John Adams Hayes, b 11 Mar 1801. (Census Strafford Co., 1790, p97; Adam's Madbury, n.p.; NHVR-Births, Deaths)

ABIGAIL, b 1760s, Barrington, d/o Ebenezer and Elizabeth (Bickford) Young; m Feb 1783, Madbury, Eleazer Cate [b ca 1750, Barrington]. Abigail was named daughter and heir, known by her married name of Cate, in Ebenezer's will written 6 May, proved 21 Jun 1786. (NHVR-Brides)

ABIGAIL, b ca 1760, Kingston, d/o Dudley Young; m 5 Jan 1789, Belmont [Upper Gilmanton], John Bond [b ca 1770, Gilmanton]. She was known by her married name of Abigail Bond in the will of her father Dudley, signed 20 May 1801, proved 10 May 1803. (NHVR-Brides)

ABIGAIL, b 1780, of Dover in 1850, age 70, single, lived at boarding house. (Census Strafford Co., 1850, p158)

ABIGAIL, b 3 Mar 1783, Barrington, d/o David and Abigail (Foss) Young, d 11 Oct 1818, home town; m 26 Nov 1799, Barrington, Joshua Otis [b 31 Jan 1773, Barrington, s/o Elder Micajah and Sarah (Foss) Otis, d 18 Jul 1839, native town]. Elder Micajah Otis was b 1747, d 20 May 1821, age 74, Barrington; he was presiding minister at their wedding; spouse Sarah (Foss) Otis was b 1748, d 20 Jan 1827, same town. Both Abigail and Joshua were buried at the Otis family plot, Pine Grove Cemetery, Barrington. Ch. b Barrington 1800s: Charlotte Otis; Polly Otis; Matilda Otis; Eliza Otis; Abigail Otis; Elmira Otis; and Lavina Otis. (Otis Gen., **Reg.** 5:218; Barrington TR, V6, p49; NHVR-Brides; Barrington Graveyards, p62)

ABIGAIL, b 1784, of Dover; in 1860 she lived with the Hawkins family in Dover, Ward 3. (Census Strafford Co., 1860, p709)

ABIGAIL, b ca 1790, Barrington; m 18 Dec 1813, Barrington, Daniel Howard [b ca 1785, Barrington]. (Hammond's Barrington TR, p35)

ABIGAIL, b 1808, Barrington, d/o Isaac and Deborah (Killey) Young, d 11 Nov 1854, age 46-2-12, Strafford; m 29 Jul 1835, Strafford, Asa Caverly [b ca 1805, Strafford]; married at Freewill Baptist Church, Strafford. Abigail, single, was to receive a marriage portion of $50.00 per her father's will of 8 Sep 1826, proved 19 Apr 1827. She was also a legatee of her sister Lucy's will drawn 30 Dec 1846, proved 2 Feb 1847. Abigail was buried at the Isaac Young family plot, Pine Grove Cemetery, Barrington. (Barrington Graveyards, p90; NHVR-Brides; Strafford Marr, **Reg.** 76:38)

ABIGAIL, b ca 1815, Dover, m 9 Sep 1835, Dover, John Gillpatrick [b ca 1805, of Dover]. (NHVR-Brides; Heritage's Dover VR, p101)

ABIGAIL, b 1826, Wakefield, d/o James C. and Ruth ( ) Young, alive 1870, Wakefield; m 17 Mar 1846, Wolfeboro, John H. Glidden [b 1826, Effingham, alive 1870, Wakefield]. Abigail and John raised a large family in Wakefield, ten children listed on both census returns for 1860 and 1870. Ch. b Wakefield: Clarence A. Glidden, b 1844; Charles L. Glidden, b 1845; Julius A. Glidden, twin, b 1846; Jerome A. Glidden, twin, b 1846; Jane A. Glidden, b 1848; Hattie S. Glidden, b 1852; Elicia A. aka Lizzie Glidden, b 30 Jun 1860; Loren J. Glidden, b 1863, m 1983, Wakefield; Sarah Glidden, b 1866; and Eugene E. Glidden, b Aug 1869, m1 1890, m2 1895, Wakefield. (Census Carroll Co., 1860, p576; 1870, p428; NHVR-Brides)

ABNER, b 1700s, of Dover Neck, d 1745 Dover; m ca 1728, Sarah ( ) [b ca 1708, of Dover]. Abner received a land grant of a one-third full share of Lot 88, Dover by vote of the legislature 8 Jul 1734. He was of Somersworth when he sold by deed signed 18 Mar 1735, rec'd 8 Apr 1737, 10 acres of Common Lands, Dover, Lot 88, 1st Div., to Samuel Walton of Somersworth, land originally given Abner Young by Town of Dover, price 30 pounds bills of credit; no dower rights were involved; witnesses Job Clements, Joseph Hanson Jr. [NH Prov. Deed 22:392]. In 1741 Abner was listed as taxpayer of Dover Parish, rated for 7 shillings-4 pence, sums collectively gathered mostly for the support of the town minister. Correspondence between Mrs. May Jarvis and Charles Wesley Tibbetts Esq., collaborators on the Tibbetts genealogy (1937), spoke of Abner Young: under "An Acct of Powder money rec'd by Theodore Atkinson according to an act of the General Assembly In May 1727," said Atkinson sold gunpowder to thirty-seven persons [presumably storekeepers], Abner Young listed as one of them; the quantity of gunpowder he received "came to 10.10 or about fifty-two dollars worth [as rated in 1937]." They believed that Laurana† aka Lurana Young who married William

Tibbetts of Dover Neck was the daughter of Abner Young; she was b ca 1730, Dover Neck. (NHVR-Deaths; NH State Papers, V24, p697,698; Tibbetts Gen., TMs, p281-283)

ACANTHUS aka Icanthus, b 1815, of Portsmouth, d 30 Jun 1877, Barnstead, farmer; m ca 1840, Harriet Nutter [b 1818, of Portsmouth, d 28 Apr 1882, Barnstead]. He and Harriet were residents of Barnstead from 1860-1870. In 1860 they lived alone; in 1870, member of family was child Hattie, age 8 [b 1862]. Merrill's Barnstead, p329, stated "Icanthus lived in the Knowles farm over on the Herndon corner in 1856." Admin. Papers on his estate in Barnstead were filed by widow Harriet N. Young on date of 11 Oct 1877; approved same date [Belknap Co. Probate #3180]. Icanthus and spouse were buried at the old Parade Cemetery, North Barnstead. (Barnstead Cemeteries, p10; Census Belknap Co., 1860, p335; 1870, p7)

ADALINE, b ca 1820, of Dover, m 11 Oct 1840, Dover, Ephraim Lord [b ca 1815, of same town]. (NHVR-Brides)

ADDIE B., b 1857, Gilmanton, d/o James H. and Abigail (Barker) Young; m 29 May 1882, Gilmanton, Ralph W. Osborn [b ca 1855, of Farmington]. (NHVR-Brides)

ADDIE C., b ca 1860, New Market, d/o Joseph Young of Dover [no main entry]; m 26 Jan 1879, Dover, George P. Burleigh [b ca 1855, of Dover]. (NHVR-Brides)

ADDIE F., b 1860s, Barnstead, d/o David L. and Annie (Aikens) Young; m 12 Oct 1889, Barnstead, George M. Bunker [b ca 1865, of same town]. (NHVR-Brides)

ADDIE R., b 1851, New Durham, d/o Jonathan B. and Hannah D. (Stevens) Young; m 17 Nov 1867, New Durham, George H. Leighton [b ca 1850, of same town]. (NHVR-Brides; New Durham VR, p55)

ADDIE R., b 7 Jul 1865, Farmington, d/o Alamander W. and Martha J. (Keniston) Young of Middleton; m 21 Feb 1884, Middleton, Samuel W. Kimball [b 1860s, of Middleton]. (NHVR-Brides)

ADELAIDE, b 1832, Ossipee, d 6 Oct 1853, age 21, single, Ossipee. (NHVR-Deaths)

ADELINE MEHITABLE, b 1820s, Wakefield, d/o Joseph and Nancy (Young) Young; m 1840s, Wakefield, Moses Colby Nay [b ca 1810, of Wakefield]. Adaline and spouse later moved to the Boston area. Daughter Almena was accepted for membership in the D.A.R in April 1897; her deposition stated she was descendant of Capt. Joseph and Anna (Folsom) Young, Joseph and Dorcas M. (Ewer) Young, and James and Mary (Kimball) Young. Ch. b Boston: Almena Nay, b ca 1840, single in 1897, Boston, MA; Cordelia Nay, b 1856, d 1859, Boston, buried in Old Young Cemetery, Wakefield beside grave sites of parents and grandparents James and Mary (Kimball) Young. (D.A.R Lineage #18022, V19, p10; Twombly's Wakefield Cem., TMs)

ADELINE P., b 1820s, Upper Gilmanton, d/o Bailey and Polly (Rundlet) Young, alive 26 Jan 1863, native town; m (Intentions) 24 Oct 1849, Belmont, m Nov 1849, Gilmanton, Ezekial Gilman [b ca 1825, of Meredith]. Adeline P. Gilman was named daughter and heir of Bailey Young of Upper Gilmanton by his will signed 26 Jan 1863, proved 18 Mar 1863. (LDS I.G.I. BR; NHVR-Brides; Meredith Annals, p456,457)

ALAMANDER W., b 23 Jul 1824, Alton, s/o Jonathan and Alice (Peavey) Young, d 7 Jul 1894, age 69-11-15, New Durham, widower; m (Intentions) 20 Mar 1857, m 5 Apr 1857, Alton, Lucy Jane Wilber [b 1836, Portland, ME, d late 1850s, Alton]; m2 1860s, Farmington, Martha J. Keniston [b 3 Aug 1830, Middleton, d/o John and Rebecca (Meader) Keniston, d 4 Feb 1890, age 59-6-1, Farmington]. In 1859 Alamander and Martha lived in Middleton where a son was born; in early 1861 they were residents of Farmington where a daughter was born. As resident of Farmington, Alamander enlisted in Co. K., 4th Regt., NH Volunteer Infantry 26 Aug 1861, mustered in 18 Sep, as Pvt.; reenlisted 16 Feb 1864 and mustered in 12 days later. He was wounded in the right hand [in one report in his right hip] by gun shot 16 May 1864 at Drury's Bluff, VA, suffered wounds to his left foot from a mine explosion causing him to lose a toe at Petersburg, VA 30 Jul 1864, and mustered out 23 Aug 1865 with P.O. address of Farmington. Alamander filed petition 1 Aug 1870 for an Invalid Pension, Application No. 159,163, Cert. No. 150,342, stating that he suffered great weakness and lameness in said hip and foot at times and "that said disability almost wholly disqualifies him from performing manual labor." While he received an honorable discharge, he had however been charged with "disobedience of orders" in absenting himself from action on several occasions when wounded. He was put to hard labor for three months, forfeiting $10.00 per month of his monthly pay for the same time. The probability is high that his war-time service contributed to the following Petition for Guardianship brought against Alamander on 5 Mar 1878, by friend and neighbor David F. Parker of Farmington on the grounds that Alamander was "a spendthrift and a drunkard." Samuel L. Amazeen, Peter M. Horne and Joseph L. Demeritt of Farmington were appointed to make careful inquiry; after the hearing of 2 Apr 1878, it was the recommendation of the court to appoint Daniel W. Edgerly as Alamander's guardian [Strafford Co. Probate #4655].

Ch. b Middleton by Martha J.: Charles E., b 13 Jul 1858, d 1 Mar 1862, age 3-7-19, Farmington. Ch. b Farmington by Martha J.: Addie R.+ (Young) Kimball, b 7 Jul 1865. (Alton VR, p616; NHVR-Death, Marr; LDS I.G.I. BR; Soldiers & Sailors, p205; Nat'l. Archives Milit. Recs.)

ALBERT, b 3 Feb 1836, Durham, s/o Daniel and Hannah (Chesley) Young, shoemaker, d pre 1900, home town; m 12 Jun 1864, at age 27, Durham, Mary A. Gleason [b 19 Nov 1832, Durham, d/o John and Charlotte (   ) Gleason of Madbury, d 5 Feb 1909, home town]. In 1850 Albert lived with his widowed mother Hannah. He attended Durham and Strafford Academies, was a charter member of the Christian Society in Durham, then united with the Congregational Church where at one time he held the title of Deacon. In 1860 he and sister Almira,

14

tailoress, single, age 26, formed a household. Albert owned
a shoe shop and farmed on part of the estate formerly owned
by his grandfather Benjamin Chesley. By 1870, Albert and wife
Mary A. had made their home in Durham; daughter at home was
Maryetta, single. According to the 1871 county map of Durham
their home was situated in District #8. He served as Selectman 1877-1878. As of 1900, Mary A. was widowed and lived with
son Albert Jr., single, daughter Maryetta Smart and son-in-law
Charles A. Smart [b Feb 1865]. Most members of the family
were buried at the family cemetery plot on Albert's farm in
Durham in a field bounded by Dover Road, Oyster River and
Beard Creek. Here his father's family and Chesley ancestors,
descendants of George Chesley, were buried.
    Ch. b Durham: Albert, b Feb 1865, single as of 1900, d
21 Sep 1910, Durham; Willie A., b 25 Nov 1866, d 12 Sep 1867,
age 9 mos., 17 days, Durham; and Maryetta+ (Young) Smart, b
4 Aug 1869. (Durham Graveyards No. 62; LDS I.G.I. BR; NHVR-
Births, Brides, Deaths, Marr; Census Strafford Co., 1860,
p583; 1870, p147; 1900 Soundex; Stackpole's Durham, V1,
p241,304-306,368; Sanford & Everts Maps)
    ALEXANDER, b ca 1825, Glasgow, Scotland, d pre 1870,
Rochester; m ca 1850, Scotland, Arabella McIlroy [b 1828,
Scotland, of Rochester in 1870, widow]. Arabella was listed
on census returns for Rochester as head of family in 1870;
living with her were two sons John and James, both of whom
later settled in Rochester with their families. Ch. b
Glasgow, Scotland: John+, b 1854; and James Burlington+, b
4 Mar 1864. (Census Strafford Co., 1870, p273; NHVR-Marr)
    ALFRED, b ca 1825, of Gilford; m 1850s, of same town,
Ellen (   ) [b ca 1830, of Gilford]. Ch. b Gilford, daughter
b 24 Jan 1856. (NHVR-Births; LDS I.G.I. BR)
    ALFRED A., b 1819, of Somersworth, alive in 1870, huck-
ster, shoemaker, Dover; m 12 Sep 1841, Lee, Abigail aka Abbie
E. Speed [b 1818, of New Market, d 1 Nov 1903, Augusta, ME].
In 1860 Alfred and Abbie E. were residents of Sandwich; children at home, George F., and Russell T. From May 1860/61 up
through Oct 1868, they lived in Rochester; from 1868 up
through Jan 1871, in Dover. In 1870 Alfred and spouse were
on the census returns for Ward 1, Dover; members of household
were son Russell T. and Frank L. Drew, age 21 [b 1859]. On
date of 22 Nov 1871, Abigail filed petition for a dependent's
pension based on son George F.'s military service in the Civil
War, Application No. 200,492, Cert. No. 170,992. Son George
F. enlisted from Rochester at age 20 on 30 Aug 1862 in Co. I,
15th Regt., NH Volunteer Infantry, mustered in 14 Oct 1862 as
Pvt., and died of wounds and disease 29 Jul 1863 at Vicksburg,
VA, single. In truth he died on a steamer which plied the
Mississippi River between Port Hudson and Vicksburg. Abigail's deposition stated that son George had become her sole
means of support due to the fact that her husband Alfred A.
was totally incapacitated; the property that they had owned
had been lost to fire. Character witnesses Edward L. Tebbetts

of Rochester and Joseph C. Young of Milton said they were well acquainted with both Alfred and Abigail and their straightened circumstances. Ch. b Dover: George F., b 1842 [cited above]; and Russell T., b 1850, alive 1871, Dover. (Census Strafford Co., 1860, p739; 1870, p4; Soldiers & Sailors, p760; Nat'l. Archives Milit. Recs.)

ALFRED GEORGE, b 5 Apr 1806, Wakefield, most likely s/o Moses and Mary (Chadwick) Young of Ossipee, d testate 19 Apr 1881, North Wakefield; m ca 1830, Sarah A. Seaman [b 24 Jul 1813, Bangor, ME, d 27 Jun 1899, Wakefield, widow, res. of Pine River settlement as of 1892]. From 1830-1880, Alfred and Sarah raised their family in Wakefield. In 1850 Alfred was first listed as head of household, Sarah named his spouse; members of family were his mother Mary, age 82 [b 1768], sister Lydia, age 48 [b 1802], and six children, Jane, William, Charles H., Almira M., Horace G. and Frances A. Young. In 1870 son George A. was the remaining child at home. On 10 May 1873, Alfred was listed as taxpayer of Wakefield, rated at $17.23.

Alfred's will was drawn 4 Sep 1880, proved 5 Jul 1881, naming wife Sarah as sole Exec. and principal legatee; witnesses Sanborn B. Carter, George A. Wentworth, Emily Wentworth [Carroll Co. Probate #5829]. He bequeathed $5.00 to each of his surviving children: Jane H. Mayo, William H. Young, Charles M. Young, George A. Young and Frances A. Hayward. The rest of his real and personal estate in Wakefield was devised to wife Sarah A. Young "forever." He also bequeathed $5.00 to Fred A. Young, relationship unknown. Son William H., single, served in the Civil War; as of 20 Aug 1862, he was on the roster of the Mass. Regiment. Alfred and Sarah were buried at the Sarah Young Cemetery, Haywood Brook Farm, North Wakefield.

Ch. b Wakefield: Jane H. (Young) Mayo, b 1831, alive 1880; William H., b 1834, alive 1880, Wakefield; Charles M., b 1837, alive 1880; Almira M. aka Myra M.+ (Young) Hill, b 1843; Frances A. (Young) Hayward, b 1845, alive 1880; Horace G., b 1847, not listed in will; and George A.+, b 1854. (NHVR-Brides; Census Carroll Co, 1850, p318; 1860, p580; 1870, p430; Twombly's Wakefield Cem., TMs; 1892 Saco Maps of Carroll Co., NH, p9; Banks' Wakefield, p175; Wentworth Gen., V1, p501,502)

ALICE, b 1842, of Madbury; in 1860 she lived with John and Elizabeth Ricker and family in Madbury. (Census Strafford Co., 1860, p8)

ALICE, b ca 1870, Rollingsford, d/o John and Mary (Blanchard) Young [no main entry]; m 27 Jan 1890, Rollingsford, Thomas Cox [b ca 1865, of same town]. (NHVR-Brides)

ALICE A., b ca 1850, Wolfeboro, m 26 Feb 1870, Wolfeboro, Charles F. Abbott [b 9 Dec 1849, Wakefield, s/o Charles and Betsey (Wentworth) Abbott, gr.s/o Mark and Betsey (Whitehouse) Wentworth, of Leighton's Corner, Wakefield]. (NHVR-Brides; Wentworth Gen., V2, p202,203)

ALMIRA, b ca 1805, Alton, m (Intentions) 24 May 1829, m
8 Jun 1829, Gilford, Richard Bickford [b ca 1800, of Alton].
(Alton VR, p549; NHVR-Brides)

ALMIRA, b Feb 1824, of Dover, Ward 2 in 1860, tailoress,
lived with Joseph Hartford family; of Rochester Union in 1900,
single, resided in boarding house. (Census Strafford Co.,
1860, p609; 1900 Soundex)

ALVAH aka Alva, b 19 Jul 1818, ME, s/o Moses and Dorothy
(Peavey) Young of Alton, farmer, d 8 Dec 1891, Alton; m 1 Dec
1839, Alton, Frances aka Fannie Cotton [b 1817, Gilmanton, d
25 Feb 1900, widow, Alton]. Prior to 1840 Alvah was of Rochester where his eldest son was born. He became head of household in Alton from 1840-1870. In 1840 his age was 20-30, with
bride of same age. Frances was named his spouse from 1850-
1870. In 1850 children at home were Charles and John. In
1860 son Charles E., his wife Hannah and their daughter Lydia
F. lived with them as well as son Albert. In 1870 granddaughter Lydia was member of household, age 12. Letters of
Admin. on Alvah's estate in Alton were filed 19 Jan 1892 by
widow Fanny and "only son" Charles E.; they both declined
administration of the estate, preferring to nominate Thomas
Cogswell of Gilmanton as Admin. in their stead; appraisers
named were Orrin French, Alvah Ellis and George Nute, all of
Alton [Belknap Co. Probate #4877]. Ch. b Rochester: Charles
E.+, b 1839. Ch. b Alton: John, b 1856 [not listed in 1860
finding]; and Albert, b 4 Feb 1852, d pre 19 Jan 1892. (Alton
VR, p566; Census Strafford Co., 1840, p303; Census Belknap
Co., 1850, p368; 1860, p280; 1870, p9; LDS I.G.I. BR; NHVR-
Births)

ALVIN F., b 20 Nov 1842, Gilmanton, s/o Andrew J. and
Sally (Seavey) Young, shoemaker, d 9 Dec 1872, age 30-0-19,
Northwood, drowned; m 27 Nov 1867, prob. Deerfield, Sarah R.
Doe [b 17 Aug 1841, Deerfield, d/o Joseph A. and Mary (Drew)
Doe, alive 27 Nov 1916, known as Sarah R. Goodwin, widow,
Gilmanton]. The 1870 census listed Alvin and Sarah as resi-
dents of Gilmanton; infant in family was Cora S. Sarah m2
(Intentions) 6 Nov 1875, Gilmanton, m 15 Nov 1875, Gilmanton
Iron Works, Sylvester Goodwin [b ca 1840, Gilmanton, d 6 May
1911]. As resident of Pittsfield Alvin enlisted in Co. E, 2nd
Regt., NH Volunteer Infantry 7 May 1861, Portsmouth, mustered
in 31 May, 1863 as Pvt., reenlisted 2 Feb 1864, mustered in
two weeks later, and was wounded 3 Jun 1864 at Cold Harbor,
VA. He was appointed Corp. 1 Jan 1865, Sgt. 1 Jul 1865, and
mustered out 19 Dec 1865. He first saw action at Bull Run,
VA on 21 Jul 1861. On 16 Feb 1867, Alvin filed petition for
an Invalid Pension due to debilitating disease contracted at
Warsaw, VA, Application No. 122,420; Cert. No. 95,236. Sarah
Goodwin filed petition for a Widow's Pension 27 Nov 1916,
based on Alvin's military service in the Civil War, Application No. 1,087,410, Cert. No. 854,841. Ch. b Gilmanton: Cora
S., b 1869; and Mary E., b 16 Aug 1871, m 3 Jul 1887, Gilmanton, Charles A. Johnson [b ca 1865, Strafford]. (NHVR-Brides,

Deaths, Marr; Census Belknap Co., 1870, p30; LDS I.G.I. BR;
Soldiers & Sailors, p96; Nat. Archives Milit. Recs.)

ANDREW aka Capt., b ca 1765, of Barrington, alive 1810,
Gilmanton; m 8 Jun 1789, Belmont [Upper Gilmanton], Betty aka
Elizabeth Pinkham [b ca 1770, of Loudon, alive 1810, Gilman-
ton]. Andrew and Elizabeth resided first in Barrington where
he bought six parcels of land; he was listed as head of household from 1790-1800. In 1790 Andrew's family contained one
male under 16 and two females. In 1800 his age was 26-45,
with family of one male under 10, two females under 10, one
age 10-16, and female [wife] age 26-45. Soon after selling
out their estate in Barrington they moved to Gilmanton to take
up residence on the 100-acre homestead, part of Lot 10, 7th
Range, bought previously. He was listed on the 1810 census
return for Gilmanton, age 26-45, with spouse of same age
group, four males, two under 10, one age 10-16, and one 16-
26, and three females, one under 10, one 10-16 and one age 16-
26. Lt. Andrew Young was chosen Moderator for Gilmanton town
meetings of 1809 and 1811, and in 1812 was listed as taxpayer
of District No. 3, Gilmanton with title of Capt., rated at
$7.83.

His original 32 acres land as part of the 5th Range in
the Two-Mile Streak, Barrington, n.e. by the road that leads
from Madbury upwards through Barrington [Province Road], was
bought by deed of 22 Feb, rec'd 24 Feb 1792, from Isaac and
Elizabeth Hall of Barrington for 40 pounds lawful money; witnesses John Cate, Moses Canney [Strafford Co. Deed 14:108].
This land holding was added to by the following four purchases
adjacent to his homestead: (1) two tracts of land, one containing 42 acres on the west side of the Province Road, s.e.
by Andrew's land and n.w. by Joseph Young's land, and one
other acre which Silas Drew had purchased of Joseph Young on
n.e. side of road beginning at the cross fence opposite Joseph
Young's house, from said Drew of Barrington, by deed signed
7 Feb, rec'd 22 Apr 1793, for 80 pounds-2 shillings; witnesses
John Cate, Clement Daniels [Strafford Co. Deed 15:519]; (2)
31 acres located s.e. of Andrew's 32-acre homestead, from
Aaron and Molley Leighton of Barrington for 50 pounds by deed
of 2 Sep 1793, rec'd 26 Aug 1797; witnesses Abigail Burnham,
Samuel Morrill [Strafford Co. Deed 21:446]; (3) 20 acres which
bounded the eastern side of Andrew's homestead, abutting on
the north side by the road that leads from Durham via Madbury
via Waldron's hill to Barnstead by deed signed 6 Feb 1794,
rec'd 4 Dec 1795, from John and Deborah Hall of Barrington for
60 pounds; witnesses John Horn, George Hawkens [Strafford Co.
Deed 18:64]; and (4) 40 acres of Range 7 in Two-Mile Streak,
on road leading from Durham to Gilmanton by lands of Silas
Drew, George Jaffrey Esq. and Solomon Hall, from Nathaniel
Caldwell of Lee, by deed signed 28 Feb 1795, rec'd 22 Nov
1800, for 97 pounds-10 shillings; witnesses Israel Peirce,
Curtis Peirce [Strafford Co. Deed 36:20]. His last purchase
of land in Barrington was 18 acres from Betsey Giles of Mad-

bury, single woman, on the n.e. side of road from Dover to Crown Point, for $40.00, by deed signed 26 Dec 1797, rec'd 23 Jan 1805; witnesses Thomas How, James Fowler [Strafford Co. Deed 47:151].

While still of Barrington, Andrew's purchase of land in Gilmanton, Upper Parish for $1,500.00 in 1801 signaled his decision to relocate there. He bought "a certain part" of the 100-acre Lot 10, 7th Range adjoining lands of John Smith, Samuel Smith, Moses Page and Edward Bean, from Bartholomew and Anna Gale of Gilmanton by deed signed 22 Jan, rec'd 31 Jan 1801; witnesses Andrew Woodman, Ebenezer Smith [Strafford Co. Deed 36:256]. Forty acres of the said Lot 10 in the Upper Parish, "part of the farm where I now live," were sold by Andrew and Betsey by deed signed 7 May 1808, rec'd 18 Jan 1809, for $400.00; witnesses Daniel Robertson, Lucy Young [Strafford Co. Deed 59:431].

In Andrew's sale of his property in Barrington wife Elizabeth ceded her dower rights in the three land deeds with Isaac Waldron Esq. of Barrington as grantee, date of recording in each instance, 23 Jan 1805; witnesses for Andrew were Joseph Haven Jr., John P. Hale, and for Elizabeth, Moses Page, John M. Edwards: (1) by deed signed 19 Jan 1801, sale of the 18 acres land which Betsey Giles conveyed to him by deed of 26 Dec 1797, for $20.00 [Strafford Co. Deed 47:148]; (2) by deed of 22 Nov 1803, sale of 40 acres bounded north by the Province Road leading from Durham to Gilmanton, for $500.00 [Strafford Co. Deed 47:155]; and (3) by deed signed 19 Jan 1801, sale of 125 acres in Two-Mile Streak, Barrington for $700.80, bounded north by Province Road, land "being the same land I purchased of Silas Drew except one acre and purchased of Isaac Hall, John Hall and Aaron Leighton, plus one other acre on north side of the road [Strafford Co. Deed 47:149].

Andrew's seven children enumerated in early census returns were never identified. Capt. Andrew's and Elizabeth's whereabouts after 1811 leave much to be resolved. His land holdings in the Two-Mile Streak amassed from 1792-1805 were extensive and their relocation from Barrington to Gilmanton circa 1805 seemed to be planned. Yet records of their stay in Gilmanton dropped off abruptly after 1812. Since town cemetery records revealed nothing, it is reasonable to assume they moved elsewhere. The study of land deeds after 1812 as well as the comparison between Capt. Andrew and Elizabeth of Gilmanton and the following main entry for Capt. Andrew and Betsey of Meredith might resolve some of the unanswered questions. The latter's personal records in Meredith started circa 1816. (NHVR-Marr; Census Strafford Co., 1790, p87, 1800, p157; 1810, p823; Gilmanton TR, V3, p385,410)

ANDREW, b 1769, of Meredith, d 10 Jan 1845, age 76, same town, with title of Capt.; m ca 1790, Betsey (   ) [b 1768, d 30 Jan 1833, age 65, Meredith]. Andrew became resident of Meredith in 1816, establishing a homestead there that year. In 1830 he was listed as head of family in Meredith, age 50-

60, living with one female age 60-70 and one female 20-30. This may possibly have been the Andrew of Meredith, an adult who was deemed a "distracted person" and made ward of Eleazer Young of Gilford on 1 Dec 1835; bond of $1,000.00 was given with sureties from Jonas Gordon of Meredith and Nathaniel Perkins of Gilford [Strafford Co. Probate 50:37]. James Gordon, Stephen Farrar Jr., and John Boynton, all of Meredith, were authorized to take inventory of Andrew's estate. The committee reported on 29 Feb 1836 that Andrew "holds a life lease on the farm on which he lives and has lived for the last twenty years," 80 acres located near the Center Meeting House; the yearly income was $55.00; attested to by Eleazer Young, guardian [Strafford Co. Probate 51:31]. Both Andrew and Betsey were buried at First Burying Ground in Meredith opposite the Old Pound; no known children. (Hanaford's Cem. Inscriptions, TMs, p110; Census Strafford Co., 1830, p132)

ANDREW, b 1843, ME, resident of Rollingsford in 1860, laborer, boarder. (Census Strafford Co., 1860, p220)

ANDREW BAILEY, b 29 Mar 1812, Upper Parish, Gilmanton, s/o of Joseph and Betsey (Young) Young, res. Sanbornton, d 8 Jan 1906, Belmont; m 19 Jan 1834, Belmont, Eliza J. Evans [b 5 Apr 1815, Gilmanton, d/o John and Nancy (Avery) Evans, d 29 Aug 1903, Belmont]. Both Andrew and Eliza were residents of Gilmanton at time of marriage. By 1840 he was listed as head of household in Gilmanton, age 30-40, with spouse age 20-30, and three young children, one male age 5-10, and two females under 5. Andrew and wife lived in Sanbornton by 1850; children at home Orrin D., Oliva, Elizabeth and Henry H. In 1900 they were residents of Belmont: members of family were son Henry H., daughter Oliva S. Atwood, widow, and granddaughter Lillian P. Young, age 31 [b Aug 1868]. Son Henry H. inherited the family homestead. Andrew, Eliza and Henry were buried next to grave sites of Andrew's parents at Bean Hill Cemetery, Belmont. Ch. b Gilmanton: Orrin Demeritt+, b 6 Jul 1834; Oliva Sophronia (Young) Atwood, b 18 May 1836, widow of James Monroe Atwood of Lisbon; Elizabeth Ann+ (Young) Elkins, b 17 Mar 1839; and Henry Harrison, b 23 Jul 1843, d 12 Jul 1914, single. (NHVR-Marr; Census Strafford Co., 1840, p405; Census Belknap Co., 1860, p22; 1900 Soundex; Lyford's Canterbury, p343,344; Belmont Cem., TMs, p2)

ANDREW HUCKINS, b 16 Jun 1827, Barrington, twin, s/o Aaron and Lydia (Daniels) Young, d testate, 10 Dec 1890, Dover; m 12 May 1853, Madbury, Susan Elizabeth Miles [b 27 Aug 1832, Madbury, d 15 Nov 1915, Dover]. In 1850 Andrew lived with his father in Barrington and was named one of the Co-Execs. of Aaron's will signed 2 Dec 1850, proved 2 May 1854. His legacy was a one-half share of both the homestead farm and personal estate, plus many other properties in Barrington. In 1870 he and wife Susan E. lived in Dover, Ward 3, occupation Collector for the IRS, estate valued at $12,000. Children at home were Mary K., Haldeman and Richard B. As resident of Dover, he was appointed 22 Oct 1861, Quarter

Master to Field and Staff, 7th Regt., NH Volunteer Infantry and was discharged 30 Jan 1863 to accept promotion. He served as Colonel in the U.S. Army and was later in command of Army Forts in Ohio and Kentucky.

Andrew H.'s will of 7 Dec 1890, Dover, proved 6 Jan 1891, designated his wife Susan E. as sole Exec. and residuary legatee; witnesses Aaron Young, Louisa B. Young, Daniel Hall [Strafford Co. Probate 107:150]. Bequests of $1,000.00 were made to each of his three children as cited above. In 1900 at age 67, widow Susan E. lived at Sumner Street, Dover as head of family. Grown children then at home were Mary H., age 38, Haldeman P., age 36, and Edward L., age 34. Andrew H., wife and children were buried at Pine Hill Cemetery, Dover. Ch. b Barrington: Mary Hale, b 1 Jul 1861, d 5 Nov 1939, Dover, single; Haldeman Putnam+, b 13 Nov 1863; and Richard Batchelder+, b 17 May 1869. (Ham Gen., p43,61; NHVR-Marr; Census Strafford Co., 1870, p52; 1900 Soundex; Frost's Dover Cem., V1, #535; Soldiers & Sailors, p401,1087)

ANDREW J., b 1816, Gilmanton, s/o Nathaniel B. and Martha (Tuttle) Young, d 16 May 1886, Pittsfield; m ca 1840, Gilmanton, Sally Seavey [b ca 1820, same town]. Ch. b Gilmanton: Alvin F.+, b 20 Nov 1842. (NHVR-Deaths)

ANDREW J., b ca 1835, of Durham; m ca 1855, Durham, Hannah aka Harriet M. (   ) [b ca 1835, Durham]. Ch. b Durham: daughter b 24 May 1856, and son b 25 Dec 1857. (LDS I.G.I. BR; NHVR-Births)

ANDREW J., b Jun 1838, CT, s/o Ira and Sarah (   ) Young of Belmont, alive 1900, Belmont, shoemaker; m ca 1858, Barnstead, Sarah C. Sweet [b Feb 1843, NY, alive 1900, Belmont]. They were residents of Strafford in 1864, and by 1866 had settled into the Meredith place in South Barnstead. Andrew J. was named a son and heir of Ira Young of Belmont by his will signed 25 Jun 1881, proved 20 Mar 1883; his legacy was the farm on which Ira then lived with dwelling house and all lands. Children at home in Barnstead in 1870 were Cora, age 12, and Andrew H., age 3. In 1900 Andrew J. and Sarah lived alone in Belmont. Ch. b Barnstead: Estelle C., b 2 Oct 1858, twin, d.y.; Sarah E. aka Cora, b 2 Oct 1858, twin; Andrew H., b 1867; and Irwin E., b 1872, m 8 Feb 1907, Concord, May Earle [b 1877, Tilton, d/o Nelson H. and Hattie (Dearborn) Earle]. (NHVR-Marr; Census Belknap Co., 1870, p9; 1900 Soundex; LDS I.G.I. BR; Merrill's Barnstead, p329)

ANDREW JACKSON, b 1828, Strafford, s/o Isaac and Mary (Willey) Young, alive 1863, home town; m 31 Oct 1855, Wolfeboro, Sarah Ann Stevens [b 1825, Tuftonboro, alive 1860, Strafford]. In 1835 when Andrew was under the age of seven, his mother was appointed his guardian upon the death of Isaac. In the division of his father's estate on 29 Apr 1841, Andrew received 4-1/2 acres of a piece of meadow land in Strafford lying near the Barnstead line and 12 acres of the Foss pasture adjacent to Jacob Drew's land. Andrew lived in Barnstead during the 1850s, but became head of household in Strafford in 1860, with household of wife Sarah A., daughter Sarah E., and brother Hiram, age 35 [b 1825]. Andrew was the sole Exec. and beneficiary of his brother Hiram's one-half share of the homestead farm in Strafford and all personal estate by Hiram's will drawn 22 Mar 1860, proved 5 May 1863. Ch. b Barnstead: Estelle C., b 2 Oct 1858, twin, d.y.; Sarah E., b 2 Oct 1858, twin. Ch. b Strafford: Hiram S., b 9 Jan 1864, d 15 Nov 1865, Strafford; and Herman Andrew aka Andrew H., b 1 Apr 1867. (LDS I.G.I. BR; NHVR-Births, Marr, Deaths; Census Strafford Co., 1860, p122)

ANDREW W., b 1845, of Alton, farmer; m late 1860s, Alton, Martha ( ) [b 1850, of Alton, alive 1870, same town]. Andrew and spouse were residents of Alton in 1870, no children. (Census Belknap Co., 1870, p28)

ANN, b ca 1790, of Meredith, d pre 5 Jul 1832, Boston, MA; poss. widow of Benjamin W. Young of Canterbury who m 1817, Meredith, Annie F. Jenness [b 1801, Meredith]. By will drawn 30 Oct 1828, proved 5 Jul 1832, Ann named as her Exec. Moses P. Piper of Meredith and left all her estate "wherever it may be found" to her daughter Betsey (Young) Piper, wife of said Moses; witnesses Parker Plummer, John W. Hunt, Martha A. Ambrose [Strafford Co. Probate 42:529]. Said Moses P. Piper was allowed Exec. on date of probate; bond of $1,000.00 given with sureties Parker Plummer of Meredith and Benjamin A. Chase of Northfield, Merrimack Co. [Strafford Co. Probate 30:276]. Appraisers Parker Humers, Nathaniel Plummer and Jonathan Pearson, all of Meredith, took inventory of personal estate only and made return to the court on 11 Jul 1832, approved 27 Sep same year: cash on hand set at $125.11; misc. household effects, $160.05 [Strafford Co. Probate 44:245]. (NHVR-Marr)

ANN E. aka Annie E., b 1845, Strafford, d/o John Frank and Phoebe H. (Hayes) Young; m 27 Feb 1865, Dover, George A. Webster [b ca 1840, of Dover]. Ann known by married name of Webster was to receive a legacy from her father's will signed 26 Nov 1878, proved 1 Jan 1884. Hayes Gen., p202-203, stated that Ann married George Brewster of Dover. (NHVR-Brides)

ANN F., b May 1836, age 64 in 1900; resident of Wolfeboro, 1900; other members of household at boarding house were Jane H. Johnson, b 1843, NH and Joseph Moulton, b Feb 1876, NH. (1900 Soundex)

ANN M., b 15 Sep 1852, Middleton. (LDS I.G.I. BR)

ANNA, b ca 1757, Rochester, m 24 Nov 1777, Rochester, Joseph Cook [b ca 1755, of Somersworth]. (NH Gen. Rec., V4, No.4, p148)

ANNA aka Annie, b 23 Feb 1760, Rochester, d/o Thomas and Anna (Roberts) Young, d 22 Feb 1846, widow, Milton; m 10 Nov 1796, Rochester, Enoch Wentworth [b 11 May 1764, of Rochester, s/o Benjamin and Rebecca (Hodsdon) Wentworth, his second marriage, d 1806, Milton]. Enoch m1 26 Dec 1793, Jane Leighton [b 24 Aug 1768, d 24 Dec 1794; no children]. Anna was not yet of legal age when she was named daughter and heir by

Thomas' will of 4 May, proved 30 Sep 1772. She and siblings were named as heirs-at-law of Isaac Young late of Dover; she and Enoch as co-grantors quitclaimed their title and interest in Isaac Young's estate in 1803; see James and Mary (Kimball) Young of Wakefield for details. Anna and husband Enoch were of Milton in 1835. Ch. b Milton: Thomas Young Wentworth, b 12 Dec 1798; and Susan Wentworth, b 20 Mar 1803. (NHVR-Marr; NH Gen. Rec., V5, No.2, p51; LDS I.G.I. BR; Wentworth Gen., V2, p255)

ANNA, b 19 Jan 1776, Belmont [Upper Gilmanton], d/o Joseph and Anna (Folsom) Young, d 14 Aug 1817, age 41, native town; m 30 Nov 1814, Upper Gilmanton, John Bean [b ca 1770, of Gilmanton]. Anna predeceased her father and was buried at parents' family plot in Gilmanton. No known children. (NHVR-Births, Brides; Folsom's NH Cemeteries, p126)

ANN aka Anna, b 25 Aug 1777, Tuftonboro, d/o Benjamin and 1st wife Phoebe (Allen) Young, d 29 Jan 1842, her native town; m 26 Jan 1804, Wolfeboro, John Piper [b 1760, of Wolfeboro, d 30 Apr 1830, Tuftonboro, age 90]. Piper was a well known family name in Tuftonboro, headed by this John Piper. Ann and John Piper's children were named as heirs-at-law, "the children of his late daughter Anna Piper" by Benjamin Young of Wolfeboro in his will signed 6 Nov 1843, proved 30 Feb 1849. By the terms of his will granddaughter Phebe received a bequest. John Piper enlisted from Wolfeboro in the Revolutionary War in 1776 as Adjutant, served throughout the war, and afterwards bought a huge tract of wild lands in Tuftonboro where he established his homestead. There were eight sons and thirteen daughters by wife Ann, only twelve of whom could be identified. Ch. b Tuftonboro: Phebe Piper, b 10 Aug 1804; Paul W. Piper, b 17 Sep 1805; Susan W. Piper, b 26 Oct 1806; Betsey Ann Piper, b 8 Jan 1808; Lucinda C. Piper, b 24 Jul 1809; Napoleon Piper, b 28 Nov 1810; Martha W. Piper, b 5 Feb 1812; Salley H. Piper, b 20 May 1813; Patience C. Piper, b 15 Oct 1814; John H. Piper, b 27 Dec 1815, who became Town Clerk and Representative for Tuftonboro; Benjamin Y. Piper, b 29 Apr 1816 who settled in Lee; and Vienna E. Piper, b 16 Jan 1821. (Tuftonboro TR, V1, p358-359; NHVR-Births, Brides; Merrill's Carroll Co., p441,443)

ANNA, b 1787, of Wakefield, prob. d/o Joseph and Dorcas M. (Ewer) Young of New Market, m 22 Sep 1808, Wakefield, James Garlin [b ca 1785, Wakefield]. (NHVR-Brides)

ANNA, b 1787, Milton, d/o Jonathan Young, d 21 Dec 1867, Barnstead, widow of 3rd husband John Hill; m1 21 Nov 1811, Milton, Ebenezer Garlin aka Garland [b 20 Apr 1788, Lebanon, ME, s/o Samuel Garland, d 4 Apr 1820, prob. Milton, age 32]. In 1818 Anna Garlin was widowed living with her parents and small son in Milton, mother not identified in her father's deposition for a Revolutionary War pension. Anna m2 1820s, Milton, William B. Wentworth [b 11 Jul 1801, s/o Otis and Abigail (Blaisdell) Wentworth, d 20 Oct 1850, Barnstead Center]; m3 1850s, John Hill [b 1790, of Alton, d 21 Sep 1867,

Barnstead, age 77]. Ch. b Lebanon, ME by Ebenezer: Susan
Elizabeth (Garland) Wallace, b 31 Oct 1814, d 15 Oct 1905,
Alton. Ch. b Milton by Ebenezer: Ebenezer Garland, b 1815.
(NHVR-Brides; N.H. Revol. War Pensions, V99, #14328; Wentworth
Gen., V2, p473,474; Young Family Recs., courtesy of Thomas P.
Doherty)

ANNA M. aka Marilla A., b 1854, Wolfeboro, d/o Jeremiah
L. and Mary A. (Jackson) Young of Tuftonboro; m 4 Nov 1871,
Wolfeboro, Samuel H. Gilman [b ca 1850, of Tuftonboro].
(NHVR-Brides)

ANNIE, b 1799, ME, of Wolfeboro in 1870, lived alone
keeping house. (Census Carroll Co., 1870, p445)

ANNIE, b Dec 1849, age 50 in 1900; lived in Dover, single
in 1900 as boarder at Henry R. Flagg [n.d.] home on Atkinson
Ave. (1900 Soundex)

ANNIE, b ca 1850, Dover, d/o Joseph and Elizabeth (   )
Young; m 15 Apr 1871, Dover, Ebenezer F. Faxon [b ca 1845, of
said town]. (NHVR-Brides)

ANNIE F., b ca 1870, Meredith; m 4 Jul 1893, Meredith,
Arthur O. Kelley [b ca 1870, of same town]. (NHVR-Brides)

ARAMINTA B., b 1844, Gilmanton, d/o Levi J. and 1st wife
Sally J. (   ) Young, alive 1883, prob. Farmington; m ca 1865,
Farmington, George H. Pierce [b ca 1840, of Barnstead]. She
was named Araminta B. Pierce in the will of step-mother Elizabeth E. (Gilman) Young, drawn 16 Feb 1883, proved 15 Jan
1884. Ch. b Farmington?: Walter H. Pierce, m 1892, Pittsfield. (NHVR-Brides)

ARTHUR, b 1850, New Durham, spool maker; m (Intentions)
20 Mar 1872, New Durham, Susie J. Griffen [b 1852, Danvers,
MA]. Arthur was resident of New Durham at time of marriage.
(New Durham VR, Bk4, n.p.)

ARTHUR P., b 26 Feb 1849, Ossipee, s/o Joseph and Hannah
(Chick) Young 2nd, d 31 Aug 1934, native town; m 25 Mar 1871,
Ossipee, Emma F. Kenniston [b 30 May 1852, Ossipee, d/o Sol-
oman B. and Hannah (   ) Kenniston, d 12 Jul 1931, her home
town]. Arthur and Emma made their home in Ossipee when they
married, and were listed on the 1900 census returns for Ossipee; family members at home were Howard E., John L. and Alice
P. Many members of the family were buried at Large Ossipee
Center Cemetery. Ch. b Ossipee: infant b 16 Apr 1872, d.y.;
Bertie A., b 1874, d 6 Apr 1879; Howard E., b 10 Jul 1873,
d.y.; Howard E., b Jul 1875, alive 1900; John L., b Nov 1883,
alive 1900; and Alice P., b Feb 1891, alive 1900. (LDS I.G.I.
BR; NHVR-Marr, Births; 1900 Soundex; Loud's Cem. Recs.,
p112,142)

ASA, b 16 Jul 1837, Madbury, s/o Eleazer and Kezia (Rowe)
Young, d 6 Oct 1912, age 75-2-20, Dover, farmer; m 22 Aug
1857, Barrington, Mary A. Joy [b Jun 1839, prob. Barrington,
d 26 Apr 1916, Dover]. Asa was named as son and heir of
mother Kezia by will drawn 17 Aug 1863, proved 2 Apr 1865.
In 1850 he lived with parents in Madbury. He and Mary were
listed on the census returns for Madbury from 1860-1900; in

1860 child at home was infant son Walter H.; in 1870, sons
Walter and Irving E. At age 25 Asa enlisted from Concord on
21 Aug 1862, in Co. K, 11th Regt., NH Volunteer Infantry,
mustered in 2 Sep 1862 as Pvt. and mustered out 4 Jun 1865,
giving P.O. address of Madbury. After military service, Asa
returned to his native town where he and Mary raised their
family. His homestead was the former Isaac Church farm on the
southern side of the road leading from Demeritt's Corner to
Lee Five Corners. Reflecting the esteem in which he was held
by his native town, Asa was elected one of the Selectmen for
the years 1883-84. Two children died young of scarlet fever
in 1863.
    On date of 1 Feb 1898 Asa filed petition for an Invalid
Pension, Application No. 1,203,990, Cert. No. 961,166. He
stated that his war-time service had brought about general
debility, lame back and rheumatism, his condition only worsening with age. Character witnesses for Asa were neighbors
George W. Hodgdon, George W. Meserve, Charles W. Hayes and
Charles S. Kingman. Asa and Mary were listed as residents of
Madbury in 1900; son Asa R., age 26, was at home. Widow Mary
A. filed petition for a widow's pension on 15 Oct 1912,
Application No. 994,849, Cert. No. 753,431; she stated that
as of 19 Feb 1898, children still alive were Walter H., Irvin
E. and Asa R. Young; and as of 14 Oct 1912, her address was
16 Florence Street, Dover.
    Ch. b Madbury: Walter H., b 7 Oct 1859; Charles E., b
15 Aug 1861, d 19 Sep 1863, age 2-1-4, Madbury; Charles E.,
b 31 Mar 1862, d 1863; Asa aka Alvah A., b 16 Mar 1863, d
24 Sep 1863, bur. Pine Hill, Dover; Irving E.+ aka Irvin E.,
b 4 Jul 1866; and Asa R., b 25 Apr 1874, at home 1900. (LDS
I.G.I. BR; Census Strafford Co., 1860, p4; 1870, p196; 1900
Soundex; NHVR-Births, Marr, Deaths; Hayes Gen., V1, p93;
Soldiers & Sailors, p600; Adams' Madbury, n.p.; Nat'l.
Archives Milit. Recs.)
    AUGUSTA, b 1835, ME, res. of Somersworth. In 1850 she
was carder and lived alone at boarding house in Somersworth;
in 1860 she lived with younger sister Elmira, age 19 [b 1841],
weaver. (Census Strafford Co., 1850, p243; 1860, p274)
    AUGUSTA, b 20 Aug 1855, Hill, d/o Daniel and Laura W.
(Mason) Young of Sanbornton [no main entry]; m 27 Nov 1879,
Sanbornton, Orrin G. Lakin [b ca 1850, of Sanbornton]. (LDS
I.G.I. BR; NHVR-Brides)
    AUGUSTUS, b 1828, of Freedom; in 1850 he lived with the
Ransalos Towle family. (Census Carroll Co., 1850, p164)
    AUSTIN C., b 1865, Wolfeboro, fireman, s/o Nahum G. and
Harriet H. (   ) Young of Goldsboro, ME; m 29 Sep 1888,
Wolfeboro, age 23, Mary Ferrill [b 1864, North Woburn, MA,
d/o George and Mary (   ) Ferrill of North Easton, MA].
Austin lived in North Woburn, MA before marriage. (NHVR-Marr)
    BADGER - see Nathaniel Badger
    BAILEY aka Bayley, b 1793, Belmont [Upper Gilmanton], s/o
Eleazer and Hannah (Bailey) Young, d testate pre 18 Mar 1863,

native town; m1 31 Dec 1818, Belmont, Polly aka Molly Rundlet [b 1797, Gilmanton, d 12 Jan 1851, age 54, Gilmanton]; m2 4 Jan 1853, Concord, Sarah Bradley [b 1797, of Concord, alive 1870, widow, Belmont]. Bailey was appointed Admin. of both his father's estate in Upper Gilmanton on 16 Dec 1845, and of his mother's estate in said town on date of 20 May 1851. As "only son" he fell heir to the old homestead, prospered as a farmer and became Deacon of the Third Freewill Baptist Church founded 27 Aug 1836. He and two eldest daughters Mary Jane and Louisa were baptized and received into the church on 1 Jul 1837; younger daughters Emeline and Adaline were received on 17 Jul 1839. Bailey and Polly were residents of Gilmanton from 1830-1850; they were of Upper Gilmanton in 1860. In 1830 Bailey was head of household under the age of 40, with spouse under 30, one male under 5, and three females, two age 5-10, and one 10-15. In 1840 his age was 40-50, as was his spouse, with family of four males between ages of 5-15, and six females, 2 between 10-15, 3 age 15-20, and 1 age 20-30. In 1850 he and Polly were listed on the census returns for Gilmanton; children at home were Emaline, George, Alfred and Ansel. In 1860 he and second wife Sarah lived in Upper Gilmanton with children Charlotte and Ansel, farm laborer. In 1870 Sarah B. lived alone as widow in Belmont.

Bailey made deposition 17 Mar 1848 on behalf of Hannah (Bailey) Young, widow of Eleazer Young of Gilmanton who had made application for a Revolutionary War pension in 1832; he stated that he had lived for many years within 10 rods of Eleazer's home in Gilmanton. His will was signed 26 Jan, proved 18 Mar 1863, which named Nathaniel Edgerly of Gilford as Exec., and son Ansel F. as residuary legatee; witnesses Samuel Hadbury, James E. P. Randlet, William Page [Belknap Co. Probate #1746]. Wife Sarah B. was to receive out of his real estate her right of dower and homestead as provided by law, as well as furniture and personal property which she already possessed and owned. Bailey made these bequests to his children: eldest daughter Louisa Y. Weymouth, wife of Henry A. Weymouth, $1.00; grandchildren Emma Jane Avery and Erick Avery, children of his late daughter Mary Jane Avery, $1.00 each; daughter Emeline Nutting, wife of Edwin Nutting, many household articles; daughter Adeline P. Gilman, wife of Ezekial Gilman, valuable household effects; single daughter Charlotte Melissa, household effects and the sum of $25.00; son John S., $25.00; son George B., $25.00; son Charles A., $200.00; and son Ansel F., all his real estate in Upper Gilmanton being his homestead farm and all personal property not otherwise disposed of, "provided nevertheless that whereas the said Ansel F. Young is now in the Army of the United States and if he should die, and not come in possession of said property, then in that case I devise the same to my four children, viz., Emeline Nutting, Charlotte Melissa Young, John S. Young and George B. Young." As events turned out Bailey predeceased son Ansel F., single, by two months; Ansel F. died of wounds 3 May 1863, age 22-5-24, buried 14 May 1863, Carrollton, LA. He had mustered in as Corp. 6 Oct 1862 in Co. A, 15th Regt., NH Volunteer Infantry.

It is to be noted that Mary E. Neal Hanaford's **Meredith Annals** listed Moses A.+ Young [b 1? Aug 1829] as son of Bailey and Polly Young. This does conflict with the terms of Bailey's will which did not mention Moses A., then alive. Yet Ms. Hanaford, a native of this area, seemed to be well acquainted with the family. The issue remains unresolved. Ch. by 1st wife Polly, b Gilmanton: Louisa+ (Young) Weymouth, b ca 1819; Mary Jane+ (Young) Avery, b 1820s; Harriet S., b 1822, d 2 Oct 1848, age 26; Emeline+ (Young) Nutting, b 1824; Adeline P.+ (Young) Gilman, b 1820s; John S.+, b 12 Aug 1831; George B., b 1833, married and left for St. Louis; Alfred, b 1834, at home in 1850, not listed in Bailey's will of 1863; Charles A.+, b 5 Sep 1835; Charlotte Melissa, b 1837, single in 1863, married and lived in VT; and Ansel F., b 9 Nov 1840, see above. (Census Strafford Co., 1830, p277; 1840, p408; Census Belknap Co., 1850, p77,78; 1860, p118; 1870, p5; NHVR-Marr, Deaths; Meredith Annals, p456,457; Morning Star, p375,376; Soldiers & Sailors, p759; 1900 Soundex; Baptist Church Recs., TMs, p2,4)

BELINDA, b ca 1835, Strafford, m 24 Apr 1856, Strafford, Damen Dennis [b ca 1830, of same town]. Ch. b Strafford: Dan H. Dennis, b 1860s; Martha Dennis, b 1860s, m Henry Maguire in 1886. (NHVR-Brides)

BENJAMIN, b ca 1720, of Dover; m ca 1750, Dover, Anna (   ) [b ca 1725, of Dover, d pre 26 Dec 1792, Barrington. In 1740 he was a Pvt. in Ye Second Foot Company of Dover formed 24 Jul 1740, and listed on 1741 Dover Tax List for Cochecho Parish, rated at 10 shillings-11 pence for the town's ministerial support. As early as 1740, he started to buy lands in Barrington where he would settle circa 1756. It is interesting that during the time of relocation from Dover to Barrington he had business dealings with Isaac Young and James Young of Dover and Stephen Young of Madbury. These three men were descendants of Jonathan and Abigail (Hanson) Young of Dover. Doubt is expressed that they were kinsmen. It is believed, rather, that Benjamin headed an entirely different branch, one that had affiliated with the Quakers. Early Town Papers of Barrington [N.H. State Papers, V11, p150] mentioned Benjamin in the "List of Captain William Cate's men, Relative to the Quakers, 1759 to 1761," on date of 17 Apr 1759. He was one of six men who had been "draughted." Moreover, "of the 80 men in Barrington fit to bear arms 14 are Quakers whose proportion would be between 2 & 3 of the 14 I [Cate] was ordered to raise." In 1790 he was head of household in Barrington; single member of family was one female (spouse), three sons then fully grown.

While of Dover he made two purchases of land in Barrington. The first was 50 acres of Lot 10, Two-Mile Streak at the foot of Barrington adjacent to land of John Hayes of Dover from William and Elizabeth Lock by deed signed 4 Jun 1740, rec'd 30 Oct 1765; witnesses Nathaniel Sparhawk, James Jeffrey [NH Prov. Deed 87:124].   He sold this land by deed signed 11 May 1741, rec'd 30 Oct 1765, to Isaac Young of Dover, housewright, for 100 pounds current money; witnesses Timothy Robinson, Joseph Hanson Jr. [NH Prov. Deed 87:129].   The second parcel of land was a moiety of 60 acres in the Two-Mile Streak, 6th Range which was part of the Cates Pasture, from Thomas Leighton of Dover who went in with co-grantor George Jaffrey of Portsmouth in the original purchase, for 270 pounds Old Tenor by deed signed 18 Jun 1743, rec'd 7 Sep 1744; witnesses James Young, James Kielle [NH Prov. Deed 28:90].

Benjamin was of Barrington when he bought another 15 acres in the Two-Mile Streak, by deed signed 4 Aug, rec'd 10 Aug 1756, for 150 pounds Old Tenor from Sarah Jaffrey of Portsmouth, widow of A. Macpheadris, and Mary Osborne, Atty. for John Osborn; witnesses Theodore Atkinson Sr., Theodore Atkinson Jr. [NH Prov. Deed 50:348]. He sold to Stephen Young of Madbury, 60 acres land in the Two-Mile Streak by land of James Church and the road intersecting the 7th and 8th Ranges for 250 pounds by deed signed 7 Oct 1774, rec'd 23 Sep 1790; witnesses Joshua Foss Jr., Thomas Howe [Strafford Co. Deed 12:136]. His 100-acre homestead in Barrington [later identified as located in Strafford], Lot 21, 1st Range, was purchased for 225 pounds by deed of 17 Oct 1774, rec'd 21 May 1781, from Joshua and Abigail Foss [Jr.] of said town; the Lot was bounded on the eastern end by Rochester line, north by land of Solomon Foss, west by Joshua Foss' father, and south by Julius Felker's land; witnesses John Cate, Nathaniel Roberts, Thomas How, John Church, Nathaniel Foss Jr., George Medar [Strafford Co. Deed 4:49].

He conveyed his homestead to son Jonathan who lived with him, by deed of gift written 24 Sep 1784, rec'd 26 Dec 1796, with this sentiment: "For love, and after Benjamin's and Jonathan's mother's decease, the household furniture and all the buildings and cattle will be left to Jonathan"; witnesses Joseph Hayes, Thomas Foss [Strafford Co. Deed 24:51]. Known ch. b Barrington: Winthrop+, b 1753; Jonathan+, b 16 Jun 1761; and Stephen, b 1760s. (Scale's Dover, p87,88; NH State Papers, V24, p700; Census Strafford Co., 1790, p86; Lyford's Canterbury, p341; Young Family Recs., courtesy of M. Elaine Woodward)

BENJAMIN, b 8 Jul 1756, New Market, s/o Joseph and Anna (Folsom) Young of Durham, clothier, d 13 Dec 1848, testate, Wolfeboro; m1 May 1777, Tuftonboro, Phoebe Allen [b Feb 1760, of Tuftonboro, d/o Josiah and Mary (   ) Allen of Stratham, d 10 Apr 1800, age 40-2-0, Tuftonboro]; m2 Jun 1802, or Jul 1812 [NHVR], Wolfeboro and Tuftonboro, Rebecca Bickford [bp 5 Nov 1758, Tuftonboro, d/o Jonathan and Sarah (Wilmot) Bickford, d Nov 1849, Wolfeboro].   While Fitts' Newfields indicated that Benjamin's first wife was Rachel Burleigh, d/o William Burleigh of New Market, Young family records, courtesy of Nancy L. Dodge of Colebrook, NH, attested that Phoebe Allen was Benjamin's first wife. Phoebe Allen's father Josiah Allen was born Stratham ca 1720, son of Jude and Deborah (Locke) Allen. Benjamin resided first in Durham, relocated in Tuftonboro and spent his remaining years in Wolfeboro. He was named as an heir in the division of his father's estate in 1806, receiving 10 acres in Horns Woods, Durham. By deed of 2 Mar 1807, rec'd 25 Jan 1809, he sold his one-twelfth share of Joseph's estate "in Rockingham Co. and Strafford Co., wherever the same may be found" to brother William Young of Durham for $100.00; witnesses Eliphalet Curtis, Wentworth Cheswell [Strafford Co. Deed 60:156].

He settled in Tuftonboro by 1790, where he became listed as head of household from 1790-1810: in 1790, family contained two males under 16 and five females; in 1810, his age was 45 plus with spouse of same age group, and family of two males, one age 10-16 and one 16-26, and two females both 16-26. He served as Selectman of Tuftonboro from 1797-1814, and Town Moderator almost consecutively from 1803-1818. From 1830-1840, he was resident of Wolfeboro: in 1830, his age was 70-80, with spouse of same age bracket, and one male age 15-20; in 1840, his age was 80-90, as was his spouse, with one male at home, age 20-30.

After their move to Wolfeboro, first wife Phoebe became a member of the new Congregational Church in 1793. Benjamin and second wife Rebecca were members of the First Congregational Church in Wolfeboro from the time the church was established on 17 Jun 1834. They were candidates for membership among a dozen who were examined by a council which met at the house of Daniel Pickering Esq. When Benjamin was still of Lee [Durham], he purchased 90 acres of 100-acre Lot 68, 2nd Div., Wakefield, drawn to the original right of Samuel Rendal, adjacent to Jonathan Cook's land, by deed of 7 Sep 1781, rec'd 16 Nov 1785, for 315 pounds from Samuel and Bethanay Hodgdon of Wakefield; witnesses Jonathan Norris, Mayhew Clark [Strafford Co. Deed 6:363]. He was still a resident of Lee when he sold to Samuel Glidden of Lee, miller, by deed of 24 Nov 1781, rec'd 27 May 1799, three-fourths of an acre in Lee, "in Wadley's grant so-called," with house and barn for 300 Spanish milled dollars; witnesses Joshua Wiggins, Timothy Moses [Strafford Co. Deed 30:268].

At one time Benjamin's occupation was clothier, i.e., one who dresses cloth for impurities. The following two deeds highlight the fact that a clothier required technical skills as well as terrain affording water power. This was a family trade practiced not only by Benjamin but also by his eldest brother Joseph and Joseph's son and grandson; it is highly possible other brothers were in this trade as well. In 1785 Benjamin, clothier and resident of Tuftonboro, sold his 90 acres of Lot 68 in Wakefield in two installments to Joseph Young of New Market, trader, for a total of 250 pounds, first by deed of 1 Mar 1784, rec'd 15 Sep 1785; witnesses Jeremiah

Young [brother], John Young Jr. [Strafford Co. Deed 5:536];
and second, by deed signed 17 Dec 1785, rec'd same date;
witnesses John Smith 3rd, James Smith [Strafford Co. Deed
6:439].

His initial purchase of land in Tuftonboro was by quitclaim of Jacob Sheafe of Portsmouth, Rock. Co., signed 10 Dec
1796, rec'd 30 Apr 1804, for 100 acres in the north quarter
at the s.w. corner of land belonging to Jonathan Brown on the
road leading to Moultonboro for 100 pounds; witnesses Mary
Davis, Samuel Penhallow [Strafford Co. Deed 45:208]. From
1798 on Benjamin held the title of Esquire in all deeds. By
deed signed 23 Oct 1798, rec'd 26 Mar 1800, he purchased from
Woodbury Langdon Esq. of Portsmouth, Rock. Co., one certain
island of land, seven acres being in Winnipesaukee Pond in the
19-mile bay or cove, drawn to original right of John Wentworth
Esq., deceased, for one dollar; witnesses James Hersey, Henry
Wiggin Jr. [Strafford Co. Deed 33:196]. In 1806 he purchased
the undivided one-half of Lot 16 in the west quarter of Tuftonboro, by deed of 14 May 1806, rec'd 2 Jan 1808, from Richard
Evans of Portsmouth, Rock. Co. for $139.00; witnesses Oliver
Crosby, L. K. Livermore [Strafford Co. Deed 55:507]. Part of
this, 13-1/2 acres from his share of Lot 16, was sold by deed
of 8 Apr 1807, rec'd 24 Jun 1807, to Daniel Libbey of Tuftonboro for $50.00; witnesses Ichabod Libbey, Benjamin Horne
[Strafford Co. Deed 53:473]. Benjamin bought 10 acres on the
eastern side of Winnipesaukee Pond in the s.w. quarter of
Tuftonboro, 3 acres of which were situated on the western side
of the stream running from Lewis Pond to Winnipesaukee Pond,
the other 7 acres on the eastern side, by deed of 27 Mar 1800,
rec'd 13 Feb 1808, from Woodbury Langdon of Portsmouth, Rock.
Co., for $60.00; witnesses H. S. Langdon, Abraham Tappan
[Strafford Co. Deed 56:476]. He then sold this property at
a considerable profit by deed of 19 Oct 1801, rec'd 15 Sep
1803, to Timothy W. Young [brother] of Tuftonboro for
$2,000.00; witnesses Richard and Susannah Rust [Strafford Co.
Deed 42:372].

In 1809 Benjamin held mortgage on John Furber' homestead,
Lot 11, Wolfeboro by deed of 11 Mar 1809, rec'd same date, for
$1,000.00; witnesses John Twombly, J. H. Woodman [Strafford
Co. Deed 60:398]. The mortgage papers contained an indemnity
clause given by said Furber for the protection of Benjamin:
inasmuch as Benjamin "has recognized for the appearance of
Joseph Furber of Wolfeboro at the next Superior Court at Dover
on first Tuesday of September next to answer to such things
as may be presented against Joseph Furber... John Furber made
the provision that if he shall compensate Benjamin for any
loss or protect him from liability in giving evidence in
court, then this deed will be null and void, otherwise to
remain in full force." Benjamin of Tuftonboro sold to Paul
H. Varney of Farmington, clothier, for $700.00, a certain mill
privilege in Wolfeboro on the stream running from Smith's Pond
in said town to Winnipesaukee Pond, together with the mill and

shop adjoining and all the tools and implements necessary for dressing cloth by deed of 13 Mar 1812, rec'd 28 Mar 1812; witnesses Richard L_____ and William Kent [Strafford Co. Deed 71:246].

Benjamin's will of 6 Nov 1843, proved 30 Feb 1849, named Thomas Rust his sole Exec. and residuary legatee; witnesses Gersham Bickford, Nathaniel Frost and William Weston [Carroll Co. Probate #5818]. He bequeathed $1.00 to each of the following sons, daughters and grandchildren: Jeremiah, Josiah A., Mehitable C. Lang, the children of his late daughter Anna Piper, likewise the children of his late daughter Betsy Kezar. To his son Benjamin Jr., he devised one cow and to daughter Sally Tibbetts, one cow. To his son Joseph, he devised a desk belonging to his father, all the farming utensils and stock not disposed of by legacies and the family homestead "for and during his natural life." Upon Joseph's death the homestead was to revert to grandson Mark A. Young, son of said Joseph. To his granddaughter Phebe Piper, daughter of the late Anna Piper, he bequeathed one bed and bedding. The remainder of his estate was to go to Thomas Rust.First wife Phoebe was buried at Edgerly Cemetery in Tuftonboro. Both Benjamin and Rebecca were buried at Bickford Cemetery, Dimond Corner, North Wolfeboro.

Known ch. b Tuftonboro by Phoebe: Ann+ aka Anna (Young) Piper, b 25 Aug 1777; Sally+ (Young) Tibbetts, b 1778; Betsey+ (Young) Keysar, b 20 May 1784; Jeremiah+, b May/Jul 1787; Joseph,+ b 1788; Josiah A.+, b 1794; and Benjamin+, b 1800. Ch. b Tuftonboro by Rebecca: Mehitable Clark+ (Young) Lang, b 1800s. Other child attributed to Benjamin was Phebe, n.d. (D.A.R Wolfeboro, p35-37; Census Strafford Co., 1790, p100; 1810, p741; 1830, p446; 1840, p389; NHVR-Deaths, Marr; Meredith Annals, p281; LDS I.G.I. BR; Fitts' Newfields, p383,384; Merrill's Carroll Co., p331-333,445; Young Family Recs., courtesy Nancy L. Dodge, Granvyl Hulse)

BENJAMIN, b 7 Jan 1778, Barrington, s/o Winthrop and Mary (Otis) Young, later of Canterbury, d 21 Mar 1854, Calais, ME; m 1800, Canterbury, Mary Jackson [b ca 1782, Lee, d/o Samuel and Elizabeth ( ) Jackson, d Nov 1883, Calais, ME, over 100 years old]. Ch. b Canterbury unless otherwise noted, order uncertain: Loren Whiting, b 7 Dec 1803, Wheelock, VT, d 1898; Obediah, b 1800s; Elijah, b 1800s; Benjamin, b 1800s; Harrison, b 1810s; Jackson, b 1810s; Winthrop, b 18 Sep 1817; John, b 1820s; Milo F., b 1820s; Mary, b 1820s; Deborah, b 1820s; Abigail, b 1820s; and Maria, b 1820s. (Lyford's Canterbury, p342,343)

BENJAMIN, b ca 1780, of Barrington, m 2 Feb 1812, Barrington, Abra Montgomery [b ca 1780, of Barrington]. Both were residents at time of marriage. (Barrington TR, V6, p69)

BENJAMIN, b ca 1790, Dover, most likely s/o _____ and Diadamy ( ) Young [see main entry Diadamy Young], d pre May 1839, Dover; ma ca 1815, Dover, Eleanor ( ) [b ca 1795, of Dover, alive 1840, of same town]. His spouse was probably

Eleanor Horne of Dover, born circa 1795, eighth child of Paul Horne, who married a Benjamin Young of Dover, her second marriage. In 1840 Eleanor was widow and head of household in Dover living with a female companion, both age 40-50. Children, if any, were not named in the administration of Benjamin's estate and only a tentative guess can be made of his date of birth. Admin. Papers on Benjamin's estate, filed 20 May 1839 [cited below], offer insight into kinship with other contemporary Youngs then of Dover who filed claims against the estate and link as well two family friends and/or relatives who figured prominently in the administration of the estates of both Benjamin Young of Dover and Daniel and Eleanor Young of Dover. In both cases Samuel Kimball of Dover acted as "an interested party" to protect the properties, and Oliver Horne of Dover acted as administrator. See Diadamy Young of Dover and Daniel and Eleanor Young of Dover for further information.

Oliver Horne, Admin., gave bond of $4,000.00 on 20 May 1839, with sureties Charles Ham and Sharanton Baker, both of Dover [Strafford Co. Probate 50:153]; on same date, the return of inventory on estate, the widow's allowance, and dower rights were dealt with. Inventory on Benjamin's estate in Dover was appraised by Charles Ham, Sharanton Baker and Daniel H. Watson, all of Dover, and returned 20 May 1839, approved same date [Strafford Co. Probate 54:337]: real estate included the 70-acre farm valued at $1,500.00 and 2-1/2 acres in Barrington rated at $30.00; personal estate, including household effects, furniture, tools, one watch and umbrella [but no livestock] was set at $130.75; total assets were worth $1,660.75. On same date, widow Eleanor was allowed $75.00 "for the support of life" [Strafford Co. Probate 43:134] and the said committee was appointed to set off her dower rights.

Claims against the estate were reported 17 Jun 1839 by Charles Ham, the Commissioner appointed to review said claims. Generally speaking the appointment of a commissioner meant that either assets were tight or that the estate was rated outright as insolvent. There were 26 accounts or notes of hand totaling $715.46 owed by the estate; only one claim, that of Eleanor Young in the amount of $15.00, was disallowed [Strafford Co. Probate 56:181]. Included in these claims were notes of hand owed to Amy Young [wife of Ephraim Young], $2.00; Ezra Young, $55.21; two notes of John C. Young, $14.00 and $5.00; and Ephraim and Charles Young, $83.97. Dower rights were set off to Eleanor "for the term of her natural life" on date of 16 Sep 1839, allowed same date, attended by Samuel Kimball of Dover [Strafford Co. Probate 54:426]: she was granted 34 acres, 145 rods beginning at n.e. corner of Diadamy Young's dower, with the privilege of passing and repassing to and from the assigned dower to Toll End Road through the land of Benjamin Young. Horne's final accounting of Benjamin's estate [Strafford Co. Probate 57:73, 1839] was unfortunately not to be found on microfilm among the county's probate records up through 1890. (Census Strafford Co., 1840, p531; Horne Gen., TMs, p35)

BENJAMIN aka Jr., b 1800, Wolfeboro, s/o Benjamin and 1st wife Phoebe (Allen) Young of Tuftonboro, d 7 Apr 1874, Clarksville; m1 26 Aug 1819, Moultonboro, Joanna Cate [b ca 1800, Barrington, d pre 1848, Clarksville]; m2 1848, Mary Cate [b 14 Jun 1811, Barrington, d/o Benjamin Cate, d 14 Jul 1867, age 56-1-0, Clarksville]. Benjamin [Jr.] was named a son and heir of Benjamin Young of Wolfeboro by his will signed 6 Nov 1843, proved 30 Feb 1849. Both Benjamin and Joanna were residents of Tuftonboro at time of their marriage, but by 1850, lived in Clarksville. Ch. b Wolfeboro by Joanna: Josiah+, b 14 Feb 1825. Ch. b Clarksville by Joanna: Joseph W.+, b 15 May 1828. Ch. b Clarksville by Mary: Charles W.+, b 1849. (NHVR-Births, Deaths, Marr; D.A.R Wolfeboro, p35-37)

BENJAMIN, b 1828, Wakefield, s/o Daniel and Betsey (Cook) Young; m 17 Feb 1852, Wakefield, Lucy Ann Wentworth [b 9 May 1827, Wakefield, d/o Joel and Abigail L. (Smith) Wentworth, d 16 Oct 1865, Dover, MA]. He lived at home in 1850 and later became resident of Acton, ME. Ch. b Boston, MA: Josephine, b 2 Jun 1855. Ch. b Dover: Clarence E., b 25 Oct 1857. (NHVR-Marr; Wentworth Gen., V2, p562)

BENJAMIN, b ca 1850, Dover; ma ca 1875, Dover, Olive ( ) [b ca 1850, of same town]. Ch. b Dover: Nellie, b ca 1876, m 4 Mar 1899, Dover, Freeman Dyer [b ca 1870, of Dover]. (NHVR-Brides)

BENJAMIN, b 1852, of Gilford; resident of Gilford in 1870, single, laborer, who lived with the Leonard Wilkerson family. (Census Belknap Co., 1870, p75)

BENJAMIN F., b 11 Mar 1788, Strafford, s/o Jonathan and Polly (Hill) Young, d testate 20 Dec 1839, age 51-9-0, Farmington, bur. Strafford; m1 ca 1805, Strafford, ( ) [b ca 1790, of Strafford, d 13 Aug 1824, same town]. No christian name was given Benjamin's first wife either by his will drawn when she was alive, or by cemetery records. Perhaps one of their two daughters Polly and Mercy had been the mother's namesake. Benjamin m2 12 Dec 1825, Farmington, Deborah Furber [b 1802, Strafford, d/o Benjamin and Kezia (Ash) Furber of Farmington, d 24 May 1890, New Durham]. Benjamin F. predeceased his father; his father's will signed 7 Dec 1844, proved 2 Sep 1851, named grandchildren, the children of son Benjamin F. Young, as heirs-at-law. In 1828 he was first listed as taxpayer of Farmington: he owned two parcels of land, 16 acres and 18 acres; value of buildings was rated at $150.00, value of unimproved land, $64.00. By 1830 he was resident of Farmington, age 40-50, with family containing spouse age 20-30, four males, one each under 5, 10, 15, and 30, and two other females, one a parent figure age 60-70, one under 15. In 1840 Deborah was widow and head of family in Farmington, age 30-40; other member of household was a female age 70-80. In 1850 she and her mother Kezia, age 82 [b 1768], lived with son Jonathan at his home in Farmington. The only land deed found for Benjamin was signed 5 Nov 1827, rec'd 28 Nov 1827, for the purchase of 90 acres of Lot 64, 2nd Div., Rochester [that section that is now Farmington], from Elisha and Martha Hayes of Farmington whose own title to the property was entailed with Kezia Furber's dower rights, for $200.00; thus Benjamin's and Deborah's property title was qualified; witnesses Jonathan Young, Nehemiah Eastman [Strafford Co. Deed 135:402].

Benjamin F.'s will signed 16 Dec 1839, proved 20 Jan 1840, named brother Stephen Young of Strafford as sole Exec. and the guardian of his two youngest children Furber and Andrew J. until they should reach the age of 21; the following day Stephen refused both positions of trust; witnesses Isaac Merrill, Isaac Neal, Stephen Young [Strafford Co. Probate 56:121]. Nonetheless, on 21 Jan 1840, Stephen was appointed Admin. "with the will annexed," having posted a $5,000.00 bond with sureties John F. Young of Strafford and Isaac Neal of Farmington [Strafford Co. Probate 50:179]. Benjamin wanted wife Deborah to have one-third part of all produce and would receive after his two youngest sons reached the age of 14, one-third of his real estate "so long as she remains my widow." After the decease of her mother [Kezia Furber], the bedroom in the west corner of the house was to be hers with privileges in common with his two eldest sons by his first wife, Jonathan and Benjamin F.; these sons were to share the homestead farm of 120 acres in Farmington and were named co-residuary legatees. Daughter Mary aka Mercy who was in feeble health was to receive a feather bed and all furniture he owned at time of first wife's decease, as well as support for her well being. The children by second wife Deborah, Furber and Andrew J. were to be raised at home by their mother until they reached the age of 14, each to receive $100.00 at age 21, and an additional $50.00 apiece towards their education.

Inventory of the estate was submitted 1 Feb 1840, sworn to same date, by appraisers Charles Dennett of Rochester, Levi H. Hayes, Isaac Merrill, both of Farmington [Strafford Co. Probate 56:102]: personal estate was assessed at $1,248.84; notes of account from 1836-1839 totalled $540.62; money in savings bank at Dover as of 17 Jul 1837, $100.00. Widow's allowance of $350.00 from the personal estate was granted 15 May 1840 to Deborah [Strafford Co. Probate 43:155].

Guardianship of son Benjamin F. Young, a minor, was awarded 10 Apr 1840, to Emerson Furber of Farmington by bond of $2,000.00 with sureties Levi Hayes and Mark Demeritt, both of Farmington [Strafford Co. Probate 50:181]. Charles Dennett of Rochester was appointed guardian of Deborah's sons Furber and Andrew J., minors, having given bond of $1,000.00, with sureties of said Stephen Young and Deborah F. Young of Farmington [Strafford Co. Probate 50:184]. Stephen submitted his account on the administration of the estate 3 May 1842, approved same date [Strafford Co. Probate 57:32]: debits paid for sundry legacies came to $1,428.05; total debits amounted

34

to $1,872.48. Credits included personal estate per inventory, $1,348.84; for cash collected for debts, $517.32; and for balance due Admin. from the estate, $6.32, total $1,872.48. The first petition for license to sell against the estate was presented 1 Jul 1845 by said Admin. who stated that the estate was not sufficient to pay demands against it, shy in the amount of $75.00; it was his intent to sell enough wood or timber growing on it to raise that amount; allowed same date [Strafford Co. Probate 60:51]. The last petition for license to sell against the estate was brought 5 Jul 1842 by Emerson Furber of Farmington, guardian of Benjamin F. Young, minor over 14 years, son of the deceased; said Furber stated that son Benjamin F. held one undivided half of the real estate in Farmington with buildings and it was in the son's best interests to sell, subject to widow's dower of Kezia Furber [maternal grandmother] of Farmington; license granted same date [Strafford Co. Probate 60:14].

Daughter Mercy Young, single, ill for some time and under medical care, predeceased her father; her will was signed 21 Apr 1840, proved 19 Jan 1841; she named her brother Jonathan Young as Exec. of her will; witnesses Stephen Young, Deborah F. Young, Lydia Furber [Strafford Co. Probate 55:168]. Jonathan was allowed Exec. on 19 Jan 1840, having given bond of $100.00 with surety Stephen Young of Strafford [Strafford Co. Probate 50:219]. Mercy bequeathed to her sister Polly Furber her feather bed, wearing apparel, gold ring and gold ear knobs, and devised to brothers Jonathan and Benjamin F., the rest of her household goods and furniture. Son Andrew, single, was resident of Dover from 1860-1900; as of 1860 he lived in Ward 2; in 1870 his estate in Dover was valued at $10,000; he lived alone. In 1900 he was still single, his occupation dentist.

Benjamin was buried at the Hayes Cemetery, First Crown Point Road, Strafford. Ch. b Strafford by first wife: Polly (Young) Furber, b ca 1805, alive in 1840; Mary aka Mercy, b ca 1810, d prior to 19 Jan 1841, Strafford; Jonathan+, b 20 Nov 1818; Benjamin F., b ca 1820 [a minor in 1839], named in his sister's will of 1 Apr 1840, cited above. Ch. b Farmington by Deborah: Furber+, b 19 Jan 1827; and Andrew J., b Jan 1833 [see above]. (Census Strafford Co., 1830, p64; 1840, p318; 1860, p655; 1870, p42; 1900 Soundex; Stiles' Cemeteries, p116; Farmington TR, V1, p414,770,771; NHVR-Deaths)

BENJAMIN F., b 1824, of Dover, prob. s/o Daniel and Eleanor W. (Smith) Young, shoemaker; m ca 1855, Rebecca (   ) [b 1835, MA, alive 1860, Dover]. For guardianship papers on Benjamin when his father died in 1826, see parents. He and Rebecca lived in Dover, Ward 3 in 1860, with their two young daughters Ella and Lizzie. Ch. b Dover: Ella, b 1857; and Lizzie, b Aug 1859. (Census Strafford Co., 1860, p675)

BENJAMIN GREEN, b 2 Sep 1813, Tuftonboro, s/o Joseph and Patience (Chase) Young of Wolfeboro; m1 7 Jan 1841, Wolfeboro, Caroline E. Horne aka Emily Horne [b 26 Oct 1816, Wolfeboro, youngest of ten children of Jacob Horne, d 5 Nov 1849, Conway]; m2 1850, Mary Ann Chase [b 1818, Meredith, d/o Jonathan and Polly (Tilton) Chase, d 1895, age 77, Tuftonboro]. Benjamin and Emily were residents of Wolfeboro when married, but settled later in Conway. Ch. b Wolfeboro by Emily: Anna Jane (Young) Hill, b 1840s, wife of Moses Hill; Henry S.+, b 1848; and Luther, b 1840s. (D.A.R Wolfeboro, p35-37; Meredith Annals, p151; Morning Star, p375; NHVR-Marr; Horne Gen., TMs, p36,37)

BENJAMIN S., b 14 Feb 1808, Durham, s/o George Young [no main entry]; d 5 Feb 1889, age 80-11-19, widowed, Durham. (NHVR-Deaths)

BENJAMIN W., b 1792, Canterbury, s/o John and Patience (Willey) Young of Gilford [no main entry]; m 15 Jul 1817, Meredith, at age 25, Annie F. Jenness, at age 16 [b 1801, Meredith]. See startling similarity of names to entry below. (NHVR-Marr)

BENJAMIN W., b 1858, Canterbury, s/o John and Patience (Willey) Young [no main entry], alive 1900, Meredith; m1 19 May 1893, age 35, Canterbury, Eliza H. Pickering [b Dec 1876, Meredith, d 1915, Meredith]; m2 post 1915, Elnora (   ) [b 1877, Meredith]. In 1900 Benjamin was head of household in Meredith; members of household were wife Eliza, her brother Curtis Pickering, age 25 [b 1875], Curtis' wife Annie M. (   ) Pickering, age 17 [b Oct 1882]. Benjamin, Eliza and second wife Elnora were buried at Oakland Cemetery, Meredith Center; no dates of death given for him or Elnora. Ch. b Meredith: Alfred, b 18 Nov 1894, not traced further. (1900 Soundex; NHVR-Births, Marr; Hanaford's Cem. Records, p135)

BESSIE, b ca 1855, Milton, d/o Horace F. and Annie F. (Remick) Young, m 2 Apr 1900, Milton, Thomas B. Bassett [b ca 1850, same town]. When guardianship was awarded to siblings in 1871 upon the death of their father, Bessie was over 14 years old. (NHVR-Brides)

BESSIE E., b 11 Nov 1845, Lebanon, ME, d/o Daniel and Eunice W. (Wood) Quimby; m ca 1865 _____ Young; d 22 Sep 1894, age 48-10-11, married, Dover. Bessie was buried at Somersworth. (NHVR-Deaths)

BETHIAH, b ca 1798, Sanbornton; m 1817, Sanbornton, Joseph Yeaton [b ca 1795, of said town]. (NHVR-Brides)

BETSEY, b 20 May 1784, Wolfeboro, res. of Gilmanton, d/o Benjamin and 1st wife Phoebe (Allen) Young, d 31 Jul 1839, Stewartstown; m 4 Mar 1807, Canterbury, Edmund Keysar Jr. [b 12 Apr 1780, Canterbury, s/o Edmund and Mary (Lyford) Keysar, d 14 Mar 1853, Stewartstown]. Their fifteen children were named as heirs-at-law of Benjamin Young of Wolfeboro, designated as "the children of my late daughter Betsey Kezar," by his will of 6 Nov 1843, proved 30 Feb 1849. Ch. b Stewartstown: Edmund Keysar, b 30 May 1808, d.y.; Mary Keysar, b 15 Sep 1809, d.y.; Benjamin Young Keysar, b 1810s; Joseph Young Keysar, b 1810s; Phebe Young Keysar, b 1810s; Mary Keysar, b 1810s; John Keysar, b 1810s; Betsey Keysar, b 1820s;

36

Edmund Hodgdon Keysar, b 1820s; Miles Hodgdon Keysar, b 1820s;
Mehitable Susan Keysar, b 1820s; Olive Keysar, b 24 May 1828,
d.y.; Rhode B. Keysar, b 21 May 1831, d 16 Jan 1849; Jessie
Keysar, b 1830s; and Susan Keysar, b 1830s. (Young Family
Recs., courtesy of Granvyl Hulse; NHVR-Brides)

BETSEY, b 21 Nov 1796, Wolfeboro, d/o Zachariah Young,
d 30 Oct 1859, native town; m (Intentions) 23 Oct 1817, Wolfeboro; m 13 Nov 1817, same town, Benjamin Smith [b 5 Jul 1792,
Ossipee, d 16 Oct 1859, Wolfeboro]. Betsey Smith was named
daughter and heir of Zachariah Young by his will signed 20 Nov
1842, proved 11 Feb 1851. She was to receive a one-sixth
share of her father's estate. Her husband Benjamin Smith was
also to receive a one-sixth share, part of which to be held
in trust for grandson William B. Young (parentage not known)
until he came of age. Benjamin, Betsey and sons were buried
at the Young family plot, Smith Hill Cemetery on road from
Ossipee Corner. Ch. b Wolfeboro: William B. Smith, b 2 Aug
1818, d 8 Apr 1893, Wolfeboro; and Benjamin B. Smith, b 1 Oct
1821, d 2 Sep 1859, Wolfeboro. (Loud's Cem. Records, p129;
NHVR-Brides; Parker's Wolfeboro Banns, 1789-1854, n.p.)

BETSEY, b 3 Jun 1800, New Hampton, d/o Joseph and Abigail
(Gilman) Young; m 28 Sep 1823, New Hampton, Joseph Dolloff [b
ca 1800, of same town]. (NHVR-Births, Brides; LDS I.G.I. BR)

BETSEY, b ca 1810, Dover; m 1830, Dover, Andrew Hall [b
ca 1805, Dover]. They were married by Rev. Samuel K. Lothrop
of First Unitarian Society, Dover. (Heritage's Dover VR,
p256)

BETSEY, b 12 Feb 1814, Gilmanton, d/o Joseph and Betsey
(Young) Young; m ca 1835, Gilmanton, Daniel Sweatt [b ca 1810,
Loudon]. Ch. b Belmont b 1840s: Dustin Sweatt, d.y.; Charles
Sweatt, moved to Manchester; and Daniel A. Sweatt, m 1883,
_____ Sanborn. (NHVR-Brides; Lyford's Canterbury, p343,344)

BETSEY A., b 20 Jan 1835, Wakefield, d/o John and Mary
(Berry) Farnum of Acton, ME, d 1 Aug 1898, age 63-6-12, Wake-
field, widow of _____ Young. Her mother was from Milton.
Betsey was buried at the Young Lot, Wakefield. (NHVR-Deaths)

BETSEY A., b ca 1855, Gilmanton; m 23 Apr 1874, Gilmanton, James I. Brown [b ca 1850, of same town]. (NHVR-Brides)

BETSEY JANE, b ca 1810, of Wolfeboro; m 3 Jan 1832,
Wolfeboro, Pierce L. Wiggin [b 14 Nov 1808, Wolfeboro, s/o
Thomas Brackett and Eliza (Thurston) Wiggin, gr.s/o of Mark
and Betsey (Brackett) Wiggin of Stratham, d 17 Jul 1833, home
town]. (Wiggin Gen., TMs, p56; Merrill's Carroll Co., p309)

BETSY, b ca 1855, Somersworth, d/o William and Jane ( )
Young [no main entry]; m 29 Aug 1874, Somersworth, James H.
Hammond [b ca 1850, same town]. (NHVR-Brides)

BETSY A., b ca 1830, Somersworth; m 6 May 1849, Somersworth, William Clements [b ca 1825, of Somersworth]. (NHVR-
Brides)

BETSY A., b ca 1845, Gilmanton, d/o John F. Young of Belmont; m 6 Dec 1865, Belmont, Joseph Bowdron aka Boudron [b ca
1840, Gilmanton]. (NHVR-Brides)

BETTY A. aka Bessie A., b ca 1851, Barnstead, d/o Samuel P. and Betsey A. (Merrill) Young, alive 1870, Rochester; m 24 May 1870, Barnstead, Charles W. Palmer [b ca 1840, Alton]. Bessie and Charles took up residence in Rochester at least by 1885. Ch. b Rochester: Fred R. Palmer, b 1870s, m 1897, Rochester; Harry C., b 1870s, m 1895; sixth ch., daughter, b 5 Nov 1885. (Rochester TR, Births, 1879-1891; NHVR-Brides)

BRADBURY S., b ca 1810, Upper Gilmanton, s/o Joseph and Betsey (Shaw) Young; m (Intentions) 14 May 1837, Lynn, MA, m 5 Jun 1837, Salem, MA, Susan B. Parsons [b ca 1815, of Lynn, MA]. (LDS I.G.I. VR of MA)

BYRON ROSEWELL, b Apr 1856, of Rochester, prob. s/o Horace F. and Annie F. (Remick) Young, alive 1900, Rochester; m Apr 1878, Ossipee, Ella Mary Pike [b Aug 1860, prob. ME, alive 1900, Rochester]. Byron, wife and son were residents of Rochester in 1900. Ch. b Maine: Frank R., b May 1881, at home 1900. (1900 Soundex; LDS I.G.I. VR)

CARL, b 1866, Russia, res. of Somersworth in 1900; m ca 1890s, Maggie Delan [b 1875, Russia, alive 1900, Somersworth]. Ch. b Somersworth: Carl, b 31 Aug 1900. (NHVR-Births)

CAROLINE, b ca 1820, Dover, m 17 Sep 1839, Dover, George Briggs [b ca 1815, Boston, MA] at St. Thomas Episcopal Church. (Heritage's Dover VR, p253; NHVR-Brides)

CAROLINE F., b ca 1820, New Durham; m 23 Nov 1841, New Durham, Thomas Wiggin [b ca 1815, Durham]. (NHVR-Brides)

CAROLINE H., b ca 1850, of Middleton; m 20 Nov 1870, Middleton, Cyrus D. Willey [b ca 1845, of same town]. (NHVR-Brides)

CAROLINE JANE, b 13 Feb 1822, Barnstead, d/o Stephen and Caroline (Munsey) Young; m 16 Jul 1839, Barnstead, John Clark [b ca 1815, Dover]. (NHVR-Brides, Births)

CARRIE A., b 7 Oct 1859, Barnstead, d/o George W. and Sarah A. (Bickford) Young, d 7 Apr 1897, native town; m Dec 1880, Barnstead, George H. Hawley, physician [b 26 Feb 1858, Bath, ME, s/o George and Elizabeth (Farrin) Hawley]. Carrie attended Salem Normal School and studied music in Concord, becoming organist of the Congregational Church in Center Barnstead. Her husband George attended public schools in Bath, Maine and earned his degree of Doctor of Medicine at Bowdoin Medical School, Brunswick, Maine. In 1878 he set up medical practice in Barnstead. From 1885-1886, he was chosen to represent his town in the New Hampshire State Legislature. He was a musician himself, playing violin, banjo and piano, a member of the Barnstead orchestra. (Biog. Review, XXI, p150,151)

CARRIE B., b 1860, Lynn, MA, res. of Farmington, d/o Charles and Elizabeth (   ) Young [no main entry]; m 1 Mar 1887, Rochester, Albion E. Lane [b 1855, Epping, s/o Winthrop M. and Frances (   ) Lane]. (NHVR-Brides; Rochester TR, Marr)

CARRIE M., b 24 Nov 1861, Kennebunk, ME, d/o Frank A. and Ann C. (Andersen) Noble, d 17 May 1890, age 28-5-23, Dover, married, spouse of _____ Young. (NHVR-Deaths)

CARRIE M., b Jun 1865, ME, res. of Barnstead in 1900, age 34, housekeeper for Charles A. W. Clark [n.d.] of Barnstead. (1900 Soundex)

CHARLES, b ca 1785, of Rochester; head of household in Rochester in 1840, age 50-60, poss. a widower, with family of four males, one each under 5, 10-15, 15-20, and 20-30, and one female age 15-20. Ch. b Rochester: Charles+, b 1815. (Census Strafford Co., 1840, p508)

CHARLES, b 22 Nov 1799, Dover, eldest s/o George and Sally (Randall) Young, d testate, 5 Oct 1882, native town; m1 Jan 1821, Dover, Ruth Varney [b 1799, prob. Dover, d 8 May 1827, Dover]; m2 6 May 1829, Brookfield, Mary Ann Hanson [b 6 Jul 1806, of Brookfield, d 23 Apr 1885, Dover]. Charles was land surveyor and lumber merchant in his home town, head of household from 1830-1880: in 1830, his age was under 40, spouse [2nd wife] was under 30, with family of one female under 15, and three females under 30; in 1840, his age was 40-50, spouse 30-40, with household of one male 20-30, and four females, one under 5, three age 20-30. He served as Town Clerk of Dover for the years 1830, 1836-1838, and he and Mary were listed as residents of Dover, Ward 2, from 1850-1870: child at home in 1860 was Ellen, age 22. Members of household in 1870 were daughter Ellen A., age 33, single, and child Eddie H. Young, age 2 [b 1868].

Petition for Dower was filed by widow Mary A. on 18 Jan 1883; granted 6 Feb 1883 [Strafford Co. Probate 96:452]. She stated she and Charles possessed a dwelling house on Mechanics Street which they occupied at the time of his decease; she prayed that the family homestead valued at $500.00 may be set off to her. On 6 Feb 1883, George E. Durgin, Burnham Hanson and Joseph H. Wiggin, all of Dover, were appointed to set off Mary A.'s dower rights, and by 17 May 1883, had notified heirs-at-law Jane A. Lawrence, Ellen A. Young and widow Mary A. of the appraisal of inventory [Strafford Co. Probate 82:55]. Assignment to widow was granted 5 Jun 1883: the one half of the dwelling house situated on one-sixth acre of land formerly owned by Winthrop Adams on the south side of Mechanics Street, Dover; allowed 5 Jun 1883 [Strafford Co. Probate 82:365]. Charles, his two wives Ruth and Mary Ann, and children were buried beside the grave sites of his parents at Pine Hill Cemetery, Dover.

Ch. b Dover by Ruth: Jane Augusta+ (Young) Lawrence, b ca 1821; Charles W., b 1822, d.y.; Charles Franklin, b 1825, d.y., Dover. Ch. b Dover by Mary Ann: Ellen A., b 1837. (NHVR-Births, Marr; Heritage's Dover VR, p74,77,78,102, 103,105; Frost's Dover Cem., V1, Plot #503; Census Strafford Co., 1830, p303; 1840, p562; 1860, p657; 1870, p57)

CHARLES, b 1815, Rochester, s/o Charles Young, d pre 4 May 1852, home town; m 19 Oct 1837, Durham, Pamela P. Snow [b 1815, of Rochester, alive 1852, same town]. Per 1840 census for Rochester it is believed that Charles and Pamela, both at the age of 25, lived at his father's home in Roch-

ester.   A decade later Charles and Pamela maintained their
own home in Rochester with their children.   He worked in
manufacturing.   Children at home in 1850 were Lydia H.,
Charles E., Helen F., Ann and Herbert R.   Admin. Papers on his
estate in Rochester were filed on 4 May 1852; on that date,
widow Pamela Young was appointed Admin. who gave bond of
$1,000.00, with sureties Joseph Young and Jacob H. Ela, both
of Rochester [Strafford Co. Probate 50:445].   Appraisers James
H. Edgerly, James Fassington Jr. and Silas Wentworth took
inventory of Charles' estate and made their report 6 Jul 1852,
allowed same date: furniture, $49.55, Misc., $28.42; total
$77.97 [Strafford Co. Probate 67:65].

     Petition for widow's allowance was filed 5 Aug 1852; the
amount of $54.97 was granted Pamela on 5 Oct 1852 [Strafford
Co. Probate 43:273].   On that date she returned her account
of administration [Strafford Co. Probate 67:315];   after
expenses of $77.97 were paid for widow's allowance, funeral
and administrative fees, the estate held a zero balance.   She
was "discharged from said estate."   Ch. b Rochester: Lydia
H., b 1838; Charles E., b 1841; Helen F., b 1843; Ann, b 1847;
and Herbert R., b 1849.   (Census Strafford Co., 1850, p668;
Stackpole's Durham, V1, p387)

     CHARLES, b 1835, MA, of Gilford in 1860, single, machin-
ist; lived at boarding house.   (Census Belknap Co., 1860,
p207)

     CHARLES, b Apr 1844, ME, resident of Rochester in 1900,
age 56, single, roomed with Samuel Shaw of Rochester.   (1900
Soundex)

     CHARLES, b Jan 1845, ME, resident of Rochester in 1900,
age 55, single, roomed with William E. Marginson [n.d.] family
of Rochester.   (1900 Soundex)

     CHARLES, b Oct 1857, resident of Farmingham in 1900; he
took in boarder Charles S. Burnham [n.d.].   (1900 Soundex)

     CHARLES A., b 5 Sep 1835, Upper Gilmanton, s/o Bailey and
Polly (Rundlet) Young, d 9 Jul 1918, Laconia; m 12 Aug 1855,
Gilmanton, by the Rev. John K. Young, Ellen F. aka Helen F.
Leavitt [b Sep 1839, of Upper Gilmanton, alive 1900, Laconia].
Charles A. was named son and heir of Bailey Young of Upper
Gilmanton by will drawn 26 Jan, proved 18 Mar 1863.   He and
Ellen were residents of Upper Gilmanton in 1860, with three
children at home, Dora P., Flora M. and Estella.   By 1870 they
had relocated to Gilford, children at home, Nason and Nellie.
At age 27 Charles enlisted in Co. A, 15th Regt., N.H. Volun-
teer Infantry 1 Oct 1862, mustered in five days later as
Corp., mustered out 13 Aug 1863, leaving P.O. address of
Meredith Bridge, now Laconia.   He had contracted debilitating
diseases at Port Hudson, Florida by date of 20 Jul 1863.   Four
months from the date he returned home on 16 Dec 1863, he filed
petition for an Invalid Pension, Application No. 37,517, Cert.
No. 191,987.   By 1900 they and youngest son Nason E. lived at
Fair Street, Laconia.   Ch. b Upper Gilmanton: Isadora aka
Dora P., b 24 Jan 1856, alive 11 Mar 1915; Flora M., b 12 Mar

1857, d 14 Oct 1914; Estella F., b 14 Nov 1859, d 9 Dec 1884;
Nason Elmer, b 16 Oct 1861, d 24 Aug 1901; and Nellie F., b
18 Dec 1865, alive 11 Mar 1915. (Census Belknap Co., 1860,
p118; 1870, p8; 1900 Soundex; Soldiers & Sailors, p760;
Meredith Annals, p456,457; Nat'l. Archives Milit. Recs.)

CHARLES ALBERT, b 22 Sep 1842, Barrington, s/o William
Hale and Sarah J. (Daniels) Young, d 26 Jul 1916, Roxbury, MA;
m 5 Jul 1868, MA, Hannah Merrill Cook [b 13 Apr 1846, West
Roxbury, MA, d 22 Dec 1920, Barrington]. In 1850 he was a lad
of 8 as listed on census returns for parents in Barrington.
As a young man of 20 years, he moved to Boston where he met
his bride-to-be Hannah, sister of Susan Cook,wife of his
brother Harrison. In Boston he established roots and became
a successful business man and civic leader. Ch. b Roxbury,
not traced further: Frederick Hale, b 29 Nov 1871, d 24 Jun
1934, Barrington; Clifford Harrison, b 28 May 1875, d 20 Sep
1937, Barrington. (Ham Gen., p27,35,36; N.H. Men, p288)

CHARLES B., b 4 Jun 1861, Wolfeboro, s/o Nathaniel and
Vinah M. (Lougee) Young, carpenter, d 4 Apr 1891 by accident,
age 29-10-0, Wakefield; m 14 Mar 1887, Ossipee, Addie Stevens
[b 1870, Brookfield, d/o Mark Stevens of Ossipee, widowed in
1891, Ossipee]. Charles B. and daughter Annie P. were buried
at Stevens-Burleigh Cemetery, Ossipee. Ch. b Whiteface: Anna
P., b 1890, d.y. Ossipee. Ch. b Wakefield: Annie Priscilla,
b 12 Jul 1891, d 23 Sep 1891, Wakefield. (NHVR-Births,
Deaths, Marr; Wakefield TR, V1; Loud's Cem. Recs., p127)

CHARLES E., b 1837, Alton, s/o Jonathan and Alice
(Peavey) Young; m 8 Dec 1857, Alton, Mary H. Nutter [b 1835,
Alton]. Charles was listed on the census returns of his
parents in 1850 for Farmington. In his native town he raised
a family, listed on the census returns for 1870, with wife
Mary and four children in the household. Ch. b Alton: Frank
E., b 1861; Herbert S.+, b Jan 1862; Susan E.+ (Young)
Wigglesworth, b 1864; and Janette, b 1869. (Census Belknap
Co., 1870, p28; Alton VR, p604,617; NHVR-Brides, Marr; 1900
Soundex)

CHARLES E. aka Edwin, b 1839, Alton, s/o Alvah and Fannie
(Cotton) Young, farmer, d 20 Jan 1903, Keene; m ca 1858,
Alton, Hannah (   ) [b 1838, Alton]. Charles, age 10, was
listed on the census returns for his parents of Alton in 1850.
In Admin. Papers filed on his father's estate in Alton on
date of 19 Jan 1892, Charles was named as only son. Charles
declined the administration; see parents for full details.
In 1860 he and Hannah lived in Alton with his parents and
daughter Lydia. At age 20, he enlisted under the name of
Edwin from Portsmouth 22 May 1861 in Co. A, 2nd Regt., NH
Volunteer Infantry; mustered in 31 May 1861 as Pvt.; appointed
Corp.; wounded 29 Aug 1862 at second engagement of Bull Run,
Virginia; appointed Sgt. 1 May 1863. He mustered out 21 Jun
1864, giving P.O. address of Shirley, MA. On date of 2 Jul
1866 Edwin filed petition for Invalid Pension, Application No.
111,105, Cert. No. 73,253. He deposed that he had been shot

through the stomach at the second battle of Bull Run, left on the battlefield for nine days, then taken to a hospital in Washington where in time he recovered. For many a year before his death he had been entirely incapacitated, suffering from the effects of his wounds and other complications. He had the greatest difficulty in obtaining a pension as he was unable to convince the Pension Board that a human being could survive such a wound. As a measure to restore his credibility he left instructions with certain doctors that upon his death, they were to perform an autopsy. Medical men were astonished to learn during the examination that Edwin had spoken the truth. Daughter Susan, though not listed on 1860 census return cited above, was noted as daughter of Charles E. and Hannah per NHVR-Brides. Ch. b Alton: Susan+ (Young) McIntire, b 7 Nov 1858; Lydia F.+ (Young) Clough, b 1859; and Frank E.+, b 19 Aug 1861. (LDS I.G.I. BR; NHVR-Births, Brides, Marr; Nat'l. Archives Milit. Recs.; Soldiers & Sailors, p96)

CHARLES E., b May 1861, resident of Barnstead in 1900, lived at own home and took in boarder James Ferrin, b 1875, MA. (1900 Soundex)

CHARLES F., b 14 Mar 1854, Farmington, s/o Thomas and Lavina Ellen (Beedy) Young, d 5 Oct 1870, at untimely age of 16-6-22, his home town; m 28 May 1869, Middleton, Carrie aka Caroline H. Perkins [b 1853, New Durham, d/o John D. and Harriet (   ) Perkins]. At time of marriage, Charles resided in Middleton, Caroline in New Durham. Upon the birth of their child they lived in New Durham. Ch. b New Durham: Ada E., b 28 Feb 1870. (NHVR-Births, Marr, Deaths; LDS I.G.I. BR)

CHARLES F., b 28 Oct 1856, Farmington, s/o Hiram H. and Judith A. (Davis) Young; m 13 Mar 1889, Farmington, Alice Gray [b 1867, Dover, d/o John and Clara (   ) Gray]. Charles was named a son and residuary legatee of Hiram H. Young by his will signed 25 Jul 1870, proved 8 Apr 1873. A one-fourth share of the homestead and personal property was to revert to Charles upon his mother's death. In 1870 he lived with his parents in Farmington. Alice was a resident of Haverhill, MA at time of marriage; her father John Gray was born in Dover, her mother Clara, born in Strafford. (NHVR-Marr)

CHARLES H., b 1833, Gilmanton, s/o David S. and Betsey (Avery) Young; m 20 Dec 1863, Gilmanton, Abbie A. Eaton [b 1839, Barnstead, d/o Peter Eaton]. Charles was resident of San Francisco, CA at time of marriage. (NHVR-Marr; Biog. Review, XXI, p354,355)

CHARLES H., b May 1848, Lebanon, ME, res. of Rochester; m ca 1865, Rochester, Laura P. Jones [b ca 1850, Lebanon, ME, of Rochester, d pre 1897, Rochester]. He and Laura settled in Milton before relocating to Rochester. In 1900 Charles lived in Rochester, age 52, widower, a member of his son Fred J.'s household. Son Albert married 7 Sep 1897, Wakefield, at age 17, Nellie S. Wiggin [b 1880, Acton, ME, d/o Mack and Ellen (   ) Wiggin of Milton]. Nellie Wiggin was of Acton, ME, at time of marriage, age 17. Nellie's father Mack Wiggin

was born in Milton. Ch. b Lebanon, ME: Fred J.+, b Aug 1867;
and Albert, b 1880 (see above). (1900 Soundex; NHVR-Marr)

CHARLES H., b ? May 1852, Middleton, s/o Samuel P. and
Martha A. (Stevens) Young, d pre Jun 1900, his home town; m1
26 Dec 1877, Farmington, Fannie S. York [b 15 Sep 1857, Middleton, d/o Wingate and Mary (   ) York, d 15 Dec 1885, age
28-3-0, Farmington]. Fannie's mother was from Danville, VT.
There may have been one child born by Fannie aka Annie when
place of residence was New Durham: Eddie W., b 22 Jun 1879.
Charles m2 4 Aug 1888, Farmington, Etta M. Young [b Feb 1864,
Middleton, d/o John Henry and Mary Emily (Cook) Young of Tuftonboro, alive 1900, Middleton, widow]. Upon the birth of son
Frederick in 1891, Middleton, Charles and wife Etta resided
in Bradford, MA. In early 1900 Etta was widowed and lived in
Middleton at the home of her brother Lewis F. Young with her
two young children born of Charles, Maud and Frederick. Ch.
b Middleton: Maud M., b Jan 1889, alive 1900; and Frederick
Roland, b 24 Jun 1891, alive 1900. Etta M. Young m2 15 Jun
1900, Middleton, James E. Leighton [b ca 1860, Middleton].
(LDS I.G.I. BR; NHVR-Births, Brides, Marr, Deaths; 1900
Soundex)

CHARLES H., b ca 1860, Newburyport, MA; m ca 1885, Etta
M. Hatstat [b ca 1865, Rutland, MA]. Ch. b Tuftonboro:
Hortense, b 1 Sep 1889, d 11 Sep 1889, native town].
(NHVR-Deaths)

CHARLES HENRY, b 1852, Durham, s/o Joseph and Maria
(Langley) Young of Wolfeboro; m 31 Jul 1873, Keene, Susan L.
(Brett) Hutchinson [b 1846, Keene, d/o Abial and Hannah (   )
Brett, age 27 when married]. Charles was listed in his
parents' household in Durham in 1860 at age of 8. By 1881
Charles' occupation was tailor. At that time he and Susan
lived in New Market where twin daughters were born to them.
Ch. b New Market: Luella May, b 8 Jun 1881, twin; Louisa, b
8 Jun 1881, twin, not traced further. (NHVR-Births, Marr;
Census Strafford Co., 1860, p598)

CHARLES L., b 1843, Concord, ME, mill operator, s/o Jacob
and Sarah B. (   ) Young of Rochester [no main entry], alive
1897, Gonic; m 4 Jul 1875, Rochester, Frances A. Foss [b
18 Jul 1841, Barrington, d/o Samuel D. and Katherine (Tebbetts) Foss, her 2nd marriage, d 8 Oct 1897, age 56-2-21,
Gonic, survived by husband]. Up through 1870 Charles lived
in Rochester, single, a mill operator rooming at boarding
house. (Census Strafford Co., 1870, p258; Rochester TR, Marr,
n.p.; NHVR-Deaths, Marr)

CHARLES L., b Dec 1856, Barnstead, alive 1900 Strafford,
age 43; m ca 1880, Annabell Babb [b Apr 1858, of Strafford,
d 30 Apr 1908, age 50, same town]. He and Annabell were residents of Strafford per 1900 census; child Victor B. was
listed. Annabell was buried at the Babb and Ransom Cemetery,
Second Crown Point Road, Strafford. Ch. b Strafford: child
b 29 Jan 1879; Victor Babb, b 26 Jun 1894, alive 1900. (1900
Soundex; NHVR-Births; Stiles' Cem. Records, Grid 1B-5, p2)

CHARLES SUMNER, b 1862, Dover, s/o George William and Cynthia E. (Flagg) Young, d Jul 1904, home town; m 1898, Dover, Lavinia Jeannette Hughs [b 23 Apr 1862, of Dover, d 21 May 1945, prob. Dover]. Ch. b Dover: Nettie May, b 18 Jul 1899; Cynthia, died in infancy; Theodora Ethel, b 18 Jan 1903, not traced further. (Ham. Gen., p65,79)

CHARLES W., b 23 Oct 1834, Ossipee, s/o John K. and Lydia A. (   ) Young of Dover, d 4 Sep 1905, Epping; m 12 Sep 1859, Epping, Walinda aka Malinda Smith [b 1838, of Northfield, d/o David and Harriet (   ) Smith]. Charles, at age 15, lived at home with parents in Dover in 1850, his trade, shoemaker. He pursued this trade at time of marriage when a resident of New Market. He enlisted from Exeter in Co. B, 8th Regt., NH Volunteer Infantry 6 Dec 1861, mustered in three weeks later as Pvt. and mustered out 18 Jan 1865, discharged in Concord, leaving P.O. address of Exeter. On 23 Apr 1898 Charles filed petition for an Invalid Pension based on his military service at New Orleans, Application No. 1,206,712, Certificate No. 1,065,895. After the war he was never considered a well man; he suffered from malaria and general debility up until the end, only able to work as stabler or hostler. Character witness Sgt. Charles W. Bridges of Co. B attested by date of 23 Nov 1899, to Charles' disabilities and the terrible conditions of camp in the campaign of western Louisiana. Circa 1862/1863 Charles W. was obliged to go to the camp hospital for a short time. Sgt. Bridges added: "As a rule our men had a particular aversion about going to the hospital. No one would go as long as he could stand...It looked too much like going to certain death for very few who went to such hospitals as we had in those days ever returned to duty. A sick man got better care (even as poor as that could be) in camp with his comrades than in the hospitals of those times." Other witnesses for Charles W. said that he had never married; that may be so, but after military service he did return to Epping, the reported place of marriage. No known children. (Soldiers & Sailors, p453; NHVR-Marr; Nat'l. Archives Milit. Recs.)

CHARLES W., b 1849, Clarksville, s/o Benjamin and Mary (Cate) Young of Wolfeboro, d 19 Jan 1889, age 40, home town; m 30 Jan 1888, Clarksville, Mary E. Lord [b 1863, Newport, P.Q., d/o Benjamin and Julia (   ) Lord. (NHVR-Marr)

CHARLES W., b 1849, Strafford, later of New Hampton, s/o Ira and Betsey (   ) Young [no main entry]; m 25 Jul 1881, New Hampton, Emma Johnson [b 1862, New Hampton, d/o Joshua Johnson]. Both Charles and Emma were residents of New Hampton at time of marriage. (NHVR-Marr)

CHARLES W., b ca 1850, Somersworth; m ca 1875, Somersworth, Lucy (   ) [b ca 1855, of same town]. Ch. b Somersworth: Charles W. Jr., b 5 Apr 1878, d 5 Oct 1878, same town. (NHVR-Deaths)

CHARLES WILLIAM, b 1826, Strafford, s/o Stephen and Lydia (Main) Young; alive 1870, same town; m 7 Mar 1858, Freewill Baptist Church, Strafford, Abbie F. Swasey [b ca 1833, Exeter,

alive 1870, Strafford]. In 1850 Charles W., age 24, lived
with parents in Strafford. He was head of family in Strafford
from 1860-1870. In 1860 members of household were child
Lizzie and single sister Mary A., age 30 [b 1830]; in 1870
children at home, Lizzie M., George A., and Abbie E. It
should be noted his age varied with each census: in 1850,
when at home with parents, year of birth was 1837; in 1860,
1826; and in 1870, 1837. Ch. b Strafford: Eliza M. aka
Lizzie M.+ (Young) Stanton, b 17 Apr 1859; George A., b 1862;
Abbie Emogene+ (Young) Rowell, b 20 Nov 1869, twin; and Alice
Emogene, b 20 Nov 1869, twin. (LDS I.G.I. BR; NHVR-Birth,
Brides, Marr; Census Strafford Co., 1860, p144; 1870, p383;
Strafford Marr, **Reg.** 76:43)

CHARLES WOODWARD aka Woodbury, b 17 Feb 1828, Wolfeboro,
s/o James H. and Nancy (Nudd) Young of Durham, farmer, d
17 Nov 1889, age 61-9-0, Wolfeboro; m1 1850s, Wolfeboro, Mary
A. Fowles [b 14 Aug 1831, ME, d/o Abial and Abby (   ) Fowles,
d 27 Jun 1868, Wolfeboro]; m2 8 May 1873, Wolfeboro, Mattie
M. Torrey [b 22 Aug 1838, ME, d/o Roswell Torrey, harness
maker, d 11 Dec 1927, Wolfeboro]. Charles lived in Wolfeboro,
Mattie in Ossipee at time of marriage. He was named as son
and heir of James Young of Wolfeboro by will signed 14 Jun,
proved 4 Nov 1873; James appointed him sole Exec. and residuary legatee. In 1860 Charles W. and first wife Mary A. lived
at the home of his parents in Wolfeboro; member of household
was Susan C. Young, age 18 [b 1842, MA], sibling by father's
adoption. In 1870, as widower, he still lived at the home of
his widowed father. He served Wolfeboro as Representative in
1880. Widow Mattie M. petitioned for guardianship of daughter
Maud who was under the age of 14 on date of 18 Feb, approved
6 May 1890 [Carroll Co. Probate #5836]. In 1900 Mattie was
listed as head of family in Wolfeboro, age 61; at home was
daughter Maud L., age 20, single. Charles and family were
buried at Nute Cemetery, Ossipee parents. Ch. b Wolfeboro:
Maud L., b 14 Aug 1879, d 3 Jan 1956, native town. (1900
Soundex; Loud's Cem. Recs., p85; NHVR-Marr, Deaths; Merrill's
Carroll Co., p325)

CHARLOTTE, b 1793, of Brookfield; resident of Brookfield
in 1860, age 67, a domestic. (Census Carroll Co., 1860, p542)

CLARA A., b ca 1845, of Rochester; m 22 Nov 1866, Roch-
ester, Charles W. Evans [b ca 1840, of same town]. Ch. b
Rochester: Fred A. Evans, b late 1860s, m 1895, Rochester.
(NHVR-Brides)

CLARA A., b 2 Aug 1851, East Rochester, d/o Thomas and
Sabrina (Wentworth) Young; m 25 Nov 1871, Somersworth, Charles
H. Furbish 2nd [b ca 1845, East Rochester]. (NHVR-Brides)

CLARA A., b 1862, New Durham, d/o Henry and Melissa
(Downing) Young; m (Intentions) Apr 1876, New Durham, at age
14, Charles H. Ricker, shoemaker [b 1856, of New Durham, s/o
Benjamin A. and Nancy J. (   ) Ricker]. (New Durham VR, Bk4)

CLARA B., b 1846, Barrington, d/o John B. and Mary J.
(   ) Young; m 31 Jan 1883, Manchester, Alex H. Durgin [b ca

1840, Wolfeboro]. Clara was listed in parents' household in
Barrington for 1850. (NHVR-Brides)

CLARA D., b ca 1825, Dover; m 17 Dec 1845, Dover, Henry
G. Swain [b ca 1820, of same town]. (NHVR-Brides)

CLARK, see Stephen C.

CORDELIA, b 1854, Alton, Dover, d/o James T. and Mary A.
(Nute) of Alton, m 27 Jun 1870, Dover, George W. Bennett [b
ca 1845, Dover]. Per census returns of 1870 for Dover, she
lived with parents that year. (NHVR-Brides)

CYNTHIA, b ca 1806, of Gilmanton; m 5 Dec 1826, New
Hampton, Simeon Smith [b ca 1805, of Meredith]. (NHVR-Brides)

CYNTHIA A., b ca 1827, Wakefield; m 10 Dec 1847, Wolfeboro, Thomas Danforth [b ca 1825, Wakefield]. (NHVR-Brides)

CYRUS F., b 9 Jan 1864, Canada, s/o John H. and Melissa
(Downing) Young of Farmington, d 9 Oct 1896, age 32-9-0,
Milton; m 15 Feb 1882, Rollingsford, Grace Dion [b 1865,
Canada, d/o of Charles and Mary (   ) Dion of Rollingsford].
At time of marriage Cyrus lived in South Berwick, ME, Grace,
in Rollingsford. (NHVR-Marr, Deaths)

DAN, b ca 1780, of New Hampton, alive 1813, same town;
m ca 1805, Mary M. aka Polly (   ) [b ca 1785, of New Hampton,
alive 1813, New Hampton]. Dan and wife Mary M. sold as co-
grantors 50 acres of the northern half of Lot 10, 1st Range,
New Hampton, being one-half of the farm formerly owned and
occupied by William Boyington, by lands of Jacob Tinkler, by
deed of 3 Nov 1813, rec'd 10 Feb 1814, for $800.00; witnesses
Newel Fogg, Rebecca Gilman [Strafford Co. Deed 78:224].

DANIEL, b ca 1710, of Dover; in 1762, Daniel was chosen
as one of eleven Moderators for the Dover town meetings. The
number of men selected indicated the number of town meetings
that year. Sessions would often be called to handle petty
disputes, the election of town officials and the like, and
often convened at local taverns. (Quint's Hist. Memos,
p10,11)

DANIEL, b 4 May 1713, Cochecho Point, s/o Nathaniel and
Mercy aka Mary (Hanson) Young, d pre 1775, Madbury; m ca 1738,
Dover, Temperance Bickford [b 7 Jun 1719, Parish of Madbury,
d/o Thomas and Juanna (   ) Bickford, alive 1771, age 52, Mad-
bury]. Temperance was the sister of Elizabeth Bickford who
married Ebenezer Young of Newington, and was known by her
married name of Young in the will of her father Thomas Bickford, signed 26 Jan, proved 27 Feb 1765. She was to receive
one cow; witnesses Solo Emerson, Ruben Chesley, Ebenezer
Demeritt [NH State Papers V31, p125]. When married Daniel and
Temperance settled in that section of Dover which became the
Parish of Madbury in 1755. In 1732 as resident of Dover,
Daniel signed the Petition to Samuel Belcher, was rated for
taxes of 10 shillings and 11 pence in 1741 for Cochecho
Parish, and was one of 61 petitioners who signed The Petition
to Have Madbury Set Off From Dover in 1743. At the first
parish meeting of the newly founded town of Madbury held on
23 Jun 1755, Daniel was elected one of two Commissioners, and

later selectman for 1765 and 1766. Children, if any, were not known.

Starting around 1765 Daniel and Temperance began selling parcels of land which made up their 46-acre homestead in Madbury and before 1775 had completely sold their estate. As noted above Daniel died within a few years after selling the homestead. Four land deeds recorded the sales; in all of them Daniel held title in fee simple and Temperance ceded dower rights. The first sale involved eleven acres, 67 rods adjoining Bellamy Banks River and James Young's land, by deed signed 25 Jul, rec'd 30 Oct 1765, to Robert Huckins of Madbury for 910 pounds Old Tenor; witnesses Joseph Drew, Ebenezer Thompson [NH Prov. Deed 89:199]. An additional two acres land on the eastern side of Bellamy Banks River at the northern corner of said Robert Huckins' land was sold by deed signed 31 Mar, rec'd 8 Apr 1767, to Joseph Drew of Madbury for 14 pounds; witnesses Ebenezer Demeritt, John Demeritt Jr. [NH Prov. Deed 92:123]. Thirdly, four-1/2 acres at the southwest corner of Daniel's homestead where he then dwelt, running north the whole width of land adjacent to land that belonged to the heirs of Jonathan Young, late of Dover, were sold to widow Mary Young of Dover for 22 pounds-10 shillings by deed of 1 Aug 1769, rec'd 18 Oct 1771; witnesses James Young, Ephraim Hanson [NH Prov. Deed 96:464]. The last 20 acres of their homestead farm in Madbury, adjacent to lands of the said Mary Young, Robert Huckins, James Young and Solomon Young, were sold by deed signed 7 Dec 1770, rec'd 18 Oct 1771, with buildings and livestock, for 100 pounds to James Young and Timothy Young, both of Dover, James buying a three-fourth share, Timothy, a one-fourth share; witnesses Silas Hanson, Ephraim Hanson [NH Prov. Deed 96:465]. Note that Strafford Co. Deed 3:41 signed 7 Mar 1775, rec'd 9 Jun 1777, cited that the 8-1/2 acres Stephen Young of Madbury was selling had originally been purchased from Daniel Young of Madbury, being "part of what was Daniel Young's homestead when he lived." Daniel's initial deed of sale to Stephen Young apparently went unrecorded. According to Adam's Madbury, n.p., Daniel's homestead has since changed hands many times over, for the house and farm "was later in the name of Ezra Young....Orlando Young sold the premises to Oliver Waldron 29 Nov 1865." (Heritage's Dover VR, p10; Holbrook's 1732 Census, p73-75; NH State Papers, V24, p700; Stackpole's Durham, V2, p2)

DANIEL, b ca 1720, Dover; original proprietor of 100-acre Lot 29, 1st Div. Wakefield, by Masonian Grant of 27 Apr 1749, and absentee owner of 100-acre Lots 23 and 27, 2nd Div., Wakefield, almost all of which had to be sold at public auction for delinquent taxes. All lots were most likely bought for speculation. For tax years of 1770 and 1771, Lot 27, drawn to the original right of Paul Gerrish of Dover, was sold for two pounds by tax deed of 10 Aug 1774, rec'd 6 Jan 1795; witnesses Moses Canney, Simeon Dearborn [Strafford Co. Deed 19:402]. For tax years 1770-1773, part of Lot 23, 57 acres, drawn to the original right of William Styles, was sold by tax deed dated 2 Jul 1778, rec'd 9 Aug 1794, for one pound and four shillings; witnesses David Copp, Samuel Hall [Strafford Co. Deed 19:72]. For the tax year of 1785, the whole 100-acre Lot 29 was sold: one half of Lot 29, 50 acres, was sold by tax deed of 6 Mar 1788, rec'd 10 Mar 1795, for 1-16-8; witnesses Molly Palmer, Benjamin Palmer [Strafford Co. Deed 21:58]; the other half was sold by deed signed 17 May 1793, rec'd 14 Mar 1798, for 17 shillings; witnesses Avery Hall, Daniel Perkins [Strafford Co. Deed 27:359]. For further information on ownership of Lot 23, 2nd Div., Wakefield, see Richard K. Young of Wakefield whose purchase of Lot 23 went unrecorded. (Bank's Wakefield, p10-14)

DANIEL, b ca 1750, Parish of Madbury. By deed of 3 Oct 1772, rec'd 8 Mar 1775, Daniel sold to David Durgin of Durham, the whole of Lot 47, 2nd Div., 136 acres in Middleton except for 12 acres already sold to Sawyer Chesley, and "is part of the original right of Nathaniel Young," for 30 pounds; witnesses John Griffin, John Smith [Strafford Co. Deed 1:264]. See Nathaniel and Mary (Kimball) Young of Parish of Madbury for further details.

DANIEL, b 1770s, of Effingham; resident of Effingham in 1830, age 40-50. Household was made up of spouse age 40-50, two males, one under 5, one age 5-10, and three females, one each under 10, 15 and 20. (Census Strafford Co., 1830, p397)

DANIEL, b 1770s, of Wakefield; head of household in Wakefield in 1810, age 26-45. Household contained spouse of same age group and one male under 10 [b ca 1805]. (Census Strafford Co., 1810, p595)

DANIEL, b ca 1780, of Barnstead; m ca 1805, Abigail (   ) [b ca 1800, of Barnstead]. He and Abigail owned Lots 36 and 38, 2nd Div., Barnstead in 1816. Their homestead was located on Province Road. (Merrill's Barnstead, p329)

DANIEL, b 1780s, of Ossipee; Daniel was head of household in Ossipee in 1840, age 50-60, with spouse of same age and family of two males age 5-10 and one female age 15-20. This may have been Daniel 2nd, son of John the Highlander of Ossipee. Daniel of Ossipee administered John Young's estate by probate papers dated 5 Sep 1822.

DANIEL, b 1785, Berwick, ME, eldest s/o John and Sally (Nason) Young of Ossipee, died testate pre 31 Aug 1874, Freedom; m1 2 Oct 1805, Freedom, Elizabeth aka Eliza Nason [b 1785 Ossipee, d pre 1864, Ossipee]; m2 31 May 1864, at age 79, Freedom, widow Catherine (Roberts) Hayes [b 1806, Brookfield, d/o Nathaniel and Patience (Garland) Roberts of Ossipee, alive 1874, Freedom]. Catherine was the widow of Robert Hayes [b ca 1797, Eaton, s/o Ezekial Hayes, d 17 Dec 1854, home town]; they had married 22 Apr 1827, Eaton. Daniel became a resident of Freedom at least by 1840; per census that year age was 50-60, with family of spouse of same age bracket, two males between the ages of 5-10, and one female age 15-20. He and Eliza were listed on the census returns for Freedom from

1850-1860. In 1850 estate was valued at $4,000; member of family was Lucinda Shaw, age 14 [b 1836.

From 1860-1870 he and second wife Catherine lived by themselves in Freedom. Although there were no known children of this second marriage Catherine was the mother of a large family by Robert Hayes; their children were brought up by different families in the neighborhood and in Effingham. See Hayes Genealogy for fuller story. Daniel's place of residence prior to 1840 is uncertain. He purchased many properties both in Ossipee and Wakefield and on the strength of witness Ezekial Wentworth who signed consistently for Daniel of both towns, belief is held that Daniel was one and the same person in all these land deeds. It may well be that through the redistricting of Wakefield, Ossipee Gore and Effingham from 1820 up through 1832, Daniel did not literally move lock, stock and barrel to Freedom before 1850, but rather, found his homestead situated in the jurisdiction of Freedom by 1832. Advice sought from the New Hampshire Archives, Concord, on new town lines drawn in the redistricting by 1832 came to no avail. For background on "gerrymandering" of town lines from 1820-1832, several N.H. resources stated that all that part of Wakefield on the n.e. side of Province Pond was annexed to Effingham 22 Jun 1820. With respect to Ossipee, that part of Ossipee Gore which was not included in Ossipee was annexed to Effingham 23 Dec 1820. And later, North Effingham was set off from Effingham proper 16 June 1831, only to change its name to Freedom by date of 6 Dec 1832. The compiler prays that logic is not stretched too thin to prove this point.

Daniel's first property came to him by deed of gift dated 30 Dec 1808, rec'd 25 Feb 1815, from his parents: the eastern half of 100-acre Lot 37, 2nd Div., North Wakefield. Yet he sold his half share "where he then lived" to Aaron Hanson of Ossipee who owned the other moiety by deed signed 10 Sep 1813, rec'd 24 Sep 1813, for $500.00; Eliza Young ceded dower rights; witnesses Ezekial Wentworth, Ezekial Keay [Strafford Co. Deed 76:616]. By way of trade-off he purchased from the said Aaron Hanson and his wife Mary Hanson, 50 acres in Ossipee being part of 500-acre Lot 4, adjacent to Lot 3, by deed rec'd 25 Feb 1815; witnesses Ezekial Wentworth, Ezekial Keay [Strafford Co. Deed 82:353]. It should be noted that Daniel's father's homestead was situated on 50 acres of Lot 4, Ossipee, abutting the North Wakefield line.

During the 1810s, Daniel bought several properties in North Wakefield; according to these deeds he was of Wakefield when he purchased (1) from Marston Ames of Parsonsfield, York Co., Mass. [later, Maine], by deed signed 1 Oct 1813, rec'd 25 Feb 1815, 5 acres land, part of Lot 55, Wakefield, situated on the s.w. side of the road leading from Ossipee to New-fields, for $15; witnesses Ezekial Wentworth, Thomas Randall [Strafford Co. Deed 82:349]; (2) purchased 5 acres of the 110-acre Lot 32, 2nd Div., Wakefield from Joseph Nason of Wake-field, by deed of 21 Dec 1814, rec'd 25 Feb 1815, for $26.00;

witnesses Samuel and Cornelia Burbank [Strafford Co. Deed 82:351]. For background of Lot 32, 2nd Div., Wakefield, Daniel's father John sold part of Lot 32 to the said Joseph Nason the year previous. There is no indication however that Daniel established a home on these Wakefield properties. In the 1820s Daniel was of Ossipee when he purchased more land in North Wakefield, 40 acres of Lot 39, 2nd Div., from James Roberts of Wakefield, by deed signed 14 Dec 1815, rec'd 10 Oct 1821, for $133.00; witnesses Ezekial Wentworth, Simon Foss [Strafford Co. Deed 110:620]. Daniel of Ossipee, James Young 2nd [cousin] of Wakefield, and Elias and Mark Wentworth, both of Wakefield, quitclaimed to Joseph T. Mathes of Ossipee, by deed signed 6 Jan, rec'd 15 Mar 1825, for $30.00, their shares in the Dearborn sawmill on Lot 2, Ossipee; witnesses James Young Jr., Ezekial Wentworth [Strafford Co. Deed 122:408].

Daniel's will was drawn 1 Oct 1866, proved 31 Aug 1874; he named Elias Towle as sole Exec. and wife Catherine as residuary legatee; witnesses Charles Adams, Richard Bennett, Elias Towle [Carroll Co. Probate #5842]. On date of probate when Elias Towle declined the position of Exec., widow Catherine of Freedom nominated Albert Locke of Freedom to fill this position. Daniel's three sons, John, Daniel Jr. and Stephen C., were each to receive $1.00; his married daughters Eleanor Philbrick, Perlina Moses and Mercy Allen were also to receive $1.00 each. Catherine was to receive all his real and personal estate in Freedom. Ch. b Ossipee: John+, b 23 Mar 1804; Eleanor (Young) Philbrick, b 1810s; and Pauline+ aka Perlina (Young) Moses, b ca 1810. Ch. b Freedom: Mercy+ (Young) Allen, b ca 1825; Daniel+ aka Jr., b 23 Aug 1827; and Stephen C.+, b 1830. (Ossipee TR, V1; Census Strafford Co., 1840, p246; Census Carroll Co., 1850, p154; 1860, p629; 1870, p305; Hayes Gen., V1, p331-332; NHVR-Deaths, Marr; Freedom VR, Bk 1, p50)

DANIEL, b ca 1785, Dover, d testate pre 16 Oct 1826, Dover; m 14 Jan 1819, Durham, widow Eleanor W. Smith [b 1790s, Durham, d pre 24 Jul 1832, Dover]. While single, Daniel lived on the Faxon Farm at Toll End, Dover, owned by Benjamin Church of Dover who was later to name Daniel as Co-Exec. and co-residuary legatee of his will drawn 7 Apr, proved 30 Sep 1812. Kinsmen John and Ephraim Young were the other two heirs. The common denominator between Benjamin Church of Dover and this Young family unit is most likely the mutual ancestor Mercy (Hanson) Church, widow of John Church and later the wife of Nathaniel Young of Cochecho. Benjamin Church was grandson of Mercy (Hanson) Church; these Young men could have been great-grandsons of Nathaniel and Mercy (Hanson) Young. Daniel received one-half of the Faxon farm with buildings, livestock and tools subject to widow Eunice's dower rights, and one-half of the furniture upon Eunice's demise. Daniel and John traded off shares of the Church estate with one another by numerous land deeds. Daniel's quitclaim of 2 Apr, rec'd 5 May 1814, conveyed to John Young of Dover for $100.00, one-half of the field which said Church formerly lived on by the western side of lot bounded on Toll End Road leading from Dover Meeting House to Barrington, plus 30 acres pasture land, 46 acres land elsewhere and the privilege of the falls on the river. Further John was to occupy one-half of the dwelling house with the privilege of making cider at the cider mill; witnesses Moses Neal, Eleanor Smith [Strafford Co. Deed 79:216]. Daniel ended up with full title to Church's dwelling house in Dover by John's quitclaim signed 20 Sep 1815, rec'd 20 Apr 1816. See John and Ruth Young of Dover for full particulars of Benjamin Church's will and shares traded off.

Daniel's will was signed 29 Sep 1826, proved 16 Oct 1826, naming Samuel Kimball Esq. of Dover his sole Exec.; witnesses John Young, Aaron Watson, Daniel H. Watson, all of Dover [Strafford Co. Probate 35:200]. Daniel bequeathed to his wife Eleanor the income of $20.00 per year "during her natural life at my house provided she will have the same for her dower in my estate and the same to be paid out of the income of my estate." Each of his three sons by Eleanor, Ezra, Benjamin and James, was to receive a one-third portion of his real and personal estate. When petition was filed for probate 16 Oct 1826, Eleanor "did not agree to take the provisions made for her," and wished that her Dower may be set off. On same date of 17 Oct 1826, Samuel Kimball of Dover was allowed Exec. of Daniel's will, bond of $4,000.00 with sureties Jonathan Kimball and Daniel H. Watson, both of Dover [Strafford Co. Probate 30:220], and appointed guardian of Daniel's three sons, minors under the age of 14, Ezra, Benjamin and James, with Eleanor's blessing; bond of $4,000.00 was posted by said Kimball with the same sureties given above [Strafford Co. Probate 30:138]. For inventory of property see distribution of estate.

Eleanor's petition for dower rights was not overlooked. Lands were set off to her 7 Feb 1828, by John W. Hayes, Joshua Ham and Daniel H. Watson, approved same date [Strafford Co. Probate 37:70]. In setting off Eleanor's dower rights the committee invoked the practice of "severing the estate from the Dower," rather than the Dower from the estate, upon the request of guardian Samuel Kimball who cited the recent precedent of Anna Young's dower rights being set off from the estate of her husband Ephraim Young, late of Dover [relative of Daniel]; see Ephraim and Anna Young of Dover for full details. The net result was that Eleanor received 25 acres from the homestead farm on the west side adjoining land of John Young, 15 acres from the tract purchased of Benjamin Horne by deed rec'd 5 Jan 1819, 68 square rods land in Barrington adjacent to Jonathan Kimball, the west front room in house with chamber of said room, and the whole of garret and western end of barn. License to convey deed to John Twombly Jr. of Dover on land from Daniel's estate was granted Samuel Kimball, Exec., 18 Apr 1829, "agreeably to the tenor of obligation made by Daniel"; allowed 24 Apr 1829 [Strafford Co.

Probate 39:352]. License to sell Daniel's real estate "as
will be sufficient to raise $700.00 to discharge debts" was
granted to said Kimball on 18 May 1829 (petitioned 28 Mar
1829) [Strafford Co. Probate 24:204]. Said Kimball returned
his first account 18 May 1829, allowed same date [Strafford
Co. Probate 39:268]: outstanding bills he had paid off,
widow's allowance of $100.00 and 58 other bills of account,
came to $1,223.64; balance of $124.28 was due Exec.

Admin. Papers on Eleanor's estate, filed 24 Jul 1832,
Dover, named the said Samuel Kimball as Admin; he gave bond
of $1,000.00 with sureties Charles Ham and Oliver J. Horn,
both of Dover [Strafford Co. Probate 30:318]. On 18 Sep 1832,
appraisal of Eleanor's estate was submitted by Oliver J. Horn,
Charles Ham, and Wentworth Watson, all of Dover; attested to
and approved same date [Strafford Co. Probate 44:111]: household effects were valued at $46.20. Oliver Horn was named
Commissioner of Eleanor's estate 14 Nov 1832, to review claims
of creditors [Strafford Co. Probate 46:57]: claims totalled
$30.98, report allowed 19 May 1834. As late as 21 Jan 1840,
said Kimball filed his closing account on her estate, allowed
same date [Strafford Co. Probate 55:17]: debts paid on last
illness, funeral expenses, appraisers, etc. came to $60.97;
amount of inventory of personal estate, $46.20; balance of
$14.77 due said Administrator.

Division of Daniel's estate was made actually eleven
years after his death at such time when his sons had reached
the age of 14 or over; findings presented by Oliver J. Horn,
Jonathan Kimball and John K. Ham on 15 May 1837, allowed same
date [Strafford Co. Probate 52:246]. Their determinations
were based upon inventory of Daniel's estate and presented in
court 27 Nov 1826 by Ephraim Ham, Jonathan Kimball and Daniel
Horn, all of Dover; approved 28 Nov 1826 [Strafford Co.
Probate 32:265]. Total value of real estate was set at
$4,955.00; personal estate at $660.61. Real estate consisted
of the 55-acre homestead farm in Dover, 12-1/4 acres on the
south side of road adjacent to Dudley Watson, aka the Otis-
Watson field; 80 acres with a two-third share of buildings at
Sunken Island purchased from Ephraim Young and subject to the
dower of his widow; 15 acres of Benjamin Horn pasture on north
side of Toll End Road adjacent to Daniel Horn's lands; and 2
acres woodland in Barrington. Total value of real estate came
to $4,955.00, personal estate, $660.61.

Son Ezra was to receive 34 acres of the homestead farm
with dwelling house until he arrived at age 22, and nine acres
of Ben pasture, so called, on south side of Toll End Road,
adjacent to Daniel Horn's land. Son James was to receive the
whole of the Otis-Watson field containing 12-1/4 acres, the
remaining eight acres of the Ben pasture on the western side
as well as 14 acres of Sunken Island on the north side of Toll
End Road by land of Elijah Austin to land set off as dower to
widow Amy Young as part of Ephraim Young's estate, until Ezra
reached the age of 22. And son Benjamin was to receive 72

acres, 26 square rods of Sunken Island being "all the land belonging to Daniel's estate with house and barn subject to the dower of widow Amy Young, which dower will revert to Daniel's estate at Amy's decease...and is included in the 72 acres," and two acres land in Barrington woods which was deeded to Daniel by Daniel Horn and James Kimball.

Exec. Kimball gave his second account on Daniel's estate 22 Jan 1840, approved same date [Strafford Co. Probate 55:18]: debts paid by Kimball, $770.72; assets (including sale on Real Estate per license at $639.95), at $738.25; balance due Exec., $32.47. He also returned his first account of expenses of guardianship of Daniel's three sons from Oct 1826 to Mar 1829, on date of 18 May 1829, allowed same date [Strafford Co. Probate 39:266]: expenses for Ezra which included clothing, out-of-pocket money, books and miscellaneous items came to $119.62, balance of $59.13 due Exec.; expenses for Benjamin covered same items, set at $97.46, balance of $36.97 due Exec.; expenses for James covering same items came to $163.62, balance of $103.13 due Exec. His responsibilities as guardian of the three sons extended to the care and maintenance of the homestead and as evidenced by his guardianship account of 22 Jan 1840 [Strafford Co. Probate 56:213]. He paid taxes for the years 1829-1832, 1833-1835 of $32.42; made repairs, mowed the grain, hauled and accounted for cash from produce; balance of $106.74 due from Kimball to be paid to the three sons. Kimball's account of 23 Jan 1840, approved same date, covered expenses for taxes from 1836-1838, sundry expenses for the boys and credits from produce and pasturing; balance due guardian, $145.42 [Strafford Co. Probate 56:219].

Ch. b Dover: Ezra+ aka 2nd, b ca 1820; Benjamin+, b 1824; and James, b 1820s. (Heritage's Dover VR, p160; Stackpole's Durham, V2, p384; Scale's Dover, p495; Census Strafford Co., 1830, p317; NHVR-Deaths)

DANIEL, b 1790s, Ossipee; head of household in Ossipee in 1830, age 30-40. Members of household were spouse age 30-40, three males, one under 5, one age 5-10, one 20-30, and one female under 5. (Census Strafford Co., 1830, p423)

DANIEL, b 1791, of Dover, d 6 Feb 1838, Durham; m1 pre Sep 1812, Durham, Abigail Chesley [b 2 Jan 1796, Durham, d/o Benjamin and Sarah (   ) Chesley, died in childbirth 16 Mar 1831, native town]; m2 Jul 1832, Durham, widow Hannah (Chesley) Butler [b 1 Jan 1799, Durham, sister of Abigail Chesley above, d 23 Feb 1881, age 81, Durham]. Daniel, tanner, was head of household in Durham in 1830, his age 30-40, with family of spouse of same age group, five males, one under 5, two age 5-10, and two 15-20, and three females, 1 age 60-70, one under 5 and one age 10-15. Abigail's father Benjamin Chesley was born 1751, Durham, died of measles taken in Town Meeting 21 Jul 1805, age 64 years, Durham. Her mother Sarah (   ) Chesley was born 1772, Durham, died 24 Sep 1825, age 53, burned in her house, Durham. She was 9 years old at the time her father died and was made ward on 3 Sep 1812 of kinsman

Joseph Chesley 3rd. Despite the fact she married at age 16
in 1812, said Joseph Chesley was appointed her guardian on
3 Sep 1812, becoming not only the guardian of her person but
also of her estate; bond of $1,000 was given with sureties
Valentine Smith Esq. and Daniel Chesley, both of Durham
[Strafford Co. Probate 19:176]. In the year following her
death, Daniel remarried, his second wife Hannah Chesley,
Abigail's sister. In 1840 Hannah was head of family in
Durham, age 40-50, with household of three males, one under
5, one age 10-15, one 10-20, and four other females, one each
under 10, 10-15, 15-20 and 20-30.

    Daniel's first known deed before his marriage, signed
1 Apr 1811, reveals that he was of Madbury, and before that,
of Dover, name given as "alias Daniel Young of Dover." After
their marriage he and Abigail lived in Durham. In the deed
cited above, Daniel and co-grantee Joseph Chesley 3rd of
Durham purchased 1 acre, 40 rods of land in Durham by the road
which leads to Madbury, from Ebenezer and Hannah Crummett of
Durham for $366.00; witnesses Andrew Emerson, Valentine Smith
[Strafford Co. Deed 67:161]. Early in March 1813, there were
numerous deeds between Daniel, Abigail and the said Joseph
Chesley as guardian involving properties Abigail inherited
from her father's estate. The first of these was dated 1 Mar
1813, rec'd 13 Mar same year, by which Joseph Chesley, acting
for Abigail, sold a parcel of land in Durham at public auction
to Jacob Odell of Durham for $43.13; witnesses William K.
Atkinson, Valentine Smith [Strafford Co. Deed 75:18]. On same
date of signing and recording in the former deed, said Chesley
sold to Joshua Ballard of Durham, land in Durham situated on
the eastern side of the main road leading to Dover, adjacent
to said Ballard's land, for $385.00; same witnesses [Strafford
Co. Deed 75:13]. Three days later, Daniel and bride sold to
said Chesley, by deed of 4 Mar 1813, rec'd 22 Apr 1817, the
one-half of both the 48-acre lot and buildings in Durham which
Abigail had inherited, land by the Turnpike Road, for $41.00;
witnesses Valentine Smith, George Hull [Strafford Co. Deed
95:405]. Daniel as sole Grantor sold to said Chesley by deed
of 17 Apr 1816, rec'd 22 Apr 1817, 4 acres land in Durham
adjacent to the northern side of the Turnpike Road, exclusive
of one half of the "Bank House, tan yard and lot now owned by
said Chesley," for $900.00; witnesses Valentine Smith, Philip
Chesley [Strafford Co. Deed 95:385].

    .   Daniel died intestate in 1838. Hannah was named Admin.
of her husband's estate 21 May 1838, giving bond of $1,000.00
with sureties Winthrop Smith of Durham and Paul Chesley of
Madbury [Strafford Co. Probate 50:119]. Inventory of the
estate was taken by Winthrop Smith, Paul Chesley and John
Yeaton, submitted and approved 30 Jun 1838 [Strafford Co.
Probate 52:492]. Personal estate only was reported, set at
$127.23; this included livestock, wagon, horse sled, farming
tools and equipment, furniture and household effects. On
15 Jan 1839, widow Hannah was granted an allowance of $90.98

"for the support of life" [Strafford Co. Probate 43:128].
Hannah returned her accounting on same date as widow's allowance was granted, approved same day: amount of personal
estate per inventory was $127.23 [as cited above]. Expenses
of last sickness, funeral and administration came to $127.23
[Strafford Co. Probate 53:425]. In 1860 Hannah kept a boarding house in Durham with son Albert at home. Family members
were buried at a private burial ground in Durham bounded by
Dover Road, Oyster River and Beard Creek.

   Ch. b Durham by Abigail: Abigail, b 1814, d 14 Oct 1831,
age 17, Durham; Joseph+, b 2 Mar 1827; and Sophia, b 1828, d
1 Nov 1831, Durham. Ch. b Durham by Hannah: Almira, b 6 Mar
1834, alive 1860, Durham, single, tailoress; Albert+, b 3 Feb
1836. (Stackpole's Durham, V1, p104; Durham Graveyards #62;
NHVR-Deaths; Census Strafford Co., 1830, p36; 1840, p498;
1850, p469; 1860, p583; LDS I.G.I. BR; NH Gen. Recs., V1,
No.1, p104)

   DANIEL, b 1 Jun 1795, Ossipee, most likely s/o Moses and
Mary (Chadwick) Young of Wakefield, d 21 May 1873, Wakefield;
m ca 1819, Wakefield, Elizabeth aka Betsey Cook [b 2 Jul 1799,
Wakefield, d/o Peter and Betsey (   ) Cook, d 10 Jan 1883,
home town]. Daniel became head of household in 1840, Wakefield, age 40-50, with household of spouse age 30-40, seven
males, two under 5, one 5-10, two 10-15, two 15-20, and four
females, one under 5, and one each 5-10, 10-15, and 15-20.
He and Betsey were listed as residents of Wakefield from 1850
up through 1870. In 1850 children at home were Peter, Daniel,
Benjamin, Mary, Susan, Abial, James and Charles, the last
three in school. From 1860-1870, members of their household
included son Peter C. and wife Mary; in 1860 another member
of household was gr.son Frank A. Leighton, age 8 [b 1852],
whose mother was Susan (Young) Leighton. Daniel's homestead
was located on Pine River Road, North Wakefield on Lot 75, 2nd
Div., abutting his brother James C.'s homestead [Lots 62-64].
Daniel purchased one-half of Lot 75 for $208.00, by deed of
2 Aug, rec'd 29 Aug 1825, from Otis P. Johnson of Wakefield
for $208.00; witnesses Ezekial Wentworth, John Mathes [Straf-
ford Co. Deed 127:160]; the other moiety was purchased for
$210.00 by deed of 24 Jan 1827, rec'd 28 Aug 1827, from said
Johnson; witnesses Sally Wentworth, Ezekial Wentworth [Straf-
ford Co. Deed 135:192].

   Letters of Admin. on Daniel's estate were filed by widow
Betsey 3 Feb 1874, approved same date; appraisers named were
Daniel Campernell, William B. Wentworth and Robert McDaniel
[Carroll Co. Probate #5842-A]. Daniel, Betsey and family
members were buried at Peter Young Cemetery, Pray Hill Road,
Wakefield. Ch. b Wakefield unless otherwise noted: Peter
C.+, b 12 Aug 1819; Daniel+, b 1826; Benjamin+, b 1828; Mary
A.+ (Young) Sweatt, b 1830; Olive, b 1832, twin, d.y.; Susan
A.+ (Young) Leighton, b 1832, twin; Abial+, b Feb 1833, ME;
James M.+, b 1836; Charles+, b 1838; Olive T., b 1841, d.y.;
and Sumner G., b 1842, d.y. (Census Strafford Co., 1840,

p378; Census Carroll Co., 1850, p319; 1860, p581; 1870, p429;
Twombley's Wakefield Cem., TMs; Wentworth Gen., V1, p501,502;
NHVR-Brides)

DANIEL, b 1822, Madbury, d 31 Mar 1882, Wolfeboro; m
10 Oct 1847, Madbury, Almeda Nutter [b 1826, Rochester, alive
1889, Rochester]. Widow Almeda m2 1 Jan 1889, Rochester,
Nicholas Brock [b 1824, Barrington]. Daniel and Almeda were
listed as residents of Madbury in 1850; member of household
was Betsey Jackson, age 80 [b 1770], no child listed. In 1860
Daniel, carpenter, and Almeda lived in Rochester with her
brother Alphonzo Nutter [b 1819]. In 1870 Daniel had become
merchant of Wolfeboro; the couple lived alone. Letters of
Admin. on Daniel's estate were filed by widow Almeda 18 Dec
1882, approved 2 Jan 1883 [Carroll Co. Probate #5846]. Ch.
born Madbury: Albert W., b 12 Mar 1851, d 19 Aug 1854, Madbury; and Daniel Webster, b 14 Mar 1855, d Apr 1856, Madbury.
(NHVR-Births, Brides, Deaths, Marr; LDS I.G.I. BR; Census
Strafford Co., 1850, p482; 1860, p464; Census Carroll Co.,
1870, p458; Roch. VR, Marr)

DANIEL aka Jr., b 1826, Wakefield, s/o Daniel and Betsey
(Cook) Young, d 17 Jan 1865, Woburn, MA; m 16 Apr 1854, Lydia
A. Wentworth [b 15 Nov 1822, Wakefield, d/o Mark and Betsey
(Whitehouse) Wentworth, d 24 Dec 1904, Wolfeboro]. Daniel
lived with parents in Wakefield in 1850. In 1857 he and Lydia
moved to Stoneham, Mass. Lydia m2 28 Jun 1870, Rev. Lewis
Phillips of the First Christian Church of Wolfeboro. Daniel,
Lydia and twin sons Oscar and Daniel [b 1859-d 1859] were
buried at the Peter Young Cemetery at top of Pray Hill Road,
Wakefield. (Twombly's Wakefield Cem., TMs; Wentworth Gen.,
V2, p202)

DANIEL aka Jr., b 23 Aug 1827, Freedom, s/o Daniel and
Elizabeth (Nason) Young, d 23 Mar 1895, age 67-7-0, Freedom;
m 4 Mar 1850, Eaton, Eleanor aka Ellen Jane Allard, [b Apr
1826, Eaton, alive 1900, age 74, Freedom]. Daniel Jr. was
named son and heir of Daniel Young of Freedom by his will
signed 1 Oct 1866, proved 31 Aug 1874. He and Eleanor were
residents of Freedom from 1850-1870. In 1850 the only other
member of household was Joseph Shaw, age 12 [b 1838]. In 1860
children at home were Adeline F., Jacob E., Mary E. Members
of household were Albion Thurston, age 17 [b 1843] and Austin
D. Allard, age 11 [b 1849]. In 1870 children at home were
Jacob Edgar and Mary E. aka Lizzie M. In 1900 Eleanor J., age
74, was listed twice in the census that year for Freedom: for
a time she lived with son Edgar J. and family, later in the
year, with son-in-law Joseph Tyler, husband of daughter Lizzie
M., deceased. Ch. b Freedom: Adeline F., b 18 Aug 1852;
Jacob E. aka Edgar J.+, b 26 Nov 1856; and Mary E. aka Lizzie
M.+ (Young) Tyler, b 1859. (Census Carroll Co., 1850, p154;
1860, p629, 1870, p305; 1900 Soundex; NHVR-Births, Deaths; LDS
I.G.I. BR; Freedom VR, 1878-1890)

DANIEL L., b Mar 1828, Sanford, ME, res. of Rochester,
s/o Joseph and Edna (Houston) Young of Rochester; m2 10 Oct

1886, Lebanon, ME, recorded in Rochester, Myra S. (Prescott) Shapleigh [b Oct 1846, Acton, ME, d/o of William Prescott, her 2nd marriage, alive 1900 Rochester]. In 1900 Daniel and Myra lived alone in Rochester. (NHVR-Marr; 1900 Soundex; Rochester TR, Marr, p14)

DAVID, b 1 May 1759, Barrington, d 29 Dec 1845, age 87, Barnstead; m ca 1782, Barrington, Abigail Foss [b ca 1760, Barrington, alive 1810, Barnstead]. David was listed as resident of Barrington from 1790-1800. In 1790 his household held one male under 16 and four females. In 1800 his age was 45 years plus; family members were spouse under 45 years, four males under 10, one male age 10-16, and three females, one under 10 and two 10-16. By 1804 he and Abigail had relocated in Barnstead where they lived on the George Pitman place. There David and family were members of the Freewill Baptist Church. In 1810 David was listed on the census returns for Barnstead, age 45 years plus; members of household were spouse over 45 years, four males, three 10-16, one 16-26, and four females, two under 10, one 10-16 and one 16-26. David's homestead in Barrington was 30 acres of parts of Lot 21 and 22, 1st Range, Barrington, bounded by Lot 22, by land of Richard Babb's, then running s.e. to lands of Benjamin Young and Joseph Hayes, bought by deed signed 23 May 1778, rec'd 21 May 1781, from Joshua Foss of said town for 54 pounds; witnesses Jonathan Young and Rebecca Otis [Strafford Co. Deed 4:50].

Ch. b Barrington: Abigail+ (Young) Otis, b 3 Mar 1783; Deborah+ (Young) Emerson, b 12 Dec 1785; David+, b 12 Nov 1788; Winthrop, b 12 Mar 1793; Ebenezer, b 15 May 1795, d 15 Nov 1812; Solomon+, b 14 Dec 1796; Stephen+, b 20 Jan 1798; Sarah+ (Young) Emerson, b 12 Mar 1790; and Betsey, b 10 Sep 1801. Ch. b Barnstead: Nancy, b 23 Jun 1805. (Stackpole's Durham, V2, p181,184; Census Strafford Co., 1790, p86; 1800, p155; 1810, p536; NHVR-Births, Deaths; LDS I.G.I. BR; Otis Gen., **Reg.** 5:218; Merrill's Barnstead, p333; Morning Star, p375)

DAVID S., b ca 1780, of Gilmanton, s/o Dudley Young; m 15 Nov 1798, Belmont [Upper Gilmanton], Susannah Mudget [b late 1770s, Gilmanton]. David was head of household in Gilmanton in 1810, age under 45; family held spouse whose age was under 45, one male age 10-16, and three females all under 10. In 1812 he was resident of District No. 1, Gilmanton, rated at $2.80. By mortgage deed dated 20 May, rec'd 27 Jun 1812, David S. held title to homestead farm of Dudley and Nathaniel B. Young [brothers] of Gilmanton; see Nathaniel Badger Young for full details. (Census Strafford Co., 1810, p801; Gilmanton TR, V3, p369; NHVR-Marr)

DAVID, b 12 Nov 1788, Barrington, s/o David and Abigail (Foss) Young of Barnstead, d 16 Nov 1847, age 61, Barnstead; m 25 Feb 1823, Barnstead, Eleanor M. Nutter [b 1797, of Barnstead, d 11 Oct 1879, age 82, same town]. David and family were members of the Freewill Baptist Church. He was head of household in Barnstead from 1830-1840: in 1830 his age was

40-50, with spouse age 30-40, and one male 5-10; in 1840 age was 50-60, with spouse 40-50 and one male age 5-10 years. On 16 Dec 1847 widow Eleanor filed Letters of Admin. on David's "personal estate" when she nominated John Collins of Barnstead as Admin. in her stead [Belknap Co. Probate #486]. On same day she filed petition of guardianship, requesting that William S. Nutter be appointed guardian of son John M., minor over 14 years, and daughter Mary Jane, under 14 years [Belknap Co. Probate #487]. Eleanor became head of household in Barnstead in 1850, age 53; living with her was Dorothy Nutter, age 84 [b 1766]. In 1860 son John, age 29, and daughter Mary J., age 18, both single, boarded at the home of James Foss, age 67 [b 1793] and wife Eleanor Foss, age 63 [b 1797] in Barnstead. In 1900 both siblings were single and lived in Barnstead. They took in boarder Eli E. Pendergast, age 60 [b Feb 1840]. David and Eleanor were buried at Barnstead Center Graveyard. Ch. b Barnstead: William S., b 18 Dec 1820; John M., b 5 Sep 1831; and Mary Jane, b Apr 1843. (Barnstead Cemeteries, p7; Census Strafford Co., 1830, p15; 1840, p447; Census Belknap Co., 1850, p404; 1860, p357; NHVR-Births, Marr; 1900 Soundex; LDS I.G.I. BR)

DAVID, b 1791, Barrington, s/o Isaac and Betsey (Cate) Young, d testate, 22 May 1871, Barrington, farmer; m 29 Aug 1838, Northwood, widow Prudence (Cate) Young [b 29 Jun 1793, d/o Joseph and Prudence (Marden) Cate of Northwood, former spouse of Ebenezer Young who was David's brother, d 7 Nov 1855, Barrington]. David was named one of three Execs. and residuary legatees by the terms of his father's will drawn 8 Sep 1826, proved 19 Apr 1827. From the division of his father's estate dated 5 Oct 1841, he received 112 acres, 54 rods in Barrington. He was head of household in Barrington in 1840, age 50-60, with family of spouse age 40-50, one male age 20-30, and three females, one each age 10-15, 15-20, and 20-30. In 1850 David, Prudence and unmarried daughter Betsey by Ebenezer lived as a family in Barrington. By 1860 David was widower; member of household was Betsey, age 41, estate valued at $5,000. David's will drawn 16 Jun 1869, proved 6 Jun 1871, named as his Exec., Rufus Hall, husband of niece Mary Ann Hall and designated his four nieces [cited below] as residuary legatees; witnesses Charles W. Hoyt, Lavina F. Hoitt, Ira B. Hoitt [Strafford Co. Probate 80:439]. David bequeathed to his housekeeper Abiah Twombley $300.00 for her many years of faithful service; devised to his brother Ivory, 40 acres of pasture land called "Popple Hill" adjacent to David's homestead farm. Residuary legatees were his four wards, Mary Ann Hall, wife of Rufus Hall, Lucy Maria Critchett, wife of John Critchett, Olive J. Buzzell, wife of John S. Buzzell, and Betsey C. Young. (Census Strafford Co., 1840, p471; 1850, p503; 1860, p156; NHVR-Brides, Marr; Barrington Graveyards, p90; Cate Gen., p14)

DAVID, b 25 May 1803, Barnstead, s/o Phineas and Dolly (Jacobs) Young, carpenter, d 9 Feb 1861, native town; m1 early

1820s, Barnstead, Sally Hodgdon [b ca 1805, of Barnstead, d pre 1827, said town]; m2 25 Jan 1827, Farmington, Elizabeth aka Eliza Hartford [b 22 Dec 1805, Strafford, d 30 Sep 1854, Barnstead]. He was named son and heir of Dorothy Young of Barnstead by her will signed 9 Nov 1851, proved 15 Apr 1862 [Belknap Co. Probate #1656]; actually he predeceased his mother. His homestead in Barnstead was situated on Lot 87, 2nd Div., derived from his father's estate. He was head of household in Barnstead from 1830-1950; in 1830, age was 20-30, his spouse of same age bracket, with one male and female both under 5; in 1840, age was 30-40, as was spouse, with a family of one male age 10-15 and three females each under 5, 10 and 15, respectively. David and second wife Elizabeth were listed as residents of Barnstead as of 1850, with four children at home: Anna M., Hiram A., Alvah and Francis. David and Elizabeth were buried at Barnstead Center Graveyard. No known children by first wife Sally. Ch. b Barnstead by Eliza: John H.+, b 1827; Anna M., b 1836; Hiram A.+, b 1844; Alvah, b 1845; and Francis, b 1848. (Census Strafford Co., 1830, p15; 1840, p442; Census Belknap Co., 1850, p416; Barnstead Cemeteries, p3; NHVR-Marr; Farmington TR, V1, p732; Merrill's Barnstead, p331)

DAVID, b ca 1822, of Rochester; m 22 Dec 1847, Rochester, Mary A. Mitchell [b ca 1825, of said town]. (NHVR-Marr)

DAVID H., b 28 Jan 1869, Barrington, s/o George W. and Elizabeth S. (Buzzell) Young, alive 1900, native town; m ca 1888, Mary E. Caligan [b May 1874, North Hanover, ME, alive 1900, Barrington]. David, Mary E. and their three children were listed on the 1900 census for Barrington. Ch. b Barrington except where noted: Ethel A., b 18 Sep 1889; Clarence D., b Mar 1896, MA; and Marian E., b Feb 1898, MA. (1900 Soundex; LDS I.G.I. BR; NHVR-Births)

DAVID L., b 1840s, Barnstead; m 1860s, Annie Aikens [b ca 1845, Barnstead]. Ch. b Barnstead: Addie F.+ (Young) Bunker, b 1860s. (NHVR-Brides)

DAVID M., b ca 1825, Barnstead; m 13 May 1851, Barnstead, Mary H. E. Young [b 8 Mar 1828, Barnstead, prob. d/o Aaron and Betsey (Bickford) Young]. (NHVR-Marr)

DAVID S., b 1796, Gilmanton, s/o Joseph and Betsey (Shaw) Young, d 22 Mar 1849, age 53, Barnstead, widower; m ca 1817, his home town, Betsey Avery [b ca 1800, Gilmanton, d/o Peter Avery, d before 1849 in California while with one of her sons]. David was farmer for the greater part of his life, a life-long resident of Gilmanton. His homestead was formerly his father's farm where he kept a large stock of cattle. David and Betsey raised a large family of six sons and four daughters. He was head of household in Gilmanton from 1830-1840. In 1830 his age was 30-40 as was his spouse; members of family were two males, one age 5-10, one 10-15, and three females, one each under 5, 10 and 15. In 1840 he and spouse were both age 40-50, with family of four males, two under 5, one age 5-10, one 15-20 and three females one each under 10, 15 and 20. David was buried singly at Barnstead Parade Ground Cemetery.

Ch. b Gilmanton: Jonathan+, b 16 Feb 1818; Asenath, b ca 1820, m Samuel Page of Campton, where they resided; Eliza, b 1820s, m Thomas Snell of Bridgewater, MA, which became their place of residence; Nathaniel, b 8 Mar 1824, d 1 Aug 1892, age 68-4-24, Gilmanton, married; Caroline, b 1820s, m William Haynes of Boston, MA; Joseph, b 1820s, relocated in California; Wesley, b 1820s, became rancher in California; Lovina, b early 1830s, m Quincy Snell of Bridgewater, MA whence they relocated; Charles H.+, b 1833; and Nelson C.+, b ca 1840. (Biog. Review, XXI, p354,355; Morning Star, p375; Barnstead Cemeteries, p18; Census Strafford Co., 1830, p277; 1840, p412; NHVR-Marr, Deaths)

DEADIMEY - see Diadamy

DEBORAH, b 1758, Dover, d/o Capt. Thomas Young, d Dec 1845, Acton, ME; m1 17 June 1776, Dover, Archibald Campbell [b ca 1750, Dover]; m2 20 Oct 1784, Somersworth, Daniel Horne [b 1754, Shapleigh, ME, d 19 May 1841, Acton, ME, formerly known as Shapleigh]. Deborah Horne was named a daughter and heir of Thomas Young by his will drawn 7 Apr 1791, proved 28 Apr 1795. Per N.H. Revolutionary War Pension Records [V19, p267], Daniel Horne of Shapleigh, ME, "enlisted Mar 1776, under Capt. Frederick Bell and Col. Poor. He served one year and was verbally discharged at Morristown, N.H. He had wife Deborah Young, age 63, a son age 17 and granddaughter Sally, age 10. Sgt. Daniel Horne was wounded in the arm at Hubbardton, taken prisoner by the British and moved to Ticonderoga. Doctors said the arm would have to be taken off but he received treatment and remained a prisoner for eighteen months. Fourteen pieces of bone were removed from his arm and one more was removed after he got home." By deposition of 28 Sep 1844, Deborah Horne, age 86, stated she and Daniel were married by Parson Pike [on date cited above], her maiden name being Deborah Young. Mary [Chadwick] Young of Wakefield testified that Deborah Horne was a sister to her deceased husband [Moses Young, b 1766], and the daughter of Capt. Thomas Young of Dover. Mary Young added that she well recalled visiting Deborah and Daniel Horne as newlyweds at the home of Thomas Young of Dover the day after their wedding. Daughter Hannah Waldron testified 26 Apr 1853 that she "is the daughter of Daniel Horne who died at Acton, ME and Deborah Horne who died in Dec 1845." Ch. b Acton, ME: Elizabeth Horne, b 1780s; Polly Horne, b 1780s; Hannah Horne, b ca 1793; Meshach Horne, b 22 Jun 1792, twin, m 27 Dec 1820, Anna Cloutman; Frederick Horne, b 22 Jun 1792, twin, m1 1817, Olive Nelia, m2 1819, Polly Chamberlain; Thomas Horne, b 2 Mar 1800, d 2 Jul 1880; Daniel Horne Jr., b ca 1802; George Horne, b ca 1804; John Horne, b ca 1806; and William A. Horne, b ca 1808. (Horne Family Recs., courtesy of Marjorie S. Heaney)

DEBORAH, b 1774, Barrington, d/o Winthrop and Mary (Otis) Young, d 1861, age 87, Belmont; m ca 1795, Barrington, John

Bean [b ca 1770, of Barrington, d 1836, Belmont]. Deborah and spouse lived in that section of Gilmanton that became Belmont. Ch. b Belmont: Winthrop Bean, b 1800s; William Bean, b 1800s; Sally Bean, b 1800s; John Langdon Bean, b 1800s; Harrison Bean, b 1810s; and Elijah Otis Bean, b 1810s. (Lyford's Canterbury, p341)

DEBORAH, b 12 Dec 1785, Barrington, d/o David and Abigail (Foss) Young of Barnstead, d 19 Jun 1843, Barnstead; m 2 Mar 1811, Barnstead, Solomon Emerson [b 1779, Durham, s/o Jonathan Emerson, d 15 Dec 1868, age 89, Barnstead]. Deborah and Solomon raised their family in Barnstead. Ch. b Barnstead: Abigail Y. Emerson, b 22 Mar 1812, d.y.; Thomas Emerson, b 1815; Solomon Y. Emerson, b 31 Sep 1817; Deborah Y. Emerson, b 4 Sep 1818; Paul Emerson, b 1821; Dr. George W. Emerson, b 25 Oct 1822, twin; Jefferson Emerson, b 25 Oct 1822, twin; Nancy J. Emerson, b 1826; Dr. James Madison Emerson, b 30 Jun 1827; Andrew Jackson Emerson, b 24 Jul 1830; and Sarah Emerson, b 1830s. (LDS I.G.I. VR; Stackpole's Durham V2, p181,184; NHVR-Births, Deaths)

DEBORAH, b 1788, of Barrington in 1850, single; she resided with Ichabod and Lydia Tibbetts in 1850, age 62. (Census Strafford Co., 1850, p529)

DEBORAH, b 6 Dec 1809, Strafford, prob. d/o Moses and Lucy (Whitehorn) Young, d 6 Mar 1906, native town; m 18 Nov 1828, at Freewill Baptist Church, Strafford Ira aka Asa Perkins [b 1808, d 7 May 1888, age 80, home town]. Deborah and Asa were buried at the same family plot as Moses and Lucy Young at Perkins Cemetery, Rte. 126, Strafford. (NHVR-Brides; Strafford Marr, **Reg.** 76:35; Stiles' Cemeteries, p165)

DIADAMY aka Deadimey, b 1760s, of Dover, widow of _____ Young. From 1830-1840 she was listed as head of household in Dover. In 1830 her age was 50-60, family consisting of one male each 15-20 and 20-30, and 2 females, one under 5 and one 20-30. In 1840 her age was 70-80 with family of two males, one age 20-30, one 30-40. See Benjamin Young of Dover with regard to her dower rights which were entailed in the Admin. of his estate in 1839. Ch. b Dover: prob. Benjamin+, b ca 1790. (Census Strafford Co. 1830, p317; 1840, p531)

DOLLY aka Dorothy, b 12 Jan 1791, Barrington, d/o William and Charity (Howe) Young, d 23 Oct 1847, native town; m 30 Aug 1810, Barrington, Ralph Brock [b ca 1785, of Barrington]. Ch. b Barrington: Sabrina Brock, b ca 1810; Nancy Brock, b ca 1813; James Brock, b ca 1815; Ralph Brock, b ca 1818; and Lydia Brock, b 21 Sep 1821, d 19 Jan 1892, Barrington. (Barrington TR, V6, NHVR-Brides; Ham's Gen., p25; Ham's Dover Marr, TMs, n.p.)

DOROTHY, b ca 1820, of Dover, d 10 Jan 1879, Dover; m 19 Apr 1842, Dover, Joseph P. Adams [b ca 1820, of Springfield, MA]. (NHVR-Brides, Heritage's Dover VR, p235)

DOROTHY, b ca 1825, of Somersworth; m 4 Jan 1845, Somersworth, Joel T. Sanborn [b ca 1820, of same town]. (NHVR-Brides)

DOROTHY A., b 1853, twin, Alton, d/o Henry and Sarah (Witham) Young; m 16 Dec 1867, Alton, George Horne [b ca 1850, of same town]. At age 7 she was listed under 1860 census returns for parents in Alton. (NHVR-Brides; Alton VR, p568)

DOROTHY B., b ca 1810, of Gilmanton; m 12 Oct 1832, Belmont, Silas Tuttle [b ca 1805, of Barnstead]. (NHVR-Brides)

DRUSILLA, b 6 Apr 1784, Durham, d/o Joseph and Dorcas M. (Ewer) Young of Newfields, d 29 Nov 1879, Packers Falls, age 95-7-23; m 25 Dec 1815, David Wiggin aka Jr. [b 6 Mar 1771, Durham, s/o David Wiggin, d 8 Nov 1866, Packers Falls]. This was David's third marriage. He m1 17 Nov 1796, Elizabeth Dame [b 1772, Packers Falls, d 12 Aug 1804, same town; m2 post 1804, Olive Wiggin [b 1772, Packers Falls, d 29 May 1815, same town]. Drusilla and David were buried at Wiggin Cemetery in the n.w. corner of Mill and Packers Falls Roads, Durham. Ch. b Durham by Elizabeth: Sally Wiggin, b 28 Sep 1797; Susan Wiggin, b 1799, d.y.; George J. Wiggin, b 14 Oct 1801; and Eliza Wiggin, b 1 Jul 1804. Ch. b Durham by Olive: Deborah Wiggin, b 19 Mar 1806; Thomas Wiggin, b 6 May 1808; and Frances Wiggin, b 17 Jul 1811. Ch. b Durham by Drusilla: Olive Wiggin, b 10 Feb 1817; Rhoda Ann Wiggin, b Nov 1818; and Mary D. Wiggin, b 26 Apr 1821. (Folsom's Graveyards, p76; Fitts' Newfields, p496,684; Durham Graveyards, #91, p77; Wiggin Gen., TMs, p82)

DRUSILLA E., b 1820, New Durham, d/o Levi and Phoebe (Stockbridge) Young; m 2 May 1841, New Durham, Joseph Jones [b ca 1815, of Dover]. Drusilla was single when named in her father's will of 27 Apr 1841, proved 1 Jan 1850]. Ch. b prob. Dover: Alphonso Jones, b 1840s, m 1891, Dover. (NHVR-Brides)

DUDLEY, b ca 1735, Kingston, poss. s/o Deacon Aaron and Abigail (Dudley) Young [no main entry], res. of Gilmanton, carpenter, d testate pre 10 May 1803, Gilmanton; m late 1750s (   ) [b ca 1735, of Kingston, alive 1801, Gilmanton]. Vital Records gave marriage entry for a Dudley Young and Jenne aka Margaret Smith, both of Kingston on date of 19 Oct 1758, Kingston. More background information on Kingston would be needed to connect Dudley of Gilmanton with this marriage entry. He settled in Gilmanton perhaps as early as 1762, having bought 100-acre Lot 13, 4th Div., 2nd Range, Gilmanton for 600 pounds Old Tenor, by deed signed 17 Jun 1762, rec'd 14 Oct 1777, from John Dudley of Exeter, land laid out on the easternmost side of the 40-acre lots; single witness Jonathan Gilman [Strafford Co. Deed 3:61]. He signed the Association Test Paper of 1776 for Gilmanton and raised a large family there. In 1790 he was listed as resident of Gilmanton, family containing two other males over 16 years, one male under 16 and five females. He served his town as Selectman in 1769 and was one of the original members of the First Baptist Church founded in 1773, where he held the title of Deacon. On 23 Jun 1777, he was chosen to serve on the committee which had the responsibility to "regulate the prices of things" in Gilmanton agreeably to the recommendation of the Convention. Dudley's estate in Gilmanton included the 100-acres Lot 13 cited above and Lot 14, 1st Div., 2nd Range which he bought in three sections: (1) part of 100-acre Lot 14 adjacent to Lot 13 by power of attorney for Moses Brown Nichols and Hannah Nichols of Amherst, Hillsborough Co., for 100 Spanish milled dollars by deed signed 5 Jun 1781, rec'd 21 Dec 1799; witnesses William smith, Joseph Badger [Strafford Co. Deed 32:101]; (2) "a certain part" of 100-acre Lot 14, from William Smith of Gilmanton by deed signed 17 Jan 1783, rec'd 21 Dec 1799, for 30 pounds; witnesses Sarah Foster, Joseph Badger [Strafford Co. Deed 32:92]; and (3) part of Lot 14, from said William Smith by deed signed 24 May 1799, rec'd 21 Dec 1799, for $1.00; sole witness John Gilman [Strafford Co. Deed 32:96]. One other property included in his estate was the whole of Lot 189, 4th Div., 2nd range, purchased by deed signed 19 Nov 1790, rec'd 21 Dec 1799, from Edward Gilman Jr. of Gilmanton for 6 pounds; witnesses Edward J. Long, Joseph Parsons [Strafford Co. Deed 32:103]. Dudley sold "a certain part" of Lot 14 cited above to the same William Smith, physician, for 30 pounds by deed signed 17 Jan 1783, rec'd 11 Feb 1786; witnesses Jonathan Young, Joseph Badger [Strafford Co. Deed 6:519].

Dudley's will was drawn 20 May 1801, proved 10 May 1803, naming sons Dudley and Nathaniel B. as Co-Execs. and residuary legatees; witnesses David Kimball, Thomas Cogswell Jr., William Cogswell and Joseph Badger [Strafford Co. Probate 8:113]. On date of probate Dudley and Nathaniel B. gave bond of $3,000 with sureties David Edgerly, Gent., Simon Lamper, both of Gilmanton [Strafford Co. Probate 8:202]. Dudley did not cite his wife's name but wanted his Execs. to provide care for their mother and sister Elizabeth "during the term of their natural lives," both receiving no further bequest. The remaining children were each devised $1.00: sons Joseph, Samuel and David and daughters Abigail Bond and Sarah Connor. Granddaughter Mary Clough's legacy was to be $60.00 when she became 18 years old. Inventory of Dudley's estate was taken by David Edgerly, Peter Dudley and William Smith, all of Gilmanton, submitted 17 Jun 1803, allowed 14 Jul 1803 [Strafford Co. Probate 9:210]. Real estate was valued at $2,000.00; personal estate of livestock, farming tools, household effects and carpenter's tools, rated at $313.33; grand total, $2,313.33.

Ch. b Kingston: Abigail+ (Young) Bond, b ca 1760; Sarah+ (Young) Connor, b 1760s; and Mary+ (Young) Clough, b ca 1765. Ch. b Gilmanton: Dudley+ aka Jr., b 1773; Nathaniel Badger+, b 1778; Joseph, b ca 1779; David+, b ca 1780; Samuel S.+, b 1794; and Elizabeth, b 1790s. (Census Strafford Co., 1790, p91; Assoc. Test, p122; Dudley Desc., **Reg.** 10:139; Lancaster's Gilmanton, p75,80,98,199; Gilmanton TR, V3, p369; LDS I.G.I. BR, VR)

DUDLEY aka Jr., b 1773, s/o Dudley Young, carpenter, alive 1850 Gilmanton; m 17 Mar 1799, Upper Gilmanton, Betsey

Jacobs [b 1777, of Gilmanton, alive 1850 same town, by then blind]. Dudley was named a Co-Exec. and co-residuary legatee by Dudley Sr.'s will signed 20 May 1801, proved 10 May 1803. His legacy was a one-half share of the homestead in Gilmanton which contained parts of Lot 13, 4th Div. and Lot 14, 1st Div., and the whole of Lot 189, 4th Div. Census returns from 1810-1850 for Gilmanton listed Dudley as resident. In 1810 age was under 45, with family of spouse in same age bracket, 1 son under 16 and 2 daughters under 10. In 1812 he was listed as resident of District No. 1, Gilmanton. By 1830 his age was 50-60, as was his wife, with family of three other females, one each 70-80, 15-20 and 20-30. In 1840 he and spouse were age 60-70 with one other member in family, a female parent figure age 80-90. By 1850 Dudley and Betsey lived alone. Their one son and two daughters were not identified.

Part of Lot 13, 4th Div. which Dudley and brother Nathaniel B. inherited was sold by deed signed 6 Apr, rec'd 11 Jun 1807, the other part by deed signed 6 May, rec'd 27 May 1808. See Nathaniel Badger+ for full details of these deeds of sale, and for the mortgage they took out on part of the 100-acre Lot 14 by deed signed 20 May, rec'd 27 Jun 1812. (Census Strafford Co. 1810, p801; 1830, p277; 1840, p418; Census Belknap Co., 1850, p43; NHVR-Marr; Gilmanton TR, V3, p378)

DUDLEY aka Jr. aka 2nd, b 18 Jan 1788, Gilmanton, s/o Joseph and Betsey (Shaw) Young of Barnstead, carpenter, d testate 21 Jun 1863, age 75-5-3, Gilmanton; m 1808, Barnstead, Sally Jacobs [b 1790, of Gilmanton, d 5 Sep 1877, Gilmanton]. Dudley's homestead was located near Mount Belknap in the vicinity of his parents' home. He was head of household in Gilmanton in 1810, age under 26, as was his spouse, and one male under 10. In 1812, known as Dudley Jr., he was taxpayer of District No. 2, Gilmanton, rated at $2.50. By 1830 his family had grown to three males, one under 5, one age 5-10, and one 20-30 and five females, two under 5, one 5-10 and two 10-15. In 1840 his age was 50-60, spouse's age 40-50, with family of three males, two under 5, one 5-10 and one female age 10-15. Dudley and Sally were listed from 1850-1860 as residents of Gilmanton. In 1850 members of family were sons Charles H. and Lewis, and child John H. Watson, age 11 [b 1839].

Dudley's will was drawn 20 Jun, proved 21 Jul 1863, naming eldest son John C. as sole Exec. and residuary legatee; witnesses Joseph B. Durell, Daniel Sargent, Moses Price [Belknap Co. Probate #1787]. He devised to wife Sally the income from one-third part of the homestead farm and the use and occupancy of all the buildings during her natural life, as well as all household furniture. Son John C. was to receive all the homestead farm and livestock, with the understanding he was to give his mother one-third of the yearly income produced from the farm. The remaining seven grown children were each to receive $5.00: Mary J. Johnson, wife

of Frank Johnson; Aaron B. Young; Julia A. Danford, wife of
Samuel Danford; Clarry Sawyer, wife of Frank Sawyer [one-half
balance of $5.00]; Abigail B. Weare, wife of Gardner W. Weare;
Harriet N. Davis, wife of Joseph B. Davis; Charles H. Young;
and Lewis A. Young. Widow Sally was listed as resident of
Gilmanton in 1870, age 80; she lived alone. Dudley and Sally
were buried at Smith Meeting House Cemetery, Gilmanton. Ch.
b Gilmanton: John C., b ca 1809, alive 1863; Mary J. (Young)
Johnson, b ca 1812; Aaron B.+, b 1815; Julia A. (Young)
Danford, b ca 1818; Clarry (Young) Sawyer, b ca 1821; Abigail
B. (Young) Weare, b ca 1824; Harriet N. (Young) Davis, b ca
1827; Charles H., b 1830; and Lewis A.+, b 1835. (Census
Strafford Co., 1810, p812; 1830, p277; 1840, p411; Belknap
Co., 1850, p54; 1860, p234; 1870, p21; Folsom's NH Cemeteries,
p172; Biog. Review, XXI, p354,355; Gilmanton TR, V3, p378;
NHVR-Deaths, Marr)

DUDLEY B., b 1869, Gilmanton, s/o Lewis A. and Lucy
(Rowe) Young; m 31 Aug 1891, Woodstock, Alice M. Moulton [b
1873, of Compton, d/o Darms and Julia A. (Ordway) Moulton of
Ellsworth]. Dudley was resident of Compton at time of marriage. Alice's father Darms Moulton was born 1843, Ellsworth;
her mother Julia A. Ordway was born 1843, Rumney. (NHVR-Marr)

E. FRANK, aka Elijah F., b 29 Aug 1825, Wolfeboro, s/o
Nathaniel and Martha (Roberts) Young, d 29 Apr 1894, native
town, age 68-8-0; m 20 Mar 1867, Wolfeboro, Annie F. Brockett
[b 1835, East Alton, d/o William and Eleanor A. (   ) Brockett, alive 1870, Wolfeboro]. Elijah lived with parents in
Ossipee in 1860; both he and spouse resided in Ossipee at time
of marriage. In 1870 Elijah and Ann F. made their home in
Wolfeboro with child Martha and married couple Joshua Brackett, age 65 [b 1805] and Betsey A. Brackett, age 60 [b 1810].
Ch. b prob. Ossipee: Martha, b 1868. (Census Carroll Co.,
1870, p454; NHVR-Marr, Deaths)

E. J., b 1852, Manchester, s/o J. D. and Elizabeth
(Marsten) Young [no main entry], res. of Gilford; m 6 Jun
1873, Gilford, Mary F. Carter [b 1852, Gilford, d/o Daniel and
Mary (   ) Carter]. (NHVR-Marr)

EBEN S., b Feb 1864, Gilmanton, s/o Jonathan and Martha
A. (Nelson) Young, alive 1900, native town, occupation, hub
manufacturer; m 2 Oct 1886, Gilmanton, Cora F. Lougee [b May
1863, Gilmanton per 1900 Soundex, but per marr. license b
1858, alive 1900, home town]. Eben and his parents lived in
Gilmanton in 1870. In 1900 Eben S. and spouse Cora F. resided
in Gilmanton; members of household were son Morton E. and
boarder Edward McMichael [b Jul 1875]. Ch. b Gilmanton:
Morton E., b Dec 1888, not traced further. (1900 Soundex;
NHVR-Marr)

EBENEZER, b 1724, of Dover, d testate 9 May 1786, Barr-
ington; m 21 Apr 1749, Newington, Elizabeth Bickford [b 1718,
Madbury, d/o Thomas and Juanna (   ) Bickford, d 29 May 1811,
Barrington, sister of Temperance who married Daniel Young of
Madbury]. Elizabeth, single, became a member of First Church

of Dover 9 Sep 1744. Ebenezer lived in that part of Dover that became Newington, then relocated in Barrington about the time of marriage to Elizabeth. Early Town Records of Barrington listed Ebenezer as signer of the Petition in favor of Joshua Foss Jr. [to be named Justice of the Peace for Barrington] on 19 Jul 1773, and in 1776, signed the Association Test for Barrington in addition to the Petition of Inhabitants in favor of John Garland [to be appointed as one of the Magistrates for Strafford Co., subsequently passed]. Wife Elizabeth was known by her married name in the will of her father Thomas Bickford of Newington, signed 6 Jan 1765, proved 27 Feb 1765, and received the bequest of "one Cow to be Delivered her by my Exec. two Years after my Decease" [NH Wills, p125]. As early as 1750 Ebenezer of Dover purchased 100 acres land in Barrington, Lot 269, from Timothy and Mary Emerson of Durham for 500 pounds Old Tenor, by deed dated 15 May 1750, rec'd 13 Apr 1762; witnesses John Hacknis, Moses Emerson [NH Prov. Deed 66:389]. Ebenezer served in the Revolutionary War in Capt. Samuel Hayes Company at Peirce Island.

Ebenezer's will was drawn 5 May, proved 21 Jun 1786, in which his eldest child and only son Isaac was named Exec. and residuary legatee; witnesses John B. Parshley, Simeon Starbird, Edmund Hodgdon [Strafford Co. Probate 2:227]. On date of probate, Isaac gave bond of 1,000 pounds lawful money given with sureties John B. Parshley of Barrington and Edmund Hodgdon of Nottingham [Strafford Co. Probate 2:409]. Ebenezer's bequests to wife Elizabeth included all his neat stock and household furniture, the use and enjoyment of one half of the house, three cows, eight sheep, one-third part of all the coin, grain and cider, and one half of the crop of flax. Son Isaac was to receive the "whole of my estate on land where I now live." Daughters Mary Giles and Abigail Cate were each to receive one cow, and single daughter Elizabeth to receive three cows, one at yearly intervals. Ch. b most likely Barrington: Isaac+, b 1754/5. Ch. b Barrington: Mary (Young) Giles, b late 1750s; Elizabeth Young, b early 1760s; and Abigail+ (Young) Cate, b 1760s. (Barrington TR, p195, p196; Heritage's Dover VR, p209; Barrington Graveyards, p90; Stackpole's Durham, V2, p2; NHVR-Marr; Wilson's Assoc. Test, p122; LDS I.G.I. VR; NH State Papers, V11, p151,154)

EBENEZER, b ca 1775, of Barrington; head of household in Barrington, 1840, age 60-70 with spouse of similar years; they lived alone. (Census Strafford Co., 1840, p479)

EBENEZER, b 1783, Barrington, s/o Isaac and Betsey (Cate) Young, d 19 Jan 1832, native town; m 2 Feb 1814, Northwood, Prudence Cate [b 29 Jun 1793, Northwood, d/o Joseph and Prudence (Marden) Cate, d 7 Nov 1855, Barrington]. In 1830 Ebenezer was head of household in Barrington, age 40-50, with female [spouse] age 20-30, with no other male, but four females, one under 5, one age 5-10, and two 10-15. He was named a son and heir of Isaac and one of three Execs. and residuary legatees by Isaac's will of 8 Sep 1826, proved

19 Apr 1827. Isaac's will acknowledged "the house in which my son Ebenezer lives to be his as it was built by him and the same is to remain his" and devised to Ebenezer a one-third share of the 433-acre homestead. Shortly after Ebenezer's death, Prudence was appointed guardian 16 Feb 1832 of daughter Mary Ann, a minor over the age of fourteen, and three daughters under the age of fourteen, Betsey Cate Young, Lucy Maria Young and Olive Jenny Young; bond of $2,000.00 given with sureties David Young and Henry Hill, both of Barrington [Strafford Co. Probate 30:182]. Three years later, Ebenezer's brother David of Barrington was appointed guardian on 17 Sep 1838 of Olive J. Young, Betsy C. Young and Lucy M. Young; see David and Prudence Young of Barrington for full details.

On 16 Feb 1832, Isaac Young [brother] was appointed Admin. of Ebenezer's estate, with bond of $3,000.00, sureties given by David Young and Henry Hill [Strafford Co. Probate 30:328]. Inventory of Ebenezer's estate was taken by Samuel Shackford Esq., Henry Hill, and James Dearborn, all of Barrington, attested to 27 Feb 1832, approved the following day [Strafford Co. Probate 42:398]. Real estate which included Ebenezer's one-third share of the homestead with buildings held in common with Isaac and David Young was valued at $1,525.00; a one-third share of their pew at Baptist Meeting House was set at $5.00. Personal estate amounted to $1,134.00, including notes of hand worth $646.44. Isaac, Admin., submitted his closing account of the estate 12 Sep 1832, allowed 17 Sep 1832 [Strafford Co. Probate 44:148]; inventory on personal estate, $1,149.54, which included Marsh Hill's note, payable in tailor work, and Nathaniel J. Young's note of $5.00, payable in leather. Debts of the estate totalled $510.43. Isaac paid several of these debts off; they included several notes of hand, one of $16.67 paid to Ivory Young, one of $7.77 to Lucy Young, and $389.72 to Prudence for support of four minor daughters; balance of $639.11 was paid to the widow. Concurrent with the closing account, widow Prudence petitioned 17 Sep 1832 for an allowance out of the personal estate; she was allowed $400.00 "for the support of life" [Strafford Co. Probate 51:127]. Prudence m2 29 Aug 1838, David Young of Barrington [b 1791, mentioned above]. Ebenezer's four daughters received a one-third share of their grandfather Isaac's estate from the division of property made 5 Oct 1841; they requested that they be called "joint owners" of the 166 acres, 133 rods set off to them. See will of David Young of Barrington for bequests to Ebenezer's four daughters. Family members were buried at the Isaac Young family plot at Pine Grove Cemetery, Barrington.

Ch. b Barrington: Mary Ann (Young) Hall, b ca 1817, wife of Rufus Hall by Sep 1835, alive 1841; Betsey Cate Young, b 21 Feb 1819, single, d 30 Nov 1887, age 68-9-9, Strafford Bow Lake; Lucy Maria+ (Young) Critchett, b 1822; William Cate, b 1827, d 1829, Barrington; and Olive Jenny+ (Young) Buzzell, b 1828. (Barrington Graveyards, p90; Cate Gen., p14; Stackpole's Durham, V2, p118; NHVR-Births, Deaths, Marr; Census Strafford Co., 1830, p24; Moses' Northwood, TMs, V1, p59)

EBENEZER D. aka Eben D., b 19 Apr 1777, twin, Madbury, s/o Timothy and Lydia (Demeritt) Young, d 1 Apr 1850, Madbury; prob. married ca 1805, Madbury; children not identified. He was named an heir in his father's will signed 16 Dec 1813, proved 25 Apr 1820; he and twin James H. received the homestead in Madbury upon their mother's demise in 1838. Ebenezer was elected selectman for Madbury in 1816, possibly also in 1831. In 1840 he was head of household in Madbury, age 60-70, with household of female in same age group, one male of his own age [twin James H.?], one male 30-40, and one female 15-20. He and Nathaniel Hayes, as co-grantee of Madbury, bought 27 acres, 3 rods of land in Madbury, south and west of lands of Tobias Evans, north of lands of Timothy Young and Joseph Drew, and east of the highway that leads from Joseph Drew's land to Moses Canney's, from Benjamin Connor, Gent. of Exeter, by deed of 27 Apr 1804, rec'd 4 Mar 1805, for $607.50; witnesses John French, Ebenezer Demeritt [Strafford Co. Deed 47:283]. See twin James H. as co-grantee in the purchase of 2-1/2 acres in Madbury east of Timothy Young's land by deed signed 25 Oct, rec'd 30 Oct 1816; and for the mortgage the twins took out on their homestead by deed signed 13 May, rec'd 27 Oct 1830. Eben D. was buried beside the grave sites of mother Lydia and twin James H. on the west side of Mill Hill Road, north of Bellamy River. (Census Strafford Co., 1840, 493; NHVR-Deaths; Madbury Cem., **Reg.** 87:347; Adam's Madbury, n.p.; Steuerwald's Dover Cem., TMs)

EDGAR F., b Apr 1864, resident of Rochester 1900; single, boarded at home of Annie M. Harvard, Rochester. (1900 Soundex)

EDGAR J. aka Jacob E., b 26 Nov 1856, Freedom, s/o Daniel and Eleanor J. (Allard) Young; m ca 1890, Etta M. Alley [b Apr 1860, Cornish, ME, alive 1900, Freedom). Edgar was raised in Freedom where he and wife took up residence up through 1900. In that year Etta's mother Eleanor J. ( ) Alley, age 74 [b Apr 1826], and daughter Eva were members of household. Ch. b Freedom: Eva M., b 1 Mar 1891, first child. (1900 Soundex; NHVR-Births)

EDWARD, b Jun 1865, Dover, alive 1900, native town; m early 1880s, Dover, Mary ( ) [b Feb 1864, MA, alive 1900, Dover]. Edward and Mary were on the census returns for Dover in 1900; daughters at home were Maude, Florence and Hazel. Ch. b Dover, not traced further: Maude, b Oct 1884; Florence, b Apr 1889; and Hazel, b Oct 1895. (1900 Soundex)

EDWARD AUGUSTUS, b 1846, Somersworth, saloon keeper, s/o George W. and Hannah aka Anna (Emery) Young; m 22 Sep 1881, Somersworth, Abbie F. Bumford [b 1851, Somersworth, d/o David and Dorcas ( ) Bumford]. He was named son and heir by his father's will of 25 Jul 1879, proved 14 Sep 1880. (NHVR-Marr)

EDWARD C., b 26 Dec 1844, Kittery, ME, s/o Thomas C. and Abigail (Wiggins) Young of Ossipee, d 26 Feb 1868; m 12 Oct

1867, Ossipee, Sarah A. Haley [b 1845, Center Harbor, d/o
Samuel and Elizabeth (   ) Haley of Moultonboro, d Feb 1868].
Note that Wiggin Gen., p176, gave Sarah's d-o-b as 10 Jul
1841. Note both Edward and Sarah died four months after date
of their marriage, location unknown. (NHVR-Marr)

EDWARD S., b Nov 1866, resident of Dover in 1900, single,
age 33, boarder at home of Henry R. Flagg [n.d.] of Dover.
(1900 Soundex)

EDWIN A., b 1841, Durham, s/o Joseph and Maria (Langley)
Young; m 22 Mar 1862, Durham, Lizzie J. Drew [b 1842, Durham,
d/o Nicholas and Mary (   ) Drew]. (NHVR-Marr)

EDWIN A., b 1863, Great Falls, shoemaker, s/o Simeon and
Joanna (   ) Young; m 23 Sep 1882, Dover, Mary J. Hathaway [b
1865, Fall River, MA, d/o William and Kate (   ) Hathaway].
Edwin A.'s age was 7 as listed on 1870 census returns for his
widowed mother Joanna in Dover. Both he and spouse lived in
Dover at time of marriage, ages 19 and 17-1/2 respectively.
Ch. b Dover: Simon H., b 1882, d 28 Nov 1887, Dover; Ethel
M., b 11 Oct 1884, not traced further. (NHVR-Births, Marr,
Deaths)

EDWIN R., aka Edward R., b Dec 1847, Barrington, s/o
Jonathan and Sophia Maria (Ricker) Young, alive 1900, New
Durham; m 11 May 1892, Northwood, Mary Hall [b Jun 1858, of
Nottingham, alive 1900, age 41, New Durham]. Edwin R. was a
child of 3 in 1850 census return on his parents, and was one
of three residuary legatees of his mother's estate in Barring-
ton by her will drawn 3 Sep, proved 5 Nov 1889; after sib-
ling's demise, Edwin would share in the homestead. He and
Mary resided in New Durham in 1900 and lived alone. (NHVR-
Births, Marr; 1900 Soundex)

ELEANOR, b ca 1795, of Dover; res. of Dover in 1830,
single, and lived alone, age 30-40. (Census Strafford Co.,
1830, p317)

ELEAZER, b 1691, Dover Neck, s/o Thomas and Anna
(Roberts) Young, alive 1765, Madbury; m 28 Dec 1716, Newington, Alice aka Allis Watson [b ca 1695, Dover, bp 25 Apr 1742,
at First Church, Dover, d/o Jonathan and Elizabeth (   )
Watson, residents of the "Upper Neck"]. Eleazer was listed
in 1741 Tax List of Cochecho Parish, rated for 1-6-8, for the
town's ministerial support. Named as son and heir of Thomas
Young of Dover by will signed 18 Mar 1726/27, proved 27 May
1727/28, Eleazer received a fifth share of land in Rochester;
for disposal of his share, see John and Elizabeth Young of
Dover. Alice and husband Eleazer quitclaimed their share and
interest in the estate of her father Jonathan Watson late of
Dover, by deed signed 18 Sep 1736, rec'd 29 Oct 1767, in favor
of Alice's brother Isaac Watson of Dover for 20 pounds; witnesses Jonathan Cushing, Elizabeth Waterhouse [NH Prov. Deed
92:361].

Eleazer's homestead adjoined the main road leading from
Littleworth, so called, to Barrington, s.w. on the road leading from said main road to Bellamy Banks River, and adjacent

to the lands of James Young and Solomon Young. He bought 30
acres land in Dover, situated on the easterly side of his
house and on the westerly side of Barbados Woods, from David
and Mary Watson, also of Dover, for eleven pounds and ten
shillings, the land originally laid out to David Watson on
23 Mar 1721, 40 acres in size, 10 acres of which David reserved for himself, by deed signed 21 Feb 1723, rec'd 30 Apr
1768; witnesses Ephraim Ham, Isaac Watson [NH Prov. Deed
94:207]. His next purchase of land was two acres of Common
Lands in Dover, Lot 388, 1st Div., from the Town of Dover
8 Jul 1734 [Dover TR]. These 20 acres represented two-thirds
of a whole share, which Eleazer in turn sold by deed signed
4 Jul 1748, rec'd 5 Apr 1753, to James Kielle of Dover for 120
pounds Old Tenor; witnesses Paul Harford, Joseph Hanson Jr.
[NH Prov. Deed 41:384]. He later acquired 10 more acres
Common Land in Dover, Lot 247, 1st Div., by deed signed
10 Nov, rec'd 23 Dec 1736, bought from Amos Pinkham of Dover
for 25 pounds Bills of Credit; witnesses Daniel Young, Joseph
Hanson Jr. [NH Prov. Deed 22:269]. That same year, by deed
signed 18 Nov 1736, rec'd 30 Apr 1768, Eleazer purchased five
acres more of Dover Common Lands from Simon Wingate of Biddeford, Co. of York, Province of Mass. [later, Maine] for 11
pounds Bills of Credit; witnesses John Cuck, Joseph Hanson
Jr. [NH Prov. Deed 94:162].
        Eleazer, husbandman, purchased an additional ten acres
in Dover, part of the 40-acre grant originally granted to
Jonathan Watson, late of Dover, bounded south of Jonathan
Young's land, and west and north of Eleazer's land, by deed
signed 26 May 1746, rec'd 30 Apr 1768, from Ichabod Hayes of
Dover for 80 pounds Old Tenor; witnesses Joseph Hanson Jr.,
Isaac Hanson [NH Prov. Deed 94:205]. Then in partnership with
Ebenezer Varney and William Wentworth, both of Dover, he was
granted Lot 27, Middleton by the purchasers of Mason's Right
11 April 1750; he quitclaimed his share in this tract to
Joseph Hanson of Dover for five pounds Old Tenor by deed
signed 17 Mar 1749/50, rec'd 13 Sep 1763; witnesses James
Kielle, Samuel Young [NH Prov. Deed 70:273]. This whole tract
of land in Middleton, drawn to the original right of Eleazer,
was sold for back taxes by deed of 1 Jul 1771, rec'd 12 Oct
1777, to John Tash of Lee, yeoman for 20 pounds-19 shillings;
witnesses John Gage, Joseph Cook [Strafford Co. Deed 2:125].
Lastly, Eleazer sold his homestead farm, lands and buildings
in Madbury, by deed signed 2 Oct, rec'd 22 Oct 1765, to son
Solomon of Madbury for 200 pounds legal tender; witnesses
James Kielle, Ephraim Hanson [NH Prov. Deed 89:18].
        Ch. b Dover: Solomon+, b ca 1730, bp 25 Apr 1742; and
Lucy, bp same date First Church of Dover. (Noyes et al, p724;
Ham's Dover Marr, TMs; Heritage's Dover VR, p149; LDS I.G.I.
VR; NH State Papers V24, p700, V27, p498; Scale's Dover, p352)
        ELEAZER, b 10 Nov 1714, Dover, s/o Jonathan and Abigail
(Hanson) Young, d testate pre Oct 1798, age 84, Barrington;
m 1740s, Dover, Mary Ham [b 8 Oct 1723, bp 23 Oct 1737 at

First Church, Dover, d/o Benjamin and Patience (Hartford) Ham, d 1808, age 85, Barrington]. Mary's siblings were William, John, Patience and Elizabeth. In 1741 Eleazer aka Jr. was resident of Cochecho Parish, taxed for 9 shillings and 9 pence, and was acknowledged son and heir by Jonathan Young's will drawn 1 Jul 1752, proved 29 Sep 1756, his legacy 100 pounds Old Tenor. As early as 1771, Eleazer was a freeholder of Barrington, his homestead situated in the Two-Mile Strip in a section known as Green Hill; he subscribed on 1 Apr 1771 to the Barrington Meeting House. As resident of Barrington in 1776, he signed the Association Test and in 1790, was listed as head of household with a family of three females.

Eleazer was an heir of Isaac Young, late of Dover [brother]. His share was a quarter acre of land situated at the s.e. corner of Isaac Hanson's lands, north by a road lead-ing from Bloody Point Ferry, so called, to Cochecho Meeting House; he sold his interest by deed signed 10 Nov, rec'd 1 Dec 1795, to John Wheeler of Dover for 45 pounds; witnesses Moses Canney, Sarah Young [Strafford Co. Deed 20:442]; see Isaac Young of Dover for full list of heirs and claimants. While in his prime, Eleazer built up large land holdings in Dover, Barrington and Rochester, 226 acres all told, by a significant outlay of money. He expended 2,490 pounds Old Tenor and 3,004 pounds British Sterling in the purchase of seven properties, or shares in them: (1) 100 acres, Two-Mile Streak, Barring-ton, for 155 pounds, which Eleazer bought from Joseph and Hannah Chesley by deed signed 12 Jan 1737/8, rec'd 8 Sep 1740; witnesses James Kielle, Ephraim Ham [NH Prov. Deed 24:576]; (2) 25 acres in Dover on the northern side of the heath, n.w. of Dover head line, southwest to land of Ichabod Canney and Paul Hayes of Barrington for 340 pounds Old Tenor, purchased from Joseph Roberts Jr. of Dover who had inherited the land from his father Joseph Roberts, by deed signed 6 Aug 1754, rec'd 13 Jul 1779; witnesses Ephraim Hanson, Solomon Hanson [Strafford Co. Deed 2:412]; (3) 25 acres, or one-half of a 50-acre lot in the Two-Mile Streak, for 1,400 pounds from Jethro Bickford of Rochester by deed signed 26 Jan 1761, rec'd 13 Jul 1779; witnesses Jonathan Cushing and Thomas Hayes [Strafford Co. Deed 2:413]; (4) a moiety of 15 acres land near Blind Will's Neck in Rochester from a 60-acre lot bounded on the north by Isinglass River and on the east by Cochecho River, with Paul Hayes buying the other moiety of 15 acres as co-grantor, for 1,500 pounds, from Joseph and Susannah Hanson by deed signed 15 Dec 1757, rec'd 29 May 1758; witnesses Ephraim Hanson, Stephen Hanson [NH Prov. Deed 65:508]; (5) 39 acres in the Two-Mile Streak beginning at Isinglass River and at eastern corner of John Garland's land and partly by Isaac Young's land, purchased from Job and Mary Jenness of Rye in New Castle for 1,950 pounds Old Tenor by deed signed 21 Jul 1764, rec'd 13 Jul 1779; witnesses Joshua Wingate and Ephraim Hanson [Strafford Co. Deed 3:358]. Lands in Rochester were next purchased: (6) 20 acres on the western side of Isinglass

River, part of Lot 112, 1st Div., bounded on the west by the
Barrington line, on the north by Lot 113, on the south by Lot
111, and by the river to the east, from Richard and Sarah
Bickford of Rochester for 32 pounds-10 shillings by deed of
10 Apr 1766, rec'd 13 Jul 1779; witnesses Joseph Hicks and
John Wood [Strafford Co. Deed 3:359]; (7) with co-grantees
Paul Hayes and John Hayes both of Barrington, by deed signed
20 Feb 1768, rec'd 15 Jul 1779, five acres in the Two-Mile
Streak, part of 50 acres of Lot 9, 7th Range, from Aaron Hayes
of Nottingham for 16 pounds and 13 shillings; witnesses Aaron
Hayes, Otis Baker [Strafford Co. Deed 2:418].

Eleazer's will was drawn 18 Jun 1771, proved 30 Oct 1798,
naming his only son Peter as sole Exec.; witnesses Elizabeth
Waldron, Mary Waldron, Thomas W. Waldron [Strafford Co. Probate 5:360]. Peter was allowed Exec. of Eleazer's will 13 Nov
1798, giving bond of $1,000.00, with sureties Thomas Footman,
John Wheeler, both of Dover [Strafford Co. Probate 2:408].
Wife Mary was to be provided with two rooms in the dwelling
house as well as two cows, firewood, produce of "my homestead
estate to be housed Free of charge by my sd executor," and the
free and sole use of his household goods "during her remaining
my widow and no longer, but afterwards in lieu thereof one
third of my homestead farm as the laws directs." He devised
30 pounds each to single daughters Mary, Patience and Susann-
nah. Peter was residuary legatee of Eleazer's estate, receiving the homestead and virtually all Eleazer's lands in
Barrington, Rochester and Dover. Eleazer and Mary were buried
at the Isaac Young plot, Pine Grove Cemetery, Barrington. Ch.
b prob. Dover: Peter, b ca 1750; Mary, b 1750s; prob.
Patience+ (Young) Temmy, b ca 1757; and Susannah+ (Young)
Garland, b 1760. (NH State Papers, V24, p700; NHVR-Births;
Barrington Graveyards, p90; Wilson's Assoc. Test, p122;
Barrington TR, V1, p685; Ham Family, **Reg.** 26:390; Hayes Gen.,
V1, p76; Barrington Congreg. Church, p1-250}

ELEAZER, b 1757, Barrington, d 9 Nov 1845, Upper Gilmanton; m 1 Dec 1787, Belmont [Upper Gilmanton], Hannah Bailey
aka Bayley [b 1760, of Gilmanton, d pre 20 May 1851, Upper
Gilmanton]. There appears to be no clear consensus on
Eleazer's origins. Freewill Baptist Church records stated he
was born in Madbury, went to Loudon in 1778 at age 21, and by
1790, resided in Gilmanton. His own deposition [given fully
below] stated however that he was of Barrington, which echoes
agreement with the Association Test of 1776 for Barrington
which he signed at the age of 19. Eleazer was listed as head
of household in Gilmanton on the 1790-1840 census returns.
In 1790 at age 33, his household held one male under 16 years
of age and five females; in 1810 his age was 45 plus, with
spouse of same age group, one male age 16-26, and five
females, one under 10, one 10-16, two under 26, and one 26-
45. In 1812, Eleazer was taxpayer of District No. 3, Gilmanton, at rate of $8.43. By 1830 his age was 70-80 years, with
family of spouse age 60-70, no other male, and four grown

females; in 1840 he and wife were both age 80-90, with a family of four females, one age 30-40, one 40-50, and two 50-60. In 1850 Hannah was widow and head of the family in Gilmanton with four unmarried daughters at home. In 1860 daughters Lucy, Abigail and Sarah formed their own household in Gilmanton, and by 1870, Abigail, age 80, was the last surviving member of the family.

As a veteran of the Revolutionary War, Eleazer filed petition for pension on 18 Oct 1832, age 76, stating: "that he was formerly of Barrington, enlisted there as Pvt. in Capt. Daniels' Co. of Artillery in Nov 1775, marched to Portsmouth and was stationed at Seavey's Island until some time in December and at the end of the month he enlisted under Capt. Cobb and Col. John Waldron for two months, marched from Portsmouth to Winter Hill in Massachusetts and then to Mystic where he was stationed until the last of February 1776 when he was discharged; that in November 1776, he enlisted again for three months, marched to Danbury, Connecticut and then to Peekskill, N.Y. where he was discharged at night the last of February 1777." Hannah deposed 17 Mar 1848 that she was the widow of Eleazer Young and that she remained widowed; Bailey Young attested on same date for Hannah and stated he lived within 10 rods of Eleazer's home in Gilmanton; pensioner claim allowed and Certificate No. 1191 was signed 14 Aug 1848.

While Eleazer was of Loudon, Rock. Co., he purchased part of Lot 8, 2nd Div., 10th Range, 50 acres, Gilmanton, by deed signed 18 Dec 1789, rec'd 24 Sep 1790, drawn to the original right of Archibald McPhedres, from Caleb Forster of Haverhill, Essex Co., MA, for 42 pounds; witnesses Samuel Philbrook, John Cram [Strafford Co. Deed 12:276]. Once a resident of Gilmanton, he acquired 38 acres of 100-acre Lot 9, 8th Range, by deed of 11 Dec 1795, rec'd 29 May 1801, from Stephen Prescot of Gilmanton for $134.00; witnesses Benjamin Weeks, William Gilman [Strafford Co. Deed 35:366].

Letters of Admin. on Eleazer's estate in Upper Gilmanton were filed 16 Dec 1845 by Bailey Young: he stated that Hannah Young, widow of Eleazer, "was incapable of administering the estate and that Eleazer left your petitioner, his only son and five daughters." He petitioned that he be appointed Admin. [Belknap Co. Probate Docket #337]. Letters of Admin. on widow Hannah's estate were filed 20 May 1851 also by Bailey; he stated that Hannah died leaving six children [Belknap Co. Probate #735]. Administration on the estate of daughter Polly Young, single, was handled by Moses A. Young of Upper Gilmanton, upon the petition of heirs-at-law Abigail Young, Lucy Young and Ruth Hadley, sisters of Polly, on 26 Feb 1864, requesting the same; approved 15 Mar 1864 [Belknap Co. Probate #1873]. Under NHVR-Deaths, daughter Lucy was said to have died 19 Jun 1864, Gilmanton.

Ch. b Loudon or Gilmanton: Polly, b 1779, d pre 26 Feb 1864, Upper Gilmanton, single; Lucy, b 1784, d 31 Mar 1865, single, Upper Gilmanton; Abigail, b 1790, d 10 Jul 1885, age

95, single, Loudon; Ruth+ (Young) Hadley, b ca 1792; Bailey+,
b 1793; and Sarah, b 7 Dec 1801, d 3 Dec 1863, age 61-11-27,
single, Upper Gilmanton. (Census Strafford Co., 1790, p86;
1810, p822; 1830, p277; 1840, p493; Census Belknap Co., 1850,
p77; 1860, p118; 1870, p5; Draper's NH Revol. War Pensions,
V99, #W15974; Wilson's Assoc. Test, p122; Morning Star, p375;
NHVR-Deaths, Marr; Gilmanton TR, V3, p385)

ELEAZER, b 1759, of Upper Gilmanton, d 26 Nov 1850, Upper
Gilmanton. Eleazer's earliest known purchases of land in
Upper Gilmanton involved parts of Lots 3, 4 and 12, according
to the deed signed 16 Nov 1802, rec'd 22 Feb 1803, by which
he purchased 1-1/2 acres of 100-acre Lot 12, 7th Range, 2-1/2
acres with buildings of Lot 3, 6th Range, and a one-half share
of 100-acre Lot 4, 6th Range, for $400; witnesses Samuel Burn-
ham, Joseph Young [Strafford Co. Deed 42:128]. These identical parcels of land were sold to his son Joseph Young 3rd of
Gilmanton, by deed signed 7 Apr 1806, rec'd 24 Aug 1812, for
$400.00; witnesses David Bean Jr., Joseph Young (J.P.)
[Strafford Co. Deed 72:93]. Known ch. b Gilmanton: Joseph+
aka 3rd, b ca 1780. (Morning Star, p375)

ELEAZER, b 1780s, of Barrington. Eleazer inherited two
properties in Barrington through "division of estate," origins
of real estate not specified. Both properties were to be
divided between Eleazer Young and Jonathan Young Jr., both of
Barrington, land set off by Elijah Austin of Madbury, Jacob
Foss and Francis Winkley, all of Barrington, both allowed
17 Sep 1838 [Strafford Co. Probate 53:282]. The property on
Green Hill Road was referred to as "being the homestead on
which Jonathan Jr. and Eleazer now live." Yet it would be
hard to say what kinship Eleazer and Jonathan Jr. held with
one another or be able to identify them safely. The first
division dated 2 Jun 1838 involved 15 acres adjoining the farm
of the late Joshua Hayes of Barrington; this piece of real
estate was north by said Hayes' farm, west by John Kingman's,
south by Samuel H. Waterhouse' and east by said Kingman
[Strafford Co. Probate 53:278]. The second property, set off
9 Jun 1838, contained 112 acres on the south side of Green
Hill Road, out of which Eleazer was granted 20 acres, the east
wing of the dwelling and another parcel of 33 acres on the
north side of the hill east by lands of John Hayes, north by
Joseph Ham's and west by John Ham's. Jonathan received the
west wing of the homestead and three parcels of 20 acres, 27
acres and 12 acres from the 112-acre homestead [Strafford Co.
Probate 53:282].

ELEAZER, b 8 Nov 1780, Barrington, s/o Peter and Sarah
(Hayes) Young, d 13 Oct 1844, Barrington; m1 20 Sep 1801,
Barrington, Alice Kingman [b ca 1785, of Barrington, d 1833,
same town]; m2 1837, Barrington, widow Deborah (Ham) Tibbetts,
[b ca 1800, Dover, d/o Samuel Ham]. In 1830 Eleazer was head
of household in Barrington, age 50-60, with household of
spouse of same age group, two males, one age 15-20 and one 20-
30, and two females, one each age 5-10 and 15-20. One of

Eleazer's earliest purchases of land in Barrington was made with co-grantor Daniel Ham of Barrington, by deed of 4 Sep 1800, rec'd same date, 18-1/2 acres out of Lot 101, 3rd Range, drawn to original right of Richard Waldron, adjacent to lands of William Caldwell for $122.00; witnesses Daniel Libbey, Clement Ham [Strafford Co. Deed 34:164].

From 1801-1820 he acquired acreage in Barrington and Dover by purchases from his father [for full documentation see Peter]: (1) 100 acres in the 1st Range, Barrington adjacent to Paul Hayes' land by deed of 17 Dec 1801, rec'd 17 Jan 1804; (2) 50 acres of Lot 2, Barrington with buildings at the north corner of James Hayes' land and adjacent to Green Hill Road, as well as 20 acres in Rochester which was part of Horne Lot 112, 1st Div. on west side of Isinglass River by deed of 1 Sep 1803, rec'd 26 Jan 1804; (3) 19-1/2 acres combined in four different parcels, 3-1/2 acres of Lot 2, 3-1/2 acres of Lot 1, 4-1/2 acres of Lot 3, Two-Mile Streak, and 8 acres of the farm purchased from Mark and Betty Jenness by deed signed 3 Jan 1804, rec'd 26 Jan same year; a combined 19-1/2 acres in Barrington by land deed signed 3 Jan 1804, rec'd 26 Jan 1804; [Strafford Co. Deed 43:518]; (4) 17 acres in Dover, 5 acres of which had been granted to Joseph Rankins in the Town Commons, and 12 acres that had been set off originally to James Killey of Dover by deed signed 24 Jan, rec'd 26 Jan 1804; (5) 25 acres in Dover on the north side of the Heath and on the Elseware Plains, so called, adjacent to lands of Ichabod Canney and James Hayes by deed of 3 Jan, rec'd 23 Jan 1804; and (6) 14 acres of Lot 12, 8th Range, in the Two-Mile Streak by deed signed 3 Mar 1820, rec'd same date.

Three purchases of land in the Two-Mile Streak, Barrington were all recorded on same date of 18 Mar 1806: first, by deed signed 22 Feb 1804, 25 acres from Thomas and Molley Wentworth of Dover, "and is that half of a certain 50-acre lot which Peter Young conveyed to me, deed dated 1 Sep last past, the same which Eleazer, the father of said Peter purchased of Jethro Bickford 6 Jan 1761," for $400.00; witnesses Oliver Crosby, John Lock, Jacob Wentworth and Douglas Stackpole [Strafford Co. Deed 50:391]; second, 16 acres land at Green Hill by land of James Hayes and Hezekiah Hayes, by quitclaim signed 26 Sep 1805, from William K. Atkinson Esq. of Dover and wife Abigail Atkinson for $352.00; witnesses William King, Samuel Hale [Strafford Co. Deed 50:392]; and lastly, by quitclaim signed 17 Mar 1806, 6 acres, 64 rods of land with buildings from Francis and Polly Drew of Madbury, land which had originally been set off to said Drew 15 Mar 1806 from Peter Young, for $108.00; witnesses Sarah Emerson, Hicks Richards [Strafford Co. Deed 50:394].

Eleazer seemed to be as intent in buying up land in and around Green Hill as his father had been. Four later purchases of land in the Two-Mile Streak were: (1) 39 acres at Green Hill at s.e. corner of Peter Young's land and by land of Hezekiah Hayes from Caleb Hodgdon and wife Elizabeth and

Moses Wingate and wife Joanna for $800.00, by quitclaim signed
6 May 1806, rec'd 6 Jan 1807; witnesses Oliver Crosby aka
Crosly, and John Coburn [Strafford Co. Deed 53:2]; (2) 9 addi-
tional acres by deed dated 3 Jan 1811, rec'd 27 Jan 1812, from
widow Abigail Cate of Barrington, Admin. of estate of Ebenezer
Cate, for $134.64; witnesses Paul Cate, John Cate [Strafford
Co. Deed 68:255]; (3) 36 square rods of land with dwelling
house which had been part of the homestead of Peter Young on
Green Hill adjacent to William K. Atkinson by quitclaim from
Oliver and Harriet Crosby of Dover signed 12 Mar 1807, rec'd
25 Jan 1809, for $237.31; witnesses William Twombly, Henry
Mellen [Strafford Co. Deed 60:158]; and (4) 18-1/2 acres
formerly owned by Daniel Ham on Green Hill, from James and
Lucy Rollins of Somersworth by quitclaim of 7 May 1808, rec'd
25 Jan 1809, for $325.00; witnesses Samuel and Hannah Rollins
[Strafford Co. Deed 60:160]. In the latter deed, the acreage
in question was recovered land set off to said Rollins on
execution against Peter Young. Eleazer's one known sale of
land in the Two-Mile Streak was by deed dated 3 Apr 1811,
rec'd 2 Apr 1812, by which he conveyed in fee simple to James
Marden Jr. and John Marden of Barrington for $134.00, 9-1/2
acres land, part of the farm formerly owned by David Drew, by
lands of Hickson Marden and Samuel Locks; Alice relinquished
dower rights; witnesses John Kingman, Thomas Babb [Strafford
Co. Deed 68:465]. Known ch. b Barrington by Alice: Jonathan-
+, b 28 Sep 1807. (NHVR-Marr; Barrington TR, V6, p44,82;
Hayes Gen., V1, p74-76; Census Strafford Co., 1830, p34)

ELEAZER, b 1787, Madbury, s/o Solomon and Elizabeth
(Hayes) Young, d 11 Mar 1868, age 82, native town, widower.
It is believed that Eleazer married twice; he m1 30 Nov 1817,
Durham, Sophia Meserve [b 1802, of Durham, d 2 Jun 1820, age
18, Madbury]. They resided in Madbury, but had no children.
As widower he m2 13 Nov 1823, Durham, Kezia Rowe [b 1787,
Dover, d/o John and Hannah (   ) Rowe, died testate 31 Mar
1864, Madbury]. Eleazer, with title of Fifer, served in the
War of 1812: on 12 Sep 1814 he made enlistment for 14 days
in Capt. Andrew Nute's Company, whose orders were to protect
and defend the town and harbor of Portsmouth and the adjacent
country. Eleazer was elected selectman for Madbury in 1820
and listed on the census returns for Madbury from 1830-1860.
In 1830 his age was given as 40-50, with spouse age 30-40, and
family of five males, three under 5, one age 5-10, one 15-20,
and one female 20-30. In 1840 his age was 50-60, spouse was
40-50, and other members of family were female parent figure
age 80-90, six males, one under 5, one age 5-10, three 10-15,
one 15-20 and one female age 5-10. From 1850-1860 Kezia was
named as Eleazer's spouse. Children at home in 1850 were
Harrison, Sophia, Asa, and Jeanette; in 1860, only John R. and
Jeanette.

Eleazer was named residuary legatee of his father Solomon
by will drawn 1 Mar 1811, proved 30 Jun 1813; he was to
receive the family homestead in Madbury. Through a division

of property in Madbury set off by Sergeant Hanson and Elijah Austin of Madbury and Nathaniel Young of Dover, Eleazer was one of three recipients. He received a 7/12th share or 7 acres out of the 12 acres, Sarah Demeritt, wife of Jonathan Demeritt Jr., 3 acres, and Thomas and Frances Drew, 2-1/4 acres, allowed 21 Sep 1835 [Strafford Co. Probate 49:302]. The acreage began a little below Gerrish's sawmills, s.w. of Eleazer's land.

Kezia predeceased her husband; her will of 17 Aug 1863, proved 1 Apr 1865, named son George W. as her Exec.; witnesses John Warren, Harriet R. Warren, Ezra E. Demeritt [Strafford Co. Probate 75:126]; execution of Kezia's will granted to George W. Young of Abbington, Plymouth Co., MA, on date of probate, bond of $2,000.00 given with sureties Orlando Young and Ezra E. Demeritt, both of Madbury [Strafford Co. Probate 68:347]. Bequests of money or household effects were made to children in lieu of real estate: Orlando, $1.00; John R., a note of $20.00 and all household goods remaining after other legacies were disbursed; George W., $90.00; Harrison, $140.00; Asa, $180.00; daughter Sophia Parsons, $200.00; Janette Durgin, $283.00. Sophia and Janette were "to share her best carpet, bureau, and all that may be in the bureau." Eleazer and members of family were buried at a family plot in Madbury on the east side of Mill Hill Road across from the Elm farm.

Ch. b Madbury: George W., b ca 1825, alive 1865, Abbington, Plymouth Co., MA; Orlando+, b 7 Jan 1826; John R.+, b 26 Mar 1827; Harrison, b 1834; Sophia+ (Young) Parsons, b 1835; Asa+, b 16 Jul 1837; and Jeannette aka Janette+ (Young) Durgin, b 1841. (LDS I.G.I. BR; NHVR-Brides, Deaths, Marr; Census Strafford Co., 1830, p90; 1840, p493; 1850, p492; 1860, p539; Hayes Gen., V1, p93; Madbury Cem., **Reg.** 87:347; Adam's Madbury, n.p.; Potter's Mil. Hist., V2, p155,190; Steuerwald's Dover Cem., TMs)

ELEAZER, b ca 1790, Meredith, alive 1830, Meredith; m 5 Sep 1816, Barnstead, Hannah Hodgdon [b 1790s, of Barnstead]. In 1830 Eleazer was head of household in Meredith, age 30-40, with spouse of same age group and three females, one under 5, and two 5-10. (NHVR-Marr; Census Strafford Co., 1830, p132)

ELEAZER, b ca 1795, of Gilmanton in that section which became Gilford in 1812; head of household in Gilford in 1840, his age and that of his spouse 40-50 years, with a family of one male age 5-10, and three females, two 10-15 and one under 20. He may have been the Eleazer Young of Gilford who became guardian on 1 Dec 1835 of Andrew Young of Meredith who was deemed "a distracted person"; bond of $1,000.00 was posted with sureties given by Jonas Gordon of Meredith and Nathaniel Perkins of Gilford [Strafford Co. Probate 50:37]. (Census Strafford Co., 1840, p428)

ELEAZER, b 16 Jan 1816, Gilmanton, s/o Joseph and Betsey (Young) Young; m ca 1840, Belmont, Alice Pickering [b ca 1820, of Gilmanton]. They adopted a child by the name of Emma Pickering Young, n.d. (Lyford's Canterbury, p343,344)

ELFIE, b Jun 1865, resident of Sanbornton in 1900, single; boarded at Hiram B. Philbrook's home. (1900 Soundex)

ELIAS, b ca 1792, Meredith; on 8 Mar 1808, he was a minor upwards of fourteen years who elected as his guardian John Neal of Meredith; bond of $1,000.00 was posted with sureties given by Joseph Neal and Samuel Kelley, both of Meredith [Strafford Co. Probate 12:208].

ELIPHALET, b 1760s, of Milton; widower and head of household in Milton in 1830, age 60-70, with family of two females one under 5 and one age 20-30. (Census Strafford Co., 1830, p408)

ELIPHALET, b 1761, ME, of Somersworth in 1850, age 89, resided alone. (Census Strafford Co., 1850, p301)

ELIPHALET, b ca 1785, of Milton in 1840, head of household, age 50-60; only other member of family was spouse of similar years. (Census Strafford Co., 1840, p324)

ELISA, b 1840, Barrington, d/o Ivory and Mary Ann (Seavey) Young; m 1 Jan 1862, Barrington, Joel F. Sherburne [b ca 1835, of same town]. (NHVR-Brides)

ELIZA, b 1798, Dover, youngest d/o of Ezra and Susannah (Demeritt) Young, d 21 Mar 1872, single, age 77, Dover. Lengthy probate papers and land deeds warranted a main entry on Eliza even though she remained single. She was named as daughter and heir of Ezra Young of Dover by his will drawn 20 Nov 1815, proved 23 Feb 1821. In addition she was named the beneficiary in the division of property dated 24 Mar 1845, wherein she received 33-1/3 acres land in Barrington from sister Polly's estate; see co-beneficiary James C. Young of Madbury for full details. Two months after the death of her sister Polly, Eliza became quite ill and was deemed "a person non compos mentis." On 1 Aug 1843, John Durell [cited above] was thus appointed the guardian not only of herself but of her property; bond of $2,000.00 was given with sureties David Peirce, Thomas E. Sawyer [Strafford Co. Probate 50:262].

On same date, John S. H. Durell, Nathaniel Young and John Hanson, all of Dover, were sworn in to take inventory, making their return on 5 Sep 1843 with the following appraisal: 3 shares in Strafford Bank and 7 shares in Dover Bank, $816.00; one-half of hogs house, $5.00; 66-2/3 acres in Barrington, $666.66; pew No. 111 (or No. 11) in Congregational Church, $37.50; total, $1,816.67. It is significant that the one-half shares of Polly's and Eliza's real estate holdings fit together as one whole. Two years later, 5 Aug 1845, Eliza became the ward of her [uncle] Nathaniel Young of Dover who posted bond of $3,000.00, sureties James Y. Demeritt, Thomas W. Kittridge [Strafford Co. Probate 50:291]. Nathaniel then gave New Bond as guardian in the amount of $3,000.00 on 7 Jan 1851; sureties John Trickey, Samuel Dunn, both of Dover [Strafford Co. Probate 50:412].

On her own behalf Eliza petitioned the court 6 Jul 1852 to have her guardianship revoked and have her liberty and property restored to her [Decree of Sanity, Strafford Co.

Probate 63:325]. Court hearings on Eliza's petition indicated that brother James C. Young and brother-in-law Eleazer Cate, husband of Abigail (Young) Cate, strongly objected to the petition. These hearings had to be readjourned several times inasmuch as some necessary witnesses could not attend. At one time, Eliza herself was ill and could not be present. On 6 Nov 1852, it was the decree of the court that Eliza "is restored to her right mind and it is unnecessary to continue guardianship." Guardianship papers were then revoked [Strafford Co. Probate 63:325]. Church records indicated she was dismissed 31 Aug 1856 from First Church of Dover to Belknap Church. Indeed in 1850 at age 52, Eliza lived with her nephew Jonathan T. Young and his family in Dover. (Heritage's Dover VR, p227)

ELIZA, b ca 1800, of Durham; m Sep 1824, Durham, Timothy Brewster [b ca 1800, of same town]. (NHVR-Brides)

ELIZA, b ca 1802, Strafford; m Oct 1822, Barnstead, Nicholas Otis [b ca 1800, Strafford]. (NHVR-Brides)

ELIZA aka Elizabeth, b 4 Jun 1813, Wolfeboro, d/o John C. and Sally (Smith) Young, d 4 Apr 1886, Ossipee, age 72-10-0; m (Intentions) 27 Apr 1850, Wolfeboro, m Apr 1850-Apr 1851, Wakefield, Samuel B. Sceggel [b 28 Sep 1820, Ossipee, d 2 Apr 1870, native town, age 49-6-4]. Eliza Sceggel was named a daughter and heir of John C. Young of Wolfeboro by his will signed 2 Nov 1853, proved 4 Sep 1866. Eliza and spouse Samuel B. were buried at the Stevens-Burleigh Cemetery on road from Ossipee to North Wakefield, over from Brown's Ridge and Smith Hill. (NHVR-Brides; Loud's Cemetery Recs., p124; Parker's Wolfeboro Banns, 1789-1854, n.p.)

ELIZA C. aka Alice, b 25 May 1860, Ossipee, d/o Joseph and Hannah (Chick) Young; m 2 Sep 1877, William A. Maybury [b ca 1855, of same town]. (NHVR-Brides, Marr; LDS I.G.I. VR)

ELIZA JANE, b 1805, Barrington, d/o Isaac and second wife Deborah (Killey) Young; m 29 Nov 1827, Freewill Baptist Church, Strafford, Enoch H. Pillsbury [b ca 1800, Northwood]. Eliza J. was known by her married name of Pillsbury in the will of her sister Lucy Young of Barrington, drawn 30 Dec 1846, proved 2 Feb 1847; see parents for Lucy's will. Eliza J., single, was also named an heir by her father's will signed 8 Sep 1826, proved 19 Apr 1827. (NHVR-Brides; Strafford Marr, **Reg.** 76:34)

ELIZABETH, b ca 1750, of Barrington, d/o William Young [no main entry]; m pre Apr 1774, Elisha Hall [b ca 1745, of Hopkinton, MA, Apr 1774, cordwainer]. Elizabeth (Young) Hall, was the Exec. of her father's estate in Barrington. She and husband Elisha Hall, co-grantor, sold to Samuel Hayes of Barrington one-half tract of land, the said Hayes possessing the other one-half, by quitclaim signed 1 Apr 1774, rec'd 4 Jun 1779, for $10.00; witnesses John W. Young, H. Y. Price [Strafford Co. Deed 2:375].

ELIZABETH, b ca 1755, Barrington; m 16 May 1787, Madbury, Simeon Page [b ca 1750, Epsom]. (NHVR-Brides)

ELIZABETH, b 1759, of Gilmanton, d Aug 1849, Gilmanton, age 90. (Census, Belknap Co., 1850 Mortality Schedules, n.p.)

ELIZABETH, b 22 Oct 1760, bp 3 May 1761, Dover, d/o Nathaniel and Mary (Kimball) Young, d 5 Feb 1822, Durham; m 25 May 1780, Dover, Ebenezer Demeritt Jr. [b 15 Feb 1759, Madbury, s/o Ebenezer and Hannah (Thompson) Demeritt, d 15 Jun 1808, Durham]. Ch. b Durham: Ebenezer Demeritt, b 3 Dec 1780, d.y.; Betsy Demeritt, b 15 Apr 1782, d 1797; Mary Demeritt, b 13 Nov 1784, d 22 Jun 1843; Hannah T. Demeritt, b 5 Feb 1787, twin, m 28 Oct 1821, Madbury, Ebenezer Thompson Demeritt; Ebenezer Demeritt, b 5 Feb 1787, twin, d 10 April same year; James Y. Demeritt, b 25 Dec 1788, m 27 Aug 1843, Strafford, Matilda Roe, d 18 Jul 1847; Sally Demeritt, b 21 Dec 1790, d.y.; Jacob Demeritt, b 5 Dec 1792; Clarissa Lavinia (Demeritt) Young, b 12 Nov 1796, see husband Jonathan+ Young of Dover; Harry Demeritt, b 1 Apr 1799, d Aug 1864; Oliver Demeritt, b 10 Dec 1801; Elvira Demeritt, b 25 Mar 1804, d 21 Sep 1861; and Albert Demeritt, b 19 Dec 1806, d.y. (Stackpole's Durham, V2, p118-122; NHVR-Births, Brides, Marr; Heritage's Dover VR, p80,180; LDS I.G.I. BR; Strafford Marr, **Reg.** 76:34; Demeritt Fam., **Reg.** 87:89,90)

ELIZABETH aka Eliza, b ca 1789, Madbury, d/o Solomon and Elizabeth (Hayes) Young, d 28 Aug 1854, Durham; m 1807 Durham, Joseph Chesley 3rd, widower [b 1785, Durham, s/o Philip and Abigail (Hayes) Chesley, d 17 May 1841, Durham]. Joseph Chesley m1 1 Sep 1803, Betsey Ham [b 1785, Durham, d 5 Apr 1807, age 22]. Elizabeth Chesley was named daughter and heir by Solomon's will signed 1 Mar 1811, proved 30 Jun 1813. Ch. b Durham by Eliza: Abigail Chesley, b ca 1814, m Benjamin F. Bunker, d 1879; and Mehitable Chesley, b ca 1825, m 24 Jun 1822, Durham, Samuel Furber of Boston, MA, d 1826. (NHVR-Brides; Stackpole's Durham, V2, p65,72; Hayes Gen., V1, p93)

ELIZABETH, b ca 1790, of Moultonboro; m 23 Mar 1818, Moultonboro, Manley Pierce [b ca 1785, of Ossipee]. (Moultonboro Marr, **Reg.** 59:283; NHVR-Brides)

ELIZABETH, b 18 Nov 1809, Effingham, d/o Timothy and Mary D. (Hobbs) Young; m1 16 Nov 1842, Effingham, Stephen Hayes [b 6 Sep 1818, Tuftonboro, s/o Hezekiah and Abigail (Bennett) Hayes, d 1 Jun 1881, Effingham], no known issue; m2 12 Apr 1887, Effingham, Levi Champion [b ca 1810, Drake's Corner, Effingham]. (Hayes Gen., V1, p290,291)

ELIZABETH, b ca 1813, of Alton, m (Intentions) 17 Aug 1833, Alton, m 8 Sep 1833, New Durham, Alfred Marsh [b 1810s, North Hampton]. (NHVR-Brides; Alton VR, p555)

ELIZABETH, b Oct 1823, of Durham, widow of _____ Young. In 1900 Elizabeth was head of household in Durham; at home was mother Clara Evans, widow [n.d.]. (1900 Soundex)

ELIZABETH, b ca 1835, Alton; m 1 Jul 1858, Farmington, Franklin S. Johnson [b ca 1830, Farmington]. Ch. b Alton: George H. Johnson, b 1860s, m 1900, Alton. (NHVR-Brides)

ELIZABETH, b 1842, of Dover, Ward 1, in 1870. She lived alone, cotton mill worker. (Census Strafford Co., 1870, p6)

ELIZABETH A., b Jul 1858, resident of Belmont, 1900, single, age 41, servant of Joseph T. Judkins family of Belmont. (1900 Soundex)

ELIZABETH ANN, b 17 Mar 1839, Gilmanton, d/o Andrew Bailey and Eliza (Evans) Young; m (Intentions) 27 Oct 1857, Belmont, George Elkins [b ca 1835, Gilmanton]. She lived at home in 1850 per census returns for Gilmanton. (NHVR-Brides)

ELIZABETH JANE, b 7 May 1812, Dover, d/o Nathaniel and Elizabeth (Kimball) Young, alive Jun 1863, home town; m 14 Apr 1842, Dover, John Trickey [b ca 1815, of Dover, alive 1861, same town]. Elizabeth J. Trickey was named Exec. of her sister Eveline A. Young's will signed 5 Nov 1861, proved 2 Jun 1863, Dover. For details of children's bequests, see Nathaniel and Elizabeth Young. Ch. b Dover 1840s, 1850s: Nathaniel P. Trickey, Fordyce P. Trickey, George O. Trickey, Matthew M. Trickey, Edward K. Trickey, Ellen A. Trickey, and Anna D. Trickey. (NHVR-Brides; LDS I.G.I. BR)

ELIZABETH JANE, b 1835, Farmington, d/o Hiram H. and first wife Margaret (Hall) Young; m 11 Jan 1852, Milton, George Page [b ca 1825, Farmington]. Elizabeth Jane Page was acknowledged as daughter and heir of Hiram H. Young by his by his will signed 25 Jul 1870, proved 8 Apr 1873. (Milton VR, Town Clerk, letter of 1989; NHVR-Brides)

ELIZABETH M., b ca 1860, of Dover; m 19 Oct 1881, Dover, Charles E. Allen [b ca 1855, same town]. (NHVR-Brides)

ELIZABETH S., b ca 1809, Dover, m 4 Jan 1829, Dover, Henry Dore [b ca 1805, same town]. (Heritage's Dover VR, p92)

ELLA A., b 1858, b Farmington, d/o Furber and Elizabeth (Goodall) Young; m 28 Nov 1874, Rochester, Dexter S. Foss [b 1853, Strafford, s/o Isaac B. and Mary A. ( ) Foss]. Both resided in Rochester at time of marriage. (NHVR-Brides; Rochester Marr, n.p)

ELLA CYNTHIA, b 10 Aug 1851, Barrington, d/o George William and Cynthia Ellen (Flagg) Young, d Jul 1934, Madbury; m 24 June 1880, Dover, Herman Edcil Canney [b 6 Mar 1851, of Strafford, s/o Jerome B. Canney). Ella and Herman resided for over 40 years in Dover where he established a livery stable; circa 1900, they moved to Madbury having purchased the old Paul Chesley farm. Ch. b Dover, not traced further: Mabel Etta Canney, b 3 Apr 1881; Herman Clarence Canney, b 18 May 1884; Addie May Canney, b 9 Oct 1886, d 12 Sep 1925, Madbury; Marion G. Canney, b 25 Feb 1889; and Elmer Leslie Canney, b 11 Mar 1891. (NHVR-Brides; Adam's Madbury, n.p.; Ham Gen., p25,43,65-67)

ELLEN, b ca 1845, Dover, d/o Joseph and Julia ( ) Young [no main entry]; m 3 Jul 1869, Dover, George Tanner [b ca 1840, Rochester]. She was resident of Rochester at time of marriage. (NHVR-Brides)

ELLEN A., b ca 1840, Somersworth; m 16 Mar 1861, Somersworth, J. Eaton Pray [b ca 1835, of same town]. (NHVR-Brides)

ELLEN A., b 1845, Dover, d/o John B. and Mary J. ( ) Young, m (Intentions) 25 Nov 1867, age 22, Alton, m 28 Nov

1867, Alton, Benjamin F. Grover, age 27 [b 1840, Alton].
(Alton VR, p670; NHVR-Brides)

ELLEN E. aka Frances E., b ca 1835, Wolfeboro; m 30 Oct
1858, Wolfeboro, William F. Piper [b ca 1830, Tuftonboro].
(NHVR-Brides)

ELLEN E., b 1846, Barrington, d/o Jonathan and Sophia
Maria (Ricker) Young, res. of Dover; m 15 Dec 1867, Dover,
George H. Tebbetts [b ca 1845, Barrington]. Ellen E. Tebbetts
was known as the daughter of Jonathan and Sophia by Sophia's
will drawn 3 Sep, probated 5 Nov 1889. (NHVR-Brides)

ELLEN J., b ca 1824, Somersworth; m 27 Nov 1845, Somersworth, Dennis Maloy [b ca 1820, of same town]. (NHVR-Brides)

ELLEN S. aka Eleanor S., b 1842, Boston, MA, d/o James
C. Young of Wakefield, believed to be the daughter of his
second wife, Rosemandel (Gill) Davis Young of MA; m 30 Mar
1862, Concord, at age 20, Mark Remick [b ca 1835, Brookfield].
In 1860 Eleanor S., at age 18, lived with her mother Rosemandel and step-father James Young in Wakefield. Ch. b poss.
Brookfield: Alonzo M. Remick, b 1860s, m 1895, Brookfield;
and Henry J. Remick, b 1860s, m 1895, Madison. (NHVR-Brides)

ELLEN SARAH, b 7 Oct 1844, Barrington, d/o William Hale
and Sarah J. (Daniels) Young, d 22 Jan 1839, Barrington; m
15 Mar 1870, Dover, John Langdon Winkley [b 10 Mar 1841, d
19 Dec 1888, Barrington]. Ch. b Barrington: Grace Ellen
Winkley, b 26 Jun 1873; Lillian Abbie Winkley, b 1 Jan 1877;
George Langdon Winkley, b 31 Jan 1879, m Mabel Hoyt Pinkham;
and Willard Choate Winkley, b 1 Jun 1885, not traced further.
(NHVR-Brides; Ham Gen., p27,29,39; Pinkham Gen., p35)

ELMER J., b 1862, Durham; m ca 1890, New Market, Mary L.
Hutchinson [b 1863, Durham]. Elmer and Mary were residents
of New Market when their first child was born. Ch. b New
Market: daughter, still born, b 28 Nov 1890. (NHVR-Births)

ELMIRA, b ca 1825, Dover; m 14 Oct 1848, Somersworth,
John Grant [b ca 1820, Madbury]. (NHVR-Brides)

EMELINE, b 1823, Wakefield, d/o James C. and first wife
Ruth (   ) Young, d 1842, age 19; m ca 1841, William Mills of
Freedom. Emeline Mills was buried at the Aaron Young Ceme-
tery, Pray Hill Road, Wakefield. Ch. b Freedom: Emma A.
Mills, b ca 1842, m 1860, Freedom, Augustus D. Ferren [b ca
1835, Madison]. (NHVR-Brides; Twombly's Wakefield Cem., TMs)

EMELINE, b 1824, Upper Gilmanton, d/o Bailey and Polly
(Rundlet) Young, alive 1863, Belmont; m 30 Nov 1852, Belmont,
Edwin Nutting [b ca 1825, Charlestown, VT]. She lived at home
in 1850. Emeline Nutting was named daughter and heir of
Bailey Young by his will drawn 26 Jan, proved 18 Mar 1863.
Ch. b Gilmanton: Edwin C. Nutting, b ca 1855. (NHVR-Brides)

EMILIA, b 1851, Tuftonboro, d 1 Feb 1875, age 24, her
native town, of typhoid fever, spouse of _____ Young. (NHVR-
Deaths)

EMMA A., b 1855, Strafford, d/o John Franklin and Phoebe
H. (Hayes) Young; m1 22 Dec 1874, Rochester, George W. Blaisdell [b 1848, of Rochester, s/o Joseph and Eliza (   ) Blais-

dell, d pre 1890, prob. Rochester]; m2 26 Nov 1890, Dover, Ebenezer N. Lambert [b ca 1850, Newburyport, MA]. She was known as Emma Blaisdell and heir-at-law in her father's will written 26 Nov 1878, drawn 1 Jan 1884. (NHVR-Brides; Hayes Gen., V1, p202,203)

EMMA E., b 1858, Great Falls, d/o John B. and Ellen R. (Hartford) Young of Somersworth, d 27 Dec 1936, Westbrook, ME; m 14 Jun 1884, Somersworth, Fred W. Norton [b ca 1855, Great Falls, d 30 Dec 1922, Somersworth]. Both Emma, Fred and son were buried at the family plot at Forest Glade Cemetery, Somersworth. Ch. b Somersworth: Walter W. Norton, b 1880s, d 1924, home town. (NHVR-Brides; Wooley's Somersworth Cem.)

EMMA F., b 1858, Barnstead, d/o Solomon W. and Louisa A. (Jenkins) Young; m 6 Dec 1876, Barnstead, Frank E. Shannon [b ca 1855, Gilmanton]. As a minor under 14 years 14 Emma F. was named as heir-at-law of her mother upon her death in 1867 and became ward of her father. (NHVR-Brides)

EMMA J., b ca 1850, Great Falls; m 19 Feb 1870, Dover, Edwin L. Perkins [b ca 1845, Great Falls]. (NHVR-Brides)

EMMA LOUISA, b 16 May 1860, Dover, d/o George William and Cynthia E. (Flagg) Young, d 11 Dec 1944, poss. Haverhill, MA; m 30 Oct 1895, Dover, George H. Clark [b 31 Mar 1860, Hyde Park, MA, d Dec 1923, Haverhill, MA]. Ch. b Dover, not traced further: Philip Leslie Clark, b 20 Sep 1896; Inez May Clark, b 11 Dec 1897; Helen Young Clark, b 14 Aug 1899; Margery Mabel Clark, b 5 Apr 1901. (NHVR-Brides; Ham Gen., p65,77)

EMOGENE A. aka Abbie Emogene, b 20 Nov 1869, twin, of Exeter, d/o Charles W. and Abbie (Swasey) Young of Wolfeboro; m 28 Oct 1896, Exeter, Edward E. Rowell [b ca 1865, Exeter]. (NHVR-Brides)

EPHRAIM, b ca 1775 of Dover, most likely brother of Daniel Young of Dover; d pre 1827, same town; m ca 1800, Dover, Diana aka Amy Coffin [b ca 1780 of Dover, alive 1827, same town]. Ephraim was head of household in Dover 1790-1810: in 1790, household contained one male under 16 and one female; in 1800 his age was 45 plus, as was his spouse, with family of one male age 16-26 and four females, two under 10, one 10-16, and one 26-45; in 1810 he and spouse were over 45 years of age, with family of four males under 10, two 10-16, two 16-26, and two females, one under 10 and one 16-26. Children's names were never identified. Ephraim was named as an heir, along with John Young and Daniel Young, both of Dover, by the will of Benjamin Church of Dover, drawn 7 Apr, proved 30 Sep 1812; he received six acres of Church's homestead in Dover, given the option to choose "around his house where he thinks best to take it" and 12 acres in Rochester; see John and Ruth Young of Dover for details on legacies.

By deed signed 19 Apr 1821, rec'd same day, Ephraim of Dover mortgaged six acres of his homestead to the said Daniel Young of Dover [Strafford Co, Deed 109:469]. It was learned through probate papers listed under "Daniel Young" that the dower rights of Anna aka Amy Young, widow of Ephraim of Dover, were set off to her through "the practice of first severing the estate" from her portion, rather than measuring off her one-thirds from the estate. This established precedent, cited in Admin. Papers on the estate of Eleanor W. Young, widow of Daniel, by date of 20 Apr 1827, allowed 7 Feb 1828 [Strafford Co. Probate 37:70]. Anna Young's dower was entailed with the land her husband Ephraim sold to Daniel Young 19 Apr 1821 [see above], being the same on which Ephraim then lived. Amy received two acres on the south side of the barn which formerly belonged to Ephraim, and 15 feet of the east end of house and barn and the south half of cellar. (Heritage's Dover VR, p159-160; Ham's Dover Marr, TMs; Census Strafford Co., 1790, p88; 1800, p160; 1810, p863)

ERASTUS, b 1819, Strafford, s/o Rufus and Nancy (Blodgett) Young; m1 19 Jan 1852, Strafford, Charlotte (Dustin) Purrington [b 1824, West Milan, d/o David H. and Sarah (   ) Dustin]. Erastus and Charlotte established residence in his home town. (NHVR-Marr)

ERWIN W., b Aug 1870, of Eaton; in 1900, at age 29, he and wife Mary L. (   ) Young [b Sep 1878, age 24 in 1900] lived alone in Eaton. (1900 Soundex)

ESTHER, b ca 1815, Dover; m 2 Dec 1839, Dover, Andrew J. Drew [b ca 1810, Derry]. (NHVR-Brides)

ESTHER ANN, b ca 1820, Wolfeboro, d/o Timothy W. and Esther (Libby) Young; m (Intentions) 6 Oct 1840, Wolfeboro, James Frost [b ca 1815, of same town]. Esther Ann was named daughter and heir in her father's will dated 24 Mar, proved 16 May 1834. (Parker's Wolfeboro Banns, 1789-1854, n.p.]

ESTHER DANIELS, b 12 May 1817, Barrington, d/o Aaron and Lydia (Daniels) Young, d 24 Jun 1909, home town; m 8 Jun 1848, Barrington, John E. Buzzell [b 21 Feb 1816, Lee, s/o Lemuel and Avis (Emerson) Buzzell, gr.son of Samuel and Lydia (Evans) Buzzell, d 13 Mar 1896, Durham]. She was named as daughter and heir, known as Esther Buzzell, in her father Aaron's will drawn 5 Mar 1850, proved 2 May 1854. Ch. b Barrington: Caroline Elizabeth Buzzell, b 25 Mar 1849; and Lydia Ann Buzzell, b 20 Jan 1851. (NHVR-Brides; Ham Gen., p43; Stackpole's Durham, V2, p50,51; Hammond's Barrington TR, p59)

ESTHER M., b 10 Nov 1862, Freedom, d/o George F. and Mary F. (Nason) Young; m 13 Apr 1884, Freedom, Hazen J. Godfrey [b ca 1810, of same town]. Esther's age was given as 8 years on the 1870 census returns on her parents in Freedom. (NHVR-Brides)

ESTHER SARAH, b 14 May 1868, Madbury, d/o Jacob Daniels and Sarah C. (Twombly) Young, d 15 Jul 1913, Rochester; m 8 Oct 1890, Madbury, Albert Ianson Hall [b 30 Apr 1856, Barrington, d 23 Feb 1949, Rochester]. She was taken care of in later years when an invalid in Rochester by her sister Lillian. Ch. b Madbury, not traced further: Roswell Ianson Hall, b 16 Apr 1893, d 21 Jun 1896; Irene Margurite Hall, b 13 Apr 1898; and Olive Frances Hall, b 14 Aug 1902. (Adam's Madbury, n.p.; NHVR-Brides; Ham Gen., p55,57)

ETHEL M., b 1870s, Alton, d/o George and Hannah (   )
Young [no main entry]; m 2 Sep 1899, Alton, Walter S. Dame [b
ca 1870, Farmington]. (NHVR-Brides)

EVA aka Evangeline, b 2 Nov 1862, Farmington, d/o Thomas
S. and Lovina E. (Beedy) Young; m (Intentions) 21 Sep 1874,
New Durham, m 23 Sep 1876, Farmington, Charles H. Tyler [b
1848, Rockland, ME, s/o C. A. and Eliza (Appleton) Tyler of
Brockton, MA]. At time of marriage, Eva was resident of
Farmington, Charles of New Durham. (NHVR-Brides; New Durham
VR, Bk1, p2)

EVA M., b 1860s, Wolfeboro, d/o Nahum G. and Harriet H.
(   ) Young of Goldsboro, ME; m 3 Jul 1885, Wolfeboro, Forrest
L. Leighton [b 1860s, Rochester]. (NHVR-Brides)

EZRA aka Sgt., b 6 Dec 1751, bp 24 May 1752, Dover, s/o
Nathaniel and Mary (Kimball) Young of Parish of Madbury, d
testate 2 Dec 1821, Dover; m 1 Apr 1779, Dover, Susannah
Demeritt [b 25 Dec 1755, d/o Ebenezer and Hannah (Thompson)
Demeritt, d 9 Jul 1826, age 71, Dover]. Ezra was named son
and heir by Nathaniel's will of 29 Jan, proved 26 May 1762,
his legacy, 80 acres land or one-third part of Lot 47, 2nd
Div., Rochester [that section which became Farmington]. Ezra
was also named Exec. and residuary legatee of [uncle] James
Young of Dover by will signed 9 Mar 1775, proved 21 Feb 1787.
His legacy was a one-half share of James' dwelling house, the
other half reverting to him upon James' widow's demise, and
the remainder of land in Dover and Madbury, as well as a
1/16th share in Gerrish's sawmill. A fourth-generation
descendant of Ezra, Mrs. Martha (Young) Kay deposed in her
application for membership in the Daughters of the American
Revolution that "Ezra Young served as sergeant in Capt. Caleb
Hodgdon's Company, 1775, for the protection of Piscataqua
Harbor."

Ezra and Susannah lived in the neighborhood called
Littleworth, Dover. He was head of family on the census
returns for Dover in 1800 and 1810: in 1800, his age was 45
years plus, one female also 45 plus, with one male under 26
years, and three females, one each under 10, 10-16, and 26-
45; by 1810, his age was 45 plus with a household of two
males, one 10-16, one 16-26, and four females, one 10-16, one
16-26, and two females 45 plus.

Ezra's first deed of record was dated 10 Apr 1775, rec'd
31 Mar 1794, in which he purchased from Paul Horn of Dover,
three acres in Dover which were bounded at the northern end
of James Young's land and at s.e. corner of lands belonging
to heirs of Reuben Hayes, deceased, to lands of Paul Horn, for
16 pounds-10 shillings; witnesses John Hayes, John B. Hanson
[Strafford Co. Deed 17:311]. An additional purchase of land
in Dover was 18-1/4 acres of land, adjacent to lands of Dr.
Ezra Green, abutting Ezra's farm at n.e. corner, by deed of
24 Apr 1787, rec'd 31 Mar 1794, from Daniel and Mary Ham of
Dover, for 92 pounds and 6 shillings; witnesses William
Kielle, Miles Evans [Strafford Co. Deed 17:330]. He held the

mortgage on Paul Horne's 80-acre homestead in Dover, by deed of 28 Dec 1798, rec'd 15 Jan 1799, advancing $500.00, due and payable one year hence; this land was adjacent to Dr. Ezra Green's land; witnesses Thomas Footman, William K. Atkinson [Strafford Co. Deed 29:331]. His legacy of 80 acres land, part of Lot 47, Rochester [Farmington] was sold in fee simple to Isaac Hanson of Farmington for $266.00; witnesses Israel Hanson Jr., William K. Atkinson [Strafford Co. Deed 53:441]. Purchase of the field from the estate of Silas Hanson late of Dover, 13 acres land, 140 sq. rods, was by deed signed 23 Feb, rec'd 9 May 1803, for $1,071.84; this land abutted the main road from Dover to Barrington, representing the dower rights of Patience Hanson as widow of Richard Hanson, eldest son of Silas Hanson, who had inherited the field after Silas Hanson's widow's dower had been set off to Abigail Roberts; witnesses Stephen Sawyer, Samuel Watson [Strafford Co. Deed 42:173].

He went into partnership with Elizabeth Young, widow of the said James Young of Dover, in buying up the property known as "Littleworth," Dover by a series of four deeds signed in 1790/1791 and the 200-acre Lot 176, Barrington by deed signed 6 Mar 1806, rec'd 27 May same year; for full details see James and Elizabeth Young of Dover. Ezra's wife Susannah and single daughters Polly and Eliza all received small legacies from the said widow Elizabeth Young of Dover, per her will of 30 Aug 1821, proved 17 Jun 1822. For the disposal of shares Susannah (Demeritt) Young held in common with her siblings Lydia (Demeritt) Young of Madbury and Jonathan Demeritt of Madbury in the 50-acre estate of the late Ebenezer Demeritt of Madbury in 1779, see Timothy and Lydia Young of Madbury. As heirs-at-law of Isaac Young of Dover, Ezra and co-grantors [all siblings and their spouses] Joseph and Abigail (Young) Hayes of Rochester, and Ebenezer and Elizabeth (Young) Demeritt of Madbury sold their shares in the 19 acres land in Dover from the estate of said Isaac to John Wheeler of Dover by deed signed 3 Jun, rec'd 16 Nov 1803, for $150.00; witnesses Olive Crosby, Jonathan Young [Strafford Co. Deed 43:313]. See Isaac Young for full description of estate and list of heirs-at-law.

Ezra's will of 20 Nov 1815, proved 23 Feb 1821, named son Jonathan as sole Exec. and residuary legatee; witnesses Moses Hodgdon, Timothy Young, Charles Kimball [Strafford Co. Probate 28:522]. He devised to wife Susanna one-half of the dwelling house in Dover, one-half of the livestock and furniture and one-fourth of the income from his farms in Dover and Madbury "to hold and enjoy as long as she is my widow." To daughters Polly and Eliza he gave each $500.00 with the privilege to live at home until they married. Another will of almost identical content drawn up and recorded on same dates cited above was documented as Strafford Co. Probate 25:517, with same witnesses. The only visible change was that daughters were to receive "three sheep each" rather than "one cow each." Ezra, Susannah and children were buried at the John Young Cemetery, Littleworth Rd., Dover. This was the family burial

plot for descendants of Jonathan and Abigail (Hanson) Young
through the branch headed by Ezra's parents Nathaniel and Mary
(Kimball) Young.

Due to extensive land deeds and probate papers found on
single daughters Polly and Eliza, main entries were provided
for them. Ch. b Dover: Jonathan+, b 14 Apr 1780; Polly+, b
14 Apr 1791; James, b 1792, d 29 Nov 1795, Dover; and Eliza+,
b 1798, bp 1799. (Steuerwald Dover Cem., TMs;   Heritage's
Dover VR, p80,156,227; Frost's Dover Cem. Plot #22; Demeritt
Fam., **Reg.** 87:89,90; Stackpole's Durham, V1, p118; Census
Strafford Co., 1800, p160; 1810, p863; 1840, p530; D.A.R
Lineage #36347, V37, p121)

EZRA, b ca 1765, bp 29 Jan 1792, Dover; m ca 1786, Dover,
Elizabeth (   ) [b ca 1765, bp 1792 with husband, Dover].
They became members of First Church of Dover by baptism 29 Jan
1792. Ch. b Dover: Jonathan, bp 5 Feb 1792; Polly, bp 25 Feb
1792; James, bp 11 Nov 1792; and Eliza, bp 1799. While the
their is a disturbing similarity between this couple's children and those of Ezra and Susannah (Demeritt) Young of Dover,
it must be stressed that Ezra's will, cited in preceding
entry, established that the mother of his children was Susannah Demeritt. (Heritage's Dover VR, p212,241,242)

EZRA, b 1803, of Madbury; head of household in Madbury
for 1860, single, age 57. Members of family were James W.
Young, age 82 [b 1778], and John Young, age 20 [b 1840].
(Census Strafford Co., 1860, p53)

EZRA, b ca 1815, of Dover. In 1840 he was listed as head
of household in Dover, age 20-30, with family of one female
age 20-30, one other male of same age and one male age 10-15.
This family unit seems to be made up of siblings, rather than
of man and wife with children. (Census Strafford Co., 1840,
p531)

EZRA aka 2nd, b ca 1820, Dover, s/o Daniel and Eleanor
W. (Smith) Young, d pre 5 May 1846, Dover; m 11 Dec 1836,
Dover, Catherine N. Trednick [b ca 1820, Dover, alive 1860,
Dover]. Ezra was resident of South Berwick, ME at time of
marriage. Upon the death of his father Ezra was made a ward
of Samuel Kimball of Dover on date of 17 Oct 1826. Widow
Catherine remarried in Dover, her second husband John G.
Palmer of Dover. She was dismissed from First Church, Dover
11 Apr 1860, to Washington Street Freewill Baptist Church,
Dover. Admin. Papers on the estate of Ezra 2nd were filed
5 May 1846, at which time Oliver J. Horn of Dover was named
Admin. by bond of $6,000.00, and sureties John B. Sargent and
Nathaniel Davis both of Dover; Peter Cushing of Dover was
appointed agent for Ezra's minor children, Ezra, Rebecca Ann
and Mary Ellen [Strafford Co. Probate 50:307]. On same date,
widow Catherine N. was allowed $300.00 from the personal
estate for her support [Strafford Co. Probate 43:209]; also
on same date it was decided Catherine's dower rights were to
be set off by Charles Ham, Walter Ham and Ephraim Ham Jr. [see
decision below].

Inventory on Ezra's estate was returned on date of 5 May 1846, by the committee cited above, accepted same date [Strafford Co. Probate 62:51]. The following assessments were made: the 37-acre homestead set at $1,665.00; the John Young pasture so called, $815.00; the Benjamin Horne pasture, $100.00; the Sunken Island pasture, $360.00; and wood lot in Barrington, $15.00; value of total real estate, $2,955.00. Personal estate was set at $385.99; this included livestock, produce, one sleigh, household effects, wood and trees on Waterhouse lot in Barrington [$16.50], and the lot of cordwood and limbs in Dover [$19.00]; grand total of estate, $3,340.99.

Petition on Catherine's dower rights was heard 4 Aug 1846 attended by Peter Cushing, agent for the minor children; approved 1 Sep 1846, [Strafford Co. Probate 55:431]. The said committee set off to Catherine 17 acres of the 37-acre homestead, including the west front room and parts of the barn and outbuildings, situated on Toll End Road, Dover. Said Cushing, agent, was to receive the balance of the homestead. Charles Ham, appointed Commissioner on 5 May 1846, presented the closing account on the estate 5 Jan 1847, allowed same date [Strafford Co. Probate 62:269]: the medical bill of James W. Cowan was paid in full, $66.59; 34 notes against the estate totalled $471.60; four of these were allowed in part, $30.66; one note was wholly disallowed, $30.34.

Petition for license to sell real estate in order to raise $500.00 against the demands on the estate was made by said Admin. Horn 5 Jan 1847 [Strafford Co. Probate 60:61]; license granted 2 Mar 1847 [Strafford Co. Probate 67:267]. Oliver Horn made his final accounting 1 Jan 1850; approved same date by the court and by T. E. Sawyer, guardian of Ezra, Rebecca Ann and Mary Ellen [Strafford Co. Probate 57:71]. Total debits came to $936.35. Credits included amount of personal estate per inventory, $388.99; cash received from sale of real estate, $395.00; rents of real estate, $152.36; total Credits, $936.35. Amendment to the children's guardianship was filed on 5 Aug 1851, which named Ezekial Hayes of Dover as guardian of the three children who had given bond of $3,000.00, sureties John W. Hurd, Jesse Hurd, both of Dover [Strafford Co. Probate 50:427]. Ch. b Dover: Rebecca Ann+ (Young) Varney, b ca 1840; Ezra D.+, b 1841; and Mary Ellen, b early 1840s. (Heritage's Dover VR, p103,236; NHVR-Births; Ham's Dover Marr, TMs)

EZRA, b ca 1820, of Roxbury, MA; m (Intentions) 30 Jan 1846, m 30 Apr 1846, Barrington, Louisa Meserve [b ca 1825, of Roxbury, MA]. (NHVR-Marr; Hammond's Barrington TR, p59)

EZRA D., b 1841, Dover, s/o Ezra and Catherine N. (Trednick) Young 2nd, shoemaker, alive 1870, native town; m 25 Nov 1863, Dover, Hattie M. Rogers [b 1845, Newfield, ME, alive 1870, Dover]. At the age of five on date of 5 Aug 1851, he was made ward of Ezekial Hayes of Dover upon the death of his father. Ezra, Hattie and son Eddie H., age 6, were residents of Ward 2, Dover in 1870. Ch. b ME: Edwin H., b

15 Jun 1864 [NHVR-Births], or born Dover [LDS I.G.I. BR].
(Census Strafford Co., 1870, p35)

FANNIE, b ca 1850, of Great Falls, d/o Josiah and Sarah
(Pettingill) Young [no main entry]; m 17 Jun 1876, Somers-
worth, John H. Littlefield [b ca 1845, of Great Falls].
(NHVR-Brides)

FANNIE H. aka Frances H., b 1841, New Durham, d/o Jona-
than B. and Hannah D. (Stevens) Young; m 11 Mar 1859, New
Durham, Samuel G. Jones [b ca 1840, of same town]. (NHVR-
Brides)

FANNIE H., b 10 Jan 1847, Gilmanton, d/o Thomas Jefferson
and Elizabeth C. (Hickson) Young of Canterbury [no main
entry]; m 24 Jul 1873, Concord, George H. Boardman [b ca 1840,
of Lowell, MA]. The couple took up residence in Lowell. Ch.
b Lowell, MA: Samuel Herbert Boardman, b 13 Dec 1874, not
traced further. (Lyford's Canterbury, p347)

FANNIE J. aka Frances, b 11 Mar 1856, Farmington, d/o
Furber and Elizabeth (Goodall) Young, d 14 Apr 1918, Roch-
ester; m 27 Jan 1872, Strafford, Charles Howland Hayes [b
1 Jun 1852, Gonic, s/o James Y. Hayes, d 8 Nov 1913, Concord].
They lived in Gonic where Charles worked as mill spinner.
Fannie and spouse were both buried in Rochester. Ch. b Gonic:
Herbert Charles Hayes, b 28 Jun 1876. (Hayes Gen., V2, p605;
NHVR-Brides; Rochester TR, Marr, n.p.; LDS I.G.I. VR)

FLORENCE S. aka Sarah F., b 1855, Ossipee, d/o Joseph and
Hannah (Chick) Young; m 13 Sep 1884, Ossipee, John T. D.
Whiting [b ca 1850, Parsonsfield, ME]. She was listed as a
child of 5 in the 1860 census return for her parents living
in Ossipee. (NHVR-Brides)

FOSTINA E., b 1858, Belmont, d/o Moses A. and Ann M.
(Chase) Young; m 7 Feb 1878, Gilford, Fred C. Sanborn [b ca
1850, Gilford]. She lived at home per 1870 census for Belmont
and was named Fostina Sanborn, wife of Fred C. Sanborn, in her
father's will signed 5 Sep 1882, proved 15 Apr 1890. (NHVR-
Brides)

FRANCIS A., b 1826, of Alton; m 1840s, Abigail (   ) [b
1827, of Alton]. They resided in Alton in 1850 with infant
daughter. By 1860 unknown circumstances had placed daughter
Mary L., then age 11, in the home of John and Mary Tucker of
Gilmanton. Ch. b Alton: Mary L., b 1849. (Census Belknap
Co., 1850, p367; 1860, p240)

FRANK, b 1837, of Gilmanton; res. of Gilmanton in 1870,
farm laborer, single. (Census Strafford Co., 1870, p38)

FRANK, b ca 1850, Barrington; m ca 1875, poss. Northwood,
Sarah M. Demeritt [b ca 1855, Deerfield]. It is quite possible Frank was the son of Jonathan and Sophia M. (Ricker)
Young of Barrington as their son Frank H. was b 1850, Barrington. Frank was named son and heir of Sophia Young by her
will signed 3 Sep, proved 5 Nov 1889. He and Sarah took up
residence in Northwood. Ch. b Northwood: daughter, b 7 Jul
1875; son b 6 Apr 1878; son b 26 Apr 1880; and son b 13 Nov
1882. (NHVR-Births)

FRANK, b 1853, Rochester; resident of Rochester in 1870, single, farm laborer, roomed at boarding house. (Census Strafford Co., 1870, p279)

FRANK, b ca 1855, of Milton, clergyman; m ca 1880, prob. Milton, Annie Remick [b ca 1860, of Milton]. Frank and Annie resided in Strafford when their daughter was born. Ch. b Milton: daughter, b 4 Dec 1882. (NHVR-Births)

FRANK E., b 19 Aug 1861, Alton, s/o Charles E. and Hannah ( ) Young; m1 18 Nov 1882, Alton, Lizzie A. Foss [b 1858, Farmington, d/o William W. Foss, d pre 1892, Farmington]; m2 25 Feb 1892, Gilmanton, Flora E. Shorey, divorcee, [b Nov 1865 New Durham, d/o Samuel Randall, alive 1900, Farmington]. He and second wife Flora lived alone in Farmington by 1900. (LDS I.G.I. BR; 1900 Soundex; NHVR-Marr)

FRANK H., b Sep 1854, Tuftonboro, s/o John and Hannah (Ham) Young, alive 1918, Wolfeboro; m 15 May 1880, Sophia W. Estes [b Oct 1850, Wolfeboro, d/o James and Louisa ( ) Estes, alive 1918, Wolfeboro]. In 1870 Frank H., age 16, lived with William and Susan A. Blaisdell in Tuftonboro. In 1900 he and Sophia were members of his parents' household in Tuftonboro. On 23 Mar 1918 Sophia W.'s sister Louisa M. Tutt of Brookfield filed petition for guardianship of Sophia W. Young of Wolfeboro inasmuch as the latter was deemed insane; husband Frank H. was appointed her guardian on 2 Apr 1918 [Carroll Co. Probate #8484]. During the proceedings Fred W. Prindle was authorized to take inventory of Sophia's estate, who set value at $4,150.00. Daughter Elsie M. m 15 Nov 1899, Moultonboro, Clarence F. Perry [b ca 1875, Moultonboro]. Ch. b Tuftonboro: Elsie M. (Young) Perry, b ca 1880. (1900 Soundex; NHVR-Brides; Census Carroll Co., 1870, p420)

FRANK JAMES aka Frank E., b Apr 1861, twin, Alton, s/o James H. and Hannah (Allen) Young; m 4 Jan 1896, Portsmouth, Jennie Amazeen [b 1865, New Castle, d/o William and Mary (Lear) Amazeen]. (NHVR-Marr)

FRANK K., b ca 1850, ME, d pre 1900, Dover; m ca 1875, poss. Dover, Alexine ( ) [b Dec 1856, ME; head of household in Dover, 1900, widow]. In 1900 Alexine was head of household with family of brother Frank H. _____ [b Jul 1857, ME], and her married daughter Lilla May (Young) Cate, b Oct 1879, NH. Lilla May m 12 Oct 1899, Dover, Charles A. Cate [b ca 1865, Dover]. (1900 Soundex; NHVR-Brides)

FRANK S., b 1864, Clarksville, s/o Josiah and Nancy E. ( ) Young of Wolfeboro; m 20 Jun 1885, Stewartstown, Mary J. Haynes [b 1864, Hereford, P.Q., d/o Clark and Martha A. ( ) Haynes]. (NHVR-Marr)

FRANK V., b 16 Jun 1852, Farmington, s/o Hiram H. and Judith A. (Davis) Young, alive 1900, native town; m 27 Apr 1879, Rochester, Mary E. Varney [b Oct 1856, Farmington, alive 1900, home town]. At time of marriage Mary resided in New Durham. Frank was one of four residuary legatees of Hiram H.'s estate by will drawn 25 Jul 1870, proved 8 Apr 1873; his one-fourth share of the homestead would revert to him upon his mother's demise. Frank and Mary were residents of Farmington up through 1900; in 1900 their seven children were at home. Ch. b Farmington, not traced further: Sadie, b 2 Aug 1880; Grace, b 20 Mar 1881; Grover, b 16 Sep 1883; Ella May, b 7 Nov 1885, surviving twin of Elsie; son b 29 Dec 1886, d.y.; son b 26 Oct 1888, d.y.; Fred, b Oct 1889; Nellie F., b Oct 1892; and Raymond F., b Nov 1895. (LDS I.G.I. BR; 1900 Soundex; NHVR-Births, Marr; Rochester TR, Marr, p5)

FRANK W., b 1841, of Strafford; in 1860 he labored as farmer and lodged with Patience and Rebecca Leighton in Strafford. (Census Strafford Co., 1860, p119)

FRANK W., b 24 May 1853, of Dover, saloon keeper; d 24 Nov 1882, age 29-6-0, Dover, survived by spouse. (NHVR-Deaths)

FRANKLIN, b ca 1805, of Strafford; head of household in Strafford in 1840, age 30-40, family containing a female parent figure age 50-60, one female age 20-30, and one male under 15. (Census Strafford Co., 1840, p463)

FRED A., b Aug 1866, Barnstead, s/o Aaron George and Priscilla F. (Boardman) Young, alive 1900, Laconia; m 14 Aug 1891, Laconia, Carrie B. Andrews [b Feb 1867, P.Q., Canada, alive 1900, Laconia]. He was named Exec. of his father's will signed 7 Dec 1886, proved 17 Apr 1894, as well as a residuary legatee. His one-half share in the homestead in Barnstead was contingent upon his mother's life estate of the property. He and Carrie were listed on census returns for Laconia in 1900, Carrie's nationality, Canadian-English. (NHVR-Marr; 1900 Soundex)

FRED B., b 1857, Gilmanton, s/o Nathaniel M. and Lucy A. (Prescott) Young, alive 1886, native town; m1 5 Jun 1887, Alton, Addie F. Aiken [b 1871, Grafton, d/o David Aiken]; m2 (Intentions) 30 Jun 1888, Dover, m 4 Oct 1889, Gilmanton, Ida M. Franks [b 1869, Calais, ME]. Fred B. was named a son and heir of Nathaniel Young of Gilmanton by his will signed 8 Feb 1886, proved 16 Aug 1892. (NHVR-Marr)

FRED J., b Aug 1867, Lebanon, ME, s/o Charles H. and Laura P. (Jones) Young of Milton, alive 1900, Rochester, shoemaker; m1 6 Nov 1886, Rochester, Addie B. Hall [b 1868, Strafford, d/o Charles H. and Elizabeth A. (Willey) Hall, d 2 Apr 1900, Rochester]; m2 22 Dec 1900, Rochester, Lovey J. Pike [b 1878, Rochester, d/o Charles Pike of Chelsea, MA]. Fred J. was head of household in Rochester in 1900, widower; members of family were his two daughters and widowed father. Ch. b Rochester by first wife Addie, not traced further: Clara A., b 15 Dec 1887, d.y., Rochester; Claro, b Dec 1889; and Norman, b 1890s, d Nov 1898. (1900 Soundex; NHVR-Deaths, Marr; Rochester TR, Births, p45)

FREDERICK, b 1847, MA, age 3, lived at the home of Jesse and Eleanor Hind of Dover in 1850. (Census Strafford Co., 1850, p195)

FREDERICK LAWRENCE, b 17 Nov 1847, of Dover, s/o Jacob K. and Rebecca Jane (Gove) Young, gr.s/o Richard and Lydia

(Wentworth) Gove; m 8 Aug 1872, Alice W. Sherman [b ca 1850, of Marshfield, MA]. Ch. b Dover: Avery Lawrence, b 24 Aug 1873, not traced further. (Wentworth Gen., V1, 226,227)

FURBER, b 19 Jan 1827, Farmington, s/o Benjamin F. and 2nd wife Deborah (Furber) Young, d 8 Feb 1900, age 73-0-20, Alton, shoemaker; m ca 1845, Rhoda E. aka Elizabeth Goodall [b 1823, Farmington, d pre 1872, native town]. Upon the death of his father in 1840, Furber became the ward of Charles Dennett of Rochester. In 1850 Furber and Elizabeth were on the census returns for Farmington; children at home, Clara A. and Frances. Per daughter Fannie's marriage record of 1872, Furber resided that year in Strafford, her mother not listed. Ch. b Farmington: Clara A., b 31 Jul 1846; Frances, b 11 Mar 1850, d.y.; Fannie J.+ (Young) Hayes, b 11 Mar 1856; Ella A.+ (Young) Foss, b 1858; and daughter b 26 Jun 1864. (Census Strafford Co., 1850, p639; NHVR-Births, Brides, Deaths; LDS I.G.I. BR; Hayes Gen., V2, p605; Rochester TR, Marr, n.p.)

GEORGE, b 1770s, of Dover; an adult when he purchased 24 sq. rods of land in Dover on the north side of the river from the main road to the shipyard, where he had begun to build a cellar, by deed signed and rec'd 29 Aug 1803, from Daniel Waldron of Portsmouth, Rock. Co., for $200.00; witnesses Moses Clements, J. Gilman [Strafford Co. Deed 43:135]. On same date of signing and recording, George mortgaged the said 24 sq. rods to the said Daniel Waldron for $200.00; witnesses said Clements and Gilman [Strafford Co. Deed 43:136]. Four years later by deed of 14 Jan, rec'd 1 Aug 1807, George sold this same property with buildings to Samuel Bragg Jr. and Dominicus Hanson Taylor, both of Dover, for $500.00; witnesses Hannah Dame, Jonathan Dame [Strafford Co. Deed 54:533].

GEORGE aka Capt., b 9 Sep 1771, Dover, s/o William and Susannah (   ) Young, d 12 Feb 1849, age 78, native town; m 1799, Dover, Sally aka Sarah Randall [b 1779, Dover, d 19 Sep 1849, age 80, her native town]. George was listed as resident of Dover from 1800-1840: in 1800 age was 26-45, with family of spouse under 26, and one male under 10; in 1810 age was under 45 years, with a family of one male under 16, two females under 10, and one female under 45. In 1830 his age was 50-60, with household of spouse 40-50, one male age 5-10, three males 20-30, and four females, two 5-10, and two 10-20. As of 1840 his age was 60-70, as was his spouse, with family of one male age 20-30, and three females, one age 15-20 and two 20-30. George and wife Sally were buried beside the graves of son Charles and daughter Susan E. at Pine Hill Cemetery, Dover. Known ch. b Dover: Charles+, b 22 Nov 1799; William, b 1800s; and Susannah Ela aka Susan E., b 1814, d 28 May 1857, Dover. (Ham's Dover Marr, TMs; Frost's Dover Cem., V1, Plot #507; Heritage's Dover VR, p204,234,235; Census Strafford Co., 1800, 160; 1810, p863; 1830, p305; 1840, p541; NHVR-Deaths, Marr)

GEORGE aka Jr., b ca 1775, of Dover; head of household in Dover, 1840, age 60-70, possibly widower, with family of one male age 15-20 and four females, one age 10-15, two 20-30, and one 30-40. (Census Strafford Co., 1840, p528)

GEORGE, b ca 1800, of Somersworth, d pre 4 Feb 1849, Somersworth; m ca 1825, Susan (   ) [b 1806, ME, alive 1850, Somersworth]. It is likely George was brother of Joseph C. Young of Somersworth, b 1805, ME. George was head of household in Somersworth in 1840, age 30-40, with spouse of same age group, and family of one male under 5 and six females, one under 5, one age 5-10, one 15-20 and three age 20-30. Susan was head of household in Somersworth in 1850; at home were daughters Elizabeth and Nancy Susan. Admin. Papers on his estate in Somersworth were filed 4 Feb 1849 by widow Susan who was appointed Admin., bond of $1,000.00 posted with sureties William H. Clements and Moses Rollings, both of Somersworth [Strafford Co. Probate 50:381]. Inventory was submitted 4 Sep 1849 by appraisers George W. Branbridge, Charles Horn and Stephen Ricker, all of Somersworth, allowed 1 Oct 1849 [Strafford Co. Probate 65:112]. Real estate was valued at $635.00. Personal estate was set at $541.11, containing cash on hand, bonds and notes of hand, livestock, farming tools, household furniture and misc. articles; grand total value of estate, $1,176.11. On the following day, 2 Oct 1849, widow's allowance of $110.00 was granted Susan [Strafford Co. Probate 43:245]. On 2 Oct 1849, Winthrop A. Marston Esq. was appointed Commissioner to review all claims against the estate; return was made 3 Apr 1850, accepted 3 Sep 1850 [Strafford Co. Probate 62:373]: expense of $21.82 for last sickness was allowed in full; 30 of the 33 notes against the estate were averaged out to $627.69; the three claims disallowed were set at $24.00.

Susan's dower rights were set off to her on same date of acceptance of the Commissioner's report, 3 Sep 1850, by George W. Branbridge, Charles Horn and Stephen Ricker, all of Somersworth, as well as Charles E. Bartlett, assignee of mortgage on the real estate, and Joseph C. Young, agent appointed by the court for minors and heirs-at-law Elizabeth J. Young and Mary S. Young [Strafford Co. Probate 63:296]. Susan was to receive a one-third part of the land and buildings situated on the easterly side of Union Street in the village of Great Falls in Somersworth, bounded by land of Great Falls Manufacturing Co., east by land of Daniel Garland, south by Summer Street, and west by said Union Street, also the sitting room, the s.e. corner of the house, west front chamber, eastern half of cellar and kitchen privileges; in addition Susan was to have the lot of land in Somersworth lying between the old and new roads leading from Great Falls to Dover by land of Ivory Hodgdon and Moses Stackpole, amount of acreage not specified. Petition for license to sell was submitted by Susan on 2 Apr 1850, to raise $400.00 for debts against the estate, approved 4 Jun 1850 [Strafford Co. Probate 60:92]: only the sum of $200.00 was approved]. It was not until 14 Nov 1850 when Susan actually received the license to sell at this reduced

price [Strafford Co. Probate 67:278]. She returned her final
accounting 3 Dec 1850, approved same date [Strafford Co.
Probate 57:79]: total Debits, $520.61; total Credits,
$791.87; balance of $271.26 due from Admin. to the estate.
Administration was wound up by 3 Jan 1851 when all outstanding
claims were averaged out [Strafford Co. Probate 64:325]: four
claims for last sickness in the amount of $21.82 were to be
paid in full. Other claims, 33 in all totalling $527.67, were
to be paid off in the amount of $249.44. It is to be noted
that one of these claims was in the name of Joseph C. Young
   Ch. b ME: Elizabeth J., b 1834; Nancy Susan, b 1836; and
Mary S., b 1830s. (Census Strafford Co., 1840, p568; 1850,
p352)
   GEORGE, b 1813, of Dover, brass foundry worker; m ca
1835, Deborah (   ) [b 1814, alive 1860, Dover]. He and
Deborah were residents of Ward 2, Dover in 1860, no known
children. (Census Strafford Co., 1860, p661)
   GEORGE, b ca 1845, of Somersworth; m ca 1870, Somers-
worth, Georgina (   ) [b ca 1850, of Somersworth. Ch. b
Somersworth, not traced further: George, b 28 Feb 1874;
Edmond, b 6 Aug 1887. (NHVR-Births)
   GEORGE, b 1859, of Somersworth; m ca 1885, Somersworth,
Bertha H. Allen [b 1871, Somersworth]. George and Bertha
lived in Somersworth at time of son's birth. Ch. b Somers-
worth: son b 2 Feb 1889. (NHVR-Births)
   GEORGE A., b 1821, of Meredith, alive 1850, same town;
m ca 1845, Pamela C. (   ) [b 1821, of Meredith]. George and
Pamela were listed on the 1850 census returns for Meredith;
children at home, George G. and Mary E.. Another member of
household was Joseph Young, age 19 [b 1831]. Ch. b prob.
Meredith: George G., b 1848; and Mary E., b 1850. (Census
Belknap Co., 1850, p45)
   GEORGE A., b 1854, Wakefield, s/o Alfred G. and Sarah A.
(Seaman) Young; m 21 Dec 1878, Wakefield, Laura Kimball [b
1862, Parsonsfield, ME, d/o Erastus and Abigail (Towle)
Kimball of Waterboro, ME, d 18 Jul 1881, age 19, Ossipee].
George A. lived at home up through 1870 and was listed as son
and heir of Alfred G. Young of Wakefield by will drawn 4 Sep
1880, proved 5 Jul 1881. Ch. b Ossipee: Chester, b 1874, d
21 Dec 1880, same town. (NHVR-Marr, Deaths)
   GEORGE F., b Oct 1836, Freedom, s/o John and Eunice
(Durgin) Young, alive 1900, Freedom, age 63, carpenter; m
17 Feb 1861, Freedom, Mary F. Nason [b Mar 1843, Eaton, d/o
Addison and Jane (   ) Nason, alive 1900, Freedom, age 57].
Mary F.'s father Addison was born in Northfield, her mother
Jane in Freedom. In 1850 at age 14, George lived at home with
parents. Note that NHVR stated George was born 1841. George
and Mary made their home in his native town, listed as resi-
dents from 1870-1900. In 1870 children Esther, Nellie and I.
Weston were at home. By 1900 George and Mary lived alone.
Ch. b Freedom: Mary Esther aka Esther M.+ (Young) Godfrey,
b 10 Nov 1862; Nellie F.+ (Young) Allard, b 1866; daughter,

b 24 Aug 1868, not listed in 1870 census. Ch. b Conway: Irving Weston+, b 1869. (Census Carroll Co. 1870, p306; NHVR-Births, Brides, Marr; Freedom VR, 1850-1878; LDS I.G.I. BR; 1900 Soundex)

GEORGE F., b Sep 1849, Wolfeboro, s/o Jeremiah L. and Mary Ann (Jackson) Young, carpenter, alive 1900, Tuftonboro: m1 31 Dec 1870, Tuftonboro, Emma Nutter [b 1850, Tuftonboro, d/o Jacob and Nancy (Young) Nutter, d pre 3 Feb 1880, home town]; m2 20 Oct 1884, Tuftonboro, Josephine Emma aka Josie E. Neal [b 1853, Tuftonboro, d/o Richard B. Neal, alive 1900, home town]. It is believed that George and 1st wife Emma took up residence in Tuftonboro at time of marriage; during second marriage he and Josie lived in Tuftonboro. George became Admin. of his father's estate upon Letters of Admin. filed by his mother Mary Ann Young on 11 Nov 1876, approved 15 Nov 1876. Upon the death of George's first wife Emma, George petitioned 3 Feb 1880 for guardianship of their son Royal P. who was then a minor under the age of 14; George stated "he is the father and only surviving parent of Royal," petition approved same date [Carroll Co. Probate #5815]. As of 1900 census George and 2nd wife Josie were residents of Tuftonboro with sons Royal P. and Charlie H. According to 1892 map of Tuftonboro, George F.'s homestead was located at Tuftonboro Center P.O., on the road heading north to Melvin Village P.O. Ch. b Tuftonboro by Emma: Elnora M., b 20 Nov 1871, d 1 Sep 1872, Tuftonboro; Royal P., b 7 Aug 1873, d 1950, Chickville, survived by wife Luru M. (   ) Young, both buried at Chickville Cemetery, Old Part. Ch. b Tuftonboro by Josephine: son, b 17 Oct 1885; Charlie H., b 8 Feb 1887, not traced further. (NHVR-Births, Deaths, Marr; Census Carroll Co., 1870, p720; 1900 Soundex; LDS I.G.I. BR; 1892 Saco Maps; Loud's Cemetery Recs., p54)

GEORGE F., b 1854, Leicester or Lancaster, MA, d pre 1895, Somersworth; m ca 1880, prob. ME, Amy M. aka Ann Libby [b 1858, Berwick, ME, d/o Solomon S. and Betsey F. (Fernald) Libby, d 20 Oct 1895, widow, age 37, Dover]. Ann's mother was of Newfield, ME. George and spouse lived in Somersworth where their children were born. Ch. b Somersworth: Harry E., b 22 Mar 1881, twin, d 5 Feb 1885, age 3-10-14, his native town; Myron A., b 22 Mar 1881, twin; Marvin A., b 24 Apr 1884, lived one day; 5th child Bessie M., b 14 Jan 1886; and Edwin Solomon, b 4 Nov 1888, twin; Oscar S., b 4 Nov 1888, twin; and Nettie C., b 24 Sep 1891. (NHVR-Births, Deaths)

GEORGE GAINES, b 27 Jan 1784, Newfields, youngest s/o Joseph and Mary (Foss) Young, res. of Wolfeboro, blacksmith, d 13 Aug 1856, Epsom; m 20 Mar 1806, Ossipee, Eleanor Sceggel [b ca 1790, Ossipee]. At time of marriage George lived in Wolfeboro, Eleanor in Ossipee. From the division of his father's estate in 1806 George received 10 acres land in Horne's Wood. He sold his one-twelfth share of his father's estate to brother William of Durham for $90.00, by deed signed 10 Dec 1806, rec'd 21 Jan 1807; witnesses Nancy Cheswell,

Wentworth Cheswell [Strafford Co. Deed 54:11]. George G. was head of family in Wolfeboro, listed on 1810 census, age 26-45, with spouse age 16-26, two males under 10, and one female under 10.

George bought part of Lot 10 in Wolfeboro on the road leading to Tuftonboro from Moses Hoyt of Wolfeboro by deed signed 22 May 1807, rec'd 16 Sep 1814, for $20.00; witnesses Mark Wiggin, William Rogers [Strafford Co. Deed 80:348]. On same date of signing George mortgaged this same property, with the exception of one-half acre to the said Moses Hoyt, for $150.00, deed rec'd 16 Sep 1814 [Strafford Co. Deed 68:78]. This mortgage was redeemed by date of 8 Apr 1813; witnesses Mark Wiggin, John Swasey [Strafford Co. Deed 68:78]. (Fitts' Newfields, p503,504,683,684; LDS I.G.I. BR; Ossipee TR, V1; NHVR-Marr; Census Strafford Co., 1810, p737)

GEORGE H., b 1843, Portsmouth, trader, saloon keeper, alive 1870, Wolfeboro; m ca 1865, Mary E. (   ) [b 1844, Sherborn, MA, alive 1870, Wolfeboro]. George H. and spouse were residents of Wolfeboro by 1866 when son was born and were listed on 1870 census for Wolfeboro. Children at home in 1870 were Edwin C. and Carrie. Ch. b Wolfeboro: Edwin C., b 1866; Carrie, b 1869; and Arthur W., b Nov 1871. (Census Carroll Co., 1870, p460; NHVR-Births; LDS I.G.I. BR)

GEORGE H., b ca 1845, Alton; m 22 Dec 1871, Middleton, Sarah F. Dame [b ca 1850, New Durham]. Ch. b Farmington: Herbert J., b 22 Sep 1872, not traced further. (NHVR-Births, Marr; LDS I.G.I. BR)

GEORGE H., b 27 Apr 1856, Farmington, s/o Thomas S. and Lovina E. (Beedy) Young, farmer; m1 (Intentions) 9 Mar 1875, New Durham, Ella J. Coburn [b 1857, New Durham, d/o Orin B. and Martha J. (   ) Coburn, d pre 1882, home town]; m2 29 Jun 1882, Dover, Lydia A. Elkins [b 1850, Lebanon, ME, d/o Aaron and Maria (   ) Elkins]. After his father's death in 1864 and his mother's remarriage in 1870, he was made ward of mother Lovina E. Hayes. (New Durham VR, Bk1, p2; NHVR-Marr)

GEORGE L., b 11 May 1859, Ossipee, s/o Luther and Sophronia (Chick) Young, d 27 Oct 1925, Rochester, bur. Ossipee; m ca 1877, Ossipee, Mary Stodgdon [b 29 May 1856, Ossipee, alive 1900, Rochester, d _____, bur. Ossipee]. George was listed as infant in 1860 census returns for Ossipee under his father's name, and was named a son and heir of Luther Young by will signed 13 Sep 1871, proved 1 Mar 1872. By an Agreement of Heirs in the administration of his mother's estate on 26 Oct 1898, approved 1 Nov 1898, George released his share in his mother's estate. He and Mary lived in Rochester [Gonic] in 1900; children at home were Myrtle and Elvena. George and spouse were buried at Large Ossipee Center Cemetery. Daughter Flora m 28 May 1898, Freedom, Vivian Durgin [b ca 1875, Eaton]. Ch. b Ossipee, not trace further: Flora B. (Young) Durgin, b ca 1878; Myrtle, b 24 Feb 1883; Elvena, b 16 May 1885, b 3 May 1894, d.y. (1900 Soundex; NHVR-Births, Brides, Deaths; Loud's Cem. Recs., p106)

GEORGE N., b 1838, of New Hampton; m 1860s, New Hampton, Emma J. Rollins [b 1846, of same town]. George, wife and family lived in New Hampton in 1870. Ch. b New Hampton: Adella, b 1864; Della F., b 18 Aug 1865; Georgia Augusta, b 26 May 1868; and Charles H., b 24 Sep 1870. (Census Belknap Co., 1870, p3; LDS I.G.I. BR)

GEORGE P., b 1847, Mt. Vernon, s/o John C. and Harriet C. (Villam) Young of Gilmanton; m 6 Jul 1868, Pittsfield, Mattie W. Foller [b 1848, Middleton, d/o Abijah Foller]. (NHVR-Marr)

GEORGE T., b 1834, Sandwich; at age 27 he enlisted 16 Aug 1861 in Co. G, 3rd Regt., NH Volunteer Infantry, mustered in 23 Aug 1861, as Pvt.; reenlisted and mustered in 31 Jan 1864. He mustered out 20 Jul 1865 giving P.O. address of Dover. (Soldiers & Sailors, p150)

GEORGE W., b 1801, of Meredith; m 1820s, Mary (   ) [b 1804, of same town]. George was head of household in Meredith from 1830-1850: in 1830 his age was 20-30, with spouse of similar years and family of one male under 5; in 1840 his age was 30-40, as was his spouse, with one female under 5 years of age. George and Mary were listed on the 1850 census for Meredith; children at home were George L., Charles E. and John. Ch. b Meredith: George L., b 1829; Charles E., b 1835; and John, b 1837. (Census Strafford Co., 1830, p132; 1840, p162; Census Belknap Co., 1850, p27)

GEORGE W., b 1817, ME, of Somersworth, machinist, d testate pre 14 Sep 1880, same town; m 29 Apr 1843, Somersworth, Hannah aka Anna Emery [b 1825, Sanford, ME, d 1 Dec 1913, Somersworth]. It should be noted that George's 1817 year of birth [NHVR-Births] is at variance with cemetery records, of 1823. Further, George's will was proved on date of 18 Sep 1880 as opposed to cemetery burial of 11 Feb 1886. Since all other data agrees, the later date of burial suggests that his remains were relocated to Forest Glade Cemetery. He, Anna and family were residents of Somersworth from 1850-1860. In 1850 members of family were children Ellen A., Edward A., Joseph A. and relatives Sally A. Emery, [b 1834, ME] and Louisa Emery, [b 1843, ME]. In 1860 children living with George and Hannah were Ellen A. and Edward A. His will drawn 25 Jul 1879, proved 14 Sep 1880, named wife Hannah sole Exec. and residuary legatee; witnesses William D. Knapp, Louis Guttman, William Pitt Moses [Strafford Co. Probate 94:115]; on date of probate Hannah was allowed Exec.; no bond was posted [Strafford Co. Probate 94:117]. He devised the bulk of his real and personal estate to wife Hannah and the sum of $50.00 each to surviving children Ellen Augusta Emerson and Edward Augustus Young. George, Hannah E. and all four children were buried at Forest Glade Cemetery, Somersworth.

Ch. b ME: Ellen Augusta (Young) Emerson, b 1843, m pre 1880, d 27 Jul 1881, Somersworth. Ch. b Somersworth: Edward Augustus+, b 1846; and Joseph A., b 1848, d 17 Dec 1857, Somersworth. Ch. b Great Falls: George W., b 1861, d 7 Dec

1878, Great Falls. (NHVR-Deaths, Marr; Census Strafford Co., 1850, p327; 1860, p307; Wooley's Somersworth Cem., #30)

GEORGE W., b 1820, of Dover, machinist; m 20 Jul 1845, Dover, Ann B. Perkins [b 1824, of Dover]. They lived in Dover, Ward 2 in 1860 with sons K____, Albert and George. Ch. b Dover: son, b 1846; Albert, b 1848; and George, b 1855. (Census Strafford Co., 1860, p664; NHVR-Marr)

GEORGE W., b 1829, Alton, s/o Joseph C. and Lydia (   ) Young of Somersworth, spinner, d 24 Nov 1875, age 46-6-11, Somersworth, widower; m 3 Oct 1852, Somersworth, Betsy Jane Colomy [b 1832, Farmington, d/o Richard Colomy, d 30 Mar 1870, age 38-9-8, Somersworth]. Per census returns for Somersworth in 1860, George and Betsey J.'s household contained two sons and Betsey's father Richard Colomy, age 60 [b 1800], stone mason. Both George and Betsey were buried at Forest Glade Cemetery, Somersworth. Ch. b Somersworth: Willie aka William H., b 17 Aug 1854, d 26 Oct 1879; and Charles E., b 1859, d 25 Mar 1884, age 25-11-19, Somersworth. (NHVR-Deaths, Marr; Wooley's Somersworth Cem., Plot #37; LDS I.G.I. BR; Census Strafford Co., 1860, p350)

GEORGE W., b 10 Apr 1829, Barnstead, s/o Stephen and Caroline (Munsey) Young, d 26 Aug 1864, age 33, Andersonville, GA; m 1 Jun 1853, Barnstead, Sarah A. Bickford [b 1833, of Barnstead, d/o Daniel and Abigail (   ) Bickford, d 30 May 1891, age 58, Barnstead]. At age 34, George enlisted with Co. G, 2nd Massachusetts Heavy Artillery 2 Dec 1863 for three years, mustered in 7 Dec 1863 as Pvt., captained, and died at Andersonville, GA. Widow Sarah petitioned on 16 May 1865 that her father Daniel Bickford be appointed guardian of her two children Carrie A. and Washington B., both under 14 years of age; approved same date [Belknap Co. Probate #2006]. Daniel Bickford found it necessary a year later to resign his guardianship on date of 14 Jul 1866, at which time Sarah petitioned for herself to be appointed the guardian of her children on 17 Jul 1866. Sarah m2 22 Jan 1885, Barnstead, George F. Clough [b ca 1830, Barnstead]. George and Sarah Young were buried at Barnstead Center Graveyard. Ch. b Barnstead: Carrie A.+ (Young) Hawley, b 7 Oct 1859; and Washington B., b 9 Oct 1861. (NHVR-Births, Marr; LDS I.G.I. BR; Barnstead Cemeteries, p3; Biog. Review, XXI, p150,151; Soldiers & Sailors, p1087)

GEORGE W., b 1834, Alton, s/o Jonathan and Alice (Peavey) Young of Farmington, alive 1870 Farmington; m2 1 Jun 1869, Farmington, Sarah Ellis aka Elkins [b 1844, Alton, d/o Alvah and Lydia (   ) Ellis, alive 1870, Farmington]. George and Sarah were listed as residents of Farmington in 1870. Son Herbert, laborer, m 12 Nov 1893, Dover, Mary F. Wentworth [b ca 1870, Dover, d/o George and Emma (Wallace) Wentworth]. Almost one year from date of his marriage, Herbert d 3 Nov 1894, age 23-1-13, buried at Alton. Ch. b Farmington: Herbert F., b 20 Sep 1871. (Census Strafford Co., 1870, p174; NHVR-Marr, Deaths)

GEORGE W., b 4 Oct 1843, Barrington, s/o Ivory and Mary Ann (Seavey) Young of Barrington, d 21 Nov 1935, Dover, previously res. of Lee.; m1 early 1860s, Barrington, Addie ( ) [b ca 1845, of Barrington, d pre 1867, same town]; m2 21 Dec 1867, Rochester, Elizabeth S. aka Lizzie S. Buzzell [b Jun 1846, Barrington, d 1918, home town]. According to father's will of 18 Jun 1878, proved 5 Jan 1892, George was to receive the family homestead in Barrington upon his mother's demise. While not named Exec. in the will, he was thus appointed on date of probate. At age 19, George enlisted in Co. F, 13th Regt., NH Volunteer Infantry on 15 Aug 1862, mustered in 22 Sep 1862 as Pvt., and transferred to Veteran Reserve Corp 1 Jul 1863. He was discharged 28 Jun 1864, from Co. F, V.R.C., Washington, DC, with forwarding address of Barrington. On 11 Oct 1876 George W. filed petition for an Invalid Pension, Application No. 226,423, Cert. No. 315,151. Due to military service he suffered from heart trouble, malaria and a back injury. Toward the end he became incapacitated, requiring the aid and attendance of another person. At that time he lived with a son. A petition for additional pension indicated his birth record came from his parents' bible; petition denied 22 Oct 1913. He and Elizabeth lived by themselves in Barrington as of 1900. George, Lizzie and son George Jr. were buried at Pine Grove Cemetery, Barrington. Ch. b Barrington by Addie: Mattie E.+ (Young) Waterhouse, b 1860. Ch. b Barrington by Elizabeth: David H.+, b 28 Jan 1869; and George W. aka William G.+, b 20 Nov 1870. (Census Strafford Co., 1850, p255; NHVR-Births, Brides, Marr; Soldiers & Sailors, p690; 1900 Soundex; LDS I.G.I. BR; Nat'l. Archives Milit. Recs.)

GEORGE W., b Jan 1847, Londonderry, res. of Dover, d pre 5 Aug 1922, Dover; m Madbury, 1870s, Mary A. Hanson [b Jun 1851, Lee, alive 5 Aug 1922, Dover]. At age 18, George enlisted first in the Strafford Guards, NH Volunteer Infantry 5 May 1864, mustered in same day as Pvt., and mustered out 28 Jul 1864, leaving P.O. address of Dover. He reenlisted 24 Aug 1864 for one year in Co. D, 1st Regt., NH Volunteer Heavy Artillery, mustered in 4 Sep 1864 as Pvt., mustered out 15 Jun 1865 with same P.O. address. Adam's Madbury, n.p., listed George's military service under Co. D, Heavy Artillery in "Soldiers of Madbury in the War of the Rebellion." George and Mary took up residence in Dover at least by 1874 when son was born. By 1900 they and two children Moses N. and Bell were listed on the census returns for Dover. On 1 Apr 1892 George filed petition for a Civil War veteran's Invalid Pension, Application No. 1,103,236; Cert. No. 843,217. Widow Mary E. filed for a widow's pension on 5 Aug 1922, Application No. 1,192,669. Only direct descendants of George and Mary are allowed to view these files today. George and Mary raised their family in Dover. Son Fred A. m 10 Sep 1898, Somersworth, Cora M. Clark [b 1858, Somersworth, d/o William H. and Annie M. ( ) Clark]. Cora's father William H. Clark was born in Webster, MA; her mother Annie M. ( ) in Milbury, MA.

Ch. b Dover, not traced further: Fred A., b 18 May 1874
(see above); George Albert, b 7 Aug 1876; Bell, b Oct 1877,
at home 1900; and Moses N., b Jun 1880, at home 1900. (1900
Soundex; NHVR-Births, Marr; Soldiers & Sailors, p962;991;
Nat'l. Archives Milit. Recs.)

GEORGE W., b 1848, Alton, s/o Moses and Mary H. (Thompson) Young, d 15 Mar 1880, age 32, Alton, shoemaker; m 13 Sep
1871, Freedom, Mrs. Mary H. (Jones) Nutter [b 10 Apr 1839, of
Alton, d/o Nathaniel and Mary (   ) Jones, d 19 Dec 1916,
Alton]. Mary's father Nathaniel W. Jones, shoe maker, was b
1808, of Alton, d 25 Jan 1879, age 71; her mother Mary was b
1801, of Alton, d 11 Jul 1882, age 81. Mary H. and children
were buried at private family plot in Alton. Daughter Ella
M. m 1 Apr 1890, Alton, Woodbury H. Glidden [b ca 1865, of
same town]. Ch. b Alton: Ella M. (Young) Glidden, b ca 1871;
Willie E., b 17 Mar 1872, d 10 Apr 1897, age 25, Alton; and
Nora B., b 1876, m ca 1894, A. B. Rollins, d 30 Jun 1896, age
20, Alton. (LDS I.G.I. BR; NHVR-Births, Brides, Deaths, Marr;
Hammond's Alton Cemeteries, p26)

GEORGE W. aka Jr., b 1857, Lowell, MA, prison officer,
s/o George W. and Abbie (Bailey) Young [no main entry]; m
16 Jun 1885, Rochester, Sadie E. Greenfield [b 1854, Rochester, d/o Charles and Arolind (Downs) Greenfield]. George
Jr. lived in Lowell, MA at time of marriage, his father George
a lobbyist. (NHVR-Marr; Roch. VR, Marr)

GEORGE WILLIAM, b 24 Jul 1830, Barrington, s/o Aaron and
Lydia (Daniels) Young, d 3 Dec 1904, Rochester, bur. Dover;
m 23 Oct 1850, Cynthia Ellen (Flagg) Moody [b 26 Jul 1833,
Ossipee, d/o Nathaniel and Urania (Hobbs) Moody, d 11 Oct
1904, Rochester, bur. Dover]. George's legacy from his father
was a one-half share of the house and lot in Dover located on
the corner of Atkinson and St. Thomas Streets, per Aaron's
will signed 5 Mar 1850, proved 2 May 1854. As a young man,
George settled in Dover to pursue various trades--apprentice
in the printing trade, job printing, and then grocer. Places
of residence between 1860-1865 were loosely drawn. In 1860
his occupation in Ward 3, Dover was grocer; children at home,
Cynthia, George W. Jr., Aaron Clarence and Emma L. During
this time, he was chosen to represent Ward 3, Dover on the
Board of Selectmen and afterward in the Common Council. In
1863 he served in the Quartermaster's Dept. of the U. S. Army
and remained there until the close of the Civil War, location
unknown. From 1865-1869, he and family lived in Clarksville,
Virginia; youngest child was born there in 1873. It is noteworthy that George reported for work in Virginia and traveled
considerably during the aftermath of the Civil War. He became
chief clerk and cashier of the Freedmen's Bureau in the State
of Virginia from 1 Dec 1865 until 1 May 1869. By 1870 George
was listed again as resident of Dover, occupation was asst.
assessor; children at home that year, the above four plus
Charles S. Subsequently he became Superintendent of Public
Printing and then Deputy Collector of Internal Revenue for

Virginia, which post he held for almost sixteen years. When George approached retirement age, he purchased a 25-acre farm in Rochester which became the family homestead from the 1890s on. In 1900 only member of family was son Albert S. George and Cynthia were buried at Pine Hill Cemetery, Dover. Note that census records for 1900 listed Cynthia's birthplace as Maine; genealogy cited below stated Tamworth.

Ch. b in Barrington, except as noted: Ella Cynthia+ (Young) Canney, b 10 Aug 1851; George William Jr., b 17 Aug 1853, d.y.; Aaron Clarence, b 7 Sep 1855, d 13 Nov 1901, Barrington; Emma Louisa+ (Young) Clark aka Louisa Emma Clark, b 16 May 1860, Dover; Charles Sumner+, b 1862, Dover; George William Jr., b 1863, Dover; and Albert Stowell, b 31 Jan 1873, Clarksville, VA, m 15 Jun 1892, Northwood, at age 19 and resident of Rochester, Grace A. Foss [b ca 1875]. (LDS I.G.I. BR; NHVR-Brides, Marr; 1900 Soundex; Ham Gen., p25,43,65,83; Census Strafford Co., 1850, p523; 1860, p717; 1870, p68; Frost's Dover Cem., V1, #535; Biog. Review, XXI, p89,90)

HALDEMAN PUTNAM aka Maj., b 13 Nov 1863, Barrington, s/o Andrew Huckins and Susan Elizabeth (Miles) Young, d 11 Apr ·1934, prob. San Francisco, CA; m 31 Dec 1904, San Francisco, Marie Voorhies [b 20 Jan 1867, Macon, GA]. Haldeman was named son and one of three heirs in his father's will of 7 Dec 1890, proved 6 Jan 1891. He was buried at the family plot, Pine Hill Cemetery, Dover, with title of Major, U. S. Army. (Ham Gen., p61; Frost's Dover Cem., V1, #535)

HALE, b ca 1802, of Wolfeboro; m 11 Oct 1827, Wolfeboro, Sophronia Nudd [b 1807, of same town]. See Sophronia M.+ Young, b ca 1828, of Milton as possible daughter. (NHVR-Marr)

HAMILTON, b 22 Jul 1805, d 22 Oct 1819, age 14-3-0, Durham, killed by the kick of a horse, buried at Madbury on south side of Mill Hill Road. (Madbury Cem., **Reg.** 87:347)

HANNAH, b ca 1770, of Milton; m ca 1790, Milton, Otis Pinkham [b 23 Nov 1765, Dover, s/o John and Phoebe (Tibbetts) Pinkham, d 5 Jan 1814, Milton]. Known ch. b Milton: Mary Pinkham, b 19 Dec 1800, Milton, see spouse Isaac C.+ Young of Milton. See Sarah+ Young, b 2 May 1775, poss. sister who married a brother of Otis Pinkham. (Scale's Dover, p323; Pinkham Gen., p25; NHVR-Deaths)

HANNAH, b ca 1770, Moultonboro; m 12 Mar 1791, Moultonboro, Samuel Randall [b ca 1765, of same town]. (NHVR-Brides)

HANNAH, b ca 1775, of Farmington, widow of _____ Young; m2 30 Jun 1805, New Durham, Daniel Peavey [b ca 1780, of Farmington]. (NHVR-Brides; Farmington TR, V1, p380)

HANNAH, b ca 1780, Gilmanton; m 10 Nov 1801, Belmont, John Dudley [b ca 1775, Barnstead]. (NHVR-Brides)

HANNAH, b 1810, of Meredith; she was listed as head of household in Meredith from 1850-1860. In 1850 her age was 40; member of family was George Whithers, age 14 [b 1836]. She was prob. the Hannah [age 56] who lived in 1860 at boarding house with Abbie D. Baker, n.d. (Census Belknap Co., 1850, p36; 1860, dwelling no. 176)

HANNAH, b ca 1835, Durham; m 24 Nov 1857, Durham, Hudson Peavey Esq. [b ca 1830, of Strafford]. (NHVR-Brides)

HANNAH, b 1848, of Gilmanton, single and head of household in Gilmanton in 1870; she lived with sister Nancy, age 20 [b 1850]. Both worked as domestics. (Census Belknap Co., 1870, p28)

HANNAH C., b 12 Dec 1818, Wolfeboro, d/o Joseph and Patience (Chase) Young, d 17 Oct 1885, Wolfeboro, age 67-10-5; m (Intentions) 12 Jun 1838, m1 14 Jun 1838, Wolfeboro, Phineas Johnson [b 5 Sep 1813, Brookfield, d 5 May 1858, Wolfeboro, age 44-8-0]; m2 ca 1860, _____ Stewart; m3 Greenleaf Piper, no dates. Hannah, 1st husband Phineas and their two daughters were buried at Wolfeboro Center Cemetery. Ch. b Wolfeboro by Phineas: Julia A. Johnson, b 1830, d 31 Aug 1857, Wolfeboro, age 27; and Caroline P. Johnson, b 1842, d 5 Oct 1860, Wolfeboro, age 18; (NHVR-Brides; Young Family Recs., courtesy of Nancy L. Dodge; Donigan's Wolfeboro Cems., TMs, p2; Parker's Wolfeboro Banns, 1789-1854, n.p.)

HANNAH C., b 1826, Gilmanton, d/o John T. and Betsey S. (Young) Young, res. of Milton; m 12 Aug 1850, Alton, George W. Sawyer [b ca 1825, Wakefield, of Milton]. Marriage intentions were filed in Milton on same date. In 1850 Hannah C. Sawyer, age 24, lived with her parents in Gilford. Ch. b prob. Milton: William A. Sawyer, b ca 1851, m 1872, Wakefield. (NHVR-Brides; Milton VR, correspondence of Town Clerk)

HANNAH D., b ca 1795, of Madbury; m 29 May 1815, Rochester, Jacob Nute [b ca 1790, of Milton]. (NH Gen. Rec., V5, No.4, p148)

HANNAH H., b 1813, Tuftonboro, d/o John and Hannah (Ham) Young; m 25 Oct 1835, Wolfeboro, Levi D. Ladd [b 10 Mar 1811, Melvin Village, s/o Samuel and Comfort (Dow) Ladd, d pre 1850 census, home town]. Hannah was widow in 1850, Tuftonboro known by her married name of Ladd, and lived with her parents and young daughter. Ch. b Tuftonboro: Hannah J. Ladd, b 1843. (NHVR-Brides; Ladd Gen., p54)

HANNAH L., b 1815, Wolfeboro, d/o Timothy W. and Esther (Libby) Young; m (Intentions) 16 Oct 1837; m 19 Oct 1837, Wolfeboro, Stephen A. Bickford [b ca 1810, Ossipee]. She was named as a single daughter and heir in her father Timothy's will signed 24 Mar 1834, proved 16 May that year. (Parker's Wolfeboro Banns, 1789-1854, n.p.; NHVR-Brides)

HANNAH L., b 1833, Gilmanton Iron Works, d/o Nathaniel Badger and Dorothy B. (Lamphrey) Young; m 4 Jul 1859, Gilmanton, Thomas W. Merrill [b ca 1830, Barnstead]. In 1850 Hannah L. lived at home with parents in Gilmanton. (NHVR-Brides)

HANNAH M., b May 1831, listed on 1900 census returns for Rochester; servant of Charles Jenness Jr. [n.d.]. (1900 Soundex)

HANNAH M., b Apr 1839, age 61 in 1900 census for Alton, boarded with Cyrus Coffin, age 65 [b 1834]. (1900 Soundex)

HANNAH W., b ca 1829, Alton, very poss. d/o Jonathan and Alice (Peavey) Young; m (Intentions) 15 Oct 1848, Alton, m

5 Nov 1848, New Durham, Orin Ellis [b ca 1825, Alton]. Hannah
may have been sibling to George W. Young and Martha A. Young,
both children of Jonathan and Alice of Alton; they each married into the Ellis family of Alton as did Hannah. (Alton VR,
p592; NHVR-Brides)

HANSON H., b 1 Dec 1843, Barnstead Center, s/o Samuel P.
and Betsey A. (Merrill) Young, undertaker, d 14 Dec 1923, home
town, of cerebral hemorrhage; m 29 Dec 1869, age 26, Barnstead, Priscilla aka Stella A. Sackett [b 1848, Barnstead,
d/o Noble and Ruby (   ) Sackett, d 1935, same town]. At age
19, Hanson enlisted from Barnstead in Co. G, 15th Regt., NH
Volunteer Infantry on 15 Sep 1862, mustered in 11 Oct 1862 as
Pvt. and was appointed Corp. 1 Mar 1863. He mustered out
13 Aug 1863, leaving P.O. address of Barnstead. He saw action
at Port Hudson, Louisiana. On 14 Dec 1888 [or 1898] Hanson
filed petition for a Civil War Invalid Pension, Application
No. 681,799, Cert. No. 435,592. In 1900 Hanson and Priscilla
lived alone in Barnstead. She filed for a widow's pension on
18 Jan 1924, Application No. 1,214,418; Cert. No. 945,875.
Ch. b Barnstead, not traced further: Burt, b 25 Jan 1878,
twin; daughter b 25 Jan 1878, twin, not traced further. (1900
Soundex; NHVR-Births, Marr; Soldiers & Sailors, p760; Nat'l.
Archives Milit. Recs.; Merrill's Barnstead, p332)

HARRIET A., b late 1840s, Dover, d/o Josiah B. and Mary
J. (Perkins) Young of Alton; m 20 Sep 1870, Dover, Benjamin
F. Whitehouse [b ca 1845, of same town]. (NHVR-Brides)

HARRIET B., b 1824, of Dover in 1850, single, no occupation, lived at boarding house. (Census Strafford Co., 1850,
p83)

HARRIET BOARDMAN, b ca 1840, Dover; m Oct 1859, Dover,
Jacob Jewett Smith [b ca 1835, Rowley, MA]. Harriet B. Smith
was dismissed from First Church, Dover to First Church,
Rowley, MA, 20 Jun 1877. (Heritage's Dover VR, p234,235)

HARRISON aka William Henry Harrison, b 15 May 1837, Barrington, inventor and manufacturer, s/o William Hale and Sarah
(Daniels) Young, d 1 May 1923, Boston, MA; m1 19 Apr 1863,
West Roxbury, MA, Susan Tappan Cook [b 17 Dec 1841, West
Roxbury, MA, d/o Thomas Jefferson Cook of Milton, d 16 Sep
1901, MA]; m2 10 Jan 1906, Barrington, Christabel Jukes [b
16 Dec 1876, Barrington, d/o Samuel J. Jukes, d 7 Jul 1947,
prob. MA]. Harrison witnessed the will of his father drawn
11 Mar 1889, proved 30 May 1891. Upon date of probate, his
father's second wife Sophia L. Young requested that Harrison
of Boston, MA be appointed Admin. of his father's estate with
the will annexed; this was so done 2 Jun 1891, with bond of
$1,000.00 posted, sureties William Hayes, John B. Huckins,
and Lewis H. Young [Strafford Co. Probate 108:17]. In 1858
he retired from teaching at Great Falls and Rollingsford and
turned his energies to the contracting business in Boston.
Upon the outbreak of the Civil War, he returned to Barrington
to enlist at age 25, on date of 9 Aug 1862, as Pvt. in Co. F,
13th Regt., NH Volunteer Infantry, was appointed 1st Lt.

27 Sep 1862 and mustered in to date 19 Sep 1862. He was disabled during both the Fredericksburg campaign and General Dix
expedition which caused him to resign 2 Feb 1864, giving forwarding address of Boston, MA. After the war he and his
family lived in Boston and later moved to Winthrop, MA. He
manufactured sanitary appliances of his own invention. Ch.
b Boston by Susan: Genevieve F., b 14 Dec 1864, d 20 Feb
1915; and Harry Hayward, b 16 Feb 1869. No known children by
2nd wife. (Ham Gen., p29,31; N.H. Men, p286; Soldiers &
Sailors, p690; N.E. Who's, p1047,1048)

HARVEY, b ca 1820, Dover; m ca 1845, Dover, Abby H. Dame
[b 3 Mar 1826, Dover d/o Israel and Hannah (Durgin) Dame.
(Scale's Dover, p284)

HATTIE A. aka Harriet, b 18 Aug 1851, Wakefield, d/o
James C. and Rosemandel (Gill) Young, d testate pre 10 Jun
1920, native town; m 31 Dec 1880, Wakefield, Samuel Kershaw
[b 1831, Wakefield, d 1892, native town]. In 1900 Hattie was
widow and head of household in Wakefield; with her was nephew
Samuel Kershaw Young, age 6, whom she raised as a son. He was
the son of her brother James Cameron Young and Mary A. (Doyle)
Young [deceased] of Wakefield. By Hattie's will of 12 May,
proved 10 Jun 1920, brother Obed S. Young was named as sole
Exec. and nephew Samuel K. Young of Wakefield as residuary
legatee; witnesses Harlan H. Cochran, Grunday K. Bartlett,
Herbert L. Grinnell Jr. [Carroll Co. Probate #14097]. Hattie
made the following bequests: to her sister Ruth C. Weeks of
Derry, NH, the sum of $500.00; to her sister Melissa A. Robin-
son of Fullerton, CA, $300.00 to be off-set against a note of
same amount owing to her; to her brothers, Obed S. of Wolfeboro, Aaron G. of Wakefield, and James Cameron of Wakefield,
$200.00 each; to her nephews Alden N. Young of Wakefield,
Sumner D. Young of Wolfeboro and Ralph A. Weeks of Derry,
$200.00 each. Both Hattie and Samuel Kershaw were buried at
the Aaron Young Cemetery, Pray Hill Road, Wakefield. (Twombly's Wakefield Cem., TMs; NHVR-Brides; 1900 Soundex)

HATTIE A., b 16 Sep 1867, Gilmanton, d 16 Mar 1869, age
1-6-0, Upper Gilmanton. (NHVR-Deaths)

HATTIE J., b 1864, Alton, d/o Moses and Mary H. (Thompson) Young; m 22 Mar 1884, Farmington, Sherman R. Peavey [b
ca 1860, Farmington]. Hattie was listed as age 6 on the 1870
census returns for her parents in Alton. (NHVR-Brides)

HELEN E., b 1838, Ossipee, d/o Luther and Sophronia
(Chick) Young, d pre 26 Oct 1898, home town; m 9 Oct 1855,
Ossipee, Charles F. Chapman [b ca 1830, of same town]. In
1850 census Helen E. was age 12, a member of her parents'
household in Ossipee, and was listed as a daughter and heir
of Luther by his will signed 13 Sep 1871, proved 1 Mar 1872.
Letters of Admin. were filed 26 Oct 1898 on her mother's
estate, approved 1 Nov 1898. These probate papers indicated
that Helen E. Chapman was deceased and that her son George
Chapman was an heir-at-law of Sophronia's estate. Ch. b
Ossipee: George Chapman, b 1850s. (NHVR-Brides)

HELEN E., b Jan 1850, MA, widow of _____ Young, res. of Sandwich in 1900, lived with brother Frederic H. Edgely and family. (1900 Soundex)

HENRY aka Ensign, b 23 Jul 1773, Durham, s/o Joseph and Mary (Foss) Young, d 24 Aug 1810, native town; m 13 Feb 1803, Durham, Sally aka Sarah Bennett [b 25 Aug 1779, Lubberland, d/o John Bennett, d 21 Apr 1853, widow, Packers Falls, Durham]. Henry was survived in 1810 by wife Sally and daughter Harriet. In 1810 census Sally was listed as head of household in Durham, age under 45 years, with family of one male age 16-26 and one female under 10. In 1850, Sarah was resident of Durham, widow, age 70; living with her was daughter Harriet Hayes, age 46, and son-in-law Samuel Hayes, age 56, and their family. Before his father's death, Henry became the owner of one-half of the family dwelling house in Durham and one-half acre adjoining the home by deed signed 1 May 1800, rec'd 2 Mar 1801; and upon division of his father's estate 22 Sep 1807, he was granted a share in the 32 acres of Horns Woods.

In 1801 Henry held title of Gentleman in the following deed. He sold to Joseph Young of Durham [brother] for $200.00, 12-1/2 acres land in Durham, "the same land that Zachariah Young [brother] bought of James Cram, Admin. of the estate of Jeremiah Young [brother] deceased," by deed signed 29 Sep 1801, rec'd 3 Jul 1806; witnesses Jeremy Demeritt, Valentine Smith [Strafford Co. Deed 52:24]. He bought up the one-twelfth share which his brother Timothy W. held in "all the estate both real and personal of our late father Joseph Young of Durham, Gent," by deed of 22 Jan, rec'd 27 Jan 1807; see Timothy W. and Esther Young of Tuftonboro for further information. Admin. Papers on Henry's estate in Durham were filed 29 Nov 1810 by widow Sally; she gave bond of $4,000.00 with sureties John Bennett and William Young [brother], both of Durham [Strafford Co. Probate 20:68]. On 1 Dec 1810, appraisers Wentworth Cheswell Esq. of New Market and Ebenezer Doe and Edmund Pendergast of Durham made return on the inventory of the estate; allowed 13 Dec 1810 [Strafford Co. Probate 14:512]. Real estate included one-half of the mansion house plus 80 acres valued at $1,500.00, 1-3/4 acres in Horn's Woods at $20.00, 1/4 of a saw mill and privilege at lower falls on Lamprey River at $100.00 and a 1/6th part of the "Reversion of Mrs. Mary Young's dower in the estate of Capt. Joseph Young" at $40.00; total of real estate, $1,660.00. Personal estate included sundry items such as livestock, farming tools and equipment, furniture, household effects, one loom, two spinning wheels and one pair brass candlesticks, all valued at $626.58; grand total of estate $2,286.58.

Widow Sally was one of three co-grantors in the sale of 1-1/2 acres in Durham by deed signed 10 Dec 1824, rec'd 4 Jul 1825; see in-laws William and Martha Young of Durham for details. Henry and Sarah were buried at Hayes Tomb, Packers Falls, Durham. Known ch. b Durham: Lydia Harriet+ (Young)

Hayes, b 15 Jun 1803. (NHVR-Marr, Deaths; Hayes Gen., V1, p227-228; Census Strafford Co., 1810, p548; 1860, p445; Fitts' Newfields, p683,684; Durham Graveyards, #157, p62)

HENRY, b 1815, Alton, poss. s/o Moses and Dorothy (Peavey) Young, d ca 1876, Alton, farmer, shoe maker; m 10 Nov 1840, Alton, Sarah Witham [b 1815 Ossipee, d ca 1876, Alton]. They were residents of Alton from 1860-1870. In 1860 six children lived at home: Aaron, Ivesta, Martha, Sarah C., Dorothy A., and John C. In 1870 son John, age 15, remained at home. Ch. b Alton: Susan M.+ (Young) Ellis, b 1841; Aaron W.+, b Feb 1846; Luesta aka Ivesta D.+ (Young) Swan, b 1847; Martha, b 1850; daughter b 7 Feb 1851; son b 23 Sep 1852; Sarah C., b 1853, twin; Dorothy A.+ (Young) Horne, b 1853, twin; John C.+, b Mar 1855; and Cora E., b 28 Mar 1861, d 11 Sep 1865, Alton. (Census Belknap Co., 1860, p280; 1870, p28; 1900 Soundex; NHVR-Brides, Deaths, Marr; Alton V.R., p568; LDS I.G.I. BR)

HENRY, b 10 May 1841, see John Henry

HENRY C., b Apr 1861, Alton, twin, s/o James H. and Hannah A. (   ) Young, alive 1900, home town; m 22 Feb 1898, Alton, Effelina aka Melonia F. (Buzzell) McDuffee [b Apr 1852, Gilford, d/o Aaron Buzzell, her 2nd marriage, alive 1900, Alton]. Henry and wife Melonia lived alone in Alton in 1900. (NHVR-Marr; 1900 Soundex)

HENRY E., b 14 Dec 1852, Somersworth, eldest s/o Simeon and Johanna (   ) Young, alive 1900, Dover; m 13 Sep 1877, Somersworth, Grace E. Smith [b Jul 1853, Dover, d/o Asa and Eliza J. (   ) Smith, alive 1900, Dover]. It should be noted that the 1870 census for Dover gave Henry E.'s age as 11 [b 1859] under his mother's return. At time of marriage Henry was still resident of Dover. In 1900 he and Grace lived at Park Street, Dover; members of household were daughter Cora, mother-in-law Eliza J. Smith [b Jun 1834] and servant Sarah A. Rafferty [b Sep 1875]. Ch. b Dover: Cora, b Jan 1878; daughter b 5 Feb 1880, not listed on 1900 census for Dover. (NHVR-Births, Marr; 1900 Soundex; LDS I.G.I. BR)

HENRY L., b 6 Nov 1849, Conway, s/o Benjamin Green and Emily (Horne) Young of Wolfeboro, carpenter; m 31 May 1871, Meredith, Mary A. Taylor [b 1848, Peacham, VT, d/o Leander Taylor of New Durham]. (NHVR-Marr)

HERBERT S., b Mar 1855, Upper Gilmanton, s/o John S. and Mehitable B. (Cate) Young, salesman, alive 1900, Laconia; m ca 1885, Gilford, Clara Start [b Mar 1856, Canada]. Herbert and spouse took up residence at Lake Village when married; they and their son and daughter were listed in 1900 census for Laconia. Ch. b Lake Village: Clara P., b May 1886, and John A., b 23 Jun 1890. (NHVR-Births; 1900 Soundex)

HERBERT S., b Jan 1862, Alton, s/o Charles E. and Mary H. (Nutter) Young, box maker, alive 1900, Rochester; m 25 Oct 1886, Alton, Susie E. Pettigrew [b Jan 1863, Farmington, d/o Charles E. Pettigrew, alive 1900, Rochester]. Herbert and Susie resided in Farmington where seven children were born.

Their eighth child was born in Milton, and by 1900 they had relocated in Rochester, listed on the census returns with nine children in household. Ch. b Farmington, not traced further: Alvah H., b 1 Mar 1887; Pearl M., b 1888, twin; Rubie, b 1888, twin; daughters, twins, b 18 Nov 1889, d.y.; son b 15 Sep 1891, d.y.; Freddie G., b Sep 1892. Ch. b Alton; Florence J., b 19 Jul 1893; Stanley R., b 9 Feb 1894; Millie E., b 5 Sep 1896; Willie E., b 12 Mar 1898; and Elsie E., b Feb 1900. (1900 Soundex; NHVR-Births, Marr)

HESTER ANN, b ca 1820, Wolfeboro; m 18 Oct 1840, Wolfeboro, James B. Frost [b ca 1815, of same town]. (NHVR-Brides)

HEZEKIAH, b 1770s, of Sanbornton, alive 1813, same town, house carpenter; m ca 1810, Judith (   ) [b ca 1775, alive 1813, Sanbornton]. Hezekiah sold part of 100-acre Lot 40, 2nd Div., Sanbornton, by lands of Rowell Straw, Capt. James Head, and John Abrams, to Nathan Pilsbury of Bridgewater, Grafton Co., by deed of 3 Jul 1806, rec'd 13 Sep 1814, for $875.00; wife Judith ceded dower rights; witnesses Carr Huse, Daniel Hills, Mary Fowler [Strafford Co. Deed 80:226]. He then sold to Mark Prescott of Sanbornton a certain dwelling house which he then lived in and grist mill "which I now improve" standing on said Prescott's mill brook on Lot 55, 2nd Div., Sanbornton for $100.00, by deed signed 9 Dec, rec'd 21 Dec 1813; witnesses Carr Huse, Asa Prescott [Strafford Co. Deed 77:436].

HEZEKIAH B., b ca 1805, Gilmanton, s/o Joseph and Betsey (Shaw) Young; m 11 Jul 1830, Belmont, Mahala Dame [b ca 1810, of Gilmanton]. (NHVR-Marr; Biog. Review, XXI, p354,355)

HIRAM, b ca 1795, of Barrington; head of household in Barrington in 1840, age 40-50 with spouse in same age group, household containing three males, one each age 5-10, 10-15, and 15-20 and one female age 5-10. (Census Strafford Co., 1840, p474)

HIRAM, b 24 Mar 1803, Barrington, s/o Moses and Lucy (Whitehorn) Young, d 31 Mar 1881, age 78-0-7, mechanic, Manchester; m ca 1822, Strafford, Fannie Clark [b 7 Nov 1797, Strafford, d 26 Nov 1884, age 87-0-20, home town]. Note that son Hiram P.'s death record stated that Hiram Sr. was born in Allentown; please refer also to William+ Young [b ca 1800] of Allentown who married Fanney Clark in Strafford. It is believed that Hiram and William were one and the same person. Hiram was head of household in Barrington [Strafford] in 1830, age 20-30; family consisted of spouse age 30-40, one male and one female both 5-10. He and Fannie were residents in Strafford in 1850; members of household were Mary S. Young, age 37 [b 1813], prob. Hiram's sister, and children John, Hiram and Eliza. The family's relocation to Manchester took place some time after 1850. Hiram and Fannie were buried next to grave sites of their married daughters and Hiram's parents at Perkins Cemetery, Strafford on Route 126. Ch. b Strafford: John C.+, b 29 Sep 1824; Hiram P., b 30 Mar 1835, d 12 Jun 1892, age 57-2-14, bur. at Pine Grove Cemetery, Farmington; and Eliza (Young) Barnes, b 18 Jul 1843, d 20 Jul 1905.

(Census Strafford Co., 1830, p30; 1850, p560; Styles' Cem. Rec., Grid 4E-1, p165; NHVR-Deaths)

HIRAM, b 27 Jun 1842, Barnstead, s/o Joseph and Jemima (Marston) Young of Canterbury [no main entry], d 20 Dec 1862, Virginia of battle wounds, age 20-5-23. (NHVR-Deaths)

HIRAM, b May 1854, Waterboro, ME, s/o Daniel and Eunice (Whitten) Young [no main entry]; m 21 Oct 1871, Wakefield, Mary M. Ham [b 1854, Newfield, ME, d/o Charles and Mary (Shaw) Ham, alive 1900 Milton]. Hiram's father Daniel was born Waterboro, MA, his mother Eunice born Newfields, ME. Hiram and Mary were residents of Milton in 1900 with son Edgar in household. Ch. b ME: Edgar, b Oct 1883, not traced further. (NHVR-Marr; 1900 Soundex)

HIRAM A., b 1844, Barnstead, s/o David and Eliza (Hartford) Young, of Meredith in 1860, cordwainer; m 4 Mar 1876, age 33, Concord, Mattie E. Lord [b 1849, Berwick, ME, d/o Jacob Lord]. Hiram was on the census returns of his parents for Barnstead in 1850, age given as 7; and in 1860 he boarded with Isaac and Lydia Pendergast, ages 54 [b 1804] and 50 [b 1810], respectively, in Meredith. (Census Belknap Co., 1860, p360; NHVR-Marr; Merrill's Barnstead, p331)

HIRAM H., b 16 Dec 1811, Farmington, s/o Joseph and Sarah (Pinkham) Young of Wakefield, farmer, d testate 29 Dec 1872, age 61-0-13, native town; m1 29 Aug 1833, New Durham, Margaret Hall [b ca 1815, of New Durham, d pre 1850, Farmington]; m2 (Intentions) 1 Apr 1850, New Durham, m 1 Aug 1850/51, New Durham, Judith A. Davis [b 1825, Barnstead, res. of Milton, alive 1870, Farmington]. Hiram was head of household in Farmington from 1840-1870: in 1840 he and his spouse were age 20-30, with family of one male age 5-10, one female under 5, and one female parent figure, age 60-70, who may have been his widowed mother Sarah. From 1850-1870 Judith was listed as spouse. In 1850 his children by Margaret were all at home, Elizabeth J., Thomas and Henry. The 1860-1870 census returns listed the children by second wife Judith: Sarah A., Frank B., Nathaniel H. and Charles. For Hiram's one-fifth share in Lot 64, 2nd Div., Wakefield which he and siblings purchased from Moses Young [uncle] of Wakefield in 1819, see brother Joel Young of Farmington.

Hiram H.'s will signed 25 Jul 1870, proved 8 Apr 1873, named second wife Judith A. as Exec. of his estate; witnesses Adelaide H. C. Parker, David P. Chamberlin, A. W. Shackford [Strafford Co. Probate 84:161]. On date of probate, Judith A. was allowed Exec. of Hiram's will; witnesses as cited above; no bond posted [Strafford Co. Probate 84:163]. Hiram bequeathed to second wife Judith all his property; after her death or should she remarry, the property real and personal would revert to her children Sarah Ann, Frank V., Nathaniel H. and Charles F., each to have an equal share. Hiram acknowledged the children by his "first wife" with bequests of $1.00 each: Thomas L., Elizabeth Jane Page and John H. His children by Judith were to have the right to live at the family home until the age of 21. Son Nathaniel H. lived alone in Farmington in 1900, age 45. Ch. b Farmington by 1st wife Margaret: Thomas L., b 1834; Elizabeth Jane+ (Young) Page, b 1835; and John Henry+, b 10 May 1841. Ch. b Farmington by Judith: Sarah Ann, b 21 May 1851; Frank V.+, b 16 Jun 1852; daughter b 21 Oct 1853; Nathaniel H., b 6 Jan 1855, (see above); and Charles F.+, b 28 Oct 1856. (Census Strafford Co., 1840, p313; 1850, p613; 1860, p381; 1870, p160; LDS I.G.I. BR; NHVR-Births, Marr, Deaths; 1900 Soundex; New Durham VR, Bk1, p1)

HIRAM STEVENS, b 1832, Strafford, s/o Isaac and Mary (Willey) Young, died of wounds, single, 16 Mar 1863, New Orleans, LA. His father died in 1835; see parents for guardianship papers dated 20 Jan 1835. He lived at home in 1850. In the division of Isaac's estate on 28 Apr 1841, Hiram received 10 acres of a piece of woodland in Strafford, 3rd Range, two acres land abutting land of Isaac Babb, and one acre, ten square rods, 2nd Range, which was part of the homestead farm in the northern corner. Hiram S., single, enlisted 14 Jan 1862 in Co. G, 8th Regt., NH Volunteer Infantry, mustered in 23 Dec 1861 as Pvt., and died of wounds on date cited above. He had his will drawn up 22 Mar 1860, proved 5 May 1863, in which he named brother Andrew J. as sole Exec. and residuary legatee; witnesses Richard Garland, Elbridge A. Lane, James Emerson [Strafford Co. Probate 70:5183]; execution of will granted to brother Andrew of Strafford, bond of $2,000.00 with sureties Caleb Hanson and Clark Swain, both of Strafford [Strafford Co. Probate 68:314]. Hiram devised to Andrew "the one undivided half of the homestead farm situate in said Strafford" and all his right and interest in a certain tract called Intervale in Strafford containing about nine acres. (Edgerly's VR's, TMs, n.p.; Soldiers & Sailors, p761)

HOLLIS aka Horace, b 17 Jan 1810, Wolfeboro, s/o William and Sally (Burleigh) Young of New Market, Rock. Co., res. of Dover, d 17 May 1883, age 73-4-0, Dover; m ca 1835, Wolfeboro, Betsey Ann Drew [b 13 Feb 1814, Wolfeboro, d/o John and Nancy (Wiggin) Drew, d 13 Oct 1883, age 69-8-0, Dover]. Hollis was head of household in Wolfeboro in 1840, age 20-30; family contained spouse of same age bracket, one male in his own age group and two males under 5. By 1870 Hollis and Betsey Ann had settled in Ward 2, Dover; sons at home, Thomas F. and John A., both shoe factory workers. Both sons served in the Civil War, to return to Dover after military service. Note that Vital Records stated Hollis was born in Dover. Ch. b Wolfeboro: Thomas F.+, b 16 Feb 1836; and John A.+, b 1839. (Census Strafford Co., 1840, p386; 1870, p32; NHVR-Deaths; 1900 Soundex)

HORACE F., b ca 1825, Milton, farmer, d pre Jan 1871, Milton; m 1850s, same town, Annie F. Remick [b ca 1830, of Milton, alive 1871, same town]. Upon his death late in 1870, guardianship of children Lydia B., Byron R. and Annie F., all under the age of fourteen, was awarded to their mother Annie

on 3 Jan 1871, by bond of $1,000.00, sureties given by Andrew
J. Remick and George Lyman, both of Milton [Strafford Co.
Probate 95:548]. Ch. b Milton: Bessie+ (Young) Bassett, b
ca 1855 (perhaps aka Lydia B); Lydia B., b late 1850s; Byron
R., b late 1850s; and Annie F., b 28 Nov 1860, d 5 Nov 1897,
age 36-11-7, home town]. (NHVR-Deaths, Marr, Brides)

   HORACE F., b 25 Jul 1856, Candia, s/o Aaron and Laura
(Hall) Young [no main entry], d 30 Nov 1890, age 34-4-5,
Milton, with wife surviving. (NHVR-Deaths)

   HORATIO G., b ca 1810, of Sanbornton; m 26 Jun 1836, New
Hampton, Lydia Dustin [b ca 1815, of New Durham]. (NHVR-Marr)

   ICANTHUS, see Acanthus

   IDA A., b ca 1850, of Pittsfield, d/o Andrew J. and
Dorothy (   ) Young [no main entry]; m 24 Nov 1870, Barnstead,
Frank E. Cram [b ca 1845, of Pittsfield. Ida's father may
have been the Andrew J. Young, b 1816 [main entry] who died
in Pittsfield. (NHVR-Brides)

   IDA E., b 3 Jan 1857, Alton, d/o Moses and Mary H.
(Thompson) Young, d 15 Jul 1902, bur. West Alton; m 28 Sep
1872, Farmington, Charles F. Rand [b 8 Mar 1840, Barnstead,
d ___, bur. West Alton]. Ida was a child of 3 in 1860 census
returns for her parents in Alton. Ch. b prob. Alton: Eva S.
Rand, b ca 1873, m 1891, New Durham, Philemon S. Lowell [b ca
1870, Alton]. Ida and Charles were buried at private cemetery
in Alton. (NHVR-Brides; Hammond's Alton Cemeteries, p26)

   IRA, b 1810, CT, s/o Levi Young [no main entry], d testate 19 Mar 1882, age 72, Belmont; m ca 1835, CT, Sarah (   )
[b 1813, Lynn, CT, d 4 Jan 1892, age 79, Belmont, widow, bur.
Laconia]. Ira's will was drawn 25 Jun 1881, proved 20 Mar
1883, naming wife Sarah as residuary legatee and James G. Cate
as sole Exec.; witnesses E. Gerry Ladd, Pike Davis, Josephine
Sanborn [Belknap Co. Probate #3746].   Ira bequeathed to
daughter Abby Jane Gilman, wife of Daniel S. Gilman, his
"homestead estate" which contained about one-half acre of land
with buildings; to son Andrew J. Young, "the farm on which he
now lives being all the land and buildings conveyed to me by
deed from Jacob Jewell and Freeman Ladd, excepting about one
acre of land now owned and occupied by Elking D. Sweet." Wife
Sarah was to receive all the remainder of his real and personal estate. Ch. b CT: Andrew J.+, b Jun 1838; Abby Jane
(Young) Gilman, b ca 1840. (NHVR-Deaths)

   IRA F., b 1828, Alton Bay, prob. twin of Ivory F., s/o
Joseph C. and Lydia (Smith) Young of Somersworth, fish dealer,
d 14 Nov 1899, Somersworth; m ca 1850, Martha W. Leavitt [b
Oct 1828, Pine Point, ME, d 17 Mar 1903, Somersworth]. From
1850-1870, he and Martha were listed on the census returns for
Somersworth. In 1850 they lived alone; in 1860 child Sara F.
was at home as was Alfred+ Young, peddler [b 1820], and Hannah
Webster, carder [b 1833], ME; in 1870 daughter Ida was listed.
In 1900 Martha was listed as widow and resident of Somersworth, age 71, living alone. Ira, Martha and daughter Ida M.
were buried at Forest Glade Cemetery, Somersworth.   Ch. b

Somersworth: Sarah F., b 1850; and Ida M., b 4 Sep 1864, d 18 Sep 1892, age 28-0-14, her native town. (Census Strafford Co., 1850, p178; 1860, p290; 1870, p357; Wooley's Somersworth Cem., G.A.R. Ave., No. 381; 1900 Soundex; NHVR-Deaths)

IRVING E. aka Irwin E., b 4 Jul 1866, Madbury, s/o Asa and Mary A. (Joy) Young, alive 1900, Dover; m 1 Jan 1898, Dover, Nellie F. Corson [b Dec 1866, Durham, alive 1900, Dover]. He was listed at age 3 on the 1870 census returns for Madbury under parents' entry. Irving, Nellie and son Ralph G. relocated in Dover by 1900 as shown by census returns that year. Ch. b Dover: Ralph J., b 30 Mar 1899, not traced further. (1900 Soundex; NHVR-Births, Marr; Hayes Gen., V2, p93)

IRVING WESTON, b 1869, Freedom, s/o George F. and Mary F. (Nason) Young, later res. of Conway; m1 7 Oct 1888, Freedom, Orrie L. Sawyer [b 21 Sep 1873, Eaton, d/o Daniel C. and Lydia A. (White) Sawyer, d 11 Aug 1889, Freedom]; m2 3 Jun 1894, Conway, Mary L. Sawyer [b 1878, Eaton, sister of Orrie L. Sawyer]. Ch. b Eaton by 2nd wife Mary: first child and son b 25 Mar 1899. (NHVR-Births, Marr, Deaths)

ISAAC, b 15 Mar 1716, Dover, s/o Jonathan and Abigail (Hanson) Young of Dover, d 27 Dec 1779, Dover; m 1740s, Dover, Elizabeth (   ) [b ca 1720, alive 1775, Dover, prob. predeceased her husband]. It is believed Isaac was a long-time resident of Dover despite his purchase of lands in Barrington; his last land deed signed in 1775 stated he was of Dover. In 1741 he was listed as resident of Cochecho Parish, taxed 7 shillings and 6 pence, and in 1761 was chosen one of the Town Moderators of Dover. Isaac's inheritance from his father's estate was 100 pounds Old Tenor per Jonathan's will signed 1 Jul 1752, proved 29 Sep 1756. His first purchase of land, the dwelling house and barn of Ichabod and Susannah Canney of Dover, was by deed signed 10 Mar 1752, rec'd 30 Oct 1765, for 450 pounds Bills of Credit Old Tenor; this was the same land that Canney bought of David Watson 7 Dec 1736. One stringent stipulation existed: Isaac was to own and improve the homestead, "excepting erecting any building thereon which I forbid and disapprove"; witnesses Dudley Watson, Joseph Hanson [NH Prov. Deed 87:126]. For his other purchase in 1741 of Lot 10, 50 acres land in the Two-Mile Streak, Barrington, adjacent to the Barrington/Rochester headlines, see Benjamin+ Young of Dover [b ca 1720], grantor. Isaac and Elizabeth sold this same lot to Peter Young of Barrington [nephew, son of Eleazer] by deed of 20 Dec 1774, rec'd 5 Dec 1778, for 200 pounds; witnesses John Gage, John Hanson [Strafford Co. Deed 3:207].

Isaac and Elizabeth also sold "a certain piece of land" in Dover, taken from the south end of the lot where he lived beginning at northern corner of the Dames dwelling house and adjacent to the estate of Colonel John Gage, Esq., deceased, by deed signed 26 May 1775, rec'd same date, to Theophilus Dame of Dover for 12 pounds and 12 shillings; witnesses John Wentworth Jr., Nathaniel Burnham [Strafford Co. Deed 1:322].

Isaac died intestate, the administration of his estate
a long and complex one. His heirs-at-law were either siblings
or offspring of siblings, all descendants of Jonathan and
Abigail Young. There were no known children. Inasmuch as
dower rights were not involved during administration of his
estate, it can be inferred that Elizabeth predeceased him.
Prior to the division of the property, heirs-at-law quitclaimed their shares and interest in Isaac's estate in Dover,
each deed treated separately under given name: (1) nephew
Timothy of Madbury, son of brother Nathaniel and Mary Young
of Madbury; (2) nephews James Young of Wakefield, Moses Young
of Rochester, and nieces Mary Young of Rochester and Anna
(Young) Wentworth of Rochester, issue of brother Thomas and
Anna (Roberts) Young of Rochester; (6) brother Eleazer Young
of Dover; (7) sister Abigail Hayes, wife of Joseph Hayes of
Rochester, (8) nephew Peter Young of Barrington, son of
brother Eleazer; (9) nephew Ezra Young of Dover, son of
brother Nathaniel and Mary Young; (10) niece Elizabeth (Young)
Demeritt and husband Ebenezer Demeritt, daughter of said
Nathaniel and Mary Young; and (11) niece Molly Hanson, wife
of Daniel Hanson of Buxton, York County, ME, and their children, issue of youngest sister Mercy (Young) Hanson. Elijah
Hanson of Somersworth was appointed agent for the said Molly
Hanson, Daniel Hanson Jr. and Michael Hanson, both of the same
Buxton, and John Hanson of Otisfield, ME, heirs of Isaac Young
late of Dover, on date of 8 Sep 1803 [Agent for Heirs, Straf-
ford Co. Probate 8:427].

Division of the estate was set off by Richard Dame, Moses
Wingate, Stephen Sawyer, Ephraim Bickford and William K.
Atkinson, accepted 11 Jan 1804 [Strafford Co. Probate 8:372].
The estate contained two tracts of land in Dover, one of
19-1/2 acres lying on the eastern side of the Main Road leading from Dover Congregational Meeting House to Piscataqua
Bridge, and the other lying on the western side of the same
road of 17 square rods. The following abutters were to receive small allotments of the remainder, Thomas Footman, heirs
of Theophilus Dame, Esq., deceased, heirs of Jonathan Gage,
deceased, John Wheeler, Hannah Chamberlin and Timothy Young.
(Heritage's Dover VR, p24;190; NH State Papers, V24, p700;
Quint's Hist. Memos, p11)

ISAAC, b 1754/5, Dover, s/o Ebenezer and Betsey (Bickford) Young, d testate 31 Mar 1827, age 72, Barrington; m1
Apr 1782, Madbury, Elizabeth aka Betsey Cate [b 1761, of
Madbury, d 12 Sep 1800, age 39, Barrington]; m2 1 Apr 1801,
Madbury, Deborah Killey [b 1764, Madbury, d 24 Sep 1833, age
69, Barrington]. A signer of the 1776 Association Test for
Barrington, Isaac became head of household there in 1790, with
family of two males over 16 years of age, three males under
16, and one female [spouse]. In 1800 he was widower, age 45
plus, with family of three males, one each under 10, 16, and
26, and one female under 10. In 1830 second wife Deborah was
widow and head of household in Barrington, age 60-70, with a

family of three grown children all age 20-30, one son and two daughters. Isaac was Exec. of his father's will signed 6 May, proved 21 Jun 1786. His legacy was the whole of Ebenezer's real estate in Barrington, 100 acres of Lot 269. As will be seen from the division of the estate given below, Isaac had amassed 430 acres in Barrington which he had kept in tact up by the terms of his own will.

Isaac's earliest known purchase of land in Barrington was 40 acres beginning at n.e. corner of Henry Hill's land, lot number not specified, by deed of 4 May 1783, rec'd 9 May 1793, from Daniel Dellan aka Delan of Barrington for 100 pounds; witnesses Richard Sinkler, Jr., Samuel Hale [Strafford Co. Deed 16:17]. In 1797 Isaac formed a partnership with Samuel Winkley Jr. of Barrington in the purchase and mortgage of 640 acres in the 4th and 5th Range, Barrington, acreage that was part of the estate of the late Mark Hunking Wentworth Esq. of Portsmouth, Rock. Co., from Francis and Anabella Gore of Exeter, Great Britain who gave power of attorney to John Fisher Jr., for $1,700.00; signed 18 Mar 1797, rec'd 23 Feb 1803; witnesses Charles B. Elton, George Gains.[Strafford Co. Deed 41:302]. On same date of signing, he and said Winkley mortgaged the 640 acres by deed rec'd 30 Mar 1797, having signed two promissory notes, the first payable 1 Nov 1797, the second due one year hence, for the same sum of money plus interest; witnesses the said Elton and Gains [Strafford Co. Deed 23:520]. They then quitclaimed 50 acres in the 5th Range, to John Smith of Barrington for $250.00, by deed signed 30 Mar 1797, rec'd 17 Jan 1805; witnesses Robert Woodberry, Andrew Torr, Eliphalet Cloutman [Strafford Co. Deed 46:525]. In a double transaction on date of 15 Dec 1802, Isaac and partner Winkley each quitclaimed one-half of the above property for $300.00 each, agreeing that Isaac was to have the western end, by quitclaim rec'd 21 Mar 1803; dower rights ceded by Polly Winkley; witnesses John Cate, Ebenezer Young, Betty Winkley, Polly Winkley [Strafford Co. Deed 41:341]; and partner Winkley Jr. to have the eastern end of the lot by quitclaim rec'd 4 Apr 1803; dower rights ceded by Deborah Young; witnesses John Cate, Ebenezer Young Jr. [Strafford Co. Deed 41:351]. Part of Isaac's western end of the lot, 78-1/4 acres in the said 4th and 5th Range, was sold by deed signed Jan 1803, rec'd 17 Jan 1805, to Pumphry Peavey of Barrington for $369.00, with Deborah ceding dower rights; witnesses Ebenezer Young, John Waldron, Benjamin Cate [Strafford Co. Deed 47:133].

Isaac's will of 8 Sep 1826, proved 19 Apr 1827, named as Co-Execs. and co-residuary legatees sons Ebenezer, Isaac Jr. and David; witnesses John Kelly, Henry Hill, Pumphry Peavey [Strafford Co. Probate 36:324]. His three sons, all of Barrington, were allowed Execs. of Isaac's will on 24 Apr 1827; bond of $5,000.00 given with sureties Samuel Shackford and Henry Hill, both of Barrington [Strafford Co. Probate 30:231]. Isaac's bequests were: to second wife Deborah, in

lieu of her right of dower, all provisions to meet her needs
during the term of her natural life: household furnishings,
a side saddle, the use and occupation of the east front room
of their homestead dwelling, the usual household privileges,
two good cows and six sheep, and privilege in his pew in the
lower meeting house in Northwood; to daughters Lucy, Eliza,
Sophia and Abigail, $50.00 each upon their marriage; unmarried
daughters were to enjoy the use of his east front room for as
long as they chose to reside in the house; to son Ivory,
$50.00 to be paid in clothing and the "gun which was bought
for him and is considered his"; to son David, his clock; to
son Isaac, his own Bible in which is his name, and his carpenter's tools; to Isaac and David, all his personal estate; and
the acknowledgment that "the house in which his son Ebenezer
lives to be his as it was built by him and the same is to
remain his."

Division of his estate with buildings was actually set
off fourteen years later on 29 Sep 1841 in more or less
one-third equal shares by appraisers Elijah Austin of Madbury,
Winthrop Smith of Durham and John Wingate of Northwood,
attested to 5 Oct 1841 [Strafford Co. Probate 59:407]. It is
to be noted that son Ebenezer died previous to the division,
thus heirs-at-law were Isaac Young [Jr.], David Young, and
Ebenezer's daughters Mary Ann, Betsey C., Lucy M., and Olive.
Isaac [Jr.] received 124 acres, 126 rods of land beginning at
n.w. side of Canaan Road and at a place commonly called "Much
Ado Hill," abutting the Shackford lot and land of Caleb
Twombley. David's share was 112 acres, 54 rods, beginning on
north side of Canaan Road at s.w. corner of Henry Hill's land,
also one acre of orchard at n.e. corner by land of the late
Nathaniel Twombly. Ebenezer's share of 166 acres, 133 rods
bounded s.e. by the Shackford lot, n.e. to David's land, n.w.
to Isaac's land and s.w. by land of John Clark, went to his
four daughters who wished to be deemed "joint owners." The
homestead dwelling and household privileges were to be shared
equally by Isaac and David.

Daughter Lucy, single, had her will drawn up 30 Dec 1846,
proved 2 Feb 1847, in which she named her brother Isaac sole
Exec.; witnesses Henry Hill, David Young, Elizabeth Garland
[Strafford Co. Probate 55:486]. Isaac Young was allowed Exec.
of her estate on date of probate, bond of $1,000.00 posted
with sureties Henry Hill and William Hale, both of Barrington
[Strafford Co. Probate 50:322]. The following bequests were
made to siblings and relatives: to brother Isaac, her caned
rocking chair; to brother Ivory, her broad cloth _____; to
Ivory's wife Mary Ann, all the remainder of her wearing
apparel; to Ivory's only daughter [Eliza A., b 1840], three
dollars; to sister Abigail Caverly [wife of Asa Caverly], her
cloak; to sister Eliza Jane Pillsbury, her morning shawl and
black silk dress; to sister Sophia, her feather bed; to the
two daughters of Asa Caverly [named above], three dollars
each; to cousins [daughters of brother Ebenezer], Betsey C.

Young, five dollars, Olive J. Young, one cotton and wool coverlet and a pair of English table cloths, and to Lucy M. Critchett, her green silk dress and one large silver spoon; to Mary Ann Hall, her silver bead spectacles and one patchwork quilt "unquilted." Family members were buried at the Isaac Young family plot, Pine Grove Cemetery, Barrington.

Ch. b Barrington by Betsey: Ebenezer+, b 1783; Isaac+, b 1788; Solomon, b 1787, d.y.; David+, b 1791; Lucy, b 1794, d 18 Jan 1847, single, age 53; Benjamin, b 1795, d.y.; John, b 1790s, d.y. Ch. b Barrington by Deborah: Sophia, b 1800s, alive 1846; Ivory+, b 9 Mar 1802; Eliza Jane+ (Young) Pillsbury, b 1805; and Abigail+ (Young) Caverly, b 1808. (Barrington Graveyards, #6B3, p90; Wilson's Assoc. Test, p122; Census Strafford Co., 1790, p87; 1800, p156; 1830, p24; NHVR-Marr)

ISAAC, b ca 1765, of Strafford; was head of household in Strafford in 1840, age 70-80, with spouse age 60-70, no children. (Census Strafford Co., 1840, p458)

ISAAC aka Jr., b 1776, Strafford, d testate 12 Oct 1834, age 58, Strafford; m1 ca 1795, Barrington, ( ) [b ca 1775, of Strafford, d pre Apr 1826, same town; m2 13 Jun 1827, New Durham, Mary aka Molly Willey [b 27 Mar 1791, of New Durham, d 7 Jan 1858, age 66, Strafford]. Isaac and family attended the Freewill Baptist Church in Strafford; both he and second wife Mary were residents of Strafford at time of marriage. He was listed on the census returns for Strafford 1800-1830: from 1800 through 1810, the census revealed a female of his own age group who could have been spouse. In 1810 there were two males age under 10 and two females one age under 10 and one 10-16. In 1830 Isaac was age 50-60 with female younger than he (2nd spouse), age 30-40, and household of 5 males, one under 5, two age 15-20, two age 20-30, and two daughters, one age 15-20, and one age 20-30. By 1840 second wife Mary, widowed, was listed as head of family in Strafford, age 40-50, members of household were two males [her sons by Isaac], one age 5-10, and one age 10-15. In 1850 she resided in Strafford, age 57, with daughter Ana and son Hiram S.

Isaac and Mary had been married only seven years when he died in 1834. Upon his death it was discovered that he had neglected to revise his last will of 1826 which of course acknowledged only the sons and daughters by first wife who was then deceased. This error of omission, whether an oversight or not, caused second wife Mary consternation as shown by her petition below for a widow's allowance. His will was signed 1 Apr 1826, probated 15 Sep 1834, naming eldest son Jonathan as Exec. of his will; witnesses William Saunders, John Berry, Joshua Wingate [Strafford Co. Probate 46:429]; Jonathan was allowed Exec. on date of probate having posted bond of $4,000.00 with sureties Joshua Wingate and John Berry, both of Strafford [Strafford Co. Probate 30:310]. Bequests were made to surviving children by his first wife: to eldest son Jonathan all Isaac's estate both real and personal; sons Ezra, Paul and Isaac who had not yet arrived at the age of 21 were each to receive $25.00, and two daughters, unnamed and under the age of 18, were to have the use of one room at home as long as they remained unmarried.

Inventory of Isaac's estate was made on 18 Nov 1834, by John Berry, Jacob Drew and Isaac Bubb, all of Strafford [Strafford Co. Probate 48:277]: the estate included the homestead farm of 75 acres in the 2nd Range, valued at $1,000.00; sheep pasture of 25 acres at $181.64; a 10-acre wood lot at $70.00; and the Hayes meadow, so-called, of 8 acres at $220.00. The list of household goods revealed a comfortable dwelling and homestead: 2 colts, 1 old mare, livestock including sheep, lambs, hogs and pigs, a granary of 25 tons hay, 15 bushels corn, 200 bushels of potatoes still in the field, wheat and rye; 1 chaise and harness at $75.00, 1 sleigh and bells at $3.50, tea table, looking glass, 6 each dining chairs and kitchen chairs, tin ware, crockery, linens and bedding.

On 20 Jan 1835, Mary, widow, was appointed guardian of their minor children Andrew Jackson Young and Hiram Stevens Young, both under the age of seven years; $2,000.00 bond was posted with sureties given by Job Otis Esq. and Isaac Willey, both of Strafford [Strafford Co. Probate 50:10]. On same date Mary petitioned the court for an allowance from Isaac's personal estate for herself and her two small children as she was without visible means of support [Strafford Co. Probate 48:462]. She eloquently stated "that she married the deceased Isaac Young about seven years ago and that she carried at his house good furniture and new stock and in cash $436.00, part of which cash was loaned to individuals and notes taken in said Young's name and still remains unpaid and the notes are appraised to said estate, part of said money was laid out in land and appraised to the estate, the residue of the money laid out to purchase a chaise... My [live]stock and furniture were worth $150.00 when I went there." Mary was allowed same day an allowance of $400.00 "situate to her condition."

Heirs-at-law widow Mary and step-son Jonathan Jr., Admin. were notified 22 Sep 1835 that a committee would meet at the homestead with the view of appraising the estate in order to set off her dower rights. Eliphalet Nutter of Barnstead and Jacob Drew and Samuel Hall of Strafford submitted their findings 24 Sep 1835; dower allowed 19 Jan 1836 [Strafford Co. Probate 49:431]. The share set off to Mary was 22-1/2 acres from the 75-acre homestead farm bounded by lands of James Bodge and Joseph Otis and two acres from the northern corner of the homestead; two acres from the meadow land bounded n.w. by land of Sampson Babb, s.e. by land of Widow Hayes; also one other piece of land, 12 acres called the Foss pasture located n.w. of Jacob Drew's land and north of Jeremiah Foss's land. The usual household privileges were allowed as well as Mary's occupancy of the west front room and west bedroom, the use of the westerly end of the barn, the lower part of the cornhouse and hogshouse. The "first account" of the estate was submitted 16 Jan 1838 by Jonathan, Admin., approved same date [Strafford Co. Probate 54:156]; he had paid debts on the estate in the amount of $849.02. Credits of $1,070.67 were reported, balance due from Exec., $221.35. Jonathan and wife Sally quitclaimed to Mary Young, widow, by deed signed 5 Feb, rec'd 2 Mar 1842, all the right Jonathan had in the land set off to Mary as her right of dower in Isaac's estate for $200.00; see Jonathan and Sally (Saunders) Young for full details.

Division of Isaac's property to his two sons by Mary, Andrew Jackson and Hiram Stevens was delayed until 28 Apr 1841 at which time the sons were over seven years old. John Saunders, Daniel Winkley and Paul Perkins, all of Strafford, made the following determinations; approved 29 Apr 1841 [Strafford Co. Probate 59:397]. The acreage each son received was subject to Mary's dower rights. Andrew J. received 4-1/2 acres of a piece of meadow land in Strafford lying near the Barnstead line, abutting Samson Babb's line at corner of land set off to Polly Hayes, widow of Benjamin Hayes, "it being the part of land Isaac Jr. bought of said Hayes of Strafford," and 12 acres of the Foss pasture adjacent to Jacob Drew's land. Hiram's share was 10 acres of a piece of woodland in Strafford, 3rd Range, it being a part of the Brewster lot beginning at east corner of Joseph Otis' land by land of James Bodge's to land of Daniel Brewster, and two acres land abutting said Babb's land, as well as one acre, ten square rods, 2nd Range, which was part of the homestead farm in the northern corner near Isaac Babb's house.

Mary was buried at the Twombly-Gray Cemetery on Evans Mountain Rd., Strafford. Ch. b Strafford by 1st wife: Jonathan Jr.+, b ca 1795; Ezra, b ca 1810; Paul, b ca 1813; Isaac, b ca 1815; daughter b ca 1817; and daughter b ca 1819. Ch. b Strafford by Mary: Andrew Jackson+, b 1828; poss. Ana, b 1830; and Hiram Stevens+, b 1832. (Census Strafford Co., 1800, p155; 1810, p506; 1830, p46; 1840, p461; 1850, p566; Morning Star, p375; NHVR-Marr; Stiles' Cemeteries, p219)

ISAAC, b ca 1775, of Barrington. This was the third Isaac Young in the 26-45 age bracket listed in 1810 census for Barrington. From 1810-1830, Isaac was head of household in Barrington: in 1810 his spouse was of similar age, with family of three males, one each under 10, 16, and 26, and two females, one under 10, one under 16; in 1830, he was age 50-60, with spouse of same age group, no children. (Census Strafford Co., 1810, p505; 1830, p48)

ISAAC aka Jr., b ca 1785, of Barrington; head of family in Barrington in 1830, age 40-50, with spouse age 30-40, and one male age 30-40; in 1840, his age was 50-60, spouse was 40-50, with household of one male age 15-20 and one female age 30-40. (Census Strafford Co., 1830, p24; 1840, p471)

ISAAC, b 1788, Barrington, s/o Isaac and 1st wife Betsey (Cate) Young, d testate 13 Aug 1861, age 73, home town; m 27 Sep 1848, Barrington, Caroline ( ) Neal, widow [b 1812, alive 1863, of Barrington]. It is a moot question whether this was Isaac's first marriage at age 60; he may have been the Isaac of the preceding entry, b ca 1785. Isaac was named one of three Execs, and residuary legatees of Isaac Young Sr. of Barrington by his will drawn 8 Sep 1826, proved 19 Apr 1827; his legacy was a one-third share of the 430-acre homestead farm, 124 acres, 126 rods, in Barrington, set off to him 5 Oct 1841. He was also named Exec, and residuary legatee of his sister Lucy by her will signed 30 Dec 1846, proved 2 Feb 1847. Isaac and Caroline were listed as residents of Barrington from 1850-1860, with her son Jacob Neal, age 9 [b 1841] as member of household. In 1850 only, Narindon Daniels, female, age 12 [b 1838] lived with them.

Isaac's will of 12 Aug 1861, proved 6 May 1862, named his step-son Jacob S. Neal as Exec. and residuary legatee; witnesses John Caverly, Daniel Boody, Isaac L. Buzzell [Strafford Co. Probate 70:478]; execution of will granted to said Neal of Barrington; bond of $5,000.00 with sureties David Young [brother] of Barrington and John Caverly of Strafford [Strafford Co. Probate 68:305]. Isaac made provisions for wife Caroline to receive a one-sixth part of the farm produce, excepting the hay and fodder, also the use of one cow, three sheep to be kept on his farm, together with the use of a horse and carriage for her use "so long as the said Caroline shall remain my widow," and bequeathed $400.00 to his brother Ivory Young. Caroline's son Jacob S. Neal was to receive all Isaac's real and personal property. No issue by a previous marriage was cited however. Caroline accepted the provisions made for her on 24 Jun 1863, and on date of 11 Jul 1863 by her married name of Caroline Hurd withdrew her notice of waiver of the provisions [Strafford Co. Probate No. 1999]. Widow Caroline m3 11 Jul 1863, Barrington, William Hurd [b ca 1810, Needham, MA]. Ch. b Barrington by Caroline's first marriage: Jacob S. Neal, b 1841. (Barrington TR, V6, p99; Census Strafford Co., 1850, p50; 1860, p156; NHVR-Deaths)

ISAAC, b ca 1790, of Milton; m 14 Mar 1816, Milton, Mehitable Varney [b ca 1796, of same town]. In 1830, Isaac was head of household in Milton, age 30-40. His family consisted of spouse age 20-30 and two daughters, one age 5-10 and one 10-15. (Census Strafford Co., 1830, p406; NHVR-Marr)

ISAAC, b ca 1803, Strafford; m 12 Jun 1828, Strafford, Lydia Perkins [b ca 1808, Strafford]. (NHVR-Marr)

ISAAC C., b 12 Sep 1797, Alton, d 21 Apr 1885, age 87-7-9, widower, Milton, farmer and manufacturer; m ca 1825, Mary Pinkham [b 19 Dec 1800, Milton, d/o Otis and Hannah (Young) Pinkham, d 19 Sep 1884, age 83-9-0, Farmington]. He was listed on the census returns for Milton from 1840-1870: in 1840, his age was 40-50 with household of spouse age 30-40, two males one age 5-10, one age 15-20, and two females, one each age 15-20 and 20-30. From 1850-1860 spouse Mary was named, his estate valued at $3,000. From 1850-1870 son William H. lived at home, occupation in 1860, chair maker, single.

Known ch. b Milton: William H., b 19 Aug 1835, d 19 Feb 1895,
age 59-6-0, Milton, single. (NHVR-Deaths; Census Strafford
Co., 1840, p324; 1850, p119; 1860, p27; 1870, p205,206; Sinnett's Pinkham Gen., p25)

ISAAC D., b 29 Dec 1822, Gilmanton, s/o Samuel S. and
Mary (Diamond) Young, d 29 Jun 1863, age 40-6-0, native town;
m1 10 Jul 1850, Ossipee, Martha H. Dorr [b ca 1830, of Oss-
ipee]. Isaac D. was named the only son and eldest of five
children of his parents; he predeceased his father. His
second wife was Judith Eastman [b ca 1830, no vital records
available]. Isaac D.'s will was written 26 Jun, proved 21 Jul
1863, in which he named wife Judith sole Exec. and legatee of
all his real and personal estate in Gilmanton; witnesses John
L. Kelly, Rhoda J. Bodger and Susan J. Kelly [Belknap Co.
Probate #1786]. (Biog. Review, XXI, p45; NHVR-Marr)

ISAAC H., b Jul 1846, Barrington, s/o Ivory and Mary Ann
(Seavey) Young, d 1936, hometown; m 22 Apr 1873, Quincy, MA,
Adaronia aka Ada R. Ewell [b Apr 1845, Quincy, MA, d/o Jacob
A. and Sarah (   ) Ewell, d 1913, bur. Barrington]. Adaronia
was resident of Marshfield, ME at time of marriage. Isaac was
named son and heir by his father's will drawn 18 Jun 1878,
proved 5 Jan 1892. He and Adaronia made their home in Barrington, listed on the 1900 Census with daughter Landella at
home. The 1892 map of Strafford Co. showed that Isaac's home
was situated at Barrington P.O., having as neighbors A. W.
Buzzell and T. Young. Isaac H. and Adaronia were buried at
Pine Grove Cemetery, Barrington. Ch. b MA: Landella, b Apr
1880. (1900 Soundex; NHVR-Marr; Barrington Graveyards, Plot
8, Lot 5E, p132,133; 1892 Saco Maps, p20)

IVESTA D. aka Luesta, b 1847 Alton, d/o Henry and Sarah
(Witham) Young of Alton; m1 24 Nov 1866, Stephen Farnham [b
1841, Alton]; m2 13 Oct 1883, Manchester, George K. Swan [b
ca 1845, ME]. (Alton VR, p568,661; NHVR-Brides)

IVORY, b 1800s, of Strafford; head of household in
Strafford, 1840, age 30-40, as was his spouse, family containing four males, two under 5, one age 5-10, one 10-15, and two
females, one each 10-15 and 15-20. (Census Strafford Co.,
1840, p458)

IVORY, b 9 Mar 1802, Barrington, s/o Isaac and 2nd wife
Deborah (Killey) Young, d testate 15 Dec 1891, age 89-9-6,
native town; m 15 Jul 1838, Portsmouth, Mary Ann Seavey [b
13 Nov 1816, Portsmouth, d/o Elijah and Sally (Parshley)
Seavey, d 2 Apr 1893, age 76-4-19, Barrington, widow]. Vital
Records named Ivory's mother as Susan Kelley of Dover; yet son
George W.'s Civil War Invalid Pension file No. 315,151 stated
his mother was the said Mary Ann Seavey. Ivory was named as
son and heir of Isaac Young of Barrington by his will signed
8 Sep 1826, proved 19 Apr 1827, and was an heir as well of his
sister Lucy Young by her will of 30 Dec 1846, proved 2 Feb
1847. He was listed on the census returns for Barrington from
1840-1860. In 1840 his age was 30-40, spouse was age 20-30,
with family of two males, one under 5, one age 10-15. Mary

was listed as spouse from 1850-1860. Children at home in 1850
were Eliza A., George W. and Isaac H., as well as John S.
Drew, age 4 [b 1846] and George W. Seavey, age 14 [b 1836].
In 1860, children at home in addition to the three listed
above were Mary, Abbie and Frank R.
   Ivory's will was drawn up 18 Jun 1878, proved 5 Jan 1892,
which named wife Mary Ann as his Exec., and son George W. as
residuary legatee; witnesses John A. Buzzell, George A.
Chesley, Frank Hanson [Strafford Co. Probate 107:256]. Mary
Ann was to receive the dwelling and farm and the remainder of
his personal property after bequests were made for the term
of her natural life. Son George W. was to inherit the family
homestead upon the demise of his mother; son Frank R.,
$100.00; son Isaac H., $25.00; married daughters Mary Susan
Stevens, $30.00; Ann E. Sherburne, $1.00, and Abby L. Locke,
one cow. It was son George W. who became Exec. of Ivory's
will. Ivory was buried at Oak Hill Cemetery, Barrington.
Other members of family were buried at Pine Grove Cemetery,
Barrington. Ch. b Barrington: George W., b Nov 1839, d.y.;
Eliza Ann aka Ann E. (Young) Sherburne, b 1840, tailoress,
alive 1878, Barrington; George W.+, b 4 Oct 1843; Isaac H.+,
b Jul 1846; Mary Susan (Young) Stevens, b 1852, alive 1878;
Abbie+ (Young) Locke, b 1856; and Frank R., b Feb 1860, d
1936, bur. Barrington. (Census Strafford Co., 1840, p480;
1850, p509; 1860, p192; Nat'l. Archives Milit. Recs.; Barr-
ington Graveyards, Plots 11-2NW and 11-2E; NHVR-Brides,
Deaths, Marr)
   IVORY F., b 1828, Alton Bay, s/o Joseph and Lydia (Smith)
Young, prob. twin, of Sanford, ME, d 14 Nov 1899, age 71,
Somersworth; m 29 Jan 1849, Wolfeboro, Fanny A. Underwood [b
ca 1830, of Saxonville, MA]. Ivory F.'s trade was stonemason.
He was paralysed for his last eight years, and was buried at
Forest Glade Cemetery, Somersworth. (NHVR-Marr, Deaths)
   J. FRANK aka Franklin, b 1832, Barrington, s/o Jonathan
and Hannah (Hall) Young, resident of Boston, MA,; m 19 Jan
1871, Durham, Francis (Hoitt) Bean [b 1840, Lee, d/o Alfred
Hoitt of Durham, her 2nd marriage]. In 1850 he was member of
brother Stephen E.'s household in Dover, known as Franklin.
(NHVR-Marr)
   J. G., b 1820, Ossipee, d 16 Apr 1860, native town; m ca
1845, Jane S. (   ) [b 1828, d 11 Oct 1859, Ossipee]. Both
were buried at Stevens-Burleigh Plot, Ossipee Cemetery.
(Loud's Cem. Recs., p131)
   J. W., b ca 1835, of Barnstead; m ca 1860, Barnstead, M.
Carswell [b ca 1840, of Barnstead]. Ch. b Barnstead: Carrie
E., b 28 Jan 1861. (LDS I.G.I. BR; NHVR-Births)
   JACOB, b 1760s, of Conway; head of household in 1790,
Conway with household of two females and two males under 16.
(Census Strafford Co., 1790, p88)
   JACOB, b 1824, of Dover; resident of Dover in 1850, age
26, carpenter; roommate was Aaron Young, age 23 [b 1827, of
Dover], carpenter. (Census Strafford Co., 1850, p104)

JACOB DANIELS, b 28 Dec 1823, Barrington, eldest s/o
Aaron and Lydia (Daniels) Young, d 8 Nov 1901, Madbury; m
1 Dec 1856, Barrington, Sarah Caverno Twombly [b 22 Jan 1831,
Madbury, d/o Hurd and Sarah C. (Caverno) Twombly, d 14 Sep
1918, native town]. Jacob was named Co-Exec. of his father's
will signed 5 Mar 1850, proved 2 May 1854, and inherited a
one-half share of the family homestead, half of his father's
personal estate and considerable property in Barrington. In
1850 he lived with his father and siblings in Barrington. In
1860 he and wife Sarah were residents of Barrington with
children Lydia L. and Edward L. at home; estate valued at
$3,500. By 1870 Jacob and family had established a home in
Madbury where he held the office of Judge of Probate, Strafford County for seventeen years; children then living at home
were Lillian, Edwin, Lewis and Sarah E.; estate appraised at
$5,000. Jacob, spouse, three grown children Lillian L.,
Edward L. and Lewis H. and daughter-in-law Mary (Shackford)
Young were listed on the census returns for Madbury in 1900.
Jacob D. and Sarah were buried at Pine Hill Cemetery, Dover.
Ch. b Barrington: Lydia Lavina aka Lillian, b 28 Jul 1858,
d 26 May 1935, Madbury; Edward Lincoln, b 21 Jun 1860, d
16 Aug 1937, Madbury; Lewis Henry+, b 15 Dec 1863; and Esther
Sarah+ (Young) Hall, b 14 May 1868. (Ham Gen., p55,57; Census
Strafford Co., 1860, p190; 1870, p194; NHVR-Births, Brides;
1900 Soundex; Frost's Dover Cem. #535; LDS I.G.I. BR; Quint's
Hist. Memos, p317,318)

JACOB K., b ca 1820, Dover; m 25 Feb 1845, Dover, Rebecca
Jane Gove [b 21 Nov 1821, Dover, d/o Richard and Lydia (Went-
worth) Gove, gr.d/o Isaac and Eleanor (Goudy) Wentworth of
Dover]. Ch. b Dover: Frederick Lawrence+, b 17 Nov 1847;
Arabella Wentworth, b 8 May 1855; and George Howard, b 16 Nov
1860. (Heritage's Dover VR, p248; Wentworth Gen., V2, p226)

JACOB W., b Oct 1838, Dover, s/o Moses C. and Mary K.
(Nutter) Young, d 11 Jan 1913, home town, retail liquor
dealer; m2 12 Oct 1867, Dover, Betsey Addie Harris [b Oct
1837, Sutton, P.E., Canada, her 2nd marriage, d/o William and
Frances (   ) Harris, alive 1900, Dover]. A native of Dover,
Jacob enlisted 21 Aug 1862, at age 23, in Co. K, 11th Regt.,
NH Volunteer Infantry and mustered in 2 Sep 1862, as Pvt. He
mustered out 4 Jun 1865, giving P.O. address of Dover. By
1870 Jacob and Betsey lived in Ward 2, Dover with infant son
Harry and Jacob's parents. On date of 16 Aug 1890, Jacob N.
filed for an Invalid Pension, Application No. 909,897, Cert.
No. 726,714. In his latter years Jacob lived at the same
address in Dover; these records indicated Jacob W. was born
6 Sep 1839 [in contrast to the 1900 Soundex]. In 1900, Jacob,
Addie and sons Harry and Herbert W. lived at Monroe St.,
Dover. Ch. b Dover: 2nd child, Harris A., b 13 May 1869,
alive 1900, Dover; and third child, Herbert W., b 1 Apr 1879,
alive 1900, Dover. (NHVR-Marr, Births; Census Strafford Co.,
1870, p61; 1900 Soundex; Soldiers & Sailors, p600; Nat'l.
Archives Milit. Recs.)

JAMES, b 10 Sep 1718, bp 31 Jan 1742, Dover, s/o Jonathan and Abigail (Hanson) Young, d testate 12 Feb 1787, age 69, native town; m Elizabeth (   ) [b 1736, of Dover, believed to be d/o Ezra and Elizabeth (   ) Kimball, d testate 18 May 1822, age 86, Dover]. James was named son and Co-Exec. of Jonathan Young's will signed 1 Jul 1752, proved 29 Sep 1756, and shared with brother Nathaniel a moiety of the family homestead situated in the then Parish of Madbury, as well as 50 acres lying on the n.e. side of Bellamin's Bank and 6 acres Common Land in Dover. Thus began a close personal and business relationship between James and Nathaniel. While no marriage record could be found for James and Elizabeth, inference to their relationship as man and wife can be drawn from several sources: the heirs-at-law revealed in both James' and Elizabeth's wills [cited below] were the issue of James' brother Nathaniel; Elizabeth's business transactions with nephew Ezra Young, s/o Nathaniel, in buying certain properties that will be cited; and the burial record of Elizabeth Young at the John Young Cemetery, Littleworth Road, Dover, a family burial plot where all kith and kin of Nathaniel and Mary (Kimball) Young were buried.

James and spouse resided in Dover into their late years; no known children. He filled many positions of trust in town government. As a young man James served as Pvt. for Ye Second Foot Company of Dover, 24 Jul 1740, and was elected Selectman for Dover consecutively from 1755-1761, and one of the Moderator of town meetings in 1755, and then from 1759-1762. Starting in 1753, he acquired many real estate holdings both in Dover and Madbury. He and Robert Hanson of Dover bought moieties of 29-1/4 acres land (total of 58-1/2 acres) adjacent to Daniel Young's lands on the road leading to Paul Gerrish's mill, and an additional 12 acres in Madbury from Nathaniel Hanson of Dover for 1,021 pounds by deed signed 29 Dec 1753, rec'd 29 May 1754; witnesses Daniel Young, Ephraim Hanson, John Molony Jr. [NH Prov. Deed 43:526]. The same Nathaniel Hanson sold seven more acres land to James and Stephen Hanson by deed of 1 May, rec'd 25 Aug 1762, for 165 pounds Old Tenor; the property began by the road that leads to Paul Gerrish's mill, adjacent to land of John Evans, Timothy Hanson, and by the said James Young and Stephen Hanson; witnesses Ephraim Hanson, William Hanson Jr. [NH Prov. Deed 67:132]. An additional half an acre located near Daniel Young's dwelling house in Madbury was purchased from Nathaniel Hanson by James Young and Solomon Young of Dover by deed signed 28 Aug, rec'd 1 Sep 1767; see Solomon Young for full details. James then bought a three-fourth share of Daniel and Temperance Young's homestead farm of 20 acres in Madbury, Timothy Young [son of said Nathaniel] buying the other fourth share by deed signed 7 Dec 1770, rec'd 18 Oct 1771.

James' will of 9 Mar 1775, proved 21 Feb 1787, named his nephew Ezra Young [son of said Nathaniel] of Dover as his sole Exec. and residuary legatee; witnesses Samuel Evans, Nathaniel

Evans [Strafford Co. Probate 2:274]. He named no issue, devising to wife Elizabeth the one-half of the dwelling house and one half of household goods during the term of her widowhood, after which the homestead would revert to nephew Ezra. The other half of the dwelling house, remainder of land in Dover, lands in Madbury, and the 1/16 share in Gerrish's sawmill were bequeathed to Ezra. The other half of the household goods went to nephew Ezra and his sister Elizabeth; she was to receive 20 pounds cash as well. Included in the bequest to Ezra was James' moiety of 29-1/4 acres land in Madbury which abutted Daniel Young's land, transaction cited above. On 2 Jun 1787, appraisers Samuel Evans and Peter Hodgdon made their return; allowed 20 Jun 1787 [Strafford Co. Probate 2:336]. James' real estate in Dover was valued at 290 pounds, land in Madbury set at 101 pounds; personal estate was rated at 105-12-0. Found under Misc. items was his large collection of farming tools valued at 46-3-2; grand total of estate real and personal, 496-12-8.

Widow Elizabeth went into partnership in the 1790s with the said Ezra of Dover, nephew [husband of Susannah (Demeritt) Young] in the purchase of "Littleworth" on the Dover-Madbury line, involving four highly well thought-out transactions with co-grantees John Kielle, Benjamin Kielle and Ezekial Hayes. While it was common practice enough then for a married woman to quitclaim her share of a parent's or sibling's estate, or for a widow to sell at public auction her husband's estate to cover debts, this is one of a very few instances to the compiler's knowledge of a widow **purchasing** real estate, albeit with a kinsman as co-grantee. In the first execution by deed signed 14 Jul 1790, rec'd 30 Aug 1791, the said five co-grantees purchased outright the aggregate 97-3/4 acres in Dover on the road leading to Barrington by lands of Dr. Ezra Green and Stephen Hanson and on the opposite side of the road by lands of Widow Hodge, Hezekiah Cook, John Kielle and Samuel Evans, for 488 pounds-15 shillings; witnesses Stephen Sawyer, Charles Chapman [Strafford Co. Deed 13:160]. In the second deed Ezekial and Hannah Hayes quitclaimed 73 of these acres to widow Elizabeth and Ezra Young for five pounds by deed signed 9 Aug, rec'd 30 Aug 1791; witnesses Miles Evans, John Durrell [Strafford Co. Deed 13:162]. As part of the deal in favor of Elizabeth and Ezra, John and Benjamin Kielle ceded to both the 24-3/4 acres on the north side of Littleworth Road and 43-1/2 acres on the south side of the road, by deed signed 29 Aug, rec'd 30 Aug 1791, for 5 pounds; witnesses Miles Evans, John Kielle [Strafford Co. Deed 13:163]. The final transaction by deed signed 29 Aug, rec'd 30 Aug 1791, netted Elizabeth Young, Ezra Young and wife Susanna, 43-1/2 acres after their quitclaim of the other 54-1/4 acres in favor of the above parties for 5 pounds; witnesses Samuel Evans, Miles Evans [Strafford Co. Deed 13:165]. These same 43-1/2 acres on the south side of Littleworth Road became dubbed "Littleworth," and were made a gift by widow Elizabeth for "one cent in hand" by deed of gift signed 8 Nov 1806, rec'd 25 Feb 1818, to "cousin" Jonathan Young of Dover [grandnephew, son of Ezra and Susannah Young]; witnesses William Kielle, Nicholas Ricker [Strafford Co. Deed 99.411].

In 1821 widow Elizabeth quitclaimed Lot 176, Barrington by deed signed 8 Mar, rec'd 13 Mar 1821, to "cousin" Jonathan Young of Barrington for $800.00, the land being the same she purchased together with Ezra Young, late of Dover; witnesses John Wingate, Mark Ayers [Strafford Co. Deed 109:340]. Originally Elizabeth and Ezra had purchased this lot from Samuel Hale, William Hale and Isaac Waldron of Barrington by deed of 6 Mar, rec'd 27 May 1806, for $1,850.00; witnesses Isaiah Horne, Benjamin Watson [Strafford Co. Deed 50:508]. Her will was drawn 30 Aug 1821, proved 17 Jun 1822, naming as sole Exec. the said Jonathan Young of Dover; no issue listed; witnesses John Wingate, John W. Hayes, Stephen Hanson Jr. [Strafford Co. Probate 29:90]. On the above date, Jonathan was allowed Exec. of Elizabeth's will; bond of $2,000.00 posted with sureties John Wingate and John W. Hayes [Strafford Co. Probate 30:15]. The list of Elizabeth's legatees indeed helped to document the surviving heirs of her in-laws Nathaniel and Mary (Kimball) Young of Dover viz. her husband James' brother. Household effects and/or savings shares were bequeathed to niece Abigail (Young) Hayes [daughter of Nathaniel], widow of Joseph Hayes of Rochester; niece Elizabeth (Young) Demeritt [daughter of Nathaniel], widow of Ebenezer Demeritt of Madbury; Eliza Young and Polly Young, single daughters of the said Ezra Young of Dover; Elizabeth Young of Dover, wife of Nathaniel Young, her husband's great nephew viz. Timothy Young [son of Nathaniel]; Elizabeth Waldron, wife of Richard Waldron [son of Joseph Waldron of Dover]; Hannah Young, wife of Jeremiah Young of Dover, her husband's great nephew viz. said Timothy Young; Elizabeth Sanborne, mother of Sarah Sanborne; Lydia Young, widow of said Timothy Young of Madbury, her husband's nephew; Eleanor Kimball, widow of Ezra Kimball; Susanna Young, widow of said Ezra Young of Dover and their son Jonathan, her husband's great nephew. (Steuerwald's Dover Cem., TMs; Frost's Dover Cem., #22; Heritage's Dover VR, p23,24,139,142,194; Scale's Dover, p87,88,259,260; Demeritt Fam., **Reg.** 87:89,90)

JAMES, b ca 1720, Scotland, res. of Barrington; m1 ca 1745, Philadelphia, Margaret Sloan [b ca 1725, of Philadelphia], d 1760s, Barrington]; m2 1770s, Susan Wood [b 1750s, of Barrington, alive 1780s, Barrington]. James emigrated to Philadelphia before 1750, there he married and took up residence and then relocated in Barrington, exact year unknown. He was one of the earliest Youngs to settle in Barrington; son William may have been the only son to put down roots there, becoming patriarch of many generations of Youngs stemming from this town. Ch. b Philadelphia by Margaret: William+, b 1749; James, bp 1751; John Croft, b 1755; Ephraim, bp 1761; Nancy, b 1760s; and Sally, b 1760s. Ch. b Barrington by Susan:

Daniel, b 1770s, lived in Raymond; Margaret+ (Young) Woodhouse, b ca 1780; and Polly+ (Young) Brock, b ca 1780. (Ham
Gen., p25; NHVR-Brides)

JAMES, b ca 1721, bp 9 Sep 1744, Rochester, s/o Jonathan
and 1st wife Hannah (Ham) Young, d 1773, same town; m ca 1750,
Rochester, (   ). It should be noted that NHVR-Marriages
revealed an error, perhaps from transcribing records decades
ago: a duplicate marriage record was made out for one Elizabeth Monroe of Rochester who married 27 Aug 1747, James Young
and Jonathan Young, both of Rochester. Only one of these
records could be used; it was attributed to Jonathan of Rochester. Church records showed that James was the son of this
Jonathan, not a peer, and Elizabeth Monroe became James' step-
mother upon her marriage to Jonathan. James lived in Rochester where he and spouse affiliated with the First Congregational Church on or about 1757; here their children were
baptized. James' two sons Daniel and Ephraim may possibly
have been the heirs cited in Benjamin Church's will dated
1812; see John and Ruth Young of Dover for full details. Ch.
b Dover: Betty, b 19 Jan 1755; James, bp 14 Aug 1757; Daniel,
bp 29 Oct 1758; and Ephraim, bp 1 Nov 1761. (Heritage's Dover
VR, p159-161; Stackpole's Durham, V2, p291; LDS I.G.I. BR)

JAMES, b ca 1752, of Dover, d 29 Oct 1786, Dover; m
26 Apr 1777, Dover, Susannah Lyons [b ca 1757, of Dover].
(Heritage's Dover VR, p79,193; NHVR-Marr)

JAMES aka Lt., b 29 Aug 1758, Rochester, s/o Thomas and
Anna (Roberts) Young of Rochester, d 8 Jan 1857, Wakefield;
m 2 Jul 1783, Rochester, Mary Kimball [bp 7 Oct 1759, Dover,
d/o Richard and Anna (Hanson) Kimball, d 1833, age 73, Wake-
field]. As resident of Rochester James signed the petition
addressed to the General Assembly on 30 Aug 1785 to repeal
items relative to the "Lumber Act, Paper Money and other
matters." His homestead in North Wakefield was established
before 1790 in the section known as the Pine River settlement.
He was the earliest of all the Youngs who actually settled in
Wakefield. D.A.R. records credited him with four years of
military service in the Revolutionary War, 1777-1780, in the
2nd Regt., 9th Co., commanded by Col. George Reid. One of the
factors that led him to Wakefield after the war was his legacy
from his father by will signed 4 May 1772, proved 30 Sep 1772,
of a one-third share of the 100-acre Lot 69, 2nd Div., East
Town (Wakefield). The 1790 census showed him as householder
of Wakefield, with a family containing two males under 16 and
three females. Actively involved in his town and well known,
he was elected moderator of Wakefield's town meeting of March
1799, was chosen Selectman for seven terms from 1798-1817 and
Assessor in 1812, and petitioned with 18 others to be free of
the Ministerial Tax in 1808. One of the original members of
the Early Settlers' Meeting House at Leighton's Corner established circa 1808, James purchased pew #32. In 1820, Lt.
James was listed as resident of Highway District No. 4, for
the purpose of a highway tax. Per Bank's Wakefield, this

district included "all the Main Road from Jonathan Quimby's lane to the Ossipee line, also the Effingham road to the center of the river at the Clark & Robert's Mills, also the road leading from said Main Road to Brookfield line by S. Hawkins." The Town Check List used at Town Meeting of 11 Mar 1834 listed him as taxpayer eligible to vote. By 1840 he was widower, age 80-90, with household of three males, one each age 5-10, 30-40, and 40-50, and one female age 30-40. In 1850, James, age 92, lived in the household of son James Jr. and family in Wakefield, the estate valued at $5,000.00. This would seem to indicate that title to the homestead in Wakefield had been conveyed to son James within that last decade, yet no land deed to this effect could be found.

By 1804 James held the title of Gent. in deed signed 16 Mar 1804, rec'd 1 Aug 1815, when he and wife Mary sold with full title his father's legacy of the said unimproved Lot 69 to Solomon Hutchins of Wakefield for $500.00; witnesses William Sawyer, James Hutchins [Strafford Co. Deed 85:399]. No document was found however to show that siblings Thomas and Moses had quitclaimed their one-third shares to James. Inasmuch as Moses later named his brother James residuary legatee of his estate (see below), the assumption could be made that the two brothers had simply made a trade-off on land holdings. James' homestead in Wakefield comprised two parcels of land of Lot 88, 2nd Div., one of 15 acres, 133 rods, and the other of 30 acres beginning at Cook's corner on the east side of the road by Wiggin's land to Blake's corner, purchased by deed of 5 Feb, rec'd 6 Feb 1798 from Christopher and Huldah Skinner of Wakefield for $400.00, drawn to the original right of Daniel Peirce, Esq. and Mary Moore; witnesses Samuel Fellows, Noah Robinson [Strafford Co. Deed 25:399].

As heirs-at-law of Isaac Young of Dover [uncle, their father's brother], James and wife Mary, Moses Young [brother] of Rochester and Mehitable his wife, Enoch Wentworth of Milton and Anna his wife [sister], and Mary Young [sister] of Rochester, single-woman, quitclaimed for $155.00 their share and interest in the estate of Isaac Young, late of Dover, i.e., 19-1/4 acres land in Dover, situated on the road leading from the Rev. McGrays' Meeting House to Piscataqua bridge, and a fourth of an acre on the opposite side of the road, to John Wheeler of Dover apothecary by deed signed 22 Jul, rec'd 16 Nov 1803; witnesses Samuel Bragg and Ichabod Cook for James and Mary Young and Moses and Mehitable Young; witnesses John Plummer Jr. and Molley Varney for Enoch and Anna Wentworth and Mary Young [Strafford Co. Deed 43:315]. Inasmuch as sibling Thomas was not one of the principals of this quitclaim, it seems safe to assume that he was then deceased. James and Mary were buried at Old Young Cemetery, at foot of Old North Wakefield Hill, Wakefield. On a recent trip in the summer of 1978 the back country road which led to this old cemetery had to be traversed by foot, and even then it was almost impenetrable with overgrown weeds, low overhead and fallen logs.

The cemetery itself showed care and the grave site of Lt.
James revealed a commemorative Revolutionary War plaque.
Ch. b Rochester: Thomas+, b 7 Oct 1784; Nancy, b 1787
(see husband Joseph Young of New Market); and Richard Kim-
ball+, b 1789. Ch. b Wakefield: son b 1792, d 19 Aug 1797,
Wakefield; son b 1795, d 20 Aug 1797, Wakefield; and James+
aka Jr., b 1801. (Wakefield TR, V1, Marr-Deaths; Twombly's
Wakefield Cem., TMs; Census Strafford Co., 1790, p100; 1810,
p585; 1830, p458; 1840, p371; Census Carroll Co., 1850, p341;
Heritage's Dover VR, p82; Kimball Gen., p122; D.A.R Lineage
No. 18022, V19, p10; Merrill's Carroll Co., p465,477-478;
Bank's Wakefield, p14,83,679,682; Leighton's Early Settlers;
NH State Papers, V13, p341-344; NHVR-Brides)

JAMES, b ca 1775, of New Hampton; m late 1790s, New Hampton, Polly (   ) [b ca 1780, of New Hampton]. By deed signed
25 Jun 1806, rec'd 20 Nov 1806, James and Polly sold 39 acres,
84 sq. rods of Lot 6, 4th Range, New Hampton, drawn to the
original right of Philip Hooker, to Stephen Chandler of New
Hampton for $200.00; witnesses Joshua Lane, David Calley
[Strafford Co. Deed 51:457]. Ch. b New Hampton: John Folsom,
b 6 Jul 1800. (NHVR-Births; LDS I.G.I. BR)

JAMES, b ca 1790, of Dover; m 1817, Dover, Elizabeth York
[b ca 1795, of Durham]. (Ham's Dover Marr, TMs)

JAMES aka Jr. aka 3rd, b 1801, Wakefield, s/o James and
Mary (Kimball) Young; m ca 1830, Aurelia ('   ) [b 1803, ME,
alive 1850, Wakefield]. In 1830 James Jr. was head of household in Wakefield: he and spouse lived alone, their ages
20-30. As of 11 Mar 1834, James 3rd was listed as eligible
to vote at the March town meeting in Wakefield. By 1840 it
is believed he and Aurelia lived with his father in Wakefield
per census that year. The 1850 census showed James to be head
of household in Wakefield; members of family were spouse
Aurelia, son Simon, and father James, aged 92; value of estate
set at $5,000.00. In 1860 son Simon lived with them. Bank's
Wakefield indicated that in 1850 James 3rd incurred expenses
of $2.58 and $3.38 in the repairs of some bridges and roads,
work for which he was reimbursed; and by date of 15 Dec 1854
he was appointed Post Master of North Wakefield. In 1857
James II sold to John Mathews 350 acres of timberland for
$5,000, which enabled Mathews to found the Pine River Lumber
Company. For James' share in the sale of Lot 23, 2nd Div.,
Wakefield in 1835, see [brother] Richard K. and Deborah
(Fernald) Young of Rochester. Son Simon M. was elected
Representative to the General Court in 1858. Known ch. b
Wakefield: Simon M., b 1832. (Census Strafford Co., 1830,
p458; 1840, p371; Banks' Wakefield, p84,104,105,107,1044;
Census Carroll Co., 1850, p341; 1860, p567; Merrill's Carroll
Co., p467; Young Family Recs., courtesy of Alden N. Young)

JAMES, b ca 1820, Dover, prob. s/o Daniel and Eleanor W.
(   ) Young; m 19 Dec 1844, Somersworth, Ellen F. Fall [b
1822, of Portsmouth]. James and Ellen of Dover quitclaimed
by deed of 3 May 1847, rec'd 17 May 1848, 14 acres land in

Dover, on the north side of Toll End Road which was deeded originally to James by Ephraim Ham, to the said Ephraim Ham for $100.00; Ellen ceded dower rights; witnesses Charles Ham, Oliver Ham [Strafford Co. Deed 201:583]. Ch. b Somersworth: son b 11 Sep 1847. (LDS I.G.I. BR; NHVR-Births, Marr)

JAMES, b Oct 1833, of Rochester; listed on 1900 census returns for Rochester, lived with uncle James M. Edny, n.d. (1900 Soundex)

JAMES, b 1841, ME, lawyer, res. of Somersworth; in 1870, he lived in Somersworth with wife Betsey E. (   ) [b 1846, ME]; members of household were Olive D. Davis [b 1828], accountant, and Mary McKinney [b 1851, ME], domestic. (Census Strafford Co., 1870, p366)

JAMES, b 1849, of Rochester in 1870; worked for shoe manufacturer, resided at boarding house. (Census Strafford Co., 1870, p247)

JAMES, b Dec 1868, Ireland, alive 1900, Dover, printer; m ca 1890s, NH, Rose A. Donnelly [b Mar 1869, Ireland, alive 1900 Dover]. Members of James' household located at Waldron St., Dover in 1900 were wife Rose, two small children, father-in-law Francis Donnelly, age 65 [b Mar 1835, Ireland] and mother-in-law Margaret (   ) Donnelly, age 62 [b Feb 1838, Ireland]; all adults had retained Irish citizenship. Ch. b NH, not traced further: John F., b Jun 1894; Annie May, b May 1897; and Margaret, b 3 Jan 1892, d 3 days later, Dover. (1900 Soundex; NHVR-Deaths)

JAMES BURLINGTON, b 4 Mar 1864, Glasgow, Scotland, s/o Alexander and Arabella (McIlroy) Young, alive 1900, Rochester; m 24 Aug 1889, E. Rochester, Lillian J. Evans [b Sep 1864, East Rochester, d/o Henry and Isabel (   ) Evans, alive 1900, Rochester]. In 1870 as a child of 7, James lived with his widowed mother in Rochester; in 1900, he and spouse Lillian were listed as residents of Rochester who had retained their Scottish citizenship; no known children. James was educated in the Rochester public schools, served as member of the Rochester City Council for six years and went on to become Commissioner for Strafford County and Mayor of Rochester in 1918. (NHVR-Marr; Rochester VR, Marr; 1900 Soundex; Metcalf's N.H. Notables, p427)

JAMES C. aka 2nd, b 1792, Ossipee, more than likely s/o Moses and Mary (Chadwick) Young of Wakefield, d 1880, Wakefield, farmer; m1 ca 1816, Ruth (   ) [b 1794, of Wakefield, d 6 Oct 1844, same town]; m2 ca 1849, widow Rosemandel (Gill) Davis [b 17 Jul 1823, East Boston, MA, d/o Aaron Gill, sea captain, d 30 Sep 1903, Wakefield]. On 1 Feb 1813, James 2nd volunteered for one month's military service during the War of 1812 in Capt. Thomas Currier's Co., First N.H. Regt. Early that spring the regiment marched to Burlington; James was discharged 11 Mar 1813. As a young man of 24 years, James 2nd established his homestead in North Wakefield on property abutting Moses' homestead, the area designated in 1820 as Highway District No. 10, with purchase of land from said Moses Young believed to be Lot 62, 2nd Div., for $200.00, by deed signed 7 Oct 1816, rec'd 7 Jun 1824. His homestead later included parts of Lots 60, 61, and 63, 2nd Div. He was listed as head of household in Wakefield from 1830-1870. In 1830 his age was 30-40, with household of spouse of same age group, one male 10-15, and two females, one each age 5-10 and 10-15. On 11 Mar 1834 his name was on the Tax Roster which listed those men who were eligible to vote at that town meeting. In 1840 census his age was 40-50, spouse was 40-50, with family of two males, one age 10-15, one 20-30 and three females, one each age 5-10, 10-15, and 15-20.

Second wife Rosemandel was listed as his spouse on census returns from 1850-1870. In 1850 members of family were the children by first wife Ruth, Thomas and Daniel, the children by Rosemandel's first marriage, Eleanor and Myron D., and a married couple by the name of Smith and Betsey Young. In 1860 children at home in addition to the four above were the children by James and Rosemandel, Harriet, Ruth C., Abby M., and Obediah. By 1870, grown children at home were Thomas, Ruth, Melissa, Obediah, and Aaron G.

James 2nd of Wakefield, Daniel Young of Ossipee [cousin] and Elias and Mark Wentworth of Wakefield quitclaimed their shares of the Dearborn saw mill on Lot 2, Ossipee to Joseph T. Mathes of Ossipee, by deed of 6 Jan, rec'd 15 Mar 1825, for $30.00; witnesses James Young Jr., Ezekial Wentworth [Strafford Co. Deed 122:408]. He also acquired 65 acres of parts of Lots 60, 61 and 63, by his purchase from Benjamin Leavitt, Gent. of North Hampton, Rock. Co. by deed of 30 Aug, rec'd 2 Sep 1825, for $130.00; witnesses Enoch Clark, Elizabeth Clark [Strafford Co. Deed 125:158]. He quitclaimed to [son] Thomas Jr. by deed of 23 Jan, rec'd 27 Jan 1849, the one undivided half of James' homestead in Wakefield, land lying on both sides of the road leading from Pine River Bridge to the house of Elias Wentworth; also the one-half share of shingle mill and privilege on the meadow brook on Daniel Young's land which was the same James bought from Moses Young of Wakefield and Ephraim Wentworth of Wakefield in 1816, for $700.00; witnesses Amasa Copp, Joel Wentworth [Carroll Co. Deed 14:66].

On date of 10 May 1873 Rosemandel was listed as tax-payer of Wakefield; she was rated at $24.96. Title to the homestead had been conveyed to her by two land deeds cited below. In 1900 widow Rosemandel was listed as head of household in Wakefield with married daughter Ruth C. Weeks [n.d.] at home. For Rosemandel's purchase of Thomas Jr.'s share and title to the homestead, by deed signed 31 Oct, rec'd 3 Nov 1864, see Carroll Co. Deed 45:324; and for her conveyance of the homestead to her son Aaron of Wakefield, by deed signed 7 Sep, rec'd 21 Sep 1899, see Carroll Co. Deed 112:333. James C., wives Ruth and Rosemandel and members of family were buried at the family plot called Aaron Young Cemetery, Pray Hill Road, Wakefield.

Davis ch. b East Boston, MA by Rosemandel's 1st marr:
Eleanor S. Davis aka Ellen S.+ (Young) Remick, b 1842; and
Myron Davis aka Myron D.+ Young, b 1 Mar 1840. b Wake-
field by Ruth: Thomas aka Jr., b 1818, alive 1870, single,
laborer; Ann, twin, b 1823, d 1842; Emeline+ (Young) Mills,
twin, b 1823; Abigail+ (Young) Glidden, b 1826; and Daniel,
b 1830. Ch. b Wakefield by Rosemandel: Melissa A.+ aka
Melina (Young) Robinson, b 1845; Hattie A.+ (Young) Kershaw,
b 18 Aug 1851; Ruth C.+ (Young) Weeks, b 20 Feb 1852; Obediah
Sumner+ aka Obed, b Nov 1859; Aaron G.+, b Jul 1861; and James
Cameron+, b 30 May 1870. (Twombly's Wakefield Cem., TMs;
Census Strafford Co., 1830, p452; 1840, p378; Census Carroll
Co., 1850, p322; 1860, p581; 1870, p429-430; 1900 Soundex;
Soldiers & Sailors, p690; Potter's Mil. History, V2, p71-73;
Banks's Wakefield, p83,141,148,181,680; NHVR-Brides; Wentworth
Gen., V1, p501,502; Young Family Recs., courtesy of Alden N.
Young)

JAMES C., b 2 Aug 1817, Madbury, s/o Jonathan and Abigail
(Coffin) Young, d testate 31 Jul 1855, age 38, his home town;
m Apr 1840, Madbury, Mary V. Mathues aka Matthew [b 1816, Madbury, alive 1854, same town]. James C. and Mary were residents of Madbury from 1840-1850. In 1840 their ages were both
20-30, no issue; in 1850, member of household was Sarah A.
Matthew, age 26 [b 1824]. James C. received a one-fourth
share of all rights which his mother Abigail had held in real
estate in Dover, situated on both sides of Coffin Road, formerly owned by Susannah Bickford and Parnel Evans, both
deceased. He sold this share by land deed signed and rec'd
25 Feb 1843, to Benjamin Wiggin of Dover, as "heirs of my
mother and late father Jonathan Young"; Mary relinquished
dower rights; witnesses George Piper, Thomas E. Sawyer [Straf-
ford Co. Deed 191:557]. He was also named the residuary legatee of his aunt Polly Young of Dover by her will drawn
25 Apr, proved 6 Jun 1843; he had been promised one-half of
a woodlot in Barrington which had been conveyed to Polly by
Jonathan Young. When this property was set off by Elijah
Austin, Jedediah Cook and Mark Swain on 24 Mar 1845, approved
1 Apr 1845, James' share was 32-1/3 acres situated by land of
John and William Bodges on the road leading to Mark Swain's
house and by land of John Buzzell [Strafford Co. Probate
58:253]; Polly's sister Eliza Young of Dover received the
other 34-1/3 acres on the east side of the above divided lot.

James' will of 9 Jun 1854, proved 6 Aug 1855, named his
wife Mary as Exec. of his will and principal legatee; witnesses Tobias Evans, Nathaniel C. Nutter, Charles D. Henderson
[Strafford Co. Probate 66:336]; allowed on date of probate,
no bond posted. Mary was to receive and enjoy "forever" the
homestead farm in Madbury, all tools and livestock, etc., the
32 acres land in Barrington [cited above], and his share in
the homestead farm of Elizabeth Coffin, late of Dover, "it
being the fifth part, held in common and undivided with siblings Jonathan T. Young, Hannah Young, Elizabeth Corvin and

the children of Eleazer Cate" [husband of his deceased sister Mary Susan Cate], viz Abby Cate [b ca 1845] and Homer Cate [b ca 1850], and the rest and residue of his estate. He was buried at John Young Cemetery, Littleworth Road, Dover. No known children. (Census Strafford Co., 1840, p494; 1850, p485; Frost's Dover Cem., Plot #22; Steuerwald's Dover Cem., TMs; Demeritt Fam., **Reg.** 87:89)

JAMES CAMERON, b 30 May 1870, East Wakefield, s/o James C. and Rosemandel (Gill) Young of Wakefield, blacksmith, auto mechanic, d testate 20 May 1847, Wakefield; m1 8 Dec 1893, Wakefield, Mary Amanda Doyle [b 3 Mar 1873, Wakefield, d/o John and Amanda (Wentworth) Doyle, eldest of 8 children, d 19 Mar 1896, Wakefield]. Mary Amanda's father John Doyle was b 19 May 1839, New York City, NY, s/o emigrant parents who disembarked there from Cork, Ireland, d 27 Nov 1922, Wakefield, a Civil War veteran. At age 22 John Doyle enlisted from Ossipee in Co. H., 5th Regt., NH Vol. Infantry 16 Sep 1861, was wounded in action at Fredericksburg, VA 13 Dec 1863, re-enlisted at Ft. Lookout, MD 19 Feb 1864, and mustered out 28 June 1865, Alexandria, VA. Mary Amanda's mother Amanda Wentworth was b 25 Jun 1856, Milton Mills, d/o Levi and Emeline (Blaisdell) Wentworth, attended Wakefield Academy, and d 7 Jul 1894, Wakefield.

James Cameron m2 31 Dec 1905, Wakefield, Harriet aka Hattie L. Fellows [b 1874, d/o Charles S. and Ann (Sherbourne) Fellows, d 1952, Sanbornville, bur. Lovell Lake Cemetery, Wakefield]. Hattie's ancestry goes back to John Fellows, the earliest by that name who was granted land by Lovell Lake, Wakefield at the time the town was founded. Charles S. Fellows was the son of John K. Fellows who was the son of the earliest ancestor. Ann Sherbourne came from Lee. Before their marriage Hattie taught at small country schools in Wakefield. James C.'s will was drawn 6 Aug 1928, proved 3 Jun 1947, naming wife Hattie as sole Exec. and principal legatee; witnesses Lillian S. Edwards, Vincent D. Rogers, William N. Rogers [Carroll Co. Probate #13,083]. He devised $100.00 to son Samuel K., $200.00 to son Alden N., and $200.00 each to grandchildren Richard K. Young and Dorothy M. Young. The remainder of his real and personal property in Wakefield was devised to Hattie. James C. and wives Mary A. and Hattie were buried at Lovell Lake Cemetery, Wakefield.

Son Alden N. remains single, retired from the Public Utilities working out of Rochester. He has belonged to the Masons for over 60 years, and to the Odd Fellows for well nigh 50 years. Over the years he was actively involved in the Wakefield-Brookfield Historical Society and the Wakefield Corner Library. Ch. b Wakefield by Mary: Samuel Kershaw, b 12 May 1894, East Wakefield, d 3 Sep 1930, Wolfeboro; m 28 Jul 1920, Sanbornville, Viola Evelyn Richardson [b 26 Sep 1899, d/o William and Maggie (Carter) Richardson of Reading, MA, d 12 Jan 1986, Walnut Creek, CA]. Samuel was residuary legatee of his aunt Mrs. Hattie (Young) Kershaw who had raised him

almost from infancy.   Ch. b Wakefield by Harriet: Alden
Norris Young, b 12 Dec 1906, Wakefield (see above).   (Twom-
bly's Wakefield Cem., TMs; NHVR-Births, Marr, Deaths; Young
Family Recs., courtesy of Alden N. Young)

JAMES H., b 19 Apr 1777, Madbury, twin, s/o Timothy and
Lydia (Demeritt) Young, twin, d 18 Jul 1862, Madbury, prob.
single. James was one of the co-execs. of his father's will
signed 16 Dec 1813, probated 25 Apr 1820, receiving a moiety
of the family homestead in Madbury after his mother's demise.
He served in the War of 1812 in the defense of the town and
harbor of Portsmouth; he enlisted as private 2 Sep 1814 in
Capt. Andrew Nute's Company and served 19 days. In 1830 James
was head of household in Madbury, age 50-60, household made
up of another male of same age, believed to be his twin, one
female age 15-20, and one female 80-90, probably his mother
Lydia. James lived alone in Madbury in 1850, age 72, estate
valued at $5,000; and by 1860, lived with [nephew] Ezra Young,
widower, and Ezra's son John in Madbury.

By quitclaim from Nathaniel and Mary Hayes [brother-in-
law and sister] dated 1 Mar, rec'd 4 Mar 1805, James H. purchased 13-1/2 acres in Madbury, "being the one half of 27
acres that I [said Hayes] now own in common with Eben D.
Young," adjacent to lands of Timothy Young, Tobias Evans, and
Joseph Drew, for $323.75; witnesses John Wingate, Lemuel
Perkins, Timothy Young Jr. [Strafford Co. Deed 47:284]. James
and twin Eben purchased 2-1/2 acres land in Madbury which was
adjacent to Timothy Young's land and by Bellamy Banks River,
so called, by deed of 25 Oct, rec'd 30 Oct 1816, for $55.00;
witnesses John Wingate and William Hanson [Strafford Co. Deed
90:495]. The twins mortgaged the homestead and dwelling they
had inherited to [brothers] Nathaniel and Jeremy Young by deed
signed 13 May, rec'd 27 Oct 1830, paying off a $500.00 note
with interest to the said Nathaniel and Jeremy; witnesses
Moses Hodgdon, William Woodman [Strafford Co. Deed 149:331].
James H. was buried next to grave sites of mother Lydia and
twin Eben D. at family burial plot near the corner off Mill
Hill and Province Roads. (Census Strafford Co., 1830, p91;
1850, p483; 1860, p539: Steuerwald's Dover Cem., TMs; Potter's
Milit. Hist., V2, p123-127,190; Madbury Cem., **Reg.** 87:347)

JAMES H., b 22 Mar 1787, Durham, s/o Zachariah Young of
Wolfeboro, d testate 16 Aug 1873, age 86, Wolfeboro; m 27 Apr
1810, Wolfeboro, Nancy Nudd [b 19 May 1789, Greenland, d 1 May
1869, Wolfeboro]. James was named a son and heir of Zachariah
Young by his will signed 20 Nov 1842, proved 11 Feb 1851; he
was to receive a one-sixth part of his father's real and personal estate in Wolfeboro. He and family were members of the
Freewill Baptist Church. James was head of household in
Wolfeboro from 1810-1870; in 1810, his age was under 26, with
two females, one age 16-26 [spouse] and one 26-45; in 1830
his age was 40-50, with family of spouse of same age group,
two males, one each under 5 and 10-15, and three females, all
15-20; in 1840 his age was 50-60, as was his spouse; family

contained two males, one age 10-15, one 20-30, and two females both age 20-30. Nancy was listed as spouse from 1850-1860. In 1850 children at home were Lucretia and Charles W. as well as Nathaniel B. Glidden, age 13 [b 1837]; in 1860, those at home were son Charles W., daughter-in-law Mary A., and adopted daughter Susan E., age 18, formerly known as Susan C. Gorman, daughter of Daniel Gorman. In 1870 James H. was widower and head of family; living at home was son Charles W., also a widower; housekeeper was Lydia A. Hilton, age 37 [b 1833].

James's will was drawn 14 Jun 1873, proved 4 Nov 1873, which named son Charles W. as his Exec. of his will and residuary legatee of all property in Wolfeboro; witnesses Ebenezer Tibbetts, James Bickford, Joseph H. Bickford [Carroll Co. Probate #5844]. He devised to daughters Rachel Ann Young and Sally E. Libby and son James B. Young $20.00 each and one-half of his household goods. Adopted and married daughter Susan C. G. Ford was to receive $10.00, and son Charles W., the other one-half of household goods. Family members were buried at Nute Cemetery, Ossipee. Ch. b Wolfeboro: Rachel Ann, b ca 1811, alive 1873, native town; Lucretia, b 4 Sep 1814, d 24 Aug 1851, Wolfeboro; Sally E.+ (Young) Libby, b ca 1815; Charles Woodbury+, b 17 Feb 1828; James B., b ca 1829; and Susan C.+ (Young) Ford, b 1842, MA. (Census Strafford Co., 1810, p737; 1830, p440; 1840, p386; Census Carroll Co., 1850, p363; 1860, p517; 1870, p444; NHVR-Marr, Deaths; Loud's Cem. Recs., p85; Morning Star, p376)

JAMES H., b 1823, Gilmanton, shoemaker, d pre 1860, Gilmanton; m 31 Mar 1842, Belmont, Abigail A. Barker [b 1823, Barnstead, d/o _____ and Abigail (   ) Barker, of Belmont, alive 1860, Gilmanton]. They were residents of Gilmanton in 1850; members of household were children John P. and Martha J., Abigail's mother Abigail Barker, age 69 [b 1781] and Rosilla Barker, age 74 [b 1776]. Widow Abigail was head of family in 1860 in Gilmanton; members of family were Martha, Charles, Mary and Addie B. Ch. b Gilmanton: John P.+, b 26 Jun 1843; Martha J. aka Jennie M.+ (Young) Bunker, b 1847; Charles F., b 1851; Mary A., b 1853; and Addie B.+ (Young) Osborn, b 1857. (Census Belknap Co., 1850, p61; 1860, p215; NHVR-Brides, Marr, Deaths)

JAMES H., b 1835, New Durham, alive 1898, Portsmouth, grocer, widower; m 1860s, New Durham, Hannah Allen [b 1837, Brookfield, d/o Henry and Lovey (   ) Allen, d 10 Jan 1871, age 34, Alton]. James and Hannah were listed on the census returns for Alton in 1860. By 1898, James lived in Portsmouth, a widower. Admin. papers on Hannah A. Young's estate in Alton were filed by James H. Young on 16 Jan 1871; he declined the administration but nominated instead John W. Currier of Alton as Admin.; appraisers appointed were Lemuel S. Nute, Dudley Eames and Nathaniel W. Jones Jr., all of Alton; value of estate was set under $1,000 [Belknap Co. Probate #2501]. Ch. b Alton: Frank E. aka Frank James+, b Apr 1861, twin; Henry C.+, b Apr 1861, twin; Charles H., b

19 Oct 1864. (LDS I.G.I. BR; Census Belknap Co., 1860, p315; NHVR-Marr, Deaths)

JAMES H., b. 1841, New Durham, s/o Joel and Mary J. (Durgin) Young of Farmington; m 27 Aug 1890, Portsmouth, Alice M. Dennett [b 1855, Portsmouth]. (NHVR-Marr)

JAMES H., b 21 May 1855, Ossipee, s/o Thomas and Abigail (Wiggin) Young of Wolfeboro, engineer, alive 1900 Farmington; m 13 Nov 1880, Wakefield, Jennie M. (   ) Small [b Feb 1845, Scotland, her 2nd marriage, alive 1900 Farmington]. Jennie m1 ca 1870, Farmington, Isaac H. Small [b ca 1840, Farmington, d pre 1880, same town]. James H. was named sibling of Martha H. Young of Ossipee, d/o of Thomas and Abigail Young, by her will drawn 6 Feb 1888, proved 5 Mar 1889; he was to receive her interest in the house and lot in Dover, formerly owned by their aunt Mary S. Wiggin. Ch. b Farmington by Jennie's first marriage: Isaac H. Small Jr., b ca 1870, m 1893, Farmington; and Jennie A. Small, b ca 1875, m 1898, Farmington, Horatio H. Babb [b ca 1870, of same town]. In 1900 James and Jennie lived at North Main St., Rochester; members of household were son Henry S. and relative Nellie C. Small, age 37 [b Aug 1862, NY]. Jennie had retained her Scottish citizenship. Ch. b Wakefield or Farmington by James H.: Henry S., b Dec 1882, not traced further. (NHVR-Brides, Marr; 1900 Soundex; Wiggin Gen., p176)

JAMES M., b 1833, Wakefield, carpenter, s/o Richard K. and Isadore (   ) Young of Rochester; m1 3 Sep 1849, Somersworth, Emeline Keniston [b 1830, Lower Canada, d pre 1882, Somersworth]; m3 3 Jun 1882, Somersworth, Jane (Roberts) England [b 1827, Berwick, ME, her 2nd marriage, d/o Samuel and Dorethea (   ) Roberts, res. of Rochester]. James and Emeline were residents of Somersworth in 1850, no known children; living at home were Abigail Smith, age 34 [b 1816] and Nancy Smith, age 28 [b 1822]. (NHVR-Marr; Rochester TR, Marr, p4; Census Strafford Co., 1850, p349)

JAMES M., b 1835, Rochester, s/o Richard Kimball and Deborah S. (Fernald) Young, alive 1878, Rochester; m2 14 Jan 1873, Rochester, Angeline F. Abbott [b ca 1840, of Rochester]; no known children. James at age 25 lived at home with parents in Rochester in 1860. At time of marriage James M. and Angeline established residence in Rochester. Upon the hearing of the petition for guardianship brought against James M. by Selectmen and neighbors A. Parshley and John Greenfield of Rochester on date of 3 Dec 1878, the court decreed that James was "a spendthrift" and of necessity would need a guardian; he was made ward of his brother John F. Young; bond of $1,000.00 was posted with sureties William A. Kimball and John Whipple, both of Rochester [Strafford Co. Probate 95:458]. (NHVR-Marr)

JAMES M., b 1836, Wakefield, carpenter, s/o Daniel and Betsey (Cook) Young; m 21 May 1864, Farmington, Mary S. Jones [b 1846, Middleton]. In 1850 James lived at home and attended school at age 14 in Wakefield. (NHVR-Marr)

JAMES MORRILL, b 6 May 1813, Lebanon, ME, s/o Joseph and Patience (Wentworth) Young, res. of Middleton in 1850; m 9 Mar 1836, prob. Rollingsford, Susan P. Henderson [b 1815, of Rochester]. Prior to 1850, James and spouse lived in Rollingsford. The 1850 census returns for Middleton listed as residents James M., spouse Susan and children Lysander, Sarah and Melissa; he worked in manufacturing. Ch. b ME: Lysander Bascom, b 19 Jun 1836, m Martha Winn [b ca 1840, of Wells, ME], resided in South Berwick, ME; Sarah Semantha, b 12 Nov 1840, m George W. Luke of South Berwick, lived in Fitchburg, MA; and James Madison, b 4 Jun 1849. Ch. b prob. Middleton: Melissa, b Sep 1849. (Census Strafford Co., 1850, p407; Wentworth Gen., V1, p456,457; NHVR-Brides)

JAMES T., b 1808, ME; s/o James Young [no main entry], d 2 Dec 1882, age 74, Dover, Farmer; m 27 Apr 1836, Alton, Mary A. Nute [b 18 Jun 1821, Dover, d/o Stephen Nute, d 18 Apr 1890, age 69-10-0, Dover]. James, Mary and family had been residents of Gilmanton and Durham before they settled in Dover. In 1850 James T. and Mary A. lived in Gilmanton with five children in household: twins Moses and Louise, twins George and Martha, and Thomas. The 1860 census for Durham listed him and spouse as residents, estate valued at $3,150; children living at home, Martha, George and Cordelia. By 1870 they lived in Dover, Ward 2; children at home were George, shoemaker and Cordelia. Ch. b prob. Gilmanton: Moses M.+, b 1836, twin; Louise, b 1836, twin; George, b 1845, twin; Martha, b 1845, twin; Thomas, b 1848; and Cordelia+ (Young) Bennett, b 1854. (Alton VR, p560; NHVR-Brides, Marr, Deaths; Census Belknap Co., 1850, p56,57; Census Strafford Co., 1860, p573; 1870, p52)

JAMES T., b 1856, Dover, s/o Jonathan T. and Elizabeth L. (Demeritt) Young, carriage maker; m 15 Apr 1886, Dover, Mabel S. Hammond, [b 1861, Dover, d/o John P. and Susan E. (   ) Hammond]. For legacy James received from aunt Hannah S. Young by her will of 8 Jun 1880, proved 6 Jul 1880, see grandparents Jonathan and Abigail (Coffin) Young of Dover. (NHVR-Marr)

JANE, b ca 1785, Gilmanton, d/o Joseph and Betsey (Shaw) Young; m 6 Oct 1808, Belmont, Ebenezer Garmon [b ca 1780, Gilmanton]. Jane was the only daughter of ten children born to Joseph and Betsey. She and spouse moved to Lexington, MA where they raised a large family. (NHVR-Brides; Biog. Review, XXI, p454,455)

JANE, b ca 1810, Wolfeboro; ma 30 Jun 1833, Wolfeboro, Richard Abbott [b ca 1805, Effingham]. (NHVR-Brides)

JANE, b Dec 1836, ME; boarded at home of Seth F. McDuffee [n.d.] on Union Street, Rochester in 1900. (1900 Soundex)

JANE, b 1839, widow of _____ Young, lived at Central Avenue, Dover in 1900 with daughter Susan [n.d.]. (1900 Soundex)

JANE AUGUSTA, b ca 1821, Dover, d/o Charles and 1st wife Ruth (Varney) Young, alive 1883, native town; m 2 Dec 1841,

135

Dover, David Lawrence [b ca 1815, of same town]. Jane A. was
known by her married name of Lawrence in Admin. Papers of her
father's estate on date of 17 May 1883. (NHVR-Brides)

JANE S., b ca 1810, Barnstead; m 24 Dec 1834, Barnstead,
Ezra S. Nutter [b ca 1805, of same town]. (NHVR-Brides)

JANETTE aka Jeannette, b 1841, Madbury, d/o Eleazer and
Kezia (Rowe) Young; m 23 Mar 1862, Durham, Henry S. Durgin [b
ca 1835, of Epping]. She was listed at age 9 on the 1850
census for her parents in Madbury, and was named Janette
Durgin in her mother's will drawn 17 Aug 1863, proved 1 Apr
1865. (NHVR-Brides)

JARUSHA, b ca 1810, of Durham; m Oct 1830, Exeter, Joshua
A. Lunt [b ca 1805, of Durham]. (NHVR-Brides)

JENNIE M. aka Martha J., b 1847, Gilmanton, d/o James
H. and Abigail A. (Barker) Young; m 9 Dec 1865, Pittsfield,
Sidney P. Bunker [b ca 1845, Gilmanton]. The 1850 census for
Gilmanton listed her at age of 3 under her parents' return.
(NHVR-Brides)

JEREMIAH, b ca 1775, of Gilmanton; m ca 1800, Nancy (   )
[b ca 1780, of Gilmanton]. Jeremiah was head of household in
Gilmanton in 1810, age 26-45; young household contained spouse
under 45 years and one male under 10. He was taxpayer of Gilmanton, District No. 4, in 1812, rated at $1.50. He sold a
moiety of one-half acre land in Gilford, held in common with
"Theophilus Doe by deed dated 30 Mar 1807," on the east side
of the Province Road by land of the widow Nancy Chase, to
Jeremiah Rowe Jr. of Gilford for $200.00; wife Nancy conveyed
dower rights, by deed signed 21 Oct, rec'd 18 Dec 1816; witnesses Lyman B. Walker, Daniel Avery [Strafford Co. Deed
92:547]. (Census Strafford Co., 1810, p838; Gilmanton TR, V3,
p394)

JEREMIAH, b May/Jul 1787, Tuftonboro, s/o Benjamin and
1st wife Phoebe (Allen) Young of Wolfeboro, d 19 Oct 1871, age
84, Stewartstown; m1 ca 1805, prob. Tuftonboro, Susan Meder
[b 1781, of Stewartstown, d 25 Dec 1819, same town]; m2 ca
1820, Stewartstown, Sally H. York, widow of James Keysar [b
1793, Stewartstown, d 19 Apr 1860, age 67-8-5, home town].
Jeremiah was named a son and heir of Benjamin Young of Wolfeboro by his will signed 6 Nov 1843, proved 30 Feb 1849. He
settled in Stewartstown in 1814. Joseph and wives Susan and
Sally were buried at North Hill Cemetery, Stewartstown.
(Young Family Recs., courtesy of Granvyl Hulse)

JEREMIAH, b 16 Jul 1814, of Freedom, d 22 Nov 1892,
Effingham, age 78-4-6; m 26 Jan 1845, Effingham, Jane Allen
[b 1821, Eaton, alive 1870, Effingham]. They were listed on
the census returns for Freedom from 1850-1860, then by 1870,
for Effingham. In 1850 children at home were Orlando, Hannah
and Lenora; in 1860 children in addition to the three above,
Olive J., Julia A., Charles, Sherman and Cornelius. By 1870,
Jeremiah and Jane lived in Effingham; children listed that
year, Olive, Sherman, Charles, Cornelius, Ellen, Mary E. and
Nellie. Ch. b Freedom: Orlando, b 1848; Hannah A., b 1849;

Lenora, b 1851; Olive J.+ (Young) Clough, b 1852; Sherman, b
1854; Charles, b 1855; Julia A., b 1856; Cornelius, b 7 Feb
1859, twin; Orleans, b 7 Feb 1859, twin; Ellen, b 19 Oct 1861;
and Nellie, b Dec 1869.   (NHVR-Births, Marr, Deaths; Census
Carroll Co., 1850, p154; 1860, p630; 1870, p297-298; Freedom
VR, Bk1, p10; LDS I.G.I. BR)
    JEREMIAH, b 29 Apr 1817, Brookfield, carpenter, joiner,
d pre 1870, Wolfeboro; m 10 Feb 1839, Brookfield, Adeline
Warren aka Adelaide Hann [b 1811, of Brookfield, alive 1870,
Wolfeboro]. At time of marriage Jeremiah lived in Alton.
From 1840-1860 he was listed as resident of Wolfeboro.   In
1840 he and wife were age 20-30, with family of two males, one
each age 5-10 and 10-15. From 1850-1860 Adeline was named as
spouse with family of two daughters Sarah A. and Maria; in
1860, only Maria A. was at home. By 1870, Adeline was widow
at age 57 and head of family in Wolfeboro; members of household were daughter Sarah A. Warren and son-in-law Charles A.
Warren. Ch. b Brookfield: Sarah Adeline+ (Young) Warren, b
7 Apr 1839; Marie Antoinette aka Maria A.+ (Young) Runnels,
b 2 Jul 1841.   (LDS I.G.I. BR; NHVR-Marr, Births, Brides;
Census Strafford Co., 1840, p385; Census Carroll Co., 1850,
p389; 1860, p489; 1870, p456)
    JEREMIAH KINGMAN, see Kingman
    JEREMIAH L., b 15 Nov 1758, Newfields [South New Market],
s/o Joseph and Anna (Folsom) Young of Durham, d 14 Jul 1793,
Newfields; m 14 Jun 1781, home town, Sarah Cram [b ca 1760,
Newfields, d/o David and Susannah (Clough) Cram].   Jeremiah
predeceased his father. His children, although unidentified,
became heirs-at-law in the division of their grandfather
Joseph's estate in 1806. Although Jeremiah purchased properties in Durham, doubt exists that he ever resided there, but
rather remained in New Market. He purchased 10 acres land in
Durham, by deed signed 3 Nov 1785, rec'd 15 Aug 1786, from
Joseph Smith of New Market, situated at the country road at
n.e. corner of land of James Cram and west of Lamprey River,
which Smith bought of the Crommetts for 60 pounds; witnesses
John Watson, Wiggin Doe [Strafford Co. Deed 7:389]. Jeremiah
of New Market also purchased a 20-acre lot in Durham, by deed
of 9 Jan 1786, rec'd 8 Feb 1794, from Joseph Young of Durham
for 50 pounds; witnesses Jeremy Bryent, Timothy W. Young
(brother) [Strafford Co. Deed 18:36].   The 20 acres represented one-half of the land which Joseph bought of Jonathan
Willey, bounded north by land in possession of Stephen
Cogin's, east by land of Abraham Bennick, south by land of
Thomas Crommet, and west by land of Joseph Young Jr. Jeremiah
was still of New Market when he purchased 12-1/4 acres in
Durham for 36 pounds-15 shillings, by deed of 7 Jun, rec'd
10 Jun 1791, from Jeremiah Folsom of Rochester, a place called
Long Marsh, it being the western half of the tract owned by
Folsom and Stephen Cogan; witnesses Joseph Young, Joseph Smith
3rd [Strafford Co. Deed 13:91]; for sale of this tract, see
administration below. His last purchase of land was 100 acres

in Tuftonboro beginning at s.w. corner of Jonathan Brown's land on the road leading to Moultonboro, by deed signed 11 Jul 1791, rec'd 11 Oct 1798, from Woodbury Langdon Esq. of Portsmouth, Rock. Co., for 30 pounds; witnesses John Marsh, Woodbury Langdon Jr. [Strafford Co. Deed 28:435].

This same property in Tuftonboro was sold when Jeremiah's estate was administered by James Cram of New Market, by deed of 6 May 1794, rec'd 20 Jan 1796, to Jacob Sheafe of Portsmouth for 82 pounds; witnesses Daniel Smith, John Bryent [Strafford Co. Deed 21:499]. During administration of his estate, two other properties were sold: (1) the 12-1/4 acres in Durham at Long Marsh, by quitclaim signed 24 Jun, rec'd 26 Jun 1797, to Stephen Cogan of Durham, sum of money not specified; witnesses Nathaniel Kidder, John Bryent [Strafford Co. Deed 27:1], and (2) 12-1/2 acres in Durham to [brother] Zachariah Young by deed dated 25 May 1794 for $50.00 [full citation on this latter deed was not obtained in Grantor or Grantee Index 1773-1817]. See Zachariah Young of Durham for other details. (LDS I.G.I. BR; Fitts' Newfields, p481,683)

JEREMIAH L., b 1817, Wolfeboro, s/o Timothy W. and Esther (Libby) Young, d 4 Oct 1876, Tuftonboro; m (Intentions) 16 Oct 1837, m 19 Oct 1837, Wolfeboro, Mary A. aka Maria A. Jackson [b 10 Jul 1812, Holderness, d/o Solomon Jackson, d 28 Jan 1894, age 81-6-18, Tuftonboro, widow]. Jeremiah L. was namesake of his father's brother. Before his marriage he became residuary legatee of his father Timothy's will signed 24 Mar, proved 16 May 1834; he was to receive the rest of Timothy's real estate in Wolfeboro and personal effects not disposed of. He and Mary A. lived in Wolfeboro in 1850; children at home were John H., Adaline, Mary J. and George F. By 1860 he and Mary had relocated to Tuftonboro, listed on the census returns from 1860-1870; in 1860 children at home, John H., Adeline, George F. and Marilla L.; in 1870, George F. and Marilla.

Letters of Admin. on his estate in Tuftonboro were filed 11 Nov 1876, approved 15 Nov 1872; widow Mary Ann declined the administration of the estate and petitioned that son George F. Young be appointed in her stead [Carroll Co. Probate #5843]. Ch. b Wolfeboro: John Henry+, b Nov 1839, Adeline A. aka Addie A., b 4 Aug 1841, d 5 Nov 1864, age 23-3-2, Tuftonboro; Mary J., b 1844, not listed in 1860 census; George F.+, b Sep 1849; and Marilla A. aka Anna M.+ (Young) Gilman, b 1854. (NHVR-Marr, Deaths; Census Carroll Co., 1850, p355; 1860, p720; 1870, p419; 1900 Soundex; Parker's Wolfeboro Banns, 1789-1854, n.p.)

JEREMIAH SMITH, b 10 Sep 1809, Whitestown, NY, res. of Dover, d 26 Apr 1861, Somerville, MA, age 52; m ca 1835, Dover, Harriet F. (   ) [b ca 1815, of Dover, alive 1845, same town]. He was ordained at Andover, MA on 20 Nov 1839. Jeremiah and Harriet F. had been members of First Church, Dover; he was dismissed to South Church, Andover, MA on 25 Feb 1845; wife Harriet F., dismissed 23 Feb 1845. (Hurd's Strafford Co. Hist., p828; Heritage's Dover VR, p232,236)

JEREMY, b 1757, of Durham; at age 18, husbandman, he enlisted in Capt. Winborn Adam's Co. on date of 2 Jun 1775. (Stackpole's Durham, V1, p123-124)

JEREMY aka Jeremiah, b 1781, Dover, s/o Timothy and Lydia (Demeritt) Young, d 13 Dec 1848, native town; m 13 Jun 1803, Rochester, Hannah aka Anna Kimball [b 1776, Dover, d 14 Sep 1862, native town]. Jeremy was named a son and heir of Timothy Young of Dover by will signed 16 Dec 1813, proved 25 Apr 1820, and listed as resident of Dover from 1810-1840. In 1810 his age was 26-45; family contained 13 members, suggesting possibly two households under one roof: another male of same age group, two females under 45 years, five males under 10, two 16-26, and five females, two under 10, one 10-16, and two 16-26. In 1830 he was age 40-50, with household of spouse 50-60, five males, two 15-20, two 20-30, and one 30-40, and three females, one each age 5-10, 15-20, and 20-30. In 1840 his age was 50-60, household made up of spouse of 60-70 years, two males, one age 15-20, one 20-30, and four females, one age 10-15, one 15-20 and two under 30. From 1850-1860 widow Hannah was listed as head of family in Dover, Ward 3. In 1850 son Ezra D. and daughters Mary R., Lydia D. and Ellen F. lived at home. Only members of family in 1860 were daughters Lydia D. and Ellen F. In 1870 single daughters Lydia and Ellen formed their own household in Dover, Ward 3, value of estate set at $5,000.

Jeremy and brother Nathaniel worked in partnership as tanners. As co-grantors, they bought up numerous properties in Dover for their place of work by the riverside. For full listing of properties, see Nathaniel and Elizabeth Young of Dover. Jeremy and Nathaniel held the mortgage on brothers Eben D.'s and James H.'s homestead farm in Madbury by deed of 13 May, rec'd 27 Oct 1830; see James H. Young of Madbury for full details. Single daughter Ellen F.'s will of 23 May 1885, proved 24 Sep 1887, named as Co-Execs. nephew Augustus Young and niece Rebecca Young [children of brother Augustus Young]; witnesses Sarah E. Billings, Clara S. Foss, George E. Durgin [Strafford Co. Probate 86:518]. The following bequests were made: to Sarah Varney of Dover, $75.00; to Mercy Mann, wife of Joseph Mann of Dover, $50.00; to Ann Wentworth, widow of Nahum Wentworth of Rollingsford, $25.00; to her nieces, daughters of deceased brother Augustus Young, Mary Elizabeth Wentworth, Rebecca Young and Anna Young, one share each in the Cochecho Aqueduct Association and one-fourth share each in all her household goods and furniture; to her nieces' sister, Lydia Ellen Moulton, the remaining one-fourth share of the household effects; to her brother Timothy R. Young, one-third part of one half of her homestead situate in Dover; and to nephew Augustus Young, son of Augustus Young deceased, and said nieces Mary Elizabeth Wentworth, Lydia Ellen Moulton, Rebecca Young and Anna Young, all the remainder of her personal and real estate in equal shares. Jeremy, Anna and most of their children were buried at Pine Hill Cemetery, Dover.

Ch. b Dover: Ezra D., b 30 Sep 1803, tanner, d pre 1885;
William Augustus aka Augustus, b 1805, d pre 1885, Dover; Mary
R., b 12 Feb 1808, d 22 Mar 1860, Dover, age 52; Timothy
Roberts+, b 19 Nov 1810 [Bowdoin College records gave his year
of birth as 1811]; Lydia D., b 26 Jul 1815, d 27 Aug 1876,
Dover, age 61; Frances Ellen aka Ellen F., b 22 Mar 1821, d
19 Sep 1887, age 66-5-28, Dover; and Charlotte, b ___, d
17 Jun 1825, Dover. (Heritage's Dover VR, p70; NH Gen. Rec.,
V5, No.2, p114; Frost's Dover Cem., V1, #406E; Census Straf-
ford Co., 1810, p863; 1830, p304; 1840, p547; 1850, p77; 1860,
p670; 1870, p85; NHVR-Deaths; LDS I.G.I. BR; Bowdoin College
Grads., p409)

    JOANNA, b ca 1750, Belmont; m 26 Dec 1768, Belmont,
Simeon Bean [b ca 1745, of same town]. (NHVR-Brides)

    JOEL, b 1801, Farmington, s/o Joseph and Sarah (Pinkham)
Young, d 6 Sep 1865, Middleton; m (Intentions) 30 Mar 1828,
Farmington, m 27 Apr 1828, Farmington, Mary J. Durgin [b 1813,
Farmington, d/o Jeremiah and Lydia (Hodgdon) Durgin, d 29 May
1886, Alton]. Joel learned the blacksmith's trade, setting
up shop in Farmington, New Durham or Middleton. As of 1827
he was taxed on personal property in Farmington, and by the
1830 census listed as resident of this town, age 20-30, with
spouse age 15-20, and one male and one female both age under
five. By 1840 Joel was on the census returns for New Durham,
age 30-40, with spouse age 30-40 and family of four males, one
under 5, three age 5-10 and two females, one each under 5 and
10-15.   In 1850 Joel, spouse and children lived with the
family of Ebenezer Blazo [b 1809, ME] and wife Sally Blazo [b
1804] in Middleton; children at home, Sarah A., Samuel P.,
Joseph, Rosilla, Mary J. and James. As of 1860, he and Mary
had their own home in Middleton; children at home, Mary J. and
Ellen F. In 1870 widow Mary J. lived with son Samuel and his
family in Middleton.

    By deed of 14 Apr 1819, rec'd 13 Sep 1836, Joel and
younger brothers Samuel, Joseph, John K. and Hiram H., all
minors and of Farmington, purchased from [uncle] Moses Young
of Wakefield a moiety of Moses' one-half share of Lot 64, 2nd
Div., Wakefield. By quitclaim of 10 Jun 1826, rec'd 23 Jun
1827, Joel of Farmington sold back his share of 80 acres land
in his father's estate in Wakefield to his widowed mother
Sarah for $100.00 [Strafford Co. Deed 132:45]. Widow Mary J.
filed Admin. Papers 2 Oct 1865, in which she declined the
administration of Joel's estate and nominated son Samuel Young
as a suitable person for that trust [Strafford Co. Probate
#2565].   On the following day, Admin. Bond was posted for
$1,000.00, appointing Samuel Young as Admin., with sureties
John D. Roberts and Henry B. Horne [Strafford Co. Probate
77:6]. Samuel declared that "from the circumstances and conditions of said estate...that the same should be administered
as insolvent." Inventory was returned by Augustus G. Orne,
Charles L. Cook and Isaiah H. Place 30 Oct 1865, allowed 7 Nov
1865 [Strafford Co. Probate 78:2]. The 15-acre homestead farm

in Middleton was appraised at $200.00. Total amount of personal estate which included some debts, farming and mechanics tools, live stock, provisions and produce, furniture, books, maps, and misc. articles, came to $178.17. Grand total of real and personal estate, $378.17.

Petition for widow's allowance was filed 7 Nov 1865 by Mary; she was granted $100.00 from the personal estate [Strafford Co. Probate 75:218]. She filed a Homestead Petition 1 Apr 1867, stating Joel died possessed of one half of a certain dwelling house, barn and lot of land in Middleton on the north side of the highway leading from Middleton Corner to Wakefield, that Joel died 6 Sep 1865, and prayed that a "Family Homestead" at value of $500.00 (if said estate shall be of that value) be set off and granted her; approved 3 Sep 1867 [Strafford Co. Probate 60:331]. Samuel, Admin., returned his account 3 Dec 1867, allowed same date [Strafford Co. Probate 78:480]: cash on hand per inventory of personal estate and money collected from notes, $167.98; cash paid out per widow's allowance, funeral expenses, last sickness, rates and taxes, and expenses of admin., $189.78; balance due Admin., $21.80. He then petitioned on same date for partition of his father's estate in order to receive his share inasmuch as he was a tenant in common with Joel Young, late of Middleton; allowed 3 Mar 1868 [Strafford Co. Probate 60:229]. Likewise on same date Samuel brought in his counter-petition with the statement that the personal estate was not sufficient to pay the demands against the same by the sum of $300.00; and he prayed for a License to Sell as the homestead was appraised for under $200.00; approved same date [Strafford Co. Probate 60:350]. License to sell was granted to Samuel on the same date of hearing 3 Mar 1868 [Strafford Co. Probate 79:9].

Ch. b Farmington: Sara A., b 1828; Samuel P.+, b Jul 1831; Joseph, b 1834; James, b 18 Dec 1838, twin, d.y.; Rosilla, b 18 Dec 1838, twin. Ch. b New Durham: Mary J., b 1840, alive 1860; and James H.+, b 1841. Ch. b Middleton: Ellen F., b 1851. (Census Strafford Co., 1830, p60; 1840, p337; 1850, p99; 1860, p62; 1870, p203;Farmington TR, V1, p311,417; NHVR-Births, Deaths, Marr; LDS I.G.I. BR; Biog. Review, XXI, p597)

JOHN, b ca 1680-1700, Dover Neck, s/o Thomas and Mary (Roberts) Young, died pre Apr 1741, native town; m ca 1728, Dover, Elizabeth (   ) [b 1680s, alive 1756, Dover]. By father's deed of gift signed 18 Mar 1726, rec'd 20 Mar 1727/28, the 24-acre homestead in Dover was devised to John, full title to take effect upon his mother's death. It would be his home as of date of signing as long as he provided a home for his mother and reimbursed his siblings by legal money for their shares in the estate. In addition he and brothers Jonathan, Nathaniel, Eleazer, and Samuel each received a one-fifth share of land in Rochester held by Thomas as original proprietor, which the siblings except for Jonathan sold to Moses Wingate for 48 pounds by deed signed 10 Mar 1730, rec'd

6 Oct 1733; witnesses Ebenezer Downs, Robert Evans [NH Prov. Deed 19:391]. John was listed as resident on the 1732 Town Census of Dover, having signed the Petition to Jonathan Belcher. By vote of the legislature 8 Jul 1734, John was granted a two-thirds share of Lot 248, Dover.

Two personal notes on John's family life are sounded. The first is found within the baptismal records of the Rev. Jonathan Cushing of First Church, Dover: his wife Elizabeth and four children, Thomas, Ann, Mary and John [Jr.] were baptized 28 Mar 1736. Then by date of 12 Mar 1741 at John's home, indicating probably the last stages of his illness, "Mary Young and Hannah and Susanna, daughters of John," were baptized. "Mary Young" may have referred to his mother getting on in years who desired to make the Covenant, rather than a daughter Mary, namesake of the paternal grandmother. The second note, based on the three children under the age of seven cited in the administration of John's estate at which time his age would have been about 61 years, is the strong misgiving in assigning to John the status of eldest sibling. To make a very fine distinction, it would seem more credible if John had been the eldest issue by Thomas' second wife Mary, rather than the eldest son of Thomas by his first marriage.

John died intestate Mar/Apr 1741, survived by widow Elizabeth and six or seven children. Later that year Elizabeth was listed as head of household in Dover Parish [Dover Neck], taxed at six shillings and four pence towards the town's ministerial support. She was named Admin. of John's estate in Letters of Admin. filed 29 Apr 1741, wherein she applied for the support of mother-in-law Mary Young, an "ancient woman," and three children under the age of 7 [NH Prov. Probate 15:91]. Warrant for John Wingate and Stephen Roberts to appraise the estate was dated 29 Jul 1741 [NH Prov. Probate 15:116]. Inventory totalled 640-1-2; real estate included the 24-acre homestead farm, the dwelling house, barn and four acres adjoining lands of John Kenney and Samuel Willey, all assessed at 423 pounds; the estate was rated insolvent [NH State Papers 33:47]. During Admin. by deed dated 4 Nov 1751, rec'd 26 Jul 1756, Elizabeth sold a tract of 16 acres Common Lands in Rochester for 40 pounds to Samuel Varney of Dover; witnesses Nicholas Tower, Thomas Young (son?) [NH Prov. Probate 50:315]. On 11 Jun 1753, warrant was made to view the estate which was under improvement "to be shewn you by Elizabeth Young his widow & Joseph Drew who married a Daughter of the Deceased." Elizabeth's account was returned 25 July 1756, in which she mentioned three sisters of John, although not named, who received monies [NH Prov. Probate No. 1065].

Ch. b Dover, all bp 28 Mar 1736: Mary+ (Young) Drew, b ca 1720; Thomas, b 1720s; Ann, b 1720s; and John, b 1720s. Ch. b Dover, bp 12 Mar 1741: Hannah and Susannah. (Heritage's Dover VR, p142,146; NH State Papers, V24, p697; LDS I.G.I. BR; Tibbetts Gen., TMs, p283; Holbrook's 1732 Census, p73-75)

JOHN, b 1740s, of Madbury, poss. s/o Samuel and Hannah (   ) Young; an adult when he purchased land in New Durham from Jonathan Meserve of Madbury, Gent., for twenty pounds, by deed signed 19 Mar, rec'd 16 Apr 1787: Lot 49, 2nd Div, land which Meserve purchased of James Davis, drawn to original right of Ebenezer Jones; witnesses Ebenezer Tasker, Daniel Meserve [Strafford Co. Deed 7:556].

JOHN, b 1750s, of Barrington; signer of the Petition in favor of Joshua Foss, Jr., 19 Jul 1773 [to be named Justice of the Peace for Barrington] and the Association Test in 1776 for Barrington. (Wilson's Assoc. Test, p122; NH State Papers, V11, p151)

JOHN, b 1750s, of Ossipee: listed as head of household in Ossipee in 1790, with family of four males under 16 and five females. (Census Strafford Co., 1790, p95)

JOHN, b 1750s, of Ossipee. Documentary evidence is not conclusive enough to assign the 100-acre Lot 14, Ossipee to a particular settler among the four grown men of Ossipee who were known as John Young in 1796. Purchase of this lot was made by a John Young of Ossipee at public auction by tax deed of 8 Apr, rec'd 27 Oct 1796, for 1 pound-2 shillings; witnesses Enoch Danforth, Winthrop Smart [Strafford Co. Deed 23:163]. John sold these 100 acres, "the whole of lot by Thompson's survey," to William Jones of Boston, by deed signed 15 Oct 1798, rec'd 19 Aug 1799, for $150.00; witnesses Joseph Fogg, Thomas Whittle [Strafford Co. Deed 31:110]. Interestingly enough, in 1829 part of Lot 14, Ossipee was listed in the inventory of the estate of John C.+ Young's, b ca 1782, Ossipee.

JOHN, b 1751, New Market, s/o Thomas and Rebechah (   ) Young, d 9 Mar 1819, age 68, Wolfeboro [Addition]; m 26 Nov 1777, Newfields [South New Market], Mary Burleigh [b 16 May 1757, Newfields, d/o William Burleigh, d 1 Sep 1838, age 81, Wolfeboro]. John held extensive properties in New Durham, New Market and Wolfeboro, a great deal of which he inherited from his grandfather Thomas Young of New Market whose will was signed 2 May 1767, proved 27 May 1767. See also deed of John's father Thomas, signed 4 Apr 1778, rec'd 20 Dec 1786, by which Thomas conveyed to John his moiety of the "homestead plantation" in New Market and Durham, the other half of which John had possessed since the probate of his grandfather's will in 1767. For disposition of the New Market property, the Rock. Co. Grantor/Grantee Index would have to be searched. Mary Burleigh's parents were part of the contingent of homesteaders who relocated from Newfields to Wolfeboro in the 1790s. John's properties in Ossipee, parts of Lots 1, 2, 6, 7, 8, 9, were clustered at the extension of Ossipee which abutted the northern town line of Wakefield and the n.e. town line of Wolfeboro, situated in that section which was annexed to Wolfeboro and thereafter known as the Wolfeboro Addition by December 1800. A petition of protest to the annexation on date of 28 May 1795, Wolfeboro was signed by nine residents,

John Young among them: "Your petitioners pray that Your Honor would in Your great wisdom disunite said Addition of land and annex the Same land to the now town of Ossipee from which it was formerly taken." The counter-petition of 26 May 1800 won the day, wherein the feeling was expressed that the Addition had always been considered as part of and belonging to the town of Wolfeboro prior to the enactment. See Topography for full description of the Wolfeboro Addition. While early land records on the original purchases of Lots 2-7 were not accounted for in the Dover Grantor/Grantee Index, later land records showed that John, as Grantor, conveyed much of this land to his sons.

John of Ossipee purchased 100-acre Lot 9, Ossipee by deed signed 18 Apr 1791, rec'd 27 Oct 1796, from Thomas and Mary King of Conway for 60 pounds; the acreage adjoined north and n.w. of Benjamin Clark's land on the line between Lots 9 and 10 at one end and the Wolfeboro Addition or highway at the other end; witnesses Joseph Fogg, Sanborn Blake [Strafford Co. Deed 23:167]. He sold one-half of Lot 9, "divided by a straight line through the middle to the other end," to Archibald Young of Boston, trader, for $1,000.00 by deed of 24 Jul, rec'd 26 Jul 1815; witnesses Stephen Hyde, Henry Hyde [Strafford Co. Deed 85:323]; kinship to John of Wolfeboro Addition unknown. In the following month Archibald Young and wife Dorcas sold these fifty acres of Lot 9 to Archibald Augustus Webb Young of Boston.

Even though property lines concerning Lot 1 of Ossipee proper, Wolfeboro Addition, and Wolfeboro proper, can be a cause for confusion, it is believed nonetheless that John of Wolfeboro Addition was the principal in the three following transactions. Part of Lot 1, 74-1/2 acres in the Wolfeboro Addition was bought by deed of 4 Jun, rec'd 6 Jun 1801, from Jonathan Warner of Portsmouth, Rock. Co., for $240.00; witnesses Daniel Rindge, Isaac Rindge [Strafford Co. Deed 36:375]. This same acreage was mortgaged to said Warner on same date of signing, rec'd one week later, 13 Jun 1801, for $240.00, due and payable 18 months hence; witnesses the said Rindges [Strafford Co. Deed 36:420]; mortgage redeemed by deed of 4 Feb, rec'd 15 Feb 1803 for $1.00; witnesses Peter Pearse, Isaac Rindge [Strafford Co. Deed 41:272]. Fifty acres of the "original" Lot 1 in Wolfeboro, beginning at s.w. corner of land formerly owned by Michael Reade, was sold by John to John Cook Jr. of Wakefield, by deed signed 23 Feb 1813, rec'd 14 Apr 1813, for $300.00; witnesses Joseph Wiggin, Jonathan Copp [Strafford Co. Deed 75:181]. Please note that the Michael Reade family later had dealings with John's three sons William, John C. and Samuel B. Young. Purchase of 44 acres of Lot 1, Ossipee with buildings on line between Lot 1 and Lot 8 was made by deed signed 20 Jan 1814, rec'd 8 Aug 1814, from Benjamin and Rachael Taylor of Ossipee for $600.00; witnesses Mark Wiggin, John Burleigh [Strafford Co. Deed 80:67]. These 44 acres were later deeded to son William [cited below].

As early as 1799 John began to partition off his estate in Wolfeboro to sons William and Samuel B., both of Wolfeboro. He sold three parcels of land to William: (1) 50 acres of the 500-acre Lot 2 in the Wolfeboro Addition, drawn to original right of James Stootly, for $1.00, by deed dated 5 Jul 1799, rec'd 9 Feb 1802; witnesses Moses Hodgdon, Sally Burleigh [Strafford Co. Deed 39:122]; (2) a total of 15 acres taken from Lots 2, 6, and 7, by deed of 23 Mar 1801, rec'd 9 Feb 1802, for $90.00; witnesses Joseph Fogg, John Burleigh [Strafford Co. Deed 39:123]; (3) 44 acres of Lot 1 in Ossipee by deed signed 24 Mar 1818, rec'd 22 Oct 1819 [his last], for $600.00; witnesses William Sawyer, John Lang [Strafford Co. Deed 104:490]. To [son] Samuel B., he sold: (1) 116 acres in the western part of the above-mentioned Lot 2, by land of Richard Glover and Moses Brown for $470.00, by deed of 7 Mar 1806, rec'd 12 Feb 1808; witnesses Joseph Fogg, Jonathan Fellows [Strafford Co. Deed 56:461]; (2) five acres land of Lot 2 by Lot 1, by quitclaim of 18 Apr 1816, rec'd 23 Jun 1819, for $76.00; witnesses Samuel Wiggin, Mark Wiggin [Strafford Co. Deed 104:156]. John, designated as "honorable father," purchased from son John C. of Wolfeboro 18 acres, part of the 500-acre Lot 8, Ossipee, by land of Benjamin Taylor, by deed signed 18 Mar 1806, rec'd 11 Feb 1808. See son John C. for full details.

John and Mary were buried at Old Cemetery on the road from Ossipee Corner to Smith Hill, their burial sites near those of sons Samuel B. and Nathaniel. Known ch. b Newfields or Wolfeboro Addition: William+, b 8 Jan 1775; prob. Mary+ (Young) Wiggin, b 1779; John C.+, b ca 1782; Samuel B.+, b 28 Apr 1784; and Nathaniel+, b 1795. (Loud's Cemetery Recs., p126,129; Fitts' Newfields, p683; Wiggin Gen., p56; NH State Papers, V13, p740,741)

JOHN, b ca 1755, Scotland, res. of Ossipee, d pre 5 Sep 1822, Ossipee. John, known as the "Highlander," may have settled as early as 1775 in Ossipee, for he was granted 100 acres of 500-acre Lot 16, Ossipee, situated on the road from Wolfeboro to Wakefield per an agreement made by the Comm. of Masons Propriety to give to "Duncan, James & Alexander Mac-Knaughton and John Young a proper quit Claim Deed of 100 acres of Land to each one of them...a Copy of Agreemt given to the Scotch Settlers, Portsmo April 28, 1775." By way of footnote, John mortgaged the 500-acre Lot 17 and 100 acres of Lot 16 in Ossipee by deed signed 10 Jul, rec'd 13 Jul 1779, through the Mason Patent Committee, for five shillings; witnesses Daniel Rogers, John Penhallow, John Peirce [Strafford Co. Deed 2:408]. The first tax inventory on record for Ossipee in 1802 showed that John was rated at $12.37, the sixth highest rated resident: aside from livestock he owned two acres tillage, twelve mowing, fourteen pasturing, and 272 acres wild land.

John of Ossipee mortgaged to son John, by deed of 6 Apr 1809, rec'd 22 Apr 1811, part of Lot 17 bounding on Lot 16, and part of Lot 21, for the sum of $2,000.00; witnesses Joseph

Fogg, Joseph Pitman [Strafford Co. Deed 67:231]. The intent
of the deed was that John Jr. was to work it to good advan-
tage, return half the profit, and allow father to use and
occupy the dwelling; otherwise it would become null and void.
Two acres of Lot 17, Ossipee were sold to Joseph Pitman by
John of Ossipee and son John Young III, by deed signed 19 Sep
1810, rec'd 25 Dec 1816, for $100.00; witnesses John Goldsmit-
h, Samuel Quarles [J.P.]. As events turned out, son John aka
John III predeceased his father in 1816.

Administration of John Sr.'s estate was granted to Daniel
Young 2nd of Ossipee [prob. son] 5 Sep 1822; bond of $1,000
with sureties Daniel Hanson, William Reynolds [Strafford Co.
Deed 30:48]. Appraisal of the estate was made by John Burleigh, John C. Young and Frederick Cate; they made return on
8 Oct 1822, attested to same date [Strafford Co. Probate
29:201]. Real estate was not included in inventory. Personal
estate contained livestock, farming tools, furniture, miscellany, bedding, portrait of Duncan Young and one pew in the
Ossipee Meeting House all valued at $287.53; judgment recov-
ered against John Sweasey on mortgage set at $88.81; good
notes worth $309.26. Total value not including outlawed notes
of $128.95, was appraised at $685.60. As Admin., Daniel 2nd
made his accounting 16 May 1827, attested to same date [Straf-
ford Co. Probate 35:462]: inventory of estate and four notes
not originally included were worth $847.63; credit of $505.49
for the expenses paid by him for the funeral, administration
costs, surveying, appraisal, and John's highway tax for 1822;
balance due from Admin., $342.14. [Strafford Co. Probate
35:462].

Known ch. b Ossipee: John C.+ aka John III, b 1780s; and
prob. Daniel aka 2nd, b 1780s. (Ham Gen., p25; NH State
Papers, V28, p140,141; Merrill's Carroll Co., p591,594)

JOHN, b ca 1761, Dover, s/o Capt. Thomas Young, d 1 Aug
1813, Ossipee; m 7 Sep 1783, Berwick, ME, Sally Nason [b ca
1760, Berwick, ME, alive 1817, Ossipee]. John was named a son
and heir of Thomas Young of Dover by will signed 7 Apr 1791,
proved 25 Apr 1795, receiving a moiety of land in Lebanon, ME.
John was head of family in Ossipee in 1810, age 45 plus, consisting of spouse age 26-45, three males, two 10-16 and one
16-26, and six females, four under 10, two 16-26. One of
John's first purchases of land was by deed of 10 Feb 1806,
rec'd 24 Sep 1813, when he and co-grantor Aaron Hanson of
Ossipee bought from Jonathan Copp of Wakefield 110 acres of
Lot 37, 2nd Div., Wakefield, drawn to original right of Samuel
Austin of Wakefield; witnesses John Palmer, William Copp
[Strafford Co. Deed 76:614]. John conveyed his moiety of 50
acres of Lot 37, 2nd Div., Wakefield by deed of 3 Dec 1808,
rec'd 25 Feb 1815, to son Daniel of Ossipee for $100.00; Sally
ceded dower rights; witnesses Joseph Fogg, Aaron Hanson
[Strafford Co. Deed 82:347]. Before his death in 1813, John
aka John 2nd, quitclaimed to Joseph Nason of Ossipee, 55 acres
or one-half of the 110-acre Lot 32, Div. 2, Wakefield for

$110.00, by deed signed 1 Sep 1806, rec'd 28 Nov 1807; wit-
nesses Joseph Fogg, Joseph Wentworth [Strafford Co. Deed
55:471].

Letters of Admin. were filed 10 Sep 1813 on John's estate
by widow Sally who gave bond of $2,000.00, with sureties Moses
Young [brother] of Wakefield and James Dore of Newfields, York
Co., MA [Strafford Co. Probate 20:203]. Inventory of his
estate was taken by Seth Fogg, Ezekial Wentworth, both of Ossipee, and John Lang of Effingham, their return allowed 25 Dec
1813 [Strafford Co. Probate 14:552]. The homestead farm, part
of Lot 4, consisted of 50 acres with buildings rated at
$800.00; personal estate of sundry farming utensils, sleigh
and harness, neat stock, furniture, bed and bedding, etc. was
valued at $207.69. Part of the estate included two notes of
hand, one of which was signed by Moses Young of Wakefield for
$10.35, and another for $11.79 signed by William Keay, Moses'
co-grantee in the purchase of Lot 64, 2nd Div., Wakefield;
grand total of real and personal estate, $1,087.69. Sally's
dower rights were set off 5 Aug 1816 by Seth Fogg, Ephraim
Leighton and Jacob Leighton all of Ossipee, Benjamin Cook of
Wakefield and John Lang of Effingham, allowed 8 Oct 1816
[Strafford Co. Probate 18:442]: as the full third of the
estate, 15 acres, part of Lot 4 in Ossipee beginning on the
eastern side of the road leading through Ossipee to Effingham,
then running n.e. by said road by lands of Ephraim Leighton,
David Philbrook, and Daniel Young, with one-third part of the
dwelling house, cellar and barn. See Moses and Mary (Chadwick) Young of Ossipee and Wakefield for former share in Lot
4, Ossipee. License to sell at public auction that part of
the homestead to raise $400.00 to discharge debts was granted
to Sally, Admin., 30 Aug 1816 [Strafford Co. Probate 18:72].
A second license to sell to raise an additional $50.00 was
granted Sally on 18 Feb 1817, this document entitled "reversion of the widow's dower" [Strafford Co. Probate 20:148].

Six months later Sally sold at public auction John's farm
of fifty acres in Ossipee for $450.00 to James Roberts of
Ossipee and Adam Brown of Wolfeboro by deed of 2 Aug, rec'd
18 Aug 1817, witnesses Daniel Young and Joseph Nason [Straf-
ford Co. Deed 98:3]. An interesting footnote to this Vendue
was the social custom then of furnishing liquid refreshment
for the occasion, in this case, rum. Six quarts rum were an
item charged to the expenses of the Vendue at the cost of
$2.25. The account of administration from 1 Aug 1813 to Dec
1817 was returned by Sally to the court on 11 Oct 1819,
allowed following day [Strafford Co. Probate 23:490]. Credits
included $287.69 on the amount of personal estate per inven-
tory and $484.00 on the amount of sales of real estate; total
$771.69. Charges included the support of three children
[assumed to be under seven years of age] each at $3.00/week:
Rhoda for 180 weeks/$94.00; John for 150 weeks/$78.00; and
Nathaniel for 32 weeks/$16.00; and expenses incurred in admin-
istering the estate, that is, funeral charges, probate fees

and payment of notes of hand amounting to $602.98; total charges, $790.98. Balance of $19.29 remaining in the hands of the Admin. was to be divided among the heirs-at-law.

Ch. b Berwick, ME: Daniel+, b 1785. Known ch. b Ossipee: Nathaniel, b ca 1806; John+, b 26 Jul 1807; and Rhoda, b ca 1810. (LDS I.G.I. VR; NHVR-Marr; Census Strafford Co., 1810, p758; Loud's Cem. Recs., p125; Young Family Recs., courtesy of Marjorie S. Heaney)

JOHN, b 3 Dec 1760, Newfields [South New Market], s/o Joseph and Anna (Folsom) Young, d 25 Jun 1808, Eastport, Washington Co., MA; m 7 Dec 1793, his home town, Anna Mason [b ca 1765, of Newfields]. John had relocated to Eastport, Wash. Co., MA [Maine in 1820] by 1806. When of Eastport, John sold his one-twelfth share of property in Durham and New Market which he derived from the partition of his father's estate to brother Joseph of New Market for $80.00, by deed signed 1 Oct 1806, rec'd 21 Jan 1807; witnesses Paul Chapman, Wentworth Cheswell [Strafford Co. Deed 54:11]. No known children. (LDS I.G.I. BR; Fitts' Newfields, p683)

JOHN, b 1760s, New Market, most likely gr.s/o Thomas and Sarah (Folsom) Young; as an adult John purchased 420 acres land in Wolfeboro by deed signed 4 Oct 1790, rec'd 24 Apr 1794 for 300 pounds from David Chapman of New Market: according to Chapman, "100 acres of the above is what I purchased of John Emerson who lives now on said land...the remainder of land is what I purchased of Francis Matthew that lies in Wolfeboro, except 200 acres which I sold to John Emerson"; witnesses John Bryent, James Smith [Strafford Co. Deed 18:189]. On the same day of signing given above, John sold to the said David Chapman, cordwainer for 300 pounds, by deed rec'd 1 Mar 1796, 100 acres in Durham at Lamprey River Bridge and north on Lamprey River to the mouth of Piscassic River to lands of Joseph Smith and Job Savage; witnesses John Bryent, James Smith [Strafford Co. Deed 22:133]. This may be the same John Young who quitclaimed his right and title to 100 acres in Wolfeboro "on land that I now live on that lays on the west side of the main river N. 14," to Jacob Clark of Wakefield, by deed of 25 Oct, rec'd 4 Nov 1802, for $200.00; wife Mary released dower rights; witnesses John Perkins, Timothy Perkins [Strafford Co. Deed 41:100]. In the latter deed John and Mary's place of residence was given as Adams, Grafton Co.

JOHN, b 1767, Dover, d 2 Nov 1836, bur. native town; m 29 Mar 1814, Barrington, age 47, widow Ruth Morrill [b 1788, Barrington, d 30 Mar 1844, Dover, age 56, bur. Dover]. John may have been a widower himself. In 1810 he was resident of Dover, single, age 26-45; in 1830, John was head of household in Dover, age 60-70, with spouse age 40-50, and one female under 15. In 1840, Ruth was widow and head of household in Dover, age 50-60, other members of household were four females, one age 15-20, two 20-30 and one under 40. It would be safe to assume that some of these daughters were by Ruth's first marriage; they were never identified. John and kinsman

Daniel Young of Dover were residuary legatees of Benjamin Church of Dover who died childless, by Church's will drawn 7 Apr, proved 30 Sep 1812; witnesses Philemon Chandler, Dominicus Hanson, J. P. Gilman; kinsman Ephraim Young of Dover also received a "set" amount of acreage from Church's estate [Strafford Co. Probate 13:14].

For the connection between Benjamin Church of Dover and the Youngs of Dover, it should be noted that said Church was the grandson of widow Mercy (Hanson) Church of Dover who married second Nathaniel Young of Dover. Beyond that his relationship with John, Daniel and Ephraim remains obscure. As for the lineal connection between John, Daniel and Ephraim, the records do not tell the story. It is known that the three lived in close proximity on the old Church or "Faxon" farm before and after being named as heirs of Benjamin Church. Said Church devised to John one half of his homestead farm in Dover and one half of the buildings except for his wife Eunice Church's life estate in the house, also one half of all his household furniture after the decease of Eunice Church, reserving out of said farm six acres given to Ephraim Young, also twelve acres land in Rochester that was set off to Church by Execution from Stephen Evans. To Daniel Young he devised the other half of his homestead farm and buildings with the above exceptions; also all the land he bought of Otis Watson except what John Young owned, also half the stock and farming utensils and half of all the household furniture after the decease of his wife. To Ephraim Young, he bequeathed six acres land around his house "where he thinks best to take it."

Before John received this legacy, he had purchased 10-1/4 acres land at Toll End, Dover, adjacent to lands of Ezra Green and Benjamin Church, by deed signed 5 Feb 1808, rec'd 13 Nov 1811, from Samuel and Lydia Watson of Dover for $481.75; witnesses Benjamin Church, John Horne, Daniel Young, Daniel Watson [Strafford Co. Deed 69:289]. After being named heirs-at-law, John and Daniel were co-grantees in the purchase of 1-1/4 acres land in Dover which held a dwelling house on the Toll End road adjacent to William K. Atkinson, by deed signed 10 Mar, rec'd 22 Mar 1814, from Benjamin and Hannah Horn of Dover for $200.00; witnesses Benjamin Garland, William K. Atkinson [Strafford Co. Deed 78:654]. For John's purchase of Daniel's one-half share of the Church's field, dwelling house and barn on Toll End Road, plus other pasturage by quitclaim signed 2 Apr, rec'd 5 May 1814, see Daniel and Eleanor W. Young of Dover. The quitclaim stressed however that John "may have use and occupy one-half of the dwelling house with the privilege of making cider at the cider mill." By way of tradeoff with Daniel, John quitclaimed to Daniel on same date of signing and recording of the former deed, his interest in two parcels of land formerly owned by said Church, 80 acres land in Dover bounded by lands of John Garland and Joshua Ham and by the Toll End Road leading from Dover Meeting House to Barrington, plus 20 acres in Dover, for $100.00; Ruth released dower rights; witnesses Moses Neal, Eleanor Smith [Strafford Co. Deed 79:191]. In addition John quitclaimed to Daniel for $30.00, by deed of 20 Sep 1815, rec'd 20 Apr 1816, his share in the Church dwelling house in Dover; Ruth released dower rights; witnesses Aaron W. Young and Susannah Young Horn [Strafford Co. Deed 89:424]. John and Ruth were buried at Pine Hill Cemetery, Dover. (Heritage's Dover VR, p226; Frost's Dover Cem., V1, Plot #115; Census Strafford Co., 1810, p863; 1830, p317; 1840, p553)

JOHN, b 1770s, of Alton; res. of Alton in 1830, age 50-60. Members of family were female age 40-50, two males, one 5-10, one 10-15, and six females, two under 5, one 5-10, two 10-15, and one under 20. (Census Strafford Co., 1830, p105)

JOHN aka Jr., b 1770s, Dover; head of household in Dover in 1800, age 16-26, with household of four females 45 plus and one female age 10-16. (Census Strafford Co., 1800, p160)

JOHN, b 1770s, of Dover; m ca 1792, Dover, Sarah (   ) [b ca 1775, of Dover]. Ch. b Dover: Elizabeth, b 3 Mar 1793; see spouse Paul D.+ Young of Dover. (Ham's Dover Marr, TMs)

JOHN, b 1770s, of Durham; head of household in Durham in 1810, age 26-45, with spouse of same age group. Family consisted of three males and two females, all under 10. (Census Strafford Co., 1810, p544)

JOHN, b ca 1775, of Ossipee; m 16 Mar 1798, Northwood, Sarah Runnels [b ca 1780, of Barrington]. (NHVR-Marr; Moses' Northwood, V1, TMs, p51)

JOHN, b 12 Dec 1776, Dover, s/o William and Susannah (   ) Young, d 27 Sep 1854, Tuftonboro; m ca 1800, Tuftonboro, Hannah Ham [b 3 Mar 1780, Dover Neck, d/o David and Hannah (Runnels) Ham, gr.d/o Daniel Ham, d 1 Jul 1875, Tuftonboro]. John was head of household in Tuftonboro from 1810-1850. Wife Hannah was member of the First Christian Church of Center Tuftonboro that was organized 27 May 1820; it is probable that the John H. Young listed as member of the church was their son. In 1810 his age was 26-45, as was spouse, with family of one male 10-16, one female 45 plus, and four females under 10; in 1830, his age was 50-60, spouse was 40-50, and household contained one female age 90-100, two males, one 5-10 and one 10-15, and five females, one age 5-10, one 10-15, two 15-20, and one 20-30. In 1840, his age was 60-70, household containing spouse age 50-60, two males, one age 5-10, one 10-20, and two females, one age 15-20, one 20-30. In 1850 John, age 74, and wife Hannah, age 70, ran a large household in Tuftonboro which included married son Mark and his family, widowed daughter Hannah Ladd and granddaughter Hannah J. Ladd, and Asa M. Gould [b 1834], age 16. From 1860-1870 Hannah lived as widow with son John and wife Mary.

Ch. b Tuftonboro: Nancy+ (Young) Ladd, b ca 1808; Susan+ (Young) Ladd, b ca 1810; Hannah H.+ (Young) Ladd, b 1813; Mark F.+, b 1817; Dolly+ (Young) Ladd, b ca 1820; and John H.+, b Feb 1822. (Census Strafford Co., 1810, p743; 1830, p385;

1840, p365; Census Carroll Co., 1850, p332; Ham's Dover Marr,
TMs; NHVR-Births, Deaths; Ham Family, **Reg.** 26:391,392; Runnels
Gen., p193, #2264; Merrill's Carroll Co., p432; Ladd Gen.,
p54,55)

JOHN aka Jr., b ca 1780, Ossipee; head of household in
Ossipee in 1810, age 26-45; family of spouse age 26-45, two
males under 10, and four females, three under 10, one 10-16.
(Census Strafford Co., 1810, p758)

JOHN, b 1780s, of Effingham; resident of Effingham in
1830, age 40-50. Household consisted of one male and one
female both 20-30. (Census Strafford Co., 1830, p397)

JOHN, b ca 1785, of Somersworth, head of household in
Somersworth in 1840, age 50-60, with household of spouse of
similar years, one male age 10-15 and three females, two age
5-10, one 15-20. (Census Strafford Co., 1840, p576)

JOHN, b ca 1785, of Wolfeboro; resident of Wolfeboro in
1810, age under 26; household contained female [prob. mother]
age 45 plus, one male 10-16, and two females 16-26, most
likely siblings. (Census Strafford Co., 1810, p737)

JOHN aka Jr., b 1800s, of Alton, resident of this town
in 1830, single. (Census Strafford Co., 1830, p104)

JOHN, b 7 Jul 1803, Dover Neck, prob. s/o Lt. Thomas and
Nancy (Drew) Young, d 1 Oct 1872, native town, carpenter; m
14 Jun 1843, same town, Rose Tuttle Pinkham [b 31 Jan 1808,
Dover, d/o Elijah and Eunice (Tuttle) Pinkham, d 23 Jan 1891,
age 82-11-23, her native town]. More than likely John was the
younger son and heir named in the will of Lt. Thomas Young,
signed 7 Jun 1841, proved 7 May 1844. John, joiner, bought
from Thomas land bounded by the corner of Thomas' dwelling
house on Dover Neck, by deed rec'd 17 May 1827. See Lt.
Thomas Young for full details. John was head of household in
Dover from 1840-1870: in 1840, before his marriage, his age
was 30-40 with only one other member of family in his household, one female age 40-50, believed to be his elder sister
Patience [b ca 1800]. From 1850-1870, Rose was listed as
John's spouse and Roxanne listed as daughter in Dover, Ward
3. By 1870, Rose's mother Eunice Pinkham, age 83 [b 1787]
lived with them. Ch. b Dover: Roxanne P., b Nov 1846, alive
in 1900, age 53, resident of Wentworth Home for the Aged,
Central Avenue, Dover. (Scale's Dover, p324; Pinkham Gen.,
p31; Census Strafford Co., 1840, p561; 1850, p154; 1860, p744;
1870, p74; 1900 Soundex; NHVR-Deaths; Young Family Recs.,
courtesy of Marjorie S. Heaney)

JOHN, b 23 Mar 1804, Ossipee, eldest s/o Daniel and
Elizabeth (Nason) Young, d 23 Feb 1886, Freedom, NH, widower
age 81-11-0; m1 8 Jan 1827, Effingham, Eleanor aka Eunice
Durgin [b 1810, Nottingham, d 31 Mar 1869, age 70, Freedom];
m2 early 1870, Freedom, Effelinda (   ) [b 1818, of Freedom,
alive 1870, same town]. John was named son and heir of Daniel
Young of Freedom by his will signed 1 Oct 1866, proved 31 Aug
1874. He and Eunice were both of Effingham at time of marriage. He was head of family in Freedom from 1840-1870. In

1840 his age was 30-40, with spouse of same age, two males, one under 5, one age 10-15, and one female 5-10. From 1850-1860 Eleanor aka Eunice was named as John's spouse. In 1850 teenagers Sarah E. and George lived at home; value of estate set at $1,400.00; in 1860 only son George was at home. In 1870 second wife Effelinda was listed as his spouse; they lived by themselves. Ch. b prob. Effingham by Eunice: Sarah E., b 1834; and George F.+, b Oct 1836. (Census Strafford Co., 1830, p416; 1840, p246; Census Carroll Co., 1850, p154; 1860, p630; 1870, p306; 1900 Soundex; NHVR-Marr, Deaths)

JOHN, b ca 1805, Ossipee; from 1830-1840 John was head of family in Ossipee, age 20-30, with spouse of same age and one male under 5 in household. In 1840 his age was 30-40, with family of spouse age 20-30 and one female under 5. (Census Strafford Co., 1830, p416; 1840, p225)

JOHN, b 26 Jul 1807, Ossipee, s/o John and Sarah aka Sally (Nason) Young, d testate 30 Apr 1875, age 67-9-4, home town; m (Intentions) 23 May 1835, Wolfeboro, Lucinda Burleigh [b 30 Oct 1812, of Ossipee, prob. d/o Nathaniel and Betsey (   ) Burleigh, d 11 May 1878, age 65-6-12, Ossipee]. He was resident of Wolfeboro at time of marriage banns. He and Lucinda were listed on the 1850-1870 census returns for Ossipee and were members of the Freewill Baptist Church. Family members in 1850 were daughter Mary J. and child Joseph Burleigh, age 13 [b 1837]; in 1860, only Mary J.; and in 1870, Betsey Burleigh [b 1792], age 78, son-in-law Joseph T. Burleigh, widower, age 37 [b 1833], and grandson Arthur Y. Burleigh [b 1866], age 4.

John's will was drawn 13 Apr 1875, proved 1 Jun 1875, and named son-in-law Joseph T. Burleigh as his Exec.; witnesses Francis P. Adams, George W. Tibbetts, William A. Smith [Carroll Co. Probate #5841]. He devised to wife Lucinda all his real and personal estate for her natural life, and to the said Joseph Burleigh, the sum of $150.00. Joseph Burleigh was to hold in trust the balance of John's real and personal estate for his son Arthur Y. Burleigh while he was a minor under 21 years of age. John, Lucinda and daughter Mary J. were buried at the Stevens-Burleigh Cemetery, Ossipee. At same family cemetery, Betsey Burleigh, cited above, was b 21 Jun 1792, d 21 Jan 1871; she was spouse of Nathaniel Burleigh, b 20 May 1791, d 20 Apr 1874. Ch. b Ossipee: Eliza, b 1837, d 11 Jun 1843, age 6, Ossipee; and Mary J.+ (Young) Burleigh, b 1843. (Loud's Cem. Records, p125,126; NHVR-Brides, Deaths; Census Carroll Co., 1850, p208; 1860, p681; 1870, p372; Morning Star, p375; Parker's Wolfeboro Banns, 1789-1854, n.p.)

JOHN, b Feb 1826, ME; resident of Strafford in 1900, and lived with wife Lottie M. (   ) Young, age 55 [b Dec 1844, ME]. In the 1870s John and Lottie M. lived in Dover where a son was born. Ch. b Dover: William H., b 1876, resident of Dover, m 1 Jan 1897, Dover, Hattie M. Pearson [b 1876, East Rawson, N.S., Canada, d/o Andrew and Harriet (   ) Pearson]. (NHVR-Marr; 1900 Soundex)

JOHN, b 1831, of Sanbornton; m ca 1855, Sanbornton, Abby ( ) [b 1830, same town]. They were residents of Sanbornton in 1860. Ch. b prob. Sanbornton: Fred, b 1859. (Census Belknap Co., 1870, p58)

JOHN, b 1833, Dover; resident of Dover at age 30 when he enlisted in the U.S. Navy 31 March 1863 at Boston, MA for one year as Coal Heaver. He served on U.S.S. "Ohio," "North Carolina," and "Virginia" and was discharged 28 May 1864 as 2nd Class Fireman from "Virginia," term expired. (Soldiers & Sailors, p1180)

JOHN, b ca 1835, of Northwood, alive 1900, Strafford, widower; m ca 1860, Charlotte M. Trask, b 31 Dec 1839, Bradford, ME, d/o John and Rebecca (Page) Trask, d 17 Oct 1900, Strafford, buried at Pine Hill Cemetery, Dover. (NHVR-Deaths)

JOHN, b ca 1835, of Tamworth; m 16 Mar 1869, Tamworth, Athalinda Heard [b ca 1840, of same town]. (NHVR-Marr)

JOHN, b 1854, Glasgow, Scotland, s/o Alexander and Arabella (McIlroy) Young, alive 1900, Rochester, weaver and overseer in mill, naturalized citizen; m 18 Aug 1878, Rochester, Emma Lord [b Oct 1856, Tamworth, alive 1900, Rochester]. John, wife and sons Edwin B. and Stanley L. lived in Rochester in 1900. Ch. b Rochester, not traced further: daughter b 10 Aug 1883, not with parents in 1900; Edwin B., b Aug 1884; and Stanley Lord, b 31 Jan 1885. (NHVR-Marr, Births; Rochester TR, Births, p31; 1900 Soundex)

JOHN, b Sep 1859, resided in 1900 at Central St., Farmington with wife Nellie B. ( ) Young, age 40 [b Oct 1860]. (1900 Soundex)

JOHN A., b 1839, Wolfeboro, s/o Hollis and Betsey Ann (Drew) Young, shoemaker, alive 1867, Dover; m ca 1866, Dover, Anna Francis [b ca 1846, Dover]. By the 1860s, his parents had moved to Dover. As resident of Dover at age 22, John enlisted in the U.S. Navy 20 Jul 1861 for three years as a Landsman and served on the U.S.S. "Ohio" and "Satelette." He was discharged 18 Mar 1863 from "Satelette", leaving P.O. address of Biddeford, ME. Ch. b Dover: Edward Leonard, b 15 Nov 1867. (NHVR-Births; LDS I.G.I. BR; Soldiers & Sailors, p1180)

JOHN B., b 16 Feb 1819, Barrington, s/o Jonathan and Hannah (Hall) Young, d testate 1 Aug 1882, age 63-5-14, native town; m early 1840s, Dover, Mary J. ( ) [b 3 Jul 1821, Barrington, d 27 Jan 1886, age 64-6-24, her native town]. John and spouse were listed on the census returns for Barrington from 1850-1860. In 1868 John became the guardian of Herbert D. Young, half-brother. John B.'s will drawn 16 Jun 1881 and proved 3 Oct 1882, named his son Frank C. as sole Exec.; allowed on date of probate; witnesses A. W. Buzzell, Albion A. Smith, Charles W. Bumford [Strafford Co. Probate 94:77]. John B. left to his wife Mary J., the entire estate real and personal "for the rest of her life." After her death the whole property was to go to son Frank C.; what money there was after debts were paid off was to be equally divided between

the surviving children. Bequests of $50.00 were made to each
of his other children: Ellen A. Grover, wife of Benjamin F.
Grover; Clara B. Young; John W. Young; and Mary E. Young who
also was to receive his watch. John, Mary J. and children
were buried at Pine Grove Cemetery, Barrington. Ch. b Barrington: Ellen A.+ (Young) Grover, b 1845; Clara B.+ (Young)
Durgin, b 1846; Mary Elizabeth, b 1848, d 1933, Barrington;
John W., b 1851, d 1901, Barrington; James B., b 1856, d 1875,
Barrington, not named in father's will of 1881; and Frank C.,
b 1858, d 1955, age 97, Barrington. (Barrington Graveyards,
Plot 18, Lots 3E and 3W, p132,133; Census Strafford Co., 1850,
p578; 1860, p189; NHVR-Brides, Deaths)

  JOHN B., b 1836, of Somersworth, miller, d 30 Apr 1875,
age 39-5-0, same town; m1 7 Mar 1857, Somersworth, Ellen R.
Hartford, [b 1837, of Somersworth, d 23 Apr 1864, age 27-8-28,
same town]; m2 27 Aug 1864, Somersworth, Mary E. Bagley [b
1849, of Somersworth, alive 1876, Rochester]. John and Ellen
were residents of Somersworth in 1860 with daughter Emma E.
at home. Widow Mary (Bagley) Young m2 20 Nov 1876, Somersworth, Benjamin Wentworth [b 12 Jun 1822, ME, his second
marriage, res. of Rochester, s/o Samuel and Lydia (Thompson)
Wentworth]. Benjamin Wentworth m1 16 Sep 1847, prob. Rochester, Nancy Merrick [b ca 1825, of New Hampton, d Dec 1875,
Rochester; he was brother of Sabrina (Wentworth) Young, wife
of Thomas Young of Rochester]. John B., Ellen and two
daughters were buried at Forest Glade Cemetery, Somersworth.
Ch. b Somersworth: Emma E.+ (Young) Norton, b 1858; Mattie,
b 1862, d 26 June 1919, age 57-5-9, Somersworth. (Census
Strafford Co., 1860, p347; Wooley's Somersworth Cem., Plot
#13; Wentworth Gen., V2, p584; NHVR-Brides, Marr)

  JOHN B., b 1867, Belmont, prob. s/o John S. and Mehitable
B. (Cate) Young, carpenter; m ca 1885, poss. Laconia, Fannie
C. Morrison [b ca 1870, Plymouth]. Ch. b Laconia: daughter
b 22 Apr 1886. Ch. b Lake Village: John Percey, b 2 Oct
1887. (NHVR-Births)

  JOHN C. aka John III, b 1780s, Ossipee, s/o John Young
the Highlander, d pre 17 Feb 1816, home town; m 9 Jan 1811,
Ossipee, Olive Stillings [b ca 1790, Ossipee, d/o Rooke and
Olive (   ) Stillings, alive 1819, home town]. John Jr.'s
first purchase of land in Ossipee was 100 acres of Lot 39,
adjacent to the s.e. corner of Lot 38, by deed signed 8 Feb,
rec'd 3 Apr 1799, from John and Dorothy Cooley of Ossipee, for
$250.00; witnesses Joseph Pitman, Nathaniel Pitman, Joseph
Fogg [Strafford Co. Deed 31:59]. Before his marriage, John
was mortgagee on 100 acres of 500-acre Lot 17, Ossipee,
granted by his father by deed dated 6 Apr 1809, rec'd 22 Apr
1811. This date of signing became a significant factor in the
administration of John C.'s estate, particularly with regard
to the property rights of daughter Catherine after his death.
The terms of the deed itself shed much light on John Jr.'s
personal circumstances in 1809: the deed stipulated that John
Jr. was to work the farm and share both the dwelling house and

produce with his father; otherwise it would be null and void. Letters of Admin. on his estate were filed by widow Olive on 17 Feb 1816; bond of $6,000.00 posted with sureties Samuel Quarles Esq. and John Chick, both of Ossipee [Strafford Co. Probate 19:69].

Inventory of John's estate was made by Samuel Quarles, Joseph Pitman and Moses Roberts, all of Ossipee; their appraisal was submitted to the court 13 May 1816, allowed same day [Strafford Co. Probate 20:401]: personal estate was valued at $312.88; real estate included 100 acres of Lot 39, Ossipee, commonly called the Cooley Place, rated at $200.00; "the house where he lived and right in the farm he carried on" was rated at $375.00; 3 notes of hand set at $27.57; grand total of real and personal property, $887.88.

Olive became guardian of daughter Catherine on 9 Jun 1818, bond of $1,000.00 posted with sureties John Chick and Richard Stilling, both of Ossipee [Strafford Co. Probate 22:159]. This decree was amended by 8 Oct 1822, when Catherine was made ward of James Reynolds of Ossipee with bond of $1,000.00, sureties William Reynolds and Moses Colby, both of Ossipee [Strafford Co. Probate 30:97]. Olive returned her account of the estate 6 Oct 1818, attested to same date: she charged herself $340.45 by the amount of appraisal of personal estate per inventory; her credits were expenses of $229.08 paid out for funeral, probate fees and costs, sickness in the family, the widow's allowance, and the support of two children under seven years of age for 104 weeks at 50 cents/week. Balance of $111.37 was owing to heirs [Strafford Co. Probate 23:76]. Therein lay the news of an infant son born to John and Olive, who died before 1818; the son lived fifteen months after his father's death. By virtue of license to sell on date of 3 Feb 1819, Olive sold at auction in the name of her daughter and ward Catherine, to John Young of Ossipee, Yeoman, 100 acres of 500-acre Lot 17, real estate derived from the estate of John Young Jr., late father of said ward, "to contain all the land that John Young lived on by date of **6 April 1809**," by deed signed 19 Mar 1819, rec'd 16 Jul 1822, for $405.00; witnesses Richard Stillings, Samuel Poland, Samuel Quarles [Strafford Co. Deed 113:472].

Guardianship account of Catherine given by James Runnels was allowed 11 May 1824 [Strafford Co. Probate 34:101]. He recapped Olive's charges of sums paid out: balance due heirs Oct 1818, $137.87. Sales of real estate sold 15 Mar 1819, brought in $405.00, plus interest of $74.90; total $479.90. Support of Catherine from Oct 1818 to 11 Oct 1823 when she reached the age of seven, at 50 cents/week came to $130.00; misc. expenses set at $192.41; balance due from Olive, $425.36. James Runnels charged himself with the following sums received: above balance paid him by Olive, $425.36, plus interest of $91.66; "Dn", $84.86; sub total of $432.16. He credited himself with the following sums paid: 8 notes per receipt, $15.70; administrative expenses, highway taxes for

1822-1825 at $2.25/year; and boarding and schooling of Catherine for 24 weeks up to 8 May 1826; total $81.52; balance due from guardian to heir, $432.16Olive, widow, by deed of 17 Feb 1816, rec'd 18 Mar 1820, quitclaimed to her mother Olive, widow of Rooke Stillings of Ossipee, all her right to the estate of her father for $20.00; witnesses John Chicke, Samuel Quarles [Strafford Co. Deed 106:481]. Known ch. b Ossipee: son b ca 1815, d.y.; Catherine, b 11 Oct 1816. (NHVR-Marr)

JOHN C., b ca 1782, Ossipee, s/o John and Mary (Burleigh) Young of Wolfeboro Addition, d pre 10 Nov 1829, Ossipee; m 18 Feb 1807, Ossipee, Elizabeth C. aka Betsey C. Lord [b 1782, ME, alive 1860, Ossipee]. John C.'s homestead at the time of his death was 110 acres of Lot 14, Ossipee. In 1830 Betsey was widow and head of family in Ossipee, age 40-50, with household of two males age 20-30, and three females, one under 5, one age 10-15, and one 15-20. It is believed that Betsey lived with son Luther and his family in Ossipee in 1840 per census that year; this was indeed the case from 1850-1870. Betsey was appointed Admin. of John C.'s estate 10 Nov 1829; bond of $5,000.00 posted with sureties Samuel Quarles, Alvah Moulton and Moses Brown [Strafford Co. Probate 30:447].

Before he married, John C. of Wolfeboro purchased 18 acres as part of the 500-acre Lot 8, Ossipee, by land of Benjamin Taylor for $216.00, from Samuel Smith of Ossipee, by deed signed 23 Mar 1803, rec'd 12 Feb 1808; witnesses Joseph Fogg, Timothy Walker [Strafford Co. Deed 56:456]. He sold this acreage to John Young, "his honorable father" by deed signed 18 Mar 1806, rec'd 11 Feb 1808, for $260.00; witnesses Joseph Fogg, Jonathan Dodge [Strafford Co. Deed 57:59]. He also purchased 100 acres land with buildings on Lot 24, Ossipee, by lands of Richard Beacham and Thomas Wiggins, from Jonathan and Miriam Fellows of Ossipee by deed of 27 Mar 1806, rec'd 12 Feb 1808, for $1,200.00; witnesses Joseph Fogg, Joseph Wentworth [Strafford Co. Deed 56:458]. As co-grantee with brothers Samuel B. and William, all of Wolfeboro, he bought "the front 100 acres" in the Wolfeboro Addition as part of the 300 acres originally drawn to the right of Jonathan Warner, located on the eastern corner of John Young's lot, from Michael Reade, Lydia Reade, Polly Reade, Nancy Reade, and Sally Reade, all of Dover, by deed signed and rec'd 9 Feb 1815, for $700.00; witnesses Carr Leavitt, Caleb Drews [Strafford Co. Deed 82:242]. A land deed was not obtained to document John C.'s purchase of the 110-acre homestead on Lot 14, Ossipee, yet it clearly was the only piece of real estate listed in the inventory of his estate at the time of his death. Research of land deeds after 1815 could reveal the disposition of the 100 acres of Lot 24, Ossipee; his brothers Samuel B. and William may have bought up John C.'s one-third share of these 100.

Inventory of John C.'s estate was taken by appraisers Joseph V. Quarles, Moses Brown and James Sceggel, completed

2 Dec 1829; approved by the widow 12 Dec 1829; attested to by committee 28 Dec 1829 [Strafford Co. Probate 38:430]. Real estate comprised the 110-acre homestead, Lot 14, set at $1,300.00; amount of demands owing to estate deemed doubtful, $513.73; demands deemed good, $728.20; total value of real and personal property, $3,328.65. Widow Betsey and sons Wentworth L. and Luther sold by tax deed of 4 Mar 1830, rec'd 16 Mar 1831, part of Lot 14 upon the demand held by John Saunders, Collector of Taxes [Strafford Co. Deed 151:194]. Upon the petition of widow's allowance 4 Mar 1830, Betsey was allowed to choose such articles from the inventory of personal estate which pleased her up to the sum of $200.00 [Strafford Co. Probate 42:203]. The estate was rated insolvent by Commissioner Aaron Roberts of Wolfeboro on date of 12 May 1831 [Strafford Co. Probate 41:313]. Widow Betsey returned her account 16 Sep 1831; approved same date [Strafford Co. Probate 41:445]. The amount of personal estate per inventory was $2,028.65, less interest collected of $114.27 which reduced debt. Net personal estate was $1,924.00; debts on 59 accounts which she herself had paid were set at $1,924.00; balance due from Admin., $114.41.

Known ch. b Ossipee: Wentworth L.+, b 18 Feb 1808; Luther+, b 18 Feb 1809; and Patience L., b 11 Jun 1821, teacher, single, d 19 Feb 1890, age 70-8-8, Sanbornton. (Census Strafford Co., 1830, p415; Loud's Cemetery Recs., p83; NHVR-Deaths)

JOHN C., b 25 Apr 1789, Wolfeboro, s/o Zachariah Young, d 25 Jun 1866, age 77, native town; m 20 Dec 1810, Ossipee, Sally Smith [b 25 Apr 1790, Lee, d 25 Sep 1842, age 52, Ossipee]. John C. was named son and heir of Zachariah Young of Wolfeboro by his will drawn 20 Nov 1842, proved 11 Feb 1851, and designated sole Exec. He was to receive a one-sixth part of his father's real and personal estate in Wolfeboro. John, a native of Wolfeboro, was listed on its census returns from 1830-1850; he and his family became members of the Freewill Baptist Church. In 1830 his age was 40-50, with family containing a female age 50-60, one male age 10-15, and four females, one age 5-10, three 15-20. In 1840 he and his spouse were age 50-60, with family of male parent figure age 70-80 [most likely Zachariah], and two females, one age 5-10, one 30-40. In 1850 he was widower and head of household; family members were single daughter Abby A. and son John H. and daughter-in-law Catherine. By 1860 son John H. had been listed as head of household with wife Catherine and father John C. as members of household. In effect title to the homestead had been conveyed to son John H. before 1860 by the terms of John C.'s will drawn 2 Nov 1853, proved 4 Sep 1866, by which son John H. was designated sole Exec. and residuary legatee of his estate; witnesses Hollis Burleigh, Benjamin Sceggel, John Burleigh [Carroll Co. Probate #5823]. John C.'s married daughters, Elizabeth Sceggel, Sarah Cook, Mary Jane Stevens and Abigail A. Brown were each to receive a one-fourth share of the household bedding and particular pieces of furniture. The remainder of the household effects were to be equally shared among his five grown children. Both John C. and Sally were buried at the Stevens-Burleigh Cemetery on the road from Ossipee to North Wakefield, as were son John H., spouse and daughter Belinda. Ch. b Wolfeboro: Mary Jane+ (Young) Stevens, b 3 Oct 1811; Eliza+ (Young) Sceggel, b 4 Jun 1813; John H.+, b 2 Oct 1817; Belinda, b 1824, d 13 Jun 1834, Lowell, MA, bur. Ossipee; Abigail A. (Young) Brown, b 1831, m' 1850s; and Sarah+ (Young) Cook, b ca 1825. (Census Strafford Co., 1830, p436; 1840, p387; Census Carroll Co., 1850, p391; NHVR-Marr, Deaths; Loud's Cemetery Recs., p126,127; Morning Star, p375)

JOHN C., b ca 1800, Dover, m 15 Mar 1827, Dover, Lydia B. Harris [b ca 1807, Chester]. (Heritage's Dover VR, p184)

JOHN C., b 29 Sep 1824, Barrington, s/o Hiram and Fannie (Clark) Young, res. of Gilmanton, machinist, d 16 Oct 1887, age 63-0-21, Manchester; m 24 Sep 1843, Amherst, Harriet C. (Villam) Read aka Reed [b 1828, b Sandwich, d/o William and Elkinia (   ) Villam of Haverhill, MA, d 20 Mar 1867, Gilmanton, 2nd marriage]. Before 1850, John and Harriet lived in Mt. Vernon with son George P. The family then moved to Gilmanton by 1850 with one son listed on the census return, and to Sandwich by 1860 when three sons were at home. In 1870 John C. was widower living in Gilmanton with his sons. In later years he relocated to Manchester as did his parents. Ch. b Mt. Vernon: George P.+, b 1847; Charles, b 1851; and Eddie, b 1858. Ch. b Sandwich: Emma E., b 1860, d 29 Jan 1870, age 10, Gilmanton. (Census Belknap Co., 1850, p54; Census Carroll Co., 1860, p776; 1870, p21; NHVR-Marr, Deaths)

JOHN C., b Mar 1855, Alton, s/o Henry and Sarah (Witham) Young, alive 1900, native town; m1 11 Dec 1877, Rochester, Jennie aka Jane L. Bennett [b 8 Jan 1853, Sanford, ME, d/o George and Harriet M. (Farnham) Bennett, d 29 May 1889, age 36-4-21, Alton]; m2 1890s, prob. Alton, Minnie L. Cunningham [b Aug 1873, of Rochester, alive 1900, Alton]. John and Jennie raised their four children in Alton. He and second wife Minnie made their home in Alton as well, listed in the 1900 census; members of household were "two children by his first wife," George and Cora. While variance of ages were shown in NHVR-Marr for John C. and second wife Minnie, both records agree that John C. was son of Henry and Sarah Young of Alton. John's age in marriage record to first wife Jennie Bennett agrees with the 1900 Census; however, the entry on second wife Minnie L. (Cunningham) points up three discrepancies with 1900 Soundex and birth records on the four children by Jennie. It seems wise to place trust in John's first marriage record and birth records of his children for a more accurate picture. Daughter Nellie M. m 21 Sep 1898, Rochester, Frank E. Dorr [b ca 1870, Sanford, ME].

Ch. b Rochester by Jennie: Nellie M. (Young) Dorr, b 1876 (see above); George H., b 4 Apr 1882; and Cora E., b

10 Jan 1884, not traced further. Ch. b Alton by Jennie:
Chester A., b 22 Oct 1886, d 10 Aug 1889, Alton. (1900
Soundex; NHVR-Births, Brides, Deaths, Marr)

JOHN E., b 1841, Barrington, s/o Jonathan and Sophia M.
(Ricker) Young, d 5 Jan 1875, age 34, native town, survived
by wife; m 1860s, Dover, Clara A. Hodgdon [b 1842, Dover,
alive 1875, Barrington]. John lived at home at age 20 in
1860, listed under his parents' census return. He then was
listed in 1870 as head of household himself in Barrington with
spouse Clara A. and children Ruth E., Julia A. and George H.
Some of the family members, if not John, relocated to Dover
in the 1870s. This was revealed by his children's marriage
licenses which stated they were "of Dover." John predeceased
his mother Sophia in 1875; his surviving children were named
as heirs-at-law in Sophia's will signed 3 Sep, proved 5 Nov
1889: Ruth E. Furbush, Julia A. Young, George H. Young and
Helen F. Young. Daughter Helen F., resident of Dover, m 4 Oct
1890, Dover, George E. Joy [b ca 1865, of same town].

Ch. b Barrington: Edmund H., b 22 Jan 1862, not listed
in 1870 census; Julia A.+ (Young) Hanford, b 1865; Ruth E.+
(Young) Furbush, b 12 Sep 1866; George H., b 7 Aug 1868, alive
1889; Helen F. (Young) Joy, b 2 Dec 1871, see above; and 6th
child, Jonathan E., b 22 Sep 1874, not named in grandmother's
will of 1889. (LDS I.G.I. BR; Census Strafford Co., 1870,
p15; NHVR-Births, Brides, Deaths)

JOHN E., b 1855, Sherman, ME, s/o Moses C. and Mary (   )
Young of Dover [no main entry]; m 7 Oct 1880, Dover, Ella S.
Smith [b 1857, Poland, ME, d/o Thomas W. and Eliza C. (   )
Smith]. (NHVR-Marr)

JOHN F., b 1763, of Ossipee, d 20 Mar 1814, Ossipee, age
51, Revolutionary Solder, buried at Ossipee Cemetery, near
Effingham line. (Loud's Cem. Records, p141)

JOHN F., b 1790s, Ossipee, alive 1843, native town; m
4 Nov 1819, Ossipee, Sarah Saunders [b ca 1800, Effingham,
alive 1843, Ossipee]. John F. was head of household in Ossipee from 1830-1840: in 1830, his age was 30-40, with family
of spouse age 20-30, two males, one age 5-10, one 10-15, and
one female under 5; in 1840 age was 40-50, with spouse age
30-40, two males, one age 15-20, one 20-30, and one female
10-15. John F.'s will was written 2 Sep 1843, date of probate
not given; wife Sarah was named sole Exec. and legatee and was
to receive his real and personal estate in both Ossipee and
Effingham "forever"; witnesses Joseph Young, Abigail Young
[Carroll Co. Probate #5828]. (Census Strafford Co., 1830,
p425; 1840, p228; NHVR-Marr)

JOHN F., b 1810, of Gilmanton, res. of Belmont; m ca
1840, Gilmanton, (   ). As of 1870 he was resident of Gilmanton, farm laborer who lived alone. Ch. b Gilmanton: Betsy
A.+ (Young) Bowdron aka Boudron, b ca 1845. (NHVR-Brides;
Census Strafford Co., 1870, p15)

JOHN F., b 16 Sep 1816, Wakefield, s/o Richard Kimball
and Deborah S. (Fernald) Young of Wakefield, d 1 Nov 1882, age

66-1-15, by accident, Rochester, survived by widow; m 29 Sep 1853, Rochester, Abby A. Waldron [b 1831, of Rochester, d/o _____ and Rosilla (   ) Waldron, alive 1882, Rochester]. John and Abby made their home in Rochester from 1860-1870. In 1860 children at home were Herbert and Richard A. In 1870 estate was valued at $6,700; members of household included John F.'s father Richard, age 81, son Herbert, age 15, brother Samuel, age 41, and mother-in-law Rosilla Waldron, age 69 [b 1801]. On 3 Dec 1878, John F. of Rochester was appointed guardian of James M. Young [brother] of Rochester; see James M. Young for particulars. The 1892 map of Strafford Co. indicated that John F.'s home was located in District No. 2, Rochester, close to the Dover/Somersworth line. Ch. b Rochester: Herbert, b 1854; and Richard A., b 1858. (Census Strafford Co., 1860, p506; 1870, p241; NHVR-Marr, Deaths; 1892 Saco Maps, p37)

JOHN F., b 1857, Farmington, s/o Jonathan and Hannah S. (Waldron) Young of Strafford, physician, alive 1896, Dover; m 15 Oct 1896, Farmington, Hattie Ellen Barker [b 1858, Farmington, d/o John and Emily M. (   ) Barker]. As practicing physician in Dover, John applied in 1878 and 1895 for the removal of his parents' remains from Strafford for reburial in Farmington. (NHVR-Marr; Biog. Review, XXI, p350,351)

JOHN FRANKLIN, b Jan 1806, Strafford, youngest s/o Jonathan and Polly (Hill) Young, d testate 9 Dec 1883, Strafford Corners, farmer; m1 (Intentions) 22 Mar 1838, Phoebe Huckins Hayes [b 9 Nov 1813, Strafford, d/o John and Mary (Chamberlain) Hayes, d 9 Nov 1866, age 53, Strafford]; m2 pre 1870, Elizabeth C. (   ) [b 1825, ME, alive 1878, Strafford]. John was named son and residuary legatee of Jonathan Young of Strafford by will signed 7 Dec 1844, proved 2 Sep 1851; his legacy, "all his land in Strafford not disposed of by deeds." He and Phoebe were listed on the 1850 and 1860 census returns for Strafford; members of family included children John F., Ann E. and Marilla, as well as Phoebe's mother Mary Hayes, age 61 [b 1789]. In 1860 his estate was valued at $3,000; children at home in addition to the three above, Mary J., and Emma A. By 1870 John and 2nd wife Elizabeth were listed on the returns for Strafford; the two youngest daughters were at home. Per 1871 county survey map his homestead was situated in District #1, Strafford Corners.

John's will was drawn up 26 Nov 1878, proved 1 Jan 1884, naming eldest child and only son John F. as Exec. and residuary legatee; witnesses William Rand, Levi L. Dame, Hattie E. Dame [Strafford Co. Probate 94:392]. Wife Elizabeth was to receive $2,000.00. Surviving daughters Ann E. Webster, Mary J. Blaisdell, and Emma A. Blaisdell were each to receive $500.00. Family members were buried at Strafford Corners Cemetery. Ch. b Strafford by Phoebe: Victoria, b ca 1840, not mentioned in will of 1878; John Frank aka John Franklin+ aka Jr., b 7 Sep 1842; Anna E. (Young) Brewster aka Ann E.+ (Young) Webster, b 1845; Marilla A., b 1847, d 12 Sep 1867; Mary Jane+ (Young) Blaisdell, b 1850; and Emma A.+ (Young)

Lambert aka Emma A. (Young) Blaisdell, b 1855. (Census Strafford Co., 1850, p143; 1860, p575; 1870, p383; Stiles' Cemeteries, Grid 1B-3, p207; NHVR-Brides, Deaths; Hayes Gen., V1, p202,203; 1871 Sanford & Everts Map of Strafford Co.)

JOHN FRANKLIN aka Jr., b 7 Sep 1842, Strafford, s/o John Franklin and Phoebe H. (Hayes) Young, d 1911, Newburyport, MA, bur. Strafford Corners Cemetery; m 20 Oct 1887, Newburyport, MA, Hannah (Langlands) Gould [b ca 1845, of Newburyport, 2nd marriage]. John lived at home up through 1860 and was named sole Exec. and residuary legatee by his father's will drawn 26 Nov 1878, proved 1 Jan 1884. He was educated at the public schools of Strafford, attended Wolfeboro Academy, attained his medical degree at Columbia, College of Physicians and Surgeons, studied ophthalmology and gynecology; he went on for further study in 1883/1884 at the Harvard Medical School and in 1889 at New York Polyclinic. He started his medical practice actually in 1870 at Gilmanton, remained there for four years, and then relocated to Newburyport. Ch. b Newburyport: John Franklin Jr., b ca 1889, not traced further. (Stiles' Cemeteries, Grid 1B-3, p207; NHVR-Brides, Deaths; Hayes Gen., V1, p202,203; N.E. Who's, p1047)

JOHN H., b ca 1805, of Meredith; m 1830s, Meredith, Ann Maria Chase [b ca 1810, Meredith, d/o Zachias Chase]. John was head of household in Meredith in 1840, age 30-40, with household of two adult females, one age 40-50, one age 30-40, one male under 5, and one female under 5. Ch. b Meredith: Ann, b 1834; see husband Moses A. Young. (Census Strafford Co., 1840, p164; Meredith Annals, p457)

JOHN H., b 2 Oct 1817, Wolfeboro, s/o John C. and Sally (Smith) Young, d 29 Mar 1887, age 69-5-27, native town, carpenter; m (Intentions) 18 May 1846, Wolfeboro, m 27 May 1846, Wolfeboro, Catherine Y. Cook [b 29 Dec 1816, Wakefield, d/o John and Mary (Young) Cook, d 2 Sep 1898, age 82, Wolfeboro]. John H. was named sole Exec. and residuary legatee of John C. Young by will signed 2 Nov 1853, proved 4 Sep 1866; he received the family homestead. He and Catherine were listed as members of his father's household in Wolfeboro in 1850. By 1860 he was head of household in Wolfeboro, in effect the owner of the homestead; family members were wife Catherine and father John C. In 1870 John H. and spouse lived alone in Wolfeboro, no known children. Catherine's will was signed 20 Sep 1893, probated 4 Oct 1898, naming nephew Edwin H. Stevens of Ossipee as sole Exec.; witnesses Fanny Adams, Susan P. Adams, Francis P. Adams [Carroll Co. Probate #5827]. Edwin H. Stevens was the son of her husband's sister Mary Jane (Young) Stevens of Wolfeboro. She made the following bequests: to sister Jane Cook and brother William R. Cook, equal shares to her savings accounts and promissory notes; to nephew Edwin H. Stevens, the family homestead in Wolfeboro where she then dwelt; and to niece Jennie Brown and Ruth Stevens, daughter of said Edwin, family heirlooms. John H. and Catherine were both buried at Stevens-Burleigh Plot, Ossipee Cemetery. (Census Carroll Co., 1860, p525; 1870, p444; NHVR-Deaths, Marr; Loud's Cem. Recs., p126; Parker's Wolfeboro Banns, 1789-1854, n.p.)

JOHN H., b 1820s, St. George's Bay, N.F., Can., alive 1892, Middleton; m ca 1860s, poss. Middleton, Augusta L. (   ) [b 1820s, of same town]. They were residents of Middleton in the 1870s. The 1892 Strafford Co. map indicated that John H.'s home was located at Middleton P.O., east of the Reservoir. Ch. b Middleton: Charles L., b 1872, not traced further. (NHVR-Marr; 1892 Saco Maps, p19)

JOHN H., b Feb 1822, Tuftonboro, s/o John and Hannah (Ham) Young of Dover Neck, alive 1900, native town; m 9 Feb 1846, Wolfeboro, Mary Ann Gordon [b 1821, of Tuftonboro, alive 1900, same town]. John, wife and family lived in Tuftonboro from 1860-1900. In 1860 son Frank H. and John's widowed mother Hannah lived with them. In 1870 only his mother, age 90 [b 1780] was part of the household. That year son Frank H., age 16, lived with William and Susan A. Blaisdell, [b 1821 and 1831, respectively], Tuftonboro. In 1900 members of household were son Frank H., daughter-in-law Sophia W. (Estes) Young, and boarders Herbert Huntington, age 14 [b Apr 1886, MA] and Arthur W. Huntington, age 11 [b Jul 1888, MA]. Ch. b Tuftonboro: Frank H.+, b Sep 1854. (Census Carroll Co., 1860, p723; 1870, p420; 1900 Soundex; NHVR-Marr; Runnels Gen., p193, #2264)

JOHN H., b 1827, Barnstead, s/o David and Eliza (Hartford) Young, cordwainer, d 9 Mar 1905, age 77-8-0, native town; m 4 Mar 1852, Barnstead, Elizabeth A. aka Anna Caswell [b 3 Aug 1832, Barnstead, d/o Enoch and Judith (Flanders) Caswell, 3 Apr 1891, home town, age 58-8-0]. Elizabeth's mother Judith was born in Alton. John lived alone in 1850 in Barnstead as shoemaker, single, age 23. In 1856 his homestead was Lot 91, 2nd Div., Barnstead. He and Elizabeth were listed on the 1860 census returns for Barnstead with three sons at home, Warren, Alva and John. The 1892 map of Belknap Co. indicated John H. and family lived in Barnstead Parade P.O. east of Lougee Pond. Both John and Anna were buried at Barnstead Center Graveyard. Ch. b Barnstead: Warren A.+, b 10 Sep 1852; Alva A., b 1858; and John C., b Jun 1860. (Barnstead Cem. Inscriptions, p7; Census Belknap Co., 1850, p419; 1860, p327; NHVR-Deaths, Marr; Merrill's Barnstead, p331; 1892 Saco Maps, p27)

JOHN HENRY, b Nov 1839, Wolfeboro, s/o Jeremiah L. and Mary A. (Jackson) Young, shoemaker, alive 1900, Middleton; m1 2 Mar 1863, Alton, Mary Emily aka Emily Mary Cook [b 7 Sep 1841, Middleton, d/o Lewis and Nancy (Jones) Cook of Milton, d 30 Mar 1894, age 54-6-23, her home town]; m2 23 Jun 1898, Rochester, Mary M. (Cloutman) Pike [b Jan 1846 Middleton, d/o William H. and Lucinda (Stevens) Cloutman, alive 1900, Middleton]. At time of first marriage John lived in Tuftonboro. He and wife Mary E. were residents of Middleton in 1870 with two small children at home. In 1900, John and second wife

162

Mary M. lived there by themselves. Ch. b Middleton by 1st
wife Mary Emily: Etta M., b Feb 1864, see husband Charles H.+
Young, b 1852; and Lewis F.+, b Sep 1866. (Alton VR, p644;
NHVR-Brides, Deaths, Marr; Census Strafford Co., 1870, p199;
1900 Soundex)

JOHN HENRY, b 10 May 1841, Farmington, s/o Hiram H. and
Margaret (Hall) Young, d pre Nov 1879, Farmington, shoemaker;
m ca 1858, Farmington, Melissa Downing [b 1839, New Durham,
d/o Royal B. and Fanny G. Downing, her 2nd marriage, former
resident of Holderness; no issue by 1st marriage]. John Henry
was named a son and heir by Hiram H. Young's will signed
25 Jul 1870, proved 8 Apr 1873. In 1860 John and Melissa
lived in Farmington with infant daughter Henrietta, age 1.
During the 1860s they lived for a short time in New Durham
where another daughter was born, then relocated in Canada by
1864 where son Cyrus was born. As widow of Henry, Melissa m3
29 Nov 1879, New Durham, widower Jerome B. Witham [b 1832, New
Durham, s/o Moses and Lydia (   ) Witham, his 3rd marriage].
Ch. b Farmington, Henrietta, b 1859. Ch. b New Durham: Clara
A.+ (Young) Ricker, b 1862. Ch. b Canada: Cyrus F.+, b 9 Jan
1864. (NHVR-Brides, Deaths; New Durham VR, Bk4, n.p.; LDS
I.G.I. BR)

JOHN K., b ca 1805, of Ossipee; in 1840 he was head of
household in Ossipee, age 30-40, with spouse of same age.
There may have been two households listed under one roof as
there was one other male and female of same age bracket, and
four males, two under 5, one age 5-10, one 10-15, and one
female 10-15. (Census Strafford Co., 1840, p224)

JOHN K., b 1810, Ossipee, alive 1850, Dover, trader; m
ca 1829, Dover, Lydia A. (   ) [b 1810, Dover, alive 1850, of
same town]. Marriage records of offspring indicated that they
and father John K. were born in Ossipee. By 1850 census John
K. and Lydia lived in Dover, children listed at home were
Joseph A., Sarah E., Charles W., Curtis P., Henry H. and
Lowell H. Ch. b Dover: Joseph A., b 1830, shoemaker; Sarah
E.+ (Young) Corson, b 1832; Charles W.+, b 23 Oct 1834; Curtis
P., b 1837; Henry H., b 1842; and Lowell H.+, b 1844. (Census
Strafford Co., 1850, p15; NHVR-Marr)

JOHN KIMBALL, b 22 Mar 1802, Dover, clergyman, eldest s/o
Nathaniel and Elizabeth (Kimball) Young, d testate pre 14 Feb
1875, Meredith; m 19 Mar 1833, Durham, Mary Willard Smith [b
10 May 1807, Durham, d/o Ebenezer and Mehitable (Sheafe)
Smith, the youngest of 8 children, alive 28 Apr 1866, Mere-
dith]. John K. lived in Gilford (Meredith) at time of marriage and received a bequest from his sister Eveline A. Young
of Dover by her will drawn 5 Nov 1861, proved 2 Jun 1863.
Mary's father Ebenezer Smith practiced at the bar more than
forty years, was President of the Strafford County Bar Association 28 years, Councillor for Strafford Co., an aid of Gov.
Gilman, and in 1798 was made Judge of the Superior Court, an
office he declined. John graduated from Durham College in
1821, thereafter taught high school in Charleston, SC, closed

a Theological course at the Andover Seminary in 1827, and then was ordained at Meredith Bridge. In 1844, Rev. John K. Young, A.M., was invited to the Board of Visitors at Gilmanton's Theological Seminary. John and spouse were residents of Meredith Bridge in 1850; members of family were daughter Ellen A. and Sally Heuse, age 47 [b 1803]. In 1855 he was elected Superintendent of the School Committee, Meredith. John's will was written 28 Apr 1866, proved 14 Feb 1875, naming wife Mary W. Young as sole Exec.; witnesses Robert E. Merrill, Sarah Merrill, Anna E. Chattle [Belknap Co. Probate #2931]. He devised to wife Mary W. the one undivided half of all his real and personal estate for her sole use and benefit; the other undivided half of his property was to be held in trust by wife Mary W. for their daughter Ellen A. Young. If Mary W. should not be living at time of probate of his estate, then Ellen A. would receive all of the said property. If any of this property should remain unexpended upon the decease of both spouse and daughter, it was to be divided equally between Dartmouth College, The Theological Seminary at Andover, and the Trustees of the Widows' Charitable Fund of New Hampshire for the support of poor and destitute ministers. Ch. b Meredith: Mehitable Augusta, b 3 Jun, d 28 Sep 1834, Meredith, not listed in will; Ellen A., b 31 Dec 1835, alive 1866; Mary Elizabeth, b 3 Oct 1837, d 30 Jun 1840, Meredith; Nathaniel, b 5 Jun 1840, d 3 May 1842, Meredith; and John Hannibal, b 3 Nov 1843, not listed in 1850 census. (Heritage's Dover VR, p71; Ham's Dover Marr, TMs; NHVR-Marr, Deaths; Census Belknap Co., 1850, p17; Lancaster's Gilmanton, p174,175; LDS I.G.I. BR; Quint's Hist. Memos, p90; Meredith Annals, p514; Wentworth Gen., V2, p316; Hurd's Belknap, p821)

JOHN L., b 4 Apr 1865, Dover, youngest s/o Jonathan T. and Elizabeth L. (Demeritt) Young, d 20 Dec 1914, native town; m ca 1890, Frances E. Lord [b 18 Jan 1864, of Dover, d 21 Sep 1929, Dover]. John L. was an heir of his aunt Hannah S. Young of Dover by will drawn 6 Jun, proved 6 Jul 1880; see details under Jonathan and Abigail (Coffin) Young of Dover. He was also the recipient of a one-ninth share of his father's 70-acre farm in Dover on date of 6 Oct 1874; see parents for details. In 1900 he and wife lived at the home of John's brother Jacob D. in Dover. John L., Frances and daughter were buried at John Young Cemetery, Littleworth Rd., Dover. Ch. b Dover: infant daughter, b ca 1901/02, d 9 Oct 1902, Dover. (Frost's Dover Cem., Plot #22; 1900 Soundex)

JOHN P., b 26 Jun 1843, Gilmanton, s/o James H. and Abigail A. (Barker) Young, d 4 Dec 1898, Pittsfield; m1 pre 31 Mar 1866, Sandwich, age 22, Henrietta D. Smith [b 23 May 1840, Sandwich, d/o Thomas and Betsey (   ) Smith, d 2 Feb 1888, Gilford]; m2 6 Sep 1892, Middletown, Conn., Eleanor F. Polley [b 1849, Middletown, Conn., alive 1891, Pittsfield]. At time of marriage to Henrietta, John lived in Moultonboro. At age 19, he enlisted from Gilmanton in Co. A., 15th Regt., NH Volunteer Infantry 1 Oct 1862; mustered in five days later as Pvt. He was discharged to date 13 Aug 1863, giving P.O. address of Pittsfield. In 1870 Henrietta Young lived in Sandwich with her parents Thomas Smith, age 61 [b 1809] and Betsey Smith, age 59 [b 1811], her brother Hartwell Smith, age 17 [b 1853], and her infant son Thomas E. John P. was absent from household in 1870, probably receiving medical care elsewhere for the "malarial poisoning" he contracted during military service. John P. filed petition for an Invalid Pension 27 Apr 1887, Application No. 608,223, Cert. No. 457,195. Henrietta died of cancer. Note that NHVR-Marr gave her year of birth as 1847, Sandwich. Ch. b prob. Sandwich: Thomas E., b 1869. (NHVR-Marr, Deaths; Census, Carroll Co., 1870, p373; Nat'l. Archives Milit. Recs.; Soldiers & Sailors, p760)

JOHN R., b 26 Mar 1827, Madbury, s/o Eleazer and Kezia (Rowe) Young, d 20 Apr 1878, testate, age 51-0-25, Madbury; m 13 Jul 1862, Newington, Abbie M. Clay [b 1846, Madbury, d/o Alpheus and Esther (Lamos) Clay, d 1913, Boston, MA]. In 1850, John was single, a farmer, and lived with the Matilda Demeritt family in Madbury. In 1860 John, age 33, lived with parents in Madbury. By his mother's will drawn 17 Aug 1863, proved 1 Apr 1865, he was named as son and heir. In 1870, he and Abbie M. established their home in Madbury; children at home that year, Mary E., William and Lillian F. In the following year, John was elected to serve as selectman 1871-1872. By an 1871 map of Madbury surveyed by Sanford & Everts, it is shown that John's homestead was located in District No. 4 in the vicinity of Bellamy River. John's own will signed 5 Oct 1877, proved 7 May 1878, appointed Edward J. Hayes of Madbury as Exec., and named wife Abbie his residuary legatee; witnesses Edward J. Hayes, George A. Locke, Hannah Bodge [Strafford Co. Probate 89:317]. He made bequests of $100.00 to each of his surviving children, sums to be disbursed when they reached the age of 21: Mary E., William H., Lillian W., John N. and Bernice A. On 4 Feb 1879, daughter Mary E., minor above the age of fourteen, elected Abbie M. Taylor of Madbury to be her guardian; bond of $500.00 was given by sureties Martin V. B. Felker and Micajah J. Hanscom, neighbors of Madbury [Strafford Co. Probate 95:493]. On same date, guardianship of children under the age of fourteen, William H., Lillian W., John N., and Bernice A., was awarded to the said Abbie M. Taylor of Madbury by bond of $500.00 given by the said sureties Felker and Hanscom [Strafford Co. Probate 95:493].

By all rules and procedures of awarding guardianship to the surviving natural father or mother then or today, it seems more than likely that Abbie M. Taylor was the former Abbie M. (Clay) Young, the natural mother of John's children. Yet if this was the case, her marriage to said Taylor could be pinpointed to pre Feb 1879, in which case this predated her marriage to David Hayes. As widow Abbie (Clay) Young m2 (or m3) 29 Aug 1886, Madbury, David Byron Hayes [b 1843, Farmington, s/o Benjamin Furber and Elizabeth Ann (Waldron) Hayes].

David Hayes married previously in 1875, Judith A. Meserve [b ca 1850, Farmington, d/o Charles G. Meserve]. David and Judith had one son, Fred Byron Hayes. David and Abby (Clay) Young Hayes had one son, David Arthur Hayes, b 22 Jul 1886, Madbury.

Son John N. married 8 Apr 1891, Durham, Hannah E. Smart [b Aug 1871, Durham, d/o John M. Smart [b 3 Sep 1824] and Ellen Mary (Davis) Smart]. John M. Smart was the s/o Enoch and Hannah (Glover) Smart of Durham; Ellen Mary Davis was the d/o Daniel and Caroline (Teague) Davis of Durham. During the 1890s John N. and Hannah lived in Durham, listed on the census returns for Durham in 1900, with their four children, son Athold H., age 7 [b 14 Jul 1892]; Edna J., age 5 [b 1895]; Beatrice L., age 2 [b 1 Apr 1898]; and Emma E., 5 months [b 4 Nov 1899]. John N.'s marriage record stated his mother was Abby M. Hayes.

Ch. b Madbury: Mary Elizabeth, b 14 Aug 1863; William H.+, b 23 Apr 1865; Lillian W., b 25 May 1867; John N., b 1 Mar 1871 (see above); and Bernice A., b 30 Nov 1873. (1900 Soundex; Census Strafford Co., 1850, p481; 1870, p195; Hayes Gen., V1, p93; NHVR-Births, Brides, Marr, Deaths; LDS I.G.I. BR; 1871 Sanford & Everts Maps; Adam's Madbury, n.p.)

JOHN S., b 12 Aug 1831, Upper Gilmanton, s/o Bailey and Polly (Rundlet) Young, d 24 Nov 1885, age 54-3-12, Belmont, carpenter; m1 1853, Gilford, Mehitable B. (Cate) Cook aka Cole, her 2nd marriage [b 1834, Gilford, d/o John Cate, d 31 Mar 1876, Belmont]; m2 1 Nov 1882, Gilford Village, Nellie N. (Merrill) Perkins [b 1844, Gilford, d/o Charles S. and Nancy E. ( ) Merrill, her 2nd marriage]. John S. was named son and heir of Bailey Young of Upper Gilmanton by his will signed 26 Jan 1863, proved 18 Mar 1863; he was to be one of four residuary legatees of Bailey's estate in the event that sibling Ansel F. Young should die in the Civil War. As fate turned out, Ansel died of wounds received in battle. In 1870 John and Mehitable were listed on census returns for Upper Gilmanton; children at home, Herbert S., Harley A., Mary E., and John B. In 1880 and 1884, he was one of two elected supervisors for Upper Gilmanton.

Admin. Papers on John S.'s estate in Belmont were filed 15 Dec 1885 by widow Nellie; only other heir-at-law cited was son Harley A., approved same date, appraisers were J. C. Waldron, Joseph Plummer and Horace Woodward [Belknap Co. Probate #4050]. Ch. b Upper Gilmanton: Herbert S., b 1854; Harley A., b 1856, alive 15 Dec 1885, Belmont; Mary E., b 1864; and John B., b 1867. (LDS I.G.I. BR; NHVR-Marr, Deaths; Census Belknap Co., 1870, p5; Hurd's Belknap Co., p724)

JOHN T., b 1801, Gilmanton, s/o Joseph and Betsey (Shaw) Young, d 5 Aug 1882, age 81, Belmont; m1 19 Oct 1825, Belmont, Betsy S. Young [b 1804, of Gilmanton, d 26 Jun 1844, age 40, same town]; m2 30 Nov 1845, Belmont, Lucy K. Young [b 1815, ME, d 28 Mar 1870, age 55, Belmont]; m3 20 May 1879, Gilmanton, Sarah A. (Knight) Hillsgrove [b 2 Sep 1810, Portland, ME, d/o Abraham and Hannah (Woodward) Knight, res. of Loudon, her 2nd marriage, d 2 Jul 1895, age 86-10-0, Gilmanton]. John's trade was farmer as well as mechanic, listed on the census returns for Gilmanton from 1830-1860. In 1830 his age was 20-30, as was his spouse's, with one female under 5; in 1840 his and his wife's ages were 30-40, with a family of three females, one each under 5, 5-10 and 10-15. From 1850-1860 he and second wife Lucy was listed on census returns for Gilford; at home in 1850 were daughters Priscilla A., Betsey A., and Hannah C. (Young) Sawyer; in 1860 youngest Betsey A. was listed at home. John T., first wife Betsy, second wife Lucy, and married daughter Elizabeth Plummer were buried at Guinea Ridge Cemetery, Gilmanton.   Ch. b Gilmanton by Betsy S.: Hannah C.+ (Young) Sawyer, b 1826; Elizabeth A. (Young) Plummer, b 1834, wife of Levi Plummer, d 20 Jun 1870, age 36; and Priscilla A., b 1836.   (NHVR-Brides, Deaths, Marr; Census Strafford Co., 1830, p277; 1840, p411; Census Belknap Co. 1850, p285; 1860, p154; Folsom's NH Cemeteries, p141; Biog. Review, XXI, p354,355)

JOHN W., b 1810, of Alton; head of household in Alton, 1850, age 40; members of household were Martha B. Young, age 56 [b 1794], George Young, age 8 [b 1842], and Mary A. Moulton, age 16 [b 1834].   (Census Belknap Co., 1850, p364)

JOHN W., b 1843, Gilmanton Iron Works, s/o Nathaniel Badger and Dorothy B. (Lamphrey) Young, alive 1888, Lynn, MA; m1 21 Sep 1862, Laconia, Falista J. Buzzell [b 1844, Barnstead, d/o Aaron and Rhoda B. (   ) Buzzell, d Jul 1872, Lynn, MA]; m2 1871, Lynn, MA, Susan C. Staples [b ca 1850, Lynn, MA, d 12 Feb 1907, home town].   Shortly before his marriage at age 19, John enlisted in Co. A, 15th Regt., NH Volunteer Infantry 12 Sep 1862, mustered in 31 Oct 1862 as Pvt. and was appointed Corp. 29 Jul 1863. He mustered out 13 Aug 1863, giving P.O. address Lynn, MA.   It can safely be assumed that John W. established residence in Lynn, MA.   He filed for an Invalid Pension 27 Mar 1888, Application No. 477,523; Cert. No. 281,318.   By deposition he stated his father was Nathaniel Young aka Badger Young per the copy he forwarded of the 1850 census return listing his father and family as residents of Gilmanton, Belknap Co.   Ch. b Lynn, MA by second wife Susan: Fred W., b 14 Nov 1875, not traced further.   (Soldiers & Sailors, p760; NHVR-Marr; Nat'l. Archives Milit. Recs.)

JONATHAN, b 1685, Dover Neck, s/o Thomas and Mary (Roberts) Young, d pre 29 Sep 1756, Cochecho Point; m 12 May 1709, Dover, Abigail Hanson [b ca 1690, Dover, d/o Thomas and Mary (Kitchen) Hanson, alive 1752, native town].   In 1715 Jonathan was listed as one of 72 persons "being householders" who lived nearer the New Meeting House on Cochecho Point than the old on Dover Neck, and in 1732, was listed on the Town Census of Dover for having signed Petition to Jonathan Belcher.   By vote of the legislature 8 Jul 1734, Jonathan was granted a full share of Lot 118, Dover, and in 1741 was taxed as resident of Cochecho Parish for 1-3-8.   Jonathan disposed of his one-fifth share of the 12 acres land in Rochester received from his father by deed of gift signed 18 Mar 1726/27, rec'd 20 May 1727/28, quitclaiming the share in sale with cograntor Moses Wingate by deed of 6 Feb 1730/1, rec'd 28 Mar 1744, to Ephraim Tebbetts Jr. of Dover for 40 pounds Bills of Credit; witnesses John Cushing, Robert Evans [NH Prov. Deed 27:100]. His trade was carpenter. His earliest known purchase of land was 40 acres in Dover by deed signed 21 May 1729, rec'd 20 Apr 1734, from Benjamin Mason of Dover, cordwainer, for 70 pounds Bills of Credit; witnesses Samuel Young [brother], Robert Evans [NH Prov. Probate 20:61]. Part of these 40 acres, that is, 17-1/2 acres, lay on the north side of Bellamy Banks River in Barbados Woods. The remaining 22-1/2 acres, beginning at n.w. corner of Nathaniel Young's land, became his homestead farm. He made deed of gift to his eldest son Jonathan Jr. of land on Blind Will's Neck, Rochester, located near Long Marsh and Great Marsh, 2nd Div., and also "outlands in sd Rochester which remains yet undivided" by deed signed 3 Dec 1745, rec'd 18 Jun 1748; witnesses James Kielle, Joseph Hanson Jr. [NH Prov. Probate 36:91].

During the Provincial period Jonathan's will was drawn 1 Jul 1752, proved 29 Sep 1756, naming as Co-Execs. and residuary legatees, sons James and Nathaniel; witnesses Daniel Evans, Joseph Young, Silas Hanson [NH State Papers V34, p239]. Provisions for wife Abigail included the use and improvement of the westerly lower room and part of the cellar in his dwelling house, one third part of all produce, two cows and four sheep "during the term of her continuing my widow"; also firewood, feather bed and bedding, and all other household goods not disposed of "during the term of her natural life." Should she remarry, "my will is that after her second marriage, she shall have out of my estate her proper dowry only as by law allowed." Jonathan made bequests of beds and bedding, table and six chairs, and one cow each to married daughter Abigail Hayes and single daughters Mary, Elizabeth and Mercy. "If his single daughters should marry before his decease, they would each receive 20 shillings cash, old Tenor, one year after his decease." He acknowledged his deed of gift to eldest son Jonathan and devised to him an additional legacy of 5 pounds old Tenor. Bequests of 100 pounds Bills of Credit, old Tenor each were made to sons Thomas, Eleazer and Isaac. Sons James and Nathaniel were to share equally in the Dover homestead, the dwelling, barn, livestock and orchards, and 50 acres land lying on n.e. side of Bellamin's Bank, plus 6 acres Common Land in Dover; these six acres were originally bought by Jonathan's deed signed 5 Mar 1738/9, rec'd 30 May 1739, from Richard Hussey of Dover for 12 pounds; witnesses John Cook, Joseph Hanson Jr. [NH Prov. Probate 24:114].

Ch. b Dover: Jonathan+, b 5 Jun 1710; Thomas+, b 5 Jul 1712, see also 24 May 1718; Eleazer+, b 10 Nov 1714; Isaac+, b 15 Mar 1716; James+, b 10 Sep 1718; Nathaniel+, b 1 Feb 1720; Abigail+ (Young) Hayes, b 15 Sep 1723; Mary, b 30 Dec

1725, d 29 Apr 1806, Dover; and Elizabeth and Mercy, bp 31 Jan
1742, upon the occasion when the whole family "received the
covenant" by baptism at First Church of Dover. (Heritage's
Dover VR, p23,24, 36,132,148; NH State Papers, V11, p508,509,
V24, p700; Holbrook's 1732 Census, p73-75; Noyes et al, p307;
Tibbetts Gen., TMs, p283)

   JONATHAN aka Jr., b 5 Jun 1710, Dover, s/o Jonathan and
Abigail (Hanson) Young, d pre 29 May 1759, Rochester; m1 near
1739, Dover, Anna Ham [b 12 Dec 1712, Dover, d/o Joseph and
Tamson (Meserve) Ham, gr.d/o of John and Mary (Heard) Ham, d
ca 1745, Rochester]; m2 27 Aug 1747, Rochester, Elizabeth
Monroe aka Mundro [b ca 1725, Rochester, d/o Peter and Mary
(   ) Munroe, d ca 1790, same town, by name of Wentworth].
It should be noted that NHVR-Marriages attributed Elizabeth
Monroe's marriage also to James Young of Rochester on same
date. Only one record can be taken literally; her marriage
is credited to this Jonathan inasmuch as he was the father of
this James, and Elizabeth Monroe became James' step-mother
upon her marriage to Jonathan. Anna (Ham) Young was identified as the daughter of Joseph Ham of Dover by deed signed
3 Apr 1739, rec'd 14 Mar 1754, in which her brother Joseph Ham
of Dover sold his share of his father's estate to his brother
Daniel Ham, after having bought out the shares of his sisters
Ann Young, Elizabeth Ham, Libby Ham, and Tamson Spinney; witnesses Joseph Roberts, Joseph Hanson Jr. [NH Prov. Deed
42:537]. Second wife Elizabeth Monroe m2 pre 1773, Rochester,
Ebenezer Wentworth [b 9 Sep 1705, of Great Falls, s/o Benjamin
and Sarah (Allen) Wentworth, his second marriage]. Said Wentworth's first wife was Sarah Roberts [b 18 Feb 1708/9, d/o
John and Deborah (Church) Roberts, d 10 Feb 1770, the mother
of his seven children].

   Jonathan Jr. was granted a one-third share of Lot 161 in
Dover by vote taken by the Legislature 8 Jul 1734. He was of
Rochester when he purchased by deed dated 7 Jul 1738, rec'd
22 May 1739, 20 acres land in Rochester [part of 2nd Div. lot
that was originally granted to Israel Hodgin Sr.], from Israel
Hodgin Jr. of Dover for 20 pounds; witnesses Joseph Hanson,
Jr., Isaac Hanson [NH Prov. Deed 24:100]. He received from
his father by deed of gift dated 3 Dec 1745, rec'd 18 Jun
1748, land on Blind Will's Neck, Rochester which became his
homestead. By terms of his father's will drawn 1 Jul 1752,
proved 29 Sep 1756, Jonathan was to receive additional cash.
He added to his land holdings in Rochester by (1) purchase of
36 acres on Blind Will's Neck, 2nd Div., Rochester adjoining
Jonathan's own land, from John Leighton of Rochester by deed
signed 1 Jun 1742, rec'd 26 Sep 1759, for 41 pounds Bills of
Credit; witnesses James Kielle, Joseph Hanson, Jr. [NH Prov.
Probate 58:339,340]; and (2) purchase of four acres on Long
Marsh, part of Lot 5, 2nd Div., Rochester from Stephen Berry
of Rochester for 14 pounds Bills of Credit, old Tenor by deed
of 28 Dec 1744, rec'd 26 Sep 1759, witnesses John Jennes,
Joseph Hanson, Jr. [NH Prov. Probate 58:338].

When Jonathan died intestate, administration on his estate was granted to widow Elizabeth on 29 May 1759; on same date, bond of 500 pounds was given with sureties of Richard Bickford of Rochester and James Kielle of Dover. Warrant to appraise the estate was then issued [NH Prov. Probate 21:303]. Inventory taken 26 Sep 1759, was submitted by James Place and Joseph Walker, both of Rochester; real estate was assessed in the amount of 2,579 pounds-11 shillings [NH State Papers 36:419]. Ch. b Rochester by Anna, bp at First Congregational Church: Hannah and Jean, bp 29 Jun 1740; and James+, b ca 1721, bp 9 Sep 1744. Ch. b Rochester by Elizabeth, bp at First Congregational Church: Ann, bp 7 Apr 1751; Elizabeth, b 29 Sep 1751; prob. Jonathan+, b 1752; and Esther, b 4 Nov 1753. (Heritage's Dover VR, p15,152; NH Gen. Recs., V4, No.4, p145; LDS I.G.I. BR, VR; Dover Gen., **Reg.** 6:329; Ham Family, **Reg.** 26:389,390; Wentworth Gen., V1, p272; Tibbett's Gen., TMs, p283)

JONATHAN, b 1 Jan 1756, Kingston, s/o Jonathan and Mary (Lovering) Young [no main entry], wheelwright, carpenter, d 27 Mar 1807, Barnstead; m (Intentions) 12 Oct 1777, m 28 Oct 1777, at First Congregational Church, Kingston, Sarah aka Sally Clifford [b ca 1755, of Kingston, d 1816, Barnstead]. It is to be noted that William R. Cutter (cited below) doubted very much that Jonathan came from Kingston, but rather from Rochester or Durham, and was the son of Jonathan Young of Blind Will's Neck. On this side of the aisle, doubt is expressed that Jonathan came from Blind Will's Neck, but rather from Kingston in light of Kingston Vital Records up through 1788 and land deeds with Kingston-Barnstead connections up through 1783. By 1790 Jonathan and family relocated to Barnstead, at which time he was listed as head of household with family of one female and three sons under 16. Sarah was listed on the census returns for Barnstead in 1810 as widow, age 45 plus, with family of two males both 16-26 years of age. While Jonathan was of Kingston, he began to purchase land that would become his homestead in Barnstead, 50 acres or one half of Lot 88, 2nd Div., Barnstead, first deed signed 18 Jan 1783, rec'd 22 Dec 1793, from John Hook of Barnstead for 60 pounds, land drawn to the original right of Timothy Gerrish, held in common and undivided with Ephraim Tibbetts; witnesses Joseph Badger, Dudley Young [Strafford Co. Deed 19:19]. Still of Kingston, Jonathan sold by deed of 23 Oct 1783, rec'd 8 May 1797, 60 acres of Lot 105, 1st Range, excepting nine acres sold at Venue, Barnstead, to Moses Avery of Gilmanton for 50 pounds; witnesses Benjamin _____ Jr., William Smith [Strafford Co. Deed 25:109].

When of Barnstead, he purchased from Theophilus Dame of Dover, two-thirds of the 100-acre Lot 89, Div. 2, Barnstead, laid out to the original right of Moses Dame, the third part owned by Ephraim Tibbetts, for 40 pounds by deed signed 10 Dec 1793, rec'd 1 Aug 1794; witnesses Henry Mellen, Daniel Rogers [Strafford Co. Deed 19:18]; he sold part of Lot 89, acreage unspecified, to Joseph Huckins of Barnstead for $60.00, by deed signed 9 Jan 1797, rec'd 8 Aug 1806; witnesses Robert Tibbetts, Joseph Parsons [Strafford Co. Deed 52:85]. Purchase was made of 60 acres of Matthew's Common, Barnstead from Joseph Sinclair of Barnstead who had purchased these acres at public auction on 19 Mar 1793, by tax deed signed 29 Dec 1794, rec'd 7 Feb 1795, for 18 pounds; witnesses Joseph Parsons, Stephen Moody [Strafford Co. Deed 19:451]. Jonathan was also interested in acreage abutting his Lot 89, owned by the said Ephraim Tibbetts; he bought 14 rods of Lot 88, 2nd Div. out of the remaining one-third section owned by Tibbetts, by deed signed 1 Aug 1794, rec'd same date, for five pounds; witnesses John Tasker, Jonathan Nutter [Strafford Co. Deed 19:20].

Admin. Papers on Jonathan's estate were filed 14 Apr 1807 by widow Sarah; she relinquished all her right by law to administer on her husband's estate as it was "her pleasure that administration on the estate be granted to David Edgerly and son Phineas Young" (eldest surviving son). On same date David Edgerly and Phineas Young were appointed Co-Admins., bond of $5,000.00 was posted with sureties Joseph Young Esq. and Joseph Jackson, Gent., both of Gilmanton; witnesses Emerson Porter, John Ham [Strafford Co. Probate 10:437]. On 25 Apr 1807, inventory of Jonathan's estate was taken by Joseph Jackson, Ezekial Edgerley, and Ezekial Eastman, sworn to 11 May 1807 by Phineas and said Edgerly [Strafford Co. Probate 11:54]. Real estate contained homestead with buildings on Lots 88 and 89, and 60 acres land known by the name of Mathes' Commons, whose total value was $1,660.00. Personal property included livestock, farming and carpenter's tools, apparel, furniture, provisions, misc. articles, notes of hand [$149.28] and books; total personal estate, $735.87; grand total of estate, $2,395.87. One item was added to the inventory on 8 May 1807: two pews on first floor of the Western Meeting House in Barnstead, valued at $55.00.

Sarah's dower rights were set off 1 May 1807, by Joseph Jackson, Benjamin Kelley, Charles Hodgdon Jr., Ezekiel Edgerley and Ezekial Eastman, all of Gilmanton; allowed 10 Jun 1807: the whole of the dwelling house, one third of the barn, ten acres of woodland and twenty acres of the 100-acre homestead farm on Lot 88, 2nd Div., adjacent to lands of Gilman Lougee and Valentine Chatman and next to Lot 89, 2nd Div., Barnstead [Strafford Co. Probate 12:194]. Guardianship of son Jonathan, minor under twenty-one years, was awarded to David Edgerley on 11 May 1807; bond of $1,000.00 posted with sureties Samuel Shepard and Joseph Jackson, both of Gilmanton [Strafford Co. Probate 12:207]. Younger son Aaron, under fourteen years, became ward on 11 May 1807 of said Edgerly; bond of $1,000.00 posted by same sureties cited above [Strafford Co. Probate 12:207]. Edgerley, Admin., made his accounting on 21 Mar 1815, allowed same date [Strafford Co. Probate 14:208]. He charged himself with the amount of sale of the personal estate, sold by order of the court, for $271.70 and for widow's allowance of $200.00. He prayed allowance for expenses and debts of the estate he had paid off in the amount of $547.17 [last medical expenses, funeral, probate fees, and notes of hand owing]; balance of $77.22 due the Admin.

Ch. b Kingston: David, b 14 Apr 1778, d 4 May 1800, Barnstead; Phineas+, b 14 Mar 1780; and Jonathan+, b 25 Jul 1788. Ch. b Barnstead: Aaron+, b 12 Jan 1794. (Census Strafford Co., 1790, p86; 1810, p533; NHVR-Births; LDS I.G.I. VR; Cutter's Eastern Mass., p1269; Hammond's Kingston VR, p59)

JONATHAN, b 1752, of Milton, cooper, prob. s/o Jonathan and Elizabeth (Monroe) Young of Rochester, d pre 1820, Milton; m ca 1785, (   ) [b 1742, of Milton, alive 1820, same town, age 78]. He was head of household in Milton in 1810, age 45 plus, with spouse age 45 plus and family of one male and one female both age 16-26. On 4 Jul 1820 at age 68, Jonathan applied for veteran's pension making deposition to the effect that he served in the Revolutionary War having enlisted in the Continental Massachusetts Service in Manchester, MA; that his wife [unnamed] was alive, age 79 in 1820; and that married daughter Anna Garlin, widow, age 33 in 1820, and three-year old son Ebenezer resided with him. Claim was allowed 7 Sep 1819, by Cert. No. 14328. Ch. b Milton: Anna+ (Young) Garlin, b 1787. (Census Strafford Co., 1810, p771; NHVR-Brides; Draper's NH Revol. War Pensions, #S43333; Young Family Recs., courtesy of Thomas P. Doherty)

JONATHAN, b ca 1755, of Middleton, m 14 Feb 1780, Rochester, Sarah Defethering aka Trefethen [b ca 1760, of Somersworth]. (NH Gen. Rec. V4, No.4, p149; LDS I.G.I. VR)

JONATHAN, b 1760s, of Wakefield; head of household in 1790, Wakefield with family of two males under 16 and two females. He was listed on the Wakefield tax roster for 1795. (Census Strafford Co., 1790, p100; Merrill's Carroll Co., p482,483)

JONATHAN, b 1760s, of Gilmanton. Jonathan was absentee owner of Lot 155, 4th Div., Gilmanton when his property was sold at public auction for back taxes, by tax deed of 10 May, rec'd 21 Dec 1799, to Thomas Cogswell of Gilmanton for $19.29; witnesses John Bodge, Joseph Badger [Strafford Co. Deed 32:97].

JONATHAN aka Capt., b 16 Jun 1761, Barrington, s/o Benjamin and Anna (   ), d 8 Aug 1851, age 90, Strafford Corners; m 5 Feb 1785, Madbury, Mary aka Polly Hill [b 1768, of Lee, prob. d/o Edward and Mary (Willey) Hill, d 16 Nov 1852, Strafford Corners]. Jonathan was a lad of eight when his parents settled at Crown Point, Strafford, after relocating from the upper parish. He became Deacon of the Freewill Baptist Church at Crown Point and served as Captain in the Militia. Before Jonathan married, he received from his father by deed of gift signed 24 Sep 1784, rec'd 26 Dec 1796, the homestead in Barrington, Lot 21, including the furniture, cattle, etc. with this stipulation: "For love, and after Benjamin's and Jonathan's mother's decease." From 1796 on however, Jonathan's homestead was the acreage he bought from Paul Hayes of Barrington, afterwards called the Hayes-Young farm. He became a prosperous farmer as well as successful investor in real estate, recorded by sixteen land deeds. It is noted that the Hill Gen., [NH Gen. Rec, V5, No.3, p99], ascribed Hannah Hill, daughter of Edward and Mary (Willey) Hill as spouse of Jonathan, rather than her sister Mary Hill. Various land deeds cited below show that Mary aka Polly released dower rights; sister Hannah Hill will be seen as witness to one land deed.

Jonathan was head of household from 1790-1850 in that section of Barrington which became Strafford by 1820; in 1790 household contained one son under 16 and two females; in 1800 his age was 26-45, spouse of same age group, with a family of three males under 10, and three females, two under 10 and one age 10-16. In 1810, with title of Capt., his age was 45 plus with spouse under 45, five males, one 26-45, one age 16-26, two 10-16, one under 10, and two females both age 10-16; in 1830, Jonathan's age was 60-70, as was his spouse, with one male in household age 20-30. In 1840 Jonathan and spouse lived by themselves, both age 70-80. In 1850 Mary was identified as spouse; they lived at the home of their son Stephen and his family in Strafford, estate valued at $8,000.

Four of Jonathan's earliest deeds involved purchase of parts of Lot 16, 1st Range, Barrington, drawn to the original right of Joseph Holmes, and were recorded on same date of 26 Dec 1796: (1) purchase of 25-1/2 acres adjacent to the northern corner of Ebenezer Cummel's orchard, from Noah Holmes of Barrington for 70 pounds by deed signed 28 Aug 1786; witnesses Thomas Foss, Solomon Drew, Hannah Hill, Katherine Foss [Strafford Co. Deed 23:309]; (2) purchased all the remaining interest of the said Noah Holmes in Lot 16, located at the northern corner of Samuel Foss' orchard, for 15 pounds, by deed signed 18 Aug 1787; witnesses Thomas Foss, John Penny [Strafford Co. Deed 23:287]; (3) purchased from Ebenezer Cummel the whole right to that part of Lot 16 located on n.e. side of Samuel Foss's orchard which said Cunnel bought from Ephraim Holmes, for 6 pounds, by deed signed 18 Feb 1788; witnesses Thomas Foss, Samuel Foss [Strafford Co. Deed 23:283]; (4) purchase of one acre and 150 sq. rods from Samuel Foss 4th which said Foss purchased from Ebenezer Cummel aka Cunnel, for 40 pounds, by deed signed 20 Oct 1790; witnesses Stephen Otis, John Foss 4th [Strafford Co. Deed 23:284]. Sale of 33 acres of Lot 16, 1st Range, Barrington was made by Jonathan with Molly ceding dower rights by deed of 28 Nov 1796, rec'd 16 Jul 1798, to Stephen Otis Jr. of Barrington for $484.00; witnesses Joseph Peirce, [J.P.] Gilman [Strafford Co. Deed 27:599].

The following land deeds describe purchases, sales and mortgage of his homestead on Lot 24, 1st Div., 1st Range, Barrington, drawn to the original right of Richard Wiberd: purchase of 60 acres by deed signed 1 Nov 1791, rec'd 26 Dec 1796, from Aaron Wingate of Portsmouth, Rock. Co. who had inherited the property from his father by will, for 90 pounds; witnesses Stephen Chase, Samuel Hutchins [Strafford Co. Deed 23:285]. Sale of 20 acres of Lot 24 to John Foss 5th of Barrington was by deed signed 14 Dec 1792, rec'd 14 Jul 1798, for 36 pounds; witnesses Thomas Foss, John Foss 4th [Strafford Co. Deed 28:214]. Sale of an additional 20 acres, "being one-half the land I own in said lot on s.e. side of land owned by John Foss," was made by deed of 28 Nov 1796, rec'd 21 Aug 1804, to Thomas Berry of Barrington for $200.00; witnesses Paul Hayes, Stephen Otis Jr. [Strafford Co. Deed 44:333]). Purchase of an additional 100 acres of Lot 24 was made by deed signed 28 Nov 1796, rec'd 13 Dec 1796, from Paul and Abigail Hayes, "the same land my father Paul Hayes late of Barrington conveyed to me by deed dated 4 Sep 1765," bounded upon the town line of Rochester, "excepting and reserving out of the premises hereby conveyed 30 sq. feet at the place where there has been seven dead bodies buried with liberty for the said Young to bury dead within this reservation," by deed signed 28 Nov, rec'd 13 Dec 1796, for $2,000.00; witnesses Israel Hayes, Paul Hayes Jr. [Strafford Co. Deed 23:320]. Mortgage of the 100 acres purchased from Paul Hayes was transacted on same date of its purchase by deed signed 28 Nov 1796, recorded on same date of 13 Dec 1796, mortgage held by Joseph Peirce Esq., for 1,000 spanish milled dollars with interest due and payable 11 Mar 1798; witnesses Paul Hayes, Stephen Otis Jr. [Strafford Co. Deed 23:319]. The size of the homestead on Lot 24 was diminished by the sale of 20 acres adjacent to lands of Stephen Brock, with Molly ceding dower rights, to Ezra Stanton of Barrington for $200.00, by deed signed 6 Apr 1816, rec'd 24 Apr 1817; witnesses Benjamin F. Young [son], William Stanton [Strafford Co. Deed 94:408].

Other land acquired in Barrington by Jonathan was one half of 40 acres in the Two-Mile Streak west of James Church's moiety of 20 acres in the said lot, which had been willed to Benjamin Church and James Church by their father, by deed signed and rec'd 28 Feb 1803, purchased from Reubin Twombly of Madbury for $100.00; witnesses William Foss Jr. and Benjamin Garland [Strafford Co. Deed 41:315]. Jonathan sold these 20 acres by deed signed 27 Aug 1803, rec'd 19 Feb 1805, to Elijah Austin Jr. of Madbury for $104.00; Mary ceded dower rights; witnesses Tobias Evans, Jonathan Hayes [Strafford Co. Deed 47:196].

Real estate in Farmington was yet on Jonathan's agenda, with the intent to build up land holdings for his sons. Capt. Jonathan became an absentee owner of land in Farmington: on 1 Jul 1806, he was listed as freeholder for School District No. 2, but by 28 Nov 1812, two of his properties in Farmington were scheduled for sale at public auction for back taxes, "so much of their land as will pay said taxes...will be sold." These properties were Lot 69, 2nd Div., 40 acres valued at $160.00, partly improved, in the name of Shadrach Walton "alias Capt. Jonathan Young," and Lot 39, 2nd Div., 15 acres

valued at $130, in the name of "first ordained minister's lot,
unimproved, alias Capt. Jonathan Young." His first recorded
purchase of land in Farmington was by date of 1 May 1816, when
Jonathan and Polly purchased from Benjamin and Abigail Read
of Farmington for $250.00, fifty acres land in the 2nd Div.,
Farmington, bounded at s.w. corner of the Barrington line, on
s.w. side by land now owned by Jonathan, lot drawn to original
right of Shadrach Walter Esq. of Rochester; witnesses Daniel
B. Hayes, Polly Young [Strafford Co. Deed 89:485]. He was
listed on Farmington's tax lists 1825-1828: from 1825-1827,
he owned two parcels of land, each 75 acres and 30 acres,
total value $300.00; in 1828, his holdings were each 65 acres
and 20 acres, valued at $260.00, value of buildings $150.00.
   Jonathan's will was signed 7 Dec 1844, proved 2 Sep 1851,
naming son Stephen as Exec. and residuary legatee; witnesses
Enoch Plan, Ichabod Rowe, Ebenezer H. Berry [Strafford Co.
Probate 61:499]. Son Stephen was allowed Exec. of Jonathan's
will on date of probate, having given bond of $2,000.00, with
sureties Ichabod Rowe, Joshua Berry, both of Strafford [Straf-
ford Co. Probate 50:429]. Wife Mary was to receive one-third
of all his real estate "while she shall remain my widow and
no longer," and all the household furniture except the writing
desk. He bequeathed to the children of his son "Benjamin F.
of Farmington" [deceased] $1.00 each, to son "Jonathan of
Barrington" $100.00, to youngest son John F., all his land in
Strafford which was not disposed of by deeds, to oldest daughter Ann Hill, $10.00, to daughter Sally Drown, $10.00, to the
children of daughter Polly Berry, deceased [wife of William
Berry] $1.00, to grandson George W. Young [father not iden-
tified], $100.00, and to son Stephen, his writing desk and
all other property both real and personal. Inventory of the
estate was taken by Jacob B. Smith, Joseph Hall and William
Berry, submitted 4 Nov 1851, allowed same date: only furn-
iture was reported, value set at $17.14 [Strafford Co. Probate
67:50]. Jonathan and Mary were buried at Freewill Baptist
Church Cemetery on First Crown Point Road, Strafford Corners.
   Ch. b Strafford Corners: Benjamin F.+, b 11 Mar 1788;
Ann (Young) Hill, b ca 1790; Mercy, b 1790s; Polly aka Mary+
(Young) Berry, b ca 1793; Sally+ (Young) Drown, b ca 1795;
prob. Jonathan Franklin+, b 1796; Stephen+, b 19 Mar 1802; and
John Frank aka John Franklin+, b Jan 1806. (Census Strafford
Co., 1790, p86; 1800, p155; 1810, p509; 1830, p56; 1840, p463;
1850, p575; Goss' Gravestones, p130; Stackpole's Durham, V2,
p216; NHVR-Births, Marr, Deaths; Morning Star, p375; Farming-
ton TR, V1, p114,421,628-770; Stiles' Cemeteries, p116,207;
Hill Gen., NH Gen. Rec., V5, No.2, p99; Strafford Pioneers,
n.p.; Young Family Recs., courtesy of M. Elaine Woodward)
   JONATHAN, b 14 Apr 1780, Dover, s/o Ezra and Susannah
(Demeritt) Young, d 7 Jan 1843, Dover; m1 16 Jul 1810, Dover,
Nabby aka Abigail Coffin [b 24 Nov 1782, Madbury, twin, d/o
Eliphalet and Patience (Evans) Coffin of Dover, d 24 Jun 1836,
age 55, Dover]; m2 6 Aug 1837, Madbury, first cousin Clarissa

Lavinia Demeritt [b 12 Nov 1796, Durham, d/o Ebenezer and Elizabeth (Young) Demeritt who was sister of said Ezra Young, d testate 16 Jan 1846, age 49, widow, Dover]. Jonathan and family were listed on the census returns for Dover from 1830-1840: in 1830 his age was 50-60, with household consisting of two females 40-50, four sons, one each age 5-10, 10-15, 15-20, and 20-30, and five females, one age 5-10, one 15-20, two 20-30, and one 30-40; in 1840, Jonathan was age 60-70, with [2nd] spouse age 40-50 and family reduced in size to two sons, one 15-20, one 20-30, and two other females, one 15-20, one 20-30. He was named Exec. of his father's will dated 20 Nov 1815, proved 23 Feb 1821, which made him residuary legatee of Ezra's estate after his mother's dower rights were granted. Jonathan was also named Exec. of the will of Elizabeth Young of Dover [great aunt, wife of James Young], signed 30 Aug 1821, proved 17 Jun 1822, when he was known as "the son of Susanna Young, widow of Ezra Young'; on date of probate Jonathan was allowed Exec., having posted bond of $2,000, with sureties John Wingate and John W. Hayes [Strafford Co. Probate 39:15]. Before great-aunt Elizabeth Young had her will drawn up, she conveyed to Jonathan by deed of gift signed 8 Nov 1806, rec'd 25 Feb 1818, the property known as "Littleworth." For further details on Elizabeth's will and deed of gift, refer to James and Elizabeth Young of Dover.

When Abigail Coffin married Jonathan, she quitclaimed her share of the home farm of her late father Eliphalet Coffin to her twin Tristam. When he died intestate in 1825, she became one of his heirs and received 35-1/2 acres adjacent to the river. By quitclaim of 15 Nov 1826, rec'd day after, Jonathan and the following list of heirs of the late Eliphalet Coffin of Dover, wife Abigail (Coffin) Young, Hannah Coffin, Mary Coffin, William Hodgdon and Susannah Hodgdon his wife, and Elizabeth Coffin, deeded land belonging to Eliphalet Coffin that abutted the company's present dam at head of Cochecho Falls and "the right to flow thereto" to Dover Manufacturing Co., (the forerunner of Cochecho Manufacturing Co. which was incorporated in 1827) for $100.00; each and severally acknowledged their signing of the instrument to be their voluntary act [Strafford Co. Deed 129:169]. And by deed signed 1 Dec 1827, rec'd 13 May 1828, Jonathan and Abigail Young, John Hanson and Hannah Coffin, single woman, all of Dover sold to Cyrus Cates of Barrington for $108.00, 9 acres land of Lot 106, 3rd Range, Barrington; witnesses Wingate Hayes, Joshua Cates [Strafford Co. Deed 136:447]. A farm in Littleworth, so called, was quitclaimed by the heirs of Patience Coffin and Hannah Coffin--Jonathan, "in right of my wife," and Abigail Young, William and Susannah Hodgdon, and Mary Copp and Elizabeth Coffin, single women, all of Dover--to John Hanson of Dover for $1,750.00 by deed signed 19 Dec 1832, rec'd the day after,; on date of recording each co-grantor acknowledged the signing of the instrument to be their voluntary act [Strafford Co. Deed 155:94].

After Abigail's death and Jonathan's remarriage, son Jonathan T., age 19, was made ward of his father; bond of $1,000.00 posted with sureties William Hodgdon and Benjamin Wiggin [Strafford Co. Probate 50:232]. Jonathan and Clarissa were married scarcely six years when he died, Clarissa, three years later. There was no issue by this marriage. After Jonathan's death, son Jonathan T. was made a ward of Nathaniel Young of Dover [uncle]; bond of $2,000.00 with sureties Jeremy Young, James Y. Demeritt [Strafford Co. Probate 50:262]. Admin. of Jonathan's estate was Thomas W. Kittredge of Dover, appointed 7 Feb 1843; bond of $16,000.00 posted with sureties James Y. Demeritt of Madbury and Israel Hanson and James W. Cowan, both of Dover [Strafford Co. Probate 50:250]. Inventory of Jonathan's estate in Dover ran seven legal-size pages long, depicting a life-style of inherited wealth. It was appraised by Andrew Peirce, John S. Durell and Daniel Hussey, all of Dover, return made 3 Mar 1843, attested to same date, total value set at $25,832.48 [Strafford Co. Probate 59:194]. Goods and chattel were valued at $6,109.32. Real estate holdings were assessed at $17,800.00: 100-acre homestead farm with buildings in Dover subject to the encumbrance of legacy to Mary aka Polly Young and Eliza Young [Jonathan's sisters], $7,700.00; 70 acres field and pasture opposite house of J. S. Durell, $4,000.00; 18 acres in Eastman's lot in Madbury, $700.00; 100-acre farm in Madbury occupied by James C. Young, $1,500; 50-acre woodlot in Barrington, a one-fifth share of first wife Abigail, derived from deceased son Ezra K.'s legacy, $800.00; and one-fifth part of the right of said Ezra K. in his mother's share in the Bickford place, $100.00. Last item was notes of hand exclusive of interest, $1,923.16.

His estate was divided seven months later on 3 Oct 1843, allowed next day; the reversion of Clarissa's dower rights was a factor in the division where boundaries of the estate were viewed in effect at the time of Jonathan's and Clarissa's marriage [Strafford Co. Probate 61:370]. Distributions of lands were made by Winthrop Smith of Durham, William W. Rollins of Somersworth and Elijah Austin of Madbury. James C. Young received 95 acres, 28 rods, with buildings in Madbury, located on both sides of road from Barrington to Dover, 48 acres of woodland in Barrington and $50.00 paid by Mary Susan Young. Hannah S. Young, eldest daughter, received one half of the late homestead, 37 acres, 58 rods on the north side of the highway and the west end of dwelling house and 11 acres, 29 rods of the western end of woodland called the Eastman lot, also reserving to Eliza Young [Jonathan's sister] and Clarissa Young household privileges. Mary S. Young received 68 acres, 105 rods of the Hodgdon land in Dover. Jonathan T. Young, a minor, and his guardian were given the other half of the homestead farm, 37 acres, 58 rods, along with 11 acres, 29 rods at the eastern end of the woodland in Madbury.

Set off to Clarissa as dower rights were the 75 acres of the homestead farm along with two other tracts of land in

Dover, the Hodgdon land of 68 acres, 105 rods, and the Eastman lot in Madbury of 22 acres, 58 rods land respectively, the 95-acre farm in Madbury with buildings where James C. Young then lived in Madbury, and 48 acres, 19 rods of timberland in Barrington. Upon Clarissa's death, the reversion of her dower rights would take effect: these lands would revert to Jonathan's surviving children. Admin. Kittredge made his accounting 2 Jan 1844, approved same date [Strafford Co. Probate 58:124]. Amount of personal estate allowed widow and heirs, $5,698.79; various and sundry administrative costs, funeral expense, parish subscription for 1842, Dover tax for 1843, and probate fees came to $750.94. Credits were set at $6,109.32, including amount of personal estate and dividends on Dover Bank shares and R.R. stock; balance of $358.63 due from Admin.

Clarissa's will of 18 Jan 1845, proved 3 Feb 1846, named as her Exec. Jonathan Thompson Young, son of her husband by Abigail; Jonathan T. and his sister Hannah S. were named co-residuary legatees; witnesses Thomas W. Kittredge, James W. Cowan, Nathaniel Young [Strafford Co. Probate 61:244]. On date of probate, Jonathan was allowed Exec.; bond of $10,000 posted with sureties Nathaniel Young and Thomas W. Kittredge [Strafford Co. Probate 50:301]. She made the following bequests: to niece Eliza L. Demeritt, daughter of brother Jacob Demeritt, $100.00; to son of her husband, James C. Young of Madbury, $50.00; to Mary Susan [Young] Cate, wife of Eleazer Cate, daughter of her husband, $50.00; and to Hannah S. Young and Jonathan T. Young, all the remainder of the estate to be equally divided between them.

Eldest daughter Hannah S. remained single, and as joint tenant in the family homestead in Dover, held close ties throughout the years with her brother Jonathan T. and his wife Elizabeth. From 1850-1860, she was listed on the census returns as a member of their family. All of Jonathan T.'s surviving children were remembered in her will drawn 8 Jun, proved 6 Jul 1880; she designated nephew Tristam A. Young as Exec. and residuary legatee; witnesses John H. White, Mabel G. Hammond [wife of nephew James T. Young] and Charles W. Ayers [Strafford Co. Probate 94:83]. Nephews Tristam A. Young, Ezra K. Young and Jacob D. Young were devised equal shares of 33 shares in the Boston & Maine R.R.; nephews James T. Young, George A. Young and John L. Young, 37-1/2 acres, "set off to me on the division of my father's homestead in Dover" and one-half of the buildings and garden lot; niece Lizzie C. Young, household effects in her front chamber, two silver spoons marked "C. L. Demeritt," six silver tea spoons marked "A.C.", her gold locket, and one-half share of nine shares in the Strafford National Bank; niece Anna A. Young, household effects in her back chamber, two large silver spoons marked "E.Y." and "J.Y.", six silver tea spoons marked "H.S.Y.", her gold watch and chain, and one-half share of nine shares in the Strafford National Bank; Martha S. Kay, one share in the Dover National Bank; Mrs. Elizabeth Young, widow of her brother Jonathan T., four shares in the Dover National Bank, and all household effects in her sitting room, wearing apparel to go to Lizzie C. and Anna A. Jonathan, first wife Abigail and their children were buried at John Young Cemetery, Littleworth Road, Dover.

Ch. b Dover by Abigail: Ezra K., b 1811, d 10 Oct 1841, Dover; Hannah S., b 11 Mar 1814, d 20 Jun 1880, age 66, Dover; James C.+, b 2 Aug 1817; Mary Susan+ (Young) Cate, b 4 Sep 1820; Elizabeth aka Lizzie C., b 1820s, alive 1880; and Jonathan Thompson+, b 7 Dec 1822. (NHVR-Marr; Heritage's Dover VR, p85,216,226; Stackpole's Durham, V2, p118-122; Quint's Hist. Memos, p285-291; Census Strafford Co., 1830, p315; 1840, p530; 1860, p818; Frost's Dover Cem., Plot #22; Steuerwald's Dover Cem., TMs; Demeritt Fam., **Reg.** 87:89,90)

JONATHAN, b 24 Jul 1785, Barrington, s/o Winthrop and Mary (Otis) Young, d 13 Jul 1859, Stewartstown, age 73-10-0; m 13 Dec 1807, Canterbury, Dolly aka Dorothy Tirrell [b 1789, of Canterbury, d 27 Sep 1863, Stewartstown]. Ch. b Stewartstown: Mary, b 13 May 1808; Hiram, b 23 Jan 1810; Madison, b 3 Jun 1813; Winthrop, b 14 Nov 1815; Edna, b 3 Jun 1818; Esther, b 1 Jan 1820; Otis, b 5 May 1822; Hannah T., b 7 Dec 1823; Deborah K., b 13 Jun 1826; Jonathan W., b 17 May 1829; Samuel A., b 17 Feb 1833; and Amanda M., b 25 Jun 1835. (LDS I.G.I. BR; Lyford's Canterbury, p341; Young Family Recs., courtesy of Nancy L. Dodge)

JONATHAN aka Jr., b 25 Jul 1788, Kingston, s/o Jonathan and Sarah (Clifford) Young, d 1 Apr 1861, Barnstead, age 72; m 24 Feb 1814, Barnstead, Susan aka Sukey Pitman [b 1792, Barnstead, d/o Samuel and Sarah (Small) Pitman, d 5 Jan 1883, age 91, widow, Barnstead]. Jonathan was just a young child when his parents relocated in Barnstead. Upon the death of his father, Jonathan at age 19 was made ward of David Edgerly of Gilmanton 11 May 1807. Jonathan kept his residence in Barnstead where he inherited a one-third share of his father's estate, parts of Lots 88 and 89. He became head of family there from 1830-1850. In 1830 his age was 40-50 years, household containing spouse age 30-40, one male age 5-10, one male 10-20, one female under 5, two females 5-10, and one female 10-15. In 1840 his age was 50-60, spouse was 40-50, with family of one male age 10-20 and three females one each 5-10, 10-15, and 15-20, respectively. Interestingly enough the 1850 census for the town of Strafford listed a Jonathan, age 63, and Susan, age 58, who lived alone. Even though their ages were identical to this Jonathan and spouse Susan, it would be hard to say whether they were one and the same couple. However, Jonathan and members of the family were buried at Barnstead Center Cemetery. Ch. b Barnstead Center: Samuel P.+, b 12 Nov 1814; Martha, b 8 Feb 1817; Jonathan Jr., b 19 May 1819; Oliver H. P.+, b 22 Mar 1824; Sarah L., b 15 Jan 1827; and Sophia F., b 15 Sep 1832, d 1891, Barnstead Center. (Barnstead Cem. Inscriptions, p6; NHVR-Births, Marr, Deaths; Census Strafford Co., 1830, p15; 1840, p444; 1850, p534,575;

LDS I.G.I. BR; Cutter's Eastern Mass., p1269,1270; Merrill's Barnstead, p332; Pitman Gen., TMs, p3)

JONATHAN, b 1792, of Alton, d 12 May 1853, farmer, Farmington; m ca 1820, Alton, Alice Peavey [b 8 Oct 1800, Alton, d/o Daniel and Mary (   ) Peavey, d 8 Apr 1874, age 73-6-0, Milton]. He was head of household in Alton in 1830, age 30-40, with spouse age 20-30 and family of one male and one female both under 5. In the late 1830s he relocated to Farmington where he became head of family from 1840-1850. In 1840 his age was 40-50, with spouse age 30-40 and family of one male under 5 and two females, one under 5 and one age 5-10. In 1850 he and Allis were listed on the census returns for Farmington with eight children: Alamander, Emaline, George W., Rosanna M., Charles H., Adeline, Mary E. and Martha A. Widow Alice of Farmington m2 11 Sep 1853, Alton, Moses Young, widower of Alton [b 1778, Lebanon, ME, res. of Alton, prob. brother of this Jonathan; see main entry on Moses Young of Alton]. As widow of Moses Young, Alice m3 7 Oct 1865, Alton, Joseph Wiggins [b 1804, Upper Gilmanton].

Ch. b Alton: Alamander W.+, b 23 Jul 1824; Emaline, b 1827; and prob. Hannah W.+ (Young) Ellis, b ca 1829. Ch. b Farmington: Rosanna M., b 1831; George W.+, b 1834; Charles E.+, b 1837; Adeline, b 1840; daughter b 4 Apr 1843; Mary E., b 1846; Martha A.+ (Young) Ellis, b 6 Apr 1847; and daughter b 25 May 1851. (Alton VR, p604,616,652,654; Census Strafford Co., 1830, p105; 1840, p316; 1850, p641; NHVR-Births, Brides, Deaths)

JONATHAN, b ca 1795, of Barrington, an adult when he purchased from Elizabeth Young of Dover, widow, 200 acres land, Lot 176, in Barrington, plus three other acres in said town by deed signed 8 Mar, rec'd 13 Mar 1821; he was designated "cousin" of Elizabeth. For full details see Elizabeth Young of Dover, widow of James Young.

JONATHAN, b ca 1795, of Gilmanton; head of household in Gilmanton in 1840, age 40-50, as was his spouse, with family of six sons, two under 5, two age 5-10, and two 10-15. (Census Strafford Co., 1840, p415)

JONATHAN, b 1799, of Wakefield, d testate pre 3 Apr 1883, Wakefield; m 1859, Wakefield, Judith K. Davis [b 23 Oct 1825, Fa ington, d/o Timothy and Ann (Applebee) Davis of Wakefield or Milton, d 25 Nov 1890, age 65-1-2, Farmington]. Judith's father Timothy Davis came from Wakefield, her mother Ann Applebee from Milton. He and Judith lived in Wakefield with their one child as of 1860, per census returns which indicated that he was unfortunately deaf and dumb. He was listed as inhabitant and taxpayer of Wakefield on date of 10 May 1873, taxed at the rate of $5.66. Jonathan's will was drawn 14 Jan 1880, proved 3 Apr 1883, in which he named wife Judith K. Young as sole Exec. and residuary legatee; witnesses Albert Meserve, Mayhew Davis [Carroll Co. Probate #5813]. Jonathan also named two daughters, Lizzie May Frye, wife of Frank O. Frye of Dover, and Belinda D. Young, both of whom were to

receive $5.00. He and wife Judith K. were buried at Young
Cemetery by Chipmunk Lane and Leighton Corner Road, Wakefield.
Ch. b Wakefield: Lizzie (Young) Frye, b 1859; Belinda Davis
Young, b 1860s. (Census Carroll Co., 1860, p580; 1870, p430;
NHVR-Marr, Deaths; Bank's Wakefield, p181; Twombly's Wakefield
Cem., TMs)

JONATHAN, b ca 1805, of Alton; m 21 Oct 1827, Alton,
Polly Doe [b ca 1807, of same town]. (NHVR-Marr; Alton VR,
p547)

JONATHAN, b ca 1805, of Barrington; head of household in
Barrington for 1840, age 30-40, with family containing female
age 20-30, two males, one under 5 years, one age 15-20, and
one female age 10-15. (Census Strafford Co., 1840, p478)

JONATHAN, b ca 1805, of Milton; m 6 Jun 1830, Alton,
Alice Knox [b ca 1815, of Alton]. This date may have indicated when they filed intentions of marriage since there is a
second date of marriage for them on 27 Jul 1838, New Durham.
Originally of Milton, the couple moved to Farmington in the
early 1840s. Ch. b Milton: daughter b 30 Nov 1838. Ch. b
Farmington: daughter b 4 Apr 1843, and daughter b 11 Sep
1847. (Alton VR, p551; LDS I.G.I. BR; NHVR-Marr)

JONATHAN, b ca 1805, of Somersworth; head of household
in Somersworth in 1840, age 30-40, with family of spouse age
20-30, and two females both under 5. (Census Strafford Co.,
1840, p575)

JONATHAN aka Jr., b ca 1805, Strafford, s/o Isaac Young
Jr. and 1st wife (   ), alive 1842, native town; m 18 Dec
1834, Freewill Baptist Church, Strafford, Sally Saunders [b
ca 1810, of Strafford, alive 1842, same town]. Jonathan was
named son and heir of Isaac Young Jr. and Exec. of his
father's will signed 1 Apr 1826, proved 15 Sep 1834. In 1840
he was head of household in Strafford, age 30-40, as was his
spouse; they lived alone. He quitclaimed to [step-mother]
Mary Young, widow, [2nd wife of Isaac Jr.], all his right in
the land set off to her as her right of dower in the estate
of Isaac Young Jr. of Strafford, by deed signed 5 Feb 1842,
rec'd 2 Mar same year, for $200.00; Sally ceded dower rights;
witnesses Benjamin Foss, Robert W. Foss [Strafford Co. Deed
190:369]. (NHVR-Marr; Strafford Marr, NEHGS **Reg.** 76:37;
Census Strafford Co., 1840, p461)

JONATHAN, b 21 Dec 1805, Effingham, s/o Timothy and Molly
D. (Hobbs) Young, d testate, pre 6 Mar 1888, age 82, native
town; m 29 Jan 1835, Effingham, Sarah Buzzell [b 1808, Effingham, alive 1860, predeceased her husband, native town]. Jonathan and Sarah lived in Effingham up through 1860 on the
family homestead which Jonathan inherited from his father.
It is believed Jonathan and Sarah lived with his parents in
1840, when both he and Sarah were age 30-40 with one daughter
age 5-10. In 1860 Sarah was listed as his spouse; members of
household were sons Timothy B. and Jonathan L. as well as
Abigail Cotton, age 62 [b 1798, ME]. The 1870 census listed
Jonathan as widower; family members at home were son Timothy

B. and his bride Sarah M., age 24 [b 1846]. Upon the death
of his son Lyman J., Jonathan declined the administration of
Lyman's estate on date of 1 Mar 1870, and petitioned that
Lyman's brother Timothy B. Young be appointed as Admin.;
approved same date [Carroll Co. Probate #5825]. Jonathan's
will was drawn up 30 Jan 1871, proved 6 Mar 1888; witnesses
Martin V. Ricker, Kirk B. Neal, Sanborn B. Carter [Carroll Co.
Probate #5814]. He named son Timothy B. as his sole Exec. and
residuary legatee and bequeathed the sum of $10.00 to each of
his grandchildren Sarah Susan Hobbs and Albert W. Hobbs, the
children of his late daughter Amanda M. Hobbs. Ch. b Effingham: Amanda M. (Young) Hobbs, b ca 1835, wife of Daniel W.
Hobbs of Effingham; Timothy Benjamin+, b 10 Nov 1840; and
Jonathan L. aka Lyman J., b 1847, d 31 Jan 1870, Effingham,
farmer. (Census Strafford Co., 1840, p350; Census Carroll
Co., 1860, p594; 1870, p292; Stearn's N.H. Gen., V3, p1284;
NHVR-Deaths)

JONATHAN, b 28 Sep 1807, Barrington, s/o Eleazer and
Alice (Kingman) Young, d Aug 1873, Dover, bur. Barrington,
farmer; m 20 Sep 1835, Durham, Sophie aka Sophia Maria Ricker
[b 13 Jun 1815, Madbury, d/o _____ and _____ (Ham) Ricker, d
testate pre 5 Nov 1889, poss. Dover, bur. Pine Hill Cemetery,
Dover]. Jonathan and Sophie raised their eleven children in
Barrington, listed as residents on census returns from
1850-1870. In 1850 children at home were John E., Alice A.,
Elizabeth E., Sarah F., Edwin R., and Frank H.; other members
of household were Elizabeth Roberts, age 65 [b 1785], James
Campbell, age 47 [b 1803], and Joseph Ham, age 54 [b 1796].
By 1860 four younger children were listed in addition to the
six children cited above: Eliza, Jeremiah K., Irwin and
Charles. All children were at home in 1870 except for John
E. and Elizabeth; newest member of family was Mary S., age 8.

On 3 Feb 1874, widow Sophia was appointed guardian of
their three youngest sons Jeremiah Kingman Young, Irvin R.
Young and Charles S. Young, all minors above the age of 14
[Strafford Co. Probate 77:547]; sons Frank H. and Edwin R.,
both of age, gave surety for Sophia in the amount of $1,000.
Sophia's will, drawn 3 Sep, proved 5 Nov 1889, named no executor but named three grown children as residuary legatees,
Alice A. Young, Edwin R. Young and Irving R. Young; witnesses
Levi G. Hill, Thomas McKee, Ephraim H. Bradley [Strafford Co.
Probate 100:156]. Sophia made the following bequests to
daughters: to Ellen E. Tebbetts, $5.00; Fannie S. Grover,
$5.00; to Eliza R. Small, $5.00; and to Mary S. Kenniston,
$250.00. To son Frank Herbert Young she gave $5.00; to her
other surviving son J. Kingman, she bequeathed the use during
his lifetime of the house and field surrounding it which he
then occupied, with the stipulation that after his death the
property shall revert to her three residuary legatees [see
above]. To her grandchildren, the children of son John E.,
deceased, she gave the sum of $1.00 each: Ruth E. Furbush,
Julia A. Young, George H. Young and Helen F. Young. Legatees

Alice A. and son Irving received title to their parents' homestead in 1895 upon the death of sibling Kingman. By 1900 both remained single and were listed on the census that year as residents of Barrington, Alice A. as head of household; living with them was servant Dennis McCarthy, age 52 [b Dec 1848, Canada, nationalized citizen]. Alice affiliated with the First Congregational Church in Barrington at least by 1900. Family members were buried at Pine Grove Cemetery, Barrington. Ch. b Barrington: John E.+, b 1841; Alice A., b Jun 1844, d 3 May 1917, single, bur. Barrington; Sarah F., b 1846; Elizabeth E. aka Ellen E.+ (Young) Tebbetts, b 1846, twin?; Edwin R.+, b Dec 1847, twin; Frank Herbert, b 1850, d 1914, Barrington; Eliza R. (Young) Small, b 1851, alive 1889; Jeremiah Kingman aka Kingman+, b 20 Jul 1855; Charles S., b 1858, not mentioned in mother's will of 1889; Irving R., b Dec 1860, alive 1900 (see above); and Mary S.+ (Young) Kenniston, b 7 Jan 1862. (Ham's Dover Marr, TMs; 1900 Soundex; Stackpole's Durham, V1, p387; Census Strafford Co., 1850, p527; 1860, p180; 1870, p29; Frost's Dover Cem., V2, Plot #1311; Barrington Congreg. Church, p251; Barrington Graveyards, p132,133; LDS I.G.I. BR; NHVR-Births, Brides, Deaths)

JONATHAN, b ca 1815, of Farmington; head of household in Farmington in 1840, age 20-30, with family of spouse age 20-30, and three males, one age 5-10, one 10-15, one 15-20. (Census Strafford Co., 1840, p318)

JONATHAN, b 16 Feb 1818, Gilmanton Iron Works, eldest s/o David S. and Betsey (Avery) Young, d 2 Apr 1900, widower, his native town; m 13 Feb 1851, Belmont, Martha A. Nelson [b 1827, Gilmanton, d/o Capt. Dudley Nelson, d 1883, home town]. At time of marriage, Jonathan lived in Lowell, MA, occupation mill worker. By 1870 he held full title to his father's 200-acre homestead, probably having bought out his siblings' shares. That year he and Martha were listed on the census returns for Gilmanton, estate valued at $4,000; children at home in 1870 were Eben S., Frank D., Ella and Wilber. He was a Deacon of the Freewill Baptist Church at Gilmanton Iron Works. Son Frank D., age 43, single, was head of household in 1900 for Gilmanton, members of household, servant Mary J. Chase and her sons Burt Chase and Arthur Chase. Jonathan's daughter Ellen was buried at private cemetery on Iron Works Road, Gilmanton. Ch. b Belmont: Jonathan, b 1850s, d.y.; Ellen, b 20 Apr 1852, d 18 Sep 1854, 2 yrs., 4 months, Gilmanton; Eben S., 7 Feb 1854, d.y.; and Frank D., b Jun 1856, alive 1900, Gilmanton. Ch. b Gilmanton: Ella, b 4 Aug 1858, d 1881, Gilmanton; Eben S.+, b Feb 1864; Wilbur, b 1866; and William N.+, b 1867. (Census Belknap Co., 1870, p33; 1900 Soundex; NHVR-Births, Marr, Deaths; LDS I.G.I. BR; Folsom's NH Cemeteries, p135; Bio. Review, XXI, p354-356)

JONATHAN, b 20 Nov 1818, Strafford, s/o Benjamin F. Young by 1st wife (   ), d 14 Dec 1895, East Rochester; m 13 Apr 1847, Rochester, Hannah S. Waldron [b 10 Jan 1820, Rochester, d 10 Apr 1878, age 58-3-0, Farmington]. By the terms of his

father's will signed 16 Dec 1839, proved 20 Jan 1840, Jonathan
was to receive a one-half share of the family homestead farm
of 120 acres in Farmington, to be shared with brother Benjamin. By the time the will was probated, Jonathan was entitled
to both moieties of the farm inasmuch as sibling Benjamin predeceased their father. Jonathan was also named Exec. of his
sister Mercy Young's will drawn 21 Apr 1840, proved 17 Jan
1841. He and Hannah were listed on census returns for Farmington from 1850-1870. In 1850 there were no children, but
household included Jonathan's stepmother Deborah, age 48 [b
1802], Anna Young, age 18 [b 1832], kinswoman, and maternal
step-grandmother Kezia Furber, age 82 [b 1768]. From 1860-
1870 children at home were Elizabeth M., Preston B., Maria and
John. It is worthy of note that their two sons became well-
known physicians and surgeons; it was son Dr. John F. Young
who as practicing physician requested in 1878 and 1895 that
his parents' last remains be removed from Crown Point Cemetery, Strafford to be interred at Pine Grove Cemetery, Farmington. Ch. b Farmington: daughter b 25 May 1851, d.y.;
Elizabeth M. aka Lizzie M.+ (Young) Forsaith, b 26 Oct 1853;
Maria Ellen, b 1855; John F.+, b 1857; and Preston B.+, b
1 Jun 1858. (LDS I.G.I. BR; NHVR-Births, Brides, Deaths,
Marr; Census Strafford Co., 1850, p639; 1860, p398,399; 1870,
p182; 1900 Soundex; Biog. Review, XXI, p350,351)

JONATHAN, b 1821, ME, of Somersworth in 1860, single,
teamster; lived at boarding house. (Census Strafford Co.,
1860, p282)

JONATHAN, b ca 1830, of Rollingsford; m 11 Jun 1857,
Rollingsford, Martha Masfield [b ca 1835, of same town].
(NHVR-Marr)

JONATHAN, b ca 1830, of Rollingsford; m 29 Apr 1858,
Somersworth, Eunice Jones [b ca 1835, of same town].
(NHVR-Marr)

JONATHAN B. aka Lt., b 18 Feb 1805, prob. Alton, s/o Levi
and 1st wife Sally (Barker) Young of New Durham, d 4 Aug 1891,
age 86-5-15, widower, farmer, Alton; m 22 Jun 1834, New
Durham, Hannah D. Stevens [b 1812, New Durham, d/o Durrell and
Nancy (Hill) Stevens, d 12 May 1875, age 63, her native town].
Jonathan was named Exec. of his father's will of 27 Apr 1841,
proved 1 Jan 1850, and received the homestead in New Durham
with the stipulation that he was to provide a home for his
mother and sisters. At the time of his marriage Jonathan
lived in New Durham where he became listed as head of household from 1840-1870. In 1840 his age was 30-40, with spouse
age 20-30 and family of one male age 5-10 and one female under
5. Hannah was named as his spouse on the census returns for
New Durham from 1850-1870. In 1850 his estate was valued at
$3,000; children at home, Joseph D., Marilla M., and Frances
H; in 1860, those at home were Joseph D., Marilla and youngest
daughter Addie R. By 1870 Jonathan and Hannah lived alone.

Admin. Papers on Jonathan B.'s estate in Alton were filed
12 Aug 1891 by daughter Marilla M. Ricker of Dover who stated

that her father died 4 Aug 1891, that there was no widow and
that the estate did not exceed $1,500.00; appraisers named
were Amos L. Rollins, Charles C. Mooney and D. Melvin, all of
Alton [Belknap Co. Probate #4830]; on same date she gave bond
of $3,000.00 with sureties Joseph Jones and Daniel Hall, both
of Dover. Ch. b New Durham: Joseph D.+, b 1835; Marilla M.
(Young) Ricker, b 1839, known by· married name of Ricker in
1891; Frances H. aka Fannie H.+ (Young) Jones, b 1841; and
Addie R.+ (Young) Leighton, b 1851. (Census Strafford Co.,
1840, p336; 1850, p581; 1860, p99; 1870, p236; NHVR-Brides,
Marr, Deaths; Jennings' New Durham, V2, n.p.)

JONATHAN FRANKLIN aka Jr., b 1796, Barrington, prob. s/o
Jonathan and Mary (Hill) Young, d 23 Oct 1850, native town;
m1 27 Aug 1818, Freewill Baptist Church, Strafford, Hannah
Hall aka Hannah Johnson [b ca 1800, Jackson, d 1847, Barring-
ton]; m2 18 Jul 1848, Dover, Martha F. Gray [b 1821, ME, alive
1850, Barrington]. Jonathan was listed on the census returns
for Barrington from 1830-1850. In 1830, his age was 30-40
with a household containing one female [spouse] of same age
group, and four males, one under 5, two age 5-10, and one 10-
15. In 1840 his age was 40-50, as was his spouse, with family of an elderly female age 70-80 [poss. Hannah's mother],
five males, two age 5-10, one each 10-15, 15-20 and 20-30, and
three females, two under 5 and one age 10-20. According to
1850 Census taken that summer or early fall, Martha was named
as his spouse when household contained six young children by
his previous marriage, whom Martha was to raise single-
handedly when widowed: Lewis, Hannah, Mary A., twins Benjamin
and Charles E., and Herschel C.. That year Rebecca Daniels,
age 86 [b 1764], lived with them.

Jonathan was named Exec. of the will of Stephen Young of
Barrington, signed 15 Oct 1824, proved 19 Jan 1826; curiously
enough, it was Jonathan's wife Hannah who received a legacy
from Stephen of a one-half share of the remainder of his real
estate after bequests; see Stephen and Kezia Young of Barrington. Jonathan's and Hannah's relationship with Stephen
remains obscure. It is rather more likely that Hannah, not
Jonathan, was the off-spring of Stephen. By late 1850, Martha
was widowed. On 5 Nov 1850, son Stephen E. Young of Dover was
appointed Admin. of Jonathan's estate; bond of $3,000.00 was
given with sureties Ezra Berry and John H. Winkley Jr., both
of Barrington [Strafford Co. Probate 50:406]. Yet the court
found it necessary to re-appoint an administrator, Ezra M.
Drown [husband of Sarah Drown] of Strafford, on 7 Jan 1851,
inasmuch as Jonathan's estate "had not before been administered on"; bond of $3,000.00 was given by the said sureties
above [Strafford Co. Probate 50:411]. On 3 Dec 1850, widow
Martha F. was allowed $200.00 for her support [Strafford Co.
Probate 43:255]; on same date of session, inventory of Jonathan's estate was returned by George McDaniel, Hatevil Rumford
and Samuel Chesley: amount of real and personal estate,
$1,210.00; personal estate of $1,244.22 included debts of

$474.86; grand total of estate, $2,454.22 [Strafford Co. Probate 67:22].

On 1 Dec 1852 at Rochester, guardianship of Herschel C., minor under 14 years of age, was awarded to Enoch P. Young of Lawrence, Essex Co., MA; bond of $1,000.00 was given with sureties given by John B. Young and Samuel Chesley, both of Barrington [Strafford Co. Probate 50:459]. This was amended on 1 Apr 1857 when Martha was appointed guardian of Herschel C., under the age of fourteen; bond of $1,000.00 was posted with sureties Samuel Chesley and Moses Pierce, both of Barrington [Strafford Co. Probate 50:418]. Another son, Herbert D., under the age of fourteen, was made ward of Moses Pierce of Barrington on 7 Feb 1854 by posting bond of $1,000.00 with sureties from Hall Pierce of Barrington and the said John B. Young [Strafford Co. Probate 68:51]. At a later date, 7 Jul 1868, the same John B. Young was appointed guardian of Herbert, a minor upwards of fourteen years, by bond of $1,000 with sureties given by Charles H. Bunker of Durham and William J. Chesley of Dover [Strafford Co. Probate 77:431].

The administration of Jonathan's estate neared completion upon the Petition to Sue [and/or sell] brought by Sarah Drown, Admin. [wife of the said Ezra Drown, d/o Jonathan and Mary (Hill) Young], dated 23 Sep 1869, granted 2 Nov 1869 [Strafford Co. Probate 60:345]. She petitioned that the personal estate was exhausted, leaving unpaid demands in the amount of $200.00. Inasmuch as the estate still held 30 acres in two tracts of land, one lot of 29 acres by land of John B. Young, the other, one acre, she prayed allowance to sell the whole of the estate as the property would be more than sufficient to pay the demands. Jonathan, Hannah and son Stephen were buried at Pine Grove Cemetery, Barrington. Some family records were obtained from son Lewis Augustus' application for Invalid Pension, having been disabled in the Civil War [see main entry], Pension No. 69,938. Ch. b Barrington by Hannah: John B.+, b 16 Feb 1819; Stephen E.+, b 1824; prob. Enoch P., b 1828, J. Frank+ aka Franklin, b 1832; Lewis Augustus+, b 1834; Hannah, b 1837; Mary A., b 1839; Benjamin A., b 1842, twin; Charles E., b 1842, twin; and Herschel C., b 1846. Ch. b Barrington by Martha: Herbert D., b ca 1850 [not listed in 1850 Census]. (NHVR-Deaths, Marr; Census Strafford Co., 1840, p481; 1850, p517; Barrington Graveyards, Plot 3W; Strafford Marr, **Reg.** 76:29; Nat'l. Archives Milit. Recs.)

JONATHAN THOMPSON, b 7 Dec 1822, Dover, s/o Jonathan and Abigail (Coffin) Young, d 23 May 1866, Dover; m 1 Oct 1846, Woodstock, Elizabeth Lucinda Demeritt [b 25 Jun 1825, North Woodstock, d/o Jacob B. and Martha V. (Barron) Demeritt, d 27 Feb 1894, age 68-8-2, Dover; Jacob Demeritt was brother of Clarissa L. (Demeritt) Young, Jonathan T.'s step-mother]. Since Jonathan was made a ward of Nathaniel Young of Dover [uncle] at the time of his father's death, both he and said Nathaniel received title to one-half of the family homestead farm in Dover, 37 acres, 58 rods, held in joint tenancy with

elder sister Hannah S. Young. His legacy also included 11
acres, 29 rods of woodland in Madbury. He and Elizabeth
raised their family in Dover on this 70-acre homestead farm
located on the northern side of Littleworth Road and Boston
& Maine R.R., bounded west by land of said Hannah S. Young and
Joseph Winkley, north by land of heirs of Peter Cushing, east
by Thomas J. Willey, and south by said Littleworth Road. In
1850 Jonathan and Elizabeth were listed on the census returns
for Dover; members of household in addition to their children
Abigail C. and Tristam, were the said Hannah S., single, age
35, and aunt Eliza Young, single, age 52 [b 1798]. From 1860
to 1870, the family were listed as residents of Ward 3, Dover;
in 1860 children at home were Abigail C., Tristam, Ezra K.,
Jacob D., Martha S., James F., George A., and Clara L. as well
as kinswoman Hannah. In 1870 members of household were children Ezra K., Jacob D., Martha, James F., George, Elizabeth,
Annie, and John L., the last six in school; estate valued at
$7,000. For Jonathan T.'s fifth share in the homestead farm
of Elizabeth Coffin, late of Dover, see [sibling] James C. and
Mary Young of Madbury.

By 3 Sep 1867, Elizabeth was widowed; on that date she
was appointed guardian of her six minor children under the age
of fourteen, Martha S., James T., George A., Lizzie C., Anna
A., and John L., by bond of $20,000.00, sureties given by
Hannah S. Young of Dover and Alaric B. Demeritt of Durham
[Strafford Co. Probate 77:459]. In 1870 she was listed as
head of household in Dover, estate valued at $7,000.00. On
25 Aug 1874, Elizabeth petitioned for a License to Sell at
public auction the 70-acre farm with the intent that each
child would receive a one-ninth part from the sale; license
was granted 6 Oct 1874 [Strafford Co. Probate 60:393]. In
1880 Elizabeth and all surviving children, Tristam A., Ezra
K., Jacob D., James T., George A., John L., Martha S. Kay,
Lizzie C. and Anna A. were heirs of Hannah S. Young of Dover,
cited above; for further details of Hannah's will, see Jonathan and Abigail (Coffin) Young of Dover. In 1900 son Jacob
D. was head of household in Dover, single; living at home were
sister Clara L., single, brother John L. and his wife Frances
E. (Lord) Young. Daughter Martha S. (Young) Kay, wife of
Edward Kay, became member of the D.A.R. as fourth-generation
descendant of Ezra and Susannah (Demeritt) Young of Dover.

Jonathan T., wife Elizabeth and children were buried at
the John Young Cemetery, Littleworth Road, Dover. Ch. b
Dover: Abigail C., b 1848, d 27 Jun 1863, age 15, Dover;
Tristam A.+, b 7 Jan 1849; Ezra K. aka George K., b 2 Jun
1850, d 13 Apr 1900, Dover; Jacob D., b 6 Jan 1852, d 1 Dec
1927, Dover; Martha S., b 1854, m pre 1880, Edward Kay; James
T.+, b 1856; George A., b 27 Nov 1857, d 1 Feb 1887, age
29-2-4, Dover; Clara Elizabeth, b 1 Jul 1859, d 23 Dec 1930,
Dover; John B., b 29 May 1861, d.y.; Anna aka Hannah, b 14 Aug
1863; and John L.+, b 4 Apr 1865. (NHVR-Births, Marr, Deaths;
Census Strafford Co., 1850, p167; 1860, p818; 1870, p100,101;

1900 Soundex; Frost's Dover Cem., Plot #22; Demeritt Fam., **Reg.** 87:89,90; Steuerwald's Dover Cem., TMs; LDS I.G.I. BR; D.A.R Lineage #36348, V37, p121; 1871 Sanford & Everts Maps)

JOSEPH aka Capt. aka Gent., b 24 Aug 1726, South New Market [Newfields], s/o Thomas and Sarah (Folsom) Young, res. of Durham, d 11 Apr 1806, age 78, Durham; m1 ca 1753, New-fields, Anna Folsom [b Aug 1731, Newfields, d/o Jeremiah Folsom, d Oct 1763, Newfields]; m2 1764, Durham, Mary Foss [b 25 Nov 1739, d/o Zachariah and Sarah (Gaines) Foss, d 1 May 1822, age 82, Durham]. He served in the French and Indian Wars on the expedition to Crown Point and at Fort William Henry in 1757, earning the rank of Captain 31 Jan 1777 in the Revolutionary War. In 1767, Joseph, innholder of New Market, was named son and heir of Thomas Young of New Market and Exec. of his father's will drawn 2 May, proved 27 May 1767; his legacy was the 140 acres "now in his possession" on the n.w. side of Piscassic River, with a one-half share of the sawmill and mills privileges on both sides of the river, and all the remainder of Thomas' real and personal estate.

There were two distinct phases in Joseph's life, resi-dence in New Market with first wife Anna, and from ca 1760 on, residence with wife Mary on the Durham side of Piscassic River which later became known as Packers Falls. The land he inher-ited from his father straddled this river so to speak, as part of it lay in Newfields and partly in Durham. Durham town records indicated that Capt. Joseph was a town officer in 1786, head of household in 1790, with family of two males over 16, one male under 16, and three females, elected Selectman for 1791, and appointed 13 Apr 1792 to a town committee whose goals were to locate a site for building their church; church pews sold for as little as 19 pounds up to 34 pounds. In 1800 Capt. Joseph was listed as resident of Durham, 45 years plus, with spouse of same age group, four sons, one 10-16, two 16-26, and one 26-45, and two females, one age 16-26 and one 26-45. He was survived in 1806 by second wife Mary and a robust family of nine sons and two daughters derived from both wives, one son having predeceased him.

Joseph's ventures into land speculation in Eaton were made in partnership with citizenry from New Market, many of whom would later bear witness to many of his land deeds or be involved in the administration of Joseph's estate, i.e., John Burley aka Burleigh, John Meed Jr., Joshua Frost, John Folsom, Thomas Bennett, Esq. and Walter Bryent Jr. Joseph was listed on the Schedule of the Proprietors of Eaton on 21 Oct 1768 but became absentee owner of three lots in Eaton, one of many co-grantees in the sale of these lots. These three lots were sold for delinquent taxes for the years 1786, 1795, and 1798. Tax deeds on the sale of these lots at public auction were recorded in Strafford Co. Deeds (1) Deed 23:238, signed 10 Nov 1790, rec'd 17 Jan 1797; (2) Deed 31:267, signed 17 May 1797, rec'd 29 Oct 1799; and (3) Deed 34:442, signed 27 Dec 1800, rec'd 30 Apr 1801.

While still of New Market, Joseph made the following land transactions: (1) purchase of 5 acres or one-half of a tract of land near Durham Falls, north by land of Thomas Bickford in part, and partly by land of the late Deacon Benjamin Wheeler, west by the highway that leads from Durham Falls to "Lamprele" River, south by the Parsonage lands and east by Ichabod Chase's land, from Rebechah Adams of New Market, widow of Samuel Adams, physician for 10 pounds-5 shillings, by deed signed 30 Dec 1766, rec'd 19 Mar 1787; witnesses Walter Bryent and John Marsten [Strafford Co. Deed 8:181]; (2) quitclaimed this tract near Durham Falls to John Sullivan of Durham for 10 pounds by deed signed 4 Jul 1772, rec'd 19 Aug 1780; witnesses illegible [Strafford Co. Deed 4:23]; (3) purchase of Lot 45, 2nd Div., New Durham by Joseph and co-grantee Joseph Smith, also of New Market, for speculation, by deed signed 5 Jun 1772, rec'd 30 Jan 1777, from Wentworth Cheswell of New Market for 25 pounds-12 shillings; witnesses Thomas Young, Jonathan Folsom [Strafford Co. Deed 1:470]. By way of footnote, Cheswell purchased this lot from Thomas Young of New Market by deed dated 7 May 1772 [NH Prov. Probate 90:522].

As resident of Durham, Joseph and the said Joseph Smith sold this same Lot 45 in New Durham by deed signed 9 Jan, rec'd 30 Jan 1777, to John Mason, Esq., of Stratham for 39 pounds; witnesses Walter Bryent, Hubartus Neal Jr. [Strafford Co. Deed 1:471]. Joseph with co-grantee John Bennett of Durham, purchased 15 acres in Durham, and "is the same land that was granted to Abraham Stevenson, and by him sold to my honorable father Joshua Crommett, late of Durham," bounded south, east and north by lands of Joseph Young and John Bennett, for 22 pounds-10 shillings by deed signed 13 Jul, rec'd 14 Jul 1787; witnesses David Chapman, John Griffen [Strafford Co. Deed 8:398]. Within six months by deed of 18 Dec 1787, rec'd 30 Mar 1789, John Bennett quitclaimed to Joseph for 20 pounds his share in these 15 acres; witnesses John Folsom, Eliphalet Smith [[Strafford Co. Deed 10:352]. He was also one of seven principals all of New Market who quitclaimed their interests in 100 acres, 1st Div. in New Durham, land drawn to the original right of Thomas Young Esq., to Joseph Young of New Market, merchant [believed to be Joseph Jr.] for 40 pounds, by deed signed 20 Jun 1786, rec'd 8 Sep 1795; witnesses Eliphalet Smith, Thomas Young Jr. [Strafford Co. Deed 20:325].

Joseph also acquired 20 acres land adjacent to the north corner of his dwelling house in Durham on the road leading from Lamprey River Landing to Packer's Falls, from Joseph Chesley of Durham for $300.00, by deed signed 11 Jun 1800, rec'd 27 Jul 1801; witnesses Joseph Young Jr., Dan Smith [Strafford Co. Deed 35:435]. The only sale of land which conveyed Mary's dower rights was by deed signed 9 Jun, rec'd 18 Sep 1800, when Joseph and Mary sold 19 acres, 62 sq. rods of land in Durham by lands of John Bennick aka Bennett, Major Joseph Young [son] and David Chapman, to Shadrach Robinson of

Greenland, Rock. Co. for $400.00; witnesses James Smith, Daniel Smith [Strafford Co. Deed 34:207].

Ten years before his death, Joseph began to partition off his estate to several adult sons. The first such conveyance was to [son] Jeremiah of New Market by deed signed 9 Jan 1786, rec'd 8 Feb 1794, 20 acres in Durham which represented one half of the land Joseph bought of Jonathan Willey by lands of Stephen Cogin, Abraham Bennick, Thomas Crommet and Joseph Young Jr., for fifty pounds; witnesses Jeremy Bryent, [son] Timothy W. Young [Strafford Co. Deed 18:36]. He conveyed to son Henry of Durham by deed signed 1 May 1800, rec'd 2 Mar 1801, for $200, the one half of the house that he then dwelt in, together with one-half acre land adjoining the house and full liberty of passing and repassing from the house to the main road called Packers Falls Road; witnesses Sally Bryent, John Bryent [Strafford Co. Deed 35:295]. In addition, he sold to Henry 79 acres of the farm where Joseph then lived, beginning at the river joining Joseph Chesley's woodland, south to a small brook which lets into Lamprey River, for $500.00; witnesses Jeremy Demeritt, Valentine Smith [Strafford Co. Deed 39:250]. He sold 80 acres of the southern part of his farm where Joseph then lived, adjacent to lands of Samuel Foss and David Davis, except for his dwelling house, to son William of Durham by deed of 29 Sep 1801, rec'd 2 Jan 1802, for $500.00; witnesses Jeremy Demeritt, Valentine Smith [Strafford Co. Deed 38:56].

Widow Mary filed Admin. Papers on Joseph's estate 8 May 1806, giving bond of $4,000.00 with sureties Ebenezer Doe and Henry Young [son], both of Durham [Strafford Co. Probate 10:144]. Inventory of the estate was permitted 3 Jun 1806 and taken by Wentworth Cheswell Esq., Samuel Joy and Ebenezer Doe; report filed 14 Jun 1806, attested to by Mary on 26 Jul 1806 [Strafford Co. Probate 10:175]. Real estate was rated at $1,554.00, which included Joseph's share of mansion house plus one acre, $300.00; see division of property below for full description of real estate. Personal estate was valued at $316.10. Mary's dower rights were set off 30 Jul 1807 by the said appraisers as well as Andrew Simpson and Valentine Smith; allowed 27 Nov 1807 [Strafford Co. Probate 11:316]. She received Joseph's half of the mansion house and his right in 1-1/2 acres of land reserved by the decease out of his deed to William Young, together with 20 acres that the deceased bought of Joseph Chesley, also the marsh and thatch bed which belonged to the estate near the fish creek on Exeter River, and one-third share of the deceased' pew in the Durham meeting house for her use "during her natural life." Distribution of Joseph's estate was made 22 Sep 1807 to sons and daughters by Ebenezer Smith, Samuel Joy, Jeremiah B. Mooney, Ebenezer Doe and Valentine Smith: Joseph Jr., 1 acre land in New Market on west side of Lamprey River; Benjamin, 10 acres land in Durham in Horns Wood; John, 4 acres in New Market on west side of Lamprey River by land of David Chapman; Zachariah, 1-1/2 acres in New Market by land of Paul Chapman, and 8 acres in Horns Woods; Thomas, 1/4 part of sawmill in New Market on west side of Lamprey River at lower falls; Timothy W., 1/4 part of a sawmill in New Market on western side of Lamprey River lower falls; Henry, 1-3/4 acres from Horns Wood by land of Joseph Smith; William, 2-1/4 acres in Horns Woods; George Gaines, 10 acres in Horns Woods; Sarah Meder, w/o Ebenezer Meder, 6-1/2 acres in New Market; Mary Young, four acres in New Market; the children of Jeremiah, deceased, the wharf in New Market on west side of Lamprey River [Strafford Co. Probate 11:66]. As noted in many a land deed later on, the telltale "one-twelfth share" each legatee received made it possible to trace the later movements of Joseph's children. Ch. b New Market by 1st wife Ann: Joseph Jr.+, b 5 Apr 1754; Benjamin+, b 8 Jul 1756; Jeremiah L.+, b 15 Nov 1758; John+, b 3 Dec 1760; and Sarah+ (Young) Meader, b 25 Mar 1763. Ch. b Durham by 2nd wife Mary: Zachariah+, b 9 Feb 1765; Thomas+, b 18 May 1767; Timothy W.+, b 23 Aug 1769; Lovina (Young) Chapman, b 7 Dec 1771, wife of James Chapman [s/o David Chapman]; Henry+, b 23 Jul 1773; William+, b 11 Sep 1777; Mary, b 11 Nov 1779, d 1 May 1820; and George Gaines+, b 27 Jan 1784. (Census Strafford Co., 1790, p90; 1800, p161; Durham Graveyards, p62,63; Folsom Fam., **Reg.** 30:214; Fitts' Newfields, p503,505,683,684; NHVR-Deaths; Stackpole's Durham, V1, p201-203,362,376,396; LDS 1.G.I. BR; D.A.R Lineage #18022, V19, p10; NH State Papers, V27, p222)

JOSEPH, b ca 1730, prob. Parish of Madbury, joiner, alive 1790, Barrington; m 1750s, Barrington, Anne (   ) [b ca 1735, of Barrington, alive 1768, same town]. Joseph had connections with Barrington as early as 1768, signed the Association Test there in 1776 and was listed as resident in 1790, with one female in household, no children. It is noteworthy that when he lived in Barrington he sold off five properties located in the Two-Mile Streak; however no equivalent deed of purchase could be found for him as co-grantee on any of the five parcels of land. When of Barrington he sold to Silas Drew of same town, 10 acres by lands of Benjamin Young and Francis Drew, which Joseph had purchased from Sarah Jaffrey and Mary Osborn 4 Aug 1756, by deed signed 2 Jun 1768, rec'd 4 May 1793, for 30 pounds; witnesses Ephraim Hanson, Nathaniel Twombly [Strafford Co. Deed 15:539]. Another sale of 10 acres adjacent to the n.w. corner of land bought by William Fowler, easterly to the highway leading from Madbury into the Two-Mile Streak, was made by deed signed 20 Apr 1771, rec'd 13 Apr 1778, to Aaron Leighton of Madbury, cordwainer, for 50 pounds; witnesses Edward Butler, Joseph Drew [Strafford Co. Deed 2:177]. By two deeds signed 14 Jun 1773, Joseph sold two parcels of land to Silas Drew of Barrington: 14-1/4 acres land in the 5th Range bounded by land owned by Francis Drew, Terry Hixon and Silas Drew by deed rec'd 4 May 1793, for 15 pounds; witnesses Peter Young, Joshua K___ [Strafford Co. Deed 6:1]; and 50 acres in the 5th Range for 35 pounds, by deed rec'd 4 May 1793; sole witness Peter Young [Strafford Co. Deed

16:2,3]. His last sale was 1-3/4 acres land in Madbury to Ebenezer Drew of Madbury for 20 pounds by deed signed 10 Aug 1780, rec'd 8 Apr 1793; Anne ceded dower rights; witnesses Andrew Young, Samuel Drew [Strafford Co. Deed 15:487]. Known ch. b Barrington: Benjamin, b 5 Apr 1756. (Census Strafford Co., 1790, p87; Wilson's Assoc. Test, p122; D.A.R Wolfeboro, p35-37)

JOSEPH aka Esq., b 20 Jun 1749, Belmont, s/o Joseph and Sarah (Brown) Young of Kingston [no main entry], d testate 21 Sep 1821, age 72, Gilmanton; m 24 Feb 1771, both Exeter and Belmont [one town, the filing of intentions], Anna Folsom [b 25 Feb 1748, Exeter, d/o Peter and Mary (Folsom) Folsom, d 1 Nov 1812, age 64-8-5, Gilmanton]; m2 pre Apr 1814, Belmont, prob. Hannah (   ) Morrill [b 1750s, of Belmont, widow of Micajah Morrill of Gilmanton in 1810, alive 1821, Gilmanton]. One tradition has it that Joseph as a youth was put out to a trade in Kensington and at the age of 21 [1770] came to Gilmanton. Yet LDS I.G.I. BR indicated he was born in Belmont [i.e., Upper Gilmanton] and his earliest purchase of land in Gilmanton was dated 1789. Hannah, as widow of Micajah Morrill of Gilmanton, was named Admin. of Micajah's estate on 21 Nov 1810, having given bond of $1,000.00 with sureties John Shepard Esq. of Gilmanton and Ebenezer Lowell of Loudon, Rock. Co. [Strafford Co. Probate 20:68]. In 1790 Joseph was head of household in Gilmanton, with two males over 16 years, no male under 16, and three females. In 1810 he was head of household there, age 45 plus with household of two females 45 plus, three males, one under 10, two 16-26, and one female 26-45. As resident of District No. 3, Gilmanton in 1812, he was taxed at $13.42, the highest tax rate of any of the eleven Young property owners of Gilmanton for that year. He was elected for nine years as Representative and eleven years as Selectman, and chosen ruling elder in the Baptist Freewill Church. It was his choice not to sign the Association Test Paper of 1776 on the grounds of being a conscientious objector.

Joseph's first purchase of land in Gilmanton was by quit-claim from Samuel Gilman of Exeter on part of 100-acre Lot 2, 7th Range, for five shillings, "in the last laying out of the township, drawn to the original right of Joseph Baker," by deed signed 10 Jun 1789, rec'd 23 Feb 1793, witnesses Ebenezer Gilman, Josiah Gilman [Strafford Co. Deed 15:385]. In 1793, he erected the tavern house and store in Academy Village which were later occupied and managed by son William Henry up until his death in 1797. Joseph also played a significant role in founding the Gilmanton Meeting House; he and co-grantees Simeon Bean and Stephen Bean purchased one acre land "for the purpose of building a meeting house thereon," by deed signed 20 Jun 1793, rec'd 2 Mar 1797, from Josiah and Abigail Weeks of Gilmanton for 5 pounds and 8 shillings; witnesses Dudley Young, Jonathan Young [Strafford Co. Deed 25:84]. One-half acre land in the n.w. corner of Lot 49, "which said half acre is now occupied by said Young," was purchased by Joseph from Stephen and Jemima Bean of Gilmanton for five shillings by quitclaim signed 9 Dec 1794, rec'd 2 Mar 1797; witnesses Ezekial Hoit, George Wentworth [Strafford Co. Deed 25:73]. Part of 100-acre Lot 8, 1st Range, Upper Div., beginning at s.w. side of the Province Road, was sold to Samuel French of Gilmanton for $900.00 by deed of 1 Aug, rec'd 5 Sep 1799; witnesses Isaac Bean, Levi Bean Jr. [Strafford Co. Deed 34:126]. He purchased one acre, 23 rods of land with buildings near the Academy House, by deed of 12 Mar 1801, rec'd 23 Aug 1802, from [son-in-law] Allen Hackett of Gilmanton, tanner, for $300.00; witnesses Benjamin Weeks, Henry Wadley [Strafford Co. Deed 40:116], and sold 1-1/4 acres near the Academy by deed of 4 Feb 1802, rec'd 26 Nov 1805, to the said Benjamin Weeks for $350.00; witnesses Samuel Burnham, Mathias Weeks 3rd [Strafford Co. Deed 49:273].

Through two purchases Joseph became owner of Lot 8, 6th Range, Gilmanton, by land of Stephen Swett: (1) 68 acres of this lot were purchased for $300.00 from Enoch Clark of Gilmanton, by deed signed 2 Jan, rec'd 23 Aug 1802; witnesses Samuel Clark, Nicholas Folsom [Strafford Co. Deed 40:105]; (2) part of Lot 8, 6th Range was purchased for $32.00 from Stephen Swett of Gilmanton by deed of 2 Dec 1802, rec'd 22 Feb 1803; witnesses Noah Burnham, Josiah Ladd [Strafford Co. Deed 42:130].

Joseph's will, written 12 Sep, proved 12 Oct 1821, illuminated the fact that he had remarried and that his second wife was named Hannah, believed to be the widow Hannah Morrill who received lands from the estate of her late husband Micajah. The sale of these lands by Hannah and Joseph is cited below. He designated wife Hannah as sole Exec. of his will, naming daughter Polly Hackett as residuary legatee; witnesses David Bean, Charles Smith, Daniel Pulsifer [Strafford Co. Probate 28:43]. On that date, Polly and husband Allen Hackett waived all objections to probate of Joseph's will, and concurrently, widow Hannah was allowed Exec.; bond of $5,000.00 was given with sureties Josiah Copp and David Bean of Gilmanton [Strafford Co. Probate 30:16]. Joseph bequeathed to his wife Hannah $200.00 in money "in consideration of money I received when I sold her place, for her use and disposal," all the produce of the homestead farm but not the livestock, one-half of his personal property "for ever," and the one-third part of his real estate during her natural life. It is shown by deed signed 25 Apr, rec'd 7 Sep 1814, that Hannah and Joseph sold her dower rights to 21-3/4 acres that had been part of Micajah Morrill's estate in Gilmanton to Benjamin Kelley, physician of Gilmanton, for $435.00; witnesses Samuel Shepard, John Bean [Strafford Co. Deed 80:282]. Polly Hackett, "his only child and heir-at-law," was to receive the remainder of his real and personal estate in Gilmanton.. Inventory of his estate was taken by Ezekial Hoit, Ebenezer Eastman, and William Hutchins, returned on 27 Oct 1821, approved same date [Strafford Co.

Probate 28:231]. Real estate was rated at $3,300.00: his homestead contained 100 acres of Lot 1, 7th Range in Upper Parish, 75 acres adjacent on south side of Lot 2, 25 acres on west side of Province Road purchased from Simeon Bean, and a small piece of land off of the north corner of the James Lot, adjacent, with buildings, were appraised at $2,400.00; also part of Lot 2, 5th Range and part of Lot 15, 4th Range in Upper Parish, containing in all 100 acres, were set at $900.00. Personal estate was appraised at $1,804.16, comprising livestock, tools, produce, furniture, beds and bedding, apparel, 7 notes of hand valued at $331.34, lumber and 3 pews at Meeting House; grand total of estate, $5,104.16.

Dower rights were set off to Hannah 11 Oct 1822 by Daniel Gale, Esq., Abraham Parsons Jr., Noah Leavitt, Samuel B. French and Joseph Weymouth based on petition of 7 Dec 1821 [Strafford Co. Probate 32:346]: one-third of 100-acre Lot 1, 7th Range, the middle front room and back bedroom of the home, the spinning house, and privileges of using the dairy, cellar, cider house and garden. Hannah's account as Exec. of Joseph's estate was filed and attested to 28 May 1824 [Strafford Co. Probate 34:133]. Personal estate per inventory was worth $1,820.63. Indebtedness paid off and administrative expenses which she had incurred including the legacy of $200.00 and the amount of "execution in favor of Allen Hackett recovered at Sep Court of $76.44," came to $938.39; balance of $882.24 was due from Exec. Joseph, Anna, and children William Henry and Anna were buried at a private cemetery in Gilmanton. Known ch. b Upper Gilmanton: William Henry+, b 5 May 1772; Anna+ (Young) Bean, b 19 Jan 1776; and Polly+ (Young) Hackett, b 13 Apr 1780. (LDS I.G.I. BR; NHVR-Births, Marr, Deaths; Census Strafford Co., 1790, p92; 1810, p823; Goss' Gravestones, p56; Gilmanton TR, V3, p385; Lancaster's Gilmanton, p93,98,136,246; Folsom's NH Cemeteries, p126; Hammond's N.H. Gazette, p169)

JOSEPH, b 1750s, of Alton; Joseph of Alton mortgaged property in Tuftonboro, 100 acres of Lot 12 which was part of a larger lot owned by John Peirce of Portsmouth, Rock. Co., and was the same land that said Peirce conveyed to Joseph concurrently when mortgage was signed 11 Apr 1799, rec'd 2 Jun 1799, for $600.00, payable in gold or silver with interest over the next 30 months; witnesses John Gains, George Gains [Strafford Co. Deed 30:290].

JOSEPH, b 1750s, of Gilsum, Cheshire Co., alive 1840, Gilmanton; m 2 Jan 1777, Swansey, Margaret Parsons [b ca 1755, Swansey, alive 1840, Gilmanton]. By 1783, Joseph was land owner in Gilmanton, listed on the census returns for both 1790 and 1840. In 1790 family contained one other male over 16 years, one male under 16, and two females. In 1840 he was senior of all the Joseph Youngs of Gilmanton, age 80-90, with spouse age 70-80; they lived by themselves. He was of Gilmanton when he purchased all that part of the homestead farm of Simeon Bean in Gilmanton on the n.w. side of the Province Road

for 10 pounds by deed signed 12 Feb, rec'd 24 Feb 1783; witnesses John Judkins Jr., Ebenezer Smith [Strafford Co. Deed
5:16]. Known ch. b Gilsum, Cheshire Co.: Joseph, b 18 Apr
1782. (Census Strafford, 1790, p91; 1840, p411; NHVR-Marr;
LDS I.G.I. BR)

JOSEPH aka Jr. aka Major, b 5 Apr 1754, Newfields, eldest
s/o Joseph and 1st wife Anna (Folsom) Young of Durham, gr.son
of Thomas and Sarah (Folsom) Young, trader, poss. res. of
Wakefield, d post Mar 1812, Newfields; m 16 Jun 1774, Newfields, Dorcas Margaretta Ewer [b ca 1750, Barnstable, MA, d/o
Nathaniel and Drusilla (Covill) Ewer, d pre 1810, Newfields].
In 1806 Joseph Jr. was an heir in the division of his father's
property, receiving a one-twelfth share and/or one acre of
land in New Market on the west side of Lamprey River.   He
earned the rank of Major by serving from 1776-1780 in the
Revolutionary War in the 2nd Regt., 8th Co., under the command
of Col. George Reid; this company saw action at Ticonderoga
and the James River. In 1788, he served in the State Militia.
[For the full account of his military service, one would have
to obtain the deposition, merely cited below, of descendant
Almena Nay, member of the D.A.R.

Joseph made two separate purchases of land in Durham of
approximately 35 acres from Thomas Crommett of Durham, Gent.:
(1) 12 acres adjacent to lands of Joseph Smith, Capt. Joseph
Young [father] and Benjamin Smith for 74 pounds by deed of
9 Jul 1784, rec'd 15 Sep 1785; witnesses [brother] Jeremiah
Young and James Smith [Strafford Co. Deed 5:535] and (2) 7
acres or one half of two small pastures once part of the dower
of Thomas Crommett's mother, situated east of the country road
leading from Exeter to Dover, for 43 pounds by deed of 5 Dec
1785, rec'd 13 Apr 1786; witnesses John Bryent, James Smith
[Strafford Co. Deed 6:535]. He sold to Walter Bryent Esq. the
second parcel of "six acres land, the same being all the land
I bought of Thomas Crommett by deed 5 Dec 1785" for 33-7-5,
by deed signed 19 Jun 1786, rec'd 20 May 1790; single witness
Edward Smith, J.P. [Strafford Co. Deed 12:62].

Although Joseph bought lands in Wakefield 1784/1785,
there is no clue that he took up residence there, or put these
lands to good use. The purchase of Lot 68, 2nd Div., Wakefield from [brother] Benjamin of Tuftonboro, clothier, indicated some interest on Joseph's part in the development of a
fulling mill and more than a passing acquaintance of the
requirements and technique of running a fulling mill; see
Benjamin and Phoebe (Allen) Young of Tuftonboro for full
details of land deeds. Disposition of Lot 68 is left unresolved as it was not listed in the inventory of Joseph's
estate. The only inference that can be drawn from Joseph ac-
quiring this lot is that it influenced son Joseph Jr. to purchase adjacent Lot 67, 2nd Div., Wakefield where he established a fulling mill and homestead ca 1805.

Joseph, merchant, became the owner of 100 acres land in
the 1st Div., New Durham, drawn to the original right of

Thomas Young Esq. [grandfather], through purchase from his
father Joseph [Sr.] of Durham, by deed signed 20 Jun 1786,
rec'd 8 Sep 1795; for full particulars see his parents' entry.
An additional 100 acres of this lot in the 1st Div., New
Durham with buildings was purchased from Thomas and Rebecca
Young of New Durham, lands which said Thomas inherited from
his father Thomas Young Esq. of New Market, by quitclaim
signed 6 Jun, rec'd 29 Dec 1787; see Thomas and Rebecca Young
for full details. He added to this acreage in New Durham by
purchase of 5 acres, 28 rods by deed signed 3 Jan 1788, rec'd
8 Sep 1795, from Ichabod Bussell of New Durham, for 18 pounds;
witnesses Benjamin Dow, James Smith [Strafford Co. Deed
20:321]. This very same land in New Durham with buildings was
conveyed to Joseph's eldest son Levi of New Durham through two
sales: (1) 150 acres or one half of all Joseph's real estate
in New Durham then occupied by Levi, by deed signed 14 Jun
1802, rec'd 16 Jan 1805, for $1,000.00; witnesses Reuben
French, Nathaniel Kidder [Strafford Co. Deed 47:122]; (2) the
other half of the farm in New Durham where Levi then dwelt,
by deed signed 14 Mar, rec'd 10 Jul 1812, for $800.00; wit-
nesses Wentworth Cheswell, Thomas Young [Strafford Co. Deed
70:529]. On same date of signing of the former deed, 14 Jun
1802, rec'd 16 Mar 1812, Joseph and Dorcas signed a life-lease
with Levi on this property, "for and during their natural life
and the life of the survivor of them," for $500.00; witnesses
Reuben French, Nathaniel Kidder [Strafford Co. Deed 71:182].
    Joseph bought up two of his brothers' properties: when
of Durham he purchased from Henry 12-1/2 acres of land in
Durham which had formerly been part of brother Zachariah's
estate, by deed of 29 Sep 1801, rec'd 3 Jul 1806; and when of
New Market, purchased by deed signed 1 Oct 1806, rec'd 21 Jan
1807, his brother John's one-twelfth share of their father's
estate in Durham and New Market. See Henry and Sarah (Bennett) Young of Durham and John and Anna (Mason) Young of
Wolfeboro for both transactions. Ch. b New Market: Levi+,
b 1775; Drusilla+ (Young) Wiggin, b 6 Apr 1784; Joseph+, b
1785; Nathaniel, b 1796, who m Newfields, Mary Cram [b ca
1800, Newfields, d/o David Cram], d 20 May 1880, native town];
Thomas, b ca 1798, settled in Wolfeboro, but returned to New
Market where he died; Mary, b 1799, d 14 Feb 1881; and "other
daughters." (LDS I.G.I. BR; NHVR-Marr; Fitts' Newfields,
p495,684; Bank's Wakefield, p111,119; Durham Graveyards, p77;
D.A.R Lineage No. 18022, V19, p10)
    JOSEPH, b 1758, Dover, d by drowning 8 Sep 1798, age 40,
Barrington. (Heritage's Dover VR, p201)
    JOSEPH, b ca 1760, Dover, m 21 Apr 1783, Madbury, Sarah.
Commody [b ca 1765, Dover]. (NHVR-Marr)
    JOSEPH aka Jr., b 1760s, Kingston, d prob. pre 1850,
Gilmanton; m 29 Mar 1787, Upper Gilmanton [Belmont], Betsey
Shaw [b 1777, Barnstead, res. of Loudon, alive 1860, Gilman-
ton]. Joseph settled in Gilmanton at the foot of Mount
Belknap. The homestead consisted of 160 acres, a large part

of which he cleared himself. In 1810 Joseph Jr. was head of a large household in Gilmanton, age 45 plus, with spouse of same age group, and eleven children in Gilmanton, eight sons, 4 under 10, 1 age 10-16, and 3 age 26-46; three females, one under 10, one age 16-26, and one 26-45. By 1830 Joseph of Gilmanton and spouse, both age 60-70, had one male [son] at home, age 20-30. As of 1860 Betsey, widow at age 83, lived with son Nathaniel B. and his family in Gilmanton. Ch. b Gilmanton: Janet (Young) Garmon, b ca 1785; Dudley+, b 18 Jan 1788; Samuel S.+, b 18 Jan 1794; Joseph+, b ca 1795; David S.+, b 1796; Nathaniel Badger+, b 1799; John T.+, b 1801; Hezekiah B.+, b ca 1805; Bradbury S.+, b ca 1810. (NHVR-Marr; Deaths; Census Strafford Co., 1810, p812; 1830, p277; Biog. Review, XXI, p454,455; Census Belknap Co., 1860, p215)

JOSEPH, b 1760s, Wolfeboro, s/o _____ and Lydia Allard Young [no main entry]. By deed signed 5 Dec, rec'd 6 Dec 1805, Joseph and sister Elizabeth Young, both of Tuftonboro, sold their share in land that belonged to their late mother Lydia Allard of Wolfeboro to Benjamin Evans and Samuel Conner of Wolfeboro for $50.00; witnesses Daniel H. Wiggin, Henry Wiggin, J.P. [Strafford Co. Deed 49:298].

JOSEPH, b ca 1764, Dover, s/o Capt. Thomas Young of Dover Neck, d pre 20 Apr 1816, Farmington; m Nov 1791, Madbury, Sarah Pinkham [b ca 1770, of Rochester, d pre Jul 1838, Farmington]. Joseph was named a son and heir of Capt. Thomas Young of Dover by will signed 7 Apr 1791, proved 25 Apr 1795. From 1794-1810 he lived in Rochester where he held joint tenancy on a homestead farm. During that time he signed the petition addressed to the General Court on 6 Jun 1798 relative to the incorporation of the North-West Parish; the petition was granted 1 Dec that year whereby the west parish was set off and became known as Farmington. His farm fell within this West Parish. He was listed as resident of Rochester from 1800-1810: in 1800 age was 26-45, with family of spouse of similar age and two sons under 10; in 1810 he and spouse were 26-45 years old, with family consisting of five males, three under 10 and two age 10-16. In 1820 widow Sarah was listed as resident of Highway District No. 10, Farmington, land owner and taxpayer in 1826, owning a parcel of 50 acres land with buildings valued at $20.00 and $100.00 for unimproved land; likewise for 1828, same acreage and values. In 1830 Sarah was head of household in Farmington, age 50-60, with one son still at home, age 15-20.

Joseph became co-grantee with Samuel Pinkham Jr. of Rochester in the purchase of 140-acre Lot 99, 3rd Div., Rochester [that part which became Farmington] from Samuel and Elizabeth Langdon of said town for $560.00, by deed signed 4 Nov 1794, rec'd 19 Jan 1796; witnesses Samuel Langdon, R. Langdon [Strafford Co. Deed 21:486]. He also purchased a moiety of Lot 64, 2nd Div., Wakefield from [brother] Moses Young of Wakefield by deed signed 24 Nov 1808, rec'd 22 Apr 1816. Joseph's five sons, when minors, later purchased the other moiety of this lot from Moses Young by deed signed 14 Apr 1819, rec'd 13 Sep 1836. It must be noted that Moses originally held this lot in joint tenancy with co-grantee William Keay, but Moses sold in fee simple Joseph's moiety. See eldest son Joel Young of Farmington for the full transaction.

By quitclaim of 5 July 1808, rec'd same date, Joseph purchased from John Wingate Jr. of Farmington 23-1/3 acres, or 1/6th part of Lot 98, 3rd Div., Milton for $100.00, the same land said Wingate purchased of Amos Place of Milton; witnesses Benjamin Canney, John H. Walker [Strafford Co. Deed 58:245]. Concurrent with the date of signing of the above, rec'd 5 Jul 1808, Joseph granted bond to Amos Place of Milton on the 1/6th part of Lot 98, 3rd Div., in the amount of $136.38, which said Place acknowledged that he was "held and stand firmly bound to Joseph Young of Farmington" for that amount, and that if the bond is paid on 5 Jul next with interest, then "Joseph will make a good deed of trust"; witnesses for Joseph, John Wingate, Benjamin Canney; witnesses for Amos Place, J. P. Hale, Benjamin Libby [Strafford Co. Deed 60:260]. The following year Joseph quitclaimed his 1/6th share in Lot 98 to Edward Tebbetts of Rochester for $136.00, by deed of 30 Mar, rec'd 12 Apr 1809; witnesses John Wingate Jr., Benjamin Canney [Strafford Co. Deed 60:526]. Joseph's last purchase of land was with co-grantor Samuel Pinkham Jr. of Farmington for two parcels of land in Farmington from Joseph and Abigail Hodgdon of Rochester, the first being a "piece" in the 3rd Div., to the original right of John Burnham, and the second, 25 acres in the 3rd Div., bounded by lands of George Leighton and Jeremiah Waldron Esq., for $300.00; witnesses John Haven, Richard Dame [Strafford Co. Deed 63:348].

Admin. Papers on Joseph's estate were filed 20 Apr 1816, by widow Sarah, having posted bond of $2,000.00 with sureties Samuel Pinkham Jr. and Stephen French, both of Farmington [Strafford Co. Probate 19:80]. Inventory on Joseph's estate was made by John Wingate Jr., Nehemiah Eastman and Stephen French, all of Farmington; appraisal was presented to the court 14 Jun 1816, allowed 20 Jul 1816 [Strafford Co. Probate 18:181]. The 165-acre homestead farm in Farmington, held "in Common and undivided" with Samuel Pinkham Jr., was rated at $700.00. Personal estate included "1-1/2 days at Waldron's saw mill" at $75.00; total figure for personal and household effects came to $400.00. Three guardianship petitions on date of 21 Jan 1817, were granted to Sarah for their five sons, all minors; each petition required $1,000 bond, sureties the said Samuel Pinkham Jr. and Stephen French. In the first two cases sons Joel and Samuel P., upwards of the age of fourteen, elected their mother as guardian [Strafford Co. Probate 21:76; 21:78]; in the third case, sons Joseph, John K., and Hiram H., were all minors under fourteen years [Strafford Co. Probate 21:79]. For Sarah's dower rights in Lot 64, 2nd Div., Wakefield, see Moses and Mary (Chadwick) Young of Wakefield. For son Joel's quitclaim of 10 Jun 1826, rec'd 23 Jun 1827, of his

share in Joseph's estate in Wakefield to his mother Sarah, see
Joel and Mary (Durgin) Young.

Ch. b Farmington: Joel+, b 1801; Samuel P.+, b ca 1802;
Joseph+, b ca 1804; John K., b ca 1806; and Hiram H.+, b
16 Dec 1811. (NHVR-Marr, Deaths; Census Strafford Co., 1800,
p163; 1810, p790; 1830, p60; Farmington TR, V1, p117,770,771;
NH State Papers, V13, p346-348; Young Family Recs., courtesy
of Marjorie S. Heaney)

JOSEPH, b ca 1765, of Dover, d pre 14 Apr 1809, Dover.
Son Thomas Young, minor upwards of fourteen years of age [b
1789-1794, Dover], was made ward of John Baker of Rochester
on above date; bond of $1,000 was given with sureties Benjamin
Tibbetts of Rochester and William Twombly of Dover [Strafford
Co. Probate 12:119].

JOSEPH, b ca 1765, of Dover, d pre 31 Aug 1811, Dover.
Guardianship of his son Shadrach H. Young, minor upward of
fourteen years [b 1791-1796], was awarded on above date to
Thomas Young, Gent. of Dover; bond of $2,000 was posted with
sureties Andrew Pierce and James B. Varney, both of Dover
[Strafford Co. Probate 19:162]

JOSEPH aka Jr., b 1770s, of Gilmanton; proprietor of 110
acres which was made up of eleven ten-acre lots in Gilmanton;
he may well have been absentee owner. Through four separate
deeds, Joseph, yeoman of Gilmanton, became the owner of Lots
135-137, Lots 139-142, and Lots 145-148, 2nd Div. By date of
recording, 4 Dec 1800, the first three deals were made: first
deed for Lots 135 and 136 was signed 27 Sep 1786, purchased
from Dudley Gilman of Gilmanton for 12 pounds; witnesses
Stephen Dudley, Thomas Cogswell [Strafford Co. Deed 36:108];
second deed for Lot 137 signed 27 May 1793, from Edward Wade
of Gilmanton for $16.00; witnesses Joseph Shaw, Joseph Badger
[Strafford Co. Deed 36:117]; and third deed for Lots 139-142,
signed 4 Feb 1791, from Samuel Brown Jr. of Gilmanton for 90
pounds; witnesses Joseph Osgood, Joseph Badger [Strafford Co.
Deed 36:103]. The fourth deed for Lots 145-148 was signed
16 Nov 1789, rec'd 18 Mar 1799, with co-grantee John Hook of
Barnstead from Benjamin Stevens of Gilmanton for 45 pounds;
witnesses Ezekiel Eastman, Joseph Badger [Strafford Co. Deed
31:28]. Full title to these last four lots was acquired when
Joseph bought out John Hook's share for $300.00, by deed
signed 2 Dec, rec'd 4 Dec 1800; witnesses Thomas R. Swett,
Joseph Parsons [Strafford Co. Deed 36:75].

JOSEPH aka Jr., b 21 Nov 1771, of Deerfield, Rock. Co.,
s/o Joseph Young [no main entry], d 2 Oct 1849, age 77-2-19,
New Hampton]; m ca 1790, New Hampton, Abigail Gilman [b 8 Jun
1772, of New Hampton, d 8 Oct 1849, New Hampton, age 77]. In
1796, Joseph Jr. resided in New Hampton [formerly named
Moultonboro Addition]; he and Abigail became members of the
Freewill Baptist Church. Joseph was head of household in New
Hampton from 1800-1840. In 1800 his age was 16-26, with family of spouse of similar age, three males under 10 and one
female under 10. In 1830 his age was 50-60, as was his

wife's, with family of one male age 10-15 and two females, one under 5, one 20-30. In 1840 his and his wife's ages were 60-70, with one male age 10-20 and four females, two age 10-15, one each 15-20 and 20-30. Joseph's father deeded to him when of New Hampton, a moiety of 80 acres of Lot 6, Range 4, New Hampton, by deed signed 8 Mar, rec'd 29 Aug 1796, for $200.00; witnesses Deli Glines and Thomas Simpson, J.P. [Strafford Co. Deed 23:97]. His father was of Deerfield when he bought the 160 acres from Thomas Leavitt Esq. of North Hampton, Rock. Co., by deed signed 9 Jan 1794, rec'd 12 Apr 1796, for 100 pounds; witnesses Jeremiah Marston, Thomas Simpson, J.P. [Strafford Co. Deed 22:214].

As will be noted above, Joseph and Abigail died within one week of each other. Admin. Papers on Joseph's estate in New Hampton were filed by surviving daughters Sarah Ward and Hannah Young on 16 Oct 1849; declining the administration, they nominated Hiram French of Meredith in their stead [Belknap Co. Probate #629]. Nathaniel Jones, Samuel P. Smith and Benjamin S. Huckins were appointed appraisers of the estate. Joseph, Abigail and grandson Joseph Young Ward [b 11 Feb 1844, d 20 Mar 1926] were buried at Young Cemetery, a "private cemetery in New Hampton on the old road which leads off from the present main road, on the westerly side of the old road in a declivity." Known ch. b New Hampton: Joseph Gilman, b 4 Jan 1797; Betsey+ (Young) Dolloff, b 3 Jun 1800; Sally (Young) Ward, b 25 Aug 1802, alive 1849, New Hampton; and Hannah, b 4 Apr 1809, d 3 Nov 1896, age 87-7-0, single, Meredith, buried at Blossom Hill. (Census Strafford Co., 1800, p169; 1830, p217; 1840, p148; LDS I.G.I. BR; Morning Star, p375; NHVR-Deaths; New Hampton Cems., TMs, p27)

JOSEPH, b 1773, Dover, s/o William Young [no main entry], d 1840, native town; m 1800s, Dover, Elizabeth Saltmarsh [b 1780, Dover, d 24 Oct 1851, home town]. From 1830-1840, he was listed on the census returns for Dover: in 1830, his age was 50-60, with family of spouse of like age, five males, one age 5-10, three 15-20, and one 20-30, and five females, one 10-15, one 15-20, and three 20-30. In 1840 his age was 60-70 as was his spouse, with one male at home, age 15-20. Both Joseph and Elizabeth were buried at Pine Hill Cemetery, Dover. Known ch. b Dover: Moses C.+, b 9 Apr 1809. (Ham's Dover Marr, TMs; NHVR-Deaths; Census Strafford Co., 1830, p302; 1840, p540; Frost's Dover Cem., V1, Plot #596)

JOSEPH aka 2nd, b 1781, of Gilmanton, d 14 Dec 1843, age 62, Belmont; m 16 Jun 1808, Canterbury, Betsey Young [b 29 Jul 1788, Canterbury, d/o Winthrop and Mary (Otis) Young, d 22 Feb 1877, age 89, Belmont]. Joseph and Betsey raised their children in Upper Gilmanton. He was head of family from 1830-1840 in Gilmanton. In 1830 he and spouse were age 40-50, with household of seven children, three males, one under 5, one age 10-15, and one 15-20; four females, one age 10-15, two 15-20 and one 20-30. In 1840 both Joseph and spouse were 50-60, with household of two males, one age 10-15, one 30-40 and one female age 20-30. Widow Betsey filed Admin. Papers on Joseph 2nd's estate on date of 15 Jan 1844; approved same date [Belknap Co. Probate #203]. She nominated as appraisers Peter Clark and Samuel French, both of Gilmanton, and Lemuel Mason of Sanbornton. Joseph, Betsey and two sons were buried at Bean Hill Cemetery, Belmont. Note that Lyford's Canterbury gives Joseph's date of birth as 13 Mar 1778, Belmont. Ch. b Belmont: Sophronia+ (Young) Bradbury, b 8 May 1809; Lavonia (Young) Dashwood, b 5 Dec 1810, wife of Henry Dashwood of Boston, d 1858, Boston; Andrew Bailey+, b 29 Mar 1812; Betsey+ (Young) Sweatt, b 12 Feb 1814; Eleazer+, b 16 Jan 1816; Nancy (Young) Currier, b 1810s, wife of John Currier of Gilmanton; Ann F., b 18 Apr 1822, d.y.; and Peter Clark, b 1827, d 18 Apr 1842, age 15, Belmont. (Census Strafford Co., 1830, p277; 1840, p405; Lyford's Canterbury,m p343,344; Belmont Cems., TMs, p2; NHVR-Brides, Marr)

JOSEPH aka 3rd, b ca 1785, Upper Gilmanton, s/o Eleazer Young; m ca 1805, Gilmanton, Hannah (   ) [b ca 1790, of Gilmanton, alive 1818, same town]. As son of Eleazer, Joseph was deeded a one-half share of the family homestead on 100-acre Lot 4, 6th Range, 1-1/2 acres of Lot 12, 7th Range, and 2-1/2 acres with buildings on Lot 3, 6th Range, Gilmanton per deed signed 7 Apr 1806, rec'd 24 Aug 1812. In 1810 he was head of household in Gilmanton, age 26-45, with female (spouse) age 16-26, and one female age under 10. In 1812 Joseph 3rd was taxpayer of Gilmanton in District No. 3, rated at $4.68. He disposed of 2-1/2 acres of Lot 3, 6th Range, Gilmanton which he had purchased from his father, by deed signed 21 May 1818, rec'd 19 Apr 1819, to Jude Bean Jr. of Gilmanton for $195.00, with Hannah ceding dower rights; witnesses Samuel Shepherd, Stephen Coffin [Strafford Co. Deed 105:275]. Daughter not identified. (Census Strafford Co., 1810, p822; Gilmanton TR, V3, p385)

JOSEPH aka Major, b 1785, New Market, s/o Joseph and Dorcas M. (Ewer) Young, d 1 Jan 1850, Wakefield; m 14 Aug 1806, Wakefield, Nancy Young [b 1787, Rochester, "only daughter" of James and Mary (Kimball) Young, d 22 Jun 1844, Wakefield]. Both Joseph and Nancy were members of the Freewill Baptist Church. As of 1804/05 he established his homestead on Lot 67, 2nd Div., in the Pine River settlement of North Wakefield, the land adjacent to father's Lot 68. He set up a fulling business which his own son Joseph B. would operate from 1834 on. Maj. Joseph was listed as resident and taxpayer of Highway District No. 4, Wakefield in 1820. Per Bank's Wakefield, "This highway district included all the main road from Jonathan Quimby's lane to the Ossipee line, also the Effingham road to the center of the river at the Clark & Roberts' Mills, also the road leading from said main road to Brookfield line by S. Hawkins." He was resident of Wakefield from 1830-1840: in 1830, age was 40-50, family consisting of spouse of same age group, five males, one age 5-10, two 10-15, one 15-20 and one 20-30; and four females, one under 5, two age 15-20 and one 20-30. In 1840 Joseph was age 50-60, with spouse age 40-50 and a family of two males, one age 15-20, one 20-30, and three females, one age 5-10 and two 15-20. He was listed as eligible to vote at the Wakefield Town Meeting of 11 Mar 1834.

Joseph's trade was clothier as early as 1804. His own Lot 67, 2nd Div., abutted his father's Lot 68 at Pine Brook off of Pine River, North Wakefield, whose streams enabled the operation of a fulling mill. The process of fulling involved dressing the cloth. According to Bank's Wakefield, "It removed the oil and impurities from wool or woolen cloth." He formed a partnership with Robert Barber, clothier of Wakefield, which was concluded no later than 1809. Joseph's mill was listed as one of twenty-six operating in Wakefield in 1827. The partners initially acquired 12 acres, part of Lot 66, 2nd Div., Wakefield, beginning at Pine Brook where the brook crosses the north and south range line, by deed signed 18 Aug, rec'd 22 Aug 1804, from Stephen Hawkins of Wakefield for $200.00; witnesses Thomas Bickford, Nathaniel Young [Strafford Co. Deed 45:377]. To this they added an additional one-half acre of Lot 66 for $10.00, located east of the above property and on the eastern side of the winter road from Pine Brook Bridge to Hawkin's dwelling house by deed signed 12 Sep 1805, rec'd 14 Jul 1813, from the same Stephen Hawkins; witnesses Spencer Wentworth, John Emerson Jr. [Strafford Co. Deed 76:58]. That same year, they acquired Lot 67, 2nd Div., Wakefield, drawn to original right of Eliphalet Cromwell, by deed signed 6 Dec 1805, rec'd 13 Jan 1809, from Paul and Thomas Garvin of Shipleigh, York Co. [Maine in 1820], for $450.00; witnesses Avery Hall, Jacob Welch [Strafford Co. Deed 60:70]. Concurrently with this latter deed, Joseph bought out the one-half share of his said partner Barber, then of Andover, Hills. Co., of Lot 66 for $290.00, by deed signed 6 Dec 1805, rec'd 13 Jan 1809; this deal gave Joseph full title to the fulling mill, dam, utensils, house, barn and clothier shop, plus the one-fourth part acre of land said shop stood on; witnesses James Young, Paul Dame [Strafford Co. Deed 60:71].

In 1810 with title of Gent., Joseph purchased 3-1/2 acres of Lot 53, Wakefield, drawn to the original right of Ebenezer Wentworth and bounded on the check line between Lots 52 and 53, from Daniel Welch of Wakefield for $35.00, by deed signed 13 Apr 1810, rec'd 28 Nov 1812; witnesses Benjamin Cook, Edward Dearborn [Strafford Co. Deed 72:415]. These 3-1/2 acres were sold to John Cook of Wakefield, by deed of 24 Oct 1811, rec'd 28 Nov 1812, for $30.00; witnesses Benjamin Cook, Paul Dame [Strafford Co. Deed 72:417]. He also acquired 10 acres, 146 square rods of land in Wakefield which were adjacent to the northern check line of land owned by Peter Cook, purchased from Nathaniel Roberts of Wakefield, by deed signed 17 Jun 1811, rec'd 26 Jan 1814, for $21.00; witnesses Benjamin Cook, John Wingate [Strafford Co. Deed 78:174]. Joseph sold 12 acres land in Wolfeboro, part of Lot 1 in the Wolfeboro

Addition, on the old line of Wolfeboro adjoining the town of Brookfield, by deed dated 30 May 1816, rec'd 20 Feb 1817, sold in fee simple to Samuel Tibbetts of Brookfield for $120.00; Nancy Young ceded dower rights; witnesses Benjamin Cook, Nathaniel Cook Jr. [Strafford Co. Deed 93:389].

As late as 1819, Joseph and former partner Barber still held land jointly, but by deed signed 27 Aug, rec'd 20 Oct 1819, Barber sold his one-fourth of an acre of Lot 67, 2nd Div., Wakefield which the partners had bought of Stephen Hawkins, for $40.00; witnesses Thomas Young, Sarah Ann Barber [Strafford Co. Deed 104:484]. The following item appearing in Bank's Wakefield could well signify a change in Joseph's physical health: on 22 Aug 1834, Joseph B. Young [believed to be son] advertised in the local town paper that "he has taken the old Fulling Mill at Pine Brook, so-called, in Wakefield, which has been for many years occupied by Joseph Young where he intends to dress cloth at the reduced price of 12-1/2 cents per yard cash down--other pay as parties can agree."

Upon Joseph's death in early 1850, Cyrus Sanborn of Wakefield was appointed Admin., and then having petitioned on 12 Feb 1850 that Joseph's estate was rated insolvent, was appointed Commissioner to review and decide on all claims; on date of 21 Feb 1850, he was granted license to sell at public auction the dwelling house, personal effects, live stock and grains on 12 Feb 1850 [Carroll Co. Probate #5822]. Upon daughter Dorcas' death in 1892, sibling Adaline M. Nay of East Boston, MA filed Admin. Papers on Dorcas's estate on 30 Apr 1892, approved 3 May, 1892 [Carroll Co. Probate #5816]. Joseph and Nancy were buried at Old Young Cemetery on Long Ridge Road, Wiggin Hill, Wakefield, beside the graves of Nancy's parents. It is to be noted that Rev. James Hill Fitts stated in his History of Newfields that although Joseph "went to Wakefield, [he] died Exeter, 6 Aug 1849." That may well have been the case, but Joseph, Nancy and children were buried at Wakefield.

Known ch. b Wakefield: Mary+ (Young) Mathews, b 25 Mar 1807; Joseph B., b ca 1809, alive 1834, native town; Dorcas Margaretta Ewer, b 27 Jun 1811, d 26 Apr 1892, 80-10-0, single, bur. Wakefield; prob. Nancy+ (Young) Nutter, b ca 1820; and Adeline Mehitable+ (Young) Nay, b 1820s. (Wakefield TR, V1; NHVR-Marr, Deaths; Twombly's Wakefield Cem., TMs; Census Strafford Co., 1830, p458; 1840, p371; Morning Star, p375,376; D.A.R Lineage #18022, V19, p10; Fitts' Newfields, p683,684; Young Family Recs., courtesy of Gerald Ortell; Bank's Wakefield, p119,176,679,682)

JOSEPH, b ca 1785, of Wolfeboro, alive 1840, same town; m 2 Sep 1821, Tuftonboro, Susannah Keay [b ca 1800, of Wolfeboro, alive 1840, same town]. Joseph was head of household in Wolfeboro from 1830-1840: in 1830 his age was 40-50; household of spouse age 30-40, three males, two under 5, one age 15-20, and one female age 10-15; in 1840 he was 50-60 years with spouse age 40-50, and household of three males, one under 5 and two age 15-20. (Census Strafford Co., 1830, p446; 1840, p386; NHVR-Marr)

JOSEPH, b 7 Aug 1788, of Lebanon, ME; d 14 Apr 1871, Somersworth or Rollingsford, age 83; m1 4 Mar 1812, Lebanon, ME, Patience Wentworth [b 9 Aug 1790, of Somersworth, d/o Samuel and Rosanna (Hill) Wentworth, gr.d/o Samuel and Patience (Downs) Wentworth, d Sep 1845, Milton]; m2 ca 1850, Sarah Ricker [b ca 1795, of East Lebanon, ME]. At time of marriage Joseph lived in Dover, Patience in Somersworth. After their children were born in Lebanon, ME, they resettled in Somersworth. Ch. b Lebanon, ME by Patience, place of death unknown: James Morrill+, b 6 May 1813; Sarah Ann+ (Young) Clements, b 14 Sep 1815; Sophia Jane, b 28 Jul 1818, d Apr 1839, Somersworth; Caroline Elizabeth, b 24 Nov 1821, m Benjamin Ayres Fernald of Lebanon, ME, settled in ME, d 24 Sep 1856, ME; Joseph Charles Wentworth, b 9 Oct 1824, d Jul 1846; Shadrach Hill, b 15 Jul 1827, d 27 Apr 1832; Patience Adeline, b 30 May 1831, d Apr 1843; and Harriet Augusta, b 7 Apr 1835, ME, single in 1900, resided in Rollingsford with nephew Nicholas A. Abbott and family. (1900 Soundex; NHVR-Marr; Wentworth Gen., V1, p456-458; LDS I.G.I. BR; Young Family Recs., courtesy of Marjorie S. Heaney)

JOSEPH, b 13 Aug 1788, Rollingsford, d 13 Apr 1871, age 82-8-0, Rollingsford or Somersworth, buried at Old Town Cemetery, Salmon Falls. See preceding entry for strong similarities of vital records. (Dover Cemeteries; NHVR-Deaths)

JOSEPH, b 20 Apr 1789, Tuftonboro, s/o Benjamin and 1st wife Phoebe (Allen) Young of Wolfeboro, d 26 Mar 1861, Wolfeboro; m 12 Nov 1812, Moultonboro, Patience Chase aka Choate [b 20 Feb 1794, of Tuftonboro, d/o _____ and Hannah (   ) Chase, d 7 Aug 1868, Wolfeboro]. Joseph was named son and heir by his father's will of 6 Nov 1843, proved 30 Feb 1849: he was to receive the improvement and income of his real estate, being the family homestead in Wolfeboro "for and during his natural life time." Thereafter it would revert to Joseph's son Mark A. Young. He also received a family heirloom desk, the farming utensils and livestock. At time of marriage Joseph was resident of Moultonboro, but as early as 1850, he and Patience relocated in Wolfeboro, listed on the census returns for that year: members of household were children Mark A., Joseph Lang. and Phoebe E. as well as Patience's mother Hannah Chase, age 82 [b 1768] and Alonzo Whitehouse, age 9 [b 1841]. In 1860, Joseph and Patience's household contained married son Mark A., his spouse Caroline P. and their infant son Joseph L., age 1 month, as well as Alonzo Whitehouse, age 18. Joseph, Patience and sons Mark A. and Joseph L. were buried at Wolfeboro Center Cemetery.

Ch. b prob. Wolfeboro: Benjamin Green+, b 2 Sep 1813; Hiram C., b 12 Dec 1817; Hannah C.+ (Young) Johnson, b 12 Dec 1818; Mark Allen+, b 1827; Joseph Lang, b 1830, d 1854, Wolfeboro; and Phoebe Emeline+ (Young) Piper, b 1836. (D.A.R Wolfeboro Chapter, p2,35-37; NHVR-Deaths, Marr; Census Carroll

Co., 1850, p356; 1860, p521,522; Moultonboro Marr, **Reg.**
59:287; Young Family Recs., courtesy of Nancy L. Dodge)

JOSEPH, b 1790, Wolfeboro, d testate pre 5 Jun 1866,
native town, widower; m (Intentions) 12 Dec 1816, Wolfeboro,
Betsey Hodgdon [b 1794, ME, d pre 1866, Wolfeboro]. Joseph
was head of household in Wolfeboro from 1830-1860: in 1830
his age was 40-50 years, with spouse age 30-40 and family of
three males, two age 5-10, one 15-20, no daughter; in 1840 his
age was just 50 [age 40-50], with household of spouse age
30-40, two males both age 15-20 and one female 5-10. In 1860
census Betsey was named his spouse; they shared the homestead
with married son Joseph Jr. and spouse Susan. Joseph's will
was drawn 8 Apr 1865, proved 5 Jun 1866; witnesses John T.
Burleigh, John W. Young, and James A. Goldsmith [Carroll Co.
Probate #5837]. He named son Joseph Jr. as Exec. of his will
and residuary legatee, devised $5.00 to eldest son William and
$50.00 to grandson George F. Young [parentage unknown], the
money to be held in trust until he reached the age of major-
ity. Known ch. b Wolfeboro: William, b ca 1818; Joseph+, b
30 Jan 1822; and Daniel, b 1836. (Census Strafford Co., 1830,
p434; 1840, p389; Census Carroll Co., 1860, p518; NHVR-Deaths;
Parker's Wolfeboro Banns, 1789-1854, n.p.)

JOSEPH aka 2nd, b ca 1795, of Durham; m 29 Jul 1821,
Durham, Mary Tibbetts [b ca 1800, of same town]. It is quite
probable that this is the Joseph who was voted Selectman of
Durham for the years 1842, 1844, 1848 and 1853-1854. (Stackpole's Durham, V1, p366,384; NHVR-Marr)

JOSEPH aka 3rd, b ca 1795, Gilmanton, s/o Joseph and
Betsey (Shaw) Young, d pre 1840, at age 40, farmer; m 13 Mar
1816, Loudon, Sally Diamond [b ca 1800, of Loudon, alive 1830,
Gilmanton]. By 1830 census he was known as Joseph 3rd, householder in Gilmanton, age 30-40, with family of female [spouse]
age 30-40, two males, one age 10-15, one 20-30; two females,
one age 5-10 and one 10-15. (Census Strafford Co., 1830,
p277; NHVR-Marr; Biog. Review, XXI, p354,355)

JOSEPH, b ca 1800, Sanford, ME, d pre Oct 1885, Rochester; m ca 1825, Sanford, ME, Edna Houston [b ca 1805,
Sanford, ME, d pre Oct 1885, Rochester]. Joseph and Edna
relocated to Rochester some time after the birth of their
second son; both were deceased in 1885 at time of son Daniel
L.'s marriage. Ch. b Sanford, ME: Daniel L.+, b Mar 1828;
and I. Thomas, b 1830s, d 5 Nov 1885, Rochester, with spouse
surviving. (NHVR-Marr, Deaths; Rochester TR, Marr, p14)

JOSEPH aka Jr., b 1800s, Strafford; head of household in
Strafford 1830, age 20-30, with spouse of same age group, one
male age 20-30, and one son under 5. (Census Strafford Co.,
1830, p52)

JOSEPH, b 1803, Ossipee, s/o Thomas and Abigail (   )
Young of Durham, d pre 4 Jun 1881, Ossipee; m 1839, Effingham,
Hannah Allen [b 17 Dec 1816, Bartlett, d/o Jacob and Ada (   )
Allen of Effingham, d 11 Aug 1884, age 67-7-25, Wolfeboro,
widow]. At age 21 Joseph purchased part of Lot 13, Ossipee

by quitclaim of Josiah Dearborn of Effingham signed 11 Dec 1824, rec'd 22 Mar 1825, for $1.00, land deeded to said Dearborn by Thomas Young on 21 Feb 1823; witnesses Carr Leavitt, Thomas Young [Strafford Co. Deed 122:412]. He was head of household in Ossipee from 1840-1870. In 1840 his age was 30-40, with household of spouse age 30-40, an elderly female figure age 60-70, one male under 5 and one female age 20-30. From 1850-1870 Hannah was named as his spouse; children at home were Thomas, Sarah A., Abby and Eldora; in 1860, Thomas, Ruth Addie, Emma A. and Joseph M.; in 1870, John F., Addie Ruth, Emma A. and Joseph.

Widow Hannah of Wolfeboro declined the administration of her husband Joseph's estate on 4 Jun 1881 and prayed that their eldest son Thomas be appointed as Admin.; allowed 7 Jun 1881 [Carroll Co. Probate #5820]. Inventory of estate was taken by Isaac Chadbourne, Joseph Young Jr. and C. S. Demeritt on 7 Jun 1881, approved 5 Jul 1881. Real estate was assessed at $280.00. This included the 60-acre homestead in Ossipee and 30 acres unimproved land in Effingham; total value of real estate, $388.50. Ch. b Ossipee: Thomas+, b Feb 1842; Sarah A., b 1843, d.y.; John F., b 1846; Abby, b 1848, d.y.; Eldora A., b Jul 1850; Ruth Addie, b 11 Jul 1851; daughter b 2 Jun 1852; Emma A., b 1853; son b 15 Jun 1853, twin?; daughter b 26 Feb 1855; daughter b 19 Oct 1857; Joseph Melvin, b 4 Apr 1859, d 14 Sep 1891, age 32-5-10, Dover; and Nathan Burleigh, b 4 Oct 1867. (NHVR-Births, Deaths, Marr; LDS I.G.I. BR; Census Strafford Co., 1840, p228; Census Carroll Co., 1850, p223; 1860, p644; 1870, p362; 1900 Soundex)

JOSEPH aka 2nd, b ca 1804, Farmington, s/o Joseph and Sarah (Pinkham) Young, d pre 18 May 1838, Wakefield; m ca 1825, Sally Ann Blaso [b 1800s, North Hampton, alive 1840, Wakefield]. As a minor and resident of Farmington, Joseph and his four brothers purchased one half of Lot 64, 2nd Div., in Wakefield from Moses Young of said town by deed signed 14 Apr 1819, rec'd 13 Sep 1836; see brother Joel Young of Farmington for details. Joseph 2nd was resident of Farmington in 1830, age 20-30, with household of spouse under age 30, one male and one female both under 5. In the early 1830s he and family relocated in Wakefield; he was listed as eligible to vote on the Wakefield Check List Used in Town Meeting on date of 11 Mar 1834. In 1840 Sally was widow and head of household in Wakefield, age 30-40, with family of four males, one age 5-10, one 10-15, one 30-40, one 40-50, and two females, one under 5 and one age 5-10.

Admin. Papers on Joseph 2nd's estate in Wakefield were filed 18 May 1838 by Sally; bond of $2,000 was posted with sureties Elias Wentworth of Wakefield and Isaac·Small of Ossipee [Strafford Co. Probate 50:416]. Inventory on his estate was returned 4 Jul 1838, attested to same day by Elias Wentworth, John Wentworth and John T. Wentworth, all of Wakefield [Strafford Co. Probate 52:459]; real estate "with incumbrance of two widows' dower before the late widow Sally Young" was valued at $500.00; livestock, furniture, farming tools and household effects were set at $182.73. A living allowance of $100.00 was granted to Sally on 14 Sep 1838, to be taken from the personal estate [Strafford Co. Probate 43:119]. Sally's dower rights were determined 29 May 1839, by freeholders Henry Tibbetts of Brookfield, Jacob Leighton of Ossipee and John L. Wentworth of Wakefield; allowed 22 Jan 1840 [Strafford Co. Probate 56:188]. The homestead contained about 55-1/2 acres with buildings on Lot 64, 2nd Div. From this 14 acres were set off to Sally, beginning at n.e. picket corner of lot, running s.w. on Ossipee line the whole length of lot, also 4-1/2 acres land from same lot beginning at the southerly picket corner of the lot adjoining land of John Mathis and Elias Wentworth and running n.e. by said Wentworth's land, the eastern end of the barn "reserving a privilege for the owner or owners of the other two thirds of said farm," and the eastern end of the house.

License to Sell was granted to Sally as Admin. 13 Sep 1839, in order to raise $400.00 to cover debts; the sale was to be subject to the right of dower of Mary Young, widow of Moses, Sarah Young, widow of Joseph, and Sally, widow of Joseph 2nd [Strafford Co. Probate 67:210]. Sally was able to raise $400.00 from the sale by deed signed 13 Sep, rec'd 30 Nov 1839, to John Wentworth of Wakefield; witnesses Jacob Leighton, Elias Wentworth [Strafford Co. Deed 184:103]; see Moses and Mary (Chadwick) Young of Wakefield for dower rights involved. Closing account of Joseph's estate was returned 13 Sep 1839, attested to same date, by Jacob Leighton Esq. of Ossipee who presented the list of all claims "by me allowed or disallowed" [Strafford Co. Probate 54:421]; there were twenty-three sundry accounts against the estate totalling $330.68. Sally's account of administration was returned and accepted 21 Jan 1840 [Strafford Co. Probate 56:222]: she had charged herself with expenses of $184.06 incurred in administrative fees, travel, cost of petition, funeral expenses and the like; amount of estate per inventory and sale of real estate came to $382.23; amount of debt brought up, $184.01; amount in hands of Admin., $198.22. By instructions from the court per averaging schedule dated 23 Mar 1840,, $190.22 from the balance of $198.22, was to be divided among the 21 creditors whose claims against the estate totalled $338.68 [Strafford Co. Probate 56:190]. Known ch. b Farmington: Sarah Ann+ (Young) Blazo, b 1828; and Joseph A.+, b 1833. (Census Strafford Co., 1830, p60; 1840, p378; NHVR-Marr; Morning Star, p35; Bank's Wakefield, p84)

JOSEPH, b 1810, of Belmont; m2 25 Mar 1873, Belmont, at age 63, Hannah (   ) Morrill [b ca 1850, of Belmont, her 2nd marriage]. (NHVR-Marr)

JOSEPH, b 22 Mar 1810, Durham, s/o William and Martha (Bennett) Young, d 1 Apr 1864, age 54, farmer, native town; m ca 1844, Martha D. Bassett [b 28 Nov 1821, Jackson, d/o David and Ann (Burnham) Bassett, d 21 Dec 1898, age 77,0-23,

Durham]. Martha's father David came from Jackson, her mother Ann from Gilmanton. Joseph and wife Martha lived in Durham per census returns from 1850-1860. In 1850 children at home were William H. and Mary E. During this interval Joseph's mother and sister Sarah C. lived with them; in 1860 daughter Josephine was a toddler, age 2. In the partition of his father's estate on 6 Dec 1859 Joseph received an 11/24th share of the house and land, which in effect made him joint tenant with mother and sister Sarah C. He received 20 acres of wood and pasture land east by Lamprey River, 19 acres of field land by said railroad, 8 acres by lands of David Davis, and 1-1/2 acres south by land of George A. Bennett and George Hilton. Joseph was named as an heir in his mother's will signed 6 Sep 1860, proved 6 May 1862. He was killed by cars on the Boston & Maine R.R. Admin. Papers on his estate were granted to widow Martha on 3 May 1864; bond of $500.00 posted, sureties of Nathan H. Harvey and L. Dow Creighton, both of New Market, Rock. Co. [Strafford Co. Probate 68:486]. Sanford & Everts' 1871 map of Durham indicated that widow Martha D.'s home was located in District No 9, in close proximity to the New Market town line, Lamprey River and the railroad. Their children who died young were buried at the Young plot, David Davis Farm, Packers Falls, Durham.

Ch. b Durham: William Henry, b 1845, drowned 29 Aug 1862, age 17, Durham; Mary E.+ (Young) Clark, b 1849; Martha Ann, b 1855, d 6 Jun 1857, age 2, Durham; and Josephine, b 1857, d 1 Oct 1865, age 8, Durham. (Census Strafford Co., 1850, p446,447; 1860, p571; Durham Graveyards, No. 158; Stackpole's Durham, V2, p15; NHVR—Brides, Deaths; Fitts' Newfields, p683,684; Folsom's NH Cemeteries, p47)

JOSEPH aka Jr. aka Capt., b 1811, Dover, carpenter, seaman, d testate 10 Apr 1868, Capt., lost at sea, bur. Dover; m ca 1820, Caroline Spurlin [b 1815, New Durham, d/o Thomas and Lydia (Lamos) Spurlin, d testate 22 Feb 1890, age 75, widow, Dover]. Caroline's father Thomas Spurlin was a sailor born in Madbury, Lydia Lamos born in Dover. In 1850 Joseph lived as carpenter in Dover with wife and son Moses F. In 1860 he was seaman on leave, living in Dover, Ward 2 with wife only. Joseph's will was drawn 14 Nov 1865, proved 5 May 1868; he named wife Caroline sole Exec. of his will and sole legatee; no issue mentioned; witnesses James Hanson, E. H. Nutter, Sarah B. Whitehouse [Strafford Co. Probate 80:121]. In 1870 Caroline was head of household in Dover, Ward 2, without occupation; brother Thomas Spurlin, age 53 [b 1817, Dover] and his family lived with her. Her will signed 22 Feb, proved 4 Mar 1890, appointed said Thomas Spurlin her sole Exec.; witnesses M. C. Lathrop, John R. Ham, Roscoe G. Blanchard [Strafford Co. Probate 107:26]. She provided $100.00 for her cemetery lot at Pine Hill Cemetery [Dover], and bequeathed to Manning A. Drew of Boston, MA, all her government bonds. Proceeds from sale of her real estate were to be divided equally among her surviving siblings; the remainder of her personal property was to go to sisters-in-law Esther B. Drew and Lorania Hough. Both Joseph and wife were buried at Pine Hill Cemetery, Dover. Ch. b Dover: Moses F., b 1836, at home in 1850 only. (Census Strafford Co., 1850, p78; 1860, p662; 1870, p63; NHVR-Deaths; Frost's Dover Cem., VI, Plot #536)

JOSEPH, b 27 Jul 1811, Wolfeboro, s/o Thomas and Elizabeth (   ) Young, alive 1870, Durham; m 13 Sep 1832, Wolfeboro, Maria Langley [b ca 1810, Wolfeboro, alive 1870, Durham]. By 1840 Joseph and Maria had relocated to Durham. There he was listed as head of household from 1840-1870. In 1840 his age was 20-30, with spouse of same age group and family of three other females, one age 50-60, one under 5, and one age 5-10. From 1850-1870 Maria was listed as his spouse. Children at home in 1850: Melissa, Marie E., Edwin A., Frances D., Josephine and Adelade; in 1860, Ada C., Charles, Frank and Fred. In 1870 estate was valued at $5,000, children at home, Josephine, Fred and Melissa, school teacher. Ch. b Wolfeboro: Melissa, b 1835, at home 1870; Maria E., b 1838; Edwin A.+, b 1841; Frances D., b 1846; Josephine F., b 1847; Adelade, b 1849; Charles Henry+, b 1852; Joseph Frank, b 1855, at home 1870; and Fred W., b 1858, at home 1870. (LDS I.G.I. BR; Census Strafford Co., 1840, p502; 1850, p448; 1860, p598; 1870, p152; NHVR-Births, Marr)

JOSEPH aka Jr., b ca 1815, Dover; m 1840s, Dover, Mary (   ) [b ca 1815, of Dover]. In 1840 Joseph was head of household in Dover, age 20-30, with spouse of same age group; they lived alone. Ch. b Dover: Julia A.+ (Young) Brock, b ca 1855. (Census Strafford Co., 1840, p541; NHVR-Brides)

JOSEPH, b 1820, Sanbornton, d 12 Aug 1881, Hill; he was resident of Hill when he enlisted at age 42 in Co. D, 12th Regt., NH Volunteer Infantry 15 Aug 1862, mustered in 5 Sep 1862 as Pvt., was wounded 3 May 1863 at Chancellorsville, VA and discharged wounded 12 Aug 1863, Concord. (Soldiers & Sailors, p647)

JOSEPH aka 2nd, b Oct 1821, Ossipee, very poss. s/o John F. and Sarah (Saunders) Young, d 1910, native town; m 5 Dec 1844, Waterboro, ME, Hannah Chick [b 28 Jul 1821, Waterboro, ME, d/o Noah and Mary (Hanson) Chick, d 28 Jan 1895, age 73-6-0, Ossipee]. Joseph was listed as resident of Ossipee from 1850-1900. Hannah was named his spouse from 1850-1870. Children at home in 1850 were John F., Willard A. and Arthur P.; in 1860, the first three plus Roswell Byron, Sarah F., Clarissa A., and Alice C.; in 1870, the first seven children plus toddler Walter H., age 2. In 1900 Joseph was widower in Ossipee with two grown children and granddaughter Grace Wilkinson, age 21 [b Feb 1879] at home. He and family members were buried at Young Cemetery at Center and South Effingham Road from Granite on east side of the road, Ossipee. Ch. b Ossipee: John F. aka Frank, b 1845; Willard A.+, b 1846; Arthur P.+, b 26 Feb 1849; Roswell Byron, b 1853; Sarah F. aka Florence S.+ (Young) Whiting, b 1855; Clarissa A. aka Clara, b 1857, d 1934, Ossipee; Alice C. aka Eliza C.+ (Young) May-

bury, b 25 May 1860; and Walter H.+, b 19 May 1868. Note that
1900 Census gave Clara A.'s d-o-b as Jan 1863, and Walter H.'s
as Apr 1868. (Census Carroll Co., 1850, p223; 1860, p645;
1870, p363; Loud's Cem. Recs., p112,142; LDS I.G.I. VR for NH
and Maine; NHVR-Deaths; 1900 Soundex)

JOSEPH aka 3rd, b 30 Jan 1822, Wolfeboro, s/o Joseph and
Betsey (Hodgdon) Young, d 10 Nov 1888, native town; m 18 Apr
1847, Newburyport, MA, Susan D. Cookson [b Feb 1828, ME, d/o
Josiah and Mary (   ) Cookson, alive 1900, Farmington, widow].
Joseph was named sole Exec. and residuary legatee of his
father's estate by will drawn 8 Apr 1865, proved 5 Jun 1866.
He and Susan lived at his parents' home in 1850, Wolfeboro.
Per 1860 census for Wolfeboro, he was head of family; members
of family were wife Susan, his parents Joseph and Betsey,
Susan's parents Josiah Cookson [b 1794] and Mary Cookson [b
1793], and her sister Julia A. Cookson [b 1844]. In 1870 he
and Susan lived in Wolfeboro with George Young, age 14 [b
1856], not listed as member of household in 1860. In 1900
widow Susan was resident of Farmington; member of family was
George W. Cookson, nephew [n.d.]. (Census Carroll Co., 1860,
p518; 1870, p446-447; 1900 Soundex; NHVR-Deaths)

JOSEPH, b ca 1825, Dover; m ca 1850, Elizabeth (   ) [b
ca 1830, Dover]. Ch. b Dover: Annie+ (Young) Faxon, b ca
1850; and Lillian Maybelle+ (Young) Wentworth, b ca 1869.
(NHVR-Brides)

JOSEPH, b 2 Mar 1827, Durham, s/o Daniel and Abigail
(Chesley) Young, d 16 Mar 1894, age 67-0-14, Rochester; m
19 Sep 1847, prob. Rochester, Elvira (   ) [b 1822, Rochester,
d 25 Feb 1919, home town]. In 1850 Joseph and Elvira lived
alone in Rochester per census returns; he worked in the woolen
mills. In 1860 there was a gap in their residence, but in
1870 they were once again living in Rochester; member of
household that year was Sally Foss, age 74 [b 1796]. Joseph
was age 37 when he enlisted from Rochester in Co. D, 1st
Regt., NH Volunteer Heavy Artillery 31 Aug 1864 for one year,
mustered in 4 Sep 1864 as Pvt. and mustered out 15 Jun 1865.
Joseph filed for an Invalid Pension 12 Nov 1887, Application
No. 628,855; Cert. No. 529.873. These papers indicated his
year of birth was 1813, date of death 14 May 1894 [this may
have been the date of burial in Rochester]. His widow Elvira
filed petition for a widow's pension 23 Jul 1894, Application
No. 599,472; Cert. No. 471,688. Elvira resided at 23 Union
Street, Rochester. (Census Strafford Co., 1850, p663; 1870,
p271; Soldiers & Sailors, p962; NHVR-Deaths; Nat'l. Archives
Milit. Recs.)

JOSEPH, b 1833, resident of Somersworth in 1850, single,
shoemaker. (Census Strafford Co., 1850, p243)

JOSEPH, b 1835, of Dover; single resident of Dover, Ward
3 in 1860, roomed at boardinghouse. (Census Strafford Co.,
1860, p706)

JOSEPH, b 1842, Dover, s/o Moses C. and Mary K. (Nutter)
Young, d 19 Nov 1870, age 28, Dover, survived by widow; m

19 Aug 1865, Dover, Lizzie Spurlin [b 1846, Dover, alive 1870, native town]. Joseph lived at the home of his parents in 1860, occupation shoemaker. As resident of Dover at age 22, Joseph enlisted 24 Jun 1861 for three years as Landsman in the U. S. Navy. He served on the U.S.S. "Ohio," "Pensacola," and "Thomas Freeborn," was discharged 23 Jun 1864 as 1st Class Fireman from the latter ship, term expired. Ch. b Dover: Lizzie M., b 13 Jun 1869. (LDS I.G.I. BR; NHVR-Births, Marr, Deaths; note that Soldiers & Sailors, p1180, gave his y-o-b as 1839)

JOSEPH A., b 1833, Wakefield, s/o Joseph and Sally (Blaso) Young, d 17 Jul 1908, Newburyport, MA, baker; m 19 Nov 1866, North Hampton, Nellie aka Ellen Jane (Blaso) Moulton [b 1814, North Hampton, d/o David P. and Phebe (   ) Blaso, her 2nd marriage, d 27 Nov 1922, Newburyport, MA]. Both were residents of North Hampton at time of marriage after his completion of three years military service in the Civil War. As resident of Rye at age 27, he enlisted 9 Aug 1861 in Co. D, 3rd Regt., NH Volunteer Infantry, mustered in 23 Aug 1861 as Pvt. and mustered out 23 August 1864 leaving P.O. address of Newburyport, MA. Concurrently on date of 9 Aug 1861, Joseph enlisted in the Winnacunnet Guards for three years as Pvt.; paid to 18 Aug 1861, giving same P.O. address. Joseph A. filed petition for Invalid Pension on 19 Jan 1891, Application No. 984,138; Cert. No. 793,996. (NHVR-Marr; Soldiers & Sailors, p150,1221; Nat'l. Archives Milit. Recs.)

JOSEPH C., b ca 1793, Sanford, ME, res. of Alton; m (Intentions) 17 Oct 1824, Alton, m 15 Nov 1824, Middleton, Lydia Smith [b 1800, Alton Bay]. Ch. b Alton Bay: Ivory F.+, b 1828; prob. Ira F.+, b 1828, if so, twins. (NHVR-Marr; Alton VR, p542)

JOSEPH C., b 11 Dec 1799, Barnstead, eldest s/o Phineas and Dolly (Jacobs) Young, d 1 Apr 1862, home town, farmer; m 31 Oct 1819, Barnstead, Lydia Lougee [b 1800, Barnstead, d 1882, native town]. Joseph C. was named Exec. and sole legatee of his mother's estate in Barnstead by her will drawn 9 Nov 1851, proved 15 Apr 1862. He was to receive the house and lands where she then dwelt. As can be seen both mother and son died practically within the same month and year. In 1825 Joseph and spouse lived on the Rufus Ewers place next to his father's homestead; he was listed on the Barnstead census reports for 1830-1860: in 1830 he was under the age of 40, as was his spouse, with one other male at home, age 10-15; in 1840 his age was 40-50, with household of spouse of same age bracket, one male age 20-30 and two females, one under 5 and one age 5-10. From 1850-1860 Lydia was named as his spouse; household included two daughters, Jane and Laura A. In 1860 Joseph and Lydia lived alone. Both were buried at Lougee Cemetery, Barnstead. Ch. b Barnstead: Francis Blake, b 18 Jan 1820, d 1846; Isaac Watts, b 16 Jul 1822; Jane, b 1832; and Laura A.+ (Young) Caswell, b 1839. (NHVR-Births; Brides, Deaths, Marr; LDS I.G.I. BR; Merrill's Barnstead, p331; Rev.

Leighton's Death Recs., TMs, n.p.; Census Strafford Co., 1830, p15; 1840, p441; Census Belknap Co., 1850, p420; 1860, p330)

JOSEPH C., b 1805, ME, stonemason, d 8 Mar 1888, Somersworth; m ca 1828, prob. ME, Lydia (   ) [b 1810, of Somersworth, d 22 Jan 1888, same town]. Before 1840 Joseph C. and spouse travelled extensively from Maine to Canada and then to Somersworth via Alton. He and wife Lydia were residents of Somersworth 1840-1860. In 1840 his age was 30-40, with spouse of similar years and family of five males, one under 5, two age 5-10, two 10-15 and two females, one age 5-10 and one 10-15. In 1850 children at home were John, Richard, Eliza, and Lydia L.; in 1860, son Richard, machinist, and Mary A. Joseph and Lydia were buried at Forest Glade Cemetery, Somersworth. For possible kinships see George+ and Susan Young of Somersworth. Ch. b Alton: George W.+, b 1829. Ch. b Canada: Richard+, b Mar 1831; Simeon+ aka Simon D., b 1833; and John, b 1838. Ch. b Somersworth: Eliza, b 1843. Ch. b ME: Mary A., b 1848, at home 1860. Ch. b Somersworth: Lydia L.+ aka Fannie (Young) Doughty, b 1849. (NHVR-Brides; Census Strafford Co., 1840, p575; 1850, p359; 1860, p295; Wooley's Somersworth Cem., Plot #37; 1900 Soundex)

JOSEPH D., b 1835, of Dover, Ward 2 in 1860, shoemaker, roomed at boarding house. (Census Strafford Co., 1860, p658)

JOSEPH D., b 1835, of Dover, Ward 3 in 1860, a boarder. (Census Strafford Co., 1860, p766)

JOSEPH D., b 1835, New Durham, s/o Jonathan B. and Hannah D. (Stevens) Young, d 13 Jun 1862 of wounds, Edisto Island, South Carolina; m 9 Jul 1859, New Durham, Emma M. Perkins [b 30 Nov 1841, Deerfield, d/o Joseph and Lovey (   ) Perkins, d 30 Mar 1860, age 18-3-30, New Durham, survived by husband]. After the death of his wife, Joseph, age 26, enlisted at New Durham on 15 Aug 1861 in Co. I, 3rd Regt., NH Volunteer Infantry and mustered in nine days later as Corp. He died of wounds at Secessionville, SC on date given above. (New Durham VR, Bk1, p55; NHVR-Marr. Deaths; Soldiers & Sailors, p150,152)

JOSEPH E., b 1852, d 2 Dec 1892, age 40 years, Ossipee, buried at Large Ossipee Cemetery. (Loud's Cem. Recs., p112)

JOSEPH G., b 1819, New Hampton; he enlisted at age 44 in the U.S. Navy 19 Dec 1863 at New York for one year as 1 Class Fireman and served on the U.S.S. "North Carolina" and "Galatia," from which he deserted 1 Feb 1864. (Soldiers & Sailors, p1180)

JOSEPH G., b 1824, New Hampton, poss. s/o Joseph Gilman Young [b 4 Jan 1797] and gr.s/o Joseph and Abigail (Gilman) Young. He enlisted at age 37 in the U.S. Navy on 19 Jun 1861 at Boston, MA for two years as Coal Heaver. He served on the U.S.S. "Ohio" and "Susquehanna" and was discharged from latter ship 25 Aug 1862. He reenlisted at age 38 in the U.S. Navy on 2 Jun 1863 at Boston, MA for one year as 1st Class Fireman; served on the U.S.S. "Ohio." (Soldiers & Sailors, p1180)

JOSEPH S., b 1843, Kittery, ME, twin, s/o Thomas C. and Abigail (Wiggin) Young of Wolfeboro, d pre 6 Feb 1888; m 7 Dec

212

1865, Durham, Mary Ann Thompson [b 1849, Boston, MA, d/o Alfred Thompson of Durham]. The will of Joseph's sister Martha H. Young of Ossipee, drawn 6 Feb 1888, proved 5 Mar 1889, listed her surviving siblings as heirs-at-law; Joseph S. was not named. He was resident of New Market at time of marriage. It should be noted that the Wiggin Gen., p176, attributes Mary Ann Thompson's marriage to John T. Young, twin of Joseph S., date of marriage 5 Nov 1865, Durham. The earlier date would signify filing of "intentions of marriage" but does not serve to clear up the confusion as to which twin married Mary Ann Thompson. (NHVR-Marr)

JOSEPH S., b ca 1845, of Gilmanton; m ca 1870, Jennie Martha Clough [b ca 1850, of Gilmanton]. Ch. b Gilmanton: Frank W., b 13 Jul 1871, not traced further. (LDS I.G.I. BR)

JOSEPH S., b 14 Aug 1854, Portsmouth, s/o Emerson and Caroline (Small) Young of Scotland [no main entry], d 8 Sep 1895, Belmont; m ca 1880, prob. Belmont, Elizabeth A. Morrell [b ca 1860, Gilmanton, alive 1890, Belmont]. Joseph's mother Caroline came from Nashua. His will was drawn 14 Jul 1890, proved 17 Sep 1895, naming wife Elizabeth A. Young as sole Exec. and legatee; witnesses Edwin P. Thompson, Marietta Kendall, William C. Belder [Belknap Co. Probate #5464]. Joseph S. devised all his real and personal estate to Elizabeth "wherever found." Ch. b Gilmanton: Caroline M., b 9 Oct 1892. (NHVR-Births, Deaths)

JOSEPH W., b 15 May 1828, Clarksville, s/o Benjamin and Joanna (Cate) Young of Wolfeboro, d 15 Nov 1893, Clarksville; m2 5 Sep 1880, Stewartstown, Lois E. Holden [b 1861, Stewartstown, d/o Joseph and Sabra (   ) Young of same town [no main entry], her 2nd marriage]. Lois' father Joseph Young was born in Stewartstown, her mother Sabra born in Whitefield. (NHVR-Marr, Deaths)

JOSEPHINE, b 1853, of Barrington; in 1860 at age of 7 she lived at the home of William Berry [b 1787], age 73, his wife Rebecca Berry [b 1801], age 59, and Martha L. Berry [b 1838], age 22. (Census Strafford Co., 1860, p184)

JOSHUA, b 1760s, of Sandwich, non-resident proprietor of Lot 6, 5th Range; Lot 30, 11th Range; and Lot 13, 10th Range, Sandwich. All these lots went for sale at public auction because of unpaid taxes. For tax year 1785, Jacob Smith Esq. of Sandwich bought two parcels of the 100-acre Lot 6, 5th Range: (1) by tax deed signed 4 Aug 1788, rec'd 4 Jun 1796, 29 acres of Lot 6 for two shillings-4 pence; witnesses John Clement, Oliver Hubbard [Strafford Co. Deed 22:474]; (2) on same date of signing and recording, 30 acres for 3 shillings-3 pence; witnesses Winthrop Marston, Sarah Gilman [Strafford Co. Deed 19:493]. For tax year 1799, by tax deed of 10 Oct 1801, rec'd 4 Feb 1804, another parcel of land from Lot 6, 5th Range was sold for back taxes to Daniel Little of Sandwich for $15.00; witnesses J. P. Gilman; James Otis Freeman [Strafford Co. Deed 43:4]. For the year 1804, 100 acres of Lot 30, 11th Range, Sandwich was sold to Jacob M. Currier of Dover by tax deed of 7 Jun 1804, rec'd 25 Sep 1804, for 88 cents; witnesses Daniel Little, James Otis Freeman [Strafford Co. Deed 45:392]. And for tax year 1801, 100-acre Lot 13, was sold by tax deed of 17 Feb, rec'd 22 Feb 1804, to John Goddard and Jonathan Goddard, both of Portsmouth, Rock. Co., for $1.32; witnesses Benjamin Cook, Ezekial French [Strafford Co. Deed 42:529].

JOSIAH, b 16 Aug 1821, New Durham, d 17 Sep 1894, native town, age 73-1-1, widower; m 1840s, Stacy (   ) [b 1818, prob. New Durham, alive 1860, same town]. Josiah and wife lived in New Durham in 1860 with children George and Harriet. Ch. b prob. New Durham: George, b 1845; and Harriet, b 1855. (Census Strafford Co., 1860, p83; NHVR-Deaths)

JOSIAH, b 14 Feb 1825, Wolfeboro, s/o Benjamin and Joanna (Cate) Young, d 29 Aug 1885, age 60-6-15, Clarksville, survived by widow; m 1860s, Nancy E. aka Mary E. (   ) [b ca 1840, Loudon, alive 1885, Clarksville]. Josiah and spouse later relocated to Clarksville, Coos Co. in the 1860s. Ch. b Clarksville: Louisa A., b 3 Apr 1862; Frank S.+, b 1864; Norman B., b 12 Dec 1866; son b 29 Mar 1869; Alman J., b 29 Jun 1871; daughter b 14 Oct 1873; and son b 29 Mar 1876. (NHVR-Births, Marr, Deaths; LDS I.G.I. BR; Young Family Recs., courtesy of Granvyl Hulse)

JOSIAH A., b 1794, Tuftonboro, s/o Benjamin and 1st wife Phoebe (Allen) Young of Wolfeboro, d 31 Aug 1860, Clarksville; m 19 Mar 1818, Stewartstown, Betsey Hurlburt [b 1794, Stewartstown, d/o Daniel and Susannah (   ) Hurlburt, d 27 Oct 1870, Clarksville]. Josiah was named a son and heir by his father's will of 6 Nov 1843, proved 30 Feb 1849. He was voted Selectman of Clarksville for the years 1830, 1834, 1836-1839, 1844-45, 1855 and 1860; Treasurer for 1859-1860; and Town Clerk for 1840. The following entry was found in the Stewartstown town records on date of 7 Oct 1817: "I authorize Mr. Josiah A. Young to engage rations for the soldiers of this town and I will pay for the same when...taxes is collected which probably will be within four or five months. Edmund Thorn, Selectman of Stewartstown." Josiah A. and Betsey were buried at Ben Young Hill Cemetery, Clarksville. Ch. b Clarksville: Edmund K., b 1820; and Allen B., b 1820s. (Young Family Records, courtesy of Nancy L. Dodge, Granvyl Hulse)

JOSIAH B., b ca 1820, of Dover; m 19 Oct 1844, Alton, Mary J. Perkins [b ca 1825, of Dover]. Ch. b Alton: Harriet A.+ (Young) Whitehouse, b late 1840s. (NHVR-Brides, Marr; Alton VR, p581)

JOSIAH B., b 1823, of Gilford, laborer, alive 1870, Barrington; m ca 1845, Mary J. (   ) [b 1824, ME, alive 1870, Barrington]. In 1850 Josiah and Mary lived in Gilford; members of family included Lovina A. Young, [b 1833], probably Josiah's sister, and children George W. and Mary A. By 1870 Josiah and Mary J. moved to Barrington; child at home, Hattie A. Ch. b prob. Gilford: George W., b 1846; Mary A., b 1848; and Hattie A., b 1856. (Census Belknap Co., 1850, p160; Strafford Co., 1870, p22)

JUDITH, b ca 1805, Strafford, prob. d/o of Moses and Lucy (Whitehorn) Young, d Strafford Corners, n.d.; m 29 Nov 1827, Strafford at Freewill Baptist Church, Nicholas Otis [b ca 1800, same town]. Judith was buried at Perkins Cemetery, Route 126, Strafford, at Young family plot containing graves of Moses and Lucy Young. Judith's spouse Nicholas Otis may have remarried; this marriage entry was found from the same church records: Nicholas Otis married 2 June 1831, Melinda Leighton of Strafford. (NHVR-Brides; Strafford Marr, **Reg.** 76:34,36; Stiles' Cemeteries, p165)

JUDITH, b 1832, of Somersworth; in 1900, she lived at Broad St., Somersworth with sister Belinda Young, age 35 [b 1865]. Boarder Abigail Goodwin was born Sep 1881, ME. (1900 Soundex)

JUDITH C., b 17 Nov 1806, Ossipee, d 17 Mar 1870, age 63-8-0, native town; m 7 Jul 1831, Wolfeboro, John T. Burleigh [b Dec 1806, of Ossipee, d 23 Mar 1873, same town]. Judith, John and children were buried at the Stevens-Burleigh Cemetery on the road from Ossipee to North Wakefield over from Brown's Ridge and Smith Hill. Ch. b Ossipee: Nancy M. Burleigh, b 1832, d 1 Nov 1848, wife of Cornelius Wilson; and Alonzo Burleigh, b 1833, d 4 Nov 1847, Ossipee. (NHVR-Brides; Loud's Cem. Recs., p127)

JULIA A., b ca 1815, Gilmanton; m 13 Apr 1836, Belmont, Jonathan B. Hilliard [b ca 1810, Gilmanton]. (NHVR-Brides)

JULIA A., b ca 1855, of Dover, d/o Joseph and Mary (   ) Young; m 30 Sep 1876, Lebanon, ME, James W. Brock [b 1851, Strafford, res. of Rochester, s/o Elijah and Nancy H. (   ) Brock]. (NHVR-Brides; Rochester TR, Marr, n.p.)

JULIA A., b 1865, Barrington, d/o John E. and Clara A. (Hodgdon) Young, res. of Dover; m 21 Dec 1889, Dover, Albert B. Hanford [b 1860s, of Rochester]. Julia A. was named the daughter of John E. Young and granddaughter of Jonathan and Sophia M. (Ricker) Young by Sophia's will of 3 Sep, proved 5 Nov 1889. (NHVR-Brides)

JULIA E., b 1850s, Rochester, d/o Nathaniel M. and Hannah M. (   ) Young; m 16 May 1870, Alton, James A. Rollins [b ca 1845, Alton]. (NHVR-Brides)

JULIA M., b ca 1850, Rochester, d/o Richard and Ann (Rollins) Young [no main entry]; m 13 Mar 1871, Farmington, Maynard Russell [b ca 1845, Rochester]. (NHVR-Brides)

KATIE, b 1842, ME; lived in Dover, Ward 2 in 1860, carder, with her sister Hannah, age 16 [b 1844, ME], spinner. (Census Strafford Co., 1860, p612)

KINGMAN aka Jeremiah Kingman, b 20 Jul 1855, Barrington, s/o Jonathan and Sophia Maria (Ricker) Young, d 5 Nov 1895, age 40-3-16, native town; m ca 1875, Fanny A. Locke [b 1859, Dover, d/o Oliver B. and Martha A. (   ) Locke, d 1932, Barrington]. Fannie A., as widow, m2 3 Jan 1897, Dover, Charles A. Grover [b 1867, Eliot, ME, d 1932, Barrington]. Jeremiah K. was known within the family as Kingman and was devised the homestead in Barrington by his mother's will of

3 Sep, proved 5 Nov 1889, with the stipulation that upon his death the estate would revert to three siblings named residuary legatees. Jeremiah and children were buried beside his parents' grave sites at Pine Grove Cemetery, Barrington. Fannie and second husband Charles were buried at the Locke family plot at the same cemetery. Ch. b Barrington, not traced further: Lewis E., b 7 Nov 1878, d 29 Jul 1900, age 21-8-22, single; Stella I., b 1880, d 1961; Flavius, b 10 Jan 1882; Herman E., b 1887, d 1964; Dora F., b 28 Mar 1889, d ___; and Fred L., b 1892, d 1965. (Census Strafford Co., 1850, p527; NHVR-Births, Brides, Deaths; Barrington Graveyards, p127,132,133, Plots 13-1E, 13-1W)

LAFAYETTE M., b Dec 1865, Somersworth, s/o John and Mary ( ) Young [no main entry], alive 1900 Rochester; m 24 Aug 1889, Rochester, Annie M. Wiggin [b 1866, Somersworth, d/o Enoch and Mary ( ) Wiggin of Parsonsfield, ME, d pre 1900]. Lafayette was resident of Berwick, ME at time of marriage. In 1900 he lived alone at Grove St., Rochester. (NHVR-Marr; 1900 Soundex)

LANCE, b 1825, of Gilford; head of household in Gilford in 1870, laborer. Members of household were Sarah Young, age 51 [b 1819] and Lucium Folsom, age 16 [b 1854], painter. (Census Belknap Co., 1870, p33,34)

LAURA A., b ca 1820, of Freedom; m 1840s, Freedom, Francis Fisher [b ca 1815, of Kennebunk, ME]. Ch. b Freedom or Somersworth: Frank Young Fisher, b 1840s, m 1863, Somersworth. (NHVR-Brides)

LAURA A., b 1839, Barnstead, d/o Joseph C. and Lydia (Lougee) Young; m pre 1860, Barnstead, Samuel D. Caswell [b ca 1835, of same town]. Laura A. was raised in Barnstead, listed at age 11 on 1850 census for her parents. Ch. b Barnstead: Orlando L. Caswell, b 1860s, m 1885, Barnstead; and Mary E. (Caswell) Nutter, b 1860s, m2 1893, Barnstead, Albert D. Walker [b 1860s, of same town]. (NHVR-Brides)

LAURA A., b 20 Apr 1860, Alton, d/o Moses and Mary H. (Thompson) Young; m 30 Jan 1877, Alton, Frank P. Woodman [b ca 1855, of same town]. (NHVR-Brides; LDS I.G.I. BR)

LAURANA aka Lurana, b ca 1730, Dover, poss. d/o Abner and Sarah ( ) Young; m 1755, Dover, William Tibbetts [b ca 1730, Dover]. (LDS I.G.I. VR; Tibbetts Gen., TMs, p269)

LAVINA, b ca 1795, of Moultonboro; m 5 Feb 1815, Moultonboro, Henry Collins [b ca 1790, of same town]. (NHVR-Brides)

LAVINA J., b 1828, ME, d/o Moses and Dorothy (Peavey) Young of Alton; m (Intentions) 30 Apr 1853, Alton, m 23 Jun 1853, Belmont, Jacob Ellis Jr. [b ca 1815, Alton]. Lavina lived with her parents in 1850 in Alton. (NHVR-Brides; Alton VR, p603)

LAVINA J. aka Lurana Jane, b 31 Jan 1835, Barrington, d/o William Hale and Sarah (Daniels) Young, d 1 Feb 1903, native town; m (Intentions) 17 May 1859, Somersworth, m 20 May 1850, Dover, John Charles Hanson [b 19 Feb 1829, Somersworth, s/o Benjamin and Clarissa ( ) Hanson, d 22 Feb 1863, prob.

Barrington]; m2 1870s, Barrington, Samuel Caverno Ham [b 18 Dec 1828, d 12 Mar 1894, Barrington]. Lurana taught school for 14 years in Dover, becoming principal of a grammar school. There were two Hanson children who died in infancy. Both Lurana Jane and second husband Samuel C. Ham and sons William H. Ham and George S. Ham were buried at Barrington, Plot 12, Lots 2E, 2W. Ch. by Samuel C. Ham, b Barrington: Thomas Caverno Ham, b 29 May 1874; William Hale Ham, b 31 Aug 1875, d 1962, Barrington; and George Samuel Ham, b 11 Feb 1877, d 1952, Barrington. (NHVR-Brides; Ham Gen., p29; Barrington Graveyards, p15,27,29,127)

LEO aka Leon, b Sep 1814, alive 1900, resident of Alton, age 85. Boarder was Charles A. Barr [n.d.]. (1900 Soundex)

LESTER A., b Apr 1860, prob. Middleton, s/o Samuel P. and Martha A. (Stevens) Young, res. of Middleton, d pre 1932, Farmington; m 17 Feb 1881, Farmington, Cora Bell Hayes [b 1862, Dover, d/o Ezra and Clarissa Drew (Coleman) Hayes, d pre 1932]. Both were buried at Pine Grove Cemetery, Farmington; no known children. (NHVR-Marr; Hayes Gen., V2, p515,516)

LEVI, b 1775, Newfields [South New Market], eldest s/o Joseph and Dorcas M. (Ewer) Young of Wakefield, d testate Dec 1849, while felling trees, New Durham; m1 ca 1800, Alton, Sally aka Sarah Barker [b 1783, Epping, d 1815, South Alton]; m2 31 Oct 1816, New Durham, Phoebe Stockbridge [b 1782, of New Durham, d 1862, Durham]. Levi was active in the Parish of Newfields up through 1793, resided for a short while in Alton, and thereafter was head of family in New Durham from 1830-1840. In 1830 his age was 50-60 years, spouse's age was 40-50, with household of two males both age 20-30, and five females, two age 5-10, two 10-15, and one 15-20. In 1840 he was 60-70, with household of spouse age 50-60 and three females all 15-20 years. In 1850 Phoebe was widowed and head of household in New Durham; living with her was granddaughter Emily A. Frost, age 13 [b 1837]. By 1860 Phoebe, age 78, lived in Durham at boarding house with twin Ruth Stockbridge [b 1782], age 78.

Levi established his 150-acre homestead in New Durham circa 1802, his father having conveyed this land to him by two deeds. In the first instance by deed of 14 Jun 1802, rec'd 16 Jan 1805, Joseph conveyed a moiety stating that this property was "where son Levi then lived." On same date of signing, 14 June 1802, Levi granted a life-lease [tenancy] to his parents on this same property, "for and during their natural life and the life of the survivor of them," deed rec'd 16 Mar 1812, for $500.00; witnesses Reuben French, Nathaniel Kidder [Strafford Co. Deed 71:182]. The second moiety was granted by Joseph by deed signed 14 Mar, rec'd 10 Jul 1812; see parents for full details on deeds of homestead. His will was signed 27 Apr 1841, proved 1 Jan 1850; witnesses Joseph Boodey, John Chamberlin, Durrell S. Chamberlin [Strafford Co. Probate 61:405]. He named his only [surviving] son Jonathan B. as Exec. and residuary legatee; on date of probate, Jonathan B. was allowed Exec. having posted bond of $2,000.00; sureties Joseph Evans, Thomas Bennett, both of New Durham [Strafford Co. Probate 50:388]. Levi provided for wife Phoebe's care by allowing her the use of the home while she remained his widow, stipulated that their daughters could live at home until they married, and made these bequests to their children: to Sally B. Davis+, $1.00; to Eliza B. Horne, $100.00; to Mary Ann Frost, $1.00 and the privilege to live at their home "while she is destitute of a home as she now is"; to Drusilla E. Young, $1.00 in addition to what shall be delivered to her on the day of her marriage; to Clarissa D. Young, $100.00 upon her marriage; and to Jonathan B. Young, all his real estate, utensils, and live stock in New Durham.

Inventory on Levi's estate was submitted 29 Jan 1850 by Joseph Boodey, Thomas Bennett and Edmund S. Furber, allowed same date [Strafford Co. Probate 674]. Real estate was valued at $1,075.00; debts came to $241.88; and personal estate which included live stock, provisions and produce, farming tools, furniture, apparel, and miscellany came to $315.40. Grand total of estate real and personal was $1,632.28. Levi, his two wives, and Sally Davis' infant children were buried at Chamberlain Cemetery, South Alton.

Ch. b prob. Alton by Sally: Levi, b 1801, d.y.; Joseph, b 1803, d 1832, New Durham; Jonathan B.+, b 18 Feb 1805; Sally B.+ (Young) Davis, b ca 1807; and Mary Ann, b 1812, d 1815, New Durham. Ch. b New Durham by Phoebe: Mary Ann+ (Young) Frost, b ca 1816; Drusilla E.+ (Young) Jones, b 1820; Eliza B. (Young) Horne, b 1820s, w/o Henry B. Horne; and Clarissa D., b 1820s. (NHVR-Deaths, Marr; Census Strafford Co., 1830, p83; 1840, p336; 1850, p581; 1860, p567; New Durham TR, n.p.; Hammond's Alton Cem., p10; Fitts' Newfields, p683,684; Census Strafford Co., 1850 Mortality Schedules)

LEVI B., b May 1834, ME; resident of Effingham in 1900, lived at home of Lucy A. Danforth [n.d.]. (1900 Soundex)

LEVI G., b 1823, Pembroke, s/o George G. and Abigail ( ) Young of Ossipee [no main entry]; d 19 Dec 1862, Falmouth, VA, age 39, blacksmith, survived by spouse. See main entry for George Gaines Young of Wolfeboro, blacksmith, for possible parentage. (NHVR-Deaths)

LEVI J., b ca 1800, Wolfeboro, s/o Timothy W. and Esther (Libby) Young, alive 1834, native town; m ca 1825, Wolfeboro, Elizabeth ( ) [b ca 1805, of Wolfeboro, alive 1830, same town]. Levi was named a son and heir in the will of Timothy W. of Wolfeboro, dated 24 Mar, proved 16 May 1834. He and Elizabeth made their home in Wolfeboro; no known children. By deed signed 26 Oct, rec'd 27 Oct 1830, Levi and Elizabeth mortgaged 50 acres that were part of Lot 14, Wolfeboro to Timothy W. Young of Tuftonboro for $150.00; single witness Esther Young [Strafford Co. Deed 149:326].

LEVI J., b Sep 1814, Wolfeboro, alive 1900 Gilmanton, widower; m1 ca 1844, Gilmanton, Sally J. ( ) [b 1822, of Gilmanton, d 21 Mar 1846, same town]; m2 22 Aug 1847, Gilmanton, Elizabeth E. Gilman [b 1825, of Gilmanton, d testate 28 Dec 1883, age 58, same town]. First wife Sally was member of the Freewill Baptist Church. Levi and Elizabeth were residents of Gilmanton in 1860; children at home were Araminta B., Sally J., Ann M., Lucy J. and Junette. Levi lived in Gilmanton in 1900, widower, age 85; boarder was John W. Rollins [n.d.]. Second wife Elizabeth E.'s will was drawn up 16 Feb 1883, proved 15 Jan 1884, naming husband Levi J. as sole Exec. and residuary legatee of her estate in Gilmanton; witnesses Joseph Brown, John W. Rollins, Frank J. Brown [Belknap Co. Probate #3846]. She devised $5.00 to each of her daughters, Sally J. Lovett, Anna M. Snow, Lucy J. Young, and Nettie L. Young; bequest of $5.00 to "daughter-in-law" [step-daughter] Araminta B. Young. Levi's two wives Sally and Elizabeth were buried at Smith Meeting House Cemetery, Gilmanton. Ch. b Gilmanton by Sally: Araminta B.+ (Young) Pierce, b 1844. Ch. b Gilmanton by Elizabeth: Sally J. (Young) Lovett, b 1848, alive 1883; Anna M. (Young) Snow, **b 1850**, alive 1883; Lucy J., b 1853, alive 1883; and Junette aka Nettie L.+ (Young) Brown, b 1856. (NHVR-Marr; Census Belknap Co., 1860, p221; 1900 Soundex; Folsom's NH Cemeteries, p159,160; Morning Star, p376)

LEWIS, b ca 1850, Gilmanton; m ca 1875, Laura ( ) [b ca 1855, Effingham]. Ch. b Effingham: Bertie, b 13 Dec 1876, d 13 Apr 1878, age 1-4-0, Effingham]. (NHVR-Deaths)

LEWIS A., b 1835, Gilmanton, s/o Dudley and Sally (Jacobs) Young, alive 1890, Stanstead Plains, Canada; m 1860s, Lucy Rowe [b ca 1840, Compton, alive 1890, Canada]. Lewis lived at home in Gilmanton in 1850, age 15. He was named a son and heir of Dudley Young of Gilmanton by his will signed 20 Jun, proved 21 Jul 1863. Lewis and Lucy were reported to be of Stanstead Plains at time of son's marriage in 1890. Ch. b Gilmanton: Dudley B.+, b 1869. (NHVR-Marr)

LEWIS AUGUSTUS, b 1834, Barrington, s/o Jonathan F. and Hannah (Johnson) Young, d 28 Jan 1912, Melrose, MA, bur. Edgewood Cemetery, Nashua; m1 5 Apr 1872, Boston, Malvina (Morrill) Pearson [b ca 1840, Boston, her 2nd marriage, d pre Jun 1905, Melrose, MA]; m2 7 Jun 1905, Laconia, Addie L. ( ) Vittum, [b 20 Apr 1868, Laconia, her 2nd marriage, alive 1916, Melrose, MA]. Addie m1 1 Oct 1890, Laconia, Stephen Vittum [b ca 1865, of Sandwich, s/o Will and Abbie ( ) Vittum, d 13 Apr 1903, ?]. Lewis lived with father and stepmother Martha in 1850, age 15, Barrington. On 7 Aug 1862, as resident of Dover age 28, Lewis enlisted in Co. K, 11th Regt., NH Volunteer Infantry, mustered in 2 Sep 1862 as Pvt. and was wounded 13 Dec 1862 at Fredericksburg, Virginia, appointed Corp. He was wounded severely 12 May 1864 at Spottsylvania, VA, mustered out 4 Jun 1865 giving P.O. address of Chelmsford Center, MA. Two weeks after returning to civilian life Lewis filed petition for an Invalid Pension, Application No. 73,221, Cert. No. 64,938. His widow Addie L. filed for a Widow's Pension 9 Oct 1916, Application No. 1,082,829, Cert. No. 829,773. Her deposition stated Lewis died of Addison's decease and angina pectoris. No known children. (NHVR-Marr; Census Strafford Co., 1850, p517; Soldiers & Sailors, p600; Nat'l. Archives Milit. Recs.)

LEWIS F., b Sep 1866, Middleton, s/o John Henry and Mary Emily (Cook) Young, alive 1900, native town; m 27 Mar 1896, Farmington, Effie A. Leighton [b Jun 1877, Middleton, d/o Charles H. and Lovey A. (Drew) Leighton, alive 1900, native town]. Effie's father Charles H. Leighton was born in Middleton, her mother Lovey A. Drew, in Eaton. In 1900 Lewis F. and Effie were listed as residents of Middleton; members of household were son Perley L., sister Etta M. Young and her children by her late husband Charles H. Young--Maud M. Young [b Jan 1889] and Frederick Roland Young [b 24 Jun 1891]. Ch. b Middleton, not traced further: Perley L., b Jun 1891; Lewis P., b 5 Jun 1898, not listed in 1900 Census; and Chester, b 4 Jan 1900, d 11 May 1900, Middleton. (NHVR-Births, Marr, Deaths; 1900 Soundex)

LEWIS HENRY, b 15 Dec 1863, Barrington, s/o Jacob Daniels and Sarah C. (Twombly) Young, d 28 Feb 1949, Madbury; m 31 Oct 1899, Barrington, Mary Shackford Hale [b 31 Mar 1872, Barrington, d/o Samuel S. and Adaline M. (Roberts) Hale, d 16 Jun 1947, Madbury]. Samuel S. Hale was b 1831, Strafford; Adaline M. Roberts was b 1837, Dover. Newly-weds Lewis and Mary lived with his parents in 1900 at the family homestead in Madbury. He served as a member of the Madbury School Board and town clerk from 1916-1920. Lewis and Mary were buried at Pine Grove Cemetery, Plot 12-8E, Barrington. Ch. b Madbury, not traced further: Esther Hale, b 2 Dec 1900; Adaline Roberts, b 24 Feb 1903; Edward Hale, b 8 Apr 1904; and Louise Shackford, b 17 Feb 1909. (Ham Gen., p55; Barrington Graveyards, p133; NHVR-Marr; 1900 Soundex; Adam's Madbury, n.p.; Scale's Dover, p308)

LEYANDER, b 9 Feb 1850, Barnstead Center, s/o Oliver H. P. and Emily J. (Tuttle) Young, physician, alive 1888, Haverhill, MA; m 29 Aug 1877, Pittsfield, Abbie A. Ring [b 20 Sep 1851, Pittsfield, d/o Stephen F. Ring, alive 1888, Haverhill, MA]. He lived with his parents in 1870, then a medical student; attended Pittsfield Academy and Northwood Seminary, later a medical student at Dartmouth Medical School, completing studies at the University of Vermont. There he earned his M.D. degree 26 June 1877, two months before his marriage. For a while he practiced medicine in Candia, only to relocate 1 Oct 1883 with his family in Haverhill, Mass. Ch. b Barnstead or Candia: Velma May, b 5 May 1878, d 10 May 1880, age 1-11-27, Candia; Viva N., b 18 Aug 1880, d 4 Feb 1903; Lester R., b 9 Jul 1882, d 9 Apr 1884. Ch. b Haverhill: Lester I., b 13 Oct 1884; and Merton P., b 7 Sep 1888, all not traced further. (NHVR-Marr, Deaths; Cutter's Eastern Mass., p1270)

LILLIE E., b 1850s, Farmington, d/o Daniel and Deborah (   ) Young [no main entry]; m 6 Sep 1877, Farmington, Fred D. Johnson [b 1850s, Farmington]. Lillie E. was of Newport, ME at time of marriage. (NHVR-Brides)

LILLIAN MAYBELLE, b ca 1869, Dover, d/o Joseph and
Elizabeth (   ) Young; m 17 Aug 1889, Dover, Byron P. Wentworth [b ca 1865, Dover]. (NHVR-Brides)

LIZZIE A., b 1865, Somersworth, d/o Richard and Mary A.
(Frost) Young, d 15 Jun 1892, native town; m 6 Oct 1886,
Somersworth, Fred E. Chesley [b Sep 1862, of Somersworth,
alive 1900, same town. Lizzie A. Chesley was buried at Forest
Glade Cemetery, Somersworth at family plot. (NHVR-Brides;
Wooley's Somersworth Cem., Bk 3, p121)

LIZZIE H., b 1857, Dover, d/o Nathaniel M. and Hannah
M. (   ) Young; m 5 May 1879, Rochester, Frank J. Drew [b
1858, Gilmanton, shoemaker, s/o Charles and E. A. (   ) Drew].
Ch. b Rochester: Gertrude May Drew, b ca 1880, m 1899,
Middleton, Leander E. Tibbetts [b ca 1880, Rochester].
(NHVR-Brides)

LIZZIE M., b 26 Oct 1853, Farmington, d/o Jonathan and
Hannah S. (Waldron) Young; m 17 Jul 1890, Farmington, Samuel
S. Forsaith [b ca 1850, of same town]. (NHVR-Brides)

LIZZIE M., b 1859, Freedom, d/o Daniel and Eleanor
(Allard) Young, d pre 1900, native town; m 3 Jun 1882, Freedom, Joseph A. Tyler [b 1856, Freedom, s/o Wentworth and Mary
M. (   ) Tyler, alive 1900, same town]. There were no children as far as is known. In 1900 Joseph Tyler [n.d.], widower,
lived with widowed mother-in-law Eleanor J. Young in Freedom.
(NHVR-Brides; Freedom VR, 1878-1890; 1900 Soundex)

LIZZIE M., b 17 Apr 1859, Strafford, d/o Charles W. and
Abbie (Swasey) Young of Exeter; m 31 Aug 1881, Exeter, Fred
T. Stanton [b ca 1855, Strafford]. Lizzie M. lived at home
in Strafford up through 1870. (NHVR-Brides)

LIZZIE N., b 1830s, Dover, d/o Moses and Mary R. (   )
Young [no main entry]; m 27 Nov 1862, Somersworth, John N.
Matthew aka Mathes [b 1830s, Durham]. (NHVR-Brides)

LOUISA, b ca 1819, Upper Gilmanton, d/o Bailey and 1st
wife Polly (Rundlet) Young, alive 26 Jan 1863, Belmont [native
town]; m 1 Jan 1844, Belmont, Henry A. Weymouth [b ca 1820,
Andover, alive 1863, Belmont]. Louisa Weymouth was named wife
of Henry A. Weymouth and eldest daughter and heir of Bailey
Young of Gilmanton by his will signed 26 Jan, proved 18 Mar
1863. Ch. b Belmont: George W. Weymouth, b 1840s, m 1884,
Laconia. (NHVR-Brides; Meredith Annals, p456,457)

LOUISA J., b ca 1825, of Somersworth; m 9 Dec 1847,
Dover, Benjamin Steavens [b ca 1820, of Somersworth].
(NHVR-Brides)

LOUISA W., b ca 1815, of Tuftonboro; m 17 May 1837,
Tuftonboro, Simon F. Beacham [b ca 1810, of Ossipee].
(NHVR-Brides)

LOVINA ADELINE, b 19 May 1858, Rochester, d/o Thomas S.
and Sabrina (Wentworth) Young, gr.d/o of Samuel and Lydia
(Thompson) Wentworth, d 1 May 1928; m (Intentions) 11 Apr
1874, m 12 Sep 1874, New Durham, Franklin Pierce Hayes, twice
widower [b 3 Mar 1853, Alton, s/o Samuel and Mary (   ) Hayes
of New Durham, d 14 Jan 1900, Farmington, of pneumonia]. This

was Franklin's third marriage; he m1 23 Aug 1869, New Durham, Abbie F. Willey [b 1851, New Durham, d/o Alfred S. and Mary J. (Young) Willey, d Jul 1871, of consumption, New Durham]; m2 17 Nov 1871, New Durham, Hannah Frances Webster [b 1853, New Durham, d/o Jonathan S. and Comfort (   ) Webster, d 5 Jan 1874, New Durham, of consumption]. Franklin aka Frank was a resident of Farmington at time of marriage, occupation knife maker; Adeline resided in New Durham at time of marriage. In 1899, Frank ran the Elmore Inn in Farmington. He and former wives were buried at Pine Grove Cemetery, Farmington. (Hayes Gen., V2, p720; New Durham VR, 1850-1867; NHVR-Brides, Deaths, Marr; LDS I.G.I. B.R.; Wentworth Gen., V2, p583,584)

    LOWELL H., b 1844, Ossipee, s/o John K. and Lydia A. (   ) Young, d 26 Oct 1910, Exeter; m1 4 Feb 1870, Exeter, Mary Greenough [b 1853, Bath, ME, d/o William Greenough, d pre 1877, Exeter]; m2 1 Apr 1877, Newfields, Ida Miranda (Young) Fogg [b ca 1850, of Newfields, her 2nd marriage]. He and parents were residents of Dover in 1850. He enlisted from Exeter at age 19 in Co. E, 13th Regt., NH Volunteer Infantry on 2 Aug 1862 and mustered in 15 Sep 1862 as Pvt. He was wounded 15 Jun 1864, Battery Five, Petersburg, Virginia and was discharged 16 May 1865 giving P.O. address of Exeter. Lowell H. filed petition for an Invalid Pension 20 May 1865, Application No. 67,568; Cert. No. 69,678. Ch. b Exeter: Frank P., b 30 Sep 1877, alive 15 Jan 1898, native town. (NHVR-Marr; Soldiers & Sailors, p690; Nat'l. Archives Milit. Recs.)

    LUCETTA, b 1834, ME, of Rollingsford in 1850; she and sister Cynthia, age 15 [b 1835, ME], lived with the Sylvanus Bunker family in Rollingsford in 1850. (Census Strafford Co., 1850, p375)

    LUCINDA, b 1828, ME, resident of Rollingsford in 1850; carder, lived with Lydia Twombly, age 44 [b 1806]. (Census Strafford Co., 1850, p372)

    LUCIUS, b ca 1825, of Somersworth; m 6 Sep 1852, same town, Jeanna Ricker [b ca 1830, of same town]. (NHVR-Marr)

    LUCY, b ca 1750, Barrington; m 14 Nov 1771, Dover, Andrew Twombly [bp 26 Sep 1753, Madbury, s/o Joseph and Martha (Wentworth) Twombly, d ME]. Andrew's mother Martha Wentworth Twombly was d/o Ephraim and Mary (Miller) Wentworth, one of nine children. Andrew m2 Mary Frost [b ca 1755, of Dover]. Wentworth Genealogy stated that Andrew "removed to Maine and died there, having had a large family of children." (LDS I.G.I. BR; Heritage's Dover VR, p172; Wentworth Gen., V1, p160,168,169)

    LUCY, b ca 1785, of Wolfeboro; m (Intentions) 25 Aug 1816, Wolfeboro, John Tuttle [b ca 1780, of same town]. (Parker's Wolfeboro Banns, 1789-1854, n.p.)

    LUCY, b ca 1805, of Meredith, poss. d/o Joseph and Abigail (Gilman) Young of New Hampton; m 18 Mar 1827, New Hampton, Capt. Stephen Farrer Jr. [b ca 1800, of Meredith]. If this parentage was correct she would have predeceased

Joseph who died in 1849 per Admin. Papers on his estate in New Hampton. (NHVR-Brides)

LUCY MARIA, b 1822, Barrington, d/o Ebenezer and Prudence (Cate) Young, d 2 Dec 1912, age 89-10-26, home town; m 9 Feb 1843, Barrington, John S. Critchett [b 1819, Barrington, d 27 Dec 1905, age 86-11-14, home town]. As a minor under 14 years, Lucy was made a ward on 17 Sep 1838 of her uncle David Young of Barrington. David named her as an heir and niece by married name of Chritchett in his will drawn 16 Jun 1869, proved 6 Jun 1871. Lucy, husband and sons were buried at Pine Grove Cemetery, Plot 4A-2, Barrington. Ch. b Barrington: Frank Chritchett, b 1851, d 18 May 1872, Barrington; and J. Loring Chritchett, b 29 Aug 1854, d 8 Oct 1919, Barrington. (NHVR-Brides; Barrington Graveyards, p28; Barrington TR, V6, p89)

LUCY MARIA, b 10 Apr 1836, Stark, ME, d/o _____ and Lucy Maria ( ) Witham; d 15 Jan 1890, age 53, Dover, survived by husband _____ Young. (NHVR-Death)

LUCY W., b ca 1815, of Dover; m 2 Feb 1839, Dover, John W. Brock [b ca 1810, of same town]. (NHVR-Brides)

LURANA, b ca 1810, of Dover; m 14 Jul 1833, Dover, Nathaniel Hobbs [b ca 1805, of same town]. (NHVR-Brides; Heritage's Dover VR, p99)

LUTHER, b 18 Feb 1809, Ossipee, s/o John C. and Betsey C. (Lord) Young, d testate, 3 Dec 1871, native town, farmer; m ca 1835, Sophronia Chick [b 1 Jan 1816, Effingham, d/o John Chick, d 9 Oct 1898, Ossipee]. Luther was head of household in Ossipee from 1840-1870, Sophronia listed as his spouse from 1850-1870. In 1840 his age was 20-30, with family of two females both age 20-30, one elderly female age 50-60 [prob. widowed mother Betsey], one male age 5-10 and one female under 5. Luther's mother Betsey was listed as member of their household from 1850-1860; in 1850 her age was 68 [b 1782, ME]. In 1850 children at home were Helen E., Jane E., Charles C., and Susan A. In 1860 all children were at home with the exception of Helen E., then married; newest additions were Annette and George. By tax deed signed 4 Mar 1830, rec'd 16 May 1831, Luther and brother Wentworth S., along with mother Betsey, relinquished their title to their late father's estate which had to be sold at auction.

Luther's will was drawn 13 Sep 1871, proved 1 Mar 1872, in which he named wife Sophronia his sole Exec. and residuary legatee of his homestead in Ossipee and "all other real estate situate in the county of Carroll" as well as all personal property; witnesses Frank Weeks, J. Sinclair, Jacob A. Haines [Carroll Co. Probate #5831]. Bequests of $1.00 were made to each of his six children: Helen E. Chapman, Jane E. Smith, Charles C. Young, Susan A. Young, Annette Young, and George L. Young. Letters of Admin. on Sophronia's estate were filed 26 Oct 1898, approved 1 Nov 1898, which listed surviving children Jane E. Smith of Vermillion, South Dakota, Charles C. Young of Goodland, Kansas, Susan A. Hodgkins of Tamworth,

Nettie Nute of Wolfeboro, George L. Young of Gonic, and
grandson George Chapman, son of Helen E. Chapman, deceased;
these heirs-at-law petitioned that sister Nettie Nute of
Wolfeboro be appointed administrator [Carroll Co. Probate
#5830]. An Agreement of Heirs was reached on 1 Nov 1898 with
the understanding that each heir would release his or her
share of their mother's savings deposit at the Strafford
Savings Bank at Dover, in favor of said Nettie Nute [Carroll
Co. Probate 46:370]. Luther and Sophronia were buried at
Large Ossipee Center Cemetery. Ch. b Ossipee: Helen E.+
(Young) Chapman, b 1838; Susan A.+ (Young) Fall aka Davis aka
Hodgkins, b 1840; Jane E., b 1841; Charles C., b 1843; Annette
aka Nettie+ (Young) Wiggin aka Nute, b 7 Oct 1853; and George
L.+, b 11 May 1859. (NHVR-Deaths; Census Strafford Co., 1840,
p233; Carroll Co., 1850, p204; 1860, p688; 1870, p362; Loud's
Cem. Recs., p106)

LYDIA, b 29 Nov 1694, Dover Neck, d/o Thomas and Mary
(Roberts) Young, alive 1755, Dover; m ca 1715, Dover, John
Cook aka Cuck [b 5 May 1692, Dover, s/o John and Mary (Downes)
Cook, d testate 1755, Dover]. Lydia was known by her married
name of Cuck, wife of John Cuck, in her father's deed of gift
signed 18 Mar 1726/27, proved 20 May 1727/28. John Cook pre-
served his children's dates of birth in his capacity as Town
Clerk of Dover. His will was written 1752, probated 1755,
which named wife Lydia and their seven children [Noyes et al,
p160]. Ch. b Dover: Marcy Cook, b 21 Jun 1716; Hessekiah
Cook, b 1 Jan 1717; Mary Cook, b 1 Apr 1720; John Cook, b
6 Nov 1725; Richard Cook, b 21 Dec 1727; Phebe Cook, b 17 Mar
1729/30; and Daniel Cook, b 11 Sep 1732. (Heritage's Dover
VR, p16,17,43)

LYDIA, b ca 1785, of Alton; m 6 Jul 1806, Barnstead,
Jonathan Witham [b ca 1780, of Alton]. (NHVR-Brides).

LYDIA, b 1800, Barnstead, d 2 Mar 1882, age 82, single,
her native town. (NHVR-Deaths)

LYDIA, b ca 1810, Somersworth; m 2 Jan 1833, Somersworth,
Charles H. Abbott [b ca 1805, of same town]. (NHVR-Brides)

LYDIA, b 1847, resident of Dover, Ward 3, in 1850, age
23; she was music teacher and roomed at boarding house.
(Census Strafford Co., 1870, p90)

LYDIA ABIGAIL, b 26 Mar 1847, Barrington, d/o William
Hale and Sarah (Daniels) Young, d 4 Jan 1929, Wichita, KA; m1
25 Dec 1873, Barrington, Cyrus True Daniels [b 30 Jan 1841,
Presque Isle, ME, d 28 Apr 1882, Lyons, KA]; m2 2 Jul 1884,
?, John Edward Davies [b ca 1845, England, d 12 Apr 1918].
No known children from either marriage. (Ham Gen., p41)

LYDIA F., b 1859, Alton, d/o Charles E. and Hannah (   )
Young; m 9 Jan 1875, Rochester, Daniel B. Clough [b 23 Jul
1845, Alton, s/o Daniel and Sally H. (Caverly) Clough]. Lydia
and spouse made their home in Alton. Ch. b Alton: Fannie E.
Clough, b 1870s, m 1900, New Durham, John L. Berry [b 1870s,
Alton]. (NHVR-Brides; Rochester TR, Marr, n.p.; LDS I.G.I.
VR)

LYDIA HARRIET aka Harriet, b 15 Jun 1803, Durham, d/o Henry and Sarah (Bennett) Young, d 22 Oct 1892, Somerville, MA; m 17 Dec 1818, Packers Falls, Durham, Deacon Samuel Hayes Jr. [b 19 Apr 1792, Green Hill, Barrington, second s/o Samuel and Hannah (Demeritt) Hayes, d 21 Jun 1852, Packers Falls, Durham]. According to the Hayes Gen., "Deacon Hayes settled in Durham about 1817 where he bought a farm on the banks of the Lamprey River at Packers Falls near the New Market line." He joined the Congregational Church both at New Market and Durham where he served as Deacon. Lydia, husband Samuel, and most of their children were buried at Hayes Tomb at cemetery on Packers Falls Road directly at end of Bennett Road and north of Lamprey River. Ch. b Packers Falls, Durham: Henry Young Hayes, b 16 Sep 1819, d 14 Apr 1882, Dover; John Samuel Hayes, b 13 Jul 1823, d 5 Jul 1825, Dover; Hannah Demeritt Hayes, b 7 Jun 1828, d 31 Mar 1869, Packers Falls; Sarah Elizabeth Hayes, b 9 Jul 1833, died in New Market; Charles William Hardy Hayes, b 2 Jan 1836; James Frederick Hayes, b 13 Sep 1838; and John Samuel W. Hayes, b 5 Jun 1841. (Hayes Gen., V1, p227-228; NHVR-Births, Brides; Durham Graveyards, Hayes Tomb #157, p62; Stackpole's Durham, V1, p382; Wentworth Gen., V1, p677,678)

LYDIA L. aka Fannie, b 1849, Somersworth, d/o Joseph C. and Lydia (   ) Young; m 26 Jun 1872, Somersworth, Julius H. Doughty [b ca 1845, of Great Falls]. Lydia lived at Great Falls at time of marriage. (NHVR-Brides)

MABEL, b 1869, Standish, ME, d/o Frank and Mary (   ) Young [no main entry], m 19 Feb 1885, Rochester, Melburn E. Maybery [b 1864, So. Windham, ME]. Mabel was resident of No. Gorham, ME before marriage. (Rochester TR, Marr, p3)

MAHALA, b ca 1820, of Strafford; m 10 Jul 1842, Northwood, William Dame [b ca 1815, of Strafford]. (NHVR-Brides)

MARGARET, b ca 1780, Barrington, d/o James and Susan (Wood) Young, res. of Dover; m 29 Mar 1801, Dover, John Woodhouse aka Woods [b ca 1775, of same town]. (NHVR-Brides)

MARGARET, b ca 1825, Dover; m 31 Mar 1845, Dover, Charles Smith [b ca 1820, of same town]. (NHVR-Brides; Heritage's Dover VR, p248)

MARGARET B., b ca 1825, of Dover; m 15 Jul 1849, Dover, Samuel Bussell 2nd [b ca 1820, of Sandwich]. (NHVR-Brides)

MARIE, b 1840s, of Wolfeboro; m 1860s, Wolfeboro, Clarence Alonzo Nutter [b 1840s, of same town]. Marie may have been widow of Orlando J. Runnels who died 6 Jul 1862; see next entry. Ch. b Wolfeboro: Nellie M. Nutter, b ca 1860s, m 1899, Wolfeboro, Ralph C. Mitchell [b 1860s], Wolfeboro; Clarence Nutter, b 1860s, m 1899, Wolfeboro. (NHVR-Brides)

MARIE A. aka Marie Antoinette, b 2 Jul 1841, Wolfeboro, d/o Jeremiah and Adelaide (Hann) Young; m 8 Mar 1860, New Durham, Orlando J. Runnels, shoemaker [b 1835, of New Durham, s/o James Runnels, d 6 Jul 1862, New Orleans, LA]. Maria lived at home in Wolfeboro from 1850-1860. Orlando died of disease contracted while serving in the 8th Regt., Co. No. I,

NH Vol. Infantry, in which he mustered 7 Dec 1861. (LDS I.G.I. VR; NHVR-Brides; Runnels Gen., p233, #2957)

MARIA E., b 1827, Alton; m (Intentions) 27 Sep 1867, Alton, at age 40, Hiram Cook of Milton, age 55 [b 1812, Milton]. (Alton VR, p669)

MARK, b ca 1780, res. of Ossipee; m ca 1805, prob. Ossipee ( ) [b ca 1785, of Ossipee]. When of Ossipee, Mark purchased 62 acres of Lot 36, 2nd Div., Wakefield, from Shadrach Folsom of Wakefield for $400.00, by deed signed 3 Feb, rec'd 30 Apr 1819,; witnesses Nathaniel F. Mason, John Roberts [Strafford Co. Deed 105:318]. By 1820 Mark lived in Wakefield, listed as taxpayer of Highway District No. 10, and was of Wakefield when he sold in fee simple this same land, 60 acres more or less "being my homestead farm and same piece of land I purchased of Shadrach Folsom with all the buildings," by deed signed and rec'd 10 Nov 1821, for $200.00, to Jedediah Abbott of Ossipee and John Roberts and Paul D. Young [s/o Thomas and Nancy (Drew) Young], both of Wakefield; witnesses Jonathan Locke, H. L. Neal [Strafford Co. Deed 112:92]. From all accounts he had not mortgaged this property; yet he repurchased the shares of Lot 36, 2nd Div., from Jedediah Abbott and Paul D. Young for $200.00, on date of 23 Feb, rec'd 25 Feb 1822, "it being the same land that the said Mark Young deeded to us by his deed bearing date November 10th 1821"; witnesses Ezekial Wentworth, Joseph Bickford [Strafford Co. Deed 112:549]. Ch. b Ossipee: Iretus, b 1810, d 19 Jan 1900, age 90, Stratford, survived by wife, buried at Center Cemetery, Stratford. (NHVR-Deaths; Bank's Wakefield, p680)

MARK ALLEN, b 1827, Tuftonboro, s/o Joseph and Patience (Chase) Young, gr.s/o Benjamin and 1st wife Phoebe (Allen) Young of Wolfeboro, d 9 Jan 1884, Wolfeboro; m1 ca 1860, Wolfeboro, Caroline J. Johnson [b 1824, Brookfield, d 1868, Wolfeboro]; m2 17 Feb 1870, Cornish, ME, Anna L. Sawyer [b Nov 1834, Porter, ME, d/o Lemuel Sawyers, reported from Wolfeboro, d 1914, widow, Wolfeboro]. Mark A. was named an heir-at-law of grandfather Benjamin Young of Wolfeboro by his will drawn 6 Nov 1843, proved 30 Feb 1849; the family homestead in Wolfeboro was to revert to Mark A. upon the death of his father Joseph. He was member of parents' household in Wolfeboro in 1850, age 23. In the 1860 census he, first wife Caroline and infant son Joseph L. lived at his parents' home in Wolfeboro. This was situated in the eastern part of Wolfeboro where they became members of the Second Christian Church established 10 Jan 1822. At one time Mark was elected Elder of the church. By 1870, Mark, second wife Annie and son Joseph, age 10, maintained residence in Wolfeboro.

Admin. Papers on Mark A.'s estate in Wolfeboro were filed by widow Annie L. on 5 Feb 1884, at which time she declined the administration of the estate and petitioned that Daniel A. Wiggin of Tuftonboro be granted this position of trust; approved same date [Carroll Co. Probate #5845]. Petition for guardianship of daughter Cara M., minor under 14 years, was filed by Anna L. on 1 Dec 1885; granted same date [same docket #]. In 1900 Annie, still widow, was head of household in Wolfeboro; at home were step-son Joseph L., age 40, single, and daughter Carrie M., single. Mark and members of family were buried at Wolfeboro Center Cemetery. Ch. b Wolfeboro by 1st wife Caroline: Joseph Lang, b 13 Apr 1860, d 17 Aug 1927, Wolfeboro. Ch. b Wolfeboro by 2nd wife Annie: Carrie May, b 28 Nov 1871; and Carolyn M., b 28 Dec 1872 who married Ralph Samuel Parker. (LDS I.G.I. VR; NHVR-Births; Marr; Deaths; Census Carroll Co., 1870, p467; 1900 Soundex; D.A.R Wolfeboro Cem., TMs, p2,35-37; Merrill's Carroll Co., p339; Young Family Recs., courtesy of Nancy L. Dodge)

MARK F., b 1817, Tuftonboro, s/o John and Hannah (Ham) Young, d 10 Apr 1876, age 59, Stratham, survived by spouse; m ca 1845, Olive L. (   ) [b 1823, of Tuftonboro, d 2 Feb 1886, age 63, Stratham]. Mark and Olive lived with his parents in 1850 in Tuftonboro; as of 1853, they were of Stratham, Rock. Co. Mark F., Olive and daughters Mary C. and Sarah L. were buried at Old Cemetery, Stratham. Ch. b Tuftonboro: John, b 1846; Hannah A., b 1848; son b 6 Nov 1850, twin; and Mary C., b 6 Nov 1850, twin, d 9 Dec 1898. Ch. b Stratham: son b 28 Jul 1853; child b 26 Jan 1855; daughter b 4 Dec 1860; and Sarah L., b 7 Feb 1863, d 25 Apr 1895, home town. (NHVR-Births; Deaths; LDS I.G.I. BR; Stratham Cemeteries, p236)

MARTHA, b 1787, of Wakefield, d 26 Jul 1814, age 27, Wakefield; m 26 Oct 1810, Wakefield, Edmund Wentworth [b 9 Apr 1787, s/o Spencer and Sarah (Stiles) Wentworth, d 17 Sep 1868, Wakefield]. Edmund Wentworth m2 14 Feb 1819, Eliza Lang [b ca 1800, of Lee]. Martha and Edmund raised their family in Wakefield. Ch. b Wakefield by Martha: Mary Wentworth, b 14 Jul 1812; and Ethelinda Wentworth, b 6 Dec 1814, d 25 Sep 1831. Ch. b Wakefield by Eliza: Martha Ann Wentworth, b 17 Oct 1821, d 14 Mar 1833; Thomas Lang Wentworth, b 29 Nov 1823, m 27 May 1849, Olive Farnham of Wakefield, residents of Ossipee. (LDS I.G.I. BR; Wentworth Gen., V2, p184)

MARTHA, b 1798, of Wolfeboro in 1870, lived alone. (Census Carroll Co., 1870, p455)

MARTHA, b ca 1810, of Tuftonboro; m 15 Mar 1829, Moultonboro, Asa Lee [b ca 1805, of Moultonboro]. (NHVR-Brides)

MARTHA, b 1819, of New Hampton in 1860, widow of _____ Young; head of household that year with family of three children in New Hampton. Ch. b Dover: prob. Martha E.+ (Young) York, b 1842; James, b 1845; and Mary E., b 1847. (Census Belknap Co., 1860, p96; NHVR-Brides)

MARTHA A., b ca 1825, Alton; m 1860s, poss. Dover, John H. Cooke [b ca 1820, Milton]. Ch. b Dover: Weston Cooke, b 1860s, m 1891, Dover. (NHVR-Brides)

MARTHA A., b 6 Apr 1847, Farmington, d/o Jonathan and Alice (Peavey) Young; m (Intentions) 2 Dec 1865, Alton, Isaac Ellis [b 1830, Alton]. In 1860 she lived with her mother Alice and step-father Moses Young in Alton. (Alton VR, p652)

MARTHA ANN, b ca 1825, Dover; m 16 Jan 1848, Dover, James M. Ryan [b ca 1820, of same town]. (NHVR-Brides; Heritage's Dover VR, p250)

MARTHA E., b 1842, Dover, prob. d/o ____ and Martha ( ) Young of Dover/New Hampton; m 16 Jun 1866, Dover, George T. York [b ca 1840, of Sandwich]. (NHVR-Brides)

MARTHA F., b ca 1830, of Barrington; m 5 Oct 1853, Barrington, Moses Pierce [b ca 1825, of same town]. (NHVR-Brides)

MARTHA L., b 15 Dec 1803, Ossipee, d/o Hubbard and Lydia (Roberts) Goldsmith, d 6 Jul 1893, age 89-7-22, Exeter, widow of ____ Young. (NHVR-Deaths)

MARY, b 1699, Dover Neck, d/o Thomas and Mary (Roberts) Young, d pre 1736, Dover; m (Intentions) 30 Jan 1719/20, Dover, m 22 Feb 1719/20, Dover, Stephen Otis [b 22 Jun 1698, Dover, s/o Richard and Susannah (Hussey) Otis of Dover, d pre 29 Aug 1759, Madbury]. They were married by James Davis, J.P., Stephen's occupation weaver. Mary was known by her married name of Otis, wife of Stephen Otis, in her father's deed of gift signed 18 Mar 1726/27, proved 20 May 1727/28. She and Stephen lived in that part of Dover before it became Madbury. After Mary's death Stephen married twice more; m2 30 Jul 1736, Dover, Catherine Austin [b 12 Jan 1715, d/o Nathaniel and Catharine N. ( ) Austin]; m3 Elizabeth ( ), alive 1759. Stephen's will was signed 2 May, proved 29 Aug 1759, in which he bequeathed to his [present] wife Elizabeth the rest of his property for life. Upon her death his children were to receive it. He gave "something" to each of his sons. Third wife Elizabeth was with child when Stephen died in 1759; daughter born to them that year was Susanna Otis. Ch. b Dover by Mary: Joshua Otis, b ca 1720; Stephen Otis, b 1731; and John Otis, b pre 1736. Ch. b Dover by Elizabeth: Susanna Otis, b 1759. (Heritage's Dover VR, p8; Otis Gen., **Reg.** 5:185,196; Noyes et al, p521)

MARY, b ca 1720, bp 28 Mar 1736, Dover Neck, d/o John and Elizabeth ( ) Young; believed to have married ca 1740, Joseph Drew [b 8 Apr 1717, Dover, s/o Francis and Ann ( ) Drew, d 1757, Dover]. In 1753 Joseph Drew was designated son-in-law in the Admin. Papers of John Young's estate in Dover. Four children were born to Joseph Drew of Dover. Ch. b Dover: Francis Drew, b 24 May 1741, twin; Elijah Drew, b 24 May 1741, twin; Mary Drew, b 9 Jun 1745; and Joseph Drew, b 30 Aug 1748. (Heritage's Dover VR, p38,146,152,154; Noyes et al, p206)

MARY, b 30 Dec 1725, Dover, d/o Jonathan and Abigail (Hanson) Young, d 29 Apr 1806, prob. Northwood; m 1753/54, Durham, John Tasker Jr. [bp Mar 1736, Dover, s/o John Tasker]. Mary and John Tasker took up residence in Northwood at least by 1754 when first child was born. Mary, single, was named in her father's will signed 1 Jul 1752, proved 29 Sep 1756. Ch. b Northwood: Abigail Tasker, bp 20 Nov 1754. Other children [n.d.] attributed by Moses' Northwood [TMs, V3, p311]: Abigail Tasker; Samuel Tasker; Joseph Tasker; Matthew

Tasker. (LDS I.G.I. VR; Heritage's Dover VR, p23,24,142,158;
NH State Papers 35:239,241)

MARY, b ca 1750, of Dover; m 4 Jun 1770, at First Church,
Dover, Moses Brown [b ca 1745, of Portsmouth, Rock. Co.].
(Heritage's Dover VR, p52,171; NHVR-Brides)

MARY, b ca 1765, Gilmanton, d/o Dudley Young, d pre 1801,
native town; m 19 Apr 1785, Belmont, Josiah Clough [b ca 1760,
Northwood]. Mary predeceased her father. Dudley's will drawn
20 May 1801, proved 10 May 1803, named granddaughter Mary
Clough as heir-at-law who was to receive $60.00 at age 18.
Ch. b Gilmanton: Mary Clough, b ca 1786. (NHVR-Brides)

MARY, b ca 1765, Madbury; m Mar 1787, Madbury, Jedediah
Hanson [b ca 1760, of Dover]. (NHVR-Brides)

MARY, b 28 Sep 1774, Madbury, d/o Timothy and Lydia
(Demeritt) Young, d 6 Aug 1860, native town, age 85; m 27 Dec
1798, Madbury, Nathaniel Hayes [b 14 Mar 1773, Madbury, s/o
Daniel and Sarah (Plummer) Hayes, d 19 Sep 1832, native town].
Mary was named as daughter by her married name of Hayes in her
father's will signed 16 Dec 1813, proved 25 Apr 1820. Nathaniel, Mary and their seven children lived on the homestead
inherited from his father Daniel Hayes, situated in Littleworth just this side of the Dover line. Their property was
adjacent to the old homestead of Mary's parents. Daniel Hayes
bought the original house and 28 acres of land for a thousand
pounds. Nathaniel Hayes was selectman and also Justice of the
Peace. The Hayes owned a private burial ground on the homestead where Mary and Nathaniel were buried. This later came
to be called the George O. Hayes land. Ch. b Madbury: Daniel
Hayes, b 8 Apr 1799; Timothy Young Hayes, b 17 Aug 1801; Ira
Hayes, b 28 May 1804; Plummer Hayes, b 8 Jul 1806, d 8 Feb
1846, Madbury; Jeremy D. Hayes, b 29 Jun 1810, d 14 Feb 1826,
Madbury; Sarah Plummer Hayes, b 24 Dec 1812, d 3 Nov 1846,
Madbury; and Oliver Kimball Hayes, b 22 Apr 1816 who m Eliza
Ham [b 13 Aug 1813, d/o Ephraim and Hannah (Kelley) Ham].
(Hayes Gen., V1, p84,170,171; Madbury Cem., **Reg.** 87:348;
Wentworth Gen., V1, p166)

MARY, b 1779, of Wolfeboro, d 27 Aug 1865, age 86,
Wolfeboro; m 18 Feb 1829, Durham, Thomas Brackett Wiggin [b
9 May 1770, Stratham, s/o Mark and Betsey (Brackett) Wiggin,
d 24 Feb 1839, Wolfeboro]. This was Thomas Wiggin's third
marriage. Thomas's father Mark Wiggin was b 25 Oct 1746,
Stratham; Thomas' mother Betsey Brackett, b 26 Nov 1748, of
Stratham. Mark Wiggins settled in Wolfeboro before 1797,
having been commissioned Lt. Col. in the First Regiment of
N.H. militia during the Revolutionary War. As resident of
Wolfeboro he became a farmer, taught school and went into
public service, a highly respected member of the community.
Thomas Wiggin m1 2 Dec 1794, Stratham, Eliza Thurston [b ca
1775, of Stratham, d 15 Jul 1822, prob. Stratham]; m2 ca 1824,
Judith Bickford [b 1 Jun 1779, prob. Stratham, d 19 Mar 1828,
prob. Wolfeboro]. Ch. b Stratham by first wife Eliza: Joseph
Wiggin, b 30 Jul 1795; Brackett Wiggin, b 27 Oct 1798; Eliza

Wiggin, b 1 Nov 1800; and Pierce L. Wiggin, b 14 Nov 1808 [see spouse Betsey Jane+ Young]. (NHVR-Brides; Wiggin Gen., TMs, p56; Merrill's Carroll Co., p309)

MARY, b 23 Dec 1783, Milton, d/o Samuel and Phebe (   ) Nute, d 9 Jan 1861, age 77-0-17, survived by husband _____ Young. Mary's parents were both born in Dover. Mary Nute was possibly spouse of Thomas Young of Wakefield [b 7 Oct 1784] who married a Mary Nute of Milton. However there are variants to be considered: death certificate does not give place of death and cemetery records of Wakefield gave her d-o-b as 22 Dec 1777. (NHVR-Deaths; Twombly's Wakefield Cems., TMs)

MARY aka Polly, b ca 1793, Barrington [Strafford], d/o Jonathan and Mary (Hill) Young, d pre Dec 1844, native town; m 28 Dec 1813, at Freewill Baptist Church, Strafford, William Berry Jr. [b ca 1790, Barrington, alive 1851, native town]. Polly Berry was named the late daughter of Jonathan Young of Barrington by his will signed 7 Dec 1844, proved 2 Sep 1851; her unnamed children as heirs-at-law were each to receive $1.00. Her husband William Berry was one of the appraisers of Jonathan's estate by probate papers dated 4 Nov 1851. See entry on child Josephine+ Young, b 1853, of Barrington who lived at home of William Berry in 1860. (Strafford Marr., **Reg.** 76:28; Census Strafford Co., 1860, p184)

MARY, b ca 1793, prob. Durham, d/o Zachariah Young of Wolfeboro, alive 20 Nov 1842, Wolfeboro; m 18 Feb 1813, Wolfeboro, Benjamin Sceggel Jr. [b ca 1790, of Ossipee]. Mary Sceggel was named the wife of Benjamin Sceggel and the daughter and heir of Zachariah Young of Wolfeboro by the latter's will drawn 20 Nov 1842, proved 11 Feb 1851. (NHVR-Brides)

MARY, b 1800s, Wolfeboro, d/o Timothy W. and Esther (Libby) Young, alive 1834, most likely Wolfeboro; m (Intentions) 4 Jan 1820, Wolfeboro, James Smith [b ca 1795, of Wolfeboro]. Mary Smith was named daughter and heir of Timothy W. Young of Wolfeboro by his will signed 24 Mar, proved 16 May 1834. (Parker's Wolfeboro Banns, 1789-1854, n.p.)

MARY, b ca 1805, of Dover; head of family in Dover in 1840, age 30-40, with one other female in household, age 20-30. (Census Strafford Co., 1840, p543)

MARY, b ca 1805, of Dover; m 18 Sep 1825, Dover, Joseph Gould [b ca 1800, Dover]. (Heritage's Dover VR, p183)

MARY, b ca 1805, of Dover; m 23 Dec 1827, Dover, Paul Clark [b ca 1800, of Dover]. (Heritage's Dover VR, p185)

MARY, b ca 1805, of York, York Co., Mass. [later, Maine]; m 18 Jan 1827, Dover, Sherburn Sleeper [b ca 1800, Dover]. (Heritage's Dover VR, p184)

MARY, b 25 Mar 1807, Wakefield, eldest child and d/o Joseph and Nancy (Young) Young; m 4 Mar 1824, Wakefield, John Mathews [b ca 1800, of Wakefield]. As a child of 13, Mary embroidered a sampler in which she stitched the date of 1820. This survives today as a family heirloom among Mary's descendants in the branch headed by the Ortells of Bellerose Terrace, NY. Ch. b Wakefield: prob. John W. Mathews Jr., b

1826, d 17 Jan 1927, Wakefield, age 100-11-17, a life-long resident of Wakefield who won posthumously the Boston Post Gold Cane award in 1927 for being eldest citizen; Mary Catherine Mathews, b 7 Jul 1831, m 8 Nov 1854, Wakefield, Reuben Wichter Randall [b ca 1825, of Wakefield]. (Young Family Recs., courtesy of Gerald Ortell; Bank's Wakefield, p294).

MARY, b ca 1810, of Effingham; m 27 Feb 1833, Wolfeboro, John F. Cotton [b ca 1805, of Wolfeboro]. (NHVR-Brides)

MARY, b ca 1810, of Ossipee; m (Intentions) Wolfeboro, John Cotter [b ca 1805, of Wolfeboro]. (Parker's Wolfeboro Banns, 1789-1854, n.p.)

MARY, b ca 1810, of Somersworth; m 1 Mar 1829, Dover, Samuel A. M. Moulton [b ca 1805, of Somersworth]. They were married by the Rev. Benjamin R. Hoyt of the Methodist E. Church. (NHVR-Brides; Heritage's Dover VR, p92)

MARY, b ca 1820, Dover; m 4 Jul 1842, Dover, Charles Hazeltine [b ca 1815, Newburyport, MA]. Mary, single, was member of First Church, Dover by 2 May 1830. (Heritage's Dover VR, p218)

MARY, b 1846, Limington, ME, res. of Raymond, ME; m 6 Aug 1876, Freedom, Charles York [b 1846, Bangor, ME]. (Freedom VR, Bk1, p65)

MARY A., b 6 Jul 1806, Brookfield, d/o Reuben and Hannah (Trickey) Nason of Dover, d 23 Apr 1885, age 78-9-17, Dover, wife of _____ Young. Mary's mother was born in Rochester. (NHVR-Deaths)

MARY A., b 21 Dec 1829, Gilmanton, d/o Samuel S. and Mary (Diamond) Young, d 4 Mar 1922, widow, home town; m 27 Feb 1861, Gilford, Charles H. Lougee [b 22 Jul 1840, Gilmanton, s/o Dudley Lougee, d 1863, Washington, DC, buried 8 Jan 1868, Gilmanton]. In 1860 Mary lived at home in Gilmanton. Mary A. Lougee was named daughter and residuary legatee of her father's estate in Gilmanton by his will drawn 29 Jan 1868, proved 19 Mar 1889. During her teens Mary attended Laconia Academy achieving a teacher's certificate. She taught school for 21 years in her native town. Charles Lougee served in Co. B, 12th Regt., N.H. Volunteers and died from disease contracted in 1863 during the Civil War. Mary, Charles and daughter were buried at Guinea Ridge Cemetery, Gilmanton. Ch. b Gilmanton: Abbie L. Lougee, b 21 Sep 1862, d 17 Sep 1915, native town. (NHVR-Brides; Folsom's NH Cemeteries, p141,2; Biog. Review, XXI, p45)

MARY A., b 1830, Wakefield, d/o Daniel and Betsey (Cook) Young; m 21 Mar 1863, Ossipee, Moses Sweat [b ca 1825, Parsonsfield, ME]. (NHVR-Brides)

MARY ANN, b ca 1815, of Somersworth; m 20 Jan 1839, Somersworth, Joseph F. Warren [b ca 1810, of New Market]. (NHVR-Brides)

MARY ANN, b ca 1816, New Durham, d/o Levi and Phoebe (Stockbridge) Young, alive 1841, home town; m 22 Dec 1836, New Durham, Hiram B. Frost [b ca 1810, Middleton]. Mary Ann Frost was named in her father's will signed 27 Apr 1841, proved 1 Jan 1850]. Ch. b New Durham: Emily A. Frost, b 1837, lived with grandmother Phoebe Young in 1850 in New Durham. (NHVR-Brides; Census Strafford Co., 1850, p581)

MARY ANN, b ca 1820, of Milton; m (Intentions) 29 Jan 1844, Wolfeboro; m 4 Feb 1844, Milton, Nathaniel Banfield [b ca 1815, of Wolfeboro]. (NHVR-Brides; Parker's Wolfeboro Banns, 1789-1854, n.p.; Milton VR, Town Clerk)

MARY ANN, b ca 1825, of Rochester; m 5 Jul 1847, Somersworth, James Edny aka Eddy [b ca 1820, of Rochester]. (NHVR-Brides)

MARY ANN, b 1 Jan 1827, Barnstead, d/o Stephen and Caroline (Munsey) Young; m 25 Nov 1847, Barnstead, George L. Merrill [b ca 1820, of Barnstead]. (LDS I.G.I. VR; NHVR-Births)

MARY C., b 1800s, of Farmington; m (Intentions) 17 Jul 1824, Farmington, m 15 Aug 1824, New Durham, Elder Nathaniel Berry [b 1800s, of Farmington]. (NHVR-Brides; Farmington TR, V1, p413)

MARY D., b Apr 1824, ME; resident of Dover in 1900, age 76, address New York Street. She lived alone. (1900 Soundex)

MARY E., b ca 1820, Farmington; m 8 Jun 1840, Farmington, Stephen French [b ca 1815, of same town]. (NHVR-Brides)

MARY E., b 1849, Durham, d/o Joseph and Martha D. (Bassett) Young; m 19 Jun 1888, Exeter, George W. Clark [b ca 1845, Durham]. Mary E. was listed as infant of one year on 1850 census returns of parents for Durham. (NHVR-Brides)

MARYETTA, b 4 Aug 1869, Durham, d/o Albert and Mary A. (Gleason) Young, alive 1900, native town; m 24 Apr 1893, Durham, Charles A. Smart [b Feb 1865, Durham, alive 1900, native town]. In 1900 Maryetta and husband lived with her widowed mother at her brother Albert's home in Durham; no child listed. Charles was elected Selectman for Durham 1877-1878. Ch. b Durham: Albert Monroe Smart, b 5 Dec 1907. (NHVR-Brides; 1900 Soundex; Stackpole's Durham, V1, p306-307,369)

MARY H., b 11 Dec 1852 Alton, d/o Moses and Mary H. (Thompson) Young; m 23 Aug 1868, Alton, Lewis D. Collins [b ca 1850, of same town]. In 1860 Mary H. was a child of 7 at her parents' home in Alton. Ch. b Alton: James Collins, b ca 1870, m 1895, Alton. (NHVR-Brides; LDS I.G.I. BR)

MARY J., b 22 Jul 1800, of Strafford, d 22 Dec 1891, age 91-5-0, Strafford, single, buried Center Strafford Cemetery. (NHVR-Deaths)

MARY J., b 1825, resident of Rochester in 1860, tailoress; boarded at rooming house in Rochester. (Census Strafford Co., 1860, p455)

MARY J., b 1843, Ossipee, d/o John and Lucinda (Burleigh) Young, d 16 Oct 1866, native town; m 6 Dec 1865, Ossipee, Joseph T. Burleigh [b 1833, Ossipee, alive 1870, native town]. In 1850 Mary J. was then age 6 at her parents' home in Ossipee. In 1870 her husband Joseph, widower age 37, and son Arthur F., age 4, lived at the home of her parents in Ossipee.

Mary J. Burleigh was buried at the Stevens-Burleigh Cemetery, Ossipee. Ch. b Ossipee: Arthur F. Burleigh, b 1866. (Loud's Cemetery Recs., p125; NHVR-Brides)

MARY JANE, b 3 Oct 1811, Wolfeboro, d/o John C. and Sally (Smith) Young, d 11 Jul 1875, native town, age 63-9-8]; m 16 Apr 1834, Wolfeboro, William B. Stevens [b 15 Apr 1806, of Wolfeboro, d 15 May 1882, same town, age 75-11-0]. Mary Jane Stevens was named the spouse of William B. Stevens and the daughter and heir of John C. Young of Wolfeboro by father's will drawn 2 Nov 1853, proved 4 Sep 1866. She and William were buried at the Stevens-Burleigh Cemetery, on the road from Ossipee to North Wakefield. Son Edwin Stevens was named the sole Exec. and legatee of the estate of sister-in-law Catherine Y. Young, wife of Mary Jane's brother John H. Young of Wolfeboro, then deceased, by her will drawn 20 Sep 1893, proved 4 Oct 1898; Edwin Stevens was to receive Catherine's homestead. Ch. b Wolfeboro: Edwin H. aka Edward H. Stevens, b 1830s. (Parker's Wolfeboro Banns, 1789-1854, n.p.; Loud's Cem. Recs., p124)

MARY JANE, b 1820s, Gilmanton, d/o Bailey and Polly (Rundlet) Young, d pre 18 Mar 1863, Gilmanton; m 16 Sep 1849, Gilford, John F. Avery [b ca 1820, of Gilmanton]. Mary Jane Avery was named the late daughter of Bailey Young of Gilmanton by his will signed 26 Jan, proved 18 Mar 1863; her children Emma Jane Avery and Erick Avery became heirs-at-law of her father's estate. (Meredith Annals, p456,457; NHVR-Brides)

MARY JANE, b 1850, Strafford, d/o John Frank and 1st wife Phoebe H. (Hayes) Young; m 30 Jul 1876, Alton, Newell Blaisdell [b ca 1850, East Rochester]. Mary J. Blaisdell was named as daughter and an heir in her father's will drawn 26 Nov 1878, proved 1 Jan 1884. She and husband took up residence in Newburyport, Mass., as did her brother John F. and sister Emma A.+ Blaisdell. (NHVR-Brides; Hayes Gen., V1, p202,203)

MARY L., b 3 Jul 1855, Rochester, d/o Thomas and Sabrina (Wentworth) Young; m 1 Aug 1886, E. Rochester, at age 31, Frank Willand aka Willard [b 1866, Lebanon, ME, age 29, shoemaker, s/o Enoch and Phebe (   ) Willard of Rochester]. (NHVR-Brides; Births; Rochester VR, Marr)

MARY S., b 7 Jan 1862, Barrington, d/o Jonathan and Sophia M. (Ricker) Young; m 16 Mar 1886, Dover, Leonard F. Kenniston [b ca 1860, Dover]. Mary S. Kenniston was named daughter of Jonathan and Sophia, and heir by Sophia's will drawn 3 Sep, proved 5 Nov 1889. (NHVR-Brides; Census Strafford Co., 1870, p29)

MARY SUSAN, b 4 Sep 1820, Dover, d/o Jonathan and Abigail (Coffin) Young, d 24 Sep 1853, age 33, native town; m 11 Apr 1844, Dover, Eleazer Cate [b ca 1815, d 12 Mar 1865, Dover]. For the one-fifth shares which the Cate children held in the estate of Jonathan and Abigail Young as of 1854, see James C. and Mary Young of Madbury. Mary Susan Cate and son Joseph H. Cate were buried at the John Young Cemetery, Littleworth Rd., Dover. Ch. b Dover: Abby Cate, b ca 1845; Homer Cate, b ca

1850; and Joseph H. Cate, b 1851, d 13 Mar 1851. (Frost's Dover Cem., Plot #22; NHVR-Brides; Steuerwald's Dover Cem., TMs; Demeritt Fam., **Reg.** 87:89,90)

MARY SUSAN, b 1824, Strafford, d 29 Mar 1891, age 67, native town; m 7 Nov 1844, Strafford, Hiram Perkins [b 1820, of Strafford, d 6 Dec 1891, age 71, same town]. There are variants of age between cemetery record and 1850 census: she lived with Hiram and Fannie Young in 1850, single, age 37 [b 1813]; and burial record noted above. She and spouse Hiram Perkins were buried at Perkins Cemetery, Route 126, Strafford, at the Young family plot where Samuel and Betsey Young, their son Moses and wife Lucy, and Hiram and Fannie Young were buried. Susan's kinship with this branch of the family is not all that clear. (NHVR-Brides; Stiles' Cemeteries, Grid 4E-1, p165)

MATTIE E., b 1860, Barrington, d/o George W. and Addie (   ) Young; m 27 Sep 1899, Barrington, Arthur C. Waterhouse [b 1860s, of same town]. (NHVR-Brides)

MATTIE W., b 2 Apr 1847, of Alton, d/o David and Patience (Thompson) Wilkinson, d 2 Jul 1889, age 42-3-0, Alton, survived by spouse _____ Young. Mattie's father was born in Ossipee, her mother in Dunbarton. (NHVR-Deaths)

MEHITABLE CLARK, b 1800s, Tuftonboro, d/o Benjamin and 2nd wife Rebecca (Bickford) Young, d Feb 1863, native town; m 10 Jun 1824, Tuftonboro, Joseph Whidden Lang [b 21 Jun 1798, Portsmouth, s/o Josiah and Sarah (Whidden) Lang, the eldest of three sons, d 1886, Meredith]. Mehitable C. Lang was named as daughter and heir of Benjamin Young of Wolfeboro by his will signed 6 Nov 1843, proved 30 Feb 1849. Joseph Lang's parents settled in Tuftonboro in 1815. Up through 1826, Mehitable and Joseph lived in Tuftonboro. Their relocation to Meredith came about through his acceptance of an offer to work in a chain of stores operated by Joseph Smith of Dover. He became a successful and prominent businessman of Meredith, eventually owning the store he started out in. In the State Legislature of 1856-57, he represented the town of Meredith. Joseph Lang married again in 1866, Meredith, Mrs. Julian (Perkins) Taylor, widow of Jonathan H. Taylor [b 1810, Meredith, d/o John B. and Comfort (Sanborn) Perkins]. At the time of Joseph's death, he was President of the Meredith Village Savings Bank and Director of the old Boston, Concord and Montreal R.R. No known children by either marriage. (Meredith Annals, p279,281; Lang Family, Hurd's Belknap Co., p862-863; Young Family Recs., courtesy of Nancy L. Dodge, Granvyl Hulse)

MELISSA A., b ca 1835, of Barnstead; m 3 Jul 1855, Barnstead, Henry J. Munsey [b ca 1830, of same town]. (NHVR-Brides)

MELISSA A. aka Melina, b 1845, Wakefield, d/o James 2nd and Rosemandel (Gill) Young, alive 1874, home town; m1 16 May 1864, Wakefield, Levi B. Johnson [b ca 1840, Strafford, d pre 1874]; m2 19 Dec 1874, Ossipee, George F. Robinson [b ca 1840,

Eastport, ME]. Melissa and George later settled in Fullerton, CA. Ch. b Wakefield by 1st husband Levi Johnson: Addie M. Johnson, b ca 1865, m 1898, Chester, Frank A. Bryant [b ca 1860, of Chester]. Ch. b CA by George Robinson: Clifford Robinson, b 1880s, not traced further. (NHVR-Brides; LDS I.G.I. VR)

MERCY, b ca 1825, Freedom, d/o Daniel and Elizabeth (Nason) Young, alive 1 Oct 1866; m 28 Jan 1844, Effingham, Samuel Allen [b ca 1820, of Parsonsfield, ME]. Mercy Allen was named the daughter and heir of Daniel Young of Freedom by his will drawn 1 Oct 1866, proved 31 Aug 1874. (NHVR-Brides)

MOSES, b 11 Oct 1763, Barrington, s/o Samuel and Elizabeth ( ) Young, d Nov 1830, Strafford; m 18 Mar 1790, Northwood, Lucy Whitehorn [b ca 1770, Barrington, d 1 Jan 1844, Strafford]. The 1790 census for Barrington showed that Moses lived alone. Upon marriage he and Lucy were affiliated with the Freewill Baptist Church. He was resident from 1800-1830 in that section of Barrington which became known as Strafford. In 1800 his age and that of his wife were 26-45, with family of two females under 10 years; in 1830 his age was 60-70, with spouse of same age, and household of one male age 40-50, one male under 5 and one female under 10. By 1840, Lucy was widow and head of family in Strafford, age 60-70; living with her was one female age 50-60. Moses' first purchase of land in Barrington was for 48 acres land or the whole of Lot 130, 3rd Range, drawn to the original right of John Ham, by deed signed 17 Feb, rec'd 8 Apr 1786, from Joshua 3rd and Elizabeth Foss of Barrington for 20 pounds, witnesses Clement Meserve, Mark Foss Jr. [Strafford Co. Deed 7:160]. He sold this same property to his brother Samuel of Barrington for ten pounds by deed signed 27 Apr 1787, rec'd 27 Mar 1801; witnesses Mark Foss Jr., Jonathan Montgomery [Strafford Co. Deed 34:369].

Letters of Admin. on Moses' estate in Strafford were filed 21 May 1832; John Perkins of Strafford was appointed Admin. [Strafford Co. Probate 30:321]. Inventory of the estate was submitted 17 Aug 1832 by William Jones, Francis Winkley and Asa Perkins [prob. son-in-law]; allowed same date [Strafford Co. Probate 44:13]. Real estate of 35 acres land "being the homestead and dwelling house and barn" and 25 acres of wild land held value of $275.00. Household effects, furniture and one cow were appraised at $53.50. Moses, wife Lucy and children were buried at Perkins Cemetery, Route 126, Strafford. Known ch. b Strafford: Lucy, b 1790s, d Jan 1844, Strafford; Hiram+, b 24 Mar 1803; prob. Judith+ (Young) Otis, b ca 1805; and prob. Deborah+ (Young) Perkins, b 6 Dec 1809. (Census Strafford Co., 1790, p87; 1800, p155; 1830, p48; 1840, p458; Barrington TR; NHVR-Marr; Stiles' Cemeteries, Grid 4E-1, p165; NHVR-Deaths; Moses' Northwood, V1, TMs, p49)

MOSES, b 1766, Dover, youngest s/o Capt. Thomas Young, d 5 Dec 1836, age 70, Wakefield; m ca 1790, Ossipee, Mary aka Molly Chadwick [b 23 Nov 1769, Berwick, ME, twin, d/o William and Elizabeth (Goodwin) Chadwick, alive 1850, Wakefield]. He was named as son and heir of Thomas Young of Dover by his will drawn 7 Apr 1791, proved 25 Apr 1795. Molly's father William Chadwick was s/o William and Abra (Wentworth) Chadwick of Somersworth, b 25 Sep 1745; Molly's mother Elizabeth Goodwin was b ca 1750, of Eliot, ME, one of ten children of Elisha Goodwin of Berwick, ME. Molly's maternal grandmother Abra Wentworth was born 14 Feb 1718, d/o Benjamin and Sarah (Allen) Wentworth of Somersworth; Molly's great-grandfather Benjamin Wentworth was youngest son of Elder William Wentworth, emigrant ancestor of Dover.

Freewill Baptist Church records stated that Moses lived in Dover as a young man. Young family records obtained through the courtesy of Marjorie S. Heaney attested to the fact that Moses of Dover and Wakefield was the son of Capt. Thomas Young. Depositions of Daniel Horne of Shapleigh, ME, wife Deborah (Young) Horne and Deborah's sister-in-law Mary (Chadwick) Young were given in "New Hampshire Pension Records" [V19, p267] to prove Daniel's and Deborah Horne's identities, and by reflection, Moses' identity. Mary [Chadwick] Young of Wakefield testified that Deborah Horne was a sister to her deceased husband [Moses Young, b 1766] and the daughter of Capt. Thomas Young of Dover. Mary Young added that she well recalled visiting Deborah and Daniel Horne as newlyweds the day after their wedding at the home of Thomas Young of Dover. For full deposition dated 28 Sep 1844, see Deborah (Young) Horne.

Moses next lived in Ossipee where his homestead, part of 500-acre Lot 4, Ossipee was adjacent to brother John Young. Probate papers showed that Moses was one of two sureties who posted bond 10 Sep 1813 in the Admin. of the estate of John Young of Ossipee. He sold his Ossipee property in the early 1800s to take up residence in North Wakefield where he became listed on census returns from 1810-1830. In 1810 his age was 26-45, with a family of spouse of like age, seven males, three under 10, three 10-16, and one 16-26; and three females, two under 10 and one 10-16. In 1830 Moses was 50-60 years old, with a household of female in 60-70 year range, two males, one under 5 and one 5-10, and one female 26-40. He was taxed as resident of Highway District No. 10, North Wakefield in 1820, the homestead situated on Lot 64, 2nd Div., abutting the Province Line between Ossipee and North Wakefield in the area known as the Pine River settlement. He was also listed on the 11 Mar 1834 Check List (of taxpayers eligible to vote at that town meeting). By 1840 widow Molly was head of household in Wakefield, age 60-70; family included two females, one age 40-50, one under 5. In 1850 Mary, age 82, and daughter Lydia, age 48, single, lived with son Alfred G. and his family in Wakefield.

In two transactions Moses of Ossipee bought up 100 acres land in the 500-acre Lot 4, Ossipee. The first purchase of 50 acres was adjacent to David Philbrick's land, by line of Lot 3, parallel with line between Wakefield and Ossipee, from

Robert and Mary Brown, by deed signed 20 Feb, rec'd 23 Feb 1795, for 60 pounds; witnesses Moses Hodgdon, John Shorey, Stephen Tasker, Ephraim Leighton [Strafford Co. Deed 19:503]. The other 50 acres of Lot 4 on the eastern side of Effingham Road were purchased from the said Robert and Mary Brown by deed signed 14 Feb, rec'd 16 Feb 1799, for $300.00; witnesses Moses Hodgdon, Ephraim Leighton [Strafford Co. Deed 29:446]. In turn Moses sold 50 acres of this lot abutting the n.w. corner of David Philbrick's land for $400.00, by deed of 13 Jun, rec'd 14 Nov 1803, to Jonathan Brown Jr. of Kensington, Rock. Co.: wife Mary ceded dower rights; witnesses Joseph Fogg, Turner Hanson [Strafford Co. Deed 43:302]. His next purchase of land with co-grantee William Keay, both of Ossipee, was 100-acre Lot 64, 2nd Div., Wakefield, drawn to the original right of Joseph Hicks, by quitclaim signed 11 Jun 1803, rec'd 24 Nov 1808, from John Haven of Lancaster, Grafton Co. for $500.00; witnesses Jonas Baker, Joseph Willard [Strafford Co. Deed 60:59]. The said Keay then quitclaimed to Moses, then of Wakefield, the western half of the lot for $1.00, by deed of 23 Nov, rec'd 24 Nov 1808; witnesses James Young, Thomas Young [Strafford Co. Deed 60:17]. Also on same date of signing and recording with said witnesses, Moses quitclaimed his interest in the eastern half of Lot 64 for the token $1.00 to the said Keay [Strafford Co. Deed 60:18].

It will be seen that Moses twice conveyed "one-half shares" of Moses' western half of Lot 64, 2nd Div., Wakefield, held in joint tenancy with said Keay as of 1808. Land deeds did not indicate that Moses ever bought Keay's eastern half of the lot, so Moses' moieties referred to in each case must have contained 25 acres, that is, if said Keay was still alive in 1808. The day after purchase, Moses sold a one-half share of Lot 64 to Joseph Young of Farmington [brother] for $200.00, by deed signed 24 Nov 1808, rec'd 22 Apr 1816; witnesses John Wingate Jr., Dolly Wingate [Strafford Co. Deed 88:531]. The other half share of this lot was sold to the five minor sons of the said Joseph and Sarah Young of Farmington, Joel, Samuel, Joseph Jr., John K., and Hiram H., for $722.00 by deed signed 14 Apr 1819, rec'd 13 Sep 1836; witnesses Jeremiah Waldron, Eliza Waldron [Strafford Co. Deed 170:316]. It also should be noted in the transfer of title of Moses' homestead to Joseph Young and his five minor sons, that the dower rights of the following three spouses were entailed in the ensuing sale of this property: of Mary Young, widow of Moses, of Sarah Young, widow of Joseph Young [Sr.], and of Sally Young, Admin. and widow of Joseph Young 2nd. The property was sold at public auction for $400.00 to discharge debts of the estate of Joseph Young 2nd who died intestate, by deed signed 13 Sep, rec'd 30 Nov 1839, to John Wentworth of Wakefield; witnesses Jacob Leighton, Elias Wentworth of Wakefield (Molly's brother-in-law) [Strafford Co. Deed 184:103]. Other Wakefield land which Moses purchased was 23 acres, 124 rods adjacent to the homestead of grantor Ephraim Wentworth, for $50.00, by deed

signed 18 Jan, rec'd 22 Mar 1813; witnesses Ezekial Wentworth,
Catey Mathes [Strafford Co. Deed 75:79]. He sold these 23
acres to James Young [believed to be son] of Wakefield, by
deed signed 7 Oct 1816, rec'd 7 Jun 1824; witnesses William
Haslett, Ezekial Wentworth [Strafford Co. Deed 121:264].

Family tradition has it that the following were children
of Moses and Mary: Mary, Sallie, Moses, Lydia, James C.,
Alfred G. and Daniel. Known ch. b Ossipee: James C.+ aka
James 2nd, b 1792; Daniel+, b 1 Jun 1795; Lydia, b 1802, lived
with brother Alfred in 1850, Wakefield. Ch. b Wakefield:
Alfred George+, b 5 Apr 1806. (Census Strafford Co., 1810,
p595; 1830, p452; 1840, p378; Twombly's Wakefield Cem., TMs;
Banks' Wakefield, p83,680; Morning Star, p376; Wentworth Gen.,
V1, p169,282,501-502; Young Family Recs., courtesy of Alden
N. Young)

MOSES, b 9 Jul 1767, Rochester, s/o Thomas and Anna
(Roberts) Young of Rochester, d 1 Jul 1835, native town; m
13 Mar 1798, Rochester, Mehitable Varney [b 1773, Dover, d/o
of Elijah and Anna (Hayes) Varney, d 2 Feb 1843, Rochester].
Moses was named son and heir of Thomas Young of Rochester by
his will drawn 4 May, proved 30 Sep 1772, his legacy, a one-
third share of Lot 69, 2nd Div., East Town (Wakefield). Of
more than passing interest is the fact that Moses and sibling
James became principal legatees of their father Thomas' estate
since eldest sibling Jonathan predeceased their father; sibling Thomas was presumed dead by 1804. Moses was also named
heir-at-law in the division of the estate of Isaac Young of
Dover as were his surviving siblings in quitclaim signed
22 Jul, rec'd 16 Nov 1803; wife Mehitable was one of the co-
grantors. See James and Mary (Kimball) Young of Wakefield for
full details of the division of Isaac's estate.

Moses was head of household in Rochester from 1790-1830:
in 1790, before he married, there was only one female in
household; in 1800 his age was 26-45, with spouse of like
years and one son under 10; in 1810 his age was 45 plus, with
household of two females 45 plus, two males 10-16, and one
female 10-16; in 1830 his age was 60-70, with spouse of same
age group, two males, one 15-20, one 20-30, and one female 20-
30. In 1840 Mehitable was listed as widow and head of household in Rochester, age 60-70, with family of two females, one
age 10-15, one 30-40.

When Moses' estate was administered in 1835, his homestead in Rochester consisted of 70 acres on the west side of
the road and 140 acres on the eastern side. The following
land deeds will account for some of this acreage. Moses purchased 18 acres of Lot 9, 2nd Div., Rochester, s.w. by part
of John Place's lands, n.e. by John Nute's lands, by deed of
2 Nov 1780, rec'd 7 Apr 1798, from William Hodgdon of Rochester for 30 pounds; witnesses Alexander Hodgdon, Moses Hammet
[Strafford Co. Deed 28:87]. Purchase of 62 acres in Rochester
formerly owned by Richard Henderson, from John and Elizabeth
Nute of Rochester, was drawn up by deed of 20 Nov 1794, rec'd

25 Nov 1794, for $580.00; witnesses Samuel Nute, Benjamin Heard [Strafford Co. Deed 19:337]. Title to this same acreage was mortgaged on same date of Moses' purchase, to Richard Furber Jr., Esq. and Alexander Hodgdon, both of Rochester, by deed signed 24 Nov 1794, rec'd 25 Nov 1794, for 100 pounds, or thirty pounds annually until debt was discharged; witnesses Simon Torr, Samuel Nute [Strafford Co. Deed 19:253]. With reference to Lot 9, 2nd Div., Moses sold 26-1/2 acres of this lot by deed signed 19 Jan 1796, rec'd 8 Mar 1802, to Stephen Whitehouse of Rochester for $130.00; witnesses Joshua Holmes, William McNeal [Strafford Co. Deed 39:291]. He and Mehitable quitclaimed land in Rochester once owned by Henry Tebbetts, deriving his title from said Tebbetts by deed rec'd 11 Nov 1823, to John Plummer Jr. of Rochester for $300.00; witnesses Hannah March, Jonathan Heard [Strafford Co. Deed 122:294]. Moses' last known purchase of land, by deed signed 19 Dec 1826, rec'd 26 May 1827, was 21-1/2 acres land in Dover from John Plummer of Rochester formerly owned by said Plummer's father John Plummer Esq. for $450.00; witnesses Wentworth Hayes, Mary Hoyt, Lewis Hoyt [Strafford Co. Deed 134:348].

Both Moses' and Mehitable's wills revealed significant details of their status in life. They held a bountiful estate in Rochester with other lands in Dover. Neither mentioned offspring as heirs-at-law. Also, it would appear that Moses and sibling James of Wakefield had reached some private understanding in the division of their father's real estate both in Rochester and Wakefield. It was brother James of Wakefield who sold in fee simple [unqualified title] the brothers' legacy of Lot 69, 2nd Div., Wakefield in 1804; it was Moses who kept and lived on their father's homestead in Rochester. And Moses' will drawn 3 Sep 1825, proved 19 Sep 1835, named his brother James as sole Exec. and residuary legatee; witnesses Hatevil Knight, William Cook, Stephen Whitehouse [Strafford Co. Probate 49:249]. James was allowed Exec. on date of probate, bond of $10,000.00 given with sureties Hatevil Knight and Stephen Whitehouse, both of Rochester [Strafford Co. Probate 50:30]. Moses bequeathed to wife Mehitable all the notes, demands and money on hand, all the furniture of every kind, and one half of all the stock "for her use and benefit forever." She was to receive also the use and occupation of one half of the homestead farm and buildings, except one room, "during her natural life," which was to satisfy Mehitable's right of dower. Brother James was to receive the other half of the stock and all the remaining property; at the time of Mehitable's decease her share of the homestead would revert to James.

On 20 Nov 1835, James attested to the truth of both the inventory and appraisal submitted that day by Hatevil Knight, Jonathan Hussey and Samuel Stackpole, all of Rochester [Strafford Co. Probate 49:385]. Real estate holdings were valued at $5,300.00: homestead farm of 70 acres on the west side of the road with buildings at $2,000.00; 140 acres on the eastern

side of the road, $2,100.00; the Adams lot of 14 acres at
$300.00; 128-1/2 acres in Dover adjoining Eli Varney and Will-
iam Cook at $400.00; and 20 acres of a wood lot on Dry Hill,
Rochester; grand total of real estate, $5,300.00. Personal
property was appraised at $1,215.68: wearing apparel, $38.00,
net worth of bank stock, $600.00, and 28 notes of hand owing
to his estate, $2,415.21; total personal and real estate
valued at $9,568.89. Beds and bedding suggested either a
large household or a truly comfortable one: 5 feather beds
with bedsteads and under-beds, 19 pairs sheets, 17 blankets,
4 comforters, 1 bedquilt and 1 coverlet. Moses' wearing
apparel contained 3 pairs of pantaloons along with 16 shirts,
1 hat and 2 coats. The closing account on Moses' estate was
presented by said James, on 16 Sep 1839, allowed same date
[Strafford Co. Probate 54:462]. Credits, including inventory
of personal estate, cider mill and press, additional miscellaneous items and 20 yards check wool cloth amounted to
$4,711.63. Debts totalled $4,636.15; among these were James'
expenses as Exec. at $97.50, crops taken by devisees to whom
land was devised at $295.00, personal property devised to
widow, $3,929.25, stock devised, one half to Exec., one half
to widow, $138.00; a balance of $177.16 was due from Exec.

     Mehitable's will was written 30 Jan 1843, proved 7 Mar
1843, naming Samuel Stackpole of Rochester as her Exec.; witnesses Richard Kimball, John F. Young and Mary Ann Young
[Strafford Co. Probate 59:308]. She made numerous bequests
of her personal property or sums of money to brothers George
Varney, Jacob Varney, Enos Varney and Israel H. Varney and
respective families. On 7 Mar 1843, Samuel Stackpole of Rochester submitted the will for probate; bond of $7,000 posted
with sureties William B. Smith, Thomas Stackpole, both of
Dover [Strafford Co. Probate 50:253]. On 24 May 1843, inventory of Mehitable's estate was returned and attested to by
Richard Kimball, Nicholas Whitehouse and John Folsom, all of
Rochester [Strafford Co. Probate 59:207]: the residue of her
real estate after bequests included two small lots of pasture
on Dry Hill, Rochester adjoining James Young's pasture, valued
at $8.00. Inventory of her personal estate included a ward-
robe of 14 dresses whose fabrics were broadcloth, merino,
cambet, bombazine, black silk, pongee, cotton print and ging-
ham, 5 flannel skirts, 4 flannel waistcoats, 27 aprons, 10
nightgowns and 13 chemises; net worth of personal estate,
$2,258.16. Her one-half share in the Congregational Meeting
House and a pew in the Gonic Meeting House, both in Rochester,
was set at $37.00; notes of hand owing to estate, $2,298.57;
total of real and personal estate, $4,593.73.

     Samuel Stackpole submitted his first account 1 Sep 1846,
approved same date [Strafford Co. Probate 55:425]. After
legacies of $3,296.36 per Mehitable's will and sundry debts
of $546.68 were paid, there was a balance due from Exec. of
$1,325.33; credits included amount of personal estate exclus-
ive of demands per inventory, $2,258.16; cash collected from

persons owing, $2,727.39; discount allowed by legatees paid
before due, $133.42; gain on sale of personal estate, $49.40;
grand total $5,168.37. Stackpole reported on 3 Nov 1846 that
there was a balance of $800.00 ready to be distributed among
residuary legatees and declared his intent to advertise the
hearing scheduled for 5 Jan next [Strafford Co. Probate
55:488]. Each niece and nephew was to receive $100.00: Enos
Varney of Charlestown, MA, Elijah Henderson of Savannah, GA,
Franklin Varney of Dover, Moses Henderson, residence unknown,
the legal representative of Benjamin Henderson, Abigail H.
Clark, wife of Smith Clark of Rochester, Sarah Varney of
Rochester and Samuel Varney of Lowell, Mass. After the
hearing, one claim for appeal on the decree of distribution
was filed on date of 4 Mar 1847 by George and Susan How of
Rochester [Strafford Co. Probate 55:512]; their appeal was
denied by date of __ Dec 1848 [Strafford Co. Probate 62:238].
Exec. Samuel Stackpole petitioned for License to Sell 8 Feb
1849, granted 3 Apr 1849, inasmuch as the estate was short
$40.00 to pay all demands against it [Strafford Co. Probate
60:84]. His second accounting of Admin. was dated 2 May 1848,
approved same date [Strafford Co. Probate 63:1]: sums paid
out totalled $1,364.08; money due from Admin., $1,315.33.
Moses and Mehitable were buried at Haven Hill Cemetery,
Rochester at the Young family plot. (Goss's Gravestones,
p116; Hayes Gen., V2, p172; NH Gen. Rec., V5, No.2, p52;
Census Strafford Co., 1790, p96; 1800, p170; 1810, p645; 1830,
p360; 1840, p521; Varney Gen., TMs, p165)

MOSES, b ca 1775, of Alton; in 1810, Moses was head of
household in Alton, age 26-45, with spouse of same age group,
one male and two females all under 10. (Census Strafford Co.,
1810, p615)

MOSES, b 1778, Lebanon, ME, res. of Alton by way of Rochester, d 13 May 1865, age 87, Alton; m 15 Dec 1808, Lebanon,
ME, Dorothy Peavey [b 1789, ME, alive 1850, Alton]; m2 11 Sep
1853, Alton, Alice (Peavey) Young, widow of Jonathan Young of
Lebanon, ME or Farmington [b 8 Oct 1800, Alton, d/o Daniel and
Mary ( ) Peavey, d 8 Apr 1874, Milton]. In 1830 Moses, age
40-50, was head of a large household in Alton, consisting of
spouse age 40-50, and twelve children: five males, one age
5-10, two 10-15, two 15-20, and seven females, three under 5,
one age 5-10, one 10-15 and two 15-20. In 1840 he and his
wife were age 50-60; family still at home were one male age
15-20 and a female age 10-15. From 1850-1860 Moses was listed
on census returns for Alton, which gave Maine as his place of
birth. In 1850 Dorothy was named as his spouse, her place of
birth was also Maine, as was the case for daughter Lavina;
member of family was Mary Peavey [b MA]. In 1860 Alice was
named as Moses' spouse; member of family, Martha A.+ Young,
b 25 May 1847, youngest daughter of Jonathan and Alice. Widow
Alice Young, age 62, m3 7 Oct 1865, Alton, Joseph Wiggins [b
1804, of Upper Gilmanton]. Alice spent her remaining years
in Milton. Known ch. b ME by Dorothy: Alvah+, b 19 Jul 1818,

twin; Henry, b 19 Jul 1818, twin, d 11 May 1882, age 63-11-4, Alton with wife surviving; and Lavina J.+ (Young) Ellis, b 1828. (NHVR-Deaths; Census Strafford Co., 1830, p104,105; 1840, p303; Census Belknap Co., 1850, p368; 1860, p280; Alton VR, p604, 654; Lebanon, ME V.R., p168,224)

MOSES aka Jr., b Jan 1824, Alton, alive 1900, home town, farmer; m ca 1843, prob. Alton, Mary H. Thompson [b Jul 1824, Ossipee, alive 1900, Alton]. Moses and Mary were listed as residents of Alton from 1850-1900 where they raised a family of six children. In 1850 children at home were Laura A. and George W.; in 1860, George, Mary H., Ida E. and Laura [2 months old]; and in 1870, Ida, Laura A. and Hattie J. In 1900 grandson Eddie W. Coffin, age 17 [b Jan 1883] lived with them. Ch. b Alton: Laura A., b 1845, d.y.; George W.+, b 1848; Mary H.+ (Young) Collins, b 11 Dec 1852; daughter b 9 Sep 1855; Ida E.+ (Young) Rand, b 3 Jan 1857; Laura A.+ (Young) Woodman, b 20 Apr 1860; and Hattie J.+ (Young) Peavey, b 1864. (Census Belknap Co., 1850, p368; 1860, p279; 1870, p9; 1900 Soundex; NHVR-Births, Brides, Marr, Deaths; LDS I.G.I. BR; Hammond's Alton Cemeteries, p26)

MOSES, b 1825, ME, res. of Rollingsford, druggist; m ca 1854, prob. ME, Martha ( ) [b 1826]. Moses, Martha and son Rufus D. made their home in Rollingsford as of 1860. Ch. b prob. Rollingsford: Rufus D., b 1855. (Census Strafford Co., 1860, p234)

MOSES, b 1840, of Dover; he lived in Ward 2, Dover in 1870, single; worked in shoe factory and roomed at boarding house. (Census Strafford Co., 1870, p41)

MOSES A., b 17 Aug 1829, Upper Gilmanton, stone cutter and farmer, d 9 Apr 1890, age 60-7-23, Belmont [native town]; m 4 Aug 1853, Gilmanton, Ann M. Young [b 1834, of Meredith, d/o John and Ann Maria (Chase) Young, gr.d/o Zachias Chase, alive 1870, Belmont]. Moses and Ann were listed on the 1870 census returns for Belmont; children at home, Oscar F., Fostina E., Charles S., and Ansel C. It is worthy of note that Meredith Annals stated Moses A. Young was the son of Bailey and Polly (Rundlet) Young of Upper Gilmanton; yet Bailey's will of 26 Jan, proved 18 Mar 1863, did not confirm this. Curiously enough Moses A. was appointed Admin. of the estate of Polly Young, eldest daughter of Eleazer and Hannah (Bailey) Young and sister of Bailey, on 15 Mar 1864. The kinship, if any, between Bailey Young and Moses A. Young remains a conundrum.

Moses A.'s own will was drawn 5 Sep 1882, proved 15 Apr 1890, naming wife Ann M. Young his sole Exec.; witnesses N. B. Gale, A. L. Bean and F. W. Reeves [Belknap Co. Probate #4659]. Wife Ann M. was to receive the use and income of all real and personal estate during her natural life. Son Oscar T. was devised $50.00; daughter Fostina Sanborn, wife of Fred C. Sanborn, was to receive $100.00. The balance of the estate upon the death of Ann M. Young was to be equally divided among son Charles S. and single daughters Abbie M. and Amy Ann.

Moses A. specifically requested guardianship for son Charles
S. Young, then a minor at age 19 [b 1871]. However, Charles'
year of birth of 1871 raises hob with several other sources.
It is a fact he was namesake of elder brother who was born in
1861 and died young. However, according to NHVR-Marr, Charles
S., son of Moses A. Young of Belmont, was age 28 [b 1861] when
he married 26 Sep 1889, Belmont, Elma C. Heath, age 30 [b
1869, Belmont, d/o J. S. Heath]. Moreover, the 1900 Soundex
for Belmont compounds discrepancies on date of birth and name
of bride: Charles S., b Jun 1862, and wife Elena C., b Feb
1859, lived in Belmont in 1900; member of household was Mary
A. Fidler, mother-in-law, b Feb 1834. An educated guess would
say that there were perhaps two Charles S. Youngs in question.
    Ch. b Belmont: Oscar T., b 1855; Fostina E.+ (Young)
Sanborn, b 1858; Charles T., b 30 Jun 1861, d.y.; Ansel C.,
b 6 Aug 1869, d 6 May 1879, age 9-9-0, Belmont; Charles S.,
b 7 May 1871; Abbie M., b 23 Apr 1872; May Anna, b 17 Apr
1874, twin, d 5 May 1879, Belmont; and Amy Ann, b 17 Apr 1874,
twin.   (LDS I.G.I. 8R; NHVR-Births, Brides, Deaths, Marr;
Census Belknap Co., 1870, p19; Meredith Annals, p456,457; 1900
Soundex)

    MOSES C., b ca 1806, Ossipee, s/o _____ and Nancy ( )
Young [no main entry], poss. eldest son of Samuel B. and Nancy
(Burleigh) Young of Ossipee; m 20 May 1845, Ossipee, Mary
Tibbetts [b ca 1810, of same town]. Moses C. and wife Mary,
later of Township No. 3 Range, Aroostock Co., ME, sold by deed
signed 13 Apr, rec'd 10 Aug 1853, their interest and title to
4 acres land in Ossipee which was "the whole of the lot on
which the said Nancy Young, Moses' mother, resided for years"
[Aroostock Co., ME, Deed 22:474]. (NHVR-Marr)

    MOSES C., b 9 Apr 1809, Dover, s/o Joseph and Elizabeth
(Saltmarsh) Young, d 9 Feb 1890, age 80-10-0, widower, home
town, boatman; m 21 Apr 1831, Dover, Mary K. Nutter [b 1808,
Wolfeboro, d pre 1890, Dover, bur. Dover, n.d.]. Moses was
head of household in Dover from 1840-1860 where he raised a
family first in Ward 3, and then in Ward 2, Dover. In 1840
his age was 30-40, spouse of same age group with family of
three sons, two under 5 and one age 5-10. From 1850-1870 Mary
was named as spouse. In 1850 children at home were George E.,
Moses F., shoemaker, Jacob N., seaman, Joseph, shoemaker,
Nancy E., tailoress and Theodore S. In 1860 son Franklin who
was not listed in 1850 was member of family, as well as the
four other children, save George E. who was then deceased.
In 1870, Ward 2, Dover, he and Mary lived at the home of son
Jacob and wife Addie. Moses C., wife Mary K. and son George
E. were buried at Pine Hill Cemetery, Dover. Ch. b Dover:
George E., b 1832, d 19 Oct 1855, Dover, age 23, title of
Capt.; Moses Franklin+, b 1835; Jacob W.+, b Oct 1836;
Joseph+, b 1840; Nancy E., b 1845, tailoress; and Theodore
L.+, b Sep 1850. (Heritage's Dover VR, p95; Census Strafford
Co., 1840, p530; 1850, p84; 1860, p688; 1870, p61; Frost's
Dover Cem., V1, Plot #1117; NHVR-Deaths, Marr; 1900 Soundex)

MOSES FRANKLIN, b 1835, Dover, s/o Moses C. and Mary K. (Nutter) Young; m 4 Oct 1862, Rochester, Anna L. Varney [b 1832, Rochester, d/o G. C. and Ann (   ) Varney, alive 1871, Dover]. Moses and Ann resided in Dover. Ch. b Dover: Anna M., b 21 Jun 1867; and Charles T., b 7 May 1871. (NHVR-Marr; Births; LDS I.G.I. BR)

MOSES M., b 1836, Gilmanton, twin, s/o of James T. and Mary A. (Nute) Young; m 1858, Dover, Jane Bole [b 1839, Dover]. He was listed as member of his parents' household in Gilmanton in 1850, age 14. (NHVR-Marr)

MOSES N., b 1838, Dover, d 1879, age 41, native town; m ca 1860, Dover, Mary J. (   ) [b 1842, of Dover, d 1930, age 88, Dover]. Moses N. and Mary J. were buried at Pine Hill Cemetery, Dover. (Frost's Dover Cem., V1, Plot #401D, #482)

MYRA M. aka Almira M., b 1843, Wakefield, d/o Alfred G. and Sarah A. (Seaman) Young, d 5 Jul 1875, native town, age 33; m 14 Jun 1873, Wakefield, Thomas W. Hill [b ca 1840, Wakefield]. She was age 7 on 1850 census return for parents who lived in Wakefield. Myra was known by her married name of Hill in her father's will of 4 Sep 1880, proved 5 Jul 1881, but she predeceased her father. She was buried in the family plot at the cemetery back in the field on the Hayward farm. (NHVR-Brides; Ossipee Cemeteries, TMs, p9)

MYRON DAVIS, b 1 Mar 1844, East Boston, s/o _____ and Rosemandel (Gill) Davis, adopted by mother's second husband James C. Young of Wakefield, d 10 Mar 1928, Malden, MA; m ca 1870, prob. Boston, Annie N. Moore [b ca 1850, Boston, alive 6 Jun 1928, Malden, MA]. Myron lived with mother and step-father in Wakefield from 1850-1860. He enlisted from Wake-field at age 18, in Co. A, 13th Regt., N. H. Volunteer Infantry, 11 Aug 1862, mustered in 18 Sep 1862, as Pvt. and was discharged disabled, 3 Jun 1863, at Fort Monroe, VA. His regiment's first engagement was at Fredericksburg, VA. Places of residence upon his return to civilian life were North Wakefield, Boston and Malden. On 20 Nov 1866 Myron D. filed petition for an Invalid Pension due to debilitating diseases contracted from military service in the Civil War, Application No. 119,116, Cert. No. 148,947. Lacking a birth certificate, Myron stated that his parents had often told him "he had first seen the light of day in East Boston on 1 Mar 1844." He later became totally incapacitated from typhoid fever and arterio-sclerosis. His widow Annie N. Young filed for a Minor's Pension 24 Mar 1928, Application No. 1,608,694 on son Wayland S. Davis. At this time she was known as Annie D. Laudrie. Ch. b Malden, MA: Wayland S. Davis, b ca 1910. (Nat'l. Archives Milit. Recs.; Young Family Recs., courtesy of Alden N. Young)

NAHUM G., b 22 May 1814, Goldsboro, ME, s/o John and Betsey (   ) Young [no main entry], res. of Wolfeboro, d 13 Nov 1884, age 70-5-22, Wolfeboro; m 1850s, Wolfeboro, Harriet H. (   ) [b ca 1820, of Goldsboro, ME]. Nahum's occupation was sailor. Ch. b Wolfeboro: Eva M.+ (Young)

Leighton, b 1860s; and Austin C.+, b 1865. (NHVR-Brides, Deaths, Marr)

NANCY, b 1787, New Market, d/o William and Comfort (   ) Smith, d 1859, Wolfeboro, age 72, widow of _____ Young. (NHVR-Deaths)

NANCY, b ca 1795, of Ossipee; head of household in Ossipee per 1840 census, age 40-50; members of family included two males age 15-20. (Census Strafford Co., 1840, p219)

NANCY, b ca 1795, of Wolfeboro; m (Intentions) 24 Jun 1816, Wolfeboro, Ezekial Keay [b ca 1790, of same town]. (Parker's Wolfeboro Banns, 1789-1854, n.p.)

NANCY, b ca 1800, of Ossipee; m 2 Jul 1819, Ossipee, Zachariah Hock [b ca 1795, of same town]. (NHVR-Brides)

NANCY, b ca 1808, Tuftonboro, d/o John and Hannah (Ham) Young; m 24 Jun 1830, Wolfeboro, Samuel Ladd Jr. [b 12 Dec 1803, Melvin Village, s/o Samuel and Comfort (Dow) Ladd]. It is fascinating to learn that three of Nancy's sisters married brothers of her spouse Samuel Ladd Jr. Ch. b Wolfeboro: John A. Ladd, b 1830s, m 1899. (NHVR-Brides; Ladd Gen., p54,55)

NANCY, b ca 1810, of Somersworth; m 14 Jan 1829, Barnstead, John Merrill [b ca 1805, of same town]. (NHVR-Brides)

NANCY, b ca 1815, of Alton; m 19 Jul 1835, Moultonboro, Samuel Emerson 2nd [b ca 1810, of Moultonboro]. They may have filed intentions of marriage in Northwood on same date. (NHVR-Brides; Moses' Northwood, TMs, V3, p245)

NANCY, b ca 1820, Wakefield, prob. d/o Joseph and Nancy (Young) Young; m 31 Jan 1839, Wakefield, Jacob Nutter [b ca 1815, Tuftonboro]. Ch. b Tuftonboro: Anna M. Nutter, b 1840s, m 1865, Tuftonboro, Alvah E. Dow [b 1840s, Tuftonboro]; Emma Nutter, b 1850, see spouse George F.+ Young of Wolfeboro. (NHVR-Brides)

NANCY, b ca 1845, Milton, widow of _____ Young; m2 25 Nov 1888, Milton, Rev. James Rines [b 1840s, of same town]. (NHVR-Brides)

NATHANIEL, b 1682, Dover Neck, s/o Thomas and Mary (Roberts) Young, d 16 Dec 1741, Cochecho Point; m ca 1712, Dover, Widow Mercy aka Mary (Hanson) Church [b ca 1680, d/o Thomas and Mary (Kitchen) Hanson of Dover, widow of John Church of Dover]. Mercy Hanson and John Church were m 1 Dec 1699, Dover; he and neighbor Thomas Downes were killed by Indians on their way home from church in the spring of 1711. John Church was survived by wife Mercy and five children: Abigail Church, b 16 May 1702; John Church, b 7 Apr 1704; Elizabeth Church, b 2 Dec 1706; Jonathan Church, b 25 Jul 1708; and Mercy Church, b 4 Aug 1710. Widow Mercy was named Admin. of John Church's estate 5 Dec 170h. 25 Apr 1715 Nathaniel was listed as one of the 72 inhabitants who lived nearer the New Meeting House on Cochecho Point than the old on Dover Neck. By vote of the legislature 8 Jul 1734, he was granted one full share of Lot 80, Dover. He purchased for 3-10-0 a parcel of 20 acres in Dover by deed of 21 May 1713, rec'd 14 Apr 1730, from Jonathan Watson of Dover, land by

Fresh Creek Neck that fronted upon Fore River above Pine Point, granted by Dover to Jonathan Watson 2 Apr 1694; witnesses Benjamin Peirce, Nathaniel Hanson [NH Prov. Probate 21:559]. In 1741, he was again listed on the Cochecho Parish Tax List, rated at 13 shillings-11 pence. He and his four brothers received a one-fifth share of land in Rochester by their father's deed of gift dated 18 Mar 1726/27, proved 27 May 1727; he disposed of his share by deed signed 10 Mar 1730, rec'd 6 Oct 1733; for full details of sale, see John and Elizabeth Young of Dover. Ch. b Dover: Daniel+, b 4 May 1713; and Mercy aka Mary, b 24 May 1718. (Scale's Dover, p495; Noyes et al, p142,307; Heritage's Dover VR, p10,130,146; NH State Papers, V11, p508, V24, p700; Tibbetts Gen., TMs, p283)

NATHANIEL, b 1 Feb 1720, Dover, s/o Jonathan and Abigail (Hanson) Young, d pre 26 May 1762, Madbury; m ca 1750, Dover, Mary Kimball [bp 4 Oct 1730, Dover, d/o Ezra and Elizabeth ( ) Kimball, d 10 Sep 1768, Madbury, widow]. Nathaniel and brother James were named Co-Execs. of their father's will signed 1 Jul 1752, proved 29 Sep 1756, each to receive an equal share in the family homestead, livestock, etc. in Dover, and 50 acres land lying on N.E. side of Bellamin's Bank. He was listed as a resident of Cochecho Parish in 1741, rated at 13 pounds-11 shillings. In 1750 when the town of Middleton [offshoot of Rochester] was chartered, Nathaniel was one of the original proprietors from Draft of Lots, 11 Apr 1750; he drew Lot 47. [For disposal of this lot, see Daniel Young of Madbury and Nathaniel's son Ezra.]

Nathaniel and Mary sold to Richard Kimball of Dover all their share in the real and personal estate of said Richard's late brother Ezra Kimball, for 270 pounds by deed dated 15 Feb 1753, rec'd 30 Oct 1765; Mary was the daughter of said Ezra Kimball; witnesses Nehemiah Hanson, John Hanson [NH Prov. Probate 87:53]. Perhaps his last known purchase of land was the 80 acres, a third share of Lot 47, 2nd Div., in Rochester from Jethro Bickford of Rochester for 320 pounds Old Tenor by deed signed 6 Jan, rec'd 5 Jun 1756; witnesses Joseph Hanson, Benjamin Hayes [NH Prov. Probate 47:416].

Nathaniel's will was dated 29 Jan, proved 26 May 1762, and named his brother James as sole Exec.; witnesses Daniel Evans, Reuben Hayes, and Samuel Evans [NH State Papers 37:262]. He made provision for wife Mary, allowing her "the full and whole privilege in my dwelling house and barn," for as long as she remained his widow, but "in case she shall marry then she shall have her proper dowry, or thirds as by law established." In addition she received most of the livestock and the use and improvement of all his household goods. In case she married, she would then receive one-third of the household effects and their daughters would receive equal shares from the remaining two-thirds. As will be seen all Nathaniel's children were minors at the time his will was drawn and probated. Son Timothy was to receive the homestead

farm with dwelling house and barn, Nathaniel's gun, and all
the land in the Parish of Madbury when he came of age. When
Ezra reached the age of 21, he was to receive all 80 acres of
the land in Rochester, or 1/3 part of Lot 47, 2nd Div., which
Nathaniel purchased of Jethro Bickford. Farm tools and his
wearing apparel were to be equally divided between the two
brothers. Daughters Abigail and Elizabeth were each to
receive 50 pounds old Tenor "as it now passeth, viz at six
pounds the dollar" when they arrived at the age of 18 years,
also one cow apiece, and were to share in the household
effects with their mother Mary. Warrant of 26 May 1762
authorized Ephraim Hanson and Daniel Evans, both of Dover, to
appraise the estate; they submitted their inventory of the
estate 23 Aug 1762, valued in the amount of 10,615.9.9 [NH
State Papers 37:263].

Ch. b Dover: Timothy+, bp 30 Sep 1750; Ezra+, b 6 Dec
1751; John, bp 13 Jul 1755, not mentioned in father's will;
Abigail+ (Young) Hayes, bp 23 Oct 1757; and Elizabeth+ (Young)
Demeritt, b 22 Oct 1760, bp 3 May 1761. (Hayes Gen., V1,
p132; LDS I.G.I. BR; Heritage's Dover VR, p10,24,139,211,155-
156,158,159,161,211; NH State Papers, V24, p700, V27, p498;
Tibbetts Gen., TMs, p283)

NATHANIEL, b ca 1780, of Gilmanton; m 1805, Barnstead,
Patty Tuttle [b ca 1785, of Barnstead]. He was probably the
head of household of Gilmanton in 1810, age 26-45 years, with
family of two females, one under 45, the other 45 plus, one
male under 10, and one female under ten. (NHVR-Marr; Census
Strafford Co., 1810, p801)

NATHANIEL, b 1795, Wolfeboro [Addition], s/o John and
Mary (Burleigh) Young, d 15 Dec 1862, Wolfeboro; m 1 Apr 1818,
Wolfeboro, Martha Roberts [b 1798, Ossipee, d 16 Sep 1877,
home town, age 80]. He was head of household in Wolfeboro in
1830, age 30-40, with spouse age 40-50, and family of five
males, two under 5, two age 5-10, one 10-15, and two females,
one age 10-15, one 20-30. Before 1840 Nathaniel and family
relocated in Ossipee; he was listed as resident of this town
from 1840-1860. In 1840 his age was 40-50, with spouse of
same age group and household containing four males, two age
10-15, one 15-20, one under 20-30, and one female age 5-10.
Martha was named as his spouse from 1850-1860. In 1850 the
estate was valued at $1,200; children at home were Basel P.,
Franklin, David and Susan; in 1860 members of family were
daughter Susan, son Elijah F., Alice A., age 10 [b 1850, VT],
and Sarah L. Edgerly, age 5.

Nathaniel of Wolfeboro quitclaimed to Adam Brown of same
town part of Lot 2 in Wolfeboro Addition, which he bought of
Samuel B. Young [brother] of same town, for $90.00 by deed of
19 Mar 1826, rec'd 3 Dec 1829; wife Martha ceded dower rights;
witnesses John C. Young, Moses P. Brown [Strafford Co. Deed
139:398]. Title to 64 acres of Lot 23, Ossipee, adjacent to
Lot 24, was purchased by deed signed 21 Mar, rec'd 28 Mar 1825
from Adam F. and Sally Brown of Ossipee for $175.00; witnesses

Jacob Leighton, Elijah Roberts [Strafford Co. Deed 124:354]. Four acres of this lot linked by land of John C. Young and once owned by Adam F. Brown were sold by deed signed 11 Jan 1828, rec'd 14 Jan that year to Isaac Pray of Parsonsfield for $800.00; witnesses Moses Colby, Louisa W. Roberts [Strafford Co. Deed 135:533].

Nathaniel and Martha were buried at a private family cemetery in Ossipee on the road leading to North Wakefield. Ch. b Wolfeboro [Addition]: Basel P., b 1825, at home 1850; Elijah F. aka E. Frank+, b 29 Aug 1825; Franklin aka George Frank, b 1825, twin, d 29 Apr 1894, widower, Wolfeboro; David, b 1829, at home 1850; and Susan, b 1834, at home 1860. (NHVR-Marr, Deaths; Census Strafford Co., 1830, p436; 1840, p228; Census Carroll Co., 1850, p212; 1860, p686; Loud's Cem. Recs., p129)

NATHANIEL, b 1805, ME, of Dover; in 1860 he was head of household in Ward 3, Dover, laborer, age 55. Member of family was Mary Young, age 70 [b 1790, ME]. (Census Strafford Co., 1860, p688)

NATHANIEL, b 1810, of Somersworth, laborer; m ca 1830, ME, Adaline (   ) [b 1816, ME, alive 1850, Somersworth]. Nathaniel and Adaline resided in Maine in the early 1830s where their first two children were born. Thereafter they lived in Somersworth up through 1850. In 1840 his age was 20-30, with household of spouse age 30-40 and four females, one under 5, two age 5-10, and one 10-15. In 1850 he and Adaline were listed on the census returns for Somersworth; children at home, Eleanor, Sarah, Elizabeth, and twins John and Nathaniel. Son Nathaniel was age 19 and resident of Dover when he enlisted in Co. H, 6th Regt., NH Volunteer Infantry 5 Nov 1861, mustered in 28 Nov 1861 as Pvt., reenlisted and mustered in 31 Dec 1863. He was wounded 12 May 1864 at Spottsylvania, Virginia, appointed Corp., appointed Sgt. 15 Mar 1865 and mustered out 17 Jul 1865. Known ch. b ME: Eleanor, b 1832; and Sarah L., b 1834. Ch. b Somersworth: Elizabeth, b 1836; John, b 1842, twin; and Nathaniel, b 1842, twin. (Census Strafford Co., 1840, p576; 1850, p303; Soldiers & Sailors, p346)

NATHANIEL, b 27 Oct 1810, Wolfeboro, s/o Samuel B. and Nancy (Burleigh) Young, d 5 Feb 1896, Ossipee; m1 3 Jun 1860, Wolfeboro, Vinah M. Lougee aka Vianna M. (Lougee) Harmon [b 1830, Effingham, d/o Moses and Joanna (   ) Lougee, her 2nd marriage, d 5 Mar 1862, Ossipee]; m2 pre 1870, Wolfeboro, Sarah F. (   ) [b Jan 1837, Ossipee, d 1922, Wolfeboro]. After his father's accidental death in 1834 and previous to his marriage, Nathaniel, age 30-40, became head of household in Wolfeboro per 1840 census; members of family were female parental figure age 50-60, two males age 20-30, and one other male age 30-40. After they married, they made their home in Wolfeboro, listed on census returns of 6 Jun 1860, and by the same token he and 2nd wife Sarah lived in Wolfeboro as of the 1870 census. In 1870 son Charles B. was listed on parents' census returns, age 9. Nathaniel's brothers John and Alonzo, both single adults, were members of his household from 1860-1870.

Son Charles B. was an infant when his mother Vinah died in 1862. Nathaniel filed petition for guardianship on 2 Dec 1862, granted same date [Carroll Co. Probate #6819]. Letters of Admin. on Nathaniel's estate in Ossipee were filed by widow Sarah F. Young on 7 Jul 1896; granted same date [Carroll Co. Probate #5834]. In 1900 Sarah F., age 63, was widow and head of household in Ossipee; brother-in-law Alonzo, age 76 and single, boarded at her home. Nathaniel and wives Vinah and Sarah, as well as son Charles and two brothers cited above were buried at Stevens-Burleigh Cemetery, Ossipee. Cemetery records gave Sarah's year of birth as 1839. Ch. b Wolfeboro by 1st wife Vinah: Charles B.+, b 19 May 1861. (Census Strafford Co., 1840, p386; Carroll Co., 1860, p527; 1870, p468; 1900 Soundex; Ossipee TR, V1; Loud's Cem. Recs., p127; NHVR-Marr, Deaths)

NATHANIEL, b 1824, Gilmanton, s/o Nathaniel and Eliza P. (Mathews) Young [no main entry], d testate 1 Aug 1892, Gilmanton; m 13 Sep 1851, Lowell, MA, Lucy A. Prescott [b 1831 or Feb 1833, Grafton, d/o Richard Prescott, d 23 Jan 1916, Gilmanton Iron Works, widow]. In 1870 Nathaniel was head of household in Gilmanton with wife Lucy and son Fred B. At age 38, Nathaniel enlisted from Concord in Co. A, 15th Regt., NH Volunteer Infantry on 13 Sep 1862, mustered in 6 Oct 1862 as Corp. and mustered out 13 Aug 1863. Pension papers gave date of death as cited above. Soon after the war Nathaniel filed for an Invalid Pension 11 Sep 1869, Application No. 147,957; Cert. No. 102, 215. He suffered a permanent disability and reapplied two months later for an increase of pension due to his worsening condition.

Nathaniel's will was drawn 8 Feb 1886, proved 16 Aug 1892, naming wife Lucy A. sole Exec. and principal legatee of his estate in Gilmanton; witnesses John W. Ham, James A. Hurd, Thomas Cogswell [Belknap Co. Probate #4970]. Son Fred B. was to receive $1.00. Widow Lucy filed for a widow's pension 12 Oct 1892, Application No. 561,699; Cert. No. 378,433; witness Frank D. Young. In 1900 Lucy A. lived alone in Gilmanton, widow age 67. Ch. b Gilmanton: Fred B.+, b 1857. (NHVR-Births; Marr; Deaths; Census Strafford Co., 1870, p31; 1900 Soundex; Nat'l. Archives Milit. Recs.)

NATHANIEL B., b 1778, Dover, s/o Timothy and Lydia (Demeritt) Young, tanner, d 26 Jun 1854, home town; m 1801, Dover, Elizabeth aka Betsey Kimball [b Feb 1774, Dover, d/o John and Mary (Roberts) Kimball, d 16 Oct 1831, home town]. From 1830-1850, Nathaniel was head of household in Dover: in 1830 his age was 40-50, with household consisting of spouse of same age group, four males, one age 5-10, one 15-20, two 20-30, and three females, one 15-20, and two 20-30 years of age; in 1840, Nathaniel was widower age 60-70, with household of two males, one age 15-20, one 30-40 and two females, one age 20-30, the other 30-40. In 1850, at age 76, Nathaniel was widower living with unmarried daughter Eveline, age 42; estate valued at $6,000.00.

He and brother Jeremy established a tannery at Dover Landing which flourished for some time. Nathaniel's earliest land deed was signed 4 May 1804, rec'd 7 Jan 1805, on the purchase of 56 sq. rods of land in Dover, from Dominicus Hanson of Dover, "it being the same and all the lands I bought of John P. Gilman on 18 Aug 1803," for $290.00; witnesses Paul Harford Jr., John P. Gilman [Strafford Co. Deed 47:46]. The partners' earliest joint purchase was by deed of 4 Nov 1806, rec'd 26 Sep 1807, for two lots of land on the west side of the river adjoining the building yard and land of Col. Amos Cogswell, formerly owned by Thomas Footman of Dover, from Oliver and Harriet Crosby of Dover, for $115.25; witnesses Henry Miller, Aaron Waldron [Strafford Co. Deed 55:302]. In 1809, they jointly bought 90 feet of land at Dover Landing beginning at the Cochecho River by the crossroad and land of Daniel Waldron, by deed of 3 Apr, rec'd 6 Apr 1809, from Ezekial Hayes Jr. of Dover for $450.00; witnesses D. M. Durell, M. L. Neal [Strafford Co. Deed 60:504]. The partners quitclaimed to Abigail Kittredge of Dover for the sum of $150.00, land in Dover on the road leading from Dover Bridge to Portsmouth by deed of 7 May, rec'd 9 Jun 1814,; witnesses Moses Hodgdon, Michael Reade [Strafford Co. Deed 79:389]. With John Durell of Dover as co-grantee, Nathaniel purchased by deed of 21 Apr 1818, rec'd same date, thirteen acres land in Dover, from William Kimball of Dover [brother-in-law], north by lands of Joseph Waldron, east by Jonathan Kimball, south by Nathaniel Horn, and by the road that leads from Dover Landing to Rochester called Scatuate Road, plus 100 acres land from William Kimball's farm, which said William inherited from his father John Kimball; total price, $2,200.00; witnesses Moses Hodgdon, Sargent Patton [Strafford Co. Deed 101:24].

Nathaniel held mortgages on two properties. The first was by deed of 8 Jul, rec'd 12 Jul 1824, whereby he and Asa Trueman, both of Dover, became mortgagees to land in Dover belonging to Joseph Young Jr., machinist of Dover and wife Mary; see Joseph and Mary Young of Dover for details. The other property title was held by Nathaniel and Jeremy, by deed signed 13 May, rec'd 27 Oct 1830, on the homestead farm in Madbury of brothers Eben D. Young and James H. Young; see James H. Young of Madbury for full details. Admin. Papers were filed on Nathaniel's estate on 5 Jul 1854, by John Trickey [son-in-law]; bond of $30,000.00 was given with sureties George Mathewson and William W. Meader, both of Dover [Strafford Co. Probate 68:46]. Inventory of his estate was taken by Asa Freeman, Thomas E. Sawyer and William A. Young, return made 31 Aug 1854; attested to same date [Strafford Co. Probate 67:122]. Nathaniel's real estate was valued at $10,325.00. Personal estate including stock in trade at $4,095.69, came to $7,804.97; grand total, $18,129.97. As is evident Nathaniel's estate was large for those times but it was decreed insolvent by Commissioner Thomas E. Sawyer Esq. of Dover on 5 Nov 1856; said Sawyer presented on that date the list of 114 approved claims against the estate totalling $13,006.91; accepted same date [Strafford Co. Probate 69:504].

Daughter Eveline A., single, predeceased her father, her will drawn 5 Nov 1861, proved 2 Jun 1863, naming her sister Elizabeth J. Trickey as Exec. of her will, witnesses Charles H. Trickey, George W. Avery, Thomas E. Sawyer [Strafford Co. Probate 70:528]. However, Admin. Papers on date of 3 Nov 1863, with will annexed passed to Thomas E. Sawyer of Dover; bond of $3,000.00 was given with sureties of Walter Sawyer and William Stevens, both of Dover [Strafford Co. Probate 68:473]. She bequeathed to her brother John K., $50.00, and to each of her five nephews [the sons of Elizabeth J.], Nathaniel P. Trickey, Fordyce P. Trickey, George O. Trickey, Matthew M. Trickey and Edward K. Trickey, $20.00; to each of two nieces [daughters of Elizabeth J.], Ellen A. Trickey and Anna D. Trickey, one-eighth part of her personal property; to sister Elizabeth J., all her wearing apparel, household goods and furniture; and to the Calvinistic Baptist Society in Dover the sum of $10.00. Nathaniel, Elizabeth and children were buried at Pine Hill Cemetery, Dover.

Ch. b Dover: John Kimball+, b 22 Mar 1802; Thomas J., b 2 Aug 1804, d 24 Jan 1850, Dover; Fordyce R., b 10 Jul 1806, d 10 Oct 1822, Dover; Effalina aka Eveline A., b 21 Feb 1809, d testate 7 May 1863, single, Dover (see above); Elizabeth Jane+ (Young) Trickey, b 7 May 1812, alive 1861, Dover; Nathaniel Jr., b 16 Oct 1815, d 30 Oct 1815, Dover; and Roxary Augusta aka Lurana Augusta, b 19 Apr 1819, d 20 Dec 1833, Dover. (NHVR-Births; Census Strafford Co., 1830, p296; 1840, p556; 1850, p73; Heritage's Dover VR, p71; Frost's Dover Cem., V1, #'s 75,166; LDS I.G.I. BR; Morning Star, p376; Kimball Gen., p123)

NATHANIEL B., b 1778, Gilmanton, s/o Dudley Young, d 15 Aug 1853, age 75, native town; m ca 1800, Gilmanton, Martha Tuttle [b 1780, Barnstead, d 1 Mar 1848, age 68, Gilmanton]. Nathaniel B. was named Co-Exec. of the will of Dudley Young, signed 20 May 1801, proved 10 May 1803, and co-residuary legatee of Dudley's real and personal estate which included parts of Lots 13 and 14, Gilmanton. His father stipulated that Nathaniel was to provide a home for their mother and sister. From 1830-1840, Nathaniel was head of family in Gilmanton: in 1830 his age was 50-60, with spouse of similar years and family of two males, one age 15-20, one 20-30, and three females, one age 5-10, one 15-20, and one 20-30. In 1840 he and spouse lived alone, their ages 60-70. The identity of but one child was uncovered. Nathaniel B. and brother Dudley Jr. were co-grantors in the sale of 10 acres of 100-acre Lot 13, 4th Div., 2nd Range, Gilmanton, called Interval land, to Theophilus Gilman of Gilmanton for $100.00, by deed of 6 Apr, rec'd 11 Jun 1807; single witness David

Edgerly [Strafford Co. Deed 53:440]. In the following year the brothers sold another 50 acres of Lot 13 "on the eastern side of the 40-acre lots in the parish...and is part of the land where we now live," to John Maloney of Northfield, Rock. Co., by deed of 6 May 1808, rec'd 27 May 1808, for $300.00; witnesses James and Sally Hersey [Strafford Co. Deed 58:62]. Mortgage of part of the 100-acre Lot 14 by Nathaniel and brother Dudley was taken out by deed signed 20 May 1812, rec'd 27 Jun 1812, title conveyed to [brother] David S. Young of Gilmanton for $150.95; if paid by 1 Nov next [1812], then the mortgage would become null and void; witnesses Peter Dudley, David Edgerly [Strafford Co. Deed 70:472].

Nathaniel and Martha were buried at Smith Meeting House Cemetery, Gilmanton. Known ch. b Gilmanton: Andrew J.+, b 1816. (NHVR-Deaths; Census Strafford Co., 1830, p277; 1840, p418; Folsom's NH Cemeteries, p159)

NATHANIEL BADGER, b 1799, Gilmanton, s/o Joseph and Betsey (Shaw) Young, alive 1860, native town; m 4 Jul 1822, Barnstead, Dorothy B. Lamphrey [b 1800, of Barnstead, alive 1860, Gilmanton]. A life-time resident of Gilmanton, Nathaniel was head of household there from 1830-1860: in 1830 his age was 20-30, with spouse of similar years, two males 5-10, and one female under 5; in 1840 his age was 40-50, spouse's age 30-40, with family of two females, one age 5-10, one 10-15. In 1850 he was then known as Badger and Dorothy was named as spouse; children at home, Hannah L. and John W., and child Rosswell Davis, age 4 [b 1846]. In 1860 Nathaniel, Dorothy, daughter Sarah, son William aka John W. and mother Betsey Young, age 83, formed a household. Ch. b Gilmanton Iron Works: Parsons C.+, b Oct 1823; Sarah J., b 1828, alive 1860; Hannah L.+ (Young) Merrill, b 1833; and John W.+, b 1843. (Census, Strafford Co., 1830, p277; 1840, p418; Belknap Co., 1850, p43; 1860, p215; NHVR-Brides, Marr; 1900 Soundex; Biog. Review, XXI, p354,355)

NATHANIEL M., b 1826, of Rochester, tanner; m 1850s, prob. Rochester, Hannah M. ( ) [b 1833, of Rochester, alive 1870, same town]. Nathaniel and Hannah lived in Rochester by 1870; children at home, Lizzie and Lucy. Ch. b prob. Rochester: Julia E.+ (Young) Rollins, b 1850s; Lizzie H.+ (Young) Drew, b 1857; and Lucy, b 1862. (Census Strafford Co., 1870, p261; NHVR-Brides)

NELLIE A., b Sep 1837, of Dover; alive 1900, lived alone at Mechanics Street, Dover. (1900 Soundex)

NELLIE F., b 1866, Freedom, d/o George F. and Mary F. (Nason) Young; m 16 Oct 1886, Freedom, Carl D. Allard [b ca 1860, of Freedom]. She was a child of four under the census returns of her parents in 1870 for Freedom. (LDS I.G.I. VR; NHVR-Brides)

NELLIE M., b ca 1855, of Farmington; m 6 Jun 1878, Farmington, Frank E. Leighton [b ca 1850, poss. s/o Susan (Young) and Jacob Leighton of Wakefield whose son Frank was b Oct 1851]. (NHVR-Brides)

NELSON C., b ca 1840, Upper Gilmanton, s/o David S. and
Betsey (Avery) Young, d pre Jun 1888, Belmont; m 1870s,
Belmont, Estelle aka Stella J. Sweatt [b ca 1850, Belmont, d/o
J. C. and S. J. (Twombly) Sweatt]. Stella, widow, m2 2? Jun
1888, Belmont, Jethro K. Page [b ca 1860, of same town]. Ch.
b Belmont: Mabelle E., b ca 1875, m 6 Aug 1895, Belmont,
Elbridge F. Akeley [b ca 1870, of same town]. (NHVR-Brides;
Biog. Review, XXI, p354,355)

NELSON E., b ca 1850, Gilmanton; m ca 1870, Eugenia (   )
[b ca 1850, Baltimore, MD]. Ch. b Pescadera, CA: Imogene
Lillian, b 9 Apr 1872, d 1 Nov 1872, age 0-6-22, Gilmanton.
(NHVR-Deaths)

NETTIE aka Annette, b 7 Oct 1853, Ossipee, d/o Luther and
Sophronia (Chick) Young, d 2 Oct 1927, native town; m1 3 Apr
1874, Wolfeboro, Edwin D. Wiggin [b ca 1850, Tuftonboro, d pre
1898, Ossipee]; m2 at least by 1898, Wolfeboro, Charles L.
Nute [b 29 Aug 1841, of Wolfeboro, d 5 Nov 1927, Ossipee].
Nettie, single, was named as daughter and heir of Luther Young
of Ossipee by his will drawn 13 Sep 1871, proved 1 Mar 1872.
Nettie Nute of Wolfeboro was chosen by her siblings per an
Agreement of Heirs on 26 Oct 1898, to be Admin. of the estate
of their mother Sophronia Young, approved 1 Nov 1898. All her
siblings then released to her their shares in a deposit held
at the Strafford Savings Bank at Dover. Both Nettie and
Charles were buried at Large Ossipee Center Cemetery by her
parents' family plot. No known children. (NHVR-Brides;
Loud's Cem. Recs., p106)

NETTIE L. aka Junette, b 1856, Gilmanton, d/o Levi J. and
2nd wife Elizabeth E. (Gilman) Young; m 18 Sep 1884, Gilmanton, Frank J. Brown [b ca 1855, of same town]. Nettie L.,
single, was named daughter and heir of Elizabeth (Gilman)
Young of Gilmanton by her will signed 16 Feb 1883, proved
15 Jan 1884; Frank J. Brown was one of three witnesses to the
will. (NHVR-Brides)

NEWELL H., b 8 Jun 1867, Newfield, ME, alive 1900, Dover,
carriage painter; m ca 1880, Ella M. (   ) [b 12 Aug 1861,
Berwick, ME, alive 1900, Dover]. Newell, spouse and daughter
Inez lived at Folsom Street, Dover in 1900. Ch. b NH: Inez
May, b 19 May 1882, not traced further. This was a rare
instance of the 1900 Soundex giving full dates of birth.
(1900 Soundex; NHVR-Births)

NOAH, b ca 1732, Parish of Madbury, s/o Samuel and Hannah
(   ) Young; m ca 1755, Dover, Abigail Perkins [b ca 1735,
Dover, d/o Joseph Perkins]. Noah was eldest son and heir as
given in Samuel's will dated 4 Jun 1755, proved 27 May 1761;
he received one-half of father's share of land in the Middle
Township at the head of Rochester and a 1/16th share in Paul
Gerrish's sawmill. He and Abigail sold their interest in the
estate of her father Joseph Perkins of Dover to Timothy
Perkins for 50 pounds by deed of 1 May 1762, rec'd 21 Jan
1763; witnesses Joseph Smith, Daniel Meserve Jr. [NH Prov.
Probate 67:303]. Noah, in partnership with brother Samuel,

purchased 120 acres land, Lot 202, 5th Range in Barrington by deed signed and rec'd 12 Mar 1760, from Edward and Elizabeth Pendexter of Portsmouth for 200 pounds New Tenor; witnesses Cutt Shannon, Zachariah Foss [NH Prov. Probate 61:69]. Two years later, the brothers legally divided the property between themselves with no exchange of money, by deed signed and rec'd 22 Mar 1762, Noah to have 60 acres on the s.w. part next to the 6th Range; witnesses Thomas Packer, William Earl Treadwell [NH Prov. Probate 64:399]. On same date of signing and recording, Noah sold his 60 acres to Moses Caverly Jr., barber of Barrington, for 600 pounds Old Tenor; Noah's wife Abigail ceded her dower rights; witnesses Thomas Packer, William Earl Treadwell [NH Prov. Probate 64:400].

Noah served in the N.H. Militia from 1 May to 13 Nov 1756, in Capt. Samuel Gerrish's Co. No. 10. He served once again in Samuel Gerrish's Co. No. 1, as did his brothers, from 8 Mar to 27 Nov 1760 on the expedition to invade Canada. And by deed of 3 Nov 1762, rec'd 13 Dec 1763, he sold in fee simple his interest in his father's homestead farm in Madbury and the 1/16th share in Paul Gerrish's sawmill "as it descended to me as an heir to my said father or otherwise as it fell to me by the death or as an heir to my late brother Jonathan Young of Madbury," to Benjamin Evans of Dover for 300 pounds Old Tenor; witnesses Moses Ham, Ephraim Hanson, [NH Prov. Probate 71:342]. Noah's last deed was as co-grantor with his mother Hannah, signed 9 Nov 1762, rec'd 21 Mar 1771, in the sale of his share in the Rochester land inherited from his father's estate; John Gage and Ephraim Hanson were personal witnesses for Noah; for further details of deed, see parents' entry. No known children. [Potter's Mil. History, p173,237].

OBEDIAH SUMNER aka Obed, b Nov 1859, Wakefield, s/o James C. and Rosemandel (Gill) Young, d 1937, Wolfeboro; m ca 1900, Wolfeboro, Fanny (Darling) Horne [b 1870, Wolfeboro, father a Wolfeboro dentist, d 1938, native town]. Obed was single in 1900, age 40, and lived in Wolfeboro; boarder was Alvah H. Bickford [n.d.]; he and Fanny made their home there also. Family members were buried at Lake View Cemetery, Lot 2, Wolfeboro. Ch. b Wolfeboro: Sumner D., b 1903, d 1946, Wolfeboro. (Young Family Recs., courtesy of Alden N. Young; Wolfeboro Cem. Records, Part III, p12; 1900 Soundex)

OLIVE J., b 1852, Freedom, d/o Jeremiah and Jane (Allen) Young; m 23 Feb 1871, Effingham, Albion Clough [b ca 1845, of same town]. Olive J. lived with her parents in Freedom and Effingham up through 1870. Ch. b prob. Effingham, not traced further: Ethel Clough, b 1870s; and Bert Clough, b ca 1875. (NHVR-Brides)

OLIVE JENNY, b 1828, Barrington, d/o Ebenezer and Prudence (Cate) Young, alive 1869, native town; m (Intentions) 27 May 1848, Barrington, m 27 Aug 1848, Northwood, John S. Buzzell [b 1822, of Barrington, d 8 Feb 1898, same town]. Olive, minor, was made ward 17 Sep 1838 of uncle David Young of Barrington upon her father's death and was named Olive J.

Buzzell in David's will of 16 Jun 1869, proved 1871; see David
Young of Barrington for full details. Olive was heir-at-law
in the division of their grandfather Isaac's estate in Barrington, receiving along with her sisters a one-third share in
the estate on 5 Oct 1841; see Isaac and Betsey (Cate) Young
for details. Olive, John and son were buried at the Buzzell
family graveyard, Barrington, Plot 5C-2. Ch. b Barrington:
William C. Buzzell, b 1850, d 11 Jan 1865, Barrington. (Barrington Graveyards, p14; NHVR-Brides; Hammond's Barrington TR,
p60)

OLIVE L., b 1833, ME, resident of Somersworth in 1850;
roomed at boarding house, occupation unknown. (Census
Strafford Co., 1850, p323)

OLIVER, b 1804, most likely ME, d testate 17 May 1830,
age 26, Somersworth; m 30 Mar 1828, Somersworth, Hannah E.
Gordon [b ca 1805, Berwick, ME]. Not quite two years after
their marriage, Oliver died, survived by wife and young son.
He had been member of the Freewill Baptist Church. His will
was drawn 22 Mar, proved 17 May 1830, appointing Nathaniel
Grant of Berwick, York Co., ME, as his sole Exec.; witnesses
W. A. Marston, Richard Shapleigh, Artemas Pratt [Strafford Co.
Probate 41:6]. Nathaniel Grant of Berwick, York Co., ME was
allowed Exec. of Oliver's last will on date of probate, bond
of $3,000.00 given with sureties James Martin, Joseph Stack-
pole, Ezra Harthern and John T. Nute [Strafford Co. Probate
30:259]. Said Grant was named the guardian of his infant son
Oliver Martin Young until he reached the age of 14, when he
would be old enough to elect his guardian. He devised to wife
Hannah one-half of his real estate and almost all his personal
property; his son Oliver Martin Young would receive the other
half of the real estate and his patent lever watch, both
bequests to be reserved to him until he reached the age of
twenty-one. His half-sister Joanna Young was to receive one
half of any disposable property remaining after bequests; the
other half was to be held in trust by the Exec. to be laid out
by him for the benefit of Oliver's father if he should stand
in need of assistance. Oliver gave his Exec. full power of
attorney to manage all his real estate and to sell properties
if necessary to pay all his just debts: a parcel of land in
Levant, Penobscot Co., ME which he purchased of Moses and Amos
Patten, William Emerson, Robert Waterston and Isaac C. Pray;
another piece of land in Dalton in said Penobscot Co. which
he purchased of William Sullivan, another piece of land in
York, ME, and a mortgage deed on property in Dover, executed
1 Jan 1830, by Sherburne Sleeper.

Inventory was taken by Charles E. Bartlett, James Cristie
and Thomas T. Edgerly, returned and attested to 11 Jun 1830
[Strafford Co. Probate 40:115]: total worth of estate including furniture, apparel, pew at Congregational Meeting House,
one horse, and amount of demands deemed good was set at
$1,553.84. On 20 Sep 1830, Hannah E. was granted an allowance
of $300.00 from the estate [Strafford Co. Probate 43:13].

Thomas Edgerly of Somersworth was appointed Commissioner 19 Mar 1831 to review and allow various claims against the estate [Strafford Co. Probate 41:327]. Said Edgerly made his return 16 May 1831 with the following list of legitimate claims: 15 notes of hand at $652.14; last sickness, $104.43; admin. expenses of Nathaniel Grant, $423.39 per order of the judge. Exec. Grant submitted his account 20 Jun 1835, approved same date [Strafford Co. Probate 48:445]: starting from 23 Apr 1830 through 3 Jun 1835, expenses for probate fees, licenses, recording of deeds, the moving of goods, journeys to Dover, storing goods and the time and expenses in selling land in York came to $978.37; amount of inventory of personal property except demands decreed bad and doubtful, $1,553.84; balance of $1,032.96 due from Exec. Petition for License to Sell was submitted by Nathaniel Grant 28 Dec 1833, approved 21 Jan 1834, to raise $700.00 to discharge debts [Strafford Co. Probate 24:300]. Said Grant submitted the list of claims on 22 Mar 1835, [Strafford Co. Probate 49:1]: balance of $1,032.96 due from Grant to be divided among thirteen creditors per averaging schedule. Among these claims was the private account for the Exec. in the amount of $423.39, and expenses during Oliver's last sickness incurred by Noah Martin in the amount of $104.43. Ch. b Somersworth: Oliver Martin, b ca 1830. (NHVR-Marr; Morning Star, p376)

OLIVER H. P., b 22 Mar 1824, Barnstead Center, s/o Jonathan and Susan (Pitman) Young, d 7 Dec 1897, age 73-8-16, home town; m 20 May 1849, Barnstead, Emily J. Tuttle [b 2 Oct 1828, Barnstead, d/o John J. and Betsey (Jacobs) Tuttle, d 19 Apr 1899, age 70-6-17, widow, native town]. At age 37, Oliver enlisted from Gilmanton Iron Works in Co. B, 12th Regt., NH Volunteer Infantry on 19 Aug 1862 and mustered in 30 Aug 1862 as Corp. He was discharged as disabled 12 Jan 1864, Concord leaving P.O. address of Barnstead Center. In 1870 he and Emily were listed on the census returns for Barnstead; son Leyander and daughter Sarah H. lived at home. The family attended the Congregational Church. He learned the carpenter's trade and while involved with town affairs, always declined to accept public office of any kind. One year before his death, Oliver suffered senile debility requiring Oscar Foss [son-in-law] to be appointed guardian on 15 Dec 1896. On date of 17 Jan 1898, Emily applied for a Widow's Pension based on Oliver's military service, Application No. 669,223, Cert. No. 480,769. She stated that since her husband's death she was without means of support and held no real estate, adding that his death had been brought about by diseases contracted during the war. Oliver and Emily were buried at Barnstead Center Cemetery. Ch. b Barnstead Center: Leander J. aka Leyander+, b 9 Feb 1850, and Sarah U.+ (Young) Foss, b 3 Dec 1852. (Barnstead Cem. Inscriptions, p6; Biog. Review, XXI, p492,493; NHVR-Brides, Deaths, Marr; Census Belknap Co., 1870, p19; Soldiers & Sailors, p647; Cutter's Eastern Mass., p1269,1270; Nat'l. Archives Milit. Recs.)

ORLANDO, b 7 Jan 1826, Madbury, s/o Eleazer and Kezia (Rowe) Young, d 27 Aug 1895, age 69-7-20, his native town, carpenter; m 11 Nov 1849, Dover, Kezia A. Peavey [b Jan 1834, Dover, d 1916, native town, by married name of Frye]. He was named son and heir by Kezia Young's will signed 17 Aug 1863, proved 1 Apr 1865, and served as Selectman for Madbury 1856-1857. He and spouse Kezia were listed in the 1850-1860 census returns for Madbury. In 1850 they lived alone; in 1860 children at home were Joseph W. and Edgar D., estate valued at $3,500. In 1900 widow Kezia lived at South Pine St., Dover, with boarder Maud V. Young, age 16 [b Mar 1884, MA]. Orlando, Kezia and three children were buried at Pine Hill Cemetery, Dover. Ch. b Madbury: Joseph W., b 28 Feb 1851, d 1862, Dover; Edgar B., b 25 Sep 1856, d 1862, Dover; daughter Edna Joshe, b 25 Sep 1863; and Cora Bell, b 20 Sep 1868, d 1869, Madbury. (Census Strafford Co., 1850, p482; 1860, p539; 1900 Soundex; NHVR-Births, Marr, Deaths; Frost's Dover Cem., V1, Plot #554; LDS I.G.I. BR; Adam's Madbury, n.p.)

ORRIN, b ca 1845, Kennebunkport, ME; ma ca 1870, Anna R. (   ) [b ca 1850, ME]. Ch. b Farmington: Arthur G., b 1 Jul 1872. (NHVR-Births)

ORRIN DEMERITT, b 6 Jul 1834, Gilmanton, s/o Andrew Bailey and Eliza J. (Evans) Young, d 7 Mar 1904, Lyndonville, VT; m (Intentions) 7 May 1857, Belmont, m 11 May 1857, Manchester, Sophia Jones [b 1840, Canada]. Orrin D. lived with his parents in Sanbornton in 1850. (NHVR-Marr)

ORRIN J., b 1864, Lawrence, MA, s/o John W. and Abbie W. (   ) Young [no main entry]; m 9 Apr 1888, Rochester, Mary A. McDonald [b 1870, of Rochester, d/o James McDonald]. (Rochester TR, Marr, p25; NHVR-Marr)

OTIS, b 1779, Barrington, s/o Winthrop and Mary (Otis) Young, d 27 Dec 1870, Canterbury, age 91; m1 25 Oct 1804, Canterbury, Catharine Johnson [b 1783, Canterbury, d 2 Nov 1845, home town, age 62]; m2 16 Apr 1846, Canterbury, Mrs. Lois (Miner) Waldron [b ca 1810, of Canterbury]. Ch. b Canterbury by Catharine: Thomas Jefferson, b 10 Mar 1805; Winthrop, b Mar 1809; Stephen, b 2 Sep 1810; John Langdon, b 22 Mar 1812; William H., b 1814, d 27 Nov 1841, Canterbury, age 27, single; Mary O., b 13 Jul 1818; and Catharine J., b 1 Jul 1823. (Lyford's Canterbury, p341,342)

OTIS, b 1830, of Sanbornton, merchant; m ca 1860, May (   ) [b 1831, of Sanbornton]. Otis and wife were residents of Sanbornton in 1860. (Census Belknap Co., 1860, p58)

PAMELA, b 1820, ME, resident of Somersworth in 1850, widow. Ch. b ME: Sarah, b 1840. (Census Strafford Co., 1850, p300)

PARSONS, b 1824, of Alton; in 1850, he lived with the Coffin family in Alton, farmer. (Census Belknap Co., 1850, p366)

PARSONS C., b Oct 1823, Gilmanton Iron Works, s/o Nathaniel Badger and Dorothy B. (Lamphrey) Young, d 1 Apr 1910, Somersworth; m1 1 Aug 1847, Belmont, Abigail E. Smith [b

22 Sep 1825, Gilmanton, s/o Josiah and Olive (Towle) Smith, d 29 Jun 1885, age 59-9-7, Somersworth]; m2 17 May 1897, Manchester, Matilda Hall [b 1837 (NHVR) or Feb 1833 (Census), Strafford, her 2nd marriage, d/o John and Abigail (Drew) Jones, alive 1900, Barnstead]. Abigail's mother Olive Towle was born in Chichester. In 1900 he and 2nd wife Matilda lived in Barnstead with boarder Charles Hill [n.d.], no known children. Both Parsons C. and 1st wife Abigail were buried at Forest Glade Cemetery, Somersworth. (NHVR-Deaths; Marr; 1900 Soundex; Wooley's Somersworth Cems., n.p.)

PATIENCE, b ca 1757, Barrington, prob. d/o Eleazer and Mary (Ham) Young of Barrington; m 9 Aug 1777, Barrington, John Tenny Jr. [b ca 1755 Rowley]. Eleazer of Barrington named as daughter and heir, Patience Young, in his will drawn 18 Jun 1771, proved 30 Oct 1798. (NHVR-Brides; Hammond's Barrington TR, p11)

PATIENCE, b ca 1775, Rochester; m 15 Nov 1795, Rochester, Oliver Peavy [b ca 1770, Rochester]. (NH Gen. Recs., V5, 1908, p51)

PATIENCE, b 1800, of Dover in 1850, single, poss. d/o Lt. Thomas and Nancy (Drew) Young of Dover Neck. Lt. Thomas' daughter Patience was single at the time he wrote his will, drawn 7 Jun 1841, proved 7 May 1844. Patience was without occupation and roomed at boarding house in 1850, Dover. (Census Strafford Co., 1850, p154)

PAUL, b ca 1750, of Barrington, alive 22 Nov 1806, Davistown, Lincoln Co., MA; m ca 1775, Rebecca (   ) [b ca 1754, of Barrington, alive 1800, same town]. Paul was an early inhabitant of Barrington having signed there in 1776 both the Association Test and the Petition of Inhabitants in favor of John Garland [said Garland to be appointed as one of the Magistrates for Strafford Co., subsequently passed]. He was head of household in Barrington from 1790-1800: in 1790 family contained three other males in family, under the age of 16, and two females; in 1800 there was one male age 16-26, three females aged 10-16 years, two females 16-26 years, and a female 45 years plus. Paul's original homestead farm in Barrington was 120-acre Lot 70, 2nd Div., the upper half of which he sold with the notation "on which I now live," by deed signed 11 Nov 1790, rec'd 13 Dec 1796, to John Pearl of Barrington for 165 pounds "legal money"; witnesses William Hale, Isaiah Felker [Strafford Co. Deed 24:54]. On same date of sale on Lot 70, Paul then purchased his new homestead of 72 acres of Lot 195, 5th Range, being the whole of said lot where Reuben Gray then lived, by deed signed 11 Nov 1790, rec'd 19 Dec 1791, from Reuben and Martha Gray of Barrington, for 150 pounds; witnesses Isaiah Felker, Samuel Winkley Jr. [Strafford Co. Deed 14:7]. He next purchased 96 acres of Lot 194, 5th Range, Barrington, by deed of 27 Jun 1791, rec'd 13 Mar 1800, from the heirs-at-law of John Bradford for 30 pounds; witnesses Elizabeth Richards and Betsey Coney for John and Mary Bradford of Roxbury, MA; witnesses Katharine Barton and Mary Kenstran for Samuel and Ann Bradford of Boston; witnesses Ruthey Hunt and Gideon Bassett for William and Sarah Bradford of Boston [Strafford Co. Deed 33:165]. Paul's last purchase of Barrington land before selling out most of his estate was 58 acres of Lot 160, 4th Range, by deed of 9 Aug 1797, rec'd 13 Mar 1800, from the heirs of Richard Parsley for $500.00; witnesses Samuel Hale, Samuel Winkley Jr. for George Parsley; witnesses Robert Woodbury, Samuel Winkley for Elizabeth Parsley [Strafford Co. Deed 32:286].

As early as 1791, Paul began disposing his estate in Barrington by the sale of 24 acres of Lot 194, 5th Range, originally laid out to John Bradford, by deed signed 6 Oct 1791, rec'd 16 Dec 1796, to Garland Smith of Barrington for 15 pounds; witnesses Isaac Waldron, Samuel Hale [Strafford Co. Deed 23:304]. He completed the process of selling what appears to be the remainder of his estate in Barrington, 72 acres of Lot 195, 5th Range, 96 acres of Lot 194, 5th Range and 58 acres of Lot 160, 4th Range by deed signed 11 Mar, rec'd 13 Mar 1800, to Jonathan Hill of Barrington for $1,000, Rebecca releasing dower rights; witnesses Joshua Foss Jr., John Pearl [Strafford Co. Deed 32:299]. As a follow-up to this sale on same date of signing, son Isaac 3rd quitclaimed to his mother Rebecca by deed rec'd 23 Mar 1804, his share in the land which his parents had just sold to Jonathan Hill, "the one-third part of the estate I have this day received of Jonathan Hill which is the estate the said Hill now lives on and is part of the original right of John Lear and part of the right of Jethro Furber in the 2nd Range, Barrington" for $300.00; witnesses Joshua Foss Jr., John Pearl [Strafford Co. Deed 44:180].

Paul relocated in Davistown, Lincoln Co., MA, as shown by deed signed 22 Nov 1806, rec'd 23 Jan 1807, which empowered Jonathan Roberts of Barrington with Power of Attorney for "various considerations"; witnesses John Foss 5th, Jonathan Bailey [Strafford Co. Deed 53:170]. Known ch. b Barrington: Isaac 3rd, b ca 1775. (Census Strafford Co., 1790, p86; 1800, p155; NH State Papers, V11, p154; Wilson's Assoc. Test, p122)

PAUL D., b 23 Aug 1792, Dover, s/o Lt. Thomas and Nancy (Drew) Young, d 11 January 1864, Madbury, bur. Dover; m ca 1815, Dover, Elizabeth Young [b 3 Mar 1793, Dover, d/o John and prob. Sarah (   ), d pre 1860, poss. Madbury]. Paul D. was acknowledged as son and heir of Thomas Young of Dover by will signed 7 Jun 1841, proved 7 May 1844. In 1830 he was head of household in Dover, age 30-40, with family of spouse of same age group, two males, one under 5, one 10-15, and six females, one under 5, four 5-10 and one 10-15. Paul enlisted in the N.H. Militia in Capt. Horace Parmelee's Co. 11 Sep 1814 and was discharged 28 Sep 1814. He was still of Dover when he purchased 32 acres of Lot 47, 2nd Div., Wakefield, next to land of James Quimby by deed of 18 May 1819, rec'd 1 Sep 1820, from James Dore of Wakefield for $237.00; witnesses Joseph Burbank, Cornelia Burbank [Strafford Co. Deed 107:431]. As of 1820, he was listed as resident and taxpayer of Highway District No. 19, Wakefield. As co-grantees Paul D., Jedediah Abbott of Ossipee and John Roberts of Wakefield purchased 60 acres of Lot 36, 2nd Div., North Wakefield, abutting Lot 63, 2nd Div. owned by James Young 2nd, and Lot 37, 2nd Div., owned by Daniel Young of Ossipee [first cousins]; for full details see quitclaim of Mark Young of Wakefield, signed and rec'd on same date of 10 Nov 1821. Paul was then of Wakefield when he and said co-grantee Jedediah Abbott reconveyed to Mark Young of Wakefield title to the very same 60 acres of Lot 36, 2nd Div. which Mark heretofore sold to them, for $200.00, by deed signed 23 Feb, rec'd 25 Feb 1822; witnesses Ezekial Wentworth, Joseph Bickford [Strafford Co. Deed 112:549]. It should be noted that although the latter deed did not specify "mort-gage," the intent would appear to be the same; if so, the mortgage was redeemed. Then by deed of 14 Dec, rec'd 19 Dec 1826, Paul D. of Wakefield sold in fee simple, 45 acres of Lot 47, 2nd Div., Wakefield, to Amasa Copp of Wakefield for $300.00; witnesses William Copp, John Wingate [Strafford Co. Deed 131:285].

It is certain that Paul at least relocated in Madbury some time after 1826, inasmuch as the 1860 census indicated that he lived there as widower, at age 67, at the home of Benjamin Stevens. The Admin. of single daughter Mary Ann's estate was Louisa Young of Dover, appointed by the court 7 Jan 1845; bond of $1,000 posted with sureties Winthrop A. Marston and Benjamin F. Preble, both of Dover [Strafford Co. Probate 50:286]. Known ch. b prob. Dover: Mary Ann, b 1818, d 14 Sep 1844, Dover, buried Pine Hill Cem., Dover. (Frost's Dover Cem., V1, #108F; Potter's Mil. History, V2, p205; Census Strafford Co., 1830, p313; 1860, p10; Banks' Wakefield, p681; Ham's Dover Marr, TMs)

PAULINE aka Perlina, b ca 1810, Ossipee, d/o Daniel and Elizabeth (Nason) Young, alive 1866, Freedom; m (Intentions) 11 Nov 1833, Freedom, m 14 Dec 1833, Eaton, Horace Moses [b ca 1805, Eaton]. Perlina Moses was named daughter and heir of Daniel Young of Freedom by his will drawn 1 Oct 1866, proved 31 Aug 1874. Ch. b Eaton or Freedom: William I. Moses, b ca 1835, m 1871, Freedom. (NHVR-Brides)

PEGGY, b ca 1780, of Ossipee; m 18 Nov 1801, Wolfeboro, Henry Hide [b ca 1775, of Ossipee]. (NHVR-Brides)

PERLEY E., b Aug 1868, Wolfeboro, eldest s/o Thomas and Maria S. (Bodge) Young, d pre 25 Jan 1936, native town, widower; m 12 Dec 1896, Milton, Lillian A. Black [b Dec 1868, Meredith, d/o O. A. and Mellisa A. (Drew) Black of Tuftonboro, alive 1900, Wolfeboro]. In 1900 Perley, wife and son lived in Wolfeboro. Letters of Admin. on Perley E.'s estate in Wolfeboro were filed by J. Clifton Avery on date of 25 Jan 1936, no heir-at-law cited [Carroll Co. Probate #10828]. Ch. b Wolfeboro: Carl L., b Jul 1897. (NHVR-Marr; 1900 Soundex)

PETER, b ca 1750, Dover, s/o Eleazer and Mary (Ham) Young, d 1828, Green Hill, Barrington; m as early as 1776, first cousin Sarah Hayes [bp 14 Feb 1751, Barrington, twin, d/o Benjamin and Abigail (Young) Hayes, alive 1803, native town]. Peter was named as only son and residuary legatee of Eleazer Young of Barrington by his will written 18 Jun 1771, proved 30 Oct 1798; he was also designated Exec. Peter was to receive all his father's real estate not conveyed by deed: the homestead in Barrington and other land in the Two-Mile Streak, Rochester and Dover. On 3 Sep 1776 Peter signed the Association Test for Barrington and from 1790-1810 was listed as resident of the town. In 1790 his family consisted of two males over 16, one male under 16, and two females; in 1800 his age was 45 plus as was his spouse, with household of two males, one age 16-26, the other 26-45, and two females age 10-16; in 1810 both he and spouse were over 45 years, with a family of two males, one age 26-45, one under 10, and one female age 26-45. He served as Selectman of Barrington from 1795-1797, and in 1803, subscribed to the Barrington Meeting House.

Peter was also named an heir of Isaac Young late of Dover [uncle, his father's brother], receiving a one-ninth share of Isaac's estate. The property in question was 19-1/2 acres in Dover, north of lands of John Wheeler and Dominicus Hanson on the road from the Dover Meeting House to Piscataqua Bridge, as well as a quarter acre bounded by said road by land of Jonathan Gage, deceased, north of Thomas Footman. Peter's share was sold to Thomas Footman of Dover by deed signed 22 Apr 1803, rec'd 19 May 1808, for $150.00; witnesses William K. Atkinson, Francis Footman [Strafford Co. Deed 58:40].

Aside from inherited properties, Peter amassed a considerable network of real estate, having invested heavily on up through 1820. There are 38 deeds in all for Peter, many of which are presented in "digest" form for the sake of brevity. Although the census returns indicated Peter had three sons, only one was named to whom he conveyed properties. In seven land deeds, some of which held connections with the Ham and Hayes families of Barrington, Peter conveyed these lands to son Eleazer: (1) 100 acres in Barrington adjacent to Paul Hayes' land which he had purchased from Maul Hanson, by deed signed 17 Dec 1801, rec'd 17 Jan 1804 for $500.00, witnesses Joseph Waldron, John Kingman [Strafford Co. Deed 43:459]; (2) 50 acres of Lot 2 with buildings beginning at north corner of James Hayes' lands, then to lands of Hezekiah Hayes, adjacent to Green Hill Road, as well as 20 acres in Rochester on west side of Isinglass River, part of Horne Lot 112, 1st Div. and by Lot 113 for $2,000.00; witnesses Simeon Jenks, Isaac Bickford, by deed signed 1 Sep 1803, rec'd 26 Jan 1804 [Strafford Co. Deed 43:514]; (3) a combined 19-1/2 acres in Barrington by land deed signed 3 Jan 1804, rec'd 26 Jan 1804: 3-1/2 acres of Lot 2 formerly owned by Shadrach Ham, 3-1/2 acres of Lot 1 formerly owned by Joseph Ham Jr., 4-1/2 acres in Lot 3, Two-Mile Streak, "part of Randal's homestead farm set off to Shadrach Ham", thence to land of Benjamin Hayes, from John and

Sarah Randal of Rochester, and 8 acres in the same farm purchased from Mark and Betty Jenness of Barrington at north side of the road by land of Joseph Ham and west to land of Benjamin Hayes, for $300.00; witnesses Simeon Jenks, Isaac Bickford [Strafford Co. Deed 43:518]; (4) two properties of 17 acres of Dover Common Land, 5 acres of which were situated on the n.e. corner of James Killey's grant by the road that leads to Isinglass Bridge above Log Hill, and 12 acres, 7 rods of which were part of Col. Paul Gerrish's right, late of Dover, by deed signed 24 Jan 1804, rec'd 26 Jan 1804, $120.00; witnesses Simeon Jenks, Isaac Bickford [Strafford Co. Deed 43:517]; (5) 50 acres of Lot 12, Two-Mile Streak, beginning at n.e. corner of Lot 11 owned by James Hayes adjacent to lands of David Drew and Joshua Hayes by deed signed 1 Jan, rec'd 26 Jan 1804, for $860.00; witnesses Simeon Jenks, Isaac Bickford [Strafford Co. Deed 43:515]; (6) 25 acres in Dover on north side of the Heath and on the Elseware Plains, so called, n.w. on Dover headline next to lands of Ichabod Canney and now James Hayes for $200.00, signed 3 Jan 1804, rec'd 23 Jan 1804; witnesses Simeon Jenks, Isaac Bickford [43:518]; (7) [actually Peter's last known deed] 14 acres of Lot 12, 8th Range, Two-Mile Streak, for $110.00, signed 3 Mar 1820, rec'd same date; witnesses A. Chadbourne, Oliver Crosby [Strafford Co. Deed 106:433].

Lands not disposed of by 1820 represent the estate that son Eleazer and possibly two siblings would have received upon Peter's death, notwithstanding the absence of will or official division of estate. The following land deeds with Peter as grantee are given: (1) purchased 50 acres, of Lot 10, Two-Mile Streak, from Isaac and Elizabeth Young of Barrington for 200 pounds, signed 20 Dec 1774, rec'd 5 Dec 1778 [Strafford Co. Deed 3:207]; (2) purchased 46 acres with buildings at no. corner of Lot 9, on the line between Barrington and Rochester, formerly known as Acerman's Commons, from Joshua Foss Jr. of Barrington, for 69 pounds; witnesses Levi Landers, Benjamin Winkley, signed 1 Jun 1790, rec'd 11 Dec 1797 [Strafford Co. Deed 26:446]; (3) purchased 19 acres adjacent to Dover head line at east corner of lands of Benjamin Hayes, parallel with the line between Barrington and Rochester, from Stephen and Mary Hanson and John and Mary Hanson for $120.00; signed 12 Oct 1792, rec'd 11 Dec 1797 [Strafford Co. Deed 26:445]; (5) purchased 40 acres at s.w. end of Lot 56, Barrington, formerly owned by Joshua Foss Esq., from James Rowe of Barrington for 60 pounds; witnesses Thomas Footman, John Drew, signed 11 Nov 1795, rec'd 2 Mar 1796 [Strafford Co. Deed 21:539]; (6) purchased 122-1/2 acres, 3rd Div., Rochester, and a piece of land 23' x 34' at Dover Landing, by two deeds signed and rec'd 30 Jan 1799, from Ebenezer Tebbetts of Dover for 200 pounds, witnesses David Copp Jr., Paul Willand Jr. [Strafford Co. Deed 29:353,354]; (7) purchase of 196 acres in four parcels of land in Barrington by deed signed 1 Jun 1801, rec'd 16 Nov 1801: (i) 116 acres at east end of Lot 101, 3rd

Range (ii) 20-1/2 acres off the west end of Lot 90, 2nd Div., adjoining; (iii) 32 acres off the west end of Lot 89, 2nd Range adjacent aforesaid lot, and (iv) 27 acres off the south corner of Lot 88, 2nd Range which was formerly the homestead of Simeon Jenks, from William and Maria Lang of Boston, Suffolk Co. for $1,400.00; witnesses Joseph Gardner, Samuel Gardner [Strafford Co. Deed 37.317]. Scarcely four months later Peter mortgaged these four properties combined, by deed (31) signed 11 Sep 1801, rec'd 16 Nov 1801, to the said William Lang, with three promissory notes as collateral security, each in the amount of $466.66, the last note payable within three years; witnesses Moses Hodgdon, William K. Atkinson [Strafford Co. Deed 37:370]).

For properties inherited from father Eleazer which Peter sold between 1803-1804, see appendix (1).

Mortgage deed signed 12 Sep, rec'd 13 Sep 1806, conveyed Peter's title to James Carr Esq. of Somersworth on lands and buildings which had been the homestead farm of Abraham Waldron late of Barrington, and all the lands which he purchased from William Lang, excepting a small one-story dwelling formerly owned by Simeon Jenks with 4 acres adjoining for $700.00; witnesses William K. Atkinson, Peggy Gage [Strafford Co. Deed 52:272]. The mortgage held an indemnity clause in favor of said Carr: on the condition that Peter pay all costs and damages and take upon himself the whole "burthen" of the defense of action that may arise to him or them from a court case pending in the Superior Court on 14 Sep 1806, which Peter had agreed to do, then the deed shall be void.

Known ch. b Barrington: Eleazer+, b 8 Nov 1780. (Barrington TR, V6; Wilson's Assoc. Test, p122; Hayes Gen., V1, p74-76, Census Strafford Co., 1790, p86; 1800, p155; 1810, p494; Barrington Congreg. Church, p1-250)

PETER, b 1770s, of York, York Co., Mass. Bay Colony [Maine in 1820]; spouse was Mary (   ) [b 1770s, of York, Mass. Bay Colony]. Peter became land owner in Alton in the purchase of 43 acres of Lot 8, 6th Div., 2nd Range in Alton, drawn to original right of John Thomlinson and John Tufton Mason, from Francis Piper of Alton by deed signed 31 Mar, rec'd 2 Aug 1806, for $350.00; witnesses James McDuffee, John Walker [Strafford Co. Deed 52:77]. On same dates of signing and recording, he mortgaged this property back to the said Francis Piper for $250.00, sum due and payable 1 Dec 1807; above-named witnesses [Strafford Co. Deed 52:78]. Two years later 40 acres of Lot 8, 2nd Range, Alton were quitclaimed by Peter still of York, York Co., by deed signed 9 Mar, rec'd 10 Mar 1809, to Francis Piper of Alton for $350.00; spouse Mary released dower rights; witnesses William Frost, Jacob Frost [Strafford Co. Deed 60:395].

PETER, b ca 1807, of Acton, ME; m 2 Dec 1832, Wakefield, Mary Garvin [b ca 1812, of Wakefield, d 27 Jun 1841]. Place names are lacking in reference source cited. One can speculate that Peter was a lineal descendant of Sarah (Hayes)

Young, spouse of Peter Young of Barrington. Richmond's Hayes Genealogy [V1, p75,76] stated that a branch of the Hayes settled in Acton, ME. Ch.: Betsey Garvin, b 3 Apr 1834, lived at Acton, ME; Joshua Moody, b 9 Apr 1836, lived at Acton, ME; John William, b 7 May 1838, d at Andersonville, GA, 8 Sep 1864, prisoner of war; Sarah Hayes, b 8 Jun 1840. (Wentworth Gen., V1, p89; NHVR-Marr)

PETER, b 1865, Canada, alive 1900, Somersworth; m ca 1885, NH, Melvina (   ) [b Jan 1867, Canada, alive 1900, Somersworth]. Peter, spouse and five children lived at Union Street, Somersworth in 1900; he and Melvina had retained their French-Canadian citizenship. Ch. b ME, not traced further: George, b Aug 1886. Ch. b NH: Leonora, b Jul 1887; Delia, b Jan 1889; Alfred, b Sep 1890. Ch. b ME: Joseph, b 1898. (1900 Soundex)

PETER C., b 12 Aug 1819, Wakefield, s/o Daniel and Betsey (Cook) Young, d 23 Oct 1902, native town; m 31 Mar 1868, Wakefield, Mary A. Farnum [b 1825, ME, res. of Concord, d pre 1900, Wakefield]. Peter, single, lived with his parents up through 1860; by 1870, he and wife Mary made their home with his parents. On date of 10 May 1873, Peter C. was listed as taxpayer of Wakefield, assessed at $15.74. In 1900 Peter was widower and resident of Wakefield; at home was daughter Ollie L., age 16. He and Mary were buried at Peter Young Cemetery at top of Pray Hill Road, Wakefield. Ch. b Wakefield: Ollie L., b Aug 1874, not traced further. (NHVR-Marr; Census Carroll Co., 1870, p429; Twombly's Wakefield Cem., TMs; Banks' Wakefield, p181; 1900 Soundex)

PHINEAS, b ca 1760, of Barnstead; in 1810 Phineas was head of household in Barnstead, over 45 years of age. His family consisted of spouse of same age group, four males, one under 10, one 10-16, one 16-26, one 26-45, and two females, one under 10, and one age 26-45. (Census Strafford Co., 1810, p532)

PHINEAS, b 14 Mar 1780, Kingston, s/o Jonathan and Sarah (Clifford) Young, d 1848, Barnstead, shipwright; m 11 Oct 1798, Belmont, Dorothy aka Dolly Jacobs [b 1782, Barnstead, d testate pre 15 Apr 1862, native town]. Phineas was head of household in Barnstead from 1830-1840: in 1830 his age was 40-50, as was his spouse, no children listed; in 1840 he and Dolly lived by themselves, ages 60-70 and 50-60, respectively. Dorothy, widow, lived alone in Barnstead from 1850-1860. At his mother's request Phineas was named Co-Admin. of his father's estate in Barnstead 14 Apr 1807, and was to receive a one-third share of the family homestead situated on parts of Lots 88 and 89, which were disposed of later by quitclaim. Phineas' earliest purchase of land in Barnstead was by deed signed 13 Oct 1800, rec'd 7 Feb 1806, for one acre land out of the s.e. corner of Lot 87, Div. 2, from Ezekial Eastman of Barnstead for $12.00; witnesses Moses Allard, John Stephens [Strafford Co. Deed 50:234]. In the sale of this one acre by deed signed 7 Jan, rec'd 7 Feb 1806, Phineas and Dolly received $200.00 from grantee Jonathan Allard of Barnstead; witnesses Nathaniel Hale, Henry Reed [Strafford Co. Deed 50:236]. Phineas and Dolly quitclaimed their one-third part of his father's estate in Barnstead as well as the one-third share of his mother's dower rights and "pews in the western meeting house in Barnstead" to David Edgerly of Gilmanton for $400.00, by deed signed 29 Jul 1807, rec'd 7 Sep 1808; witnesses for Phineas, Charles Hodgdon Jr., John Ham; witnesses for Dolly, Henry Parker, John Ham [Strafford Co. Deed 58:507]. "A certain lower pew in the western meeting house in Barnstead, being the first pew on the floor of broad alley on the left hand as you go in...which belonged to the heirs of Jonathan Young late of Barnstead," was quitclaimed by Phineas about two weeks later to Thomas Williams of Barnstead for $30.00, by deed signed 15 Aug, rec'd 29 Dec 1807; witnesses Benjamin Hodgdon, Jonathan Nutter [Strafford Co. Deed 56:230].

Widow Dorothy's will was drawn 9 Nov 1851, proved 15 Apr 1862, which devised the family homestead in Barnstead where she then dwelt to son Joseph C., and $5.00 to youngest son David; witnesses Oliver Dennett, Eunice Dennett, and Augustus Dennett [Belknap Co. Probate #1656]. Known ch. b Barnstead: Joseph C.+, b 11 Dec 1799; and David+, b 25 May 1803. (Merrill's Barnstead, p331; Jewett's Barnstead; Census Strafford Co., 1830, p15; 1840, p441; Census Belknap Co., 1850, p420; 1860, p330; NHVR-Marr)

PHOEBE EMELINE, b 1836, Wolfeboro, d/o Joseph and Patience (Chase) Young; m 9 Feb 1858, Tuftonboro, Stephen Piper [b ca 1835, Tuftonboro]. Known ch. b Tuftonboro: Sadie C. Piper, b ca 1860, m Joseph Blake; and Emma Jane Piper, b 1860s, m John Sanborn Bennett. (NHVR-Brides; Young Family Records, courtesy of Nancy L. Dodge)

PHOEBE J., b Apr 1824, ME, alive 1900, resident of Rochester, age 76. Her boarder was David W. Horam, b Jun 1853, MA, age 46. (1900 Soundex)

PLACENTIN, b 1822, of Meredith; head of household in Meredith in 1850, lived at resident-hotel. Members of his household may have been spouse and siblings: Emma A. Young, b 1825; Benjamin F. Young, b 1833; and Alexis E. Young, b 1843. (Census Belknap Co., 1850, p13)

POLLY, b ca 1780, of Dover, d/o James and Susan (Wood) Young; m (Intentions) 3 Jul 1802, m 6 Jul 1802, Barrington, Isaac Brock [b ca 1775, of Barrington]. (Ham Gen., p25; Hammond's Barrington TR, p27; NHVR-Brides)

POLLY, b 13 Apr 1780, Upper Gilmanton, d/o Capt. Joseph and Anna (Folsom) Young, alive 1821, native town; m 19 Feb 1800, Gilmanton, Allen Hackett [b ca 1775, of same town]. By Joseph Young's will drawn 12 Sep, proved 12 Oct 1821, Polly Hackett was named a daughter and heir-at-law; her husband Allen Hackett was also named a principal in probate. Polly was to receive the balance of the estate upon her mother's demise. For the parcel of land near the Academy House which Allen sold to Joseph Young by deed signed 12 Mar 1801, rec'd

23 Aug 1802, see entry on Polly's parents. (NHVR-Brides; NH Gazette, p169)

POLLY, b ca 1785, of Wolfeboro; m (Intentions) 29 Dec 1808, Wolfeboro, Tobias Pray [b ca 1780, of Brookfield]. (NHVR-Brides; Parker's Wolfeboro Banns, 1789-1854, n.p.)

POLLY, b 14 Apr 1791, Dover, d/o Ezra and Susannah (Demeritt) Young, d 9 May 1843, single, native town. Inasmuch as extensive documents were found on Polly, it was deemed feasible to provide a main entry for her. Polly aka Mary, single, became head of household in Dover in 1840, age 40-50; her household contained one other female of same age group, believed to be her sister Eliza. In failing health, Polly had her will drawn 25 Apr, proved 6 Jun 1843, in which she named John S. Durell her Exec. and [nephew] James C. Young to be residuary legatee; witnesses Nathaniel Young, Harry B. Buzzell and I. S. Durell [Strafford Co. Probate 59:1]. Admin. Papers on her estate in Dover were granted 6 Jun 1843 "with the will attached" to John S. H. Durell of Dover; bond of $2,000.00 was posted with sureties Nathaniel Young and John Hanson, both of Dover [Strafford Co. Probate 50:258]. She left these bequests: sister Eliza, one share of N.H. Strafford Bank, all interest from two other shares in said bank; [niece] Hannah S. Young the two shares in said bank after decease of Eliza; [niece] Mary Susan Young, two shares in said bank after Eliza's decease; [nephew] Jonathan T. Young, the same bequest; [said] James C. Young, the mahogany secretary and table, brass fire set, chaise and harness, feather bed, bolster, pillows, underbed, eight pr. sheets, 1 pr. blankets, 4 quilts, 6 table-cloths, large looking glass, high case of drawers, 7 silver spoons. One-half of a woodlot in Barrington was to be conveyed after Eliza's decease, "it being held in common and undivided with Eliza Young and was conveyed by Jonathan Young." Inventory of Polly's estate was made by John Durell, Nathaniel Young and John Hanson, all of Dover, returned 5 Sep 1843, accepted same date. Personal estate was assessed at $1,088.41. Real estate contained one half of hogs' house, $5.00; half of 66-2/3 acres land in Barrington, $666.67; and half of Pew No. 11 in the Congregational Meeting House, $37.50; total real estate, $1,797.57 [Strafford Co. Probate 59:495].

PRESTON B., b 1 Jun 1858, Farmington, s/o Jonathan and Hannah S. (Waldron) Young, d 31 Jul 1900, home town; m 14 Sep 1895, Farmington, Jennie C. Clark [b Jul 1859, Berwick, ME, d/o Hiram Clark, alive 1900, Farmington]. Preston lived with his parents in Farmington up through 1870. He had a varied career, at first taught school, then became physician and surgeon. He attended Austin Academy in Strafford which led to his teaching credential, teaching school for several terms. He then enrolled at Eastman's National Business College in Poughkeepsie, NY, after which he taught commercial school in Biddeford, ME. Preston later entered the University Medical College of New York City where he was graduated in 1888. He

started his practice of medicine in Berwick, ME where he lived
for six years, returning to Farmington by August of 1894 to
set up practice. Shortly thereafter, he and Jennie Clark were
married in his home town. In 1900 Preston, wife Jennie, and
young son John lived in Farmington; in household was servant
Bertha M. Lane, age 18 [b Mar 1882]. Ch. b Farmington: John
W. C., b Apr 1896, not traced further. (1900 Soundex; Biog.
Review, XXI, p350,351; NHVR-Deaths)

REBECCA, b ca 1825, of Dover; m 22 Apr 1847, Dover, James
S. Read [b ca 1820, of same town]. (NHVR-Brides)

REBECCA ANN, b ca 1840, Dover, d/o Ezra and Catherine N.
(Trednick) Young 2nd; m 19 Mar 1863, Dover, Edwin H. Varney
[b ca 1835, of Dover]. For guardianship papers of Rebecca Ann
and siblings see Admin. of her father's estate in 1846.
(NHVR-Brides)

REUBEN H., b ca 1790, Barrington, m 31 Aug 1813, Hannah
Simpson [b ca 1795, Barrington]. (NHVR-Marr; Barrington TR,
V6, p66)

RICHARD, b 1779, of Farmington; d 25 Nov 1854, age 75,
Farmington. (NHVR-Deaths)

RICHARD, b 1780s, of Alton; resident of Alton in 1830,
age 40-50, with spouse of same age group, and family of three
males, one each age 5-10, 10-15, 15-20, and six females, two
under 5, one age 5-10, one 10-15, and two 15-20. As early as
1816, Richard was resident of Alton. He and co-grantee Thomas
Perkins, both of Alton, bought 125 acres, a one undivided
fourth part of 500-acre Lot 14, Alton from Edward Minchen,
resident of England whose attorney was William Sheafe of
Portsmouth, Rock. Co., for $250.00 by quitclaim signed 28 Sep,
rec'd 28 Nov 1816,; witnesses Samuel Fernald, Nathaniel Pitman
[Strafford Co. Deed 93:15]. For Richard's mortgage and other
related deeds on Lot 14, refer to Strafford Co. Deeds 92:365;
92:417; and 92:422, which were not researched. (Census Strafford Co., 1830, p105)

RICHARD, b 1780s, of Dover; head of household in Dover
in 1840, age 50-60, family containing spouse age 50-60, and
three females, two age 10-15 and one age 15-20. (Census
Strafford Co., 1840, p554)

RICHARD, b 1789, of New Durham; resident of New Durham
in 1850, age 61, widower. Members of family were Mary Young,
age 27, Charlotte Young, age 7 [b 1843], and Richard Young,
age 5 [b 1845], the youngsters probably Richard's grandchildren. In 1860, Richard, age 15, shoemaker, lived with Daniel
and Rebecca Colomy in New Durham. Ch. b prob. New Durham:
Mary, b 1823. (Census Strafford Co., 1850, p586; 1860, p87)

RICHARD, b ca 1815, of Somersworth; m 9 Apr 1840, Somersworth, Mrs. Betsey (   ) Neally [b ca 1820, of same town].
(NHVR-Marr)

RICHARD, b ca 1825, of New Durham; m 26 Dec 1848, New
Durham, Mary Sophia Witham [b ca 1830, of same town]. Richard
and spouse resided in New Durham at time of their twins'
births. Ch. b New Durham: daughter, b 18 May 1852, twin, and

son, b same date, twin. (NHVR-Births, Marr; New Durham TR, 1791-1868, n.p.; LDS I.G.I. BR)

RICHARD, b Mar 1831, Canada, s/o Joseph C. and Lydia (   ) Young of Somersworth, d 25 Mar 1915, age 86-0-12, Somersworth, iron foundry worker; m 12 Mar 1859, Somersworth, Mary A. Frost [b Jun 1839, ME, poss. d/o Oliver Frost, d 12 Feb 1900, Somersworth]. Richard lived with his parents in 1860, age 20. By 1870, he was head of household, age 40; family members were spouse Mary and children Freddie and Lizzie, as well as George Horne, age 21 [b 1849], carpenter from Maine, and Annie E. Horne, age 18 [b 1852]. In 1900 he, wife Mary, son Fred, and granddaughter Celia, age 20 [b Feb 1880] resided at Union Street, Somersworth; Richard had kept his English-Canadian citizenship. It should be noted that dates of birth for Richard and Mary were derived from the 1900 Soundex, but cemetery records gave Richard's d-o-b as 1829, and Mary's as 1837. Richard and members of family were buried at Forest Glade Cemetery, Somersworth. Ch. b Somersworth: Mary J., b 1862, d 25 Apr 1935, age 73-11-19, Somersworth; Fred, b Sep 1862, twin?, alive 1900; and Lizzie A.+ (Young) Chesley, b 1865. (NHVR-Brides, Marr; Wooley's Somersworth Cemeteries, Bk 3, p121; Census Strafford Co., 1870, p357; 1900 Soundex)

RICHARD, b 1843, Parsonsfield, ME. As resident of Farmington at age 18, Richard enlisted in Co. K, 4th Regt., NH Volunteer Infantry on 3 Sep 1861 and mustered in 15 days later as Pvt. He reenlisted 15 Feb 1864, mustered in 28 Feb 1864, was captured at Drury's Bluff, VA, 16 May 1864, escaped 26 Feb 1865, and was discharged 15 Aug 1865 at Raleigh, NC. (Soldiers & Sailors, p205)

RICHARD BATCHELDER, b 17 May 1869 Barrington, s/o Andrew Huckins and Susan Elizabeth (Miles) Young, d 12 Apr 1927, NY.; m 23 Oct 1894, Dover, Flora E. Miller [b 15 Apr 1869, of Newport, KY, d 27 May 1933, Dover]. Richard was named a son and heir in Andrew H. Young's will signed 7 Dec 1890, proved 6 Jan 1891. He graduated from Dover High School, became an alumnus of the University of Ohio and Cincinnati Law Schools and made a career for himself in investment banking in New York City. He and Estella were buried at Pine Hill Cemetery, Dover. (Ham Gen., p61; Frost's Dover Cem., V1, #535)

RICHARD K., b ca 1808, of Wakefield; m ca 1830, Isadore (   ) [b ca 1813, of Wakefield]. Ch. b Wakefield: James M.+, b 1833. (NHVR-Births)

RICHARD KIMBALL, b 1789, Rochester, s/o James and Mary (Kimball) Young of Wakefield, alive 1870, Rochester, farmer; m 27 Nov 1817, Wolfeboro, Deborah S. Fernald [b 1793, Wolfeboro, d/o John Fernald, d pre 1870, Rochester]. As early as 1820, Richard was taxpayer of Wakefield, listed in Highway District No. 4 in the same neighborhood as his father, and on 11 Mar 1834, was listed as an eligible voter for the town meeting that spring. In 1830 he was listed on the census returns for Wakefield, age 40-50, with spouse age 30-40, two males under 5, three females, two age 5-10, one 10-15, and one female age 50-60. In the following decade Richard and family settled in Rochester where he was listed as head of household in 1840 and 1860: in 1840 his age was 40-50, with spouse of similar years, and family of three males, one age 5-10, two 10-15, and two females, one age 15-20, one 20-30. In 1860 Deborah was named as his spouse; children at home, Samuel N., James and Mary E. In 1870, Richard K., widower, was member of son John F.'s household in Rochester.

Wife Deborah and her siblings John W. Fernald, William Fernald, Abigail Nute, Sally Cotton of Wolfeboro and James Fernald of Durham purchased from their father John Fernald, 200 acres comprising the family homestead in Brookfield by the Wolfeboro line where their father then lived for $3,000.00, daughters to have three-ninths shares and sons, six-ninths shares, by deed signed 6 Jan 1824, rec'd 24 Jan 1828; witnesses William Cotton, Hannah Lucas [Strafford Co. Deed 135:555].

Richard bought Lots 23 and 24, 2nd Div., Wakefield, which he sold in turn. With respect to Lot 24, "the one undivided moiety of land in Wakefield, south by Lot 23, 2nd Div., being one-half of the land and buildings of the farm on which I formerly lived" adjacent to neighbors Nathaniel Mescove, Joshua Hall and John Campernell, was sold to James Young Jr. [brother] of Wakefield for $500.00 by deed signed 4 Mar 1830, rec'd 21 Nov 1831; witnesses William Sawyer, Lewis Dearborn [Strafford Co. Deed 152:185]. With respect to Lot 23, Richard K., wife Deborah F., James Young III [brother] and wife Aurelia, and Paul Young, all of Wakefield, quitclaimed this lot to Ezra Wentworth of Farmington for $975.00; original title to Grantors was dated 19 Jun 1822, said deed not rec'd [Strafford Co. Deed 114:416]; Deborah F. conveyed dower rights by deed signed 11 Mar 1835, rec'd day after; witnesses Benjamin Cook, James Young [Strafford Co. Deed 164:82]. When of Wakefield he purchased Lot 44, 2nd Div., Brookfield from Thomas Young of Wakefield by deed signed 29 Sep 1823, rec'd day after; see Thomas and Mary Young of Wakefield for details.

Ch. b Wakefield: John F.+, b 16 Sep 1816; and Samuel N.+, b 1832. Ch. b Rochester: James+, b 1835; and Mary E., b 1841. (NHVR-Marr, Deaths; Census Strafford Co., 1830, p458; 1840, p521; 1860, p506; 1870, p241; Banks' Wakefield, p83,679; under 1870 Census Records, son John F.'s y-o-b was given as 1827)

RICHARD PEACOCK, b ca 1778, of Wakefield; m 1 Mar 1803, same town, Rebecca Cheney [b ca 1783, Wakefield]. (Wakefield TR, V1)

ROBERT A., b Mar 1856 [Census] or 1854 [Cem. Rec.], England, s/o James and Mary (Oldcroft) Young [no main entry], painter, d 1931, Dover, naturalized citizen; m 12 Jun 1895, Dover, Mary Anna Bowser [b Mar 1872, Nova Scotia, d/o George E. and Charlotte L. (   ) Bowser, d 1948, Dover]. Robert, Mary and infant sons lived at Pierce St., Dover in 1900; their home held five lodgers, names not given. They and sons were buried at Pine Hill Cemetery, Dover. Ch. b Dover, not traced further: Robert H. aka Harold R., b 27 Dec 1896, d 1942, Dover; and James H., b 9 Dec 1898, d____, Dover. (NHVR-Marr; Births; Frost's Dover Cem., V2, Plot #1606; 1900 Soundex)

ROBY B., b Apr 1869, RI. Roby was resident of Barnstead in 1900, age 31, and lived with boarder Charles E. Rand [n.d.]. (1900 Soundex)

RODOLPHA, b 1780s, of Ossipee. She was head of household in Ossipee in 1830, age 40-50. Household contained male age 40-50, three males, two under 5, one 5-10, and two females, one 10-15, one 15-20. (Census Strafford Co., 1830, p421)

ROLAND V., b May 1865, ME, alive 1900, Belmont; m ca 1885, ME, Lomena (   ) [b Dec 1869, ME, alive in 1900, Belmont]. In 1900 Roland, Lomena and their three children lived in Belmont. Ch. b ME: Howard M., b Dec 1889; Julia B., b Feb 1892; and Marshie E., b Sep 1894. (1900 Soundex)

ROSE ELLEN, b 22 Jan 1863, Freedom, d 22 Sep 1865, age 2-8-0, Freedom, buried at Lake View Cemetery. (NHVR-Deaths)

ROWLAND aka Jr., b ca 1648, York, York Co., MA [Maine in 1820], s/o Rowland and Johanna (Knight) Young, d testate pre 2 Jan 1721/22, York; m ca 1669, Oyster River [Durham Point], Susannah Mathews [b ca 1655, Oyster River, d/o Walter and Mary (   ) Mathews, alive 14 Sep 1719, York]. Either Roland Sr. or Roland Jr. became the progenitor of the York County branch of Youngs. Rowland Jr. received a "tract adjoining the home-stall of their father [maternal grandfather] Robert Knight," by deed of Roland Sr., rec'd 25 Aug 1685. He was named heir-at-law of his mother by her will probated 20 Jun 1698. Walter Mathews was son of emigrant Francis and Thamarsin (   ) Mathews from England, one of the earliest families to settle in Dover. Susannah and three children Joseph, Matthew and Mary were named as heirs-at-law of Walter Mathews by his will drawn 15 Apr 1678, proved 25 Jun 1678; witnesses Amey Downe, Richard Gumer [NH State Papers, V31, p211]; Susannah's spouse was not named. Rowland and family lived on the Isles of Shoals for a time and then returned to York. Rowland's will of 14 Sep 1719, proved 2 Jan 1721/22, named wife Susannah, the three children cited above, and their fourth and youngest child Susannah as heirs-at-law. Ch. b York: Mary, b ca 1670; Joseph, b ca 1672; Mathews, b ca 1674; and Susannah, b ca 1678. [Noyes et al, p469,776,777; Quint's Hist. Memos, p80; Pope's Pioneers, p244)

RUFUS, b 1769, Ossipee; m ca 1815, Ossipee, Nancy Blodgett [b 1789, Strafford]. Ch. b Strafford: Erastus+, b 1819. (NHVR-Marr)

RUTH, b ca 1792, Upper Gilmanton, d/o Eleazer and Hannah (Bailey) Young, alive 26 Feb 1864, Belmont; m 5 Sep 1813, Belmont, Bradford Hadley [b ca 1785, of Gilmanton]. Ruth Hadley was referred to as sister and heir-at-law in Admin. Papers on Polly Young's estate on 26 Feb 1864; Polly was d/o Eleazer and Hannah cited above. (NHVR-Brides)

RUTH C., b 20 Feb 1852, Wakefield, d/o James C. and Rose-mandel (Gill) Young, d 13 Nov 1932, Methuen, MA; m 24 Dec 1885, Brookfield, John S. Weeks [b 24 Oct 1850, Brookfield, s/o Nathan C. and Anna J. ( ) Weeks, d 12 Mar 1916, Derry]. Ch. b Brookfield: Ralph A. Weeks, b 1888, d 1969, Wakefield; m ca 1915, Wakefield, Maude W. Pike [b 1880, Wakefield, d 1963, home town]. Both Ralph and Maude were buried at Lovell Lake Cemetery, Wakefield. (NHVR-Brides; Twombly's Wakefield Cem., TMs; Young Family Recs., courtesy of Alden N. Young)

RUTH E., b 12 Sep 1866, Barrington, d/o John E. and Clara A. (Hodgdon) Young, alive Sep 1889, Dover; m 27 Sep 1884, Dover, George H. Furbush [b ca 1860, of same town]. Ruth E. Furbush was named as daughter of John E. and granddaughter of Jonathan and Sophia (Ricker) Young by Sophia's will of 3 Sep, proved 5 Nov 1889. (NHVR-Brides)

SALLEY, b ca 1805, of Meredith; m 23 Mar 1829, Gilford, Asa D. Peabody [b ca 1800, of Meredith]. (NHVR-Brides)

SALLY, b 1778, Wolfeboro, d/o Benjamin and 1st wife Phoebe (Allen) Young, d 1850, native town; m 9 Oct 1798, Wolfeboro, Richard Tibbetts [b ca 1775, of same town]. Sally Tibbetts was named a daughter and heir of Benjamin Young of Wolfeboro by his will signed 6 Nov 1843, proved 30 Feb 1849. (NHVR-Brides; Young Family Recs., courtesy of Nancy L. Dodge)

SALLY, b ca 1778, Barrington; m 29 Jan 1798, Barrington, Israel Tasker [b ca 1775, Barrington]. (Barrington TR, V6, p42; NHVR-Brides)

SALLY, b ca 1795, Strafford, d/o Jonathan and Mary (Hill) Young; m 3 Jul 1816, at Freewill Baptist Church, Strafford, Ezra M. Drown [b ca 1790, Rochester]. Sally Drown was named an heir in Jonathan Young [Sr.]'s will of 8 Dec 1844, proved 2 Sep 1851. Husband Ezra M. Drown was named as Admin. of the estate of her brother Jonathan Young [Jr.] on 7 Jan 1851, inasmuch as Jonathan's estate "had not before been admin-istered on." (Strafford Marr, **Reg.** 76:28)

SALLY, b 30 Nov 1801, Barnstead; m 27 Nov 1821, Barn-stead, Isaac Jacobs [b ca 1795, of same town]. (NHVR-Brides)

SALLY, b 1 Jul 1807, Middleton. (LDS I.G.I. BR)

SALLY, b ca 1825, of Somersworth; m 10 Feb 1848, Somers-worth, Harrison Drew [b ca 1820, of Somersworth]. (NHVR-Brides)

SALLY B., b ca 1807, prob. Alton, d/o Levi and 1st wife Sally (Barker) Young, res. of New Durham; m 24 Nov 1825, New Durham, Alva B. Davis [b ca 1800, of Middleton]. Sally was known by her married name of Davis in Levi Young's will drawn 27 Apr 1841, proved 1 Jan 1850. (NHVR-Brides)

SAMUEL, b ca 1700, Dover Neck, s/o Thomas and Mary (Roberts) Young, d pre 27 May 1761, Parish of Madbury, Dover; m ca 1725, Dover, Hannah ( ) [b ca 1705, Dover]. Samuel was named as son and heir of Thomas Young of Dover by deed of gift dated 16 Mar 1726/7, rec'd 27 May 1727/8, and received a one-fifth share of land in Rochester, held in common with four brothers; for disposal of his share in 1730, see John and

Elizabeth Young of Dover. He was listed on the 1732 Town Census of Dover, having signed Petition to Jonathan Belcher, and on date of 8 Jul 1734, was granted a two-thirds share of Lot 136, Dover by a vote of the legislature. He and Hannah lived in that section of Dover that became the Parish of Madbury. He was one of the original proprietors of Middleton, drawing Lot 25 by Draft of Lots dated 11 Apr 1750. Military service saw him in the N.H. 5th Regt., captained by Paul Gerrish, on the expedition to Crown Point made in early Fall, 19 Sep through 1 Dec 1755. Potter's Military History gave this account of the expedition: "This regiment marched to Albany by way of Number Four but was in no active service, being discharged in December, at which time the campaign ended."

Samuel's will was written 4 Jun 1755 because he was mindful of "Being bound on the Expedition to Crown Point and not knowing whether I may return to my family again," will proved 27 May 1761; witnesses Joseph Hanson, Solomon Hanson and John Hanson [NH State Papers 35:307]. His wife Hannah was named Exec. of the estate and was to receive the use and improvement of his whole estate real and personal during her widowhood or "at least until she shall marry another man, then to share only as the law directs as to widow's dower." Eldest son Noah received a 1/16th share of Paul Gerrish's sawmill and a one-half share in the Middle Township at the head of Rochester; sons Samuel and Jonathan to receive the homestead farm where the family then dwelt in Dover; and sons Moses and John, each a fourth share of the land in the Middle Township, held in common with Noah. Daughters Lydia Perkins, Kezia Young and Susanna Young were each to receive 150 pounds Old Tenor and shares of the household goods and furniture at the discretion of their mother. Inventory on the estate was taken by Paul Gerrish and Solomon Hanson 18 Aug 1761, rated at 4,044 pounds and 15 shillings [NH Prov. Probate 22:209].

Widow Hannah, son Samuel and his wife Elizabeth sold in fee simple their share and interest in 15 acres land that was part of Samuel Young Sr.'s estate in the Parish of Madbury, bounded by lands of Daniel Young, James Young and John Bussell, to Benjamin Evans of Madbury for 1,150 pounds, Hannah Young and Elizabeth Young both ceding dower rights, by deed signed 26 Mar 1762, rec'd 13 Dec 1763; witnesses Humphrey Hanson and Ephraim Hanson who "gave evidences" for Samuel Young [Jr.] and Mrs. Hannah Young [NH Prov. Probate 71:340]. Samuel Young Sr.'s whole share of land in Rochester was sold by deed signed 9 Nov 1762, rec'd 21 Mar 1771, by those who then held share and interest in it for 70 pounds Old Tenor: Hannah, widow of Samuel, John Young and Noah Young, son Moses presumed to be deceased as of that date. Those who gave evidences for Hannah Young in latter deed were Moses Ham and Jonathan Hayes [NH Prov. Deed 90:359]. Widow Hannah and son Samuel, yeoman of Madbury, sold in fee simple to Benjamin Evans of Dover, yeoman, all their interest and title in the estate of Samuel [Sr.], 14 acres land, orchards and buildings in Madbury where they then dwelt, by deed signed 16 Feb, rec'd 22 Oct 1765, for 433 pounds Old Tenor; witnesses Ebenezer and Hannah Demeritt [NH Prov. Deed 82:179].

Son John, alive 1762, apparently single, sold during the administration of his father's estate his one-fourth share of the land in Middleton by deed dated 9 Nov 1762, rec'd 21 Mar 1771; Daniel Young, witness, gave "evidence" for John Young that he was an heir of Samuel Young. In 1760 John served in the N.H. Militia as a family point of honor. His brother Jonathan had enrolled in Capt. Samuel Gerrish's Co., No. 1, which was part of the regiment sent on the invasion of Canada on 8 Mar 1760. When Jonathan deserted 19 July at the "15-mile post," John joined the regiment in Jonathan's stead, beginning in September that year, then mustered out 27 Nov 1760 at the close of the campaign. Ch. b Parish of Madbury: Noah+, b ca 1732; Samuel+, b 25 Apr 1734; and the following b 1730s, Jonathan, Moses, John, Lydia (Young) Perkins, Kezia, and Susannah. (NHVR-Births; Potter's Mil. Hist., V1, p237; Tibbetts Gen., TMs, p283; Holbrook's 1732 Census, p74,75; Charters, NH State Papers, V27, p498)

SAMUEL, b 25 Apr 1734, Parish of Madbury, s/o Samuel and Hannah (   ) Young of Dover, alive 1790, Barrington, bur. Strafford, n.d.: m ca 1762, Dover, Elizabeth aka Betsey (   ) [b ca 1740, of Dover, bur. Strafford, n.d.]. Named as son and heir in his father's will drawn 4 Jun 1755, proved 27 May 1761, Samuel received a one-half share of the family homestead in Dover. By 1763, Samuel and Elizabeth had relocated in Barrington [that section that became Strafford in 1820] where they raised six children. In 1790 he was head of household in Barrington with one son over 16 years of age, two sons under 16, and two females [one, his wife]. Samuel and spouse sold their share and interest in land in Madbury that was adjacent to James Young's land during Admin. of Samuel Sr.'s estate, by deed signed 26 Mar 1762, rec'd 13 Dec 1763. Samuel then disposed of his share in his father's homestead by deed signed 16 Feb 1765, rec'd 22 Oct 1765. For further details see parents' entry.

Samuel and brother Noah were co-grantees in the purchase of 120 acres land in Barrington, Lot 202, 5th Range by deed signed and rec'd 12 Mar 1760. In a later deed signed and rec'd 22 Mar 1762, the brothers divided the property, Samuel receiving 60 acres at the n.e. part lying next to the 4th Range; see Noah Young for both deeds. Samuel of Madbury sold his land holding in Barrington, Lot 201, 5th Range, drawn to the original right of Samuel Winkley, to Stephen Hawkins of Barrington for 450 pounds Old Tenor, by deed signed 14 Apr, rec'd 9 May 1761; witnesses Arthur Danielson, Daniel Young [NH Prov. Deed 62:505]. For Samuel's purchase of the 48-acre Lot 130, Range 3, Barrington from brother Moses in 1787, see Moses and Lucy Young of Barrington. Samuel mortgaged these 48 acres by deed signed 27 Apr 1789, rec'd 9 Dec 1793, to Joshua Foss

3rd of Barrington for 27 pounds-18 shillings, payable within four years; witnesses Jonathan Montgomery, Mark Foss [Strafford Co. Deed 17:106]. Mortgage on Lot 130, Range 3 was redeemed by deed of 23 Dec 1793, rec'd 27 Mar 1801, for 27 pounds-18 shillings; witnesses George Foss 3rd, Samuel Hale [Strafford Co. Deed 34:367]. On the following day, by deed of 24 Dec 1793, rec'd 27 Mar 1801, he sold the whole of 48-acre Lot 130 to the said George Foss for 81 pounds; witnesses Samuel Hale, Joshua Foss [Strafford Co. Deed 34:368]. Samuel and Betsey were buried at Perkins Cemetery, Route 126, Strafford, no dates given, in family plot where Samuel's son Moses and grandchildren were buried.

Ch. b Barrington: Moses+, b 11 Oct 1763, Susannah, b 7 Oct 1766, Elijah, b 24 Apr 1769, Isaac, b 8 May 1772, Jonathan, b 9 Nov 1774, and John, b 17 Nov 1778. (Barrington TR, V6, p681; NHVR-Births; Census Strafford Co., 1790, p87; Stiles' Cemeteries, Grid 4E-1, p165)

SAMUEL aka Jr., b ca 1766, of Barrington; head of family in Barrington in 1810, age 26-45, household consisting of spouse under 45 years, two males, one age 10-16, one 16-26, and three females, one age 10-16 and two 16-26. (Census Strafford Co., 1810, p504)

SAMUEL, b 1852, Standish, ME, s/o George Young [no main entry], res. of Rochester, mechanic; m 14 Feb 1873, Rochester, Annie McNerton aka McThornton [b 1854, Boston, MA]. (Rochester TR, Marr, n.p.; NHVR-Marr)

SAMUEL BURLEIGH, b 28 Apr 1784, prob. Wolfeboro [Addition], s/o John and Mary (Burleigh) Young of Newfields, d 2 Apr 1834, of exposure, Wolfeboro, age 50; m (Intentions) 10 Mar 1807, m 12 Mar 1807, Ossipee, Nancy Burleigh [b 1787, Wolfeboro, d/o William and Nancy (   ) Burleigh, d 31 Mar 1860, Ossipee]. Samuel was born in that part of Ossipee which became known as the Wolfeboro Addition ca 1800, and attended the Freewill Baptist Church. From 1810-1830, he was listed as head of family on census returns for Wolfeboro. In 1810 his age was 16-26 years, with spouse of similar years, one male under 10, and one female age 10-16; in 1830 both he and wife were age 40-50, household containing six males, one under 5, one age 5-10, three 10-15, and one 15-20. Nancy as widow in 1840 most likely lived with son Nathaniel who was head of family in Wolfeboro. In 1850 Nancy and sons Nathaniel, John and Alonzo lived with her sister Sally (Burleigh) Young and brother-in-law William Young in Wolfeboro.

One of Samuel's earliest purchases of land was 116 acres in the western part of 500-acre Lot 2, Wolfeboro by lands of Richard Glover and Moses Brown from his father John by deed signed 7 Mar 1806, rec'd 12 Feb 1808; see John and Mary Young of Wolfeboro for more details. His next purchase was 100 acres of land in the Wolfeboro Addition abutting the s.w. corner of John Young's farm [believed to be his father], by deed signed 14 Jul 1807, rec'd 12 Feb 1808, from Michael Reade of Dover for $500.00; witnesses A. Baker, Michael Reade Jr.

[Strafford Co. Deed 56:460]. His next land deed conveyed 50 acres of Lot 5, Wolfeboro by s.e. corner of land of John C. Young [brother], then running n.w. by the Wolfeboro old line by land of William Young [brother] by deed signed 6 Nov 1809, rec'd 17 Apr 1811, to grantee James Burleigh of Wolfeboro for $300.00; witnesses Mark Wiggin, Moses Humton [Strafford Co. Deed 67:214]. Samuel B. was also co-grantee with brothers John C. and William in the purchase of "the front 100 acres" in the Wolfeboro Addition as part of the 300 acres drawn to the right of Jonathan Warner by deed signed and rec'd 9 Feb 1815; see John C. Young, b ca 1782 for full details.

The following three land transactions by Samuel B. are representative land deeds from 1810-1822: sale of 25 acres of Lot 1, Wolfeboro, adjacent to lands of John Bickford, Michael Reade, William Young and Joseph Hawkins, to Nancy Keay of Ossipee for $100.00, by quitclaim signed 4 Mar 1820, rec'd 30 Apr 1827; witnesses Thomas B. Wiggin, Mark Wiggin [Strafford Co. Deed 133:51]; sale of 87 acres of land in Ossipee which belonged to the heirs of William Burleigh as laid out to Nancy Burleigh [Nancy's mother], with Nancy ceding dower rights, by deed signed 6 Jun 1822, rec'd 12 Dec 1824, to John Sceggel Jr. of Ossipee for $155.00; witnesses Mark Wiggin, John Young [Strafford Co. Deed 123:173]; and purchase of an additional 11 acres of Lot 2, Wolfeboro, next to land of Adam Brown and between lands owned by Joseph Young and himself, from the said Joseph Young for $56.00, by deed signed 6 Jul 1822, rec'd 17 Feb 1825; witnesses Aaron Roberts, Samuel Tebbetts [Strafford Co. Deed 124:268].

Admin. Papers on Samuel B.'s estate were filed 3 May 1834 by John Burleigh of Ossipee, having given bond of $3,000 with sureties George Stevens and Nathaniel Burleigh [Strafford Co. Probate 30:298]. The homestead farm consisted of 250 acres valued at $1,500.00; personal estate was set at $554.00, per inventory and appraisal made on 14 May 1834 by John C. Young and Aaron Roberts, both of Wolfeboro, and Nathaniel Ambrose of Ossipee; allowed same date [Strafford Co. Probate 48:11]. The home possessed a loom and linen wheel and one looking glass. An allowance of $250.00 was granted to widow Nancy on 16 May 1834 after she had petitioned two days earlier [Strafford Co. Probate 43:59]. Nancy's dower rights were determined by Aaron Roberts, John C. Young and Daniel Martin, all of Wolfeboro, on 10 Jun 1834, allowed 20 Jan 1835 [Strafford Co. Probate 49:290]; out of Samuel's 225-1/2 acre homestead farm in Wolfeboro bounded s.w. by land of William Young, John W. Fernald and Timothy Watson, s.e. by land of Joseph Hawkins and Michael Reed, n.e. by land of John W. Bickford, Adam Brown and Moses P. Brown, and n.w. by land of said Adam Brown and Joseph Young, Nancy was to receive 53 acres with part of the house and barn, the hogshouse, and household privileges [Strafford Co. Probate 49:290].

When it was established that Samuel's estate was insolvent, Aaron Roberts of Wolfeboro was sworn in as Commissioner

14 Nov 1834 to administrate all claims against the estate; he made his return 20 Jan 1835, allowed same date [Strafford Co. Probate 51:135]. 36 notes of hand totalling $829.30 were allowed in full. Petition for License to Sell was initiated 2 Dec 1834 by the said John Burleigh in order to raise $600.00 for debts against the estate, approved 20 Jan 1835 [Strafford Co. Probate 24:314]. Said Burleigh returned his account 13 May 1836, allowed same date [Strafford Co. Probate 51:55]. Debts which he charged himself with came to $1,183.59; this included the widow's allowance, sundry debts, admin. expenses and articles inventoried but not sold. Credits of personal estate per inventory, sale of real estate, cash collected on bills, gain on sale of personal estate and income for year 1834 totalled $1,231.33; balance of $47.74 due from Admin. Samuel and Nancy were buried at Old Cemetery, Ossipee.

Ch. b Wolfeboro: Nathaniel+, b 27 Oct 1810; John, b 1822, single, d 7 Aug 1890, age 68, Ossipee; and Alonzo, b Aug 1824, d 7 Jan 1911, single, age 87, Ossipee. (Census Strafford Co., 1810, p737; 1830, p436; 1840, p386; Carroll Co., 1850, p365; Morning Star, p376; NHVR-Births, Marr, Deaths; Ossipee TR, V1; Merrill's Carroll Co., p364; Loud's Cem. Records, p129; Parker's Wolfeboro Banns, 1789-1854, n.p.)

SAMUEL E., b 3 Jun 1822, of Meredith, d testate 10 Jun 1894, Laconia, widower; m 31 Oct 1853, Meredith, Katherine aka Catherine J. Parker [b 3 Oct 1824, Meredith, d/o Isaac W. and Abigail (Parsons) Parker, d 3 Jan 1887, age 63-3-0, Laconia]. Samuel E.'s will was drawn 20 Apr, proved 14 Jun 1894, naming John E. Jewett as Exec.; witnesses William A. Plummer, Idella M. Drew, and Mrs. Carrie L. Howe [Belknap Co. Probate #5253]. Samuel E.'s estate was so devised that a three-fourths share would go to Samuel's niece Mrs. Nellie M. Carter of Concord, NH, and a one-fourth share to go to his late wife's niece Ellen Parker of Sherborn, MA. Family heirlooms were devised to Marshall P. Hall of Manchester and the said Ellen Parker. Family members were buried at Meredith Bridge Cemetery, Laconia. Ch. b Meredith: Nellie Francis, b 1855, d 10 Apr 1871, Meredith. (Hanaford's Cemeteries, TMs, p22; NHVR-Marr, Deaths)

SAMUEL L., b ca 1795, of Gilmanton; head of household in Gilmanton in 1840, age 40-50, with family of spouse age 30-40, one male age 15-20, and three females, one under 5 and two age 10-15. (Census Strafford Co., 1840, p411)

SAMUEL L., b 1826, of Gilford, tailor, d pre 1900, Laconia; m 1860s, Gilford, Mary C. ( ) [b Oct 1838, of Gilford, alive 1900, Laconia]. Samuel and Mary lived in Gilford in 1870 with child Cora J. In 1900 Mary C., widow, age 61, lived at Church Street, Laconia with daughter Cora J., age 32. Ch. b Gilford: Cora J., b Mar 1868. (Census Belknap Co., 1870, p2; 1900 Soundex)

SAMUEL M., b ca 1825, of Nottingham; m 14 Aug 1856, Moultonboro, Ann R. Hanson [b ca 1830, of Moultonboro]. (NHVR-Marr)

SAMUEL M., b 1828, of Meredith in 1860, hostler; m ca 1858, Ruth A. (   ) [b 1830, of Meredith, alive 1860, same town]. Ch. b Meredith: Martin, b 1859, Meredith. (Census Belknap Co., 1860, p406)

SAMUEL N., b 1832, Wakefield, s/o Richard Kimball and Deborah S. (Fernald) Young; m 27 Nov 1859, Somersworth, Mary L. Watson [b 1839, Somersworth, d pre 1870, prob. Rochester]. In 1870 Samuel N., single, lived with brother John F.+ in Rochester. (NHVR-Marr)

SAMUEL P., b ca 1802, Farmington, s/o Joseph and Sarah (Pinkham) Young, d pre 1827, native town; m 22 Oct 1820, Farmington, Abigail B. Rand [b ca 1800, Farmington, d pre 1843, home town]. Abigail m2 3 Jun 1827, Farmington, Nathaniel Burnham Roberts, widower [b 4 Aug 1799, of Farmington, d 14 Jun 1886, same town]. Roberts' first marriage was to Leah Hayes on 29 Jun 1823 [b 16 Mar 1800, d/o Ichabod and Deborah (French) Hayes, died in childbirth 22 Nov 1825, buried in Pine Grove Cemetery, Farmington]. Nathaniel Roberts m3 26 Apr 1843, Farmington, Nancy Waldron, widow of John Thurston. There were no children by Abigail. Ch. b Farmington by Nancy Roberts: Leah Roberts, b ca 1845. (NHVR-Brides; Farmington TR, V1, p409,415; Hayes Gen., V1, p277)

SAMUEL P., b 12 Nov 1814, Barnstead Center, s/o Jonathan and Sukey (Pitman) Young, d pre 18 Nov 1873, native town, millwright; m1 6 Jan 1839, Barnstead; Betsey A. Merrill [b 1814, of Barnstead, d 1856, same town]; m2 post 1856, Barnstead, Lynthia Reynolds [b 1831, of Barnstead, d pre 1863, same town]; m3 14 Mar 1863, Barnstead, Mary J. Otis [b 1820, of Barnstead, alive 1870, same town]. In 1835 Samuel P. operated the mills on the Pieno stream. He was head of household in Barnstead in 1840, age 20-30 with bride of same age group, no child as yet. Samuel and Betsey were listed on census returns for Barnstead in 1850 with son Hanson H., age 7, and Nancy Young, age 63 [b 1787] as members of household. In 1870 Samuel P. lived with third spouse Mary J. and son by first marriage, Charles, age 13. Upon Samuel's death, son Charles M., minor over 14 years of age, elected as guardian Oliver H. P. Young of Barnstead [uncle, brother of Samuel P.] on 18 Nov 1873, approved 17 Feb 1874 [Belknap Co. Probate #2826]. Ch. b Barnstead by first wife Betsey: Hanson H.+, b 1 Dec 1843; Betty A.+ aka Bessie A. (Young) Palmer, b ca 1851; and Charles M., b 1857. (Census Strafford Co., 1840, p444; Census Belknap Co., 1850, p408; 1870, p27; Merrill's Barnstead, p332; NHVR-Births, Brides, Marr)

SAMUEL P., b ca 1830, of Middleton; m 2 May 1852, Middleton, Clara A. Stevens [b ca 1832, of Middleton]. In 1850 Samuel, single, lived at the home of Enoch York, age 65 [b 1785] and spouse Sarah York, age 63 [b 1787] in Middleton. See following entry for some similarities of background. (NHVR-Marr; Census Strafford Co., 1850, p101)

SAMUEL P. aka Jr., b Jul 1831, New Durham, s/o Joel and Mary J. (Durgin) Young of Farmington, alive 1900, Middleton, age 69; m1 3 Nov 1850, Middleton, Martha A. Stevens [b 1836, Middleton, alive 1870, same town]; m2 4 Jan 1874, Middleton, Sarah W. (Coleman) Stevens, [b 1832, Dover, d/o Oliver J. and Mehitable (   ) Coleman, d 6 Feb 1892, Middleton, her 2nd marriage]; m3 29 Sep 1892, Mary A. (Parsons) Lougee, widow [b Jul 1828, Acton, ME, d/o William Parsons, alive 1900, Middleton]. Before his first marriage in November 1850, the census that year listed Samuel as member of household of Ebenezer and Sally Blazo of Middleton. Samuel and first wife Martha were listed as residents of Middleton from 1860-1870: in 1860 children at home were Charles, Susan A., Alvina and Alberto; in 1870 members of family were Samuel's widowed mother Mary J. and children Charles, Ella E. and Lester. In 1900 he and third wife Mary A. lived by themselves in Middleton. Ch. b Middleton by Martha: Charles H., b 1852; Alvina, b 14 Oct 1854, d.y.; Susan A., b 1855, d.y.; Ella E., b 1858; and Alberto aka Lester A.+, b Apr 1860. (Census Strafford Co., 1850, p99,100; 1860, p58; 1870, p203; 1900 Soundex; LDS I.G.I. BR; NHVR-Births, Marr, Deaths)

SAMUEL S., b 18 Jan 1794, Gilmanton, carpenter, s/o Joseph and Betsey (Shaw) Young, d testate 18 Feb 1889, age 95-1-0, Gilmanton, widower; m 28 Feb 1822, Loudon, Mary Diamond aka Dimond [b 1794, Loudon, d/o Isaac Diamond, d 24 Jan 1880, Gilmanton]. Samuel and Mary began their married life with a homestead farm in Gilmanton. Family tradition has it that in order to pay off encumbrances on the farm, Samuel and spouse relocated in Lowell, MA, where he found steady work as a carpenter, only to return to Gilmanton by 1830 where he was able to accumulate other property. He was head of household in Gilmanton from 1830-1870. In 1830 he was 30-40 years, with spouse of same age group and family of one other female 50-60, one male age 5-10, and three females, two under 5, one age 5-10. In 1860 Mary was named as his spouse; single daughter Mary A., school teacher lived at home. In 1870 they lived alone.

Samuel S.'s will was drawn 29 Jan 1868, proved 19 Mar 1889, naming wife Mary D. his Exec. and daughter Mary A. Lougee his residuary legatee; witnesses Thomas Cogswell Jr., Rufus W. Lamprey, Charles G. Tibbetts [Belknap Co. Probate #4475]. He devised to wife Mary D. the use and income of all real and personal estate during her natural life; after her death the property would revert to daughter Mary A. Lougee. Daughter Sarah Davis was to receive $500.00; her children Samuel Y. Davis and George H. Davis were each to receive $100.00. It is to be noted the only surviving heirs identified during probate were daughters Mary A. Lougee and Sarah Davis. Samuel, Mary, daughters Judith B. Young and Abbie C. Davis were buried at Guinea Ridge Cemetery, Gilmanton.

Ch. b Gilmanton: Isaac D.+, b 29 Dec 1822; Judith B., b 1823, d 28 Dec 1832, Gilmanton; Mary A.+ (Young) Lougee, b 21 Dec 1829; Sarah (Young) Davis, b ca 1830, wife of H. A. Davis of Laconia, d 20 Mar 1896; and Abbie C. (Young) Davis,

b 1832, wife of George N. Davis of Farmington, d 11 Jun 1862.
(Census Strafford Co., 1830, p277; Census Belknap Co., 1860,
p233; 1870, p15; Folsom's NH Cemeteries, p142; Bio. Review,
XXI, p45,454,455; NHVR-Brides, Marr, Deaths)

SAMUEL T., b 10 Aug 1852, Rochester, s/o Thomas and
Sabrina (Wentworth) Young, shoemaker, alive 1888, Portsmouth;
m1 1870s, Farmington, Dorcas J. Furbush [b 1851, Lebanon, ME,
alive 1882, Rochester]; m2 30 Sep 1888, Portsmouth, Nellie M.
Foss [b 1858, Madbury, d/o Horace and Betsey (   ) Foss]. Son
Sidney S. m 1894, Rochester, Shuella Towle [b 1875, Farming-
ton, d/o John W. and Mary (Goldsmith) Towle of New Durham].
Ch. b Lebanon, ME by Dorcas: Sidney S., b 1874. Ch. b Farm-
ington: daughter, b 2 Jan 1875. Ch. b Rochester: daughter
M. C., b 2 Jan 1878; Winnie L., b 17 Jul 1882, d 1 Nov 1884,
age 2-3-15, Rochester. (Rochester TR, Deaths, p45; LDS I.G.T.
BR; NHVR-Births, Deaths, Marr)

SARAH, b ca 1755, Dover; m 5 Nov 1775, Dover, Duncan
Campbell [b ca 1750, of Dover]. (Ham's Dover Marr, TMs]

SARAH, b 1760s, Kingston, d/o Dudley Young of Gilmanton;
m 1 Nov 1792, Belmont, Noah Connor [b 1760s, Gilmanton].
Sarah Connor was named daughter and heir of Dudley Young of
Gilmanton by his will drawn 20 May 1801, proved 10 May 1803.
(NHVR-Brides)

SARAH, b 25 Mar 1769, poss. Durham, d/o Joseph and Anna
(Folsom) Young, d 25 Apr 1844, Wolfeboro; m Jan 1806, poss.
Durham and poss. her 2nd marriage, Ebenezer Meader [b ca 1760,
of Durham]. Sarah Meader was listed as daughter and heir in
the division of Joseph Young's estate in 1806. Please note
that Stackpole's Durham gave another set of vital records for
Sarah: b Mar 1769, d 25 Apr 1855, Wolfeboro. (Fitts' Newfields, p503,505,683,684; Stackpole's Durham, V2, p278)

SARAH, b ca 1770, Dover; m 1791, Dover, John Wentworth
[b ca 1765, Dover]. (LDS I.G.I. VR)

SARAH, b 2 May 1775, poss. of Milton; m ca 1800, Tufton-
boro, Joseph Pinkham [b 18 Jan 1772, twin, Dover, s/o John and
Phoebe (Tibbetts) Pinkham, d 18 Apr 1842, Tuftonboro]. It is
worthy of note that Otis Pinkham, another son of John and
Phoebe Pinkham, married Hannah+ Young of Milton [b ca 1770].
It may well have been that Sarah and Hannah were sisters.
Sarah and Joseph settled in Tuftonboro. Ch. b Tuftonboro:
Enoch Pinkham, b ca 1805, later resided on Dover Neck.
(Scale's Dover, p323,324; Pinkham Gen., p31; Quint's Hist.
Memos, p136)

SARAH, b 1785, Dover, d 1832, age 47, Dover; m near 1804,
Dover, Joseph Ham [b 28 Jan 1779, Dover]. (Ham's Dover Marr,
TMs)

SARAH, b 12 Mar 1790, Barrington, d/o David and Abigail
(Foss) Young of Barnstead; m 1 Mar 1816, Barnstead, Jonathan
Emerson [b ca 1785, of same town]. (NHVR-Brides; Merrill's
Barnstead, p333)

SARAH, b ca 1805, of Somersworth; m 24 Sep 1826, Dover,
John Tuttle [b ca 1800, of Durham]. (NHVR-Brides)

SARAH, b ca 1825, of Wolfeboro, d/o John C. and Sarah (Smith) Young; m (Intentions) 18 May 1846, Wolfeboro, John A. Cook [b ca 1820, of same town]. Sarah Cook was named daughter and heir of John C. Young of Wolfeboro by his will drawn 2 Nov 1853, proved 4 Sep 1866. It is of interest that Sarah's brother John H. Young filed intentions of marriage to Catherine Cook on identical date as her own. (Parker's Wolfeboro Banns, 1789-1854, n.p.)

SARAH, b 1835, of New Hampton; in 1860 she lived as student in New Hampton. (Census Belknap Co., 1860, p109)

SARAH A., b 8 Sep 1816, Ossipee, d/o John and Mary H. (Hammond) Upton of Bow, d 8 Feb 1889, age 74-5-0, Alton, widow of _____ Young. (NHVR-Deaths)

SARAH ADELINE, b 7 Apr 1839, Wolfeboro, d/o Jeremiah and Adeline (Hann) Young; m 6 Feb 1856, Wolfeboro, Charles A. Warren [b ca 1830, of same town]. Sarah was member of parents' household in 1850 but was away from home in 1860 as married woman. By 1870 she and spouse Charles Warren lived at the home of her widowed mother Adeline in Wolfeboro. (NHVR-Brides)

SARAH ANN, b 14 Sep 1815, Lebanon, ME, d/o Joseph and Patience (Wentworth) Young of Somersworth; m 15 Feb 1838, Somersworth, Samuel Clements [b ca 1810, of same town]. Ch. b prob. Somersworth: Charles A. Clements, b 2 Dec 1838; Frank P. Clements, b 26 Nov 1850; Mary E. Clements, b 30 Sep 1852, d 11 Apr 1872, Somersworth; and Almira A. Clements, b 29 Sep 1854. (Wentworth Gen., V1, p456,457)

SARAH ANN, b 1828, Farmington, youngest d/o Joseph and Sally (Blazo) Young of Wakefield, d 16 Nov 1850, Middleton; m ca 1848, Middleton, Albert M. Blazo [b ca 1825, Middleton]. Sarah Ann was member of the Freewill Baptist Church. (Morning Star, p35)

SARAH B., b _____, d 30 Sep 1869, Effingham. (LDS I.G.I. VR; NHVR-Deaths)

SARAH C., b 17 Dec 1820, Durham, d/o William and Martha (Bennett) Young; m 6 Mar 1867, Durham, Otis P. Dudley [b ca 1815, of New Market]. In the partition of her father's estate on 6 Dec 1859, Sarah C. received a 11/24th share: 30 acres of field and woodland by land of Lydia Hayes and 20 acres of wood and pasture land by the Boston & Maine R.R., plus joint tenancy of the family home with her brother Joseph, to have the privilege of the east front room and north bedroom. In 1860 Sarah C., single, lived together with brother Joseph and widowed mother at the family homestead in Durham. Her mother's will signed 6 Sep 1860, proved 6 May 1862, named Sarah C. as her [single] daughter, Exec. of her will and residuary legatee. No known children by Otis Dudley. (NHVR-Brides)

SARAH C., b ca 1826, of Tuftonboro, m 3 Dec 1846, Wolfeboro, James Jenkins [b ca 1820, of Tuftonboro]. (NHVR-Brides)

SARAH E., b 1832, of Dover, prob. d/o John K. and Lydia A. ( ) Young of Ossipee; m 13 Oct 1850, Dover, John A.

Corson [b ca 1825, of same town]. Sarah E., single at age 18, lived at parents' home in 1850, Dover. (NHVR-Brides)

SARAH ELIZABETH, b ca 1830, of Milton; m (Intentions) 17 Jun 1849, Milton, m 18 Jun 1849, Durham, Horace Reynolds aka Runnels [b ca 1825, of Milton]. (NHVR-Brides; LDS I.6.1, VR; Milton VR, Town Clerk)

SARAH ELNORA, b ca 1815, Wolfeboro, d/o James H. and Nancy (Nudd) Young, alive 1873, native town; m (Intentions) 29 Dec 1834, m 1 Jan 1835, Wolfeboro, George W. Libby [b ca 1810, of Wolfeboro]. Sally E. Libby was named a daughter and heir of James H. Young of Wolfeboro by his will drawn 14 Jun 1873, proved 4 Nov 1873. (NHVR-Brides; Parker's Wolfeboro Banns, 1789-1854, n.p.)

SARAH H., b ca 1815, of Somersworth; head of household in Somersworth in 1840, age 30-40. Other members of family were two females age 20-30. It would seem to appear this family unit was made up of siblings. (Census Strafford Co., 1840, p566)

SARAH H., b ca 1855, of Great Falls; m 16 Sep 1878, Strafford, Daniel Pease [b ca 1850, of North Strafford]. (NHVR-Brides)

SARAH M., b 1832, d 9 Feb 1892, age 60, Middleton, buried Dover. (NHVR-Deaths)

SARAH U., b 3 Dec 1852, Barnstead Center, d/o Oliver H. P. and Emily J. (Tuttle) Young; m 5 Nov 1871, Barnstead, Oscar Foss [b 17 Nov 1845, Barnstead, s/o Eli H. and Mary A. (Furber) Foss, alive 1896, native town]. Sarah lived at home up through 1870. While Oscar was born on Beauty Hill, his parents moved to Barnstead Center soon after his birth. As a young man he learned the trades of blacksmith and carpenter, served three years in the 12th Regt., NH Volunteer Infantry, and thereafter went into the lumber business extensively. As resident of Barnstead, Oscar served as Town Treasurer, was elected in 1896 to the office of Supervisor, and in later years became Justice of the Peace. On date of 15 Dec 1896 Oscar was appointed guardian of father-in-law Oliver Young who was then elderly and in failing health. No known children. (NHVR-Brides; Biog. Review, XXI, p492,493; Cutter's Eastern Mass., p1269,1270)

SIDNEY H., b Sep 1838, Rochester. As resident of Westmoreland at age 24, Sidney enlisted 14 Aug 1862 in Co. A, 14th Regt., NH Volunteer Infantry, mustered in 22 Sep 1862 as Pvt., and was killed 19 Sep 1864 at Opequan, VA. (Soldiers & Sailors, p731)

SIMEON aka Simon D., b 1833, Canada, s/o Joseph C. and Lydia ( ) Young of Somersworth, d 16 Apr 1870 [age 37-0-0], Somersworth; m ca 1850, same town, Joanna ( ) [b 1833, of Somersworth, alive 1870, Dover, widow]. Before 1870 Simeon and Joanna lived in both Somersworth and Great Falls; by 1870 Joanna was head of family living in Ward 2, Dover with four small children. Simon was buried in the family burial plot at Forest Glade Cemetery, Somersworth. Ch. b Somersworth, son b 14 Dec 1852. Ch. b Great Falls: Henry E., b 1859; Frank E., b 1863; Angie, b 1865; and Edwin A.+, b 1868. (Census Strafford Co., 1870, p52; LDS I.G.I. BR; NHVR-Births; Wooley's Somersworth Cem., Plot 37)

SIMON P., b 1856, Sherman Mills, ME, res. of Dover; m 1880s, Cora Etta Ellis [b Jan 1858, Middleton, alive 1900, Dover, age 42]. Simon and Cora lived at 6th Street, Dover in 1900; members of household were Maud H. Young, called a "friend" [b 1889], and son Perley. Ch: Perley E., b 5 Dec 1887. (NHVR-Births; 1900 Soundex)

SMITH, b ca 1795, of Gilmanton, m 26 Sep 1817, Gilford, Betsey Avery [b ca 1800, of Gilmanton]. It is to be noted a married couple with same names and ages lived with James C. Young and family in Wakefield in 1850 where Smith worked as a hired hand. This may be strictly coincidental. (NHVR-Marr; Census Carroll Co., 1850, p322)

SOLOMON, b ca 1730, Dover, bp 25 Apr 1742, s/o Eleazer and Alice (Watson) Young of Madbury, alive 1787, Barrington; m ca 1756, Kezia Hanson [b ca 1735, Dover, d/o Timothy and Kezia (   ) Hanson]. Solomon was born and brought up in that section of Dover which became the Parish of Madbury, and was baptized at First Church, Dover with parents and sister. He bought out his father's homestead in Madbury by deed signed 2 Oct, rec'd 22 Oct 1765. This farm adjoined the main road leading from Littleworth to Barrington, s.w. of the road leading from said main road to Bellamon's Bank River. As a resident of Madbury he was elected in 1767 to serve a one-year term as Selectman. Solomon and wife relocated to Barrington before 1776, as did his son Stephen. He was a signer of the 1776 Association Test for Barrington; it is believed Solomon as widower lived at Stephen's home in 1790 in Barrington.

Solomon's first purchase of land was 4-1/4 acres in Dover, being part of the estate of the late Nathaniel Garland, beginning at Eleazer Young's fence on the south side on the way that leads from Littleworth to Barrington, near to where Joseph Young formerly dwelt, west to James Young's fence, and then by said Eleazer's fence, from co-grantors Ebenezer Garland, Nathaniel Garland, Sarah Garland, widow of Nathaniel Garland, and Bridget Garland, all of Dover, by deed signed 18 Apr 1763, rec'd 27 Mar 1764, for 362 pounds-15 shillings; witnesses Stephen Young, John Wingett aka Wingate [NH Prov. Probate 72:295].

Solomon bought a moiety of 29-1/4 acres [a total of 58-1/2 acres held in common and undivided with neighbor James Young of Dover], from Elijah and Martha Hanson of Dover for 2,925 pounds Old Tenor, it being the same 58-1/2 acres that Robert Hanson and the said James Young purchased of Nathaniel Hanson; by lands south of Daniel Young's, west of Isaac Twombly's and William Twombly's, north by Timothy Hanson's, and east by the road leading from Littleworth, so-called, to Madbury New Bridge, by deed signed 10 May 1764, rec'd 22 Oct 1765; witnesses Jonathan Hanson, Jr., James Hanson [NH Prov.

Probate 77;224]. Solomon and James bought an additional one-half acre from Nathaniel Hanson, by deed signed 28 Aug, rec'd 31 Aug 1767, for four pounds; the land was situated near Daniel Young's dwelling house; witnesses John Young, Timothy Young [Strafford Co. Deed 92:310].

When of Barrington he sold two tracts of land in the Two-Mile Streak, Barrington: (1) quitclaimed all his interest and title in the estate of the late John Daniels of Barrington by deed of 10 Oct 1786, rec'd 23 Sep 1790, to [son] Stephen Young of Barrington, tanner, for 250 pounds; witnesses Charles Babb, Abigail Tarlot [Strafford Co. Deed 12:138]; (2) sold 12 acres land adjacent to the land of Francis Drew of Madbury which Solomon originally bought from Daniel Meserve of Madbury, to the said Francis Drew for 15 pounds by deed signed 15 Nov 1787, rec'd 22 Oct 1788; witnesses John Tasker, John Meserve [Strafford Co. Deed 10;64].

Ch. b Parish of Madbury: Timothy+, b 1750s, Stephen+, b 1750s; and Solomon+, b ca 1755. (Wilson's Assoc. Test, p122; Dover Gen., **Reg.** 6:329,330; Heritage's Dover VR, p149)

SOLOMON, b ca 1755, Madbury, s/o Solomon and Kezia (Hanson) Young, d testate pre 30 Jun 1813, Madbury; m Feb 1782, Madbury, Elizabeth Hayes [b 24 Sep 1757, Madbury, d/o Daniel and Sarah (Plummer) Hayes, d 26 Aug 1824, home town]. Solomon was head of family in Madbury from 1790-1810. In 1790 family consisted of one other male over 16 years, three males under 16, and four females. In 1800 his age was 45 plus, with household of spouse age 26-45, four males, two under 10, two age 10-16, and two females, one under 10 and one 10-16. In 1810 his age was 45 plus as was his spouse, household containing two males, one under 10, one under 16, and one female age 10-16. Wife Elizabeth received a marriage portion of 20 pounds from her father Daniel Hayes. Richmond's Hayes Gen. stated that Hayes papers showed that from 1805-1807 Solomon was "buying shoes and felt hats for Eleazer, Joseph and Daniel, and velvet shoes for Sophy." These papers contained an indenture of Samuel Alle of Rochester as an apprentice to Solomon Young.

Solomon and brother Timothy were two of four co-grantees in the purchase of 96 acres, Lot 78, 1st Div., Barrington by deed signed and rec'd 28 Jan 1780. Ten years later this same acreage of Lot 78, plus 24 acres of Lot 79, 2nd Range, Barrington was sold by Solomon et al by deed signed 29 Dec 1790, rec'd 13 Jul 1799 year. The same four grantors sold 96 acres more of Lot 79, 2nd Div., Barrington by deed signed 29 Dec 1790, rec'd 20 Feb 1800. See Timothy Young of Madbury [b 1750s] for complete details on these three deeds. There is no indication that Solomon and Elizabeth relocated to Barrington.

Solomon's will of 1 Mar 1811, proved 30 Jun 1813, named eldest son Eleazer as Exec. of his will, and residuary legatee of his estate; witnesses Tobias Evans, Nathaniel Hayes, James H. Young [Strafford Co. Probate 13:199]. On date of probate

Eleazer was allowed Exec. having posted bond of $3,000.00 with sureties Tobias Evans and Nathaniel Hayes, both of Madbury [Strafford Co. Probate 20:199]. Solomon made provisions for his wife Elizabeth: all stock of cattle, one-half of the furniture and indoor utensils, and for her use "for and during her natural life" one-third part of all his real estate. Son Eleazer was to receive the remaining two-thirds; upon her death her share of real estate would revert to Eleazer. To his others sons he devised $100.00 each: Asa, Daniel and Joseph. Daughters Elizabeth Chesley, wife of Joseph Chesley [3rd], and Sophia Young were to receive the other one-half of the household furniture and indoor utensils and $20.00 each, Sophia to live with her mother until she married. Son Joseph received the instruction that "while he is 15," he was to live at home.

Ch. b Madbury: Eleazer+, b 1787; Asa, b 1790s; Elizabeth+ (Young) Chesley, b ca 1790; Daniel, b 1790s; Sophia, b 1790s; and Joseph, b 1796. (NHVR-Marr; Deaths; Hayes Gen., V1, p93; Census Strafford Co., 1790, p93; 1800, p164; 1810, p598)

SOLOMON, b ca 1795, of Alton; head of household in Alton, 1840, age 40-50, with spouse of same age group, and family of male parental figure age 80-90 [b ca 1775], and one male child under 5. All things considered in these early census enumerations, Solomon could have been the elder parent figure at age 80-90. (Census Strafford Co., 1840, p304)

SOLOMON, b 14 Dec 1796, Barrington, s/o David and Abigail (Foss) Young of Barnstead, d 6 Sep 1858, Barnstead; m 2 Mar 1826, Barnstead, Lucy Walker [b 1793, Barnstead, d/o William Walker, gr.d/o Seth and Nancy (Tripe) Walker of Portsmouth, alive 1850, native town]. Solomon lived in Alexandria at time of marriage and was the author of a remarkable hymnal. He and spouse were residents of Barnstead in 1850; children at home, Solomon 2nd and Lucy. Ch. b Barnstead: Solomon 2nd aka Solomon W.+, b 1835; and Lucy A., b 1841. (Census Belknap Co., 1850, p408; NHVR-Marr, Deaths; Merrill's Barnstead, p333; Quint's Hist. Memos, p319)

SOLOMON F., b ca 1825, res. of Ossipee, m (   ). Ch. b Ossipee: daughter b 21 Oct 1851, and daughter b 1 Aug 1853, Ossipee. (NHVR-Births; LDS I.G.I. BR)

SOLOMON W. aka 2nd, b 1835, Barnstead, s/o Solomon and Lucy (Walker) Young, d 23 Jan 1890, Pittsfield, widower; m 19 Jun 1856, Barnstead, Louisa A. Jenkins [b 1838, Barnstead, d/o Joseph and Lydia A. (   ) Jenkins, d pre 19 Feb 1867, native town]. Solomon and wife were listed as residents of this town in 1860; children at home were son Albert W. and Emma F. Young. Solomon enlisted at age 27 in Co. B, 12th Regt., NH Volunteer Infantry on 16 Aug 1862; he mustered in two weeks later as Pvt. and deserted 11 Nov 1862 at Hillsborough, VA. Albert W. and Emma F. were heirs-at-law of their mother Louisa A. Young upon her death in 1867; they inherited their mother's share in land conveyed to her by deed of her

284

parents Joseph and Lydia Jenkins on 24 Mar 1858, "an advance-
ment, in part her portion of our estate." Per deposition made
26 Jan 1867, Louisa's parents did not object to the whole of
the real estate being sold under license from the court. In
effect Solomon wanted to sell one acre of land upon which he
had erected a dwelling house; in view of the fact that their
two children were "both under 14 years of age and having real
estate in said county," Solomon had to petition on 19 Feb 1867
for their guardianship in order to manage their property;
approved same date [Belknap Co. Probate #2156]. Ch. b Barnstead: Albert W., b 1856; and Emma F.+ (Young) Shannon, b
1858. (Census Belknap Co., 1860, p327; NHVR-Brides, Marr;
Soldiers & Sailors, p647)

SOPHIA, b 1811, of Strafford; in 1850 Sophia was single
and worked as domestic servant for Edmond Caswell's family.
It is entirely possible the following entry [giving only
approximate ages] pertains to this Sophia. (Census Strafford
Co., 1870, p374)

SOPHIA, b ca 1855, Barrington, m 8 Feb 1877, Strafford,
Edmond O. Caswell [b ca 1850, Strafford]. (NHVR-Brides)

SOPHIA, b 1835, Madbury, d/o Eleazer and Kezia (Rowe)
Young; m 4 Oct 1857, Rochester, Bradley F. Parsons [b ca 1830,
Rochester]. Sophia was known by her married name of Parsons
in her mother's will drawn 17 Aug 1863, proved 1 Apr 1865, and
was of Rochester when she married. (NHVR-Brides; Rochester
VR, Marr)

SOPHIA ABIGAIL, b 4 Feb 1820, Barrington, d/o Aaron and
Lydia (Daniels) Young, d 21 Nov 1869, Somersworth; m 17 Jul
1849, Somersworth, George Sullivan Hanson [b 15 Sep 1826, of
Barrington, d 19 Sep 1919, same town]. Sophia Hanson was
named a daughter and heir of Aaron Young of Barrington by his
will signed 2 Dec 1850, proved 2 May 1854. Ch. b Somersworth:
Frances E. Hanson, b 9 Jul 1852, d 4 Jun 1948; Woodbury E.
Hanson, b 25 Oct 1855, d 12 May 1947; and George Harry Hanson,
b 1 Mar 1859, d 28 Nov 1889. (NHVR-Brides; Ham Gen., p43,53)

SOPHRONA, b ca 1835, New Durham; m 21 Oct 1855, New
Durham, William Stowell [b ca 1830, of New Durham]. (New
Durham VR, Bk1, p8)

SOPHRONIA, b 8 May 1809, Upper Gilmanton, d/o Joseph and
Betsey (Young) Young, d 2 May 1897, Belmont [native town]; m
19 Aug 1841, Belmont, James G. Bradbury [b ca 1815, of Con-
cord]. (NHVR-Brides; Lyford's Canterbury, p343)

SOPHRONIA JANE, b ca 1825, of Milton; m 9 Jun 1844,
Wolfeboro, Shepard Goodwin [b ca 1820, of Milton].
(NHVR-Brides)

SOPHRONIA M., b ca 1828, of Milton, poss. d/o Hale and
Sophronia (Nudd) Young of Wolfeboro, d pre 5 Feb 1850, Milton.
Admin. Papers were filed on the estate of Sophronia M.,
single, by uncle Samuel Nudd on 5 Feb 1850, requesting that
he be appointed Admin. He deposed that both father and mother
of Sophronia M. were dead, that she had never married and
"left neither brother nor sister of the whole blood but did

leave a brother of the half-blood who is a minor"; allowed
same date [Strafford Co. Probate 54:390]. On same date said
Nudd petitioned for License to Sell inasmuch as the personal
estate was not sufficient to pay demands against it by the sum
of $200.00; allowed 7 May 1850 in the amount of $150.00
[Strafford Co. Probate 60:93].

SOPHY, b 1806, of Barrington; in 1860 she resided at
boarding house in Barrington. Member of household was George
Fisher, age 11, b 1849. (Census Strafford Co., 1860, p156)

STEPHEN, b 1750s, Madbury, s/o Solomon and Kezia (Hanson)
Young, tanner by trade, d testate pre 19 Jan 1826, Barrington;
m 4 Apr 1776, Barrington, **Kezia Hanson** [b ca 1753, Madbury,
alive 1826, Barrington]. In 1776 Stephen signed the Association Test for Barrington, married and settled on or about
their date of marriage in that section of Barrington known as
the Two-Mile Streak. From 1790-1800 he was listed on the
census returns for Barrington as head of household. In 1790
family contained one male over 16 years besides himself
[believed to be his widowed father] and one female. In 1800
his age was 45 plus with household of two males age 16-26,
one female under 10, and one female age 26-45.

The earliest deed on record for Stephen of Madbury was
signed 7 Mar 1775, rec'd 9 Jun 1777, when he sold to Timothy
Young of Madbury [brother] 8-1/2 acres in said town for 20
pounds; property was located on Littleworth Road on the s.e.
corner of Solomon Young's homestead being what Stephen bought
from Daniel Young and was part of what was Daniel's homestead
"when he lived"; witnesses John Church, Elijah Austin [Straf-
ford Co. Deed 3:41]. He was still of Madbury when he purchased his first acreage in the Two-Mile Streak, Barrington,
60 acres at north corner of James Church's land by the road
between the 7th and 8th Ranges by deed signed 7 Oct 1774,
rec'd 23 Sep 1790; see grantor Benjamin Young of Barrington
for further details. In two transactions, Stephen bought two
shares of the John Daniels estate in Barrington. The first
purchase was by deed signed 14 Feb 1780, rec'd 23 Sep 1790,
from Joseph Daniel Jr. of Barrington, half of said Daniels'
interest in the estate of the late John Daniels, part of which
Joseph Daniels bought of Jacob Daniels, for 480 pounds; witnesses Abraham and Mary Waldron [Strafford Co. Deed 12:137].
The second purchase out of the Daniels estate was from
[father] Solomon Young of Barrington who quitclaimed all his
interests in said estate by deed signed 10 Oct 1786, rec'd
23 Sep 1790; see Solomon and Kezia (Hanson) for complete
transaction.

The following deed involved the purchase of the Fowler
and Daniels lands in Barrington, the names of which will
reappear in the listing of real estate belonging to Aaron
Young of Barrington who had purchased these from Stephen [not
researched]. By deed signed 27 Nov 1793, rec'd 20 Jan 1794,
Stephen purchased all the land that Daniel Fowler held title
through purchase in the estate of his father William Fowler,

which fell to the father from the estate of John Daniels, late of Barrington, for seven pounds-10 shillings; witnesses Clem Daniels, John Daniels [Strafford Co. Deed 18:74,5]. Forty acres of land in the Streak were acquired by quitclaim from Jonathan Steele of Durham signed 24 Dec 1800, rec'd day after, which Silas Drew conveyed to said Steele by deed of 23 Dec 1799, for $145.00; witnesses John Sullivan, Jonathan Chesley [Strafford Co. Deed 35:208,9]. On identical dates of the latter deed, Sarah Drew, widow of Silas Drew Sr., ceded her dower rights to the said 40 acres land to Stephen of Barrington for $100.00; witnesses Jonathan Steele, Joseph Richardson [Strafford Co. Deed 35:210]. Stephen bought 21-1/2 acres in the Two-Mile Streak from Silas Drew, Exec. of the estate of his father Silas Drew [Sr.], deceased, on the north side of the road opposite the farm on which Andrew Young lately lived, on west corner of Joseph Daniels' land, and abutting an acre of land owned by Isaac Waldron Esq. for $120.15, by deed signed 13 Dec 1802, rec'd 23 Jul 1803; witnesses John Wingate, Eliphalet Cloutman [Strafford Co. Deed 42:230].

Stephen's will was drawn up 15 Oct 1824, proved 19 Jan 1826, in which he named Jonathan Young Jr. of Barrington as sole Exec.; witnesses John Wingate, Elijah Austin, Aaron Wingate [Strafford Co. Probate 34:27]. On date of probate, Jonathan was allowed Exec. having posted bond of $5,000.00 with sureties Elijah Austin and John Wingate, both of Madbury [Strafford Co. Probate 30:225]. Wife Kezia was to receive his "clock and that part of my household furniture which is in her possession and has been for a number of years." He devised to John Bumford of Barrington the lot of land where he then lived, also 40 acres land which Stephen purchased of the heirs of Silas Drew adjoining the "Solloman Hall farm in Barrington in the Two-Mile Streak, and ten acres of woodland which he purchased of John Bruster in Barrington." To Nancy Brock, wife of Nicholas Brock, and Hannah Young, wife of Jonathan Young Jr., he devised the remainder of his real estate "wherever it may be found" and the remainder of household furniture in equal shares. Jonathan, Exec., was to receive "all the rest of the estate."

While Stephen's will did not specifically devise dower rights to his wife Kezia, these were duly set off to her 27 Apr 1827 by Tobias Evans, said John Wingate and said Elijah Austin; allowed 21 May 1827 [Strafford Co. Probate 36:270]: she was to receive about 45 acres of the homestead farm which was adjacent to Aaron Young's land [in Barrington], one piece of land containing seven acres by Hezekiah Hayes' land, another piece of 16 acres on the south side of the road leading from Barrington to Madbury Meeting House adjacent to land of Andrew Huckings, and one-half acre at the s.w. corner of the shed, plus the usual household privileges.

Stephen's homestead farm "in back of Drew's Pond on Littleworth Road" was located in the historic Two-Mile Streak; part of this was quitclaimed by [son or son-in-law?] Jonathan

Young Jr. and wife Hannah Young of Barrington to Nicholas Brock of Barrington for $1,000.00, by deed signed 18 Mar, rec'd 26 Mar 1826 [Strafford Co. Deed 129:466]. Barrington Graveyards [p91] stated "from the wording of the deed, it is assumed they [the grantors] laid out the graveyard....Nancy was probably nee Young." While it is probable that Nancy Brock and Hannah Young cited above were daughters of Stephen, it is certain that the properties bequeathed by Stephen to the said Nancy and Hannah were eventually bought by Aaron Young of Barrington [b 1793], cited above. Both women were members of First Congregational Church, Barrington; by 1835 Hannah Young was deceased, and on 15 Mar that year, Nancy Brock was dismissed from this church to the First Congregational Church in Dover. (Wilson's Assoc. Test, p122; Census Strafford Co., 1790, p86; 1800, p156; Heritage's Dover VR, p174; Barrington Congreg. Church, p251)

STEPHEN, b ca 1775, of Barrington. In 1810 Stephen was listed as head of household in Barrington, his age 26-45, with family of spouse of similar years and two females both age 16-26. (Census Strafford Co., 1810, p493)

STEPHEN, b 20 Jan 1798, Barrington, s/o David and Abigail (Foss) Young, shoe maker, d 1863, Barnstead; m 1 Nov 1821, Barnstead, Caroline Munsey [b 1802, of Barnstead, d 1854, same town]. By trade Stephen was shoemaker and was listed on the census returns for Barnstead from 1830-1840. In 1830 his age was 30-40, with spouse age 20-30, and family of two males, one under 5, one age 5-10, and two females, one under 5, and one 5-10. In 1840 his age was 40-50, spouse was age 30-40, with a large family of three males, one each age 5-10, 10-15, and 15-20, and three females, one under 5, 10-15, and 10-15, respectively. From 1841-1842 Stephen served his town as Representative to the New Hampshire State Legislature. He, Caroline and son Smith were buried at Pittsfield Cemetery. Ch. b Barnstead: Caroline Jane+ (Young) Clark, b 13 Feb 1822; Stephen Jr., b 1 Mar 1824; Mary Ann+ (Young) Merrill, b 1 Jan 1827; George W.+, b 10 Apr 1829; Mahala A., b 13 May 1831; and Smith W., b 25 Aug 1834, d 1857. (Hurd's Belknap Co., V2, p712; NHVR-Births, Marr; Census Strafford Co., 1830, p15; 1840, p451; LDS I.G.I. BR; Merrill's Barnstead, p333)

STEPHEN, b 19 Mar 1802, Strafford, s/o Jonathan and Mary (Hill) Young, d 4 Dec 1893, age 91-8-16, native town; m ca 1825, Lydia Main [b 1803, Rochester, d/o Amos Main, d 21 Nov 1881, Strafford]. Stephen and family were members of the Freewill Baptist Church, Crown Point, Strafford. He was named Exec. of elder brother Benjamin F. Young's will signed 16 Dec 1839, proved 20 Jan 1840, but as events turned out, was appointed Admin. instead. He was also named Exec. of his father's will signed 7 Dec 1844, proved 2 Sep 1851, his legacy, the family homestead called the Hayes-Young farm.

Stephen was head of household in Strafford from 1830-1870. In 1830 his age was 20-30, with spouse of same age group and family of three males, two under 5, one age 10-15,

one female age 50-60 [parental figure] and one female under
5. In 1840 his age was 30-40, as was his spouse, with family
of four males, one under 5, one age 5-10, two 10-15, and one
female age 10-15. From 1850-1870, Lydia was named as his
spouse, returns with their children. In 1850 they shared the
homestead with his parents, estate valued at $10,000; children
at home, Charles W., Mary A. and Stephen L. In 1860 members
of family were son Steven L., his wife Cynthia and children
Freeman N. and Edward W. In 1870 family members at home were
daughter Mary A. and her son Stephen, age 15 [b 1855]. Survey
maps of Strafford made in 1871 established that Stephen's
homestead was situated in District #1. According to Strafford
Pioneers: "No one has lived on the Hayes-Young farm since the
home of Stephen Young was destroyed by an explosion caused by
dynamite in the cellar." Stephen, Lydia and son Jonathan F.
were buried at Strafford Corners Cemetery.

    Ch. b Strafford: George, b 1820s, named in grandfather's
will of 1844; Charles William+, b 1826; Jonathan Freeman, b
1827, d 14 Nov 1843, Strafford Corners; Mary Ann (Young)
Mason, b 1830, at home 1870; and Stephen L.+, b 1835. (Census
Strafford Co., 1830, p56; 1840, p463; 1850, p575; 1860, p144;
1870, p382; Stiles' Cemeteries, p207; Morning Star, p375;
Strafford Pioneers, n.p.; note that under NHVR-Deaths Lydia's
date of death was 24 Nov 1880)

    STEPHEN, b 22 Oct 1854, Strafford, physician, s/o George
E. and Mary Ann (Young) Mason, gr.s/o Stephen and Lydia (Main)
Young of Strafford, alive 1900, Dover. At the suggestion of
his maternal grandfather Stephen Young, he adopted the surname
of his mother. Stephen m1 1 Mar 1882, Andover, VT, Fannie F.
Stoddard [b 1859, Warren, VT, d/o J. and Mary A. (Randall)
Stoddard, d 7 Nov 1885, Andover, VT]. There was one child by
this union, Eva M., b 1880s. Stephen m2 16 May 1888, Rochester, Lucy R. (Karl) Brown [b 9 May 1852, Rockland, ME, d/o
John and Lucy (Stam) Karl of Russia, her 2nd marriage, d 2 Jan
1897, age 34-7-24, East Rochester]; m3 10 Feb 1898, Lowell,
MA, Lilla M. aka Maud L. Cutts [b 17 Dec 1866, Gardner, ME,
d/o William and Lavina C. (Basford) Cutts, d 11 Nov 1900, age
33-10-25, Dover].

    In 1870 Stephen and his mother Mary Ann lived with her
parents in Strafford. His maternal grandfather Stephen under-
took the expenses of his education by which Stephen received
broad schooling at the Austin and West Lebanon Academies in
Strafford, Rochester High School and high school in South
Berwick, Maine, graduating class of 1875. He went on to
matriculate at Dartmouth College for two years, spent the next
two years at Dartmouth Medical School and completed his
studies at Long Island Hospital College, class of 1881. Later
he set up practice in East Rochester where he earned an excel-
lent reputation for his skill in surgery; there he served as
a member of the Board of Health. In 1900 at age 45, Stephen
lived at Silva Street, Dover with third wife Maud L.; member
of family was Lavina Cutts, b Apr 1842, ME, believed to be

Maud's mother; no known children. (NHVR-Marr; Rochester TR, Marr, p2,25, Deaths, p63; 1900 Soundex)

STEPHEN C. aka Clark, b 1830, Freedom, youngest s/o Daniel and Elizabeth (Nason) Young, alive 1894, native town; m1 ca 1855, Susan A. Patch [b 21 Dec 1833, Eaton, d 2 May 1891, Freedom, age 57-4-2]; m2 22 Aug 1894, Eaton, Mrs. Susan (Snow) Dudley [b 1829, Eaton, d/o Joseph and Sally ( ) Snow, both deceased]. Stephen C. was named son and heir of Daniel Young of Freedom by his will drawn 1 Oct 1866, proved 31 Aug 1874. The census returns of 1860 and 1870 for Freedom strongly suggest that Stephen C. and Clark were one and the same person, with Stephen using his middle name on the former census. In 1860 Stephen and Susan were residents of Freedom; child at home was Augusta; one other member of household was Thomas Lougee, age 35 [b 1825]. In 1870 Augusta was a teen-ager of 14 years. Ch. b Freedom: Augusta aka Vina A.+ (Young) Hatch, b 1856, and Ellen F., b 24 Oct 1862, Freedom, d 7 Jan 1864, age 1-2-14, buried at Lakeview Cemetery. (LDS I.G.I. BR; NHVR-Births, Marr, Deaths; Census Carroll Co., 1860, p629; 1870, p305; Freedom VR, 1878-1890)

STEPHEN E., b 1823, of Barrington; in 1860 Stephen E. was boarder at rooming house, Barrington, occupation school teacher at age 37. (Census Strafford Co., 1860, p166)

STEPHEN E., b 1824, of Dover, prob. s/o Jonathan and Hannah (Hall) Young, d 1860, Barrington; m ca 1850, Dover, Mary J. ( ) [b 1824, of Dover, alive 1860, Strafford. It is believed this is the Stephen who was named Admin. of Jona-than Young's estate in Strafford 5 Nov 1850; however, he was unable to attend to this. He was listed as head of household in Dover in 1850, occupation trader, living with wife Mary J. Members of family were two males, Enoch P. Young, b 1828, a resident of Lawrence, MA in 1852 when named legal guardian of one of Jonathan's sons, and Franklin Young, b 1831. In 1860 Mary J. was widow and head of household in Strafford, occupa-tion tailoress; she lived with son Nathaniel and boarders Ezra and Sarah Downs. Stephen was buried at Young family plot, Pine Grove Cemetery, Barrington. Ch. b Dover: Jonathan M., b 1851. (Census Strafford Co., 1850, p14; 1860, p143; Barr-ington Graveyards, p133, Plot 18, Lot 3W; NHVR-Deaths)

STEPHEN L., b 1832, Strafford, s/o Stephen and Lydia (Main) Young, shoemaker; m ca 1855, Strafford, Cynthia ( ) [b 1835, of Strafford, alive 1860, same town]. Stephen and Cynthia lived at his parents' homestead in District #1, Strafford Corners in 1860 with sons Freeman and Edward. Ch. b Strafford: Freeman N., b 1856; Edward W., b 1858. (Straf-ford Pioneers, n.p.)

SUSAN, b ca 1804, of Strafford; m 25 Nov 1824, at Free-will Baptist Church, Strafford, Joseph Roberts [b ca 1800, of Barrington]. (NHVR-Brides; Strafford Marr, **Reg.** 76:32)

SUSAN, b ca 1804, of Dover; m between Jul 1824-Jun 1825, Dover, Joseph L. Neal [b ca 1800, of same town] by Minister Jothem Horton. (NHVR-Brides; Heritage's Dover VR, p88)

SUSAN, b ca 1805, Dover; m 28 Nov 1824, Dover, David R. Stephens [b ca 1800, Dover]. (Heritage's Dover VR, p182)

SUSAN, b ca 1810, of Milton; m 8 Dec 1833, Farmington, Rufus Boles [b ca 1805, Milton]. Ch. b Somersworth: Emmons Boles, b 1830s, m 1900, Somersworth. (NHVR-Brides)

SUSAN, b ca 1810, Tuftonboro, d/o John and Hannah (Ham) Young; m 1 Feb 1838, Wolfeboro, Jonathan Ladd [b May 1808, Melvin Village, s/o Samuel and Comfort (Dow) Ladd]. (Ladd Gen., p54,55; NHVR-Brides)

SUSAN, b 7 Nov 1858, Alton, d/o Charles E. and Hannah (   ) Young; m 26 Jun 1878, Alton, Charles A. McIntire [b ca 1855, of same town]. (NHVR-Brides; LDS I.G.I. BR)

SUSAN A., b 1832, Wakefield, d/o Daniel and Betsey (Cook) Young, d 1851, home town; m 1851, Wakefield, Jacob Leighton [b Sep 1828, Ossipee, s/o Ephraim Leighton, gr.s/o Jacob and Sarah (Wentworth) Leighton, d pre 1860]. In the 1850s Susan and spouse lived in Wakefield on Pine River Road, North Wakefield. In 1860 their son Frank, age 8, lived with maternal grandparents in Wakefield. Susan Leighton was buried next to her parents' grave sites at Peter Young Cemetery, Pray Hill Road, Wakefield. Ch. b Wakefield: Frank Leighton, b Oct 1851. (Census for Carroll Co., 1850, p319; 1860, p581; Twombly's Wakefield Cem., TMs; Wentworth Gen., V2, p199)

SUSAN A., b ca 1850, of Middleton; m 11 Nov 1871, Middleton, Frank R. Marston [b ca 1845, of same town]. They took up residence in Farmington where a son was born. Ch. b Farmington: Fred B. Marston, b ca 1872, m 1893, Farmington, Hester A. Bumpus [b ca 1875, of Farmington]. (NHVR-Brides)

SUSAN AMANDA, b 1840, Ossipee, d/o Luther and Sophronia (Chick) Young, alive Oct 1898, Tamworth; m1 2 Oct 1860, Ossipee, Benjamin W. Davis [b ca 1835, Farley, VT, d pre Sep 1871, Ossipee]; m2 2 Jul 1876, Ossipee, Charles Weeley Fall [b ca 1845, of Ossipee, d pre Oct 1898, same town]; m3 ca 1898, Tamworth, _____ Hodgkins [b 1840s, of Tamworth]. Susan A. was a child of 10 at the home of her parents in 1850, Ossipee, and was named Susan A. Young, single [widow] in the will of her father written 13 Sep 1871, proved 1 Mar 1872. In the Admin. of her mother's estate in Ossipee on 26 Oct 1898, approved 1 Nov 1898, she was named Susan A. Hodgkins of Tamworth. She released her share in her mother's estate to sister Nettie Nute of Wolfeboro. Ch. b prob. Ossipee: Mae S. Davis, b 1860s. (NHVR-Brides)

SUSAN C., b 1842, MA, d/o Daniel Gorman, adopted daughter of James H. and Nancy (Nudd) Young of Wolfeboro; m 6 Feb 1865, Wolfeboro, Edwin H. Ford [b ca 1840, Pembroke, MA]. Susan C. Young was listed as member of James H.' family in the 1860 census for Wolfeboro. Susan C. G. Ford was named as an adopted daughter and heir of James H. Young in his will drawn 14 Jun, proved 4 Nov 1873. (NHVR-Brides)

SUSAN E., b 1817, of Dover; she was single in 1850, with no occupation, rooming at boarding house. (Census Strafford Co., 1850, p82)

SUSAN E. aka Susie E., b 1864, Alton, d/o Charles E. and Mary H. (Nutter) Young; m 24 Nov 1881, Farmington, Frank H. Wigglesworth [b ca 1855, of Farmington]. (NHVR-Brides)

SUSAN M., b 1841, Alton, d/o Henry and Sally (Witham) Young; m 1 Feb 1859, Alton, Lewis aka Levi Ellis [b 1835, of Alton]. (Alton VR, p619; NHVR-Brides)

SUSAN N., b 24 Nov 1817, Wakefield, d/o Thomas and Mary (Nute) Young, d 12 Apr 1893, native town; m between Apr 1855-Apr 1856, Wakefield, William Powell, trader [b 10 Oct 1801, England, d 4 Aug 1885, Wakefield]. In 1860 Susan and William lived in Wakefield; her parents were members of household. In 1870 they lived by themselves. Both Susan and William were buried at Old Young Cemetery where her parents had been buried, on Long Ridge Road, Wiggins Hill, Wakefield. No known children. (Twombly's Wakefield Cem., TMs; NHVR-Brides; Census Carroll Co., 1860, p566; 1870, p430)

SUSAN S., b ca 1830, of Somersworth; m 1 Dec 1851, Somersworth, Andrew J. Senett [b ca 1825, of same town]. (NHVR-Brides)

SUSANNAH, b 1760, prob. Dover, d/o Eleazer and Mary (Ham) Young of Barrington, d 7 Feb 1861, age 101-3-19, Northwood; m 20 Jul 1780, Dover, Nathaniel Garland [b 12 Aug 1758, Barrington, d 30 Oct 1819, Northwood]. By Eleazer's will written 18 Jun 1771, proved 30 Oct 1798, Susannah was named daughter and heir. Susanna and spouse raised their family in Northwood. Ch. b Northwood in 1780s: Patience Garland; Susanna Garland; Sally Garland; Polly Garland; Nathaniel Garland Jr.; and Elizabeth Garland. (NHVR-Marr, Brides; Moses' Northwood, V2, TMs, p124)

THEODORE L., b Sep 1850, Dover, s/o Moses C. and Mary K. (Nutter) Young, alive 1900, native town; m 5 Aug 1867, Dover, Anna aka Annie McLinn [b Jul 1850, Dover, alive 1900, home town, d/o Patrick and Mary ( ) McLinn of Dover]. Vital records indicated that twelve children were born to them in Dover. In 1900 Theodore, Annie and children Eva B., Lillie, Frank A. and Annie M. lived at Forest Street, Dover. Ch. b Dover, not traced further: Anna, b 1 Aug 1871, d 9 Sep 1885, age 15-1-8, Dover; Mary Ida, b 14 Dec 1875, not at home in 1900; Eva B., b 2 Dec 1877; daughter b 28 Jun 1879; daughter b 28 Jun 1880; Elizabeth, b 18 Jun 1882, twin, not at home in 1900; Lizzie aka Lillie, b 18 Jun 1882, twin; Frank Albert, b 2 May 1884; [eleventh child] Annie May, b 11 Apr 1888; and Joseph J., b 28 Aug 1889, d 1 Oct 1889, Dover. (NHVR-Births, Deaths, Marr; LDS I.G.I. BR; 1900 Soundex)

THOMAS, b 1653, of Dover, d pre May 20 1727/8, Dover Neck; poss. m2 ca 1700, Dover, Mary Roberts [b ca 1660, Dover, d/o Thomas and Mary (Leighton) Roberts, died "an ancient woman," 1745, Dover]. John R. Ham's "Dover Marriages" stated: "I am not certain that there were not two men named Thomas Young, instead of a second marriage." He added, however, that he thought it possible Thomas Young could have first married Susannah Mathews, daughter of Walter and Mary Mathews of

Oyster River [Durham Point]. See spouse Rowland Young of York for crucial differences on Susannah Mathews. The writer holds to the school of thought that Thomas of Dover probably married twice, but first wife remains unknown. It has been hard to accept the fact that son John was "eldest" of all his siblings simply by that status accorded him in his father's deed of gift signed 1726/27. It seems more likely that John was the eldest son of Thomas by his union with Mary as second wife for the following rationale. At the time of John's death in 1741 he was the father of six children, three of whom were under the age of seven, which places him in the prime of life. Had he in fact been the eldest of all siblings, his year of birth of necessity would have to be placed circa 1680; his age then in 1741 would have been 60 plus. The matter will remain moot of course. The fact remains that Thomas of Dover Neck was the patriarch of a long line of descendants who settled throughout Dover, Durham, Madbury, Barrington and Rochester, heavily concentrated in the branch headed by son Jonathan and Abigail (Hanson) Young.

Mary (Roberts) Young was the maternal granddaughter of Thomas and Joanna (Nutter) Leighton; by Leighton's will signed 21 Sep 1671, proved 25 Jun 1672, daughter Mary, "the wife of Thomas Roberts Jr." was named as legatee; witnesses Thomas Roberts Jr., Jonathan Reyner [NH State Papers, V31, p126,127]. Joanna Nutter was the daughter of Antony Nutter of Dover Neck; she died by 1674 shortly after her husband's death. Mary Roberts was also the paternal granddaughter of Thomas Roberts Sr., b 1600, Woolaston County, Worcester, England, who was elected Colonial Governor of Dover in 1640, serving in such office until Dover came under Massachusetts rule in 1643. It is noteworthy that Roberts Sr. took a compassionate stand for several Quaker women who were persecuted and run out of town by the then Constables of Dover, sons Thomas Roberts and John Roberts. Quint's Historical Memoranda of Dover spoke of him as "rebuking his sons Thomas and John...for the excessive virulence with which they enforced the laws against the Quakers in 1662." It is ironic that these women had been "imprisoned" at the home of one Thomas Canney of Dover, tailor, to whom Thomas Young had been apprenticed in 1769.

According to deposition made by Thomas in 1717 at age 64, he had been a servant of Thomas Canney of Dover at age 16. He attested that he worked for James Stackpole of Dover in 1680. Thomas' apprenticeship with the Canneys of Dover was documented by NH Prov. Deed V3, p20b, signed 3 Dec 1669, rec'd 9 Dec 1669, wherein Thomas Canney stated, "I do assign my servant Thomas Young unto my son Joseph Canney." As for his trade or occupation, one can speculate whether he learned the tailoring trade while indentured to the Canneys. In 1684, Thomas signed the petition against Gov. Cranfield which was taken to London by Nathaniel Weare as agent for the petitioners; he was one of the signers of a General Petition of Inhabitants (of N.H.) to Massachusetts, on 20 Feb 1689/90, to

293

set up a temporary Government. In 1693/4, Thomas was granted 30 acres in Dover and was one of the original grantees of Rochester in 1722, receiving a whole share of 53 acres land. This would seem to indicate that Thomas had then become Freeman, having long since served his apprenticeship. In 1700 Thomas was elected Town Constable of Dover and in 1715 was named one of the Surveyors of Highways. Also on 25 Apr 1715, he was listed as one of 24 persons "being householders" who lived nearer the Old Meeting House on Dover Neck than the New at Cochecho Point. There is no evidence that he ever resided in Rochester.

Thomas' one land deed was deed of gift signed 18 Mar 1726/7, proved 20 May 1727/8, naming son John as grantee. John was to receive all his estate of house and land where he then dwelt on Dover Neck, and all his goods, wares, household stuff and chattel as well as one whole right within the town of Rochester. John was to give to each of his four brothers an equal share with himself in the right of the above said Rochester, Jonathan, Nathaniel, Eleazer, and Samuel; also to pay to his three sisters five pounds each, Mary, wife of Stephen Otis, Liddiah, wife of John Cuck, and Sarah Young, to be paid within one year and one day after his decease and the decease of his wife Mary Young; witnesses Joshua Perkins, William Weymouth [NH Prov. Deed 16:69]. Widow Mary thereafter lived with son John and his wife Elizabeth at the family homestead until her death in 1745.

Ch. b Dover Neck: John+, b ca 1680-1700; Nathaniel+, b 1682; Thomas Jr., b 1684, in court for fighting 1701, d 27 Dec 1704, Dover; Jonathan+, b 1685; Eleazer+, b 1691; Lydia+ (Young) Cuck aka Cook, b 29 Nov 1694; Mary+ (Young) Otis, b 1699; Samuel+, b 1700; and Sarah, b 1700s, may have married Hicks. (Noyes et al, p777; Scale's Dover, p302-309; McDuffee's Rochester, V1, p38; Quint's Hist. Memos, p76,91,142,198; Ham's Dover Marr, TMs; Otis Gen., **Reg.** 5:185,196; Roberts Gen., TMs, p15-18; NH State Papers, V11, p509)

THOMAS, b 1691, Haverhill, MA, eldest s/o Edward and Hannah (Whittier) Young [no main entry], d testate 11 May 1767, New Market, inn keeper; m ca 1720, prob. New Market, Sarah Folsom [b 1692, New Market, d/o Ephraim and Phaltiel (Hall) Folsom, d 13 May 1768, Durham]. Early on, Thomas became land owner and resident of Durham. He was progenitor of an untold number of descendants. Various branches headed mainly by son Joseph and his two wives Anna Folsom and Mary Foss of New Market and Durham were prolific. These families helped to settle the then new towns of Durham, New Durham, Tuftonboro, Wolfeboro, Ossipee, Clarksville and Canterbury.

Thomas' parents Edward Young and Hannah Whittier were married 30 May 1683, prob. Haverhill, MA; Hannah Whittier was born 10 Sep 1683, Haverhill, MA, daughter of Thomas and Ruth (Green) Whittier. Lack of provisions in Edward's will for widow's dower would indicate that Thomas' mother Hannah was deceased in 1734. Thomas was named son and heir-at-law of

Edward Young by his will signed 12 Aug 1734; date of probate 25 Jul 1743 [Essex Co., MA Probate #30783]; he was to receive a one-fourth part of his father's estate real and personal lying in Salisbury, County of Essex, MA; his three siblings Richard, William, and Hannah Hackitt, wife of William Hackitt, were each to receive their one-fourth share of the estate. Sibling Henry was then deceased.

Young family records, courtesy of Granvyl Hulse of Colebrook, NH, stated that "Thomas purchased part of the 600 acres granted to Moses Gilman of his sons, Jeremiah, James, and Caleb 4 Sep 1720" and bought John Willey's proprietary rights in the township of Canterbury 16 Mar 1730; [listed on] committee of New Market parish on the settlement of Mr. Moody 9 Feb 1730. Other real estate Thomas acquired early, to reappear in estate inventories of sons and grandsons: (1) purchase of 30 acres land in Exeter from Abraham Bennick [Bennett] of Dover for "a valuable sum of money" by deed signed 22 Aug 1728, rec'd 5 Jan 1730/31; witnesses Joseph Smart, Samuel Ralings [NH Prov. Deed 17:401]; (2) purchase of a one-fifth interest in Common Land in Durham from Ezekial Leathers of Durham for "a valuable sum of money," by deed of 5 Mar 1732/33, rec'd 21 Feb 1733/34; witnesses Edward Hilton, Thomas Young Jr. [NH Prov. Deed 19:559]; (3) purchase of two acres of salt marsh situated in New Market on Lamperel [Lamprey] River Creek from Samuel Hilton of New Market for 25 pounds by deed signed 7 Jun, rec'd 13 Jun 1733; witnesses Nathan Johnson, Timothy Emerson [NH Prov. Deed 19:255]; (4) purchase of six acres of marsh land in the Cochecho Marshes of Dover from Abraham Bennett of Durham "for a valuable sum of money" by deed signed 21 Jul 1735, rec'd 4 Feb 1735/36; witnesses Jonathan Barber Jr., Jonathan Colcard [NH Prov. Deed 21:485]; (5) purchase of six acres of marsh land in the Cochecho Marshes of Dover from Martha Critchett of Durham for a valuable sum of money, by deed of 22 Jul, rec'd 12 Aug 1735; witnesses Nicholas Gugins, John Young [NH Prov. Deed 21:259]; and (6) purchase of the one-half part of the Carver Falls of Lamperel [Lamprey] River with the half-part of the saw mill now standing with the privileges and land attached thereto from George Jaffrey of Portsmouth for 125 pounds current money by deed of 21 Jun 1738, rec'd 21 Jul 1760; witnesses George Jaffrey, Susanna Ellison [NH Prov. Deed 62:174].

Thomas lived in Durham at least by 1746 and was rated for parish dues at Dover in 1753. By 1767 his residence was New Market, but the land and homestead actually fell half way between New Market and Durham. Thomas' will of 2 May, proved 27 May 1767, named son Joseph as Exec.; witnesses John Cooke, Jeremy Bryent, Walter Bryent [NH State Papers 39:1]. Joseph Young of New Market [son], innholder, gave bond of 500 pounds on 27 May 1767 for the execution of the will with Walter Bryent of New Market and Nicholas Duda of Lee, Gent., as sureties; witnesses, Robert Parks, Henry Foss. He devised to wife Sarah all his part of the grist mill at Lamprey River "during the whole of her natural life," as well as live stock, moveable household stuff of every kind and his ready cash or bills of credit then in his possession. He devised to son Thomas Jr. the half part of all his homestead plantation where he then lived, 100 acres lying on the s.e. side of Piscassic River, and a half part of his salt mash and thatch bed "during the whole of his natural life and no longer," as well as all his right and title in the town of New Durham, and one half of his right to the sawmill and grist mill. Thomas' title to these properties would revert upon his death to his son John, grandson of Thomas and Sarah. Thomas Sr. devised also to grandson John the other half part of the homestead plantation, the whole to be equally divided between John and his father. To son Joseph he devised about 140 acres land on the n.w. side of the Piscassic River "now in his possession" with the one half of the saw mill and mills privileges on both sides of the river, and all the remainder of his real and personal estate.

Ch. born Newfields [South New Market]: Thomas+, b 1715; Joseph+, b 24 Aug 1726; and John, b 1731. (Fitts' Newfields, p94,95,503,683; Young Family Records, courtesy of Nancy L. Dodge; LDS I.G.I. BR; Folsom Fam., **Reg**. 30:207-231)

THOMAS aka Jr., b 1715, New Market, s/o Thomas and Sarah (Folsom) Young, d 7 Jul 1791, New Durham; m 1740s, New Market, Rebecca (   ) [b 1720s, alive 1787, New Durham]. Thomas was named son and heir by his father's will signed 2 May, proved 27 May 1767, and was devised one half part of the "homestead plantation" of 100 acres in New Market, saw mill privilege and one half of the salt marsh and thatch bed "for his natural life," the moiety to revert to his son John upon his demise and all Thomas Sr.'s right and title to land in New Durham. Thomas and Rebecca originally lived in New Market, but by 1790 were residents of New Durham. He was in fact one of the original proprietors of New Durham. On 5 May 1749 at the house of widow Sarah Priest, Portsmouth, Thomas of New Market was granted Lot 45, 2nd Div., but became absentee owner. Added as a postscript to Thomas' many dealings, this lot drawn originally to Thomas was sold at public auction in 1812 for back taxes to Benjamin Libbey of New Durham for $1.41, by tax deed of 27 Jun 1814, rec'd 3 Jul 1815; witnesses Moses Davis, Samuel Runnels [Strafford Co. Deed 85:101].

New Durham town records indicated he was voted selectman for the years 1773, 1774, 1778 and 1779. The 1790 census listed him also as head of family in New Durham with only one female in the household. Thomas served two months and eleven days prior to 30 Sep 1777 in Capt. Jeremiah Gilman's Co. [NH State Papers 39:1].

In 1778, Thomas of New Durham conveyed title to the homestead plantation in New Market to son John of New Market who then occupied the estate with the buildings, bounded s.w. by land of Job Savage and Col. Joseph Smith, n.w. on the Piscassic River and easterly by Lamprey River, situated partly in New Market and partly in Durham, by deed signed 4 Apr 1778, rec'd 20 Dec 1786, for 50 pounds lawful money; witnesses Walter Bryent, Simon Dow [Strafford Co. Deed 8:63]. In 1787 Thomas quitclaimed the 100 acres in the 1st Div., New Durham with its buildings which he had inherited from his father, "the farm on which we now live....laid out to the [original] right of Thomas Young Esq. of New Market," to Joseph Young of New Market, Rock. Co., [probably brother] by deed signed 6 Jun, rec'd 29 Dec 1787, for 50 pounds; Rebechah conveyed dower rights; witnesses Benjamin Drew and Joseph Peirce [Strafford Co. Deed 8:494].

The following deeds involved the purchase and sale of 116 acres of Lot 121, 3rd Div., Rochester. Thomas Jr. bought this acreage excluding the 24 acres previously sold for back taxes, by deed signed 11 Jun, rec'd 13 Jul, 1779, from John Tolford of Chester, Rock. Co., for 180 pounds; Anna Tolford ceded dower rights; witnesses Jane Tolford, Joshua Tolford [Strafford Co. Deed 2:411]. Thereafter, Thomas sold all of Lot 121 in moieties by (1) quitclaim for the n.e. half to Jacob Joy of Durham, blacksmith, for 2,800 Continental dollars, by deed signed 17 Jun, rec'd 17 Jul 1779; witnesses Joseph Peirce and Benjamin Lear [Strafford Co. Deed 2:420]; (2) when of Durham, quitclaimed the other half, or 58 acres, to Stephen Pinkham of the Parish of Madbury for 90 pounds by deed signed 27 Nov 1779, rec'd 7 Jan 1785; witnesses Andrew Hanson, Robert Hanson [Strafford Co. Deed 6:171].

Known ch. b New Market: John+, b 1751. Known ch. b New Durham: Thomas Jr.+, b 1759. (Census Strafford Co., 1790, p94; New Durham, **Reg.** 61:359,360; Fitts' Newfields, p683,684; LDS I.G.I. VR; Jennings' New Durham, p12,13,90; Folsom Fam., **Reg.** 30:207-231; Young Family Recs., courtesy of Marjorie S. Heaney)

THOMAS, b 24 May 1718, of Rochester, poss. gr.s/o Thomas and Mary (Roberts) Young of Dover Neck, d 10 May 1772, Rochester; m 28 Jul 1745, Rochester, Anna Roberts [b 1723, bp 16 Jun 1751, Rochester, d Oct 1777, native town]. It is to be noted that Thomas' surviving children in 1803/1804 were heirs-at-law of Isaac Young of Dover who was son of Jonathan and Abigail (Hanson) Young. (For complete list of Isaac's heirs who were descendants of the said Jonathan and Abigail, see Isaac and Elizabeth Young of Dover.) While Jonathan of Dover named a Thomas as son and heir by his will drawn 1 Jul 1752, proved 29 Sep 1756, this Thomas' date of birth does not agree with "Thomas, b 15 Jul 1712, s/o Jonathan" [Heritage's Dover VR, p24]. Another possible family connection is suggested by Thomas' purchase of Lot 69, 2nd Div., Wakefield in 1770 [cited below] and the purchase in 1785 of adjacent Lot 68, 2nd Div., Wakefield by Joseph Young of the New Market branch. Whether or no Thomas was a descendant of this same branch, the records show that Thomas' granddaughter Nancy Young of Wakefield married the grandson of the said Joseph of New Market, Joseph Young of Wakefield in 1806; their homestead on Lots 66 and 67 were contiguous with Lots 68 and 69.

Thomas' earliest purchase of land was 60 acres of Lot 85, 1st Div., Rochester by deed signed 23 Oct 1741, rec'd 26 Oct 1782, from Timothy Gerrish Esq. of Kittery, York Co., Bay Colony of Mass. [later, Maine], "which fell to me [Gerrish] in the draught of the said first division lots in said Rochester," for 145 pounds; witnesses Moses Carr, Samuel Gerrish [Strafford Co. Deed 4:303]. Thomas and Anna took up residence in Rochester by the early 1750s, during which time they became members of the First Congregational Church, Rochester where Anna and children were baptized. He was listed as one of the petitioners of Rochester on 8 Feb 1762 in the town's appeal to Gov. B. Wentworth for representation at the General Assembly, and was a signer in 1770 of the petition addressed to the Assembly relative to the inconveniences of the proposed building of a bridge at Cochecho Falls in the town of Dover.

As yeoman, he bought Lot 69 in "the New Town Ship lying at the headline of Rochester commonly called the "Easternmost Township" [aka East Town aka Wakefield] and joining on Salmon Fall River" for 18 pounds, by deed signed 27 Mar 1770, rec'd 5 May 1773, from Benjamin Canney, cordwainer, and William Canney, both of Somersworth, drawn to the original right of their father Thomas Canney, late of Dover; witnesses Benjamin Varney, James Varney [Strafford Co. Deed 1:144].

Thomas's will, signed 4 May, proved 30 Sep 1772, named his eldest son Jonathan as Exec. and residuary legatee; witnesses Moses Brown, James Bickford, Avery Hall [Exeter, Rock. Co. Probate No. 3962, Old Series]. He devised to wife Anna her one-third share of both his personal and real estate "during her natural life." Son Jonathan was to receive the family homestead in Rochester and all his personal and movable estate not disposed of. Sons Thomas, James and Moses, were each to receive a one-third share of Lot 69, 2nd Div., Wakefield. He devised to single daughter Abigail Young five shillings, and to single daughters Anna, Mary and Susannah "when they arrive at lawful age, each a cow and feather bed." The administration of Thomas' estate fell to widow Anna with will annexed since son Jonathan predeceased his father; bond of 500 pounds was posted 30 Sep 1772, by widow Anna, John Plummer Esq. and Jonathan Dam, Yeoman, by which the sureties were authorized to take inventory and submit their findings at Exeter, at or before the last Wednesday of December next [Rock. Co. Deed Docket No. 3692].

Admin. papers on the estate of single daughter Mary were granted to her brother Moses of Rochester 22 Mar 1831; bond of $2,000.00 was posted with sureties Samuel Stackpole of Rochester and Joseph Cross of Dover [Strafford Co. Probate 30:465]. Inventory of her personal estate was submitted 2 May 1831, sworn to the following day by appraisers Charles Dennett, Samuel Stackpole and Benjamin Hayes [Strafford Co. Probate 40:240]: clothing and household effects were valued at $90.53; 17 notes of hand considered good, $1,144.44; 5 notes deemed doubtful, $379.45; and 4 notes considered bad,

$70.76. Moses submitted his account of his sister's estate 19 May 1832, approved same date [Strafford Co. Probate 42:323]. Lucy's personal estate was valued at $2,014.46; expenses of admin., funeral, appraisal and sundry fees came to $487.00; balance of $1,527.46 was due from Admin.

Both Thomas and Anna were buried at Haven Hill Cemetery, Rochester. Ch. b Rochester: Abigail, b ca 1750, alive 1772; Jonathan, b 1750s, d 4 Jul 1772, Rochester; Timothy, bp 16 Dec 1753, not listed in father's will; Thomas, b ca 1754, d pre 1803/04; James+, b 29 Aug 1758; Anna+ (Young) Wentworth, b 23 Feb 1760; Mary, b 1763, d 9 Dec 1830, single, age 67, Rochester; Susannah, bp 21 Apr 1765, alive 1772; Moses+, b 9 Jul 1767. (NH Gen. Recs., V4, No.4, p145; V5, No.2, p51,52; V6, No.2, p115,116; Wentworth Gen., V2, p255; Goss's Colonial Graveyards, p117; McDuffee's Rochester, p586-621; NH State Papers, V13, p332-338)

THOMAS, b ca 1720, of New Market, m 1 Feb 1749/50, Durham, Mary Huntress [b ca 1725, of Newington, that part of old Dover and Portsmouth which came to be known as Bloody Point]. (Stackpole's Durham, V1, p379; Ham's Dover Marr, TMs)

THOMAS, b 5 Dec 1728, Dover, poss. s/o John and Elizabeth ( ) Young of Dover Neck [whose son Thomas was bp 1736], d 9 Sep 1809, age 81, Dover; m ca 1759, Dover, Patience ( ) [b ca 1730, Dover]. (Heritage's Dover VR, p142; Ham's Dover Marr, TMs)

THOMAS, aka Gent. aka Capt., b 1730s, of Dover Neck, d testate 4 Mar 1795 of consumption, Dover; m 1750s, Dover ( ). He was listed as head of a large household in 1790, Dover with family of three sons over 16 years of age, one son under 16, and four females. Thomas, Gent., purchased two parcels of land in Dover, 15-1/2 acres and 7-1/2 acres, with buildings adjacent to lands of Alexander Cardwell, Adam Perkins and John Perkins, east on Berwick River, by deed of 10 Nov 1783, rec'd 21 Jul 1789, from Clement Ham of Dover for 180 pounds; witnesses Samuel Wigglesworth, Israel Ham [Strafford Co. Deed 11:57].

His will was drawn 7 Apr 1791, probated 28 Apr 1795, naming son Thomas as his Exec. and residuary legatee; witnesses Ephraim Bickford, Stephen Roberts Jr. and Moses Hodgdon, all of Dover [Strafford Co. Probate 4:246]. Son Thomas was allowed Exec. on date of probate, having given bond of $3,000.00 with sureties of said Hodgdon and Bickford [Strafford Co. Probate 4:349]; he was directed "to deliver to his mother [anonymous] her thirds as the law directs." Thomas made the following bequests: son Thomas, all his real estate in Dover where he then dwelt and elsewhere in Dover together with all stock of cattle, sheep and horses, also the bed and bedding "as it stands, whereon he usually lies"; daughters Mary Nason, Sarah Young, and Deborah Horn, each one cow; sons John and Stephen, equal halves of seventy acres of land in Lebanon; sons Joseph and Moses, each a yoke of six feet oxen and a cow.

The appraisal of Thomas' estate was returned on 15 Jul 1795, by said witnesses of Thomas' will, allowed on same date [Strafford Co. Probate 4:284]; values were given in dollars and cents. Real estate of 58 acres on Dover Neck with dwelling house was assessed at $1,900.00. Personal estate was rated at $248.14: some of the items included neat stock, farming tools, one old "gondalow" and old canoe at $8.00, one bed and bedding in the west room supposed by the appraisers to be the bed Capt. Young gave his son Thomas in his will at $10.00, three "underbeds" with bedstead and cord, pewter ware, free lock gun at $6.00, one pistol at 50 cents, one other free lock gun son Thomas lent to his brother Joseph at $6.00, one pair silver shoe buckles at $2.00, razor at $8.00 and one sermon book at 75 cents. A vivid description of "the Piscataqua gundalow" referred to in the inventory of Thomas's estate was given by Catherine B. Fahnestock in her family history of the Bickfords of New Hampshire: it was a really unique type of vessel in shipbuilding developed along the Piscataqua as early as 1697 to accommodate specific demands. "They had to be very narrow for the tributary rivers, be able to carry heavy loads in shallow waters, and so constructed that they could be handled in the dangerous currents of the 'Horse Race' off Bloody Point....Skill was required to handle a gundalow and took as much practice and experience as foreign voyages." Often gundalows were used in ferrying travelers, but more often than not, carried lumber, bricks and granite.

Son [Lt.] Thomas remained on Dover Neck at the family homestead. Sons John and Moses moved to Ossipee where they bought shares of Lots 3 and 4, Moses to move on to Wakefield; and son Joseph began homesteading in Farmington, then relocated in Wakefield. Nothing further was known of Stephen; he may well have settled in Lebanon upon receiving his legacy. Ch. b Dover Neck: Mary (Young) Nason, b ca 1754; Sarah, b ca 1756; Deborah+ (Young) Horne, b 1758; Thomas+, b 19 Dec 1759; John+, b ca 1761; Stephen, b ca 1763; Joseph+, b ca 1764; and Moses+, b 1766. (Census Strafford Co., 1790, p89; Heritage's Dover VR, p198; Ham's Dover Marr, TMs; Bickford Gen., p231; Young Family Recs., courtesy of Marjorie S. Heaney)

THOMAS aka Jr., b 1759, New Durham, s/o Thomas and Rebecca (   ) Young, gr.s/o Thomas and Sarah (Folsom) Young of Newfields, alive 1806, Alton; m 23 Dec 1784, Dover, Tamme aka Tamsen Hayes [bp 8 Aug 1762, Toll End, Dover, d/o Thomas and Hannah (Twombly) Hayes, alive Alton, 1806]. Thomas was of New Durham at time of marriage. Tamsen was named daughter and heir, a minor under 14 years, in her father's will drawn 3 Mar 1772, proved post 7 Apr 1774 [Hayes Gen., V1, p61,62]. Her father devised to her a one-fourth share of the household furniture, the sum of 25 pounds, the use of the west room of the homestead while she remained single and the privilege of hauling wood from her father's land in Green Hill, Barrington.

Throughout his adult life Thomas speculated heavily in real estate in Strafford County, astute enough to recognize

the developing areas surrounding Dover after the Revolutionary
War and to act accordingly. The earliest of Thomas' some
forty land deeds showed that Thomas and wife Tamme lived in
Dover roughly from 1783 to 1794. Despite overlapping dates,
other places of residence were New Durham from 1784 to 1801,
Barrington from 1794 to 1796, and lastly, Alton from 1801 to
last date of signing, 24 Nov 1806. Their one known homestead
was situated on part of Lot 7, 1st Div., Alton described in
one of Thomas's deeds by date of 22 Aug 1803, rec'd 24 Aug
1804, "being the same I now live on" [Strafford Co. Deed
46:266].

The presence of lot numbers, Tamme's right of dower, and
the familiar names of witnesses helped immensely in establishing not only Thomas' identity but the roads he traveled from
Dover to Alton. The records did not allude to children, nor
did purchase or sale of any of his properties name another
"Young." Full coverage of Thomas' speculative purchases of
land would not be feasible in this narrative. For the sake
of the descendants of Thomas and Tamme Young and history buffs
who would wish to delve further into the nearly four dozen
land deeds, please refer to appendix (2) which covers the time
spans and residences referred to above. (Ham's Dover Marr,
TMs; Heritage's Dover VR, p82)

THOMAS aka Lt., b 19 Dec 1759, Dover Neck, s/o Capt.
Thomas Young, d testate 13 Apr 1844, native town; m ca 1791,
Dover, Nancy Drew [b 1760, Dover, d 5 Dec 1839, age 79, home
town]. Thomas's legacy by his father's will drawn 7 Apr 1791,
proved 28 Apr 1795, was the family homestead of 58 acres on
Dover Neck, assessed in 1795 at $1,900.00. He was listed on
the census returns for Dover from 1800-1830. In 1800 his age
was 26-45, household containing another male of same age
group, one female 45 plus, one female 26-45 [spouse], four
males under 10, and three females, two under 10 and one age
10-16. In 1810 Thomas was age 45 plus, with family of spouse
in same age bracket, three males, two under 10, one age 16-
26, and three females all age 10-16. In 1830 his age was
70-80, members of household were spouse of like years, one son
age 20-30 and one daughter age 30-40.

The following land deeds of Lt. Thomas are included,
courtesy of Marjorie S. Heaney who is a direct descendant of
Thomas' line. Thomas Young and Daniel Drew, both of Dover,
purchased and then mortgaged on same date, 50 acres land in
Dover on the western side of the road leading from Dover to
Portsmouth, usually called Fields Plains, adjacent to lands
owned by Joseph Reynolds, from Nicholas Peaslee of Dover by
mortgage signed 28 Oct 1823, rec'd 4 Feb 1824, for $500.00;
witnesses Daniel Pierce, A. Pierce [Strafford Co. Deed
120:435]. Thomas, with wife Nancy ceding dower rights, sold
to Deborah Bickford, widow of Ephraim Bickford, 7 acres on
Dover Neck, bounded by lands of Joseph and Paul Pinkham and
John Nason by deed rec'd 12 Mar 1824 [Strafford Co. Deed
120:358]. He sold to son John of Dover, joiner, land bounded

by the corner of his dwelling house, by deed rec'd 17 May 1827
[Strafford Co. Deed 152:19]; purchased 2 rods land at n.e.
corner of his dwelling house from Alonzo and Mary Roberts by
deed rec'd 30 Oct 1834 [Strafford Co. Deed 162:176]. Before
Thomas drew up his will in 1841, he deeded to Alonzo Roberts
of Dover, 24 acres land in Dover Neck, north by George Nason
and east by Robert Varney, deceased, "land conveyed to my late
father Thomas Young by Clement Ham, deed dated 10 Nov 1783,"
for $1,225.00; deed rec'd 7 Sep 1835 [Strafford Co. Deed
166:126]. Thomas then sold his homestead place of 30 acres
or more where he then lived to Joshua Banfield of Dover, by
deed rec'd 7 Sep 1835 [Strafford Co. Deed 166:135]. By two
deeds rec'd on same date of 27 Jan 1838, Thomas settled his
remaining properties: (1) Thomas and co-grantor John P. Hale
of Dover quitclaimed 24-1/2 acres land on Dover Neck to Alonzo
Roberts of Dover for $1.00; this land abutted land of Robert
Varney, George Nason, Andrew Varney and other lands of Aaron
Roberts and George Nason; Lucy Hale, wife of John P., ceded
her dower rights; witnesses Timothy R. Young, Joseph H. Smith
[Strafford Co. Deed 176:504]; (2) for these considerations
Alonzo Roberts stated in second deed that he was "held firmly
bound to Thomas Young of Dover, to be paid to said Thomas
Young in sum of $2,000.00 or his heirs...said Roberts obli-
gates himself to provide and support Thomas...provide him with
food, drink, wood, clothes, nursing needs and all other things
necessary and convenient...." [Strafford Co. Deed 176:499].
    Thomas' will of 7 Jun 1841, proved 7 May 1844, left all
of his real and personal estate to his sole Exec., Alonzo
Roberts of Dover; witnesses Ezekial Hurd, J. Richardson,
Andrew Peirce Jr. [Strafford Co. Probate 58:195]. Each of his
surviving children, Paul D., Patience, and John, received the
token legacy of $1.00. In ailing health, Thomas spent his
last days at the home of the said Alonzo Roberts where he
died. Ch. b Dover Neck: Paul D.+, b 23 Aug 1792; Patience,
b ca 1800; and John+, b prob. 7 Jul 1803. (Census Strafford
Co., 1810, p863; 1830, p313; NHVR-Deaths; Ham's Dover Marr,
TMs; Gaz. & Strafford Adv. Obit, p3)
    THOMAS, b 1760s, of Rochester. He was absentee owner of
80 acres in 2nd Div., Rochester; this acreage was sold for
back taxes for the year 1780, by tax deed signed 25 Jan 1781,
rec'd 3 Mar 1797, to Samuel Robinson of Rochester for 48
pounds; witnesses William and Elizabeth Palmer [Strafford Co.
Deed 23:523].
    THOMAS, b ca 1760, of Wakefield; head of household in
Wakefield in 1810, age 45 plus, with spouse of same age group,
and family of four males, one under 10, two age 10-16, one age
16-26, and two females, both age 10-16. (Census Strafford
Co., 1810, p586)
    THOMAS, b 18 May 1767, Durham, s/o Joseph and Mary (Foss)
Young of New Market, cordwainer, d 30 Jul 1845, Ossipee; m ca
1790, Abigail (   ) [b ca 1770, of Ossipee, alive 1815, same
town]. Thomas was named son and heir of Joseph Young of New

Market in the division of property determined in 1806, receiving what came to be termed by all siblings as their "one-twelfth share" in Joseph's estate. Thomas received a one-fourth part of a sawmill in New Market on the western side of Lamprey River at the lower falls. When first married Thomas and Abigail made their home in Durham. They became landowners in Durham, Wolfeboro and Ossipee. It is likely that they returned to Durham in their later years.

After Thomas married and while still of Durham, he bought 50 acres land in Wolfeboro from John and Molly Emerson, situated at n.w. corner of Waldron Hennison's land to s.e. corner of acreage said Emerson sold to James Suthern, by deed of 23 Feb 1792, rec'd 13 Jun 1793, for 30 pounds; witnesses John Young, Samuel Burleigh [Strafford Co. Deed 16:169]. Another of Thomas' earliest purchases, probably with speculation in mind, was a piece of land in Dover Commons, acreage not specified, on east side of Province Road between Israel Huckings' land and that of Jabax Davis by deed signed 7 May 1796, rec'd 15 Aug 1798, from William Evans Jr. of Barrington, for nine pounds; witnesses Joshua Foss Jr., Moses Canney [Strafford Co. Deed 28:238]. Sale of the Wolfeboro land, with Abigail ceding dower rights, was conveyed by deed signed 19 Apr 1800, rec'd 18 Oct 1804, to Moses Brown of Wolfeboro for $300.00; witnesses Joseph Fogg, Thomas Rogers [Strafford Co. Deed 45:421]. Concurrent with this sale, Thomas bought 50 acres of the 500-acre Lot 12, Ossipee, drawn to the original right of Thomas Wallingford Esq., from Moses and Lydia Brown of Wolfeboro for $300.00, by deed signed 19 Apr 1800, rec'd 25 Jan 1809; witnesses Joseph Fogg, Thomas Rogers [Strafford Co. Deed 60:154].

Circa 1807 Thomas settled in Ossipee when he sold his "one-twelfth share" of his father's estate in New Market and Durham to [brother] William Young of Durham by deed of 14 Jul 1806, rec'd 21 Jan 1807, for $80.00; witnesses Nathaniel Kidder, Wentworth Cheswell [Strafford Co. Deed 54:13]. Per 1802 tax polls of Ossipee, Thomas was taxed as resident; besides livestock, he owned 2 acres tillage, 4 acres mowing, 4 acres pasturing, and 41 acres wild land. The census records for Ossipee listed him as head of family from 1810-1830 only. In 1810 Thomas was under 45 years, with spouse of same age group, and family of two males, one under 10, one age 16-26, and three females, one under 10, two age 10-16. In 1830 he and spouse were age 60-70, and had family of one male age 20-30 and two females, one age 20-30, and one age 30-40. When of Ossipee, he sold the 50 acres of 500-acre Lot 12, Ossipee "where I now live," by deed signed 18 Sep 1815, rec'd 24 Nov 1815, to Elijah Hodgdon of Ossipee for $700.00; Abigail ceded dower rights; witnesses Charles Bickford, Ezekial Wentworth [Strafford Co. Deed 87:231]. One of Thomas' last known deeds when of Wolfeboro was the sale of 50 acres of Lot 1, Wolfeboro [Addition] to Joseph Young of Wakefield, clothier [nephew] for $200.00, by deed of 19 Jun, rec'd 24 1823; witnesses Ezekial Wentworth, John Wentworth [Strafford Co. Deed 118:263].

Known ch. b Ossipee: Thomas Jr.+, b 1790 and Joseph+, b 1803. (Census Strafford Co., 1810, p758; 1830, p425; Fitts' Newfields, p683,684; Merrill's Carroll Co., p592)

THOMAS, b 1770s, of Wakefield. Thomas was landowner in the Wolfeboro Addition in 1807. Based on the following two land deeds, proper identification could not be made on this Thomas. The deeds pertained to large Lot 1, Wolfeboro Addition. Two men come to mind: (1) Thomas+, b 18 Mar 1767, son of Joseph and Mary (Foss) Young of Durham, or (2) Thomas+, b 7 Oct 1784, s/o James and Mary (Kimball) Young of Wakefield. While of Wakefield, Thomas bought 50 acres of Lot 1, Wolfeboro [Addition], from Samuel Jennes of Wolfeboro for $300.00, by deed signed 3 Aug 1807, rec'd 16 Sep 1807; witnesses Mark Wiggin, Thomas B. Wiggin [Strafford Co. Deed 55:265]. Sale of part of Lot 1, Wolfeboro Addition by Thomas of Wakefield, land Thomas "recovered of Samuel Jennes by execution," was by quitclaim signed 10 Feb, rec'd 17 Feb 1810, to James of Wolfeboro for $1.00; witnesses James Young, Joseph Hawkins [Strafford Co. Deed 63:78]. It is to be noted that John+ Young, b 1751, held title to 74-1/2 acres, Lot 1, Wolfeboro Addition as of 1801.

THOMAS, b 1780s, of Wolfeboro; head of household in Wolfeboro in 1830, age 40-50, with family of two females age 30-40, one male age 15-20 and two females, one age 5-10 and one 15-20. (Census Strafford Co., 1830, p443)

THOMAS, b 7 Oct 1784, Rochester, s/o James and Mary (Kimball) Young, d 10 Oct 1864, North Wakefield; m 23 Dec 1813, Wakefield, Mary Nute [b 22 Dec 1777, Milton, d 7 Jan 1861, Wakefield]. He was listed as resident of Wakefield from 1830-1860. In 1830 Thomas's age was 40-50, spouse was 50-60; their family held three females, one age 5-10 and two 10-15. In 1840 his age was 40-50, with family of spouse, age 50-60 and three females age 15-20. On date of 11 Mar 1834 Thomas was listed as taxpayer of Wakefield by Check List Used in Town Meeting, and on date of 15 Jun 1848 was appointed Post Master for North Wakefield. In 1850 Thomas and Mary lived by themselves; in 1860, with daughter Susan and her husband William Powell; both Thomas and Mary were blind. Thomas bought 6 acres, 5 rods with buildings on the n.e. part of Lot 44, Brookfield at the line between Brookfield and Wakefield from Nathaniel Roberts of Brookfield for $120.00, by deed signed 24 Jul 1810, rec'd 11 Aug 1813; single witness Joseph Young [Strafford Co. Deed 76:281]. This self-same property was sold by Thomas to Richard K. Young of Wakefield [brother] by deed signed 29 Sep 1823, rec'd 30 Sep 1823, for $150.00; witnesses Ezekial Wentworth, Spencer Wentworth [Strafford Co. Deed 119:54]. Thomas and spouse were buried at Old Young Cemetery on Long Ridge Road, Wiggins Hill, North Wakefield. Known ch. b North Wakefield: Susan N.+ (Young) Powell, b 24 Nov 1817. (Twombly's Wakefield Cem., TMs; NH Gen. Recs., V5, No.4, p147; Census Strafford Co., 1830, p458; 1840, p371; Census Carroll Co., 1850, p318; 1860, p566; Bank's Wakefield, p84,1044)

THOMAS, b 1790s, of Dover; head of household in Dover in 1840, age 40-50, with large household of female age 50-60 and nine other females, four age 15-20, five age 30-40. This family profile suggests a breadwinner and spouse, several teenage daughters and adult female siblings. (Census Strafford Co., 1840, p543)

THOMAS aka Jr., b 1790, Ossipee, s/o Thomas and Abigail (   ) Young, alive 1860, Durham, soap boiler; m ca 1810, Wolfeboro, Elizabeth (   ) [b 1790, alive 1860, Durham]. Thomas and Elizabeth raised their family in Wolfeboro but returned to Durham late in life. He was head of household in Wolfeboro from 1830-1840, and then in Durham from 1850-1860. In 1830 his age was 30-40; young household contained spouse age 20-30, one male age 5-10 and two females, one under 5 and one 10-15. In 1840 his age was 40-50, with spouse age 30-40, and family of two females, one under 5 and one age 10-15. By 1850 Thomas and Elizabeth had relocated to Durham where he became head of household in Durham from 1850-1860. Youngest daughter Aloria aka Alvina was sole child at home during this time span. In 1850 other member of household was Mary Fernald, age 22 [b 1828, ME].

Ch. b Wolfeboro: Joseph+, b 27 Jul 1811; Ann C., b 2 Jul 1813; Thomas C.+, b 30 Apr 1815; Elizabeth, b 15 Sep 1816; Caroline E., b 18 Sep 1820; and Aloria aka Alvina, b 1821. (Census Strafford Co., 1830, p434; 1840, p387; 1850, p449; 1860, p598; NHVR-Births; LDS I.G.I. BR)

THOMAS, b 1790, of Wakefield, shoemaker; m 1820s, Anna (   ) [b 1800, ME, alive 1860, Wolfeboro]. Thomas and Anna were residents of Wakefield in 1850 with child Ellen at home. By 1860 Thomas and spouse had taken up residence in Wolfeboro where they lived alone. Ch. b Wakefield: Ellen, b 1837. The following main entry strikes a note of similarity with this Thomas. (Census Carroll Co., 1850, p347; 1860, p525)

THOMAS, b ca 1795, of Lebanon, ME, d pre 1891, prob. Dover Neck; m 4 Jul 1818, Lebanon, ME, Anna Furbush [b 1798, Kittery, ME, d/o Joseph and Martha (Lord) Furbush, d 30 Jan 1891, widow, age 93, Dover Neck]. (NHVR-Deaths; Lebanon, ME V.R., p168,224, courtesy of Marjorie S. Heaney)

THOMAS, b 1806, of Dover; he lived alone in Ward 2, Dover as of 1870, retired at age 64. (Census Strafford Co., 1870, p56)

THOMAS, b 1812, Ossipee, d 9 May 1890, native town, single. (NHVR-Deaths)

THOMAS, b 1822, of Dover; in 1850, he roomed at boarding house, his trade carder. (Census Strafford Co., 1850, p41)

THOMAS, b Dec 1823, of Farmington, poss. s/o Samuel P. and Abigail B. (Rand) Young, alive 1900, Rochester; m 9 Jun 1850, Somersworth, Sabrina Wentworth [b Jan 1826, Berwick, ME, d/o Samuel and Lydia (Thompson) Wentworth of Rochester, one of ten children, alive 1900, Rochester]. Note that Wentworth Gen. gave Sabrina's d-o-b as 3 Jan 1827. Thomas and Sabrina lived in Farmington in 1850 when eldest daughter Martha A. was born. By 1900 their place of residence was Rochester; members of household were daughter Mary L. Willand, husband Frank Willand and grandson George Willand. Ch. b Farmington: Martha A., b Aug 1850, d 28 Dec 1853, Farmington; daughter b 12 Jan 1854. Ch. b Rochester: Clara A.+ (Young) Furbush, b 2 Aug 1851; Samuel T.+, b 10 Aug 1852; Mary L.+ (Young) Willand, b 3 Jul 1855; and Lovina A.+ (Young) Hayes, b 19 May 1858. (NHVR-Births, Marr, Brides, Deaths; Census Strafford Co., 1850, p644; 1900 Soundex; Wentworth Gen., V2, p583,584; LDS I.G.I. BR; Rochester TR, Marr)

THOMAS, b ca 1825, of Lebanon, ME, res. of Milton and Rochester; m ca 1850, ME, Lavinia (   ) [b ca 1830, ME]. Thomas and Lavinia were residents of Lebanon in 1859 where daughter Susan F. was born. They lived for a short time ca 1874 in Milton where a son was born, and upon the death of their children they lived in Rochester. Ch. b Lebanon, ME: Susan F., b 1859, d 18 Dec 1874, age 15 of scarlet fever, Rochester. Ch. b Milton: Benjamin W., b 24 Mar 1874, d 24 Feb 1875, age 11 mos., of scarlet fever, Rochester. (Rochester VR, Deaths, p193)

THOMAS, b 1826, of Lebanon, ME, manufacturer, res. of Rochester; m ca 1850, prob. Lebanon, Sophia (   ) [b 1826, of Lebanon, ME, alive 1870, Rochester]. Thomas and Sophia were listed on the 1870 census returns for Rochester with a family of three children, Samuel, Clara and Mary S. Ch. b Rochester: Samuel, b 1852; Clara, b 1854; and Mary S., b 1855. (Census Strafford Co., 1870, p287)

THOMAS, b Feb 1842, Ossipee, s/o Joseph and Hannah (Allen) Young, drayman, d 27 Oct 1919, Wolfeboro, widower; m 1867, Wolfeboro, Maria S. Bodge [b Sep 1848, Ossipee, alive 1900, age 51, Wolfeboro, predeceased her husband]. Thomas lived at parents' home in Ossipee up through 1860. He and Maria raised their family in Wolfeboro, listed as residents from 1870-1900. In 1870 sole child at home was Perley E. Thomas was appointed Admin. of his father Joseph's estate in Ossipee on 7 Jun 1881. In 1900 children Mabel C., Addie C. and Bertha M. lived at home as well as nephew John H. Bodge, age 13 [b Feb 1887]. Letters of Admin. on Thomas' estate in Wolfeboro were filed by heirs-at-law Perley E. Young, Mabel E. Humphrey, Ruth Adelaide Young and Bertha M. Young, all of Wolfeboro, on 26 Dec 1921; approved 7 Feb 1922 [Carroll Co. Probate #8486]. They petitioned that Sewall W. Abbott of Wolfeboro be appointed Admin. Value of real estate was set at $3,000.00; personal estate, $1,000.
    Ch. b Wolfeboro: Perley E.+, b Aug 1868; Dana, b 12 Jun 1871, d 29 Dec 1874, Wolfeboro; Mabel E. (Young) Humphrey, b Apr 1873, alive 1921; Addie aka Ruth Adelaide, b Aug 1875, alive 1921, single; Dana E., b 6 May 1878, d 31 Mar 1879, Wolfeboro; Bertha M., b 9 May 1882, alive 1921, single; Dana E., b 19 Mar 1884; and Harry M., b 1889, d 26 Sep 1891, Wolfeboro. Note that Vital Records gave d-o-b on son Leslie as __ Mar 1884, d 22 Nov 1884, Wolfeboro, most likely twin of

Dana E. born that year. (Census Carroll Co., 1870, p464; 1900 Soundex; NHVR-Births, Deaths, Marr; LDS I.G.I. BR)

THOMAS C., b ca 1815, of Moultonboro; head of household in Moultonboro in 1840, age 20-30, with spouse of same age group, no children. (Census Strafford Co., 1840, p237)

THOMAS C., b 30 Apr 1815, Wolfeboro, s/o Thomas and Elizabeth (   ) Young of Durham, d 31 Aug 1887, Ossipee; m 25 Feb 1839, Ossipee, Abigail Wiggin [b 2 Feb 1815, Ossipee, d/o Isaac Wiggin, d 15 Oct 1896, native town, age 81-8-14]. Thomas and Abigail lived in Kittery, ME up through 1844 where a number of their children were born. By 1860 at least, Thomas, wife and family lived in Wakefield as listed on the census returns for that year; children at home, John C., Edward C., Martha, Henry aka James H., and Abby M. By 1870 Thomas and Abigail had resettled in Ossipee; the three young-est children lived at home.

Daughter Martha H. Young of Ossipee wrote her will 6 Feb 1888; date of probate 5 Mar 1889; witnesses Melvin A. Harmon, Nellie Harmon, Aldo M. Rumery [Carroll Co. Probate #5835]. She named sister Abby M. Young Exec. of her will and residu-ary legatee of her share in the homestead farm and personal property deeded to both Martha and Abbie by their father Thomas by deed signed 2 Jul 1886, "provided she shall be single and unmarried at the time of my decease." She stipul-ated further that if Abby were married [at time of probate], she then would receive the remainder of her estate "except the money that I may have deposited in any savings bank, which said bank deposits I bequeath to my brother James H. Young after the death of my mother." Brother John T. Young was to receive $1.00; John's daughters Sarah A. Young and Leona M. Moynihan were each to receive $50.00, Sarah when she reached the age of 21. If Sarah did not attain that age, then her share would go to her sister Leona. Brother James H. Young was to receive her interest in the house and lot in Dover formerly owned by Martha's aunt Mary S. Wiggin. Martha's mother Abigail was to receive the interest and income of any savings deposits she may have.

Ch. b Kittery, ME: Phebe E., b 11 Sep 1841, d 6 Apr 1842, ME; infant, b 1842, d same year, ME; John T., b 1843, twin, alive 1898; Joseph S.+, b 1843, twin; Edward C.+, b 26 Dec 1844. Ch. b Ossipee: Mary E., b 20 Jun 1848, d 20 Dec 1855, Ossipee; Henry A., b 26 Jan 1850, d 12 Oct 1855, Oss-ipee; Martha H., b 15 Apr 1853, d pre 5 Mar 1889, age 35, Ossipee; J. Henry aka James H.+, b 21 May 1855; and Abby M.+ (Young) Nute, b 10 May 1858. (NHVR-Births, Marr, Deaths; Census Carroll Co., 1860, p583; 1870, p366; LDS I.G.I. BR; Wiggin Gen., TMs, p176)

THOMAS F., b 16 Feb 1836, Wolfeboro, s/o Hollis and Betsey Ann (Drew) Young, d 7 Aug 1900, age 64-5-20, Dover; m 28 Nov 1867, Exeter, Mary Dermody [b May 1842, Ireland]. Thomas was a resident of Dover by the early 1860s on up through 1900. At age 24 as resident of Dover, Thomas enlisted

307

18 Jun 1861 for three years as Landsman in the U.S. Navy as
did his brother John A. two days later; he served on the
U.S.S. "Ohio," "Pensacola," and "Thomas Freeborn" and was dis-
charged 21 Jun 1864 as Quartermaster on his last ship, term
expired; he gave P.O. address of Dover. In 1900 Thomas F.,
Mary and son George lived at Ham Street, Dover. Ch. b Dover:
George P., b 27 Mar 1869. (NHVR-Births, Deaths, Marr; LDS
I.G.I. BR; 1900 Soundex; Soldiers & Sailors, p1180)

THOMAS J., b 1807, of Dover; d Jan 1850, same town, age
43. (Census, Strafford Co., 1850 Mortality Schedules, n.p.)

THOMAS S., b 1834, Farmington, d 23 Oct 1864, VA, of war
wounds; m 26 Aug 1855, Milton, Lovina E. aka Ellen L. Beedy
[b 1838, Berwick, ME, alive 1870, Farmington]. He and Lovina
were listed as residents of Farmington in 1860; children at
home, Charles, George H., and Adeline. Thomas enlisted from
New Durham, 21 Aug 1862 in Co. I, 10th Regt., NH Volunteer
Infantry, mustered in 4 Sep 1862 as Pvt., was wounded 29 Sep
1864 at Fort Harrison, VA and died of wounds 23 Oct 1864. His
widow Lovina m2 22 Dec 1870, Middleton, Levi F. Hayes [b ca
1845, of same town]. After Lovina E.' remarriage to said
Hayes, she filed guardianship papers 3 Jan 1871 for her children by Thomas; she was appointed guardian of daughters Lovina
A. and Evangeline, minors under the age of 14; bond of $600.00
was given by sureties Isaiah H. Place of Middleton, Jeremiah
S. Colbath of New Durham and Levi F. Hayes of Middleton
[Strafford Co. Probate 77:480]. On same date, George H.
Young, Thomas' son and minor above the age of fourteen,
elected the same Lovina E. Hayes to be his guardian; bond of
$600.00 with sureties given by the said three gentlemen above
[Strafford Co. Probate 77:480].

Ch. b Farmington: son b 10 Aug 1852; Charles F.+, b
14 Mar 1854; George H.+, b 27 Apr 1856; Adeline aka Lovina A.
b 1858; Eva+ aka Evangeline (Young) Tyler, b 2 Nov 1862. (LDS
I.G.I. BR; NHVR-Births, Brides, Deaths, Marr; Census Strafford
Co., 1860, p382; Soldiers & Sailors, p552)

TIMOTHY, bp 30 Sep 1750, Parish of Madbury, s/o Nathaniel
and Mary (Kimball) Young, d testate pre 25 Apr 1820, native
town; m 11 Nov 1773, Madbury, Lydia Demeritt [bp 7 Nov 1750,
Durham, d/o Ebenezer and Hannah (Thompson) Demeritt, d 5 Mar
1838, buried on Mill Hill Road, north of Bellamy River,
Madbury]. Timothy was elected selectman for Madbury in 1780,
1786, and from 1797-1798. He was listed on their census
returns from 1790-1810. In 1790 Timothy's household contained
five males under 16 years and four females; in 1800 his age
was 45 plus with household of two males under 16, two females
over 45 years and two females age 10-16. And in 1810 he and
spouse were over 45 years with household of two males age 16-
26 and two females 10-16.

Lydia, daughter and heir of Ebenezer Demeritt late of
Madbury, and husband Timothy relinquished their title and
interest in the 50-acre Demeritt estate in Madbury to her
mother, widow Hannah Demeritt in 1779; see co-grantors Ezra

and Susannah (Demeritt) Young for details. Timothy, as an heir-at-law of the late Isaac Young of Dover, received upon the division of the estate filed 1804, one acre land on the east side of the Main Road leading from the Dover Congregational Meeting House to Piscataqua Bridge by land of John Wheeler [Strafford Co. Probate 8:372]. This acreage was sold by Timothy by deed signed 18 Apr 1804, rec'd 17 Mar 1809, to Thomas Footman of Dover for $50.00; Lydia Young ceded dower rights; witnesses Thomas Hanson, J. P. Gilman [Strafford Co. Deed 60:422].

In 1804 Timothy added to his homestead by the purchase of 14 acres, 27 rods of land, "in moiety, being part of land I [Tobias Evans] purchased of John Twombly" in Madbury at the s.w. corner of Solomon Young's land and west by Timothy's to the river, from Tobias and Sarah Evans of Madbury for $314.00, by deed signed 3 Apr that year, rec'd 15 Sep 1806; witnesses Joseph Hussey, Elijah Austin Jr. [Strafford Co. Deed 52:288]. He then bought an additional 13 acres of land that lay north of his homestead, east by lands of Nathaniel Hayes [brother-in-law], south by lands of Jonathan Demeritt and west of Gerrish's river, from Jonathan and Elizabeth Chesley for $143.00, by deed of 30 May 1806, rec'd 15 Sep 1806; witnesses Maul Hanson, Paul Gerrish, Benjamin Moulton, Franklin Chesley [Strafford Co. Deed 52:283].

Timothy's will drawn 16 Dec 1815, proved 25 Apr 1820, named as Co-Execs. and residuary legatees his eldest sons, twins Eben D. and James H.; witnesses Benjamin Thompson, Stephen Bordman, Ebenezer Thompson [Strafford Co. Probate 23:494]; on date of probate, Eben D. and James H. gave bond of $5,000.00 with sureties Maul Hanson of Madbury and Nathaniel Ham of Dover [Strafford Co. Probate 25:103]. He devised to wife Lydia one-third of the homestead and dwelling, one-third of the farm income, and all household furniture for and during her natural life. Sons Ebenezer D. and James H. would receive full title to the homestead in Madbury upon their mother's demise, and were to have 40 acres woodlot in Barrington and his right in Gerrish's sawmill. Each of the following children were to receive $5.00: Nathaniel, Jeremy, Timothy, daughter Mary Hayes [wife of Nathaniel Hayes], and Hannah. Daughter Lydia would receive a $100.00 marriage portion, and the household furniture after the decease of their mother. Lydia and family members were buried at the family burial plot on west side of Mill Hill Road, Madbury, on land owned by William H. Knox.

Ch. b Madbury: Mary+ (Young) Hayes, b 28 Sep 1774; Ebenezer D.+ aka Eben D., b 19 Apr 1777, twin; James H.+, b same date, twin; Nathaniel B.+, b 1778; Jeremy+, b 1781; Timothy+, b 1780s; Lydia, b 1785, d 6 Nov 1829, age 44, Madbury, single; Hannah, b 1780s. (Heritage's Dover VR, p155,173; Census Strafford Co., 1790, p93; 1800, p164; 1810, p568; Hayes Gen., V1, p118,170; Demeritt Fam., **Reg.** 87:347; Adam's Madbury, n.p.; Steuerwald's Dover Cem., TMs)

TIMOTHY, b 1750s, Parish of Madbury, s/o Solomon and Kezia (Hanson) Young, alive 1796, native town. In all land deeds attributed to Timothy of Madbury up through 1796 no mention was made of spouse ceding dower rights, or conveyance of property to son or daughter. His earliest land deed was dated 2 Sep, rec'd 17 Oct 1774, when he purchased from James and Margaret Molony of Canterbury, Rock. Co., for 2 pounds and 16 shillings, three acres land in Madbury which was part of the real estate of John Molony, schoolmaster late of Madbury, the father of said grantors; it bounded the n.e. corner of the road that ran by Solomon Young's land; witnesses Archelaus Moore, Obediah Mooney [Strafford Co. Deed 1:195]. Timothy as co-grantee bought a one-fourth share of Daniel and Temperance (Bickford) Young's homestead in Madbury by deed signed 7 Dec 1770, rec'd 18 Oct 1771; see co-grantors Daniel and Temperance for full details. Timothy then consolidated his land holdings in Madbury adjacent to Daniel Young's former homestead with the purchase of 8-1/2 acres on Littleworth Road in 1775; see grantor Stephen Young [brother] and Kezia Young of Madbury for details.

Timothy, brother Solomon and Hezekiah Cook, all of Madbury, bought lands in Barrington. The first of these was 96 acres, Lot 78, 1st Div., in the 2nd Range drawn to the original right of Timothy Davis of Portsmouth, from Benjamin Bodge of Lee for 720 pounds lawful money by deed signed 28 Jan 1780, rec'd same date; witnesses John Wentworth Jr., Solomon Perkins [Strafford Co. Deed 2:478]. Ten years later, Timothy et al as co-grantors sold the same 96 acres of Lot 78, and 24 acres, part of Lot 79, 2nd Range, Barrington, drawn to original right of Jonathan Stootly, to Eleazer Cate of Barrington for $50.00, by deed signed 29 Dec 1790, rec'd 13 Jul 1799; witnesses John Cate, Joseph Cate [Strafford Co. Deed 30:432]. On same date of signing 29 Dec 1790, rec'd 20 Feb 1800, Timothy and co-grantors Solomon Young, Jeddiah Cook, and Hezekiah Cook Jr., disposed of 96 acres more from said Lot 79, 2nd Div., for 30 pounds lawful money; witnesses John Cate, Eleazer Cate [Strafford Co. Deed 31:540]. As sole grantee Timothy bought 34 acres of Lot 103, 3rd Range, Barrington, which was part of the original right of Samuel Sherburne, from Silas Caldwell of Barrington for $170.00, by deed signed 19 Mar, rec'd 31 Mar 1796; witnesses John Cate, William Caldwell [Strafford Co. Deed 22:209]. Another purchase from said Silas Caldwell was 24 acres situated partly in Lot 102, 3rd Range, and partly in Lot 103, 3rd Range, Barrington at n.e. corner of Timothy Young's land for $144.00, by deed signed 4 Feb 1801, rec'd 25 Mar 1802; witnesses John Cate, John Cate Jr. [Strafford Co. Deed 39:313].

TIMOTHY, b 13 Apr 1776, of York Co., MA [later Maine], s/o Jonathan and Mercy (   ) Young of England, d 10 Apr 1841, Effingham; m 27 Apr 1802, Effingham, Molly aka Mary D. Hobbs [b 1775, Effingham, sister of Jonathan Hobbs, d 6 May 1845, native town, widow]. Timothy's father Jonathan was b 11 Jul

1721, England, d 2 Nov 1807, York, Maine; his mother Mercy
(   ) was b 1736, England, d 29 Jun 1800, York, Maine. Circa
1805 Timothy and Mary took up residence in Effingham where
they became members of the Freewill Baptist Church. He was
listed as householder of Effingham from 1810-1840. In 1810
his age was 26-45 with spouse of same age group and family of
two males, one under 10, one age 10-16 and two females both
under 10. In 1830 he and spouse were age 50-60, with family
of one male age 20-30 and three females, one age 5-10 and two
age 20-30. By 1840 Timothy's age was 60-70, as was his
spouse's; household contained one male age 30-40 and four
females, one age 5-10, one 20-30, and two 20-40.

Timothy's father Jonathan of York Co., Mass. Bay Colony
[later Maine], made deed of gift to Timothy, age 21, of 60
acres of Lot 62, 1st Div, Effingham by deed signed 15 Aug
1797, rec'd 18 Jun 1804; witnesses John Kingsbury, Benjamin
Kingsbury [Strafford Co. Deed 45:275]. Jonathan of York Co.
bought these 60 acres by deed signed 15 Dec 1791, rec'd 18 Jun
1804, from Dudley Atkins Tyng, Admin. of estate of Patrick
Tracy, late of Newburyport, MA, for 27 pounds lawful money;
witnesses Benaiah Titcomb, Billing Putnam [Strafford Co. Deed
45:274]. There is no indication that Timothy's parents left
York Co., Mass. By 1808 Timothy owned parts of Lots 60, 61,
62 and 63, all in the 1st Div., Effingham. As a minor at age
20, even before his father's deed of gift, Timothy of York,
York Co., MA purchased 8 acres of Lot 63, 1st Div., Effingham
at corner of Lot 62 to line between Ossipee and Effingham from
John Buzzell of Effingham for $40.00, by deed signed 16 Aug
1796, rec'd 18 Jun 1804; witnesses Moses Hodgdon, Samuel
Tucker [Strafford Co. Deed 45:276]. He then bought part of
Lot 62, 1st Div., by quitclaim signed 11 Nov 1805, rec'd
10 Feb 1806, from John Leavitt, Simon Leavitt, Morris Leavitt,
Gent., Abraham Marston and John S. Dearborn, all of Effingham,
for $12.00; witnesses Gideon Rust, Isaac Lord [Strafford Co.
Deed 50:245].

He added to his homestead in the purchase of a one-half
share of 60-acre Lot 61, 1st Div., Effingham, drawn to the
original right of Josiah Marston, from Moses and Dorcas
Hodsdon and Moses Hodsdon Jr. for $125.00, by deed signed
28 Feb 1805, rec'd 16 Aug 1805; witnesses Isaac Bemis Jr.,
John Wheeler [Strafford Co. Deed 48:371]. By deed signed
28 Feb 1805, rec'd 19 Oct 1808, Timothy bought part of Lot
60, 1st Div., from Morris Hobbs of North Hampton, Rock. Co.,
for "a valuable consideration"; witnesses Morris Leavitt,
Morris Hobbs [Strafford Co. Deed 59:67]. He was empowered by
said Hobbs "at his own risk and cost to take all legal meas-
ures for procuring and holding said land by virtue of said
covenant made by us Morris and Abigail...or for obtaining cost
and damage in case of a failure of title." He was enabled to
buy 56 acres of this same Lot 61 at public auction by tax deed
of 8 Mar, rec'd 19 Oct 1808 for $1.50; witnesses Nathan Brown,
Morris Leavitt [Strafford Co. Deed 59:68].

Ch. b York Co.:   Sally, b ca 1803.   Ch. b Effingham:
Jonathan+, b 21 Dec 1805; Elizabeth+ (Young) Hayes, b 18 Nov
1809; Mercy, b 1810s; and Mary, b 1810s. (Census Strafford
Co., 1810, p765; 1830, 390; 1840, p350; Stearn's NH Gen., V3,
p1284; NHVR-Deaths; Hayes Gen., V1, p290; Morning Star, p376)
    TIMOTHY, b 1780s, of Dover, prob. s/o Timothy and Lydia
(Demeritt) Young of Madbury; m 27 Sep 1812, Rochester, Sabrina
Corson [b ca 1795, Rochester]. In 1840 Timothy was head of
household in Dover, age 50-60, with family of spouse age
40-50, one male age 10-15, and three females, one age 5-10 and
two age 10-15. (Ham's Dover Marr, TMs; Census Strafford Co.,
1840, p541; NH Gen. Rec., V5, No.4, p146)
    TIMOTHY, b 1790s, Dover; head of family in Dover in 1830,
age 30-40, with spouse of similar years, two males, one age
5-10, one 10-15, and four females, two under 5, one age 5-10,
and one 10-15. (Census Strafford Co., 1830, p313)
    TIMOTHY BENJAMIN, b 10 Nov 1840, Effingham, s/o Jonathan
and Sarah (Buzzell) Young, alive 1900, Wolfeboro; m 28 Nov
1867, Ossipee, Sarah M. Brown [b Nov 1849, of Wakefield, alive
1900, Wolfeboro]. Timothy B. was appointed Admin. of his
brother Lyman J.'s estate, father Jonathan having declined
the position of trust on 1 Mar 1870.   Inventory was taken
8 Mar 1870 by appraisers Simon P. Hill, David W. Hobbs, and
Stephen Hayes, approved 5 Apr 1870: savings accounts in Newburyport, Mass. amounted to $345.13; misc., $15.00 [Carroll
Co. Probate #5825].   By 1870 Timothy and Sarah lived with
Timothy's father Jonathan, then widower, in Effingham. Other
residences included Ossipee where a son was born, and in later
years Wolfeboro. By his father's will drawn 30 Jan 1871,
proved 6 Mar 1888, Timothy B. was named the sole Exec. and
residuary legatee of Jonathan's estate. In 1900 Timothy B.,
Sarah and son Oscar were residents of Wolfeboro; member of
household was boarder Clara E. Stanton, age 43 [b Apr 1857].
Note that Metcalf's Notables, p539, stated that Timothy B.'s
wife was Isabel S. Buzzell; no vital record on this came to
light.
    Ch. b The Pocket, Ossipee: Oscar Lyman, b 11 Sep 1874,
not traced further. (NHVR-Marr; Census Carroll Co., 1870,
p292; 1900 Soundex; Stearn's NH Gen., V3, p1284)
    TIMOTHY ROBERTS, b 19 Nov 1810, Dover, s/o Jeremy and
Anna (Kimball) Young, d 12 May 1898, Oilfield, Illinois; m
14 Jan 1852, Illinois, Margarette E. Jones [b ca 1815,
Illinois, d/o David L. W. and Frances (   ) Jones, alive 1898,
home state]. Timothy was witness to deed of co-grantors Lt.
Thomas Young and John P. Hale, both of Dover, date of recording 27 Jan 1838. He attended Phillips Academy at Exeter,
studied law in his home town and graduated from Bowdoin
College, Brunswick, ME, Class of 1835. After being admitted
to the bar while still single, Timothy relocated to Marshall,
Illinois, where he practiced law for ten years. For a few
years he went into politics, serving his district in the
thirty-first Congress but apparently did not find this con-

genial. When he retired from public life he became farmer. Other interests he pursued were merchandising wholesale tobacco and the construction of railroads before the Civil War. Ch. b Oilfield, Illinois: Kimball, b 1850s; Ellen Swepson, b 1850s, of Chicago; and Fanny J., b 1860, d 1890, home town. (Heritage's Dover VR, p70; Bowdoin College Grads., p409)

TIMOTHY W., b 23 Aug 1769, Durham, s/o Joseph and Mary (Foss) Young, d testate 28 Mar 1834, Wolfeboro; m 11 Oct 1798, Tuftonboro, Esther Libby [b 1778, Wolfeboro, d/o Reubin and Esther ( ) Libby of Wolfeboro, d 8 Jul 1858, age 80, Ossipee, seamstress]. In the division of his father's estate in 1806, Timothy received a one-fourth share of a sawmill in New Market on the western side of Lamprey River lower falls; this share came to be described among siblings as "a one-twelfth share" of their father's estate. Timothy was a resident of Tuftonboro as early as incorporation of the town 17 Dec 1795. At the first town meeting at the home of William Copp on Monday, 14 Mar 1796, Timothy was voted Town Clerk; he took minutes of that session. The 1810 census for Tuftonboro showed he was resident, age 26-45; family consisted of spouse of same age group, four males, three under 10, one age 10-16, and three females, two under 10, and one 10-16. By 1830 Timothy was householder in Wolfeboro, age 60-70, family containing spouse age 50-60, one male age 10-15, and two females, one age 5-10 and one 10-15.

His one-twelfth share of his father's estate was sold to brother Henry of Durham, by deed of 22 Jan, rec'd 27 Jan 1807, for $100.00; witnesses Edmund Layn, Wentworth Cheswell [Strafford Co. Deed 53:202]. For Timothy W.'s purchase of 10 acres land on the eastern side of Winnipesaukee Pond in the s.w. quarter of Tuftonboro by deed of 19 Oct 1801, rec'd 15 Sep 1803, see Benjamin and Phoebe (Allen) Young of Tuftonboro. He purchased 50 acres of Lot 14 "in the Masonian Proprietors' quarters of Wolfeboro," running n.w. by Lot 16 to Upper Beech River Pond so-called, from Samuel Connor of Wolfeboro for $190.00; by deed signed 26 Jan, rec'd 27 Dec 1814; witnesses Richard Rust, Benjamin Brown [Strafford Co. Deed 82:22]. Some time before 1830 Timothy must have conveyed title to these 50 acres in Wolfeboro to son Levi J.; see son Levi J. and Elizabeth Young for full details on the mortgage Timothy held on this property by deed signed 26 Oct, rec'd 27 Oct 1830.

Timothy W.'s will was drawn up 24 Mar, proved 16 May 1834, naming nephew John C. Young [s/o brother Zachariah] sole Exec. and son Jeremiah L. as residuary legatee; witnesses Thomas J. Tibbetts, David T. Livy, Paul Brown [Strafford Co. Probate 46:323]. As events turned out, widow Esther was allowed Admin. of his estate 26 May 1834; bond of $2,000.00 given with sureties Robert Wiggin and Paul Brown, both of Wolfeboro [Strafford Co. Probate 30:301]. Timothy bequeathed to wife Esther one-third of all his real estate in Wolfeboro, all the household furniture and one-third of his livestock for

313

as long as she remained his widow; if she remarried her share
of the homestead in Wolfeboro would revert to son Jeremiah L.
He made the following bequests: to sons Timothy, Joseph, and
Levi J., each $2.00; to daughter Mary Smith, $3.00; to single
daughters Sarah, $20.00; Hannah L., $10.00; and Esther A.,
$30.00; and to Jeremiah L., the rest of his real and personal
estate.

His estate contained 75 acres at the time of his death,
valued at $500.00. Personal and household effects including
1 loom, 2 spinning wheels and 1 linen wheel were set at
$349.75, appraised by John C. Young, Robert Wiggin and Paul
Brown, all of Wolfeboro; presented and allowed 23 Jun 1834
[Strafford Co. Probate 48:169]. The assessments given
Timothy's household effects, livestock and produce in 1834 are
indeed a lesson in 19th century economics. Furniture, linens,
ploughs and tools were very inexpensive. On the other hand,
livestock and farm produce, especially grains, commanded high
prices. Whereas 65 lbs. pork were worth $6.50, 3-1/2 bushels
oats cost $14.75. A handful of books were rated at $1.60, and
8-1/2 bushels wheat cost $12.75. An accounting of the estate
was made 20 Mar 1835 by John C. Young of Wolfeboro who had
been commissioned earlier on 13 Sep 1834 to draw up claims
against the estate. His report stated that claims t   d
$156.72, $13.25 of which were for expenses of Timothy's last
sickness, medical treatment given by Dr. Thomas J. Tebbetts
and Dr. David T. Levy; approved same date [Strafford Co.
Probate 49:74]. Esther, widow, made return on the estate as
Admin. 14 Sep 1838, allowed same date [Strafford Co. Probate
53:396]: under Credits, inventory of personal estate came to
$349.75, income of two-thirds of real estate, $75.00, cash
received of Jonathan Brown, $1.50; under Debts were payments
for last sickness and funeral expenses, $16.75, payments to
creditors, $152.66, payments of legacies to single daughters
Sarah, Hannah and Esther A., and payment to Jeremiah L. for
his proportion of personal estate, $172.34, debts totalling
$417.25.

Ch. b Wolfeboro: Levi J.+, b ca 1800; Timothy, b 1800s;
Sarah, b 1800s; Mary+ (Young) Smith, b 1800s; Joseph, b 1800s;
Hannah L.+ (Young) Bickford, b 1815; Jeremiah L.+, b 1817; and
Esther Ann+ (Young) Frost, b ca 1820. (Census Strafford Co.,
1810, p741; 1830, p437; NHVR-Marr, Deaths; Fitts' Newfields,
p683,684)

TRISTAM A., b 7 Jan 1849, Dover, s/o Jonathan T. and
Elizabeth L. (Demeritt) Young of Dover, d 18 Jan 1912, age
63, native town; m 2 Dec 1874, Dover, Sarah Amanda Wiggin [b
28 Aug 1840, MA, eldest child of William Wallace and Sarah
(McDuffee) Hayes Wiggin, d 14 Jul 1921, age 81, Dover]. They
had no issue. Tristam lived at home in 1870 with his widowed
mother and worked on the farm in Dover, Ward 3. He was named
Exec. and residuary legatee of the will of maiden aunt Hannah
S. Young of Dover [father's sister] drawn 8 Jun, proved 6 Jul
1880; see Jonathan and Abigail (Coffin) Young of Dover for

details. He and Amanda were listed on 1900 census return for Dover; household included sole boarder Fred E. Perkins, b 23 Apr 1882, Texas, age 18. Tristam and spouse were buried at Young Cemetery on Littleworth Road, Dover owned by John Young. (Hayes Gen., V1, p410; Dover Cem. Inscrip; 1900 Soundex; Wiggin Gen., TMs, p100)

VINA A., b 1856, Freedom, d/o Stephen C. and Susan A. (Patch) Young; m 11 Jul 1878, Freedom, Ernest L. Hatch [b ca 1850, Eaton, s/o Charles and Harriet N. (Perkins) Hatch]. (NHVR-Brides; Freedom VR, 1878-1890)

WALTER, b ca 1860, of Lee. He was widower in 1891, resident of Lee; his wife Lizzie (   ) was born 3 Mar 1863, d 2 Nov 1891, buried at cemetery on Mast Road, Lee, where Elder Osborne's Church once stood. (Folsom's Madbury Gravestones, p71)

WALTER, b ca 1862, Rochester; m ca 1885, Alice M. Tufts [b ca 1865, Rochester, alive 1888, home town]. Walter and spouse were residents of Rochester. Ch. b Rochester: Walter Jr., b 6 Apr 1888, not traced further. (Rochester TR, Births, p45)

WALTER H., b 19 May 1868, Ossipee, s/o Joseph and Hannah (Chick) Young 2nd, d____, native town; m 1890s, Ossipee, Margaret (   ) [b 1873, of Ossipee, d 1938, same town]. In 1870 he was age two on census returns for his parents in Ossipee. He and Margaret were buried at Young Cemetery, Ossipee. (Loud's Cem. Records, p142)

WARREN, b 1853, Barnstead, s/o George and Lucy (   ) Young [no main entry]; m 2 Aug 1871, Charlestown, Ella D. Graham [b 1854, Charlestown, d/o Albert G. and Sarah H. (   ) Graham of Alstead]. (NHVR-Marr)

WARREN A., b 10 Sep 1852, Barnstead, eldest s/o John H. and Elizabeth Anna (Caswell) Young, d 10 Apr 1886, age 33-7-0, Pittsfield, harness maker; m2 1 Jan 1879, Barnstead, Emma E. Stevens [b 1855, Chichester, d/o John B. and Emeline (   ) Stevens]. (NHVR-Marr, Deaths)

WENTWORTH L., b 18 Feb 1808, Ossipee, eldest s/o John C. and Betsey C. (Lord) Young, d testate 23 Mar 1870, Tuftonboro, merchant; m1 17 Feb 1831, Tuftonboro, Mary E. Wiggin [b ca 1810, Tuftonboro, d/o Gideon and Dolly (Lyford) Wiggin, d pre 1850, native town]; m2 ca 1850, Susan F. Wiggin [b 17 Feb 1808, Tuftonboro, sister of the said Mary E. Wiggin, d 8 Nov 1898, age 80, native town, widow]. It is worthy of note that there are variants on the name of the bride but not on the date of marriage in 1831: NHVR-Marr listed Mary E. Wiggin as bride; the Wiggin Gen. stated it was Susan F. Wiggin. Both of Susan's parents were born in Exeter; when married the Wiggins relocated in Tuftonboro. Wentworth was head of household in Ossipee from 1840-1850: in 1840, his age was 30-40, with family of spouse age 20-30, and one male and female both age 5-10. The 1850 census named Susan F. as his spouse; member of family was daughter Adalade, age 18. Sometime thereafter, Wentworth and spouse relocated to Tuftonboro. By

census returns taken 1 Jun 1870 for Tuftonboro, widow Susan
F. lived alone. See Luther Young, brother and co-grantor, for
details of the sale of father John C.'s homestead in Ossipee
in 1830.

Wentworth L.'s will was drawn 17 Aug 1854, proved 5 Apr
1870, naming wife Susan F. as sole Exec. and legatee of his
real and personal estate "wherever it may be found"; no other
heir-at-law was cited; witnesses John Wingate, Joshua Roberts,
J. E. Russell [Carroll Co. Probate Docket #5838]. Parents and
children were buried at Water Village Cemetery, Ossipee. Ch.
b Tuftonboro, by Mary?: Adalade C., b 10 Feb 1832, d 6 Oct
1853, Freedom; John C., b 15 Mar 1835, d 18 Aug 1846, Ossipee.
(NHVR-Marr, Deaths; Loud's Cem. Records, p83; Census Strafford Co., 1840, p224; Carroll Co., 1850, p191; 1870, p424;
Wiggin Gen., TMs, p76)

WILLARD A., b 1846, Ossipee, s/o Joseph and Hannah
(Chick) Young 2nd; m 1870s, Lottie (   ) [b 1854, of Ossipee,
d 23 Jul 1877, same town]. In 1850 Willard A. was a lad of
four at his parents' home in Ossipee and lived there up
through 1870. Lottie was buried at Young Cemetery, Center and
South Effingham Road, Ossipee. (Loud's Cem. Recs., p141)

WILLIAM, b ca 1700, of Dover; m 27 May 1722, Portsmouth,
Susannah Cotton [b ca 1700, of Portsmouth]. (NHVR-Marr)

WILLIAM, b 23 Apr 1723, Dover, d 17 Jun 1787, native
town; m ca 1770, Dover, Susannah (   ) [b 1 Oct 1740, of
Dover, d 14 Mar 1833, Dover or Tuftonboro]. This was possibly
William's 2nd marriage. In 1790 widow Susannah was head of
household in Dover with family of two males under 16 and two
females. It is believed that in 1830, at age 90-100, she
lived with son John and his family in Tuftonboro. Ch. b
Dover: prob. George+, b 9 Sep 1771; John+, b 12 Dec 1776.
(Census Strafford Co., 1790, p89; 1830, p385; Heritage's Dover
VR, p194; Ham's Dover Marr, n.d.)

WILLIAM, b 1749, poss. Philadelphia, s/o James and
Margaret (Sloan) Young of Scotland, d 1833, Barrington; m
5 Jun 1791, Barrington, Charity Howe [b 1767, of Barrington,
d 1819, same town]. William of Philadelphia and Scotland
became patriarch of a long line of descendants stemming from
Barrington. William was head of household in 1800, Barrington, age 45 plus, with spouse age 26-45, and one male and two
females all under age of 10. Ch. b Barrington: Dolly+
(Young) Brock, b 1790s; Aaron+, b 30 Nov 1793; and William
Hale+, b 14 Mar 1809. (Census Strafford Co., 1800, p156; Ham
Gen., p25; NHVR-Marr; Hammond's Barrington TR, p13)

WILLIAM, b 1750s, of Wolfeboro; listed on the 1810 census
for Wolfeboro, age 45 plus, with spouse of same age; household
of four males, two under 10, one age 16-26, one 26-45, and two
females, one under 10, one age 16-26. (Census Strafford Co.,
1810, p737)

WILLIAM, b 8 Jan 1775, poss. Wolfeboro [Addition], s/o
John and Mary (Burleigh) Young, alive 1850, Wolfeboro, gr.s/o
Thomas and Sarah (Folsom) Young of New Market; m (Intentions)

21 Sep 1801, m 22 Oct 1801, Wolfeboro, Sally Burleigh [b 8 Jan 1777, Newfields, d/o William and Comfort (Taylor) Burleigh of Ossipee, d Nov 1858, Wolfeboro]. William was resident of Wolfeboro from 1830-1850. In 1830 his age was 40-50 as was his wife, with family of three males, one age 15-20, two 20-30, and two females, one age 10-15, one 20-30. In 1840 his and his wife's ages were 60-70; no offspring at home. In 1850, Sarah was named as his spouse; members of household were daughter Drusilla, Nancy (Burleigh) Young, age 63 [b 1787], widow of Samuel B. Young [William's brother], and nephews Nathaniel, John and Alonzo, sons of Samuel B. Young.

Sarah's father William Burleigh bought 500-acre Lot 46, Ossipee in 1798, where he and spouse relocated. William Burleigh died 11 May 1801 while chopping down a dead limb of a tree. Sarah's legacy from her father was 45 acres of Lot 46 in Ossipee, which she and husband William sold by deed signed 28 Dec 1802, rec'd 29 Jan 1819, to George Stevens of New Market [husband of sister Mary Burleigh] for $150.00; witnesses Joseph Fogg, John Burleigh [Strafford Co. Deed 101:509]. See brother and co-grantee John C.+ Young, b ca 1782, for full details in the following two purchases of land: property bought in Wolfeboro by co-grantees William Young and Samuel Wiggin, both of Wolfeboro, by deed signed 13 Apr 1816, rec'd 23 Jun 1819; and "the front 100 acres" in the Wolfeboro Addition as part of the 300 acres originally drawn to the right of Jonathan Warner made with co-grantees [brothers] Samuel B. and William of Wolfeboro, by deed signed and rec'd 9 Feb 1815.

Known ch. b Wolfeboro: Hollis+ aka Horace, b 17 Jan 1810 and Drusilla, b 1817. (NHVR-Marr, Deaths; Census Strafford Co., 1830, p436; 1840, p386; Census Carroll Co., 1850, p365; 1900 Soundex; Ossipee TR, V1; Fitts' Newfields, p461,683,684; Parker's Wolfeboro Banns, 1789-1854, n.p.)

WILLIAM, b 11 Sep 1777, Durham, s/o Joseph and 2nd wife Mary (Foss) Young of New Market, gr.s/o Thomas and Sarah (Folsom) Young, d 12 Dec 1844, age 67, native town; m 19 Feb 1809, Durham, Martha Bennett [b 2 Feb 1783, Newfields, d/o John and Mary (   ) Bennett, d testate 7 Mar 1862, age 79, Durham]. William was first cousin to the preceding William of Wolfeboro. He received a one-twelfth share in the disposition of his father's property in Durham and Newfields in 1806, 2-1/2 acres in Horns Wood. He and Martha made their home in Packers Falls, Durham on 80 acres or one-half of the homestead farm deeded to him by his father Joseph on date of 29 Sep 1801, rec'd 2 Jan 1802, exclusive of the dwelling house, situated on the southern portion of the lot by lands adjacent to those of Samuel Foss and David Davis.

William was a life-long resident of Packers Falls, Durham, listed on census returns from 1810-1840. In 1810 his age was 26-45, household consisting of two females 26-45 and one son 5-10. By 1830, he was age 50-60, with family of one female age 40-50, four sons, one under 5, one age 10-15, one

15-20 and one 20-30, and two females, one under 5 and one age 5-10. In 1840 his age was 60-70, spouse was 50-60, household containing two males one age 15-20, one 30-40, and two other females, one age 10-15 and one 20-30. In 1850 widow Martha was head of family, age 66; living at home were her married son Joseph, his family and daughter Sarah C., age 31. In 1860 she and Sarah C. were members of son Joseph's household, which would indicate that title of the homestead had by then been conveyed to Joseph.

William bought out a total of three one-twelfth shares of his father's estate, two from brothers George G. of Wolfeboro and Thomas of Ossipee, both deeds recorded 21 Jan 1807, and the third, from brother Benjamin Young of Tuftonboro by deed recorded 25 Jan 1809. See entries on parents and brothers for full details. By deed signed 10 Dec 1824, rec'd 4 Jul 1825, he, wife Martha and Sally Young of Durham, [widow of his brother Henry Young] sold to Robert Channel of Durham for $55.75, 1-3/4 acres land in Durham; single witness Joseph Young [Strafford Co. Deed 127:78].

Admin. Papers on William's estate were filed 7 Jan 1845 by widow Martha and son Joseph, both of Durham, who were appointed Co-Admins.; bond of $5,000.00 posted, sureties Moses H. Wiggin, Eleazer Bennett, both of Durham [Strafford Co. Probate 50:287]. On 1 Feb 1845, inventory of William's estate was returned and attested to by Moses H. Wiggins, Edward Griffith and Samuel Hayes, all of Durham [Strafford Co. Probate 58:226]: real estate included the 80-acre homestead farm with buildings at $3,000.00; 16-1/4 acres in 20-acre lot in Durham, $240.00; 6 acres in Piscassic lot, $300.00; and 1-1/2 acres of meadow in New Market, $20.00; total value of real estate, $3,560.00. Personal estate contained goods and chattels rated at $651.46; notes of hand deemed good, $210.00; total real and personal estate valued at $4,421.46. Widow's allowance of $200.00 was granted to Martha on 4 Mar 1845 [Strafford Co. Probate 43:200]. As Co-Admins., Martha and son Joseph submitted their account 4 Nov 1845 [Strafford Co. Probate 67:321]: expenditures during Admin. amounted to $1,147.44. Amount of receipts on hand was $861.46. Balance of $285.98 was to be shared between the two administrators.

Petition for Martha's dower rights was filed 3 May 1859, surprisingly delayed for some fifteen years after William's death; allowed 6 Sep 1859 [Strafford Co. Probate 71:352]. Dower rights were set off by David Davis, Benjamin Doe and Deacon John Thompson, all of Durham: 9 acres of field land beginning at the corner of the tract by the Boston & Maine R.R. and by land of widow Lydia Hayes, 20 acres of a tract of wood and pasture land beginning at the corner of the tract by the said railroad and by land of the said widow Hayes, then south to Lamprey River, and the customary household privileges. The partition of William's estate was made on date of 6 Dec 1859 between Martha, son Joseph and daughter Sarah C., by the above committee [Strafford Co. Probate 63:472]. It made all three parties joint tenants of house and land; Martha received a 2/24th part of the real estate, Sarah C., an 11/24th part, and Joseph, an equal 11/24th share. Martha's will was drawn up 6 Sep 1860, proved 6 May 1862, which named daughter Sarah C. Young Exec. and residuary legatee; witnesses Benjamin Doe, Nancy M. Doe, Olinthus N. Doe [Strafford Co. Probate 70:479]. Sarah C. posted bond of $1,000 on date of probate, with sureties Eben J. Pearson and William Woodman, both of Durham [Strafford Co. Probate 68:304]. Martha made these bequests: to son Joseph, $5.00; to daughter Sarah C., eight acres of field land and the remainder of her estate.

Family members were buried at the David Davis Farm, Packer's Fall, Durham. Ch. b Durham: Joseph+, b 22 Mar 1810; William, b 27 Jun 1813, d 29 Aug 1839, Durham; John Henry, b 7 Feb 1816, d 2 Mar 1835, Durham; Sarah C.+ (Young) Dudley, b 17 Dec 1820; Thomas, b 28 Sep 1821, d 31 Jul 1845, Durham; and Mary Elizabeth, b 4 Jul 1826, d 16 Oct 1846, Durham. (Stackpole's Durham, V2, p15; Durham Graveyards, No. 158, p63; Census Strafford Co., 1810, p548; 1830, p44; 1840, p501; 1850, p446; 1860, p571; Fitts' Newfields, p440,683,684; NHVR-Deaths)

WILLIAM, b ca 1780, of Barrington; listed on the 1810 census for Barrington age 26-45, family containing spouse age 26-45, two males, one under 10, one age 10-16, and one female under 10. (Census Strafford Co., 1810, p493)

WILLIAM, b ca 1785, of Durham; m 1808, Durham, Patty Bennett [b ca 1790, of Durham]. (NHVR-Marr)

WILLIAM, b ca 1800, of Allentown; m 23 Jan 1823, Freewill Baptist Church, Strafford, Fanney Clark [b ca 1805, Barrington]. (Strafford Marr, **Reg.** 76:31)

WILLIAM, b ca 1810, of Somersworth; m 12 Apr 1837, Somersworth, Sarah Keniston [b ca 1815, of Somersworth]. (NHVR-Marr)

WILLIAM aka Jr., b ca 1815, of Wolfeboro; listed on 1840 census for Wolfeboro age 20-30; household contained spouse age 30-40, and three females, one under 5 and two 5-10. (Census Strafford Co., 1840, p386)

WILLIAM, b 1853, of Farmington; at age 7 in 1860, he lived at home of Isaac and Mary Kenney. (Census Strafford Co., 1860, p400)

WILLIAM C., b ca 1810, Madbury; m ca 1835, Madbury, Clemina M. ( ) [b 1817, Madbury, d 25 Jul 1855, age 38, her native town]. William C.'s homestead stood at Shadogee Corner, Madbury; the home and farm were later mortgaged, then sold to another family. Ch. b Madbury: Lucy Ellen, b 12 Jun 1855. (NHVR-Births, Deaths; LDS I.G.I. BR; Adam's Madbury, n.p.)

WILLIAM G., b 20 Nov 1870, Barrington, s/o George W. and Elizabeth S. (Buzzell) Young; m 23 May 1892, Barrington, Georgann Brown [b 1873, of same town, d/o George and Julia ( ) Brown]. (NHVR-Marr; LDS I.G.I. BR)

WILLIAM H., b 1833, of Middleton, shoemaker; in 1850, at age 17, he lived at the home of Charles York, age 29 [b 1821] and Emily F. York, age 21 [b 1829] in Middleton. (Census Strafford Co., 1850, p101)

WILLIAM H., b 23 Apr 1865, Madbury, s/o John R. and Abbie M. (Clay) Young; m 28 Aug 1897, Raymond, Florence D. Pearsons [b 1865, Londonderry, d/o David W. and Esther (Lamos) Coffin of Bethel, ME, her 2nd marriage]. William H. was named son and heir of John R. Young of Madbury by his will drawn 5 Oct 1877, proved 7 May 1878. For guardianship papers on William, petitioned on 4 Feb 1879 after father's death, see parents' entry. (NHVR-Marr; LDS I.G.I. BR)

WILLIAM HALE, b 14 Mar 1809, Barrington, s/o William and Charity (Howe) Young, d 5 May 1891, farmer, native town; m1 24 Mar 1834, Barrington, Sarah J. Daniels [b 31 Jan 1814, of Barrington, d 22 Mar 1848, same town]; m2 24 Jan 1849, Barrington, Sophie aka Sophia Locke Hall [b 2 Oct 1828, Barrington, d/o Jacob and Abigail (Foss) Hall, d 21 Oct 1898, age 70-0-19, native town, half sister of first wife]. William was listed on the 1840 census for Barrington, his age 30-40, with household of spouse age 20-30, an elderly female figure age 90-100 [poss. Sarah's mother], three males, two under 5, one age 20-30, and one female age 5-10. He and Sophie were listed as residents of Barrington from 1850-1860. In 1850 children by first wife Sarah were at home: Lorana J., William Jr., Charles, Sarah E. and Lydia A. In 1860 the three youngest children were at home, estate valued at $3,500. Sophia helped to raise her half-sisters' children and became a member of the First Congregational Church, Barrington.

According to the 1871 Strafford County Map, William H.'s home was located in District #8, fairly close to the Madbury/Dover town lines. This area would coincide with the historic Two-Mile Streak. William H.'s will was signed 11 Mar 1889, proved 30 May 1891, naming neither Exec. nor children but devised all personal estate to second wife Sophia; witnesses G. W. Davidson, W. H. H. Young, Sophia L. Young [Strafford Co. Probate 107:206]. On date of probate widow Sophia requested that [son] William H. H. Young of Boston, MA be allowed Admin. of her husband's estate. Letters of Admin. "with the will annexed" were issued to William H. H., who posted bond of $1,000.00, with sureties L. J. Ham and E. S. Winkley [Strafford Co. Docket #7357]. Ch. b Barrington: Lurana Jane aka Lavina J.+ (Young) Hanson, b 31 Jan 1835; William Henry Harrison aka Harrison+, b 15 May 1837; Ira, b 28 Nov 1839, d 16 Sep 1840, Barrington; Charles Albert+, b 22 Sep 1842; Ellen Sarah+ (Young) Winkley, b 7 Oct 1844; and Lydia Abigail+ (Young) Daniels, b 26 Mar 1847. (Census Strafford Co., 1840, p479; 1850, p523,524; 1860, p188; Barrington Church Rec., p251; NHVR-Brides, Marr, Deaths; Ham Gen., p27,29; Sanford & Everts 1871 Maps; Hammond's Barrington TR, p59; note that under NHVR-Deaths, Sophia's d-o-b was 2 Oct 1828)

WILLIAM HENRY, b 5 May 1772, Upper Gilmanton, s/o Joseph and Anna (Folsom) Young, d 26 Sep 1797, age 25-4-21, native town; m 29 Dec 1796, Belmont, Hannah Dudley [b ca 1775, of Upper Gilmanton, alive 1798, same town]. William H. was the only son of a prominent businessman and farmer. As a young man William was one of the principal merchants in Academy Village, keeping open a store and tavern from 1793-1797 until his untimely death. He bought land in Gilmanton [acreage not specified] located at the north side of the new road which led from Burn's store to Sanbornton and on s.w. side of the Province Road, from Thomas Burns of Gilmanton for 10 pounds and 10 shillings, by deed signed 11 Dec 1794, rec'd 2 Mar 1797; witnesses John Busswell, Samuel Nudget [Strafford Co. Deed 24:303]. Apparently his second and last purchase of land was by deed signed 21 May 1795, rec'd 2 Mar 1797, for 45 rods of land which was part of Lot 8, 1st Range, in Gilmanton beginning at the north corner of William's land which he had lately purchased of Thomas Burns along the Province Road, from Joseph Badger Jr. of Gilmanton for $40.00; witnesses Elizabeth Badger, Joseph Young [Strafford Co. Deed 25:83].

William died prematurely without having written a will. It is not known if he and spouse Hannah had children. At the request of Capt. Joseph Young [father], Joseph Badger Jr., Benjamin Swett and Jacob Tucker were appointed to take inventory of William's estate. Return was made on 9 Oct 1797, allowed same day [Strafford Co. Probate 5:343]. Real estate of house, barn and one-half acre were valued at $900.00. Personal estate was rated at $740.22, which included one horse at $50.00, two cows at $30.00, household goods at $89.83, one bible at 60 cents, one watch at $15.00, wearing **apparel at** $60.00 and shop goods at $54.20; grand total of real and personal estate, $1,640.22. His father Joseph, acting as Admin., submitted his account 16 Nov 1798 [Strafford Co. Probate 5:395]. Personal and real estate was rated at $1,640.22; sundry accounts on the books amounted to $100.00; grand total of estate, $1,740.22. He prayed allowance for the expenses of $869.22 which the estate had incurred; balance due to Admin., $877.00. William was buried at the family burial plot situated between Laconia and Gilmanton on Province Road. (Goss's Gravestones, p56; NHVR-Marr, Deaths; LDS I.G.I. BR; Lancaster's Gilmanton, p136,137,246; Folsom's Gilmanton Cem., p126)

WILLIAM HENRY HARRISON - see Harrison

WILLIAM J., b 1828, Gilmanton; at age 33, William enlisted 12 Aug 1861 at Boston for two years as Ordinary Seaman, U.S. Navy; he failed to appear. However, as resident of Laconia at age 34, he enlisted 8 Aug 1862, mustered in the following day as Private and deserted 25 May 1863. He was "joined from desertion" 1 Sep 1864 and discharged 1 Jul 1865 at Fort Delaware, Delaware. (Soldiers & Sailors, p96,1180)

WILLIAM N., b 1867, Gilmanton, s/o Jonathan and Martha A. (Nelson) Young; m 1 Apr 1893, Concord, Susie M. Pitman [b 1876, Barnstead, d/o John T. and Dora R. (Dyer) Pitman]. He was resident of Concord at time of marriage. (NHVR-Marr)

321

WINTHROP, b 1753, Barrington, s/o Benjamin and Anna (   ) Young, d 8 Jan 1832, age 79, Canterbury; m ca 1776, Barrington, Mary Otis [b 1751, Barrington, d/o Joshua and Jane (Hussey) Otis, d 11 Apr 1849, age 98, Canterbury]. Winthrop was one of the early inhabitants of Barrington having signed the 1776 Association Test for Barrington and the Petition of Inhabitants in favor of John Garland in the same year [Garland was subsequently appointed as one of the Magistrates for Strafford Co.]. He became Elder of the Freewill Baptist Church in his community. In the early 1780s, Elder Winthrop, wife and large family relocated to Canterbury, most likely after they sold their property in Barrington: by deed signed 25 Nov 1785, rec'd 6 Jun 1787, he and wife Mary sold 60 acres of Lot 70, 2nd Range, Barrington by land of Abraham Waldron, and eight acres of Lot 15, 1st Range, Barrington which he purchased of John Garland in 1782, to Jeremiah Berry of Rochester for 300 pounds lawful money; witnesses Joshua Foss Jr., Alexander Berry [Strafford Co. Deed 8:321].

Ch. b Barrington: Deborah+ (Young) Bean, b 1774; Benjamin+, b 7 Jan 1778; Otis+, b 1779; Winthrop+, b 1783; Jonathan+, b 24 Jul 1785. Ch. b Canterbury: Polly (Young) Hill, b 25 Aug 1786, wife of Elder Samuel Hill of Loudon; Betsey, b 29 Jul 1788, [see husband Joseph Young of Gilmanton, b 1771]; Hannah, b 25 Jun 1790; Mercy, b 1793; Solomon, b 1795, d 14 Jul 1873, age 78, widower, Canterbury; and Nancy (Young) Batchelder, b ca 1800, m 25 Dec 1822, Canterbury, Gardner Batchelder of Loudon. (Wilson's Assoc. Test, p122; NH State Papers, V11, p154; Otis Gen., **Reg.** 5:209,210; Morning Star, p376,377; NHVR-Deaths; Lyford's Canterbury, p341-344; Young Family Recs., courtesy of M. Elaine Woodward)

WINTHROP, b 1783, Barrington, s/o Winthrop and Mary (Otis) Young of Canterbury; m 25 Oct 1804, Canterbury, Polly Cochran [b ca 1785, of Canterbury]. (Lyford's Canterbury, p341)

WINTHROP, b ca 1805, of Meredith, d pre 17 Feb 1846, same town; m ca 1830, prob. Meredith, Sally C. (   ) [b ca 1810, of Meredith, alive 1846, same town]. Winthrop was head of family in Meredith in 1840, age 30-40, with spouse of same age group, and family of two females, one under 5, one age 20-30. Admin. Papers on Winthrop's estate in Meredith were filed by widow Sally C. Young on 17 Feb 1846; approved same date [Belknap Co. Probate #345]. (Census Strafford Co., 1840, p163)

ZACHARIAH, b 9 Feb 1765, New Market, eldest s/o Joseph and second wife Mary (Foss) Young of Durham, gr.s/o Thomas and Sarah (Folsom) Young of New Market, d testate 31 Jan 1851, age 86, Wolfeboro; m1 ca 1786, Durham, _____ [b ca 1770, d pre 1830]; m2 post 1830, Wolfeboro, Nancy (   ) [b ca 1770, of New Market, d pre 20 Nov 1842, Wolfeboro]. Zachariah was named as son and heir in the division of Joseph's estate in Durham on 22 Sep 1807, receiving a one-twelfth share: 1-1/2 acres in New Market by land of Paul Chapman and 8 acres in

Horns Woods, Durham. Up through 1800 he resided in Durham, thereafter in Wolfeboro as did many of his brothers, where he became a member of the Freewill Baptist Church. From 1810-1830, Zachariah was listed on the census returns for Wolfeboro: in 1810 his age was 45 plus, spouse was age 26-45 years, with family of two sons, one under 10, one age 16-26, and three daughters, one under 10 and two 16-26. In 1830 his age was 60-70, apparently a widower, with family of one son and one daughter at home, both age 20-30. In 1840 it is believed Zachariah [age 70-80] resided with only son John H. who was head of household in Wolfeboro. He was elected Selectman of Wolfeboro for 1814-1815.

While of Durham Zachariah speculated a little in real estate by the purchase of 40 acres in Gilmanton, Lot 30, 1st Div., 5th Range, drawn to the original right of Edward Hilton, from Abraham aka Abiather Sanborn of Gilmanton by deed signed 28 Jun, rec'd 1 Jul 1790, for 82 pounds-10 shillings; witnesses Jeremiah Connor Jr., Joseph Badger [Strafford Co. Deed 12:114]. In turn he sold this same acreage to Tabitha Wilkins of Gilmanton, single woman, for 60 pounds by deed signed 1 Jun, rec'd 2 Nov 1792; witnesses Joseph Badger Jr., Dudley Hutchinson [Strafford Co. Deed 15:85]. In 1794, still of Durham, he purchased 50 acres of Lot 3 in the Wolfeboro Addition, extending to the town line between Ossipee and Wolfeboro, from James and Mary Fernald of Wolfeboro for 60 pounds by deed signed 24 June 1794, rec'd 30 Jun 1808; witnesses Moses Hodsdon, Thomas Young for James Fernald; John Sweasey, Timothy W. Young for Mary Fernald [Strafford Co. Deed 58:218]. And by deed signed 30 Sep 1797, rec'd 8 Mar 1798, he sold to Henry Young [brother] of Durham, 12-1/2 acres in Durham which had belonged to brother Jeremiah, deceased, from the sale of Jeremiah's estate by James Cram, Admin. [by deed of 25 May 1794 which referred to abuts, etc.] for $50.00; witnesses Wentworth Cheswell, Nathaniel Kidder [Strafford Co. Deed 28:12]. In 1801, then of Wolfeboro, he purchased an additional 25 acres of Lot 3, Wolfeboro, from Jacob and Augusta Wiggin of Wolfeboro, for $250.00, by deed signed 3 Jun 1801, rec'd 30 June 1808; witnesses Joseph Fogg, John Brown, Joseph Bussell, Stephen Thurston [Strafford Co. Deed 58:220]. This lot became his homestead. In same year, Zachariah held a mortgage on 21 acres land of owner John Sweasey of Wolfeboro by deed dated 14 Mar, rec'd 20 Apr 1801, in the amount of $100.00; witnesses Moses Thurston, James Martin [Strafford Co. Deed 35:306]. Said Sweasey did not redeem this mortgage, but rather quitclaimed the 21 acres to Zachariah by deed signed 5 Feb, rec'd 3 Sep 1802, for $250.00; witnesses Mark Wiggin, Moses Thurston [Strafford Co. Deed 40:196]. Zachariah followed this up by selling these acres in Wolfeboro adjacent to lands of Thomas Whittle and James Sheafe, to Joseph Nudd of Wolfeboro for $283.50, by deed signed 25 Oct 1802, rec'd 13 Apr 1807; witnesses Mark Wiggin, William Nudd [Strafford Co. Deed 54:282]. One of his last known deeds quitclaimed

land in New Market to his brother William of Durham for
$50.00, by deed signed 23 Nov 1818, rec'd 21 Dec 1819; wit-
nesses Samuel Hayes, Valentine Smith [Strafford Co. Deed
106:44].

Zachariah's will was drawn 20 Nov 1842, proved 11 Feb
1851, in which he named son John C. as his sole Exec.;
witnesses John Burleigh, Hollis Burleigh, Stephen Tibbetts
[Carroll Co. Prob. #5817]. By the terms of his will he had
split up his real and personal estate into six parts and
devised them in this manner: one share each to sons James H.
and John C.; one share each to daughters Mary Sceggel, wife
of Benjamin Sceggel, and Betsey Smith, wife of Benjamin Smith;
and a one-third share to said son-in-law Benjamin Smith. The
understanding here was that Benjamin Smith was "to pay over
to my grandson William B. Young a part of the avails of said
bequest when he arrives to the age of twenty-one years provided he remains to live with him...during his minority."
Grandson William B. Young [b 1837, d 25 Jan 1862, age 25,
buried Wolfeboro, parentage not discovered] was to receive the
sum of $4.00; granddaughter Sophronia M. A. Young [b ca 1835,
parents not identified] to receive the sum of $2.00.

Zachariah and daughter Nancy were buried at Smith Hill
Cemetery, Ossipee. Ch. b Durham by 1st wife: James H.+, b
22 Mar 1787; John C.+, b 25 Apr 1789; Mary+ (Young) Sceggel,
b ca 1793; and Betsey+ (Young) Smith, b 21 Nov 1796. Ch. b
Wolfeboro by 2nd wife Nancy: Nancy, b 1804, d 23 May 1842,
Wolfeboro, age 38. (Census Strafford Co., 1810, p737; 1830,
p434; Loud's Cem. Recs., p85,126,129,130; Morning Star,
p376,377; Fitts' Newfields, p683; Merrill's Carroll Co., p324)

APPENDIX I.

LANS DEEDS OF PETER YOUNG OF BARRINGTON

(Peter Young, b ca 1750, Barrington, s/o Eleazer and Mary (Ham) Young, d 1828 Green Hill, Barrington; m ca 1776, Barrington, Sarah Hayes [ba 14 Feb 1751, of Barrington, d/o Benjamin and Abigail (Young) Hayes]). These land deeds are treated as supplementary material for the sake of historical interest. They are in addition to land deeds on Peter's own purchases and conveyances of lands to son Eleazer.)

Peter's deeds of sale on lands once owned by his father Eleazer revealed the extensiveness of his estate: (1) sold 110 acres at Green Hill, Barrington on road leading from Dover to Crown Point in Barrington, "being all the land purchased by me of Isaac Young and all that land I purchased from my father Eleazer, deceased, by Isinglass River," to William K. Atkinson of Dover for $937.64, by deed of 11 Jan, rec'd 12 Jan 1803; witnesses Lydia Tibbetts, William Twombly [Strafford Co. Deed 41:230]; (2) sold 25 acres in the Two-Mile Streak, or 1/2 of a 50-acre lot, the same which Jethro Bickford purchased of Benjamin Hayes and which said Bickford conveyed to Peter's father Eleazer on 26 Jan 1761, to Thomas Wentworth of Dover for $229.96, by deed signed and rec'd 1 Sep 1803; witnesses Joseph Clark, Hatevile Knight [Strafford Co. Deed 43:150]; (3) quitclaimed 12 acres in Rochester, "part of the real estate of Lemuel Bickford, late of Rochester" which was devised to Peter "in my favor as execution of my late father Eleazer Young against Dependence Bickford, Admin. of said Bickford 18 Jul 1804, to Elihu Hayes [father of Mehitable Hayes Young, wife of Moses Young of Rochester] for $20.00, by deed signed 16 Aug, rec'd 29 Aug 1804; witnesses John Roberts, William K. Atkinson [Strafford Co. Deed 46:273]; (4) quitclaimed 110 acres at Green Hill, Barrington located on north side of road leading from Dover to Crown Point, Barrington, "purchased by my father Eleazer, deceased, of Job Jennings, and all purchased by me of Isaac Young" to William K. Atkinson of Dover for $900.00, by deed signed 22 Dec, rec'd 28 Dec 1804; witnesses John Remick, Samuel Bragg Jr. [Strafford Co. Deed 47:22].

Appendix II.

LAND DEEDS OF THOMAS AND TAMME YOUNG
OF DOVER AND ALTON

(Thomas aka Jr., b 1759, New Durham, s/o Thomas and Rebecca ( ) Young, gr.s/o Thomas and Sarah (Folsom) Young of Newfields, alive 1806, Alton; m 23 Dec 1784, Dover, Tamme aka Tamsen Hayes [ba 8 Aug 1762, Toll End, Dover, d/o Thomas and Hannah (Twombly) Hayes, alive Alton, 1806]. Thomas was of New Durham at time of marriage.)

Abstracts of Thomas' well nigh forty speculative land deeds are presented in abbreviated form with proper citations for the sake of their descendants and history buffs who would like to acquaint themselves better with these transactions from Dover, New Durham, Barrington and Alton. Deeds of Dover era: (1) purchased by deed 9 Sep 1791, rec'd 3 Apr 1792, one-half of Lot 6, 2nd Div, New Durham from William Lord of Barnstead [Strafford Co. Deed 14:190]; (2) sold one whole proprietor's share in Eaton [date of grant 21 Oct 1768] by deed of 7 Sep, rec'd 2 Oct 1792, to Emerson Porter of Gilmanton [Strafford Co. Deed 14:526], NH State Papers (Masonian Papers, V5, p152); (3) purchased by deed 7 Sep 1792, rec'd 13 Mar 1794, 15 acres in Dover, bounded south and west by lands of Dr. Ezra Green, from Stephen Gale of Gilmanton [Strafford Co. Deed 17:240]; (4) sold the other ten acres in Dover with Tamme's dower rights ceded, by deed of 12 Mar, rec'd 9 May 1794, on the side of the new road from John Hall's to Maul Hanson's, being part of land which Thomas bought of Stephen Gale, to Henry Mellen of Dover [Strafford Co. Deed 18:101].

Deeds of the New Durham era, conveyances of Lot 4 in the Gore and Lot 7, Alton: (1) purchased by tax deed of 11 Mar 1784, rec'd 23 Jan 1804, 30 acres of 100-acre Lot 4, North Range [Strafford Co. Deed 43:500]; (2) sold these same 30 acres of Lot 4, North Range by deed of 11 Mar 1784, rec'd 23 Jan 1804, to Jacob Chamberlin [Strafford Co. Deed 43:501]; (3) purchased 265 acres of Lot 7, Alton, by deed of 10 Dec 1800, rec'd 18 Sep 1802, from Clement March of Greenland, Rock. Co. [Strafford Co. Deed 40:230]; (4) mortgaged this very same property on same date of signing, 10 Dec 1800, rec'd 23 Jan 1801 to Clement March of Greenland, Rock. Co., for $435.00 [Strafford Co. Deed 36:245]; (5) sold with co-grantor Clement March 100 acres of Lot 7, Alton to Daniel Pinkham of Madbury, by deed of 27 Jun, rec'd 14 Dec 1801 [Strafford Co. Deed

39:40]; (6) sold 100 acres of Lot 7, Alton, at the southern
line between Lots 6 and 7, ceding Tamme's dower rights, to
David Wentworth of Wolfeboro [Strafford Co. Deed 46:491]; (7)
sold 50 acres at s.e. corner of Lot 7, Alton, thence north to
a point by New Durham line by deed of 23 Sep 1801, rec'd 18
Sep 1802, to George Walker of Alton [Strafford Co. Deed
40:228].

The Barrington era with respect to Lot 97, 4th Div.,
Rochester, acreage in Dover, and part of Lot 6, 5th Range,
Barrington held seven deeds: (1) granted mortgage, by deed
of 6 Nov, rec'd 14 Nov 1794, to William Evans of Barrington,
on five acres with the dwelling house where said Evans then
lived on the north side of Province Road, due and payable by
6 Apr next [Strafford Co. Deed 19:308]; (2) mortgage redeemed
by William Evans 26 Nov 1794, rec'd 27 Jul 1799 [Strafford Co.
Deed 30:470]; (3) sold two parts of Lot 97, 4th Div, Rochester, the first one being 40 acres, drawn originally to James
Hobbs, and the second, 15 acres (one-third of the lot) to
Joseph Peirce of Dover, by deed 5 Nov 1794, rec'd 2 Jun 1801
[Strafford Co. Deed 36:448]; please note that this deed is
duplicated in all respects to Strafford Co. Deed 35:356; (4)
sold five acres of the 15 acres in Dover purchased from
Stephen Gale of Gilmanton, by deed of 9 Jun 1795, rec'd 2 Jan
1797, by lands of Ezra Green's and Col. Thomas Watson's, to
Moses Canney of Madbury [Strafford Co. Deed 23:392]; (5)
purchased 62-3/4 acres of Lot 6, 5th Range, Barrington, by
lands of Israel Huckin's and Jabish Davis', by deed of 7 May
1796, rec'd 2 Jan 1797, from Joshua Foss Jr. of Barrington
[Strafford Co. Deed 23:398]; (6) sold these very same 62-3/4
acres of Lot 6, 5th Range, with dower rights of Tammy Young
ceded, by deed of 7 May 1796, rec'd 2 Jan 1797, to Moses
Canney of Madbury [Strafford Co. Deed 23:403]; (7) purchased
on same date of signing, 7 May 1796, rec'd 15 Aug 1798, piece
of land in the Commons [Barrington], acreage not given, by
William Evans Jr.'s quitclaim [Strafford Co. Deed 28:238].

Thomas's last known address was Alton where he transacted
deals involving Lot R, Alton, Lot 193, 3rd Div., Barrington,
Lot 123, 3rd Div., Farmington, Lot 129, Farmington and further
sales of Lot 7, Alton: (1) sold part of Lot R in Alton which
was a certain piece of land he then owned on east side of the
road lead- ing from Phineas Gliddens to James Jewetts' Mills
by deed of 29 Dec 1801, rec'd 18 Sep 1802, to James Jenings
of Gilmanton, [Strafford Co. Deed 40:232]; (2) sold 150 acres
of Lot 193, 3rd Div., Barrington, by lands of John Beck and
Aaron Jenne by deed of 10 Jul, rec'd 16 Jul 1802, to Jethro
Lock Jr., Joshua Hayes, and Francis Winkley Jr., all of
Barrington [Strafford Co. Deed 38:390]; (3) purchased 74 acres
of Lot 123, Div. 3, Farmington, drawn to the original right
of Hateval Nutter, from Richard and Eliza Downing of Farmington by deed signed 10 Jul, rec'd 18 Jul 1802 [Strafford Co.
Deed 38:389]; (4) sold 40 acres from Lot 123, 3rd Div.,
Farmington, by land "that Joshua Hayes and others purchased

of me," by deed signed 21 Sep 1802, rec'd 9 Sep 1803 [Strafford Co. Deed 43:155]; (5) Thomas, "alias Richard Savory," one of the original proprietors of Farmington founded in 1798, was absentee owner of Lot 129, 3rd Div., Farmington, parts of which were slated to be sold at public auction for money sufficient to pay back taxes for 1818 and 1819, by dates of 30 Nov 1818 and 20 Nov 1819 [Farmington TR, V1, p596]; (6) sold 50 acres of Lot 7, 1st Div., to Zebulon Davis of Alton by deed 22 Aug 1803, rec'd 24 Aug 1804, "being the same I now live on" [Strafford Co. Deed 46:266]; (7) sold 50 acres of Lot 7, 1st Range, Alton, at south corner of Daniel Pinkhams' land to Judge Cogswell's land, now lands of Phineus Gliddens, by deed of 8 Jan, rec'd 12 Nov 1805, to James Treffen of Farmington [Strafford Co. Deed 49:225]; (8) sold 13 acres of large Lot 7, 1st Range, Alton, "lying upon the east side of land that said Young sold to said David Wentworth [purchaser] in the above named lot", by deed of 30 Jul 1805, rec'd 6 May 1806 [Strafford Co. Deed 51:172]; and (9) quitclaim to Stephen Davis of Alton of 65 acres of Lot 7 by land of William Pinkham by deed of 3 Apr 1806, rec'd 20 Jan 1809 [Strafford Co. Deed 59:472].

Lot 6, 1st Div., Alton is a story in itself by the sheer quantity of transactions and expenditure of $1,900.00 in the purchase of the 900 acres available to Thomas out of the 1,000-acre lot as well as the cost of two mortgages, it is considered that he came out some what ahead in the sale of 760 acres at the total price of $2,470.00 between 1802 and 1806. Thomas may have kept the remaining 140 acres for his own homestead, final transaction signed in 1806, date of recording, 5 May 1808. It is a moot question indeed as to whether that date signified that Thomas was then deceased. At any rate, what is set forth below are the citations only of Strafford County deeds detailing 13 transactions on Lot 6, Alton: (1) deed of 30 Nov 1802, rec'd 5 Mar 1808 [Strafford Co. Deed 57:180]; (2) deed of 30 Nov 1802, rec'd 11 Mar 1803 [Strafford Co. Deed 40:288]; (3) deed signed 19 Feb, rec'd 26 Sep 1803 [Strafford Co. Deed 42:378]; (4) 19 Feb, rec'd 25 Feb 1803 [Strafford Co. Deed 42:99]. The 900 acres, while mortgaged, were sold off in 100-acre increments, sometimes cited as 16,000 sq. rods, with three exceptions of sales of 60 acres or less listed last, to the following grantees: (5) deed of 23 Sep, rec'd 26 Sep 1803 [Strafford Co. Deed 42:379]; (6) deed of 23 Sep, rec'd 26 Sep 1803 [Strafford Co. Deed 42:381]; (7) deed of 16 Jan, rec'd 14 Feb 1804 [Strafford Co. Deed 45:8]; (8) deed of 1 Dec 1804, rec'd 18 Feb 1805 [Strafford Co. Deed 47:186]; (9) deed with Tamme's dower rights ceded, of 22 Sep 1806, rec'd 5 Sep 1807 [Strafford Co. Deed 55:206]; (10) deed of 10 Nov 1806, rec'd 9 Sep 1807 [Strafford Co. Deed 55:245]; (11) deed of 28 Nov 1804, rec'd 9 Jan 1807 [Strafford Co. Deed 53:17]; (12) deed of 17 Nov 1806, rec'd 5 May 1808 [Strafford Co. Deed 57:536]; and (13) deed of 24 Nov 1806, rec'd 18 Sep 1807 [Strafford Co. Deed 55:277].

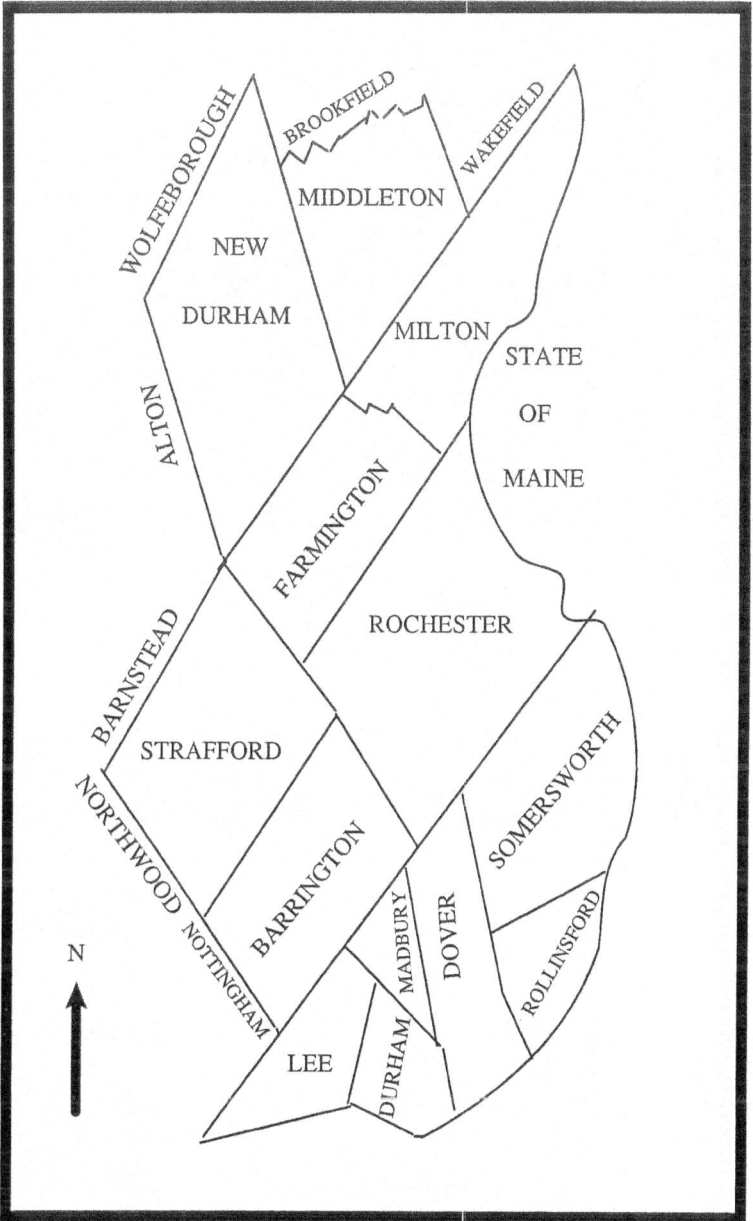

Appendix III
Map of Strafford County, N.H.
After Annexations of 1840

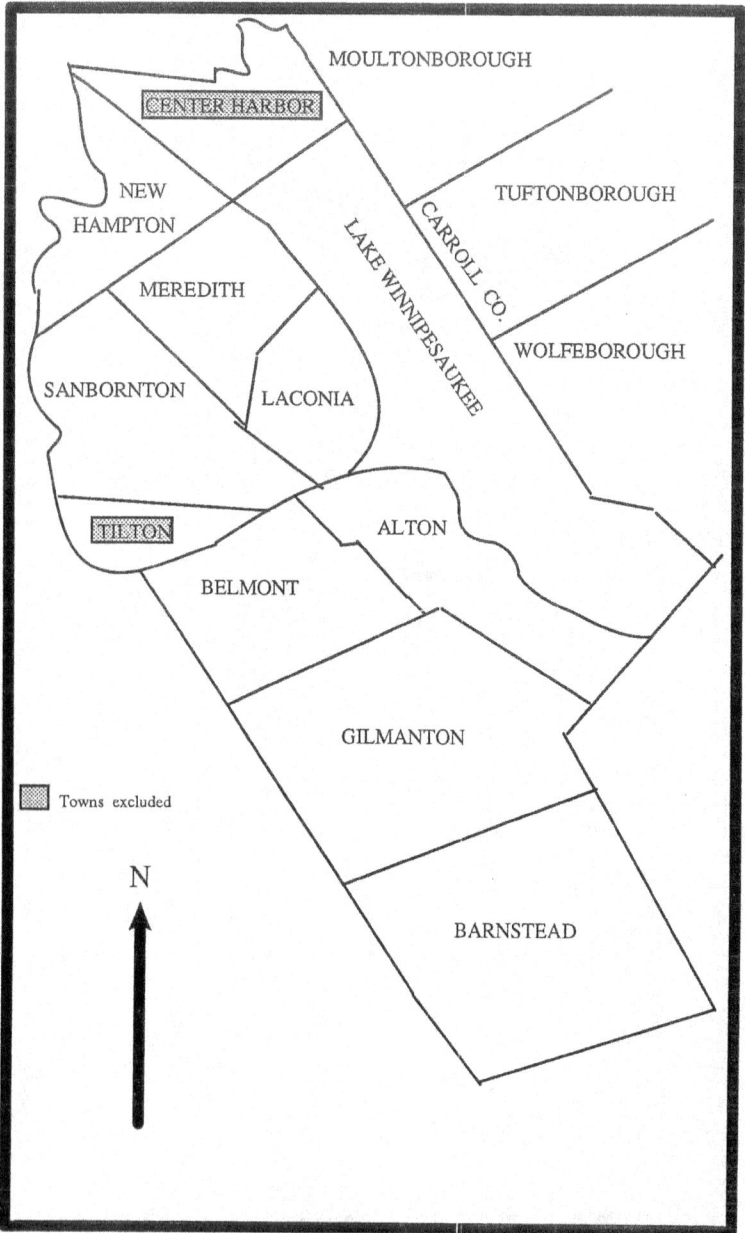

Appendix IV
Eight Towns of Belknap County, N.H.,
Originally of Strafford Co. , Containing Youngs

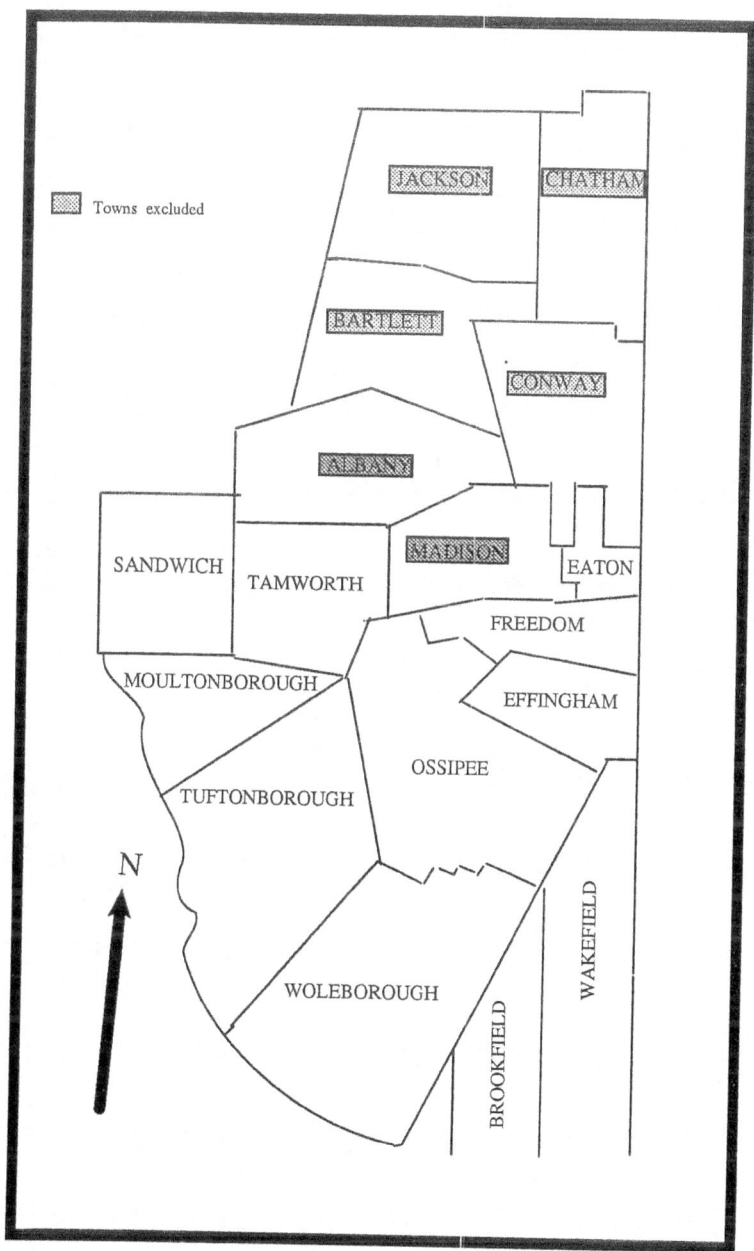

Towns excluded

JACKSON CHATHAM

BARTLETT

CONWAY

ALBANY

SANDWICH TAMWORTH MADISON EATON

FREEDOM

MOULTONBOROUGH EFFINGHAM

OSSIPEE

TUFTONBOROUGH

N

WOLEBOROUGH BROOKFIELD WAKEFIELD

Appendix V
Ten Towns of Carroll County, N.H.,
Originally of Strafford Co., Containing Youngs

BIBLIOGRAPHY BY STATE, COUNTY AND TOWN

NEW HAMPSHIRE STATE

Ayling, Augustus D. Revised Register of the Soldiers and
Sailors of New Hampshire in the War of the Rebellion, 1861-
1866. Concord, N.H.: Ira C. Evans, Public Printer, 1895.
Batchellor, Albert Stillman, Ed. Town Charters Including
Grants of Territory Within the Present Limits of New Hamp-
shire. New Hampshire State Papers, Vol.24. Concord, N.H.
_____. Town Charters Granted Within the Present Limits of
New Hampshire. New Hampshire State Papers, Vol.25, 1895.
_____. Township Grants of Lands in New Hampshire Included
in the Masonian Patent. New Hampshire State Papers, Vol.27,
1896.
_____. Township Grants of Lands in New Hampshire. New
Hampshire State Papers, Vol.28, 1896.
_____. Probate Records of the Province of New Hampshire,
V.1 (1635-1717). New Hampshire State Papers, Vol.31, 1907.
_____. Probate Records of the Province of New Hampshire,
V.2 (1718-1740). New Hampshire State Papers, Vol.32, 1914.
_____. Probate Records of the Province of New Hampshire,
V.3 (1741-1749). New Hampshire State Papers, Vol.33, 1915.
_____. Probate Records of the Province of New Hampshire,
V.4 (1750-1753). New Hampshire State Papers, Vol.34, 1933.
_____. Probate Records of the Province of New Hampshire,
V.5 (1754-1756). New Hampshire State Papers, Vol.35, 1936.
_____. Probate Records of the Province of New Hampshire,
V.6 (1757-1760). New Hampshire State Papers, Vol.36, 1938.
_____. Probate Records of the Province of New Hampshire,
V.7 (1760-1763). New Hampshire State Papers, Vol.37, 1939.
_____. Probate Records of the Province of New Hampshire,
V.8 (1764-1767). New Hampshire State Papers, Vol.38, 1940.
_____. Probate Records of the Province of New Hampshire,
V.9 (1767-1771). New Hampshire State Papers, Vol.39, 1941.
Carpenter, Georgia B. and Winifred L. Goss. New Hampshire
Gravestone Inscriptions. Typescript, New Hampshire Histor-
torical Society, Concord, N.H.
Daughters of the American Revolution. Index of the Rolls of
Honor (Ancestor's Index) in the Lineage Books of the
National Society of the Daughters of the American Revolu-
tion. Vol.1-160. Washington, D.C.: NSDAR Library.
Daughters of the American Revolution (New Hampshire). New
Hampshire Cemeteries and Bible Records. Washington, D.C.:
NSDAR Library.

Dearborn, David C. "New Hampshire Genealogy: A Perspective." New England Historical and Genealogical Register, Vol.130, p244-258 (Oct 1976).

Draper, Mrs. Amos G. New Hampshire Revolutionary War Pension Records, 1776-1850, Vols. 98,99. Filmed by Genealogical Society of Utah, No. 0887542, Items 1,2.

"Family Names in New Hampshire Town Histories, 1947-1980," Historical New Hampshire (December 1946). Concord, N.H.: New Hampshire Historical Society.

Folsom, Mrs. Wendell B. New Hampshire Graveyard Inscriptions of Early Date. Microfilm by Genealogical Society of Utah, 1951, No. 0015566.

Genealogical Library Catalog [G.L.C.]. State of New Hampshire. Counties of Belknap, Carroll, and Strafford. Microfiche by Genealogical Society of Utah [n.n.].

Goss, Mrs. Charles Carpenter. Colonial Gravestone Inscriptions in the State of New Hampshire. Dover, N.H.: Historical Activities Committee of the National Society of the Colonial Dames of America in New Hampshire, 1942.

Hammond, Isaac W. Early Town Papers Relating to Towns in N.H., "A" to "F" Inclusive. N.H. State Papers, Vol.11, 1882.

_____. Early Town Papers Relating to Towns in N.H., Gilmanton to New Ipswich Inclusive. N.H. State Papers, Vol.12, 1883.

_____. Early Town Papers Relating to Towns in N.H., New London to Wolfeboro Inclusive. N.H. State Papers, Vol.13, 1884.

Hammond, Otis G. Vital Records From Notices From the New Hampshire Gazette, 1765-1800. Lambertville, N.J., 1970.

_____. Hammond's Checklist of New Hampshire History. Edited by E. J. Hanrahan, Somersworth, N.H.: New Hampshire Publishing Co., 1971.

Holbrook, Jay Mack. New Hampshire Census, 1732. Oxford, MA: Holbrook Research Institute, 1981.

_____. New Hampshire Residents, 1633-1699. Oxford, MA: Holbrook Research Institute, 1979.

Hunt, Elmer Munson. New Hampshire Town Names and Whence They Came. Peterborough, N.H.: William L. Bauhan, 1970.

International Genealogical Index [I.G.I.]. Mormon Birth Records for State of New Hampshire: Young to Zwingge. Genealogical Society of Utah, Microfiche #0399946.

McClintock, John N. New Hampshire, Colony, Province and State. Boston: B. B. Russell, 1889.

Merrill, Eliphalet and Phineas Merrill Esq. Gazetteer of The State of N. H. Bowie, MD: Heritage Books, Inc. Ed., 1987.

Metcalf, Henry Harrison and Frances M. Abbott. One Thousand New Hampshire Notables. Concord, N.H.: Rumford Printing Co., 1919.

Moses, George H., Ed. New Hampshire Men, A Collection of Biographical Sketches. Concord, N.H.: N.H. Publishing Co., J. G. Patterson Jr., 1893.

New Hampshire Provincial Deeds, Exeter: Grantor/Grantee Index 1623-1771,Vol.1-96,solelyfortownsof Dover,Barrington, Durham, Madbury and Rochester as well as New Market.

New Hampshire Vital Records: Births — Waters to Zeumer. Records housed at Bureau of Vital Records and Health Statistics, Concord, N.H. Filmed by Genealogical Society of Utah, No. 1001057.

_____. Brides, Wright to Zogukewicz. Filmed by Genealogical Society of Utah, Microfilm No. 0975694.

_____. Deaths, Wiswall to Zadoch. Filmed by Genealogical Society of Utah, Microfilm No. 1001117.

_____. Marriages, Worthern to Young. Filmed by Genealogical Society of Utah, Microfilm No. 1001321.

_____. Marriages, Young to Zimmerman. Filmed by Genealogical Society of Utah, Microfilm No. 1001322.

Noyes, Sybil, Charles T. Libby and Walter G. Davis. Genealogical Dictionary of Maine and New Hampshire. Baltimore: Genealogical Publishing Co., 1972.

Pope, Charles H. The Pioneers of Maine and New Hampshire, 1623-1660. Baltimore, MD: Genealogical Publishing Co., 1973.

Potter, Chandler E. The Military History of the State of New Hampshire, 1623-1861, Two Parts in One Volume. Baltimore, MD: Genealogical Publishing Co., 1972.

State of New Hampshire. 1850 Mortality Schedules for Belknap, Carroll, and Strafford Counties as of 1 June 1850. New Hampshire State Library, Concord, N.H.

Stearns, Ezra S. Genealogical and Family Histories of the State of New Hampshire. Vol. 3. N.Y.: The Lewis Publishing Co., 1908.

U.S. Bureau of the Census. Heads of Families at The First Census of the United States Taken in The Year 1790, New Hampshire. Washington, D.C.: Government Printing Office, 1907.

U.S. Bureau of the Census. Heads of Families at the Second Census of the United States Taken in The Year 1800, New Hampshire. Madison, WS: John Brooks Threlfall, 1973.

Wilson, Emily S. Inhabitants of New Hampshire, 1776 (Association Test). Lambertville, N.J., 1983.

Young, David C. and Robert L. Taylor. "Death Notices From the Morning Star," Death Notices From Freewill Baptist Publications. Bowie, MD: Heritage Books, Inc., 1985.

NEW HAMPSHIRE COUNTIES

Belknap County Probate, Laconia: Probate Index, 1 Jan 1841-1 Jan 1898. Selected probate papers.

Biographical Review, Vol. XXI, "Containing Life Sketches of Leading Citizens of Strafford and Belknap Counties, New Hampshire." Boston: Biographical Review Pub. Co., 1897.

Carroll County Probate, Ossipee: Probate Index, 1841-1899. Selected probate papers.

Hurd, C. H. & Co. The Old Maps of Belknap County, New Hampshire in 1892. Fryeburg, ME: Saco Valley Printing, 1982.
_____. The Old Maps of Carroll County, New Hampshire in 1892. Fryeburg, ME: Saco Valley Printing, 1982.
_____. The Old Maps of Strafford County, New Hampshire in 1892. Fryeburg, ME: Saco Valley Printing, 1983. Hurd, D. Hamilton.

Hurd, D. Hamilton. History of Merrimack and Belknap Counties, New Hampshire, Vol.2. Philadelphia: J. W. Lewis & Co., 1885.
_____. History of Rockingham and Strafford Counties, New Hampshire, With Biographical Sketches of Many of Its Pioneers and Prominent Men. Philadelphia: J. W. Lewis & Co., 1882.

Merrill, Georgia D., ed., History of Carroll County, New Hampshire. Boston: W. A. Ferguson & Co., 1889.

Sanford, E. F. Atlas of Strafford County, New Hampshire. Drawn and published by Sanford & Everts, Philadelphia, 1871.

Scales, John. History of Strafford County, New Hampshire. Chicago: Richmond-Arnold Publishing Co., 1914.

Strafford County Deeds, Dover: Grantor/Grantee Index 1773-1812, Vols. 1-60, complete through 1809; selected land deeds thereafter.

Strafford County Probate Papers, Dover: Probate Index 1772-1863, Vols.1-70 researched in toto; all wills and guardianship papers complete Vols.71-100, 1890; after 1863, selected administrative papers.

Thompson, Lucien. Revolutionary Pension Declarations, Strafford County, 1820-1832, Comprising Sketches of Soldiers of The Revolution. Manchester, N.H.: Rumley Press, 1907.

U.S. Bureau of Census. Third Federal Census of Strafford County, New Hampshire, 1810. National Archives, Washington, D.C., Film No. M-252, R-25.
_____. Fourth Federal Census of Strafford County, New Hampshire, 1820. **Missing for entire Strafford County.**
_____. Fifth Federal Census of Strafford County, New Hampshire, 1830. National Archives, Washington, D.C. Film No. M-19, R-78.
_____. Sixth Federal Census of Strafford County, New Hampshire, 1840. National Archives, Washington, D.C. Film No. M-704, R-245; M-704, R-246.
_____. Seventh Federal Census of Belknap, Carroll and Strafford Counties, New Hampshire, 1850. Microfilm: Belknap, No. M-432, R-425; Carroll, M-432, R-426; Strafford, M-432, R-439, R-440. National Archives, Washington, D.C.
_____. Eighth Federal Census of Belknap, Carroll and Strafford Counties, New Hampshire, 1860. Film: Belknap, No. M-653, R-666; Carroll, M-653, R-667; Strafford, M-653, R-680. National Archives, Washington, D.C.
_____. Ninth Federal Census of Belknap, Carroll and Strafford Counties, New Hampshire, 1870. Microfilm:

Belknap, M-593, R-836; Carroll, M-593, R-837; Strafford, M-593, R-849. National Archives, Washington, D.C.

————. _Twelfth Federal Census of New Hampshire, 1900_. Soundex T-1059, W-856, Z-500, No. 52. National Archives, Washington, D.C.

ALTON

Church Records of Alton, N.H., 1803-1854. Typescript collected by Daughters of Founders and Patriots of America, Alton, N.H. Microfilm by Genealogical Society of Utah, 1976, No. 1007595.

Hammond, Priscilla. _Some Gravestone Inscriptions From Alton and West Alton, N.H._ Typescript, New Hampshire Historical Society.

Town Clerk. _Alton Town Records (Births, Deaths, Marriages, 1777-1870)_. Originals at State Capitol Building, Concord. Filmed by Genealogical Society of Utah, 1950, No. 0015058.

BARNSTEAD

Blaisdell, Lillian B. et al. _Death Records From Graveyards in Barnstead, N.H._ Typescript, New Hampshire Historical Society, Concord, N.H.

Holman, Mary Lovering, Winifred Holman et al. _Records From The First Book of The Smith Meeting House, Gilmanton, N.H. 1775-1819 and Cemetery Records From Barnstead, N.H._ Filmed by Genealogical Society of Utah, 1970, No. 0496849, Item 4.

Jackman, Mrs. Freeman T. _Gravestone Inscriptions of Barnstead, N.H._ Typescript, New Hampshire Historical Society, Concord, N.H.

————. _Gravestone Inscriptions, Barnstead, N.H, 1810-1921_. Collected by Daughters of the Founders and Patriots of America. Filmed by Recordak Corp., Wash., D.C., 1957, No. 0165996, Item 38.

Jewett, Jeremiah P. _The History of Barnstead From Its First Settlement in 1727 to 1872_. Ed. and Publisher Robert B. Caverly, Lowell, Mass.: Marden & Rowell, 1872.

Knowlton, David (Elder). _Barnstead Baptist Church. A Record of the First Freewill Baptist Church of Christian Barnstead Organized in 1803_. Typescript at New Hampshire Historical Society, Concord, N.H.

McQuesten, Leonora White. _Cemetery Inscriptions from Stratham, Dover, Durham, Barnstead Parade and Strafford, New Hampshire._ Filmed by Genealogical Society of Utah, 1951, No. 0015553.

Merrill, Stuart. _The History and Genealogy of the Barnstead Early Families, 1727-1970_. Typescript, 1979, New Hampshire Historical Society, N.H.

BARRINGTON

Barrington, New Hampshire Historical Society. Graveyards of Barrington, N.H. Barrington: N.H. American Revolution Bicentennial Commission, 1976.

Barrington Church Records. Congregational Church Parish Church Records, 1771-1817. Originals at Dover, N.H. Filmed by the Genealogical Society of Utah, 1976, No. 0987962, Items 1,2.

_____. First Freewill Baptist Church of Barrington, N.H. Church Records, ca. 1819-1845. Originals at Dover, N.H. Filmed by Genealogical Society of Utah, 1976, No. 0987962, Items 4,5.

Folsom, Mrs. Wendell B. Gravestone Inscriptions, Barrington, N.H. Typescript, New Hampshire Historical Society, Concord, N.H.

Hammond, Priscilla. Vital Records of Barrington, New Hampshire. Compiled from the original town records, 1934. Filmed by Genealogical Society of Utah, 1973, No. 0908584, Item 3.

Wiggin, Morton H. A History of Barrington, N.H. Barrington: Barrington, New Hampshire Historical Society, 1966.

BELMONT

Bean Hill Cemetery Records, Belmont, N.H. Typescript, N.H. Historical Society, Concord, N.H., n.d., 2 pp.

BROOKFIELD

Town Clerk. Brookfield Town Records, Family Records 1778-1826; Marriages 1821-1834. Typescript at State Capitol Building, Concord, N.H. See also Middleton.

CENTER HARBOR

Cemetery Inscriptions for Center Harbor and New Hampton From Town Records of New Hampton. Typescript, New Hampshire Historical Society, Concord, N.H.

DOVER

Dover Historical Society. Vital Records of Dover, New Hampshire, 1686-1850. Bowie, MD: Heritage Books, Inc., 1977.

Frost, J. E. Dover Graveyards, Pine Hill Cemetery, Dover, New Hampshire, Vols. 1,2. Dover, N.H.: Dover Historical Society, 1976.

Ham, John R. Dover, New Hampshire: Marriages, Births and Deaths, 1623-1825. Typescript at New Hampshire Historical Society, Concord, N.H. Filmed by the Genealogical Society of Utah, 1951, No. 015557, Item 22.

McQuesten, Leonora White. Cemetery Inscriptions from Dover,
  N.H.; see Barnstead.
Quint, Dr. Alonzo Hall. Historical Memoranda Concerning
  Persons and Places in Old Dover, N.H. Ed. by John Scales,
  Facsimile Edition, Bowie, MD: Heritage Books, Inc., 1983.
  _____. "Genealogical Items Relating to Dover, N.H.," New
  England Historical and Genealogical Register 6:329-334 (Oct
  1852).
Scales, John. History of Dover, New Hampshire. Manchester,
  N.H.: John B. Clarke Co., 1923.
Steuerwald, Emma N. Inscriptions Copied From Tombstones in
  Homestead Cemeteries in and Around Dover, N.H. TMs, 1946,
  N.H. Historical Society, Concord, N.H. Filmed by the
  Genealogical Society of Utah, 1951, No. 015557, Item 18.
Thompson, Mary P. Landmarks in Ancient Dover, New Hampshire.
  Concord, N.H.: Republican Press Association, 1892.

DURHAM

Durham Vital Records. Correspondence with Timothy MacGregor,
  Librarian, Special Collections, University of N. H., Durham,
  13 Nov 1986.
McQuesten, Leonora White. Cemetery Inscriptions from Durham;
  see Barnstead.
Stackpole, Everett S., Lucien Thompson, and Winthrop S.
  Meserve. History of the Town of Durham, N.H., (Oyster River
  Plantation) With Genealogical Notes. 2 Vols., Durham, N.H.:
  Rumford Press, 1913.
Tibbetts, Charles W. "Genealogical Records of Durham:
  Births, Marriages and Deaths," N. H. Genealogical Records,
  Vol.1, No.1.
Wilcox, Philip E. Graveyard Inscriptions of Durham, N.H.
  Durham, N.H.: Durham Historic Association, 1976.

EFFINGHAM

Cemetery Inscriptions For Effingham, N.H. Typescript, New
  Hampshire Historical Society, Concord, N.H. Filmed by the
  Genealogical Society of Utah, 1951, No. 0015558, Item 1.
First Congregational Society of Effingham, N.H. Church
  Records 1820-1893. Filmed by Genealogical Society of Utah,
  1976, No. 1003286.
Town Clerk. Leavitt's Town (Effingham) Town Records, 1748-
  1852, Vol.1, 1748-1852; Vol. 2, 1812-1852. Originals at
  State Capitol Building, Concord, N.H. Filmed by Genealog-
  ical Society of Utah, 1950, No. 015130.

FARMINGTON

Gravestone Incriptions From Farmington, N.H. Originals at New
  Hampshire Historical Society, Concord, N.H. Filmed by the
  Genealogical Society of Utah, 1951, No. 015558, Item 12.

Town Clerk. _Farmington Town Records, 1798-1828_, Vol.1,2. Originals at State Capitol Building, Concord, N.H. Filmed by the Genealogical Society of Utah, 1950, No. 0015137.

FREEDOM

Freedom Cemetery Records. Correspondence with Mr. Elliot Waterbury, Caretaker of Cemeteries, 5 May 1988.

Town Clerk. _Freedom Town Records, Vital Records: Births, Marriages, Deaths_, Book 1, 1850-1878; Book 2, 1878-1890. Filmed by Genealogical Society of Utah, 1976, No. 1003288, Items 1-5.

GILFORD

Cox, John W. _Vital Records of Gilford, N.H._ Typescript, 1938, at New Hampshire Historical Society, Concord, N.H.

Town Clerk. _Gilford Vital Records, Births, 1756-1856; Marriages, 1786-1854; Deaths, 1801-1856_. Originals at State Capitol Building, Concord, N.H. Filmed by Genealogical Society of Utah, 1950, No. 0015145.

GILMANTON

Folsom, Mrs. Wendell B. _Cemetery Transcriptions of Beech Grove Cemetery at Gilmanton Corner, Gilmanton, N.H., 1786-1938_. Collected by Daughters of Founders and Patriots of America. Filmed by Microfilming Service, Recordak Corp., Wash., D.C., 1975, No. 0165996, Item 16.

Holman, Mary Lovering and Winifred Holman et al. _Records From the First Book of the Smith Meeting House, Gilmanton, N.H., 1775-1819_. Typescript, New Hampshire Historical Society, Concord, N.H.

Lancaster, Daniel. _The History of Gilmanton, From The First Settlement To The Present Time_. Gilmanton, N.H.: Alfred Prescott, 1845.

Records of the Third Free Will Baptist Church in Upper Gilmanton, 1837, Altered to the Second Free Will Baptist Church in Upper Gilmanton (Belmont). Typescript, n.p., New Hampshire Historical Society, Concord, N.H.

Town Clerk. _Gilmanton Town Records, 1799-1868_, Vol 3, p1-357. Original records held in Belmont, N.H. Filmed by the Genealogical Society of Utah, 1950, No. 0015147.

Town Clerk. _Gilmanton Town Records, Vital Records 1772-1868_. Filmed by the Genealogical Society of Utah, 1950, No. 015147. Transcripts at Laconia, New Hampshire, originals in Belmont, New Hampshire.

MADBURY

Adams, Eloi A. _Madbury, Its People and Places_. [n.p.]. Madbury, N.H.: Madbury Historical Society, N.H., 1968.

Folsom, Mrs. Wendell B. Gravestone Inscriptions, Madbury,
N.H. Typescript, New Hampshire Historical Society, Concord,
N.H. Filmed by Genealogical Society of Utah, 1951, No.
015565, Item 1.
Shackford, Moses Austin Cartland. "Inscriptions From Grave-
stones at Madbury, N.H.," New England Historical and
Genealogical Register, Vol.87, p342-351 (Oct 1933).

MEREDITH

Hanaford, Mary E. Neal. Cemetery Inscriptions of Meredith,
N.H. Typescript, 1931, New Hampshire Historical Library,
Concord, N.H. Filmed by the Genealogical Society of Utah,
1951, No. 0015553, Item 12. See also New Hampton.
_____. Annals of Meredith, N.H. Concord, N.H.: The
Rumford Press, 1932.

MIDDLETON

Town Clerk. Middleton Town Records, 1778-1826, Vols. 1,2.
Originals at State Capitol Building, Concord, N.H. Filmed
by the Genealogical Society of Utah, 1950, No. 015083.

MILTON

Daughters of the American Revolution, Mary Torr Chapter (Rochester, N.H.). Cemetery Records of Milton, N.H. Typescript,
New Hampshire Historical Society, Concord, N.H. Filmed by
the Genealogical Society of Utah, 1951, No. 015565, Item 13.
See also Moultonboro.
Town Clerk. Milton Vital Records, correspondence 6 April
1989.

MOULTONBORO

_____. Gravestone Inscriptions of Moultonboro, N.H. Ibid,
Item 14.
Folsom, Albert A. "Marriage Records of Rev. Jeremiah Shaw of
Moultonboro, N.H., 1779-1833," New England Historical and
Genealogical Register, Vol.59, p283-289 (July 1905).
Moultonboro Cemetery Committee, Ed. The Cemetery Records of
Moultonboro, N.H. Published by the Moultonboro Cemetery
Committee, 1988. Typescript at New Hampshire Historical
Society, Concord, N.H.

NEW DURHAM

Cemetery Records of New Durham. Correspondence with Eloise
Bickford, Town Historian, 9 June 1987.
Folsom, Mrs. Wendell B. Gravestone Inscriptions From Davis
Cemetery, Runnals Cemetery, New Durham, N.H. Filmed by the
Microfilming Service, Recordak Corp., Wash., D.C., 1957, No.

0165996, Item 77. Collected by Daughters of Founders and Patriots of America.

Jennings, Ellen C. Genealogy of New Durham Families. Filmed by the Genealogical Society of Utah, 1976, No. 0987961, Item 6. Transcripts at State Capitol Building, Concord, N.H.

New Durham Town Records, Vital Records, 1850-1913. Ibid, Items 1-5.

New Durham Graveyards, N.H. Ibid, Item 7.

Palmer, William L. "A Chapter of New Durham History, N.H.," New England Historical and Genealogical Register, Vol.61, p359-371 (Oct 1907).

NEW HAMPTON

Hannaford, Mary Elizabeth Neal. New Hampton Cemetery Records. Typescript, 1931, New Hampshire Historical Society, Concord. See also Belmont, Center Harbor and Meredith.

OSSIPEE

First Congregational Society, Center Ossipee, N.H. Church Records 1806-1939; Society Record Book, 1825-1842. Filmed by the Genealogical Society of Utah, 1976, No. 1003285, Items 1-3.

Leighton, Minnie I. The Early Settlers' Meeting House at Leighton's Corner, N.H. (Four-Corner Freewill Baptist Church). Center Ossipee: Independent Press, 1933.

Loud, Eva Blake and Mabel E. Blake. Early Cemetery Records of Ossipee, N.H. Ossipee, N.H.: Bicentennial Committee, 1976. Transcript at New Hampshire Historical Society, Concord, N.H.

ROCHESTER

Cemetery Records of Rochester, N.H. Original records at New Hampshire Historical Society, Concord, N.H. Filmed by the Genealogical Society of Utah, 1951, No. 015574, Item 11.

McDuffee, Franklin. History of the Town of Rochester, N.H., From 1722-1890. Ed. Silvanus Hayward, Manchester, N.H.: J. B. Clarke Co., 1892.

Tibbetts, Charles W. "The Church Records of First Congregational Church, Rochester, N.H," N.H. Genealogical Record, Vol. 4, No. 4, p145-152 (Oct 1907); Vol. 5, No. 1, p1-8 (Jan 1908); Vol. 5, No. 2, p49-56 (Apr 1908); Vol. 5, No. 3, p113-120 (Jul 1908); Vol. 5, No. 4, p145-152 (Oct 1908); Vol. 6, No. 2, p113-120 (Apr 1909).

Town Clerk. Rochester Town Records, Vital Records 1850-1891. Microfilm by Genealogical Society of Utah, No. 0987952.

ROLLINGSFORD

Town Clerk. Rollingsford Vital Records, 1747-1778. Filmed
  by Genealogical Society of Utah, 1951, No. 015583, Item 2.

SANBORNTON

Burleigh, Mrs. Etta M. Cemetery Records of Sanbornton, N.H.
  Typescript at New Hampshire Historical Society, Concord,
  N.H.
Hooper, Edna W. The Old Horn Cemetery, Horn's Mills, San-
  bornton, N.H. Filmed by the Genealogical Society of Utah,
  1951, No. 015575, Items 9-10.
Jackman, Mrs. Freeman T. Gravestone Inscriptions of San-
  bornton, N.H. 1787-1925. Collected by Daughters of Founders
  and Patriots of America. Filmed by Microfilming Service,
  Recordak Corp., Washington, D.C., No. 0165996, Item 42.

SANDWICH

Leighton, Mrs. Harriet V. Gravestone Inscriptions of Sandwich, N.H. Originals at New Hampshire Historical Society,
  Concord, N.H. Filmed by the Genealogical Society of Utah,
  1951, No. 015575, Items 15,24.

SOMERSWORTH

Forest Glade Cemetery Records, Somersworth, correspondence
  with Frances E. Wooley, Clerk and Trustee, 22 June 1987 and
  14 Nov 1988.
Somersworth Cemetery Records. Typescript, New Hampshire
  Historical Historical Society, Concord, N.H.
Town Clerk. Somersworth Parish and Town Records, 1729-1829,
  Vols. A-E. Originals at State Capitol Building, Concord,
  N.H.

STRAFFORD

Cemetery Inscriptions of Center Strafford, N.H. Typescript,
  New Hampshire Historical Society, Concord, N.H. Filmed by
  the Genealogical Society of Utah, 1951, No. 015577, Item 2.
Crown Point Church Yard, Strafford, N.H. Ibid, Typescript,
  Item 3.
Leighton, Lena Waldron. Deaths in Strafford, N.H., From
  January 1826 to March 1865, Records Kept by Rev. Enoch
  Place. D.A.R. Else Cilley Chapter, September 1939
Garland, Caroline H. "Rev. Enoch Place's Record of Marriages,
  1813-1864." [Freewill Baptist Church, Strafford]. New
  England Historical and Genealogical Register, Vol. 76, p27-
  44 (Jan 1922).

McQuesten, Leonora White. Cemetery Inscriptions from Straf-
ford, N.H. See Barnstead.
Stiles, Corinne Foss and Neva Harvey Stiles. Strafford, New
Hampshire Cemeteries. 2nd Ed., 1985, Strafford, Typescript
at New Hampshire Historical Society, Concord, N.H.
Town of Strafford. The Pioneers, A History of Strafford, New
Hampshire. Published by Town of Strafford, N.H., 1971, n.p.

TUFTONBORO

Town Clerk. Tuftonboro Town Records, Family Records, 1796-
1829, Vol. 1. Originals at State Capitol Building, Concord,
N.H. Filmed by Genealogical Society of Utah, 1950, No.
015329, item 2.

WAKEFIELD

Banks, Elizabeth MacRury. Footsteps of Pride to The Past,
1774-1974, The First 200 Years, Wakefield, New Hampshire.
Sanford, ME: Wilson's Printers, 1987.
Marriages and Deaths in Wakefield, N.H., 1784-1834. Original
transcript found at Town Library, Wakefield. Filmed by
Genealogical Society of Utah, 1952, No. 015582, Item 4.
Town Clerk. Wakefield Cemetery Records on Youngs. Typescript
of Mrs. Frances Twombly, August 1978.

WEST ALTON - see Alton

WOLFEBORO

Daughters of the American Revolution (New Hampshire). New
Hampshire Cemeteries and Bible Records (Wolfeboro). Type-
script, New Hampshire Historical Society, Concord, N.H.
Filmed by Genealogical Society of Utah, 1971, No. 887542,
Item 5.
_____. Winnipesaukee Chapter, N.H. Wolfeboro, N.H. Family
and Bible Records. Typescript, New Hampshire Historical
Society, Concord, N.H. Filmed by Genealogical Society of
Utah, 1951, No. 015579, Item 11.
_____. Winnipesaukee Chapter, N.H. Genealogical Records.
Pembroke, N.H., 1948. Copied by Mrs. Joseph Donigan, type-
script at New Hampshire Historical Society, Concord, N.H.
Parker, Benjamin F. "Wolfeboro Banns," History of Wolfeboro,
New Hampshire. Published by Town of Wolfeboro, N.H., n.p.,
1901.

FAMILY HISTORIES

Cates, E. E. and M. Kay Sanborn. The Cate-Cates Family of New
England. Frederick, MD, 1904.
"Governor Thomas Dudley and his Descendants," New England His-
torical and Genealogical Register, Vol.10, p139, (Apr 1856).

Folsom, Rev. Nathaniel S. and Rev. Jacob Chapman. "The Folsom Family," New England Historical and Genealogical Register, Vol.30, p207-231 (Apr 1876).

French, Harry Dana. The Ancestry and Descendants of Warren Lovell Pitman, 1841-1912, of Alexandria, N.H. Typescript, at New Hampshire Historical Society, Concord, N.H.

Ham, John R. "Ham Family in Dover, N.H.," New England Historical and Genealogical Register, Vol.26, p388-395 (Oct 1872).
_____. Horne Family of Dover, N.H. Typescript (1902) at NEHGS Library, Boston.

Ham, Thomas Caverno. Genealogy of the Ham Family and of the Young Family. Arlington, Mass.: Mr. Ham, 1949.

Hardon, Henry W. The Roberts Family. Vol.1-4. Typescript circa 1920, New Hampshire Historical Society, Concord, N.H.

Jarvis, Mrs. May Tibbetts. Henry Tibbetts of Dover, New Hampshire and Some of his Descendants, Vol.1. Typescript, San Diego, CA, 1937.

Ladd, Warren. The Ladd Family, A Genealogical and Biographical Memoir of Daniel Ladd of Haverhill, MA, Joseph Ladd of Portsmouth, RI, John Ladd of Burlington, NJ. New Bedford, MA: Edmund Anthony & Sons, 1890.

Lapham, W. B. John Hill of Dover in 1649 and Some of His Descendants. Augusta, ME: Maine Farmer Job Print, 1889.

Morrison, Leonard A. and Stephen P. Sharples. The History of the Kimball Family in America, 1634-1897. Boston: Damrell and Upham, Old Corner Bookstore, 1897.

Otis, Horatio N. "The Otis Genealogy," New England Historical and Genealogical Register, Vol.5, p177-197 (April 1851).

Richmond, Mrs. Katharine F. John Hayes of Dover, New Hampshire, A Book of His Family. Tyngsboro, Mass, 1936.

Runnels, Rev. M. T. Genealogy of the Runnels and Reynolds Families in America. Boston: Alfred Mudge & Son Printers, 1873.

Sinnett, Rev. Charles Nelson. Richard Pinkham of Old Dover, N.H. and His Descendants East and West. Concord, N.H.: Rumford Printing Co., 1908.

Varney, Herbert Clarkson. A Genealogy of Some of the Descendants of William Varney of Ipswich, Massachusetts, 1649 and More Particulars of His Son Humphrey Varney of Dover, N.H., 1659. Typescript, 1949 at New Hampshire Historical Society, Concord, N.H.

Wentworth, John. The Wentworth Genealogy: English and American Descendants. Vols. 1-3. Boston: Little, Brown & Co., 1878.

Wiggin, Arthur C., Agnes P. Bartlett, Alexander Lincoln, Franklin C. Thompson. Wiggin Genealogies. Typescript, New Hampshire Historical Society, Concord, N.H.

"Wille Hill of Durham, N.H.," New Hampshire Genealogical Record, Vol. 5, No. 3, July 1908.

PERIPHERAL AREAS

Bowdoin College, Brunswick, Maine. Obituary Record of the Graduates of Bowdoin College and the Medical School of Maine for the Year Ending 1 June 1899.

Cutter, William Richard. Genealogical and Personal Memoirs Relating to the Families of Boston and Eastern Massachusetts. Vol. 3, Ed. by W. R. Cutter. New York: Lewis Historical Publishing Co., 1908.

Fitts, Rev. James Hill. History of Newfields, New Hampshire, 1638-1911. Ed. Rev. N. F. Carter, Concord, N.H.: Rumford Press, 1912.

Hammond, Priscilla. Vital Records of Kingston, N.H. Typescript, compiled from the original town records, 1935.

Latter Day Saints Family History Library. International Genealogical Index: Youngs of Massachusetts, Microfiche. (Selective search only for readily identifiable names of Youngs)

_____. International Genealogical Index, Youngs of Maine, Microfiche. (Selective search only for readily identifiable names of Youngs)

Lyford, James Otis. History of the Town of Canterbury, New Hampshire, 1727-1912. Facsimile of 1912 Edition. Canterbury: Canterbury Historical Society, 1973.

Moses, John Mark. Early Settlers of Northwood, New Hampshire, Vol.2, n.d. Typescript at New Hampshire Historical Society, Concord, N.H.

Stratham Old Cemetery Records. Collected by Daughters of Founders and Patriots of America. Filmed by Microfilming Service, Recordak Corp., Washington, D.C., No. 0165996.

TAPED RECORDINGS

Federation of Genealogical Societies Conference, Boston, MA: "New England In Your Blood," August 24-27, 1988, hosted by New England Historic Genealogical Society.

_____. What to Look for in Probates and Deeds, by William H. Schoeffler, T-19.

_____. Think You've Done the U.S. Census? Think Again, by James L. Hansen, T-31.

_____. Resolving Discrepancies: Applying Principles of Genealogical Evidence, by Cameron Allen, T-38.

_____. Additional Thoughts on the Validity of Genealogical Evidence, by Eugene A. Stratton, F-75.

Young

Abigail, b 1814 55
Abigail, b 1820s 31
Abigail, b ca 1750 299
Abigail, see Abbie E. 15
Abigail+, b 15 Sep 1723 10, 169
Abigail+, b 1760s 11, 66
Abigail+, b 1780 11
Abigail+, b 1784 12
Abigail+, b 1808 12, 115
Abigail+, b 1826 12, 130
Abigail+, b 3 Mar 1783 11, 57
Abigail+, b ca 1760 11, 63
Abigail+, b ca 1790 12
Abigail+, b ca 1815 12
Abigail+, ba 23 Oct 1757 11, 247
Abner 216
Abner+, b 1700s 12
Abra (Montgomery), b ca 1780 31
Acanthus+, b 1815 13
Ada E., b 28 Feb 1870 42
Ada R. (Ewell), b Apr 1845 119
Adalade C., b 10 Feb 1832 316
Adaline ( ), b 1816 248
Adaline Roberts, b 24 Feb 1903 220
Adaline+, b ca 1820 13
Adaronia, see Ada R. 119
Addie ( ), b ca 1845 99
Addie ( ) 234
Addie (Stevens), b 1870 41
Addie A., b 4 Aug 1841 138
Addie B. (Hall), b 1868 91
Addie B.+, b 1857 13, 133
Addie C.+, b ca 1860 13
Addie F. (Aiken), b 1871 91
Addie F.+, b 1860s 13, 59
Addie L. ( ) Vittum, b 20 Apr 1868 219
Addie R.+, b 1851 13, 185
Addie R.+, b 7 Jul 1865 13, 14
Addie, see Ruth Adelaide 307
Adelade, b 184 209

Young

Adelaide (Hann), b 1811 137, 225, 280
Adelaide+, b 1832 13
Adeline (Warren), b 1811 137
Adeline A., see Addie A. 138
Adeline F., b 18 Aug 1852 56
Adeline M.+, b 1820s 13, 203
Adeline P.+, b 1820s 14, 27
Adeline, b 1840 180
Adeline, see Lovina A. 308
Adella, b 1864 97
Alamander W.+, b 23 Jul 1824 13, 14, 180
Albert 232
Albert Stowell, b 31 Jan 1873 101
Albert W., b 12 Mar 1851 56
Albert W., b 1856 285
Albert, b 1848 98
Albert, b 1880 42, 43
Albert, b 4 Feb 1852 17
Albert, b Feb 1865 15
Albert+, b 3 Feb 1836 14, 55
Alberto, see Lester A.+ 278
Alden Norris, b 12 Dec 1906 132
Alexander 128, 153
Alexander+, b ca 1825 15
Alexine ( ), b Dec 1856 90
Alexis E., b 1843 265
Alfred A.+, b 1819 15
Alfred G. 94, 244
Alfred George+, b 5 Apr 1806 16, 238
Alfred, b 18 Nov 1894 36
Alfred, b 1820 110
Alfred, b 1834 27
Alfred, b Sep 1890 264
Alfred+, b ca 1825 15
Alice (Gray), b 1867 42
Alice (Kingman), b ca 1785 74, 182
Alice (Knox), b ca 1815 181
Alice (Peavey) Young, b 8 Oct 1800 14, 41, 98, 180

347

Young
228, 241
Alice (Pickering), b ca 1820   77
Alice (Watson) 5, 282
Alice (Watson), b ca 1695 69
Alice A., b 1850   247
Alice A., b Jun 1844   183
Alice A.+, b ca 1850   16
Alice C., see Eliza C.+   210
Alice Emogene, see Emogene A.+
Alice M. (Dennett), b 1855   134
Alice M. (Moulton), b 1873   65
Alice M. (Tufts), b ca 1865   315
Alice P., b Feb 1891   24
Alice Richardson, b 1 Mar 1858   9
Alice W. (Sherman), b ca 1850   92
Alice, see Eliza C.+
Alice+, b 1842   16
Alice+, b ca 1870   16
Allen B., b 1820s   214
Allis, see Alice
Alman J., b 29 Jun 1871   214
Almeda (Nutter), b 1826   56
Almira M., see Myra M.+   16, 244
Almira, b 6 Mar 1834   55
Almira+, b ca 1805   17
Almira+, b Feb 1824   17
Alonzo, b Aug 1824   276
Aloria, see Alvina   305
Alva A., b 1858   162
Alvah   41
Alvah H., b 1 Mar 1887   107
Alvah, b 1845   59
Alvah+, b 19 Jul 1818   17, 242
Alvin F.+, b 20 Nov 1842   17, 21
Alvina, b 14 Oct 1854   278
Alvina, b 1821   305
Amanda M., b 25 Jun 1835   179

Young
Amanda M., b ca 1835   182
Amy (Coffin), see Diana   83
Amy Ann, b 17 Apr 1874   243
Amy M. (Libby), b 1858   95
Ana, b 1830   117
Andrew   77
Andrew Bailey+, b 29 Mar 1812   20, 81, 201, 257
Andrew H., b 1 Apr 1867   22
Andrew Huckins+, b 16 Jun 1827   8, 20, 101, 268
Andrew J.   17, 110
Andrew J., b 1816   110
Andrew J., b Jan 1833   35
Andrew J.+, b 1816   21, 252
Andrew J.+, b ca 1835   21
Andrew J.+, b Jun 1838   21, 110
Andrew Jackson+, b 1828   21, 117
Andrew W.+, b 1845   22
Andrew+, b 1769   19
Andrew+, b 1843   20
Andrew+, b ca 1765   18
Angeline F. (Abbott), b ca 1840   134
Angie, b 1865   282
Ann (Rollins)   215
Ann (Sherbourne)   131
Ann B. (Perkins), b 1824   98
Ann C., b 2 Jul 1813   305
Ann E., b 1840   120
Ann E.+, b 1845   22, 161
Ann F., b 18 Apr 1822   201
Ann F.+, b May 1836   22
Ann M. (Young), b 1834   242
Ann M., b 1834   242
Ann M.+, b 15 Sep 1852   22
Ann Maria (Chase), b ca 1810   89, 161, 242
Ann R. (Hanson), b ca 1830   277
Ann, b 1720s   142
Ann, b 1823   130
Ann, b 1834   161
Ann, b 1847   40
Ann, b ca 1790   175
Ann, ba 7 Apr 1751   170
Ann, see Anna+   23
Ann+ (   ), b ca 1790   22
Ann+ (Young), b ca 1790   22

348

Young

Betsey A. (Merrill), b 1814
38, 103, 277

Betsey A.+ (Farnum), b 20
Jan 1835 37

Betsey A.+, b ca 1855 37

Betsey Ann (Drew), b 13 Feb
1814 109, 153, 308

Betsey C. (Lord), b 1782
156, 223, 315

Betsey Cate, b 21 Feb 1819
67

Betsey E. (   ), b 1846
128

Betsey Garvin, b 3 Apr 1834
264

Betsey Jane+ 230

Betsey Jane+, b ca 1810 37

Betsey S. (Young) 102

Betsey, b 10 Sep 1801 57

Betsey, b 29 Jul 1788 200

Betsey+, b 12 Feb 1814 37,
201

Betsey+, b 20 May 1784 31,
36

Betsey+, b 21 Nov 1796 37,
324

Betsey+, b 3 Jun 1800 37,
200

Betsey+, b ca 1810 37

Betsy A.+, b ca 1830 37

Betsy A.+, b ca 1845 38,
159

Betsy Jane (Colomy), b 1832
98

Betsy S. (Young), b 1804
166

Betsy+, b ca 1855 37

Betty A.+, b ca 1851 38,
277

Betty, b 19 Jan 1755 125

Bradbury+, b ca 1810 38,
197

Burt, b 25 Jan 1878 103

Byron R., b late 1850s 110

Byron Rosewell+, b Apr 1856
38

Carl L., b Jul 1897 261

Carl+, b 1866 38

Caroline (   ) Neal, b 1812
118

Caroline (Munsey), b 1802

Young

38, 98, 232, 288

Caroline (Small) 213

Caroline (Spurlin), b 1815
208

Caroline E., b 18 Sep 1820
305

Caroline E., b 24 Nov 1821
204

Caroline F.+, b ca 1820 38

Caroline H. (Perkins), b
1853 42

Caroline H.+, b ca 1850 38

Caroline J. (Johnson), b
1824 226

Caroline Jane+, b 13 Feb
1822 38, 288

Caroline M., b 9 Oct 1892
213

Caroline, b 1820s 60

Caroline+, b ca 1820 38

Carolyn M., b 28 Dec 1872
227

Carrie A.+, b 7 Oct 1859
38, 98

Carrie B. (Andrews), b Feb
1867 91

Carrie B.+, b 1860 38

Carrie E., b 28 Jan 1861
120

Carrie M.+ (Noble), b 24 Nov
1861 38

Carrie M.+, b Jun 1865 39

Carrie May, b 28 Nov 1871
227

Carrie, b 1869 96

Carrie, see Caroline H. 42

Catharine (Johnson), b 1783
257

Catharine J., b 1 Jul 1823
257

Catherine (Roberts) Hayes,
b 1806 48

Catherine N. (Trednick), b
ca 1820 87, 88, 267

Catherine Y. (Cook), b 29
Dec 1816 161, 280

Catherine, b 11 Oct 1816
156

Catherine, see Katherine
276

Celia F. (Lilley), b Mar

Young

Daniel+, b ca 1785 50
David   11, 57, 61, 108,
    162, 223, 255, 280, 284,
    288
David H.+, b 28 Jan 1869
    59, 99
David L. 13
David L.+, b 1840s 59
David M.+, b ca 1825 59
David S. 42, 183, 253
David S.+, b 1796 59, 197
David S.+, b ca 1780 57
David, b 14 Apr 1778 172
David, b 1791 67
David, b 1829 248
David+, b 1 May 1759 57
David+, b 12 Nov 1788 57
David+, b 1791 58, 115
David+, b 25 May 1803 58,
    265
David+, b ca 1780 63
David+, b ca 1822 59
Deadimey, see Diadamy+ 60
Deborah (   ) 221
Deborah (   ), b 1814 94
Deborah (Furber), b 1802
    33, 92
Deborah (Ham) Tibbetts, b
    ca 1800 74
Deborah (Killey), b 1764
    12, 79, 112, 119
Deborah K., b 13 Jun 1826
    179
Deborah S. (Fernald), b
    1793   127, 134, 160, 269,
    277
Deborah, b 1802 184
Deborah, b 1820s 31
Deborah+, b 12 Dec 1785
    57, 61
Deborah+, b 1758 60, 300
Deborah+, b 1774 60, 322
Deborah+, b 1788 61
Deborah+, b 6 Dec 1809 61,
    235
Delia, b Jan 1889 264
Della F., b 18 Aug 1865 97
Diadamy+ (   ), b 1760s
    32, 61
Diana (Coffin), b ca 1780
    83

Young

Dolly (Jacobs), b 1782 58,
    211, 264
Dolly (Tirrell), b 1789 179
Dolly+, b 12 Jan 1791 61
Dolly+, b 1790s 317
Dolly+, b ca 1820 151
Dora F., b 28 Mar 1889 216
Dora P., b 24 Jan 1856 40
Dorcas J. (Furbush), b 1851
    279
Dorcas M. (Ewer), b ca 1750
    13, 23, 62, 195, 201, 217
Dorcas M. E., b 27 Jun 1811
    203
Dorothy (   ) 110
Dorothy (Peavey),   b   1789
    17, 106, 216, 241
Dorothy A.+, b 1853 62, 16
Dorothy B. (Lamphrey), b
    1800   102, 167, 252, 258
Dorothy M. 131
Dorothy+, b ca 1820 61
Dorothy+, b ca 1825 61
Drusilla E.+, b 1820   62,
    218
Drusilla, b 1817 317
Drusilla+, b 6 Apr 1784 62,
    196
Dudley 8, 11, 57, 219, 229,
    251, 279
Dudley B.+, b 1869 65, 219
Dudley+, b 1773 63
Dudley+, b 18 Jan 1788 64,
    197
Dudley+, b ca 1735 62
E. Frank+, b 29 Aug 1825
    65, 248
E. J.+, b 1852 65
Earl B., b 3 Jun 1878 9
Eben D., see Ebenezer D.+
    68, 310
Eben D.+, b 19 Apr 1777 68
Eben S., 7 Feb 1854 183
Eben S.+, b Feb 1864 65,
    183
Ebenezer   4, 11, 58, 112,
    223, 254
Ebenezer D.+, b 19 Apr 1777
    68, 310
Ebenezer, b 15 May 1795 57
Ebenezer+, b 1724 65

354

Young

89

Fannie H.+, b 1841 89, 185
Fannie J.+, b 11 Mar 1856
  89, 92
Fannie S. (York), b 15 Sep
  1857 43
Fannie, see Lydia L.+ 225
Fannie+, b ca 1850 89
Fanny (Darling) Horne, b
  1870 254
Fanny A. (Locke), b 1859
  215
Fanny A. (Underwood), b ca
  1830 120
Fanny J., b 1860 313
Flavius, b 10 Jan 1882 216
Flora B., b ca 1878 96
Flora E. (Miller), b 15 Apr
  1869 268
Flora E. (Randall) Shorey,
  b Nov 1865 90
Flora M., b 12 Mar 1857 40
Florence A., b 1854 8
Florence D. (Coffin) Pear-
  sons, b 1865 320
Florence J., b 19 Jul 1893
  107
Florence S.+, b 1855 89,
  210
Florence, b Apr 1889 68
Fordyce R., b 10 Jul 1806
  251
Fostina E.+, b 1858 89,
  243
Frances A. (Foss), b 18 Jul
  1841 43
Frances A., b 1845 16
Frances D., b 1846 209
Frances E. (Lord), b 18 Jan
  1864 164
Frances E., see Ellen E.+
  82
Frances Ellen, see Ellen F.
  140
Frances H., see Fannah H.+
  89, 185
Frances, b 11 Mar 1850 92
Frances, see Fannie J.+ 89
Francis (Hoitt) Bean, b
  1840 120
Francis A.+, b 1826 89

Young

Francis Blake, b 18 Jan 1820
  211
Francis, b 1848 59
Frank 225
Frank Albert, b 2 May 1884
  292
Frank C., b 1858 154
Frank D., b Jun 1856 183
Frank E., b 1861 41
Frank E., b 1863 282
Frank E., see Frank James+
Frank E.+, b 19 Aug 1861
  42, 90
Frank H., b 1850 89
Frank H.+, b Sep 1854 90,
  162
Frank Herbert, b 1850 183
Frank James+, b Apr 1861
  90, 134
Frank K.+, b ca 1850 90
Frank P., b 30 Sep 1877 222
Frank R., b Feb 1860 120
Frank R., b May 1881 38
Frank S.+, b 1864 90, 214
Frank V.+, b 16 Jun 1852
  90, 109
Frank W., b 13 Jul 1871 213
Frank W.+, b 1841 91
Frank W.+, b 24 May 1853 91
Frank, b 1845 209
Frank+, b 1837 89
Frank+, b 1853 90
Frank+, b ca 1850 89
Frank+, b ca 1855 90
Franklin, b 1831 290
Franklin, see George Frank
  248
Franklin, see J. Frank+
  120, 186
Franklin+, b ca 1805 91
Fred A., b 18 May 1874 100
Fred A.+, b Aug 1866 9, 91
Fred B.+, b 1857 91, 249
Fred J.+, b Aug 1867 43, 91
Fred L., b 1892 216
Fred W., b 14 Nov 1875 167
Fred W., b 1858 209
Fred, b 1859 153
Fred, b Oct 1889 91
Fred, b Sep 1862 268
Freddie G., b Sep 1892 107

Young
103, 277
Harley A., b 1856 166
Harold R., see Robert H.
270
Harriet (Nutter), b 1818
13
Harriet A., b 7 Apr 1835
204
Harriet A.+, b late 1840s
103, 214
Harriet B.+, b 1824 103
Harriet Boardman+, b ca
1840 103
Harriet C. (Villam), b 1828
97, 158
Harriet F. (   ), b ca 1815
138
Harriet H. (   ) 25, 85
Harriet H. (   ), b ca 1820
245
Harriet L. (Fellows), b
1874 131
Harriet M. (   ), b ca 1835
21
Harriet N., b ca 1827 65
Harriet S., b 1822 27
Harriet, b 1855 214
Harriet, see Hattie 131
Harriet, see Hattie A.+
104
Harriet+, b 15 Jun 1803
225
Harris A., b 13 May 1869
121
Harrison, b 1810s 31
Harrison, b 1834 77
Harrison+, b 15 May 1837
103, 321
Harry E., b 22 Mar 1881 95
Harry Hayward, b 16 Feb
1869 104
Harry M., b 1889 307
Harvey+, b ca 1820 104
Hattie A., b 1856 215
Hattie A.+, b 16 Sep 1867
104
Hattie A.+, b 18 Aug 1851
104, 130
Hattie E. (Barker), b 1858
160
Hattie J.+, b 1864 104,

Young
242
Hattie M. (Pearson), b 1876
153
Hattie M. (Rogers), b 1845
88
Hattie, b 1862 13
Hazel, b Oct 1895 68
Helen E.+ (Edgely), b Jan
1850 105
Helen E.+, b 1838 104, 224
Helen F., b 1843 40
Helen F., b 2 Dec 1871 159
Henrietta D. (Smith), b 23
May 1840 164
Henrietta, b 1859 163
Henry 5, 9, 45, 62, 119,
158, 225, 292
Henry A., b 26 Jan 1850 308
Henry C.+, b Apr 1861 106,
134
Henry E., b 1859 282
Henry H., b 1842 163
Henry Harrison, b 23 Jul
1843 20
Henry L.+, b 6 Nov 1849 106
Henry S., b Dec 1882 134
Henry S.+, b 1848 36
Henry, b 1815 106
Henry, b 19 Jul 1818 242
Henry, see John Henry+ 106
Henry+, b 23 Jul 1773 105,
191
Herbert D., b ca 1850 186
Herbert F., b 20 Sep 1871
98
Herbert J., b 22 Sep 1872
96
Herbert R., b 1849 40
Herbert S., b 1854 166
Herbert S.+, b Jan 1862 41,
106
Herbert S.+, b Mar 1855 106
Herbert W., b 1 Apr 1879
121
Herbert, b 1854 160
Herman Andrew, see Andrew H.
22
Herman E., b 1887 216
Herschel C., b 1846 186
Hester Ann+, b ca 1820 107
Hezekiah B.+, b ca 1805

Young
  Jacob 43
  Jacob D., b 6 Jan 1852 187
  Jacob Daniels+, b 28 Dec
    1823 8, 84, 121, 220
  Jacob E., see Edgar J.+
    56, 68
  Jacob K.+, b ca 1820 91,
    121
  Jacob W.+, b Oct 1838 121,
    244
  Jacob+, b 1760s 120
  Jacob+, b 1824 121
  James 13, 82, 127, 135,
    201, 225, 235, 265, 268,
    270, 304, 316
  James B., b 1856 154
  James B., b ca 1829 133
  James B.+, b 4 Mar 1864
    15, 128
  James C. 8, 12, 79, 82,
    104, 131, 244, 254, 271
  James C.+, b 1792 128, 238
  James C.+, b 2 Aug 1817
    130, 179
  James Cameron+, b 30 May
    1870 104, 130, 131
  James H. 13, 90, 106, 136,
    164, 281, 284, 291
  James H., b 9 Dec 1898 270
  James H.+, b 1823 133
  James H.+, b 1835 133
  James H.+, b 1841 134, 141
  James H.+, b 19 Apr 1777
    132, 310
  James H.+, b 21 May 1855
    134, 308
  James H.+, b 22 Mar 1787
    132, 324
  James M.+, b 1833 134, 268
  James M.+, b 1835 134
  James M.+, b 1836 55, 134
  James Madison, b 4 Jun 1849
    135
  James Morrill+, b 6 May
    1813 135, 204
  James S. 45
  James T. 46, 244
  James T.+, b 1808 135
  James T.+, b 1856 135, 187
  James W., b 1778 87
  James, b 1792 87

Young
  James, b 18 Dec 1838 141
  James, b 1820s 53
  James, b 1845 227
  James, ba 11 Nov 1792 87
  James, ba 14 Aug 1757 125
  James, ba 1751 125
  James+, b 10 Sep 1718 122,
    169
  James+, b 1801 127
  James+, b 1835 269
  James+, b 1841 128
  James+, b 1849 128
  James+, b 29 Aug 1758 125,
    299
  James+, b ca 1720 124
  James+, b ca 1721 125
  James+, b ca 1752 125
  James+, b ca 1775 127
  James+, b ca 1790 127
  James+, b ca 1820 128
  James+, b Dec 1868 128
  James+, b Oct 1833 128
  James+, ba 9 Sep 1744 170
  Jane (   ) 37
  Jane (   ), b 1839 135
  Jane (Allen), b 1821 136,
    254
  Jane (Bole), b 1839 244
  Jane (Leighton), b 24 Aug
    1768 23
  Jane (Roberts) England, b
    1827 134
  Jane Augusta+, b ca 1821
    39, 136
  Jane E., b 1841 224
  Jane H., b 1831 16
  Jane S. (   ), b 1828 120
  Jane S.+, b ca 1810 136
  Jane, b 1832 211
  Jane+, b ca 1785 135, 197
  Jane+, b ca 1810 135
  Jane+, b Dec 1836 135
  Janette, b 1869 41
  Janette+, b 1841 77, 136
  Jarusha+, b ca 1810 136
  Jean, ba 29 Jun 1740 170
  Jeanna (Ricker), b ca 1830
    222
  Jeannette, see Janette+ 77,
    136
  Jemima (Marston) 108

Young

Jonathan
185

Jonathan Freeman, b 1827
289

Jonathan L., see Lyman J.
182

Jonathan M., b 1851 290

Jonathan T.+, b 7 Dec 1822
135, 164, 179, 186, 315

Jonathan W., b 17 May 1829
179

Jonathan, b 11 Jul 1721
311

Jonathan, b 1730S 273

Jonathan, b 1750s 299

Jonathan, b 1850s 183

Jonathan, b 19 May 1819
179

Jonathan, b 9 Nov 1774 274

Jonathan, ba 5 Feb 1792 87

Jonathan+, b 1 Jan 1756
170

Jonathan+, b 14 Apr 1780
80, 87, 175

Jonathan+, b 16 Feb 1818
60, 183

Jonathan+, b 16 Jun 1761
28, 172

Jonathan+, b 1685 167, 294

Jonathan+, b 1752 172

Jonathan+, b 1760s 172

Jonathan+, b 1792 180

Jonathan+, b 1799 180

Jonathan+, b 1821 184

Jonathan+, b 20 Nov 1818
35, 183

Jonathan+, b 21 Dec 1805
181, 312

Jonathan+, b 24 Jul 1785
179, 322

Jonathan+, b 25 Jul 1788
172, 179

Jonathan+, b 28 Sep 1807
76, 182

Jonathan+, b 5 Jun 1710
168, 169

Jonathan+, b ca 1750 311

Jonathan+, b ca 1755 172

Jonathan+, b ca 1795 117,
180

Jonathan+, b ca 1805 181

Jonathan+, b ca 1815 183

Young

Jonathan+, b ca 1830 184

Joseph 5, 13, 20, 23, 24,
28, 36, 37, 43, 56, 59,
62, 64, 69, 77, 79, 81,
89, 95, 102, 105, 107,
108, 120, 127, 135, 137,
140, 148, 166, 192, 195,
199, 201, 205, 206, 210,
211, 212, 213, 215, 217,
221, 223, 226, 230, 232,
243, 245, 252, 265,
277-280, 285, 303, 306,
313, 315-317, 321, 323

Joseph A., b 1830 163

Joseph A., b 1848 97

Joseph A.+, b 1833 207, 211

Joseph B., b ca 1809 203

Joseph B., b Jun 1897 8

Joseph C. 16, 98, 110, 216,
225, 268, 282

Joseph C. W., b 9 Oct 1824
204

Joseph C., b 1805 93

Joseph C.+, b 11 Dec 1799
211, 265

Joseph C.+, b 1805 212

Joseph C.+, b ca 1793 211

Joseph D.+, b 1835 185, 212

Joseph E.+, b 1852 212

Joseph Frank, b 1855 209

Joseph G.+, b 1819 212

Joseph G.+, b 1824 212

Joseph Gilman, b 4 Jan 1797
200, 212

Joseph J., b 28 Aug 1889
292

Joseph Lang, b 13 Apr 1860
227

Joseph Lang, b 1830 204

Joseph Melvin, b 4 Apr 1859
206

Joseph S.+, b 14 Aug 1854
213

Joseph S.+, b 1843 213, 307

Joseph S.+, b ca 1845 213

Joseph W., b 28 Feb 1851
257

Joseph W.+, b 15 May 1828
33, 213

Joseph, b 1796 284

Joseph, b 18 Apr 1782 195

367

Young

Joseph, b 1800s 314
Joseph, b 1803 218
Joseph, b 1820s 60
Joseph, b 1831 94
Joseph, b 1834 141
Joseph, b 1898 264
Joseph, b ca 1672 270
Joseph, b ca 1779 63
Joseph, b ca 1785 201
Joseph,+ b 1788 31
Joseph+, b ca 1765 199
Joseph+, b 13 Aug 1788 204
Joseph+, b 1749 192
Joseph+, b 1750s 194
Joseph+, b 1758 196
Joseph+, b 1760s 196, 197
Joseph+, b 1770s 199
Joseph+, b 1771 200, 322
Joseph+, b 1773 200
Joseph+, b 1785 196, 201
Joseph+, b 1790 205
Joseph+, b 1800s 205
Joseph+, b 1803 205, 304
Joseph+, b 1810 207
Joseph+, b 1811 208
Joseph+, b 1820 209
Joseph+, b 1833 210
Joseph+, b 1835 210
Joseph+, b 1840 244
Joseph+, b 1842 211
Joseph+, b 2 Mar 1827 55, 210
Joseph+, b 20 Apr 1789 204
Joseph+, b 21 Nov 1771 199
Joseph+, b 22 Mar 1810 207, 319
Joseph+, b 24 Aug 1726 188, 296
Joseph+, b 27 Jul 1811 209, 305
Joseph+, b 30 Jan 1822 205, 210
Joseph+, b 5 Apr 1754 191, 195
Joseph+, b 7 Aug 1788 204
Joseph+, b ca 1730 191
Joseph+, b ca 1760 196
Joseph+, b ca 1764 197, 300
Joseph+, b ca 1765 199
Joseph+, b ca 1780 74

Young

Joseph+, b ca 1785 203
Joseph+, b ca 1795 197, 205
Joseph+, b ca 1800 205
Joseph+, b ca 1804 199, 206
Joseph+, b ca 1815 209
Joseph+, b ca 1825 210
Joseph+, b Oct 1821 209
Josephine F., b 1847 209
Josephine, b 1830 8
Josephine, b 1857 208
Josephine, b 2 Jun 1855 33
Josephine+, b 1853 213
Joshua Moody, b 9 Apr 1836 264
Joshua+, b 1760s 213
Josiah 89, 90
Josiah A.+, b 1794 31, 214
Josiah B. 103
Josiah B.+, b 1823 214
Josiah B.+, b ca 1820 214
Josiah+, b 14 Feb 1825 33, 214
Josiah+, b 16 Aug 1821 214
Josie E. (Neal), b 1853 95
Judith ( ), b ca 1775 107
Judith (Eastman), b ca 1830 119
Judith A. (Davis), b 1825 42, 90, 108
Judith B., b 1823 279
Judith C.+, b 17 Nov 1806 215
Judith K. (Davis), b 23 Oct 1825 180
Judith+, b 1832 215
Judith+, b ca 1805 215, 235
Julia ( ) 81
Julia A., b 1856 137
Julia A., b ca 1818 65
Julia A.+, b 1865 159, 215
Julia A.+, b ca 1815 215
Julia A.+, b ca 1855 209, 215
Julia B., b Feb 1892 270
Julia E.+, b 1850s 215, 252
Julia M.+, b ca 1850 215
Junette, see Nettie L.+ 219, 253
Katherine J. (Parker), b 3 Oct 1824 276
Katie+, b 1842 215

Young

Kezia (Hanson) 5, 283, 286, 310
Kezia (Hanson), b ca 1735 282
Kezia (Hanson), b ca 1753 286
Kezia (Rowe), b 1787 24, 76, 136, 165, 257, 285
Kezia A. (Peavey), b Jan 1834 257
Kezia, b 1730s 273
Kimball, b 1850s 313
Kingman+, b 20 Jul 1855 183, 215
Lafayette M.+, b Dec 1865 216
Lance+, b 1825 216
Landella, b Apr 1880 119
Laura ( ), b ca 1855 219
Laura (Hall) 110
Laura (Kimball), b 1862 94
Laura A., b 1845 242
Laura A.+, b 1839 212, 216
Laura A.+, b 20 Apr 1860 216, 242
Laura A.+, b ca 1820 216
Laura P. (Jones), b ca 1850 42, 91
Laura P., b 1834 8
Laura W. (Mason) 25
Laurana+, b ca 1730 216
Lavina Ellen (Beedy) 42
Lavina J.+, b 1828 216, 242
Lavina J.+, b 31 Jan 1835 216, 321
Lavina+, b ca 1795 216
Lavinia ( ), b ca 1830 306
Lavinia Jeannette (Hughs), b 23 Apr 1862 44
Lavonia, b 5 Dec 1810 201
Leander J., see Leyander+ 257
Lenora, b 1851 137
Leo+, b Sep 1814 217
Leon, see Leo+ 217
Leonora, b Jul 1887 264
Leslie, b Mar 1884 307
Lester A.+, b Apr 1860 217, 278

Young

Lester I., b 13 Oct 1884 220
Lester R., b 9 Jul 1882 220
Levi 62, 110, 184, 232, 271
Levi B.+, b May 1834 218
Levi G.+, b 1823 218
Levi J. 253
Levi J.+, b ca 1800 218, 314
Levi J.+, b Sep 1814 219
Levi, b 1801 218
Levi+, b 1775 196, 217
Lewis A.+, b 1835 65, 219
Lewis Augustus+, b 1834 186, 219
Lewis E., b 7 Nov 1878 216
Lewis F.+, b Sep 1866 163, 220
Lewis Henry+, b 15 Dec 1863 121, 220
Lewis P., b 5 Jun 1898 220
Lewis+, b ca 1850 219
Leyander+, b 9 Feb 1850 220, 257
Lilla M. (Cutts), b 17 Dec 1866 289
Lilla May, b Oct 1879 90
Lillian A. (Black), b Dec 1868 260
Lillian J. (Evans), b Sep 1864 128
Lillian Maybelle+, b ca 1869 210, 221
Lillian P., b Aug 1868 20
Lillian W., b 25 May 1867 166
Lillian, b 28 Jul 1858 121
Lillie E.+, b 1850s 221
Lizzie ( ), b 3 Mar 1863 315
Lizzie (Spurlin), b 1846 211
Lizzie A. (Foss), b 1858 90
Lizzie A.+, b 1865 221, 268
Lizzie C., b 1820s 179
Lizzie H.+, b 1857 221, 252
Lizzie J. (Drew), b 1842 69
Lizzie M., b 13 Jun 1869 211
Lizzie M.+, b 17 Apr 1859 45, 221

Young

Lizzie M.+, b 1859 56, 221
Lizzie M.+, b 26 Oct 1853
    184, 221
Lizzie N.+, b 1830s 221
Lizzie, b 18 Jun 1882 292
Lizzie, b 1859 181
Lizzie, b Aug 1859 35
Lois (Miner) Waldron, b ca
    1810 257
Lois E. (Holden), b 1861
    213
Lomena (   ), b Dec 1869
    270
Loren Whiting, b 7 Dec 1803
    31
Lottie (   ), b 1854 316
Lottie M. (   ), b Dec 1844
    152
Louisa (Lovering), b 1815
    8
Louisa (Meserve), b ca 1825
    88
Louisa A. (Jenkins), b 1838
    83, 284
Louisa A., b 3 Apr 1862
    214
Louisa Blaisdell (Page), b
    2 Jul 1831 9
Louisa Emma, see Emma Lou-
    isa 101
Louisa J.+, b ca 1825 221
Louisa W.+, b ca 1815 221
Louisa, b 8 Jun 1881 43
Louisa+, b ca 1819 27, 221
Louise Shackford, b 17 Feb
    1909 220
Louise, b 1836 135
Lovey J. (Pike), b 1878 91
Lovina A., b 1833 214
Lovina A., b 1858 308
Lovina A.+, b 19 May 1858
    221, 306
Lovina E. (Beedy) 85, 96
Lovina, b 7 Dec 1771 191
Lovina, b early 1830s 60
Lowell H.+, b 1844 163,
    222
Lucetta+, b 1834 222
Lucinda (Burleigh), b 30
    Oct 1812 152, 232
Lucinda+, b 1828 222

Young

Lucius+, b ca 1825 222
Lucretia, b 4 Sep 1814 133
Lucy (   ) 315
Lucy (   ), b 1815 167
Lucy (   ), b ca 1855 44
Lucy (Rowe), b ca 1840 65,
    219
Lucy (Walker), b 1793 284
Lucy (Whitehorn), b ca 1770
    61, 107, 215, 235
Lucy A. (Prescott), b 1831
    91, 249
Lucy A., b 1841 284
Lucy Ann (Wentworth), b 9
    May 1827 33
Lucy Ellen, b 12 Jun 1855
    320
Lucy J., b 1853 219
Lucy Jane (Wilber), b 1836
    14
Lucy K. (Young), b 1815 166
Lucy Maria+ (Witham), b 10
    Apr 1836 223
Lucy Maria+, b 1822 67, 223
Lucy R. (Karl) Brown, b 9
    May 1852 289
Lucy W.+, b ca 1815 223
Lucy Walker, b 8 Jul 1817
    8
Lucy, b 1784 73
Lucy, b 1790s 235
Lucy, b 1794 115
Lucy, b 1862 252
Lucy, ba 25 Apr 1742 70
Lucy+, b ca 1750 222
Lucy+, b ca 1785 222
Lucy+, b ca 1805 223
Luella (Stevens) Gilkerson,
    b Aug 1853 9
Luella May, b 8 Jun 1881 43
Luesta, see Ivesta D.+ 106,
    119
Lulla, see Luella 9
Lurana Augusta, b 19 Apr
    1819 251
Lurana Jane, see Lavina J.+
    216, 321
Lurana, see Laurana+ 216
Lurana+, b ca 1810 223
Luru M. (   ), b 1870 95
Luther 96, 104, 253, 291

370

Young
    Marie A.+ 137, 225
    Marie+, b 1840s 225
    Marilla A., b 1847 161
    Marilla A., see Anna M.+
    24, 138
    Marilla M., b 1839 185
    Mark Allen+, b 1827 204,
    226
    Mark F.+, b 1817 151, 227
    Mark+, b ca 1780 226
    Marshie E., b Sep 1894 270
    Martha (   ) 228
    Martha (   ), b 1826 242
    Martha (   ), b 1850 9, 22
    Martha (Bennett), b 2 Feb
    1783 207, 280, 317
    Martha (Masfield), b ca
    1835 184
    Martha (Roberts), b 1798
    65, 247
    Martha (Tuttle), b 1780
    21, 251
    Martha (Winn), b ca 1840
    135
    Martha A. (Nelson), b 1827
    65, 183, 322
    Martha A. (Stevens), b 1836
    43, 217, 278
    Martha A., b Aug 1850 306
    Martha A.+, b 25 May 1847
    242
    Martha A.+, b 6 Apr 1847
    180, 228
    Martha A.+, b ca 1825 227
    Martha Ann, b 1855 208
    Martha Ann+, b ca 1825 228
    Martha B., b 1794 167
    Martha D. (Bassett), b 28
    Nov 1821 208, 232
    Martha E.+, b 1842 227,
    228
    Martha F. (Gray), b 1821
    185
    Martha F.+, b ca 1830 228
    Martha H. (Dorr), b ca 1830
    119
    Martha H., b 15 Apr 1853
    308
    Martha J. (Keniston), b 3
    Aug 1830 13, 14
    Martha J., see Jennie M.+

Young
    133, 136
    Martha L.+ (Goldsmith), b 15
    Dec 1803 228
    Martha S., b 1854 187
    Martha W. (Leavitt), b Oct
    1828 110
    Martha, b 1845 135
    Martha, b 1850 106
    Martha, b 1868 65
    Martha, b 8 Feb 1817 179
    Martha+ (   ), b 1819 227
    Martha+, b 1787 227
    Martha+, b 1798 227
    Martha+, b ca 1810 227
    Martin, b 1859 277
    Marvin A., b 24 Apr 1884 95
    Mary (   ) 159, 215, 216,
    225
    Mary (   ), b 1770s 263
    Mary (   ), b 1804 97
    Mary (   ), b Feb 1864 68
    Mary (   ), b ca 1815 209
    Mary (Blanchard) 16
    Mary (Burleigh), b 16 May
    1757 143, 156, 247, 274,
    317
    Mary (Cate), b 14 Jun 1811
    33, 44
    Mary (Chadwick), b 23 Nov
    1769 16, 55, 128, 236
    Mary (Cram), b ca 1800 196
    Mary (Dermody), b May 1842
    308
    Mary (Diamond), b 1794 119,
    231, 278
    Mary (Ferrill), b 1864 25
    Mary (Foss), b 25 Nov 1739
    5, 95, 105, 188, 303,
    313, 317, 323
    Mary (Garvin), b ca 1812
    264
    Mary (Greenough), b 1853
    222
    Mary (Hall), b Jun 1858 69
    Mary (Ham), b 8 Oct 1723
    70, 258, 261, 292
    Mary (Hill) b 1768 33,
    160, 172, 185, 230, 271,
    288
    Mary (Huntress), b ca 1725
    299

Young

Mary (Jackson), b ca 1782
31

Mary (Kimball) 5, 11, 13,
80, 85, 87, 127, 201,
268, 304, 308

Mary (Kimball), ba 4 Oct
1730 246

Mary (Kimball), ba 7 Oct
1759 125

Mary (Lovering) 170

Mary (Nute), b 22 Dec 1777
292, 304

Mary (Oldcroft) 270

Mary (Otis), b 1751 31,
60, 179, 200, 257, 322

Mary (Pinkham), b 19 Dec
1800 101, 118

Mary (Roberts), b ca 1660
141, 167, 224, 228, 245,
272, 293, 297

Mary (Stodgdon), b 29 May
1856 96

Mary (Tibbetts), b ca 1800
205

Mary (Tibbetts), b ca 1810
243

Mary (Willey), 27 Mar 1791
21, 109, 115

Mary A. (Farnum), b 1825
264

Mary A. (Fowles), b 14 Aug
1831 45

Mary A. (Frost), b Jun 1839
221, 268

Mary A. (Gleason), b 19 Nov
1832 14, 232

Mary A. (Hanson), b Jun
1851 99

Mary A. (Jackson), b 10 Jul
1812 24, 162, 138

Mary A. (Joy), b Jun 1839
24, 111

Mary A. (McDonald), b 1870
257

Mary A. (Mitchell), b ca
1825 59

Mary A. (Nute), b 18 Jun
1821 46, 135, 244

Mary A. (Parsons), b Jul
1828 278

Mary A. (Taylor), b 1848

Young

106

Mary A., b 1830 45

Mary A., b 1839 186

Mary A., b 1848 212, 215

Mary A., b 1853 133

Mary A.+ (Nason), b 6 Jul
1806 231

Mary A.+, b 1830 55, 231

Mary A.+, b 21 Dec 1829
231, 279

Mary Amanda (Doyle), b 3 Mar
1873 104, 131

Mary Ann 289

Mary Ann (Chase), b 1818 36

Mary Ann (Gordon), b 1821
162

Mary Ann (Hanson), b 6 Jul
1806 39

Mary Ann (Seavey), b 13 Nov
1816 78, 99, 119

Mary Ann (Thompson), b 1849
213

Mary Ann, b 1812 218

Mary Ann, b 1818 260

Mary Ann, b 1830 289

Mary Ann, b ca 1817 67

Mary Ann+, b 1 Jan 1827
232, 288

Mary Ann+, b ca 1815 231

Mary Ann+, b ca 1816 218,
232

Mary Ann+, b ca 1820 232

Mary Ann+, b ca 1825 232

Mary Anna (Bowser), b Mar
1872 270

Mary C. (   ), b Oct 1838
277

Mary C., b 6 Nov 1850 227

Mary C.+, b 1800s 232

Mary D. (Hobbs) b 1775 80,
311

Mary D.+, b Apr 1824 232

Mary E. (   ), b 1844 96

Mary E. (Bagley), b 1849
154

Mary E. (Caligan), b May
1874 59

Mary E. (Lord), b 1863 44

Mary E. (Varney), b Oct 1856
90

Mary E. (Wiggin), b ca 1810

374

Young
Mary Susan, b 1852 120
Mary Susan+, b 1824 234
Mary Susan+, b 4 Sep 1820 179, 233
Mary V. (Matthew), b 1816 130
Mary Willard (Smith), b 10 May 1807 163
Mary, b 11 Nov 1779 191
Mary, b 13 May 1808 179
Mary, b 1750s 66, 72
Mary, b 1763 299
Mary, b 1790 248
Mary, b 1799 196
Mary, b 1810s 312
Mary, b 1820s 31
Mary, b 1823 267
Mary, b 24 May 1718 246
Mary, b 30 Dec 1725 169
Mary, b ca 1670 270
Mary, b ca 1754 300
Mary, see Mercy 35
Mary, see Polly (Hill) 33
Mary+ (Nute), b 23 Dec 1783 230
Mary+, b 1699 228, 294
Mary+, b 1779 145, 229
Mary+, b 1800s 230, 314
Mary+, b 1846 231
Mary+, b 25 Mar 1807 203, 230
Mary+, b 28 Sep 1774 229, 310
Mary+, b 30 Dec 1725 228
Mary+, b ca 1720 142, 228
Mary+, b ca 1750 229
Mary+, b ca 1765 63, 229
Mary+, b ca 1793 175, 230, 324
Mary+, b ca 1805 230
Mary+, b ca 1810 231
Mary+, b ca 1820 231
Maryetta+, b 4 Aug 1869 15, 232
Mathews, b ca 1674 270
Matilda (Jones) Hall, b 1837 258
Mattie E. (Lord), b 1849 108
Mattie E.+, b 1860 99, 234
Mattie M. (Torrey), b 22

Young
Aug 1838 45
Mattie W. (Foller), b 1848 97
Mattie W.+ (Wilkinson), b 2 Apr 1847 234
Mattie, b 1862 154
Maud H., b 1889 282
Maud L., b 14 Aug 1879 45
Maud M., b Jan 1889 43, 220
Maud V., b Mar 1884 257
Maude, b Oct 1884 68
May (   ), b 1831 257
May (Earle), b 1877 21
May Anna, b 17 Apr 1874 243
Mehitable (Varney), b 1773 238
Mehitable (Varney), b ca 1796 118
Mehitable Augusta, b 3 Jun 164
Mehitable B. (Cate) Cook, b 1834 154, 166
Mehitable Clark+, b 1800s 31, 234
Mehitable, see Hittie R. (Cole) 166
Melina, see Melissa A.+ 130
Melina, see Melissa+ 235
Melissa (Downing), b 1839 45, 46, 163
Melissa A.+, b 1845 130
Melissa A.+, b ca 1835 234
Melissa, b 1835 209
Melissa, b Sep 1849 135
Melissa+, b 1845 235
Melvina (   ), b Jan 1867 264
Mercy (   ), b 1736 311
Mercy (Hanson) Church, b ca 1680 46, 245
Mercy, b 1790s 175
Mercy, b 1793 322
Mercy, b 1810s 312
Mercy, b ca 1810 35
Mercy, ba 31 Jan 1742 169
Mercy, see Mary 246
Mercy+, b ca 1825 50, 235
Merton P., b 7 Sep 1888 220
Millie E., b 5 Sep 1896 107
Milo F., b 1820s 31
Minnie L. (Cunningham), b

Young

Aug 1873　158

Molly D. (Hobbs)　181

Molly, see also Polly　26

Morton E., b Dec 1888　65

Moses　16, 17, 55, 61, 100,
104, 106, 107, 110, 128,
215, 216, 221, 232

Moses A.　89

Moses A.+, b 17 Aug 1829
27, 242

Moses C.　121, 159, 211,
244, 292

Moses C.+, b 9 Apr 1809
200, 243

Moses.C.+, b ca 1806　243

Moses F., b 1836　209

Moses Franklin+, b 1835
244

Moses M.+, b 1836　135, 244

Moses N., b Jun 1880　100

Moses N.+, b 1838　244

Moses, b 1730s　273

Moses, b 1778　180

Moses, b Jan 1824　242

Moses+, b 11 Oct 1763　235,
274

Moses+, b 1766　236, 300

Moses+, b 1770s　238

Moses+, b 1778　241

Moses+, b 1825　242

Moses+, b 1840　242

Moses+, b 9 Jul 1767　238,
299

Moses+, b ca 1775　241

Myra M.+, b 1843　16, 244

Myra S. (Prescott) Shap-
leigh, b Oct 1846　57

Myron A., b 22 Mar 1881　95

Myron D.+, b 1 Mar 1844
130, 244

Myrtle, b 24 Feb 1883　96

Nahum G.+, b 22 May 1814
25, 85, 245

Nancy　13

Nancy (　)　243

Nancy (　), b ca 1770　323

Nancy (　), b ca 1780　136

Nancy (Blodgett), b 1789
84, 270

Nancy (Burleigh), b 1787
243, 248, 274, 317

Young

Nancy (Drew), b 1760　151,
248, 274, 301, 317

Nancy (Nudd), b 19 May 1789
45, 132, 281, 291

Nancy (Young), b 1787　13,
127, 201, 230, 245

Nancy E. (　), b ca 1840
214

Nancy E. (　)　90

Nancy E., b 1845　244

Nancy Susan, b 1836　94

Nancy, b 1760s　125

Nancy, b 1787　127, 201, 277

Nancy, b 1804　324

Nancy, b 1810s　201

Nancy, b 1850　102

Nancy, b 23 Jun 1805　57

Nancy, b ca 1800　322

Nancy+ (　), b ca 1845　245

Nancy+ (Smith), b 1787　245

Nancy+, b ca 1795　245

Nancy+, b ca 1800　245

Nancy+, b ca 1808　150, 245

Nancy+, b ca 1810　245

Nancy+, b ca 1815　245

Nancy+, b ca 1820　203, 245

Nason Elmer, b 16 Oct 1861
41

Nathan Burleigh, b 4 Oct
1867　206

Nathaniel　5, 11, 41, 46,
65, 80, 81, 85, 87, 163,
249, 308

Nathaniel B.　21

Nathaniel B.+, b 1778　249,
251, 310

Nathaniel Badger　102, 167,
258

Nathaniel Badger+, b 1778
63

Nathaniel Badger+, b 1799
197, 252

Nathaniel H., b 6 Jan 1855
109

Nathaniel M.+, b 1826　91,
215, 221, 252

Nathaniel, b 16 Oct 1815
251

Nathaniel, b 1796　196

Nathaniel, b 1842　248

Nathaniel, b 5 Jun 1840　164

Young

Sally (Nason), b ca 1760
48, 146, 152

Sally (Randall), b 1779
39, 92

Sally (Saunders), b ca 1810
117, 181

Sally (Seavey), b ca 1820
17, 21

Sally (Smith), b 25 Apr
1790 157, 161, 233, 280

Sally (Witham) 292

Sally Ann (Blaso), b 1800s
206

Sally B.+, b ca 1807 218,
271

Sally C. ( ), b ca 1810
322

Sally E.+, b ca 1815 133

Sally H. (York), b 1793
136

Sally J. ( ), b 1822 219

Sally J., b 1848 219

Sally, b 1760s 125

Sally, b 25 Aug 1802 200

Sally, b ca 1803 312

Sally+, b 1 Jul 1807 271

Sally+, b 1778 31, 271

Sally+, b 30 Nov 1801 271

Sally+, b ca 1778 271

Sally+, b ca 1795 175, 271

Sally+, b ca 1825 271

Samuel 143, 235, 253, 273

Samuel A., b 17 Feb 1833
179

Samuel B.+, b 28 Apr 1784
145, 243, 248, 274

Samuel E.+, b 3 Jun 1822
276

Samuel Kershaw, b 12 May
1894 104, 131

Samuel L.+, b 1826 277

Samuel L.+, b ca 1795 276

Samuel M.+, b 1828 277

Samuel M.+, b ca 1825 277

Samuel N.+, b 1832 269,
277

Samuel P. 38, 43, 103,
217, 306

Samuel P.+, b 12 Nov 1814
179, 277

Young

Samuel P.+, b ca 1802 199,
277

Samuel P.+, b ca 1830 278

Samuel P.+, b Jul 1831 141,
278

Samuel S. 119, 231

Samuel S.+, b 1794 63

Samuel S.+, b 18 Jan 1794
197, 278

Samuel T.+, b 10 Aug 1852
279, 306

Samuel, b 1852 306

Samuel+, b 1700 294

Samuel+, b 1852 274

Samuel+, b 25 Apr 1734 273

Samuel+, b ca 1700 272

Samuel+, b ca 1766 274

Sara A., b 1828 141

Sarah ( ) 216, 259

Sarah ( ), b 1813 110

Sarah ( ), b ca 1708 12

Sarah ( ), b ca 1775 150

Sarah (Bennett), b 25 Aug
1779 105, 225

Sarah (Bradley), b 1797 26

Sarah (Brown) 192

Sarah (Buzzell), b 1808
181, 312

Sarah (Caverno) Twombly, b
22 Jan 1831 121

Sarah (Commody), b ca 1765
196

Sarah (Cram), b ca 1760 137

Sarah (Ellis), b 1844 98

Sarah (Folsom), b 1692 5,
148, 188, 195, 294, 296,
300, 317, 323

Sarah (Hayes), ba 14 Feb
1751 11, 74, 261, 264

Sarah (Keniston), b ca 1815
319

Sarah (Pettingill) 89

Sarah (Pinkham), b ca 1770
108, 140, 197, 206, 277

Sarah (Ricker), b ca 1795
204

Sarah (Runnels), b ca 1780
150

Sarah (Saunders), b ca 1800
159, 209

Sarah (Trefethen), b ca 1760

Young
        1828   210
    Susan (Meder) b 1781   136
    Susan (Park)   197
    Susan (Snow) Dudley, b 1829
        290
    Susan (Wood), b 1750s   124,
        225, 265
    Susan (Young)   253
    Susan A. (Patch), b 21 Dec
        1833   290, 315
    Susan A., b 1855   278
    Susan A.+, b 1832   55, 291
    Susan A.+, b 1840   224
    Susan A.+, b ca 1850   291
    Susan Amanda+, b 1840   291
    Susan C. (Staples), b ca
        1850   167
    Susan C.+, b 1842   45, 133,
        291
    Susan E., b 1814   92
    Susan E.+, b 1817   292
    Susan E.+, b 1864   41, 292
    Susan Elizabeth (Miles), b
        27 Aug 1832 20, 101, 268
    Susan F. (Wiggin), b 17 Feb
        1808   316
    Susan F., b 1859   306
    Susan L. (Brett), b 1846
        43
    Susan M.+, b 1841   106, 292
    Susan N.+, b 24 Nov 1817
        292, 305
    Susan P. (Henderson), b
        1815   135
    Susan S.+, b ca 1830   292
    Susan Tappan (Cook), b 17
        Dec 1841   103
    Susan, b 1834   248
    Susan+, b 7 Nov 1858   42,
        291
    Susan+, b ca 1804   291
    Susan+, b ca 1805   291
    Susan+, b ca 1810   150, 291
    Susannah (   )   150
    Susannah (   )   92
    Susannah (   ), b 1 Oct
        1740   316
    Susannah (Cotton), b   ca
        1700   316
    Susannah (Demeritt), b 25
        Dec 1755   78, 85, 175,

Young
        309
    Susannah (Keay), b ca 1800
        203
    Susannah (Lyons), b ca 1757
        125
    Susannah   (Mathews),   b   ca
        1655   5, 270
    Susannah   (Mudget),   b   late
        1770s   57
    Susannah Ela, see Susan E.
        92
    Susannah, b 1730s   273
    Susannah, b 7 Oct 1766   274
    Susannah, b ca 1678   270
    Susannah, ba 21 Apr 1765
        299
    Susannah, bp 12 Mar 1741
        142
    Susannah+, b 1760   72, 292
    Susie E. (Pettigrew), b ca
        1865   107
    Susie J. (Griffen), b 1852
        24
    Susie M. (Pitman), b 1876
        322
    Tamsen (Hayes), ba 8 Aug
        1762   300
    Temperance (Bickford), b 7
        Jun 1719 46, 65, 310
    Theodora Ethel, b 18 Jan
        1903   44
    Theodore L.+, b Sep 1850
        244, 292
    Thomas   5, 22, 42, 45, 60,
        69, 125, 134, 141, 143,
        146, 148, 151, 167, 188,
        195, 197, 205, 209, 224,
        228, 233, 236, 238, 245,
        258-260, 272, 279, 292,
        296, 297, 301, 305, 307,
        317, 323
    Thomas C.   10, 68, 213
    Thomas C.+, b 30 Apr 1815
        305, 307
    Thomas C.+, b ca 1815   307
    Thomas E., b 1869   165
    Thomas F.+, b 16 Feb 1836
        109, 308
    Thomas J., b 2 Aug 1804   251
    Thomas J.+, b 1807   308
    Thomas Jefferson   89

Young

William C.+, b ca 1810 320
William Cate, b 1827 67
William G.+, b 20 Nov 1870
  99, 320
William H., b 17 Aug 1854
  98
William H., b 1814 257
William H., b 1834 16
William H., b 1876 152
William H., b 19 Aug 1835
  119
William H.+, b 1833 320
William H.+, b 23 Apr 1865
  166, 320
William Hale+, b 14 Mar
  1809 41, 82, 103, 216,
  224, 317, 320
William Henry 6
William Henry Harrison, see
  Harrison+ 103, 321, 322
William Henry, b 1845 208
William Henry+, b 5 May
  1772 194, 321
William J.+, b 1828 322
William N.+, b 1867 183,
  322
William S., b 18 Dec 1820
  58
William, b 1800s 92
William, b 27 Jun 1813 319
William, b ca 1818 205
William+ 107
William+, b 11 Sep 1777
  191, 317
William+, b 1749 125, 316
William+, b 1750s 317
William+, b 1853 320
William+, b 23 Apr 1723
  316
William+, b 8 Jan 1775
  145, 317
William+, b ca 1700 316
William+, b ca 1780 319
William+, b ca 1785 319
William+, b ca 1800 319
William+, b ca 1810 319
William+, b ca 1815 319
Willie A., b 25 Nov 1866
  15
Willie E., b 12 Mar 1898
  107

Young

Willie E., b 17 Mar 1872
  100
Willie, see William H. 98
Winnie L., b 17 Jul 1882
  279
Winthrop 5, 31, 60, 179,
  200, 257, 322
Winthrop, b 14 Nov 1815 179
Winthrop, b 18 Sep 1817 31
Winthrop, b Mar 1809 257
Winthrop+, b 12 Mar 1793 57
Winthrop+, b 1753 28, 322
Winthrop+, b 1783 322
Winthrop+, b ca 1805 322
Woodbury, see Charles Wood-
  ward+ 45
Zachariah+, b 9 Feb 1765
  157, 191, 230, 323

INDEX II.   SURNAMES OTHER THAN YOUNG
(+ signifies main entry)

Babb
   134
Bagley
   Mary E., b 1849   154
Bailey
   Hannah, b 1760   72
Baker
   Abbie D.   101
Banfield
   Mary Ann+ (Young), b ca
      1820   232
   Nathaniel, b ca 1815   232
Barker
   Abigail (   ), b 1781   133
   Abigail A., b 1823   133
   Emily M. (   )   160
   Hattie E., b 1858   160
   John   160
   Rosilla, b 1776   133
   Sally, b 1783   217
   Sarah, see Sally   217
Barnes
   Eliza (Young), b 18 Jul
      1843   108
Barr
   Charles A.   217
Bassett
   Ann (Burnham)   208
   Bessie+ (Young), b ca 1855
      36, 110
   David   208
   Martha D., b 28 Nov 1821
      208
   Thomas B., b ca 1850   36
Batchelder
   Gardner   322
   Nancy+ (Young), b ca 1800
      322
Bayley, see Bailey   72
Beacham
   Louisa W.+ (Young), b ca
      1815   221
   Simon F., b ca 1810   221
Bean
   Anna+ (Young), b 19 Jan
      1776   23, 194
   Deborah+ (Young), b 1774
      60, 322
   Elijah Otis, b 1810s   61
   Francis (Hoitt), b 1840
   120
   Harrison, b 1810s   61

Bean
   Joanna+ (Young), b ca 1750
      140
   John Langdon, b 1800s   61
   John, b ca 1770   23, 61
   Sally, b 1800s   61
   Simeon, b ca 1745   140
   William, b 1800s   61
Beedy
   Ellen L., b 1838   308
   Lovina E., see Ellen L.   308
Bennett
   Cordelia+ (Young), b 1854
      46, 135
   Emma Jane (Piper), b 1860s
      265
   George   158
   George W., b ca 1845   46
   Harriet M. (Farnham)   158
   Jane L., see Jennie   158
   Jennie, b 8 Jan 1853   158
   John   105, 318
   John Sanborn   265
   Mary (   )   318
   Patty, b ca 1790   319
   Sarah, b 25 Aug 1779   105
Berry
   Fannie E. (Clough), b 1870s
      225
   John L., b 1870s   225
   Martha L., b 1838   213
   Mary C.+ (Young), b 1800s
      232
   Mary+ (Young), b ca 1793
      175, 230
   Nathaniel, b 1800s   232
   Rebecca, b 1801   213
   William, b 1787   213
   William, b ca 1790   230
Bickford
   Abigail (   )   98
   Almira+ (Young), b ca 1805
      17
   Alvah H.   254
   Betsey, b ca 1795   8
   Daniel   98
   Elizabeth, b 1718   65
   Hannah L.+ (Young), b 1815
      102, 314
   Jonathan   29
   Juanna (   )   46, 65
   Judith, b 1 Jun 1779   230

Bickford
  Rebecca, ba 5 Nov 1758 28
  Richard, b ca 1800 17
  Sarah (Wilmot) 29
  Sarah A., b 1833 98
  Stephen A., b ca 1810 102
  Temperance 65
  Temperance, b 7 Jun 1719
    46
  Thomas 46, 65
Black
  Lillian A., b Dec 1868 260
  Mellisa A. (Drew) 260
  O. A. 260
Blaisdell
  Eliza (   ) 83
  Emma A.+ (Young) 233
  Emma A.+ (Young), b 1855
    82, 161
  George W., b 1848 83
  John F. 233
  Joseph 83
  Mary Jane+ (Young), b 1850
    161, 233
  Newell, b ca 1850 233
  Susan A. 90
  Susan A., b 1831 162
  William 90
  William, b 1821 162
Blake
  Joseph 265
  Sadie C. (Piper), b ca 1860
    265
Blaso
  David P. 211
  Phebe (   ) 211
  Sally Ann, b 1800s 206
Blazo
  Albert M., b ca 1825 280
  Ebenezer 278
  Ebenezer, b 1809 140
  Sally 278
  Sally, b 1804 140
  Sarah Ann+ (Young), b 1828
    207, 280
Blodgett
  Nancy, b 1789 270
Boardman
  Fannie H.+ (Young), b 10
    Jan 1847 89
  George H., b ca 1840 89
  Priscilla F., b 1830 9

Boardman
  Samuel Herbert, b 13 Dec
    1874 89
Bodge
  John H., b Feb 1887 306
  Maria S., b Sep 1848 306
Bole
  Jane, b 1839 244
Boles
  Emmons, b 1830s 291
  Rufus, b ca 1805 291
  Susan+ (Young), b ca 1810
    291
Bond
  Abigail+ (Young), b ca 1760
    11, 63
  John, b ca 1770 11
Boudron
  Betsy A.+ (Young), b ca 1845
    38
  Joseph, b ca 1840 38
Boudron, see Bowdron 38, 159
Bowdron
  Betsy A.+ (Young), b ca 1845
    159
Bowser
  Charlotte L. (   ) 270
  George E. 270
  Mary Anna, b Mar 1872 270
Brackett, see also Brockett
  Betsey A., b 1810 65
  Joshua, b 1805 65
Bradbury
  James G., b ca 1815 285
  Sophronia+ (Young), b 8 May
    1809 201, 285
Bradley
  Sarah, b 1797 26
Brett
  Abial 43
  Hannah (   ) 43
  Susan L., b 1846 43
Brewster
  Anna E. (Young), b 1845 161
  Eliza+ (Young), b ca 1800
    79
  Timothy, b ca 1800 79
Briggs
  Caroline+ (Young), b ca 1820
    38
  George, b ca 1815 38
Brock

Brock
Almeda (Nutter) Young, b 1826 56
Dolly+ (Young), b 12 Jan 1791 61
Dolly+, b 1790s 317
Elijah 215
Isaac, b ca 1775 265
James W., b 1851 215
James, b ca 1815 61
John W., b ca 1810 223
Julia A.+ (Young), b ca 1855 209, 215
Lucy W.+ (Young), b ca 1815 223
Lydia, b 21 Sep 1821 61
Nancy H. ( ) 215
Nancy, b ca 1813 61
Nicholas, b 1824 56
Polly+ (Young), b ca 1780 125, 265
Ralph, b ca 1785 61
Ralph, b ca 1818 61
Sabrina, b ca 1810 61
Brockett
Annie F., b 1835 65
Eleanor A. ( ) 65
William 65
Brown
Abigail A. (Young), b 1831 158
Betsey A.+ (Young), b ca 1855 37
Frank J., b ca 1855 253
Georgann, b 1873 320
George 320
James I., b ca 1850 37
Julia ( ) 320
Lucy R. (Karl), b 9 May 1852 289
Mary+ (Young), b ca 1745 229
Moses, b ca 1745 229
Nettie L.+ (Young), b 1856 219, 253
Sarah M., b Nov 1849 312
Bryant
Addie M. (Johnson), b ca 1865 235
Frank A., b ca 1860 235
Bumford
Abbie F., b 1851 68

Bumford
David 68
Dorcas ( ) 68
Bumpus
Hester A., b ca 1875 291
Bunker
Abigail (Chesley), b ca 1814 80
Addie F.+ (Young), b 1860s 13, 59
Benjamin F. 80
George M., b ca 1865 13
Jennie M.+ (Young), b 1847 133, 136
Sidney P., b ca 1845 136
Sylvanus 222
Burleigh
Addie C.+ (Young), b ca 1860 13
Alonzo, b 1833 215
Arthur F., b 1866 233
Arthur Y., b 1866 152
Betsey ( ), b 21 Jun 1792 152
Comfort (Taylor) 317
George P., b ca 1855 13
John T., b Dec 1806 215
Joseph T., b 1833 152, 233
Joseph, b 1837 152
Judith C.+ (Young), b 17 Nov 1806 215
Lucinda, b 30 Oct 1812 152
Mary J.+ (Young), b 1843 152, 232
Mary, b 16 May 1757 143
Nancy ( ) 274
Nancy M., b 1832 215
Nancy, b 1787 274
Nathaniel, b 20 May 1791 152
Rachel 29
Sally, b 8 Jan 1777 317
William 29, 143, 274, 317
Bussell
Margaret B.+ (Young), b ca 1825 225
Samuel, b ca 1820 225
Butler
Hannah (Chesley), b 1 Jan 1799 53
Buzzell
Aaron 106, 167

Clements
   280
   Frank P., b 26 Nov 1850
   280
   Mary E., b 30 Sep 1852 280
   Samuel, b ca 1810 280
   Sarah Ann+ (Young), b 14
   Sep 1815 204, 280
   William, b ca 1825 37
Clifford
   Sally, b ca 1755 166, 170
   Sarah, see Sally 170
Clough
   Lydia F.+ (Young), b 1859
   42
   Albion, b ca 1845 254
   Bert, b ca 1875 254
   Daniel 224
   Daniel B., b 23 Jul 1845
   224
   Ethel, b 1870s 254
   Fannie E., b 1870s 225
   George F., b ca 1830 98
   Jennie Martha, b ca 1850
   213
   Josiah, b ca 1760 229
   Lydia F.+ (Young), b 1859
   224
   Mary, b ca 1786 229
   Mary+ (Young), b ca 1765
   63, 229
   Olive J.+ (Young), b 1852
   137, 254
   Sally H. (Caverly) 224
   Sarah A. (Bickford) Young,
   b 1833 98
Cloutman
   Anna 60
   Lucinda (Stevens) 162
   Mary M., b Jan 1846 162
   William H. 162
Coburn
   Ella J., b 1857 96
   Martha J. (   ) 96
   Orin B. 96
Cochran
   Polly, b ca 1785 322
Coffin
   Abigail, b 24 Nov 1782 175
   Amy, see Diana 83
   Cyrus, b 1834 102
   David W. 320

Coffin
   Diana, b ca 1780 83
   Eddie W., b Jan 1883 242
   Eliphalet 176
   Esther (Lamos) 320
   Florence D., b 1865 320
   Nabby, see Abigail 175
   Patience (Evans) 176
Coldmy, see Colomy 98
Cole
   Hittie R., b 1834 166
   Mehitable, see Hittie R.
Coleman
   Mehitable (   ) 278
   Oliver J. 278
   Sarah W., b 1832 278
Collins
   Henry, b ca 1790 216
   James, b ca 1870 232
   Lavina (Young)+, b ca 1795
   216
   Lewis D., b ca 1850 232
   Mary H.+ (Young), b 11 Dec
   1852 232, 242
Colomy
   Betsy Jane, b 1832 98
   Daniel 267
   Rebecca 267
   Richard, b 1800 98
Commody
   Sarah, b ca 1765 196
Connor
   Noah, b 1760s 279
   Sarah+ (Young), b 1760s 63,
   279
Cook
   Anna+ (Young), b ca 1757 22
   Betsey (   ) 55
   Betsey, b 2 Jul 1799 55
   Catherine 280
   Catherine Y., b 29 Dec 1816
   161
   Daniel, b 11 Sep 1732 224
   Elizabeth, see Betsey 55
   Emily Mary, see Mary Emily
   162
   Hannah Merrill, b 13 Apr
   1846 41
   Hessekiah, b 1 Jan 1717 224
   Hiram, b 1812 226
   John 161, 224
   John A., b ca 1820 280

Cook
  John, b 5 May 1692   224
  John, b 6 Nov 1725   224
  Joseph, b ca 1755   22
  Lewis   162
  Lydia+ (Young), b 29 Nov
    1694   224, 294
  Marcy, b 21 Jun 1716   224
  Maria E.+ (Young), b 1827
    226
  Mary (Downes)   224
  Mary (Young)   161
  Mary Emily, b 7 Sep 1841
    162
  Mary, b 1 Apr 1720   224
  Mehitable B. (Cate), b 1834
    166
  Nancy (Jones)   162
  Peter   55
  Phebe, b 17 Mar 1729/30
    224
  Richard, b 21 Dec 1727   224
  Sarah+ (Young), b ca 1825
    280
  Sarah+ (Young), b ca 1825
    158
  Susan Tappan, b 17 Dec 1841
    103
  Thomas Jefferson   103
Cooke
  John H., b ca 1820   227
  Martha A.+ (Young), b ca
    1825   227
  Weston, b 1860s   227
Cookson
  George W.   210
  Josiah, b 1794   210
  Julia A., b 1844   210
  Mary, b 1793   210
  Susan D., b Feb 1828   210
Corson
  John A., b ca 1825   281
  Nellie F., b Dec 1866   111
  Sabrina, b ca 1795   312
  Sarah E.+ (Young), b 1832
    163, 281
Cotter
  John   231
  Mary+ (Young), b ca 1810
    231
Cotton
  Abigail, b 1798   182

Cotton
  Fannie, b 1817   17
  Frances, see Fannie   17
  John F., b ca 1805   231
  Mary+ (Young), b ca 1810
    231
  Susannah, b ca 1700   316
Cox
  Alice+ (Young), b ca 1870
    16
  Thomas, ca 1865   16
Cram
  David   137, 196
  Frank E., b ca 1845   110
  Ida A.+ (Young), b ca 1850
    110
  Mary, b ca 1800   196
  Sarah, b ca 1760   137
  Susannah (Clough)   137
Critchett
  John S., b 1819   223
  Lucy Maria+ (Young), b 1822
    67, 223
Cuck, see Cook
Cunningham
  Minnie L., b Aug 1873   158
Currier
  John   201
  Nancy (Young), b 1810s   201
Cutts
  Lavina C. (Basford), b Apr
    1842   289
  Lilla M., b 17 Dec 1866   289
  Maud L., see Lilla M.   289
  William   289
Dame
  Abby H., b 3 Mar 1826   104
  Elizabeth, b 1772   62
  Ethel M.+ (Young), b 1870s
    85
  Hannah (Durgin)   104
  Israel   104
  Mahala, b ca 1810   107
  Mahala+ (Young), b ca 1820
    225
  Sarah F., b ca 1850   96
  Walter S., b ca 1870   85
  William, b ca 1815   225
Danford
  Julia A. (Young), b ca 1818
    65
Danforth

Dennis
  Damen, b ca 1830 27
  Dan H., b 1860s 27
Dermody
  Mary, b May 1842 308
Diamond
  Isaac 278
  Mary, b 1794 278
Dimond, see Diamond 205, 278
Dion
  Charles 46
  Grace, b 1865 46
  Mary (   ) 46
Doe
  Joseph A. 17
  Mary (Drew) 17
  Polly, b ca 1807 181
  Sarah R., b 17 Aug 1841 17
Dolloff
  Betsey+ (Young), b 3 Jun
    1800 37, 200
  Joseph, b ca 1800 37
Donnelly
  Francis, b Mar 1835 128
  Margaret (   ), b Feb 1838
    128
  Rose A., b Mar 1869 128
Dore
  Elizabeth S.+ (Young), b ca
    1809 81
  Henry, b ca 1805 81
Dorr
  Frank E., b ca 1870 158
  Martha H., b ca 1830 119
  Nellie M. (Young), b 1876
    159
Doughty
  Julius H., b ca 1845 225
  Lydia L.+ (Young), b 1849
    212, 225
Dow
  Alvah E., b 1840s 245
  Anna M. (Nutter), b 1840s
    245
Downing
  Fanny G. 163
  Melissa, b 1839 163
  Royal B. 163
Downs
  Ezra 290
  Sarah 290
Doyle

Doyle
  Amanda (Wentworth), b 25 Jun
    1856 131
  John, b 19 May 1839 131
  Mary Amanda, b 3 Mar 1873
    131
Drew
  Andrew J., b ca 1810 84
  Ann (   ) 228
  Betsey Ann, b 13 Feb 1814
    109
  Charles 221
  E. A. (   ) 221
  Elijah, b 24 May 1741 228
  Esther+ (Young), b ca 1815
    84
  Francis 228
  Francis, b 24 May 1741 228
  Frank J., b 1858 221
  Frank L., b 1859 15
  Gertrude May, b ca 1880 221
  Harrison, b ca 1820 271
  John 109
  John S., b 1846 120
  Joseph, b 30 Aug 1748 228
  Joseph, b 8 Apr 1717 228
  Lizzie H.+ (Young), b 1857
    221, 252
  Lizzie J., b 1842 69
  Mary (   ) 69
  Mary, b 9 Jun 1745 228
  Mary+ (Young), b ca 1720
    142, 228
  Nancy (Wiggin) 109
  Nancy, b 1760 301
  Nicholas 69
  Sally+ (Young), b ca 1825
    271
Drown
  Ezra M., b ca 1790 271
  Sally+ (Young), b ca 1795
    175, 271
Dudley
  Hannah, b ca 1775 321
  Hannah+ (Young), b ca 1780
    101
  John, b ca 1775 101
  Otis P., b ca 1815 280
  Sarah C.+ (Young), b 17 Dec
    1820 280, 319
  Susan (Snow), b 1829 290
Durgin

Estes
  James 90
  Louisa (   ) 90
  Sophia W., b Oct 1850 90
Evans
  Charles W., b ca 1840 45
  Clara 80
  Clara A.+ (Young), b ca
    1845 45
  Eliza J., b 5 Apr 1815 20
  Elizabeth+, b Oct 1823 80
  Fred A., b late 1860s 45
  Henry 128
  Isabel (   ) 128
  John 20
  Lillian J., b Sep 1864 128
  Nancy (Avery) 20
Ewell
  Ada R., b Apr 1845 119
  Adaronia, see Ada R. 119
  Jacob A. 119
  Sarah (   ) 119
Ewer
  Drusilla (Covill) 195
  Nathaniel 195
Fall
  Charles W., b ca 1845 291
  Ellen F., b 1822 128
  Susan A.+ (Young), b 1840
    224
Farnham
  Ivesta D.+ (Young), b 1847
    119
  Luesta, see Ivesta D.+
  Olive 227
  Stephen, b 1841 119
Farnum
  Betsey A.+, b 20 Jan 1835
    37
  John 37
  Mary (Berry) 37
  Mary A., b 1825 264
Farrer
  Lucy+ (Young), b ca 1805
    223
  Stephen, b ca 1800 223
Faxon
  Annie+ (Young), b ca 1850
    24
  Ebenezer F., b ca 1845 24
Fellows
  Ann (Sherbourne) 131

Fellows
  Charles S. 131
  Harriet L., b 1874 131
  John K. 131
Fernald
  Benjamin Ayres 204
  Caroline Elizabeth (Young),
    b 24 Nov 1821 204
  Deborah S., b 1793 269
  John 269
  Mary, b 1828 305
Ferren
  Augustus D., b ca 1835 82
  Emma A. (Mills), b ca 1842
    82
Ferrill
  George 25
  Mary (   ) 25
  Mary, b 1864 25
Ferrin
  James, b 1875 42
Fidler
  Elena C., b Feb 1859 243
  Mary A., b Feb 1834 243
Fisher
  Francis, b ca 1815 216
  Frank Young, b 1840s 216
  George, b 1849 286
  Laura A.+ (Young), b ca 1820
    216
Flagg
  Henry R. 69
Fogg
  Ida Miranda (Young), b ca
    1850 222
Foller
  Abijah 97
  Mattie W., b 1848 97
Folsom
  Anna, b 25 Feb 1748 192
  Anna, b Aug 1731 188
  Ephraim 294
  Jeremiah 188
  Lucium, b 1854 216
  Mary (Folsom) 192
  Peter 192
  Phaltiel (Hall) 294
  Sarah, b 1692 294
Ford
  Edwin H., b ca 1840 292
  Susan C.+ (Young), b 1842
    133, 291

Forsaith
  Lizzie M.+ (Young), b 26
    Oct 1853 184, 221
  Samuel S., b ca 1850 221
Foss
  Abigail, b ca 1760 57
  Betsey (   ) 279
  Charles A. 222
  Dexter S., b 1853 81
  Eleanor, b 1797 58
  Eli H. 281
  Ella A.+ (Young), b 1858
    81, 92
  Frances A., b 18 Jul 1841
    43
  Grace A. (Young), b ca 1875
    101
  Horace 279
  Isaac B. 81
  James, b 1793 58
  Katherine (Tebbetts) 43
  Lizzie A., b 1858 90
  Mary A. (   ) 81
  Mary A. (Furber) 281
  Mary, b 25 Nov 1739 188
  Nellie M., b 1858 279
  Oscar, b 17 Nov 1845 281
  Sally, b 1796 210
  Samuel D. 43
  Sarah (Gaines) 188
  Sarah U.+ (Young), b 3 Dec
    1852 257, 281
  William W. 90
  Zachariah 188
Fowles
  Abby (   ) 45
  Abial 45
  Mary A., b 14 Aug 1831 45
Francis
  Anna, b ca 1846 153
Franks
  Ida M., b 1869 91
French
  Mary E.+ (Young), b ca 1820
    232
  Stephen, b ca 1815 232
Frost
  Emily A., b 1837 217, 232
  Esther Ann+ (Young), b ca
    1820 84, 315
  Hester Ann+ (Young), b ca
    1820 107

Frost
  Hiram B., b ca 1810 232
  James B., b ca 1815 107
  James, b ca 1815 84
  Mary A., b Jun 1839 268
  Mary Ann+ (Young), b ca 1816
    218, 232
  Mary, b ca 1755 222
  Oliver 268
Furber
  Benjamin 33
  Deborah, b 1802 33
  Kezia (   ), b 1768 184
  Kezia (Ash) 33
  Kezia, b 1768 184
  Mehitable (Chesley), b ca
    1825 80
  Polly (Young), b ca 1805 35
  Samuel 80
Furbish
  Charles H., b ca 1845 45
  Clara A.+ (Young), b 2 Aug
    1851 45
Furbush
  Anna, b 1798 305
  Clara A.+ (Young), b 2 Aug
    1851 306
  Dorcas J., b 1851 279
  George H., b ca 1860 271
  Joseph 305
  Martha (Lord) 305
  Ruth E.+ (Young), b 12 Sep
    1866 159, 271
Garland
  Ebenezer, b 1815 24
  Elizabeth, b 1780s 292
  Nathaniel, b 12 Aug 1758
    292
  Nathaniel, b 1780s 292
  Patience, b 1780s 292
  Polly, b 1780s 292
  Sally, b 1780s 292
  Samuel 23
  Susan E., b 31 Oct 1814, 24
  Susanna, b 1780s 292
  Susannah+ (Young), b 1760
    72, 292
Garlin
  Anna+ (Young), b 1787 23,
    172
  Ebenezer, b 20 Apr 1788 23
  James, b ca 1785 23

Garmon
  Ebenezer, b ca 1780   135
  Jane+ (Young), b ca 1785
    135, 197
Garvin
  Mary, b ca 1812   264
Giles
  Mary (Young), b late 1750s
    66
Gilkerson
  Ernest L., b Jul 1890   10
  Harry, b Sep 1878   10
  Luella (Stevens), b Aug
    1853   9
  Lulla, see Luella   9
  William H., b Aug 1882   10
Gill
  Aaron   128
  Rosemandel, b 17 Jul 1823
    128
Gillpatrick
  Abigail+ (Young), b ca 1815
    12
  John, b ca 1805   12
Gilman
  Abby Jane (Young), b ca
    1840   110
  Abigail, b 8 Jun 1772   199
  Adeline P.+ (Young), b
    1820s   14, 27
  Anna M.+ (Young), b 1854
    24, 138
  Elizabeth E., b 1825   219
  Ezekial, b ca 1825   14
  Samuel H., b ca 1850   24
Gleason
  Charlotte (   )   14
  John   14
  Mary A., b 19 Nov 1832   14
Glidden
  Abby M. (Young), b ca 1860
    10
  Abigail (Young)   10
  Abigail+ (Young), b 1826
    12, 130
  Charles L., b 1845   12
  Clarence A., b 1844   12
  Elicia A., see Lizzie   12
  Ella M. (Young), b ca 1871
    100
  Eugene E., b Aug 1869   12
  Hattie S., b 1852   12

Glidden
  Jane A., b 1848   12
  Jerome A.   10
  Jerome A., b 1846   12
  John H.   10
  John H., b 1826   12
  John N., b ca 1860   10
  Julius A., b 1846   12
  Lizzie, b 30 Jun 1860   12
  Loren J., b 1863   12
  Sarah, b 1866   12
  Woodbury H., b ca 1865   100
Godfrey
  Esther M.+ (Young), b 10 Nov
    1862   84, 94
  Hazen J., b ca 1810   84
Goldsmith
  Hubbard   228
  Lydia (Roberts)   228
  Martha L.+, b 15 Dec 1803
    228
Goodall
  Elizabeth, b 1823   92
  Rhoda E., see Elizabeth
Goodwin
  Abigail, b Sep 1881   215
  Elisha   236
  Sarah R. (Doe) Young, b 17
    Aug 1841   17
  Shepard, b ca 1820   285
  Sophronia J.+ (Young), b ca
    1825   285
  Sylvester, b ca 1840   17
Gordon
  Hannah E., b ca 1805   255
  Mary Ann, b 1821   162
Gorman
  Daniel   133, 291
  Susan C., 133
  Susan C.+, b 1842   291
Gould
  Asa M., b 1834   150
  Hannah (Langlands), b ca
    1845   161
  Joseph, b ca 1800   230
  Mary+ (Young), b ca 1805
    230
Gove
  Lydia (Wentworth)   92, 121
  Rebecca Jane, b 21 Nov 1821
    121
  Richard   91, 121

Graham
  Albert G.   315
  Ella D., b 1854   315
  Sarah H. (   )   315
Grant
  Elmira+ (Young), b ca 1825
    82
  John, b ca 1820   82
Gray
  Alice, b 1867   42
  Clara (   )   42
  John   42
  Martha F., b 1821   185
Greenfield
  Arolind (Downs)   100
  Charles   100
  Sadie E., b 1854   100
Greenough
  Mary, b 1853   222
  William   222
Griffen
  Susie J., b 1852   24
Grover
  Benjamin F., b 1840   82
  Charles A., b 1867   216
  Ellen A.+ (Young), b 1845
    81, 154
  Fannie A.+ (Locke) Young, b
    1859   215
Hackett
  Allen, b ca 1775   266
  Polly+ (Young), b 13 Apr
    1780   194, 265
Hadley
  Bradford, b ca 1785   271
  Ruth+ (Young), b ca 1792
    74, 271
Hale
  Adaline M. (Roberts), b
    1837   220
  Mary Shackford, b 31 Mar
    1872   220
  Samuel S., b 1831   220
Haley
  Elizabeth (   )   69
  Samuel   69
  Sarah A., b 1845   69
Hall
  Abigail (Foss)   320
  Addie B., b 1868   91
  Albert Ianson, b 30 Apr
    1856   84

Hall
  Andrew, b ca 1805   37
  Betsey+ (Young), b ca 1810
    37
  Charles H.   91
  Elisha, b ca 1745   79
  Elizabeth A. (Willey)   91
  Elizabeth+ (Young), b ca
    1750   79
  Esther Sarah+ (Young), b 14
    May 1868   84, 121
  Irene Margurite, b 13 Apr
    1898   84
  Jacob   320
  Margaret, b ca 1815   108
  Mary Ann (Young), b ca 1817
    67
  Mary, b Jun 1858   69
  Matilda (Jones), b 1837   258
  Olive Frances, b 14 Aug 1902
    84
  Roswell Ianson, b 16 Apr
    1893   84
  Rufus   67
  Sophia Locke, b 2 Oct 1828
    320
Ham
  Anna, b 12 Dec 1712   169
  Benjamin   71
  Charles   108
  Daniel   150
  David   150
  Deborah, b ca 1800   74
  Eliza, b 13 Aug 1813   229
  Ephraim   229
  George Samuel, b 11 Feb 1877
    217
  Hannah (Kelley)   229
  Hannah (Runnels)   150
  Hannah, b 3 Mar 1780   150
  John   169
  Joseph   169
  Joseph, b 1796   182
  Joseph, b 28 Jan 1779   280
  Lavina J.+ (Young) Hanson,
    b 31 Jan 1835   216
  Mary (Heard)   169
  Mary (Shaw)   108
  Mary M., b 1854   108
  Mary, b 8 Oct 1723   70
  Patience (Hartford)   71
  Samuel   74

Hayes

Benjamin, b 12 Mar 1723/24 10

Catherine (Roberts), b 1806 48

Charles Howland, b 1 Jun 1852 89

Charles William Hardy, b 2 Jan 1836 225

Clarissa Drew (Coleman) 217

Cora Bell, b 1862 217

Daniel 229, 283

Daniel, b 8 Apr 1799 229

David Arthur, b 22 Jul 1886 166

David Byron, b 1843 166

David, b 28 May 1787 11

Deborah (French) 277

Ebenezer, ba 14 Feb 1751 11

Eliza (Ham), b 13 Aug 1813 229

Elizabeth 11

Elizabeth Ann (Waldron) 166

Elizabeth, b 20 Apr 1790 11

Elizabeth, b 24 Sep 1757 283

Elizabeth+ (Young), b 18 Nov 1809 80, 312

Ezekial 48

Ezra 217

Fannie J.+ (Young), b 11 Mar 1856 89, 92

Franklin Pierce, b 3 Mar 1853 222

Fred Byron 166

Hannah (Demeritt) 225

Hannah (Twombly) 300

Hannah Demeritt, b 7 Jun 1828 225

Hannah Frances (Webster), b 1852 222

Harriet+ (Young), b 15 Jun 1803 225

Henry Young, b 16 Sep 1819 225

Herbert Charles, b 28 Jun 1876 89

Hezekiah 80

Hayes

Ichabod 277

Ira, b 28 May 1804 229

James Frederick, b 13 Sep 1838 225

James Young 89

James Young, b 29 May 1797 11

Jeremy D., b 29 Jun 1810 229

Job 11

John 160

John Adams, b 11 Mar 1801 11

John Samuel W., b 5 Jun 1841 225

John Samuel, b 13 Jul 1823 225

Joseph, b 1748 11

Judith A. (Meserve), b ca 1850 166

Leah, b 16 Mar 1800 277

Levi F., b ca 1845 308

Lovina A.+ (Young), b 19 May 1858 221, 306

Lydia Harriet+ (Young), b 15 Jun 1803 106

Mary (   ) 222

Mary (Chamberlain), b 1789 160

Mary, b 23 Apr 1782 11

Mary+ (Young), b 28 Sep 1774 229, 310

Nathaniel, b 14 Mar 1773 229

Nathaniel, b 15 Mar 1776 11

Oliver Kimball, b 22 Apr 1816 229

Peter 10

Phoebe Huckins, b 9 Nov 1813 160

Plummer, b 8 Jul 1806 229

Rachel 11

Robert, b ca 1797 48

Samuel 105, 222, 225

Samuel, b 19 Apr 1792 225

Sarah (Plummer) 229, 283

Sarah (Wingate) 10

Sarah Elizabeth, b 9 Jul 1833 225

Sarah Plummer, b 24 Dec 1812 229

Johnson
  Julia A., b 1830 102
  Levi B., b ca 1840 235
  Lillie E.+ (Young), b 1850s
    221
  Mary E. (Young), b 16 Aug
    1871 18
  Mary J. (Young), b ca 1812
    65
  Melissa A.+ (Young), b 1845
    235
  Phineas, b 5 Sep 1814 102
Jones
  Abigail (Drew) 258
  Alphonso, b 1840s 62
  David L. W. 313
  Drusilla E.+ (Young), b
    1820 62, 218
  Eunice, b ca 1835 184
  Fannie H.+ (Young), b 1841
    89, 185
  Frances (   ) 313
  John 258
  Joseph, b ca 1815 62
  Laura P., b ca 1850 42
  Margarette E., b ca 1815
    313
  Mary (   ), b 1801 100
  Mary H., b 10 Apr 1839 100
  Mary S., b 1846 135
  Matilda, b 1837 258
  Nathaniel W., b 1808 100
  Nathaniel, b 1808 100
  Samuel G., b ca 1840 89
  Sophia, b 1840 257
Joy
  George E., b ca 1865 159
  Helen F. (Young), b 2 Dec
    1871 159
  Mary A., b Jun 1839 24
Judkins
  Joseph T. 81
Jukes
  Christabel, b 16 Dec 1876
    103
  Samuel J., d 7 Jul 1947
    103
Karl
  John 289
  Lucy (Stam) 289
  Lucy R., b 9 May 1852 289
Kay

Kay
  Edward 187
  Martha S. (Young), b 1854
    187
Keay
  Ezekial, b ca 1790 245
  Nancy+ (Young), b ca 1795
    245
  Susannah, b ca 1800 203
Kelley
  Annie F.+ (Young), b ca 1870
    24
  Arthur O., b ca 1870 24
Keniston
  Emeline, b 1830 134
  John 14
  Martha J., b 3 Aug 1830 14
  Rebecca (Meader) 14
  Sarah, b ca 1815 319
Kenney
  Isaac 320
  Mary 320
Kenniston
  Emma F., b 30 May 1852 24
  Hannah (   ) 24
  Leonard F., b ca 1860 233
  Mary S.+ (Young), b 7 Jan
    1862 183, 233
  Solomon B. 24
Kershaw
  Hattie A.+ (Young), b 18 Aug
    1851 104, 130
  Samuel, b 1831 104
Keysar
  Benjamin Young, b 1810s 37
  Betsey, b 1820s 37
  Betsey+ (Young), b 20 May
    1784 31, 36
  Edmund Hodgdon, b 1820s 37
  Edmund, b 12 Apr 1780 36
  Edmund, b 15 Oct 1752 36
  Edmund, b 30 May 1808 36
  James 136
  Jessie, b 1830s 37
  John, b 1810s 37
  Joseph Young, b 1810s 37
  Mary (Lyford) 36
  Mary, b 15 Sep 1809 37
  Mary, b 1810s 37
  Mehitable Susan, b 1820s 37
  Miles Hodgdon, b 1820s 37
  Olive, b 24 May 1828 37

405

407

Marsh
  1813 80
Marston
  Frank R., b ca 1845 291
  Fred B., b ca 1872 291
  Hester A. (Bumpus), b ca
    1875 291
  Susan A.+ (Young), b ca
    1850 291
Masfield
  Martha, b ca 1835 184
Mason
  Anna, b ca 1765 148
  Charles, b 1844 8
  George E. 289
  Mary Ann (Young), b 1830
    289
Mathes, see Matthew
Mathews
  Francis 270
  John W., b 1826 231
  John, b ca 1800 230
  Mary ( ) 270
  Mary Catherine, b 7 Jul
    1831 231
  Mary+ (Young), b 25 Mar
    1807 203, 230
  Susannah 293
  Susannah, b ca 1655 270
  Thamarsin ( ) 270
  Walter 270
Mathues
  Sarah A., b 1824 130
Matthew
  John N., b 1830s 221
  Lizzie N.+ (Young), b 1830s
    221
  Mary V., b 1816 130
  Sarah A., b 1824 130
Maybery
  Mabel+ (Young), b 1869 225
  Melburn E., b 1864 225
Maybury
  Eliza C.+ (Young), b 25 May
    1860 79, 210
  William A., b ca 1855 79
Mayo
  Jane H. (Young), b 1831 16
McCarthy
  Dennis, b Dec 1848 183
McDonald
  Christine, b July 1876 9

McDonald
  James 257
  Mary A., b 1870 257
McDuffee
  Melonia F. (Buzzell), b Apr
    1852 106
  Seth F. 135
McIlroy
  Arabella, b 1828 15
McIntire
  Charles A., b ca 1855 291
  Susan+ (Young), b 7 Nov 1858
    42, 291
McKinney
  Mary, b 1851 128
McLinn
  Anna, b Jul 1850 292
  Mary ( ) 292
  Patrick 292
McMichael
  Edward, b Jul 1875 65
McNerton
  Annie, b 1854 274
McThornton, see McNerton
Meader, also Meder
  Ebenezer, b ca 1760 279
  Sarah+ (Young), b 25 Mar
    1763 191, 279
  Susan, b 1781 136
Merrick
  Nancy, b ca 1825 154
Merrill
  Betsey A., b 1814 277
  Charles S. 166
  George L., b ca 1820 232
  Hannah L.+ (Young), b 1833
    102, 252
  John, b ca 1805 245
  Mary Ann+ (Young), b 1 Jan
    1827 232, 288
  Nancy E. ( ) 166
  Nancy+ (Young), b ca 1810
    245
  Nellie N., b 1844 166
  Thomas W., b ca 1830 102
Meserve
  Charles G. 166
  Judith A., b ca 1850 166
  Louisa, b ca 1825 88
  Sophia, b 1802 76
Miles
  Susan Elizabeth, b 27 Aug

413

Wiggins
    Oct 1800 180, 242
    Joseph, b 1804 180, 242
Wigglesworth
    Frank H., b ca 1855 292
    Susan E.+ (Young), b 1864
       41
Wilber
    Lucy Jane, b 1836 14
Wilkerson
    Leonard 33
    Mattie W.+, b 2 Apr 1847
       234
Wilkinson
    David 234
    Grace, b Feb 1879 209
    Patience (Thompson) 234
Willand
    Frank 233, 306
    George 306
    Mary L.+ (Young), b 3 Jul
       1855 306
Willard
    Enoch 233
    Frank, b 1866 233
    Mary L.+ (Young), b 3 Jul
       1855 233
    Phebe (   ) 233
Willey
    Abbie F., b 1851 222
    Alfred S. 222
    Caroline H.+ (Young), b ca
       1850 38
    Cyrus D., b ca 1845 38
    Mary J. (Young) 222
    Molly, b 27 Mar 1791 115
Wilson
    Cornelius 215
    Nancy M. (Burleigh), b 1832
       215
Winkley
    Ellen Sarah+ (Young), b 7
       Oct 1844 82, 321
    George Langdon, b 31 Jan
       1879 82
    Grace Ellen, b 26 Jun 1873
       82
    John Langdon, b 10 Mar 1841
       82
    Lillian Abbie, b 1 Jan 1877
       82
    Mabel Hoyt (Pinkham) 82

Winkley
    Willard Choate, b 1 Jun 1885
       82
Winn
    Martha, b ca 1840 135
Witham
    Jerome B., b 1832 163
    Jonathan, b ca 1780 224
    Lucy Maria (   ) 223
    Lucy Maria+, b 10 Apr 1836
       223
    Lydia (   ) 163
    Lydia+ (Young), b ca 1785
       224
    Mary Sophia, b ca 1830 268
    Melissa (Downing) Young, b
       1839 163
    Moses 163
    Sarah (Young), b 1815 106
Wood
    Susan, b 1750s 124
Woodhouse, see also Woods
    John 225
    Margaret+ (Young), b ca 1780
       125
Woodman
    Frank P., b ca 1855 216
    Laura A.+ (Young), b 20 Apr
       1860 216, 242
Woods
    John, b ca 1775 225
    Margaret+ (Young), b ca 1780
       225
Yeaton
    Bethiah+ (Young), b ca 1798
       36
    Joseph, b ca 1795 36
York
    Charles, b 1821 320
    Charles, b 1846 231
    Elizabeth, b ca 1795 127
    Emily F., b 1829 320
    Enoch, b 1785 278
    Fannie S., b 15 Sep 1857 43
    George I., b ca 1840 228
    Martha E.+ (Young), b 1842
       227, 228
    Mary (   ) 43
    Mary+ (Young), b 1846 231
    Sally H., b 1793 136
    Sarah, b 1787 278
    Wingate 43

ERRATA TO THE BIOGRAPHICAL DICTIONARY OF THE YOUNGS
(BORN 1653 — 1870) FROM TOWNS UNDER THE JURISDICTION OF
STRAFFORD COUNTY, NEW HAMPSHIRE BEFORE 1840

p21   ESTELLA C., aka Estelle, b 2 Oct 1858, twin, Barnstead,
        NH, d/o Andrew J. and Sarah C. (Sweet) Young, **did not
        die young**; she married in 1878, Lynn, MA. (Mass. V.R.,
        Marr, 298:225)

p34   CATHERINE (Roberts), **b 23 Apr 1802**, Brookfield, NH, d/o
        Nathaniel and Patience (Garland) Roberts of Ossipee, **d
        15 Jun 1884**, Haverhill, MA, of old age, buried at
        Freedom, NH, age 82-1-22; she was widow of Daniel Young
        [b 1785, Berwick, ME, eldest s/o John and Sally (Mason)
        Young of Ossipee]. (Mass. V.R., Deaths, 355:212)

p38   BRADBURY S[mith] was **b 30 Aug 1799**, Upper Gilmanton,
        NH, twin of Nathaniel B., sons of Joseph and Betsey
        Shaw Young, **d 21 Sep 1865**, Lynn, age 66-0-22, testate,
        widower. He and spouse Susan P. relocated in Lynn,
        Essex Co., MA, where four children were born. (Mass.
        V.R., Deaths 174:220)

p43   CHARLES H., **b 4 May 1853**, Middleton, NH, s/o Samuel P.
        and Martha A. (Stevens) Young, **d 14 Dec 1894**, Haver-
        hill, age 41-7-10, married, buried at Farmington, NH.
        (Mass. V.R., Deaths 445:435)

p62   DUDLEY, **bp 25 Feb 1738/9**, Kingston First Church, NH,
        s/o Deacon Aaron and Abigail (Dudley) Young, d testate
        pre 10 May 1803, Gilmanton, NH; m 19 Oct 1758, King-
        ston, Jenne aka Margaret Smith of Kingston. (NH
        I.G.I.; NH Gen. Recs. 3:90; 5:104)

p69   EDWIN A., **b Dec 1840**, Durham, s/o Joseph and Maria
        (Langley) Young, **alive 1900**, Newmarket, NH, married
        (1900 Mass. Soundex)

p138   HARRIET **Fletcher** (Marland), b ca 1815, Dover, w/o
        Jeremiah Smith Young of Andover, MA. They raised **two
        sons** in Andover, George Washburn and Francis Cogswell.
        Maiden name was discovered in Sarah L. Bailey's
        "Historical Sketches of Andover, Mass," p594. (Andover
        V.R., Births, p388)

p158   CHARLES A., **b 10 May 1852**, Gilmanton, NH, s/o John C.
        and Harriet C. (Villam) Young, **d 22 Aug 1888**, Haver-
        hill, MA, of consumption. He earned his own entry,
        having married in 1877. (Mass. V.R., Deaths, 391:244)

p163   ETTA Gertrude, **b 1866**, New Durham, NH, was **another
        daughter born to John Henry** and Melissa (Downing)

Young. She became resident of Lawrence, weaver, and married in 1885. (Mass. V.R., Marr, 361:246)

p170 JONATHAN, b 1 Jan 1756, Kingston, NH, who married Sarah Clifford. His parentage and background remain obscure.

p186 ENOCH P., b 1828, Barrington, under entry of parents Jonathan Franklin and Hannah Hall Young: he earned his own entry: b 1827, he settled in Lawrence, MA and married Elizabeth R. Hubbard. (Mass. V.R., Marr, 60:149)

p211 JOSEPH A., b Mar 1835, Wakefield, d 17 Jul 1908, Newburyport, MA, s/o Joseph and Sally Blaso Young. He, wife Nellie and one daughter settled in North Hampton, MA. (1900 Mass. Soundex; Nat'l Archives Milit. Recs.)

p214 JEREMIAH Copse aka Jere, b 12 Jan 1812, Alton, NH, was another son born to Moses and Dorothy (Peavey) Young; he d 12 Jun 1883, Newbury, MA, age 71-5-0, married. (Mass. V.R., Deaths, 346:265)

p243 OSCAR T., b May 1854, Belmont, NH, s/o Moses A. and Ann Maria (Chase) Young, teamster, was alive 1900, North Andover, married. (1900 Mass. Soundex)

p252 JOHN William aka John W., b Jun 1844, Gilmanton Iron Works, NH, clerk, s/o Nathaniel Badger and Dorothy B. (Lamphrey) Young, alive 1900, Lynn, age 56, twice married. (1900 Mass. Soundex; Mass. V.R., Marr)

p270 RODOLPHA, b 1780s, of Ossipee, NH, was not a distaff, but rather a male head of household as listed in the 1830 federal census for Ossipee. His wife was Nancy aka Anna Tarr of Gloucester; they resided briefly in Gloucester before their stay in Ossipee. (Young Family Recs., courtesy of Douglas Hall of Auburn, ME and David C. Young of Danville, ME)

p276 EZRA, b 1817, Walpole, MA, was another son born to Samuel B. and Nancy (Burleigh) Young of Newmarket and Wolfeboro, NH, whose second marriage took place in 1863, Raymond. (NHVR-Marr)

p277 CLARA A. (Stevens), b 31 Oct 1832, Middleton, NH, w/o Samuel P. Young of Middleton, d/o David and Maria ( ) Stevens of Middleton and Milton, NH, respectively, d 7 Sep 1882, Newburyport, married, age 49-10-7. (Mass. V.R., Deaths, 337:271)

Errata to the Biographical Dictionary of the Youngs of
Strafford County, N.H., continued

p284   ASA, **b 1785, Madbury,** entered as s/o of Solomon and
       Elizabeth Hayes Young, rated a full entry of his own.
       He and wife Lucy Maria Reed settled in Portsmouth where
       they raised a family of six children. (Young Family
       Recs. of Mildred W. Young Urban of Jacksonville, FL and
       Norman G. Parker of West Haven, CT)

p294   HANNAH (Whittier), **b 10 Sep 1660,** Haverhill, MA, w/o
       Edward Young, under entry of their son Thomas Young of
       Newmarket who married Sarah Folsom. (Desc. of Thomas
       Whittier, p15)

www.ingramcontent.com/pod-product-compliance
Lightning Source LLC
Chambersburg PA
CBHW071828270326
41929CB00013B/1924